UNITED NATIONS CONFERENCE ON TRADE AND DEVELOPMENT

INTERNATIONAL INVESTMENT AGREEMENTS: KEY ISSUES
Volume I

UNITED NATIONS
New York and Geneva, 2004

Note

UNCTAD serves as the focal point within the United Nations Secretariat for all matters related to foreign direct investment and transnational corporations. In the past, the Programme on Transnational Corporations was carried out by the United Nations Centre on Transnational Corporations (1975-1992) and the Transnational Corporations and Management Division of the United Nations Department of Economic and Social Development (1992-1993). In 1993, the Programme was transferred to the United Nations Conference on Trade and Development. UNCTAD seeks to further the understanding of the nature of transnational corporations and their contribution to development and to create an enabling environment for international investment and enterprise development. UNCTAD's work is carried out through intergovernmental deliberations, research and analysis, technical assistance activities, seminars, workshops and conferences.

The term "country" as used in this study also refers, as appropriate, to territories or areas; the designations employed and the presentation of the material do not imply the expression of any opinion whatsoever on the part of the Secretariat of the United Nations concerning the legal status of any country, territory, city or area or of its authorities, or concerning the delimitation of its frontiers or boundaries. In addition, the designations of country groups are intended solely for statistical or analytical convenience and do not necessarily express a judgement about the stage of development reached by a particular country or area in the development process.

The following symbols have been used in the tables:

Two dots (..) indicate that data are not available or are not separately reported. Rows in tables have been omitted in those cases where no data are available for any of the elements in the row;

A dash (-) indicates that the item is equal to zero or its value is negligible;

A blank in a table indicates that the item is not applicable;

A slash (/) between dates representing years, e.g. 1994-1995, indicates a financial year;

Use of a hyphen (-) between dates representing years, e.g. 1994-1995, signifies the full period involved, including the beginning and end years.

Reference to "dollars" ($) means United States dollars, unless otherwise indicated.

Annual rates of growth or change, unless otherwise stated, refer to annual compound rates.

Details and percentages in tables do not necessarily add to totals because of rounding.

The material contained in this study may be freely quoted with appropriate acknowledgement.

UNCTAD/ITE/IIT/2004/10 (Vol. I)

UNITED NATIONS PUBLICATION
Sales No.E.05.II.D.6
ISBN 92-1-112663-0
92-1-112660-6 (Volume I)
92-1-112661-4 (Volume II)
92-1-112662-2 (Volume III)

Printed in Switzerland

Table of contents

Volume I

Volume II

Volume III

Table of contents
Volume I

Boxes

Figures

Tables

Annex table

Chapter 2. International Investment Agreements: Flexibility for Development

Boxes

Figures

Chapter 3. Scope and Definition

Boxes

Table

Chapter 4. Admission and Establishment

Boxes

Table

Chapter 5. National Treatment

Boxes

Table

Chapter 6. Most-Favoured-Nation Treatment

Table

Chapter 7. Fair and Equitable Treatment

Table

Chapter 8. Taking of Property

Boxes

Table

Chapter 9. Transfer of Funds

Chapter 10. Transparency

Boxes

Tables

Chapter 11. Dispute Settlement: State-State

Boxes

Table

Chapter 12. Dispute Settlement: Investor-State

Table

Introduction: Issues in International Investment Agreements

With the ascendancy of foreign direct investment (FDI) as one of the main factors driving international economic relations in the era of globalization, international investment rulemaking has come to the forefront of economic diplomacy. It may well be that, as the second half of the 20th century was characterized by the establishment of an international trade law system, the first half of the 21st century may be characterized by the establishment of an international investment law system.

Indeed, countries' efforts to attract FDI and benefit from it increasingly take place in an environment characterized by a proliferation of investment rules at the bilateral, sub-regional, regional and multilateral levels. The resulting investment rules – laid out now in over 2,200 bilateral investment treaties (see www.unctad.org/iia), over 2,300 double taxation treaties, numerous preferential free trade agreements with investment components, and multilateral agreements – are multi-layered and multi-faceted, with obligations differing in geographical scope and coverage and ranging from the voluntary to the binding. They constitute an intricate web of commitments that partly overlap and partly supplement one another.

This web is becoming more complex almost by the day, both in number and scope. The number of investment agreements continues to grow, with, for example, almost two bilateral investment treaties added every week in 2004. In addition, investment components have now begun to be added to preferential trade agreements. The recent decision by the WTO not to pursue investment issues as part of the Doha work programme may add further stimulus to the trend towards bilateral and regional regulatory approaches.

It is this proliferation of international agreements addressing investment issues – international investment agreements (IIAs) for short – and hence the need to understand the issues that are raised in their negotiation that prompted UNCTAD's decision to develop a series of 27 booklets on *Issues in International Investment Agreements* as a means to help negotiators and decision-makers, in particular from developing countries, to come to grips with the complex matter at hand and to provide them with a basic reference tool for use in the preparation of negotiations as well as for the development of model treaties. They seek to provide balanced analyses of issues that arise in negotiations and/or discussions of IIAs. (For an analysis of the economic issues, see UNCTAD's *World Investment Report*, at www.unctad.org/wir.)

These booklets are combined in this three-volume compilation, each of them constituting a chapter. Each chapter deals with a specific issue, structured along the same lines, with particular attention to the development dimension of international rule making in its given area. Almost all chapters address a standard set of questions:[1] How is the concept/issue in question defined? How has it been used in relevant instruments to date? What are its connections with other key issues? And what are the development implications? At the same time, consideration is given to the fact that it is up to States to decide which path to pursue, which framework to use and which policy to follow. Hence, the chapters do not contain recommendations as to the formulation, conceptualization or approach to use. Rather, each chapter outlines options available to negotiators tasked with drafting the respective treaty provisions, pointing to the specific circumstances that may or may not apply in the pursuit of each.

---

[1] There are some exceptions, i.e. *Trends in International Investment Agreements*, *FDI and Development*, *Flexibility for Development* and *Lessons from the MAI*.

To increase user-friendliness, the references in each chapter have been consolidated by volume and a subject index has been added in volume III. The underlying organizing principle of the volumes follows roughly the curriculum of UNCTAD's intensive training courses on issues in IIAs, without prejudice to the importance of the individual issues at hand. Chapters dealing with overriding concerns (*Trends in IIAs* and *Flexibility for development*) are grouped at the beginning of the first volume. Virtually all the IIAs referred to in these volumes can be found either in UNCTAD's publication *International Investment Instruments: A Compendium* or at www.unctad.org/iia.

The preparation of the booklets underlying these chapters began in 1998, with the first papers being published in May 1999. Since then, of course, the world of FDI and of international investment rule-making has continued to evolve, and new developments would warrant a second look at some of the issues. For one, FDI flows have continued at a high level; for that reason, volume III complements the chapter on *FDI and development* with data from the *World Investment Report 2004: The Shift Towards Services.* For another, the universe of IIAs has grown immensely, not only at the bilateral but also at the regional and inter-regional levels; for that reason, this volume includes an updated version of the annex table 1 of the first chapter, *Trends in IIAs*, which, in its original format, listed agreements only until 1999.

The growth of FDI flows and the increase in agreements aside, the basic problematique at stake remains the same, both in its technicality as well as in its political implications – enough reason to embark on this edition of all 27 booklets after the finalization of the last one in autumn of 2004. At the same time, it is obvious that some of the changes in approach to and nature of some of the issues reviewed need to be reflected in an updating of the chapters – an undertaking that the Secretariat will consider in the near future. (Some data have been updated in the present volumes.)

The first draft of each chapter was prepared by a leading scholar in the field, as acknowledged at the beginning of each chapter. That draft, in turn, went through a rigorous and systematic peer review and revision, involving also a group of standing advisors which included, at various stages, Thomas L. Brewer, Arghyrios A. Fatouros, Sanjaya Lall, Peter Muchlinski, Patrick Robinson and Pedro Roffe. UNCTAD staff finalized the text. As a result, the final product was often quite different from the first draft – and became an UNCTAD document. Hence, the ultimate author of each chapter below is UNCTAD.

The materials were used in the various capacity- and consensus-building activities of UNCTAD's work programme in the area of international investment agreements (see www.unctad.org/iia), especially the intensive training courses for investment negotiators (and their distance-learning elements), regional and national seminars, Geneva workshops and discussions in UNCTAD's Investment Commission and its related expert group meetings, as well as the WTO Working Group on the Relationship between Trade and Investment. At the same time, their production benefited greatly from the synergies arising out of the programme's technical assistance and consensus-building elements, as authors became speakers, participants peer reviewers – "an outstanding example of the successful combination of technical assistance work, policy analysis and research and consensus-building activities".[2] Furthermore, the preparation of the texts profited from close interaction with UNCTAD's overall research and policy analysis of investment issues, including in particular the *World Investment Report* series (specifically *WIR96: Investment, Trade and International Policy Arrangements*; *WIR03: FDI*

[2] Olof Karsegard (2003). "UNCTAD work programme on capacity-building in developing countries on issues in international investment agreements: Midterm evaluation report", mimeo., p.16.

Policies for Development: National and International Perspectives; and *WIR04: The Shift Towards Services*), the *Transnational Corporations* journal, analytical studies of specific topics such as *Bilateral Investment Treaties in the Mid-1990s*, and the *Compendium of International Investment Instruments*, a compilation of investment treaties and other relevant instruments.[3] This process helped to ensure the relevance and accuracy of the materials contained in these volumes.

The volumes are addressed to government officials and negotiators, officials of international agencies, researchers, lawyers and representatives of non-governmental organizations.

Karl P. Sauvant
Director
Division on Investment, Technology and Enterprise Development
UNCTAD

Geneva, September 2004

[3] For a full list of UNCTAD work and publications on this issue, see www/unctad.org/iia.

Chapter 1. Trends in International Investment Agreements: An Overview *

Executive summary

In the past two decades, there have been significant changes in national and international policies on foreign direct investment (FDI). These changes have been both cause and effect in the ongoing integration of the world economy and the changing role of FDI in it. They have found expression in national laws and practices and in a variety of international instruments, bilateral, regional and multilateral.

While in earlier times indirect foreign investment was far more important than direct, FDI acquired increasing importance as the twentieth century advanced, and it began gradually to assume the forms prevalent today. In international legal terms, however, FDI long remained a matter mainly of national concern, moving onto the international plane, where rules and principles of customary international law applied, only in exceptional cases, when arbitrary government measures affected it.

After the end of the Second World War, attitudes towards FDI and policies and conditions in host countries were shaped by the prevalence of political support for state control over the economy and the beginnings of decolonization. Socialist countries for a long time excluded FDI from their territories, while developing countries endeavoured to regain control of their natural resources from foreign interests. At the same time, controls and restrictions over the entry and operations of foreign firms were imposed in many countries, with a view to excluding FDI from certain industries for the benefit of domestic investors (or the State), determining the specific terms under which investments were to be made, and ensuring the participation of local nationals in major industries. No international consensus on the pertinent legal norms could be reached at the time.

In the 1980s, a series of national and international developments radically reversed the policy trends prevailing until then, with an immediate impact both on national policies regarding inward FDI and on regional and world-wide efforts at establishing international rules on the subject. Now at the end of the 1990s, host countries are seeking to attract FDI, by dismantling restrictions on its entry and operations and by offering strict guarantees, both national and international, against measures seriously damaging the investors' interests. The tone and direction of international legal discourse has significantly changed. Debate among policy makers is now centred on the most efficient ways of attracting FDI and deriving benefits from it rather than on questions of jurisdiction.

An international legal framework for FDI has begun to emerge. It consists of many kinds of national and international rules and principles, of diverse form and origin, differing in strength and degree of specificity. The entire structure rests on the twin foundations of customary international law and national laws and regulations and relies for its substance on a multitude of international investment agreements (IIAs) and other legal instruments.

An extensive network of bilateral investment promotion and protection treaties has come into existence. They are highly standardized, yet they appear to be capable of adapting to special circumstances. Their principal focus has been from the very start on the protection of investments against nationalizations or expropriations and on free transfer of funds, although they also cover a number of other areas. Regional and plurilateral international arrangements, while binding on a limited number of countries in each case, are increasingly important in matters of FDI. They help to change pre-existing structures of law and policy and create important habits and patterns of expectations on a broader transnational level. Economic integration agreements are a significant subcategory of regional instruments, whose importance has grown in recent years. At the multilateral level, there is no comprehensive instrument on the subject, although a number of recent multilateral instruments of less

* The present chapter is based on a 1999 manuscript prepared by Arghyrios A. Fatouros with contribution from Victoria Aranda. The final version reflects comments received from Giorgio Sacerdoti.

comprehensive scope are directly relevant, dealing with particular aspects of the FDI process.

Legal rules of other kinds, of varying normative intensity and general applicability, are also relevant. "Soft law" texts, adopted by States or international organizations on a non-binding basis, are important elements of the framework. Corporate codes of conduct and other texts of private origin help to formulate widely accepted prescriptions. Transnational arbitration not only provides useful procedures for dispute settlement but also, through the corpus of its awards, gradually fills in the normative conceptual framework for FDI issues.

In terms of substance, the provisions of IIAs must be perceived in their constant interaction with national policies and measures. They concern two principal types of issues. A first class of provisions is linked to the process of liberalization, which, in its application to FDI, involves the gradual decrease or elimination of measures and restrictions on the entry and operations of firms, especially foreign ones; the application of positive standards of treatment with a view to the elimination of discrimination against foreign enterprises; and the implementation of measures and policies seeking to promote the proper operation of markets. A second category of issues covers provisions that concern the protection of foreign investments already made against government measures damaging to them. As to both types of issues, it is important to consider the provisions and approaches which import into the operation of IIAs the flexibility necessary for enhancing the development of the host countries concerned.

An examination of the key issues involved starts from the question of definition. In legal instruments, definitions are not neutral and objective descriptions of concepts; they form part of the instrument's normative content and determine the object to which an instrument's rules apply. The way in which a term is defined, whether by a formal definition or through the manner in which it is used, affects significantly the substance of the legal rules involved.

Government measures concerning FDI have historically often involved the exercise of controls over the admission of investments. Such controls may extend from prohibition to selective admission to mere registration. Certain key industries may be closed to foreign investment, or investment in them may be allowed subject to conditions. The screening of investments before admission was once very common but is now to be found in fewer cases and is less strict and demanding.

Once admitted in a country, foreign affiliates are subject to that country's jurisdiction. Recent efforts have focused on the elimination (or limitation) of discrimination against them, by applying with respect to entry as well as post-admission operations the relevant international standards of treatment, namely, "most-favoured-nation" treatment and national treatment, involving respectively no discrimination between foreign firms on account of their national origin and no discrimination as between foreign and domestic firms. In the application of treatment standards, a number of exceptions or qualifications are allowed, the most frequent among them being those grounded on public order and health and national security. The national treatment standard may expressly not apply to particular industries, whether through "negative" or "positive" lists.

In an increasingly integrated world economy, the proper functioning of the market depends not only on the control of government measures that seek directly to regulate the conduct of foreign investors, but also on the presence of a broader national and international legal framework protecting the market from public or private actions and policies that distort its operation. Regional and to a lesser extent multilateral instruments already embody rules and mechanisms to that effect, although the general picture is still mixed and no comprehensive regulatory framework has emerged. In the context of FDI, certain international standards may be emerging which relate to the conduct of transnational corporations (TNCs) and their affiliates. While the legal mechanisms by which such standards may become operative are complicated and at this moment still uncertain, the contents of such standards are becoming increasingly clear and definite in a number of areas, such as competition and restrictive business practices, the protection of the environment and bribery and illicit payments.

The second principal category of issues in IIAs concerns "investment protection", that is to say, the international rules and principles designed to protect the interests of foreign investors against host government actions unduly detrimental to their interests. The norms in question have their roots in customary law but in recent years they have found expression in numerous treaty provisions. The principal government measures against which investors seek protection are expropriations, nationalizations and other major cases of deprivation of property and infringement of property rights of investors. Relevant international law norms have been the object of considerable debate in the decades since the Second World War. While a number of preconditions for the legality of such takings are mentioned in relevant instruments and debates, in practice, most of the debate has centred on the requirement of compensation and the modalities of its assessment and payment. More recently, in the past two decades, concern has shifted from dealing with past situations to establishing rules for the future. Host countries appear to be increasingly inclined to provide assurances of fair treatment to future investors, including undertakings against expropriation, promises of full compensation and acceptance of dispute settlement procedures. The formulation of pertinent provisions in international instruments raises issues related to the problems of definition. Efforts to expand the scope of the notion of expropriation or "taking", by covering indirect measures or by including permits and licences in the definition of investors' assets, raise the possibility of excessively limiting generally accepted regulatory powers of the host State.

In the second place, protection provisions seek to cover other government measures, possibly less catastrophic but still seriously detrimental to an investor's interests, such as discriminatory taxation, disregard of intellectual property rights, or arbitrary refusal of licences. In this respect, the general non-discrimination standards may be invoked as well as certain broad standards, such as that of "fair and equitable treatment".

A third category of protection provisions covers measures which, although not necessarily unfair or even unpredictable, affect foreign investors in a disproportionate manner, compared to domestic enterprises, so that pertinent assurances are considered necessary. The principal such provisions concern the transfer of funds (profits, capital, royalties, etc.) by the investor outside the host country and the possibility of employing foreign managerial or specialized personnel without restrictions.

Protection provisions are supplemented by provisions concerning the settlement of disputes. Of the several types of disputes possible, those between the investor and another private party are normally left to be resolved by the host country judicial system or by voluntary arbitration between the parties. Disputes between States concerning the interpretation or application of the IIA involved are usually dealt with on the basis of State-to-State arbitration or adjudication before the International Court of Justice. Disputes between an investor and the host State are the ones where the search for a dispute settlement method has been most active in recent years. In the past, such disputes either were resolved by the host country's national courts or resulted in an interstate dispute, through espousal of the private claim by the State of the investor's nationality. Today, most IIAs contain provisions that allow investors to have recourse to international arbitration. A choice of procedures is usually provided for, ranging from ad hoc proceedings to procedures under the World-Bank-sponsored 1965 Convention on the Settlement of Investment Disputes between States and Nationals of Other States.

Developing country Governments participate in IIAs because they believe that, on balance, these instruments help them in their efforts towards economic development. The manner and extent to which this is true may vary, depending on the actual contents of the IIA involved. Since IIAs, like all international agreements, limit to a certain extent the freedom of action of the States party to them, the question arises whether and how far developing countries can retain the ability to make the choices and decisions necessary for promoting their development by influencing, through direct or indirect measures, the amount and kinds of FDI that they receive and the conduct of the foreign firms involved.

Several IIAs address such concerns by including in their text, usually in their preamble, declaratory language concerning the promotion of development. Such language may have greater impact when it is formulated in a manner that permits its utilization – in negotiations, in court, or in arbitration – so as to make development a test for the interpretation or application of the instrument's provisions. Promotion of development may also be manifested in the very structure of IIAs, where, for instance, distinctions are made between developed and developing participating countries, and the members of each category do not necessarily have the same rights and duties. There may also be general clauses allowing for special and differential (in fact, favourable) treatment of developing countries. A common device to similar effect is the inclusion of exceptions and special clauses, essentially granting developing countries increased freedom to disregard certain provisions of the instrument, with a view to taking action to promote their development. Such exceptions may take a great variety of forms.

Thus, while non-legal factors – especially economic ones – play a primary role in the determination of FDI flows and their contribution to economic development, IIAs also have an established role in the determinants matrix of FDI and, given the dynamics between economic, social and political factors, IIAs need therefore to provide for a certain flexibility for countries to follow their policies for economic growth and development.

This chapter provides both an overview of the developments in the international legal framework for FDI and an introduction to this collection of *UNCTAD's Issues Papers Series on IIA*. It sets the overall context for each of the issues separately examined in the different chapters in these three volumes.

Introduction

The growth of FDI in quantitative as well as qualitative terms, is at the core of the continuing process of global integration, usually referred to as "globalization". The total volume of FDI has kept increasing: in 2003, the world's FDI stock exceeded $8 trillion in book value, while global sales of foreign affiliates had reached $18 trillion, considerably above the level of world exports of goods and services ($9 trillion). In terms of operational forms, the relatively isolated operators of the past have been replaced by increasingly integrated TNCs. A new international actor has thus come to the fore, whose activities have been a major factor in the unprecedented degree of integration of the world economy. In fact, not only FDI but also a good part of trade, technology transfer and finance are now conducted under the common governance of TNCs. Each of these activities can best be understood today as one of several interwoven modalities of international production rather than as a separate, alternative form of operation (UNCTAD, 1999a; see also the chapter on FDI and development in Volume III).

In this transformation, legal and policy change, at the national and international levels, has been both cause and effect. The lowering of national barriers to trade and other forms of economic intercourse, throughout the half century since the end of the Second World War and at an increasing pace in the past decade, has made possible close interactions across borders and has thereby facilitated the internationalization of production. This process has put continuing pressure on national policy makers at all levels to help create a legal framework to match the needs and capabilities of the world economy, while ensuring that particular national economies share in world growth and development.

A major consequence has been that the legal regulation of FDI is now increasingly accepted as a matter of international concern. Only a few decades ago, FDI was still perceived as being governed mainly by national legal rules and principles. International law was deemed to be relevant chiefly with respect to the initial allocation of national jurisdiction and in exceptional circumstances, especially in cases of government action causing major disruptions to foreign investment operations. Today, the accepted role of international law rules and processes – customary, conventional or other – in investment matters has considerably expanded and is under constant pressure to expand further. The substance of pertinent rules is itself rapidly changing.

While there is no single legal instrument covering all aspects of FDI, a broad international legal framework is taking shape, consisting of a wide variety of principles and rules, of diverse origins and forms, differing in their strength and specificity and operating at several levels, with gaps in their coverage of issues and countries. This framework includes rules of customary international law, bilateral, regional and multilateral agreements, acts of international institutions, and authoritative texts without formal binding force, such as declarations adopted by States or resolutions of international organization organs, all in interplay with and against the background of national legal rules and procedures.[1]

This chapter seeks to present a broad overview of this international legal framework, focusing on international agreements (in force or not yet in force) that directly concern and affect FDI, while also taking into account other major components of this framework (trends in national law, non-binding international instruments, etc.)[2] (annex table 1). It is in a way a substantive introduction to these volumes. They address key concepts and issues in IIAs, seeking to present and analyse them, with a view to assisting officials from member countries, especially developing ones, who may participate in international negotiations concerning foreign direct investment (table 1).

The present chapter starts with a summary historical overview of law and policy on FDI, with an emphasis on the recent decades. It then considers the "sources" of international FDI law, reviewing the general approaches and the types of

Table 1. Topics covered by this volume

Admission and establishment	Host country operational measures	State contracts
Competition	Illicit payments	Taking of property
Dispute settlement (investor-State)	Incentives	Taxation
Dispute settlement (State-State)	Investment-related trade measures	Transfer of funds
Employment	Lessons from the MAI	Transfer of technology
Environment	Most-favoured-nation treatment	Transfer pricing
Fair and equitable treatment	National treatment	Transparency
Foreign direct investment and development	Scope and definition	Trends in IIAs: an overview
Home country measures	Social responsibility	

legal instruments in use over the years. The core of the chapter is the next section, which examines the key substantive issues of law and policy concerning FDI. The chapter concludes with a discussion of the ways in which IIAs and their provisions seek (or may seek) to take into account the need to give effect to the overriding necessity to promote the development of the developing and least developed countries.[3]

A necessary caveat should be made at the very start: law, national and international, has played a prominent role in the radical transformation of the world economy in the past 50 years. Yet, focusing on the legal dimensions of current trends concerning FDI should not obscure the primordial importance of political, economic, social and other non-legal factors. Laws and policies may facilitate and channel, sometimes indeed may make possible, business action and economic developments, but they are not, as a rule, the prime movers, the initial causes.[4] They may be necessary, but they are rarely, if ever, sufficient. Accordingly, this discussion of legal and policy aspects of FDI, while recognizing the fact that they affect outcomes in important ways, does not imply a claim to the effect that they are controlling.

Section I Historical Overview

To understand current legal approaches to FDI, it is useful to begin with a brief look at the historical evolution of national and international law and policy on the matter.[5]

A. The legal situation up to the Second World War

The rules of classical international law, i.e. public international law as crystallized by the end of the nineteenth century, were, as already noted, mainly concerned with the allocation of jurisdiction among States. Since FDI issues involve primarily relations between foreign investors and host States, they were treated in the main as matters of national law. International law dealt with related problems only in exceptional cases, in terms of the treatment of the property of aliens (foreigners) by the host State, the rules concerning the international responsibility of States for acts in violation of international law, and the exercise of diplomatic protection by the State of the aliens' nationality.

In the liberal era of the nineteenth century, States did not by and large attempt systematically to control or restrict international private capital transactions. In economic and political terms, indirect foreign investment -- loans and the floating of government bonds -- was far more important than direct (Nurkse, 1954). In the first decade of the twentieth century, multilateral efforts to address investment issues resulted in the Drago-Porter Convention of 1907 (AJIL, 1908), which imposed limitations on the use of armed force for the recovery of public debts. The FDI that did exist at that time involved in the main the exploitation of natural resources (e.g. plantations or mines) and on occasion the operation of public utilities. Roughly the same situation prevailed in colonial territories, which, however, were not treated as "foreign" in their relationship to the metropolitan country. In a few cases, disputes arose over the expropriation of the property of individual aliens to serve specific public purposes, such as road-building, or sometimes on other, less widely acceptable, grounds. Most legal debate concerning the treatment of the property of aliens arose in the context of changes of sovereignty over territories (because of the creation of new States or the cession of territory). In terms of international law doctrine, the issue of the "acquired rights" of aliens related to matters of State succession, rather than investment protection in the modern sense of the term.

FDI started acquiring increased importance and assuming the forms prevalent today as the nineteenth century neared its end. The government measures involved also began to resemble those that have been of concern in more recent times, increasingly acquiring a general rather than an individualized character (e.g. land reform). In strict legal terms, FDI remained largely a matter of national concern, moving onto the international plane only in exceptional, although less and less rare, cases, whenever rules and principles of customary international law were deemed to have been infringed.

Then as now, two fundamental principles of public international law were involved in such cases: on the one hand, the principle of territorial sovereignty, asserting each State's full and exclusive jurisdiction over persons and events in its territory, and on the other, the principle of nationality, involving each State's interest in the proper treatment of its nationals abroad.

At the turn of the century, capital-exporting States insisted on the importance of the latter principle and treated all measures causing uncompensated injury to the person or property of foreigners as violations of the international minimum standard of treatment to which aliens were entitled. Developing, capital-importing, countries, especially Latin American ones, stressed the exclusive character of territorial sovereignty and held that foreign investors were entitled to no more than equality of treatment with the host State's nationals. In legal doctrine, largely as a consequence of constitutional and other distinctions between property and contract, the taking of the property of aliens was clearly distinguished from measures affecting State contracts with aliens (usually involving public utility concessions and the like). Latin American countries, in particular, insisted that such contracts were governed solely by national law, by virtue of both general principle and express contractual provisions (Calvo doctrine and related practices) (Shea, 1955).

Later on, during the first half of the twentieth century, FDI issues came increasingly to the fore, even though disputes concerning government debt continued to be more important (Borchard and Wynne, 1951). Generalized government measures affecting foreign property started to become more common. Prominent among them were land reform efforts in the aftermath of the Mexican Revolution and in some countries of Central and Eastern Europe after the First World War; the nationalization of an entire economy, after the advent of the Soviet Union; or the nationalization of natural resources, as in Mexico. The legal questions that arose became more and more difficult to resolve on the basis of classical international law rules, which had been developed under different conditions: they were meant to deal with individual measures and to protect physical persons, often in the aftermath of civil disturbances or changes in sovereignty over territories. The diplomatic correspondence between the United States and Mexico in the 1930s over the Mexican nationalizations of land and petroleum holdings of United States nationals illustrated clearly the difficulties of reaching a generally agreed position. Mexico relied on a State's sovereign right to control its natural resources and on the lack of established rules in international law requiring payment of full compensation in the case of generalized measures; the United States, while recognizing a Government's right to nationalize property, insisted that payment of "prompt, adequate and effective" compensation was required in all cases of takings of alien property.

B. Developments since 1945: the early years

This was the general international legal picture at the end of the Second World War. At that time, in the context of the creation of a broad organizational framework for the post-war economy, an attempt was made to formulate international principles concerning FDI in the Havana Charter of 1948. The Charter was intended to establish an International Trade Organization and dealt mainly with international trade (the original General Agreement on Tariffs and Trade (GATT) was based on its trade provisions) (United Nations, 1950). It also included, however, important provisions that addressed, directly or indirectly, other issues, such as investment and competition. The initial United States proposals for the provisions on foreign investment were intended to provide protection to investors, but, during the last phase of the negotiations, important qualifications were introduced through the efforts of developing, particularly Latin American, countries. The end product (box 1) met with strong opposition by investor interests in developed countries, and this was in fact partly responsible for the Charter 's failure to enter into force. A comparable effort at the regional (inter-American) level, the Economic Agreement of Bogota of 1948 (OAS, 1961), had the same fate.

Box 1. Havana Charter for an International Trade Organization (1948)
[excerpts]

Article 12
International Investment for Economic Development and Reconstruction

1. The Members recognize that:
   (a) international investment, both public and private, can be of great value in promoting economic development and reconstruction and consequent social progress;
   (b) the international flow of capital will be stimulated to the extent that Members afford nationals of other countries opportunities for investment and security for existing and future investments;
   (c) without prejudice to existing international agreements to which Members are parties, a Member has the right:
      (i) to take any appropriate safeguards necessary to ensure that foreign investment is not used as a basis for interference in its internal affairs or national policies;
      (ii) to determine whether and to what extent and upon what terms it will allow future foreign investment;
      (iii) to prescribe and give effect on just terms to requirements as to the ownership of existing and future investments;
      (iv) to prescribe and give effect to other reasonable requirements with respect to existing and future investments;
   (d) the interests of Members whose nationals are in a position to provide capital for international investment and of Members who desire to obtain the use of such capital to promote their economic development or reconstruction may be promoted if such Members enter into bilateral or multilateral agreements relating to the opportunities and security for investment which the Members are prepared to offer and any limitations which they are prepared to accept of the rights referred to in sub-paragraph (c).

Source: UNCTAD, 1996a, vol.1, pp. 4-5.

The first post-war years were marked by large-scale nationalizations of key industries, affecting foreign as well as domestic firms, not only in the countries that became part of the socialist bloc, but also in Western Europe (e.g. France and the United Kingdom) (Foighel, 1957; Katzarov, 1960). As colonial territories began to acquire their independence, moreover, takings of foreign-owned property multiplied. For many of the countries emerging into political independence, but also for some of the economically weaker States that had been independent for some time, a principal political and economic goal was to regain national control over their natural wealth and their economy. Their Governments feared that foreign control over natural resources and key industries would deprive the countries concerned of economic benefits and compromise their newly found political independence. A sharp distinction was usually made at the time between old investments, made during the colonial period, and new ones, after independence. The number of cases of nationalization or expropriation of foreign property (chiefly in natural resources) kept increasing worldwide, reaching its peak in the early 1970s (figure 1).

Figure 1. Changing moods: the number of nationalization measures, 1960-1992[a]

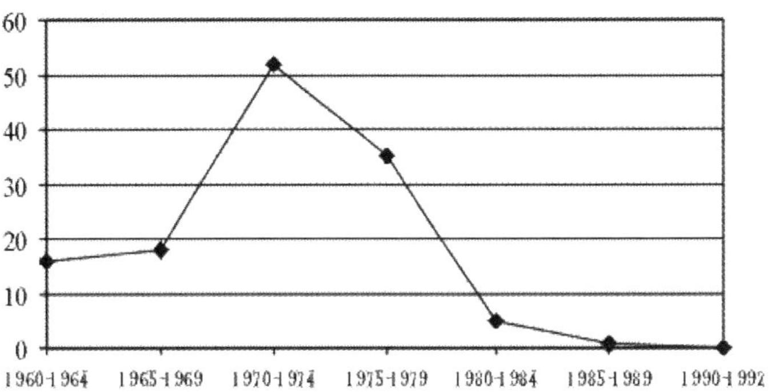

Source: UNCTAD, 1993, p. 17.

[a] Nationalization numbers refer to the average number of measures per year during the period indicated.

As a result of such conditions, throughout the first three decades after the Second World War, concerns of host countries, particularly developing ones, and foreign investors and their countries of origin focused on FDI in natural resources and in key industries. The attitude of developing host countries towards FDI generally combined a realization of the need for and possible benefits from FDI with the conviction that national controls and limitations on FDI were necessary. This attitude also found expression in United Nations resolutions and studies concerning the need for an increase in FDI flows to developing countries and the appropriate methods for bringing this about.[6] A watershed in the efforts to find common ground between developed and developing countries on the topic was Resolution 1803 (XVII) of the United Nations General Assembly, adopted in 1962, concerning the principle of permanent sovereignty over natural wealth and resources. Coming after a series of less elaborate resolutions on the same topic in the 1950s, the 1962 text (box 2) gave to the principle its definite formulation. While recognizing the rights of peoples and nations over their natural resources, including their right to exercise control over investments in such resources and to nationalize them, the resolution provided expressly for the payment of appropriate compensation for any taking of property and stressed that agreements between foreign investors and Governments should be observed in good faith (Kemper, 1976; Rosenberg, 1983).

Box 2. United Nations General Assembly Resolution 1803 (XVII) (1962): Permanent sovereignty over natural resources [Excerpts]

The General Assembly,

....

Declares that :

1. The right of peoples and nations to permanent sovereignty over their natural wealth and resources must be exercised in the interest of their national development and of the well-being of the people of the State concerned.
2. The exploration, development and disposition of such resources, as well as the import of the foreign capital required for these purposes, should be in conformity with the rules and conditions which the peoples and nations freely consider to be necessary or desirable with regard to the authorization, restriction or prohibition of such activities.
3. In cases where authorization is granted, the capital imported and the earnings on that capital shall be governed by the terms thereof, by the national legislation in force, and by international law. The profits derived must be shared in the proportions freely agreed upon, in each case, between the investors and the recipient State, due care being taken to ensure that there is no impairment, for any reason, of that State's sovereignty over its natural wealth and resources.
4. Nationalization, expropriation or requisitioning shall be based on grounds or reasons of public utility, security or the national interest which are recognized as overriding purely individual or private interests, both domestic and foreign. In such cases the owner shall be paid appropriate compensation, in accordance with the rules in force in the State taking such measures in the exercise of its sovereignty and in accordance with international law. In any case where the question of compensation gives rise to a controversy, the national jurisdiction of the State taking such measures shall be exhausted. However, upon agreement by sovereign States and other parties concerned, settlement of the dispute should be made through arbitration or international adjudication.

.....

8. Foreign investment agreements freely entered into by or between sovereign States shall be observed in good faith; States and international organizations shall strictly and conscientiously respect the sovereignty of peoples and nations over their natural wealth and resources in accordance with the Charter and the principles set forth in the present resolution.

Source: UNCTAD, 1996a, vol.1, pp. 22-23.

Initially, there was less legal concern over control of the entry of foreign firms and their routine treatment after establishment. These were left largely to the municipal law of host countries; only extreme regulatory measures, essentially tantamount to takings, were addressed by international law norms. Elaborate administrative machinery for the control of the entry and operations of foreign investments was put in place in many countries with a view to excluding such investments from certain industries for the benefit of domestic investors (or the State), determining the specific terms under which investments were to be made, and ensuring the participation of local nationals in major industries. While this trend was particularly strong in developing countries, such controls were also common, although less strict and less rigid, in many developed countries.

Several early proposals by private investor associations for the conclusion of a comprehensive international agreement were aimed primarily at the protection of foreign investments against expropriation rather than at the liberalization of the admission of investments. These proposals did not find wide support (Fatouros, 1961; Seidl-Hohenveldern, 1961). When developed country Governments took over the task, they had no greater success. In the Organisation for Economic Co-operation and Development (OECD), a draft Convention on the Protection of Foreign Property was prepared and in 1967 was approved by the Organisation's Council, but was never opened for signature. The one successful effort on a worldwide basis was directed at a specific aspect of FDI protection. This was the World Bank-sponsored Convention on the Settlement of Investment Disputes between States and Nationals of Other States, signed in 1965, initially with rather limited participation, although the number of States party to it eventually expanded considerably, especially in the 1980s and 1990s, to reach 154 by December 2004 (Broches, 1972).

Around the same time, i.e. in the early 1960s, developed countries embarked upon a process of gradual investment liberalization. The two OECD Codes of Liberalisation, of Capital Movements and of Current Invisible Operations, established binding rules for continuing liberalization and provided effective machinery for gradual implementation and expansion (OECD, 1995). The creation and growth of the European Economic Community (as it was then called), established in 1957, initiated a movement towards regional economic integration, broadly followed later by other groups of countries, developed and developing, which has affected considerably the situation of FDI.

The early 1960s also saw the beginning of the process of negotiating bilateral investment promotion and protection agreements (BITs) (UNCTAD, 1998a). The conclusion of such agreements was recommended early on, in the Havana Charter, while unsuccessful efforts were made to include investment in broader traditional international treaties (treaties "of establishment" or "of Friendship, Commerce and Navigation") (Wilson, 1960; Fatouros, 1962; Preiswerk, 1963). Specialized bilateral treaties, however, dealing solely with investment protection (and to a lesser extent with its promotion), proved more successful, although it was only later, in the late 1980s and 1990s, that they proliferated (figure 2). Through such agreements, an increasing number of developing countries subscribed to basic standards for investment protection and treatment (while rejecting them on the multilateral level), though typically not to positive rights of entry and establishment, which remained within the discretion of the host contracting party.

Figure 2. Bilateral investment treaties, 1959-2003 (cumulative number)

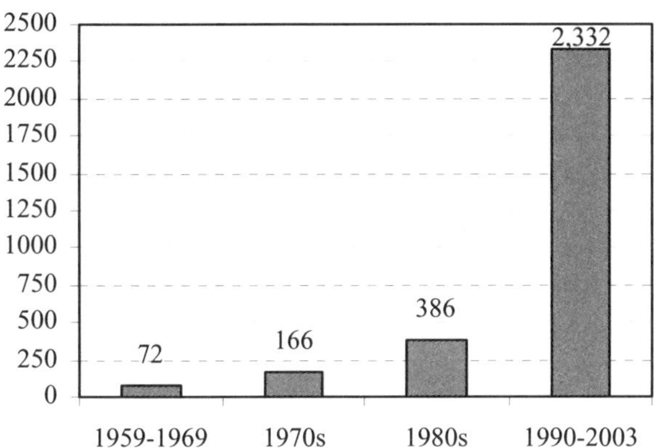

Source: UNCTAD database on BITs.

C. The decade of the 1970s

In the early 1970s, the energy crisis had a profound impact on the international environment for development and for FDI. The atmosphere in international forums became for a time more favourable to the views of the developing countries, and they were able to set the agenda -- although not to determine the eventual outcome -- in international economic organizations. Developed countries were apprehensive over the control of energy resources by what appeared to be at the time a rather solid coalition of developing countries. Before this short period was over, the developing countries sought to assert the legitimacy of their interests and perceptions on FDI issues, among others.

A direct result of the energy crisis was the Conference on International Economic Cooperation, which met in Paris from 1975 to 1977. Within its framework representatives from 27 developed and developing (including oil-exporting) countries conducted negotiations concerning energy, trade and financing, including FDI. While there was agreement on a significant, and wide-ranging, agenda of issues, no common ground was reached on several critical points. Around the same time, the developing countries' demands for a radical restructuring of the world trading and financial system, under the banner of the creation of a New International Economic Order, found formal expression in a series of programmatic texts embodied in General Assembly resolutions, adopted by large majorities, but not without dissent. The most relevant for present purposes are the 1974 Declaration on the Establishment of a New International Economic Order and its accompanying Programme of Action (Resolutions 3201(S-VI) and 3202(S-VI)) and the Charter of Economic Rights and Duties of States (Resolution 3281(XXIX)), also adopted in 1974 (box 3). The latter, in particular, sought to restate the basic legal principles governing international economic relations, focusing attention on developing country demands for economic independence and stressing the legitimacy of their concerns. The Charter's provisions on the treatment of FDI emphasized the role of host country Governments and insisted on the exercise of host country jurisdiction and national controls over foreign investment and specifically over TNCs (Virally, 1974; Flores Caballero et al., 1976; Meagher, 1979).

The structure and role of TNCs had first been described by business administration experts and economists in the late 1950s and early 1960s. However, there was no universal agreement as to what the economic and social effects of such firms were. Some saw TNCs as a means of improving the well-being of the societies in which they operated, especially in their function as transferors of productive technology and know-how across borders. Others saw a different picture: they tended to view TNCs as monopolistic entities that grew through the exploitation of their competitive advantage in technology and know-how at the expense of host country competitors, bringing economic dislocation and dependency in their wake. More worryingly, some began to see TNCs as a threat to local political and cultural freedoms, given their power to influence the direction of local social and political development. The result was a polarization of views as to the costs and benefits of FDI. However, such polar opinions did not survive the growth in knowledge and experience about the actual operations of TNCs, with the result that now the study and discussion of TNCs have moved into a more informed and less partisan setting.

Box 3. United Nations General Assembly Resolution 3281 (XXIX) (1974): Charter of Economic Rights and Duties of States [Excerpts]

Article 1

Every State has the sovereign and inalienable right to choose its economic system as well as its political, social and cultural systems in accordance with the will of its people, without outside interference, coercion or threat in any form whatsoever.

Article 2

1. Every State has and shall freely exercise full permanent sovereignty, including possession, use and disposal, over all its wealth, natural resources and economic activities.
2. Each State has the right:
   (a) To regulate and exercise authority over foreign investment within its national jurisdiction in accordance with its laws and regulations and in conformity with its national objectives and priorities. No State shall be compelled to grant preferential treatment to foreign investment;
   (b) To regulate and supervise the activities of transnational corporations within its national jurisdiction and take measures to ensure that such activities comply with its laws, rules and regulations and conform with its economic and social policies. Transnational corporations shall not intervene in the internal affairs of a host State. Every State should, with full regard for its sovereign rights, cooperate with other States in the exercise of the right set forth in this subparagraph;
   (c) To nationalize, expropriate or transfer ownership of foreign property, in which case appropriate compensation should be paid by the State adopting such measures, taking into account its relevant laws and regulations and all circumstances that the State considers pertinent. In any case where the question of compensation gives rise to a controversy, it shall be settled under the domestic law of the nationalizing State and by its tribunals, unless it is freely and mutually agreed by all States concerned that other peaceful means be sought on the basis of the sovereign equality of States and in accordance with the principle of free choice of means.

Source: UNCTAD, 1996a, vol. 1, p. 61.

On the national level, and occasionally on the regional one as well, elaborate structures of control over the entry and operations of TNCs were established in many developing countries. In order to ensure that TNCs would serve on a concrete and immediate basis the development needs of the host country, as determined by its Government, entry of foreign firms or investment of foreign capital was allowed on the basis of sometimes quite elaborate approval procedures. A characteristic regional instrument that reflected national approaches and methods was Decision 24 of the Andean Pact, adopted in 1970, which imposed screening procedures and other controls on FDI and on technology transfer, including a "fadeout" provision, requiring the disinvestment of foreign firms after a number of years. At the national level, "investment laws" (or "codes") provided for screening procedures, frequently combined with tax incentives and other measures intended to attract as well as regulate FDI.

At the same time, the efforts to establish standards for the conduct of TNCs led to negotiations for the adoption in legally non-binding forms of "international codes of conduct" for TNC activities (Horn, 1980; Metaxas, 1988). The lead was taken by the OECD. In 1976, the Organisation's Council adopted a Declaration on International Investment and Multinational Enterprises that included a set of voluntary Guidelines for Multinational Enterprises. They consist of recommendations addressed to enterprises, not to Governments, which, while requiring respect of host country laws and policies, also establish international standards of proper conduct. They cover both general issues and specific topics, such as employment and industrial relations and the disclosure of information. The Guidelines are complemented by institutional machinery charged with two principal tasks: on the one hand, providing "clarifications" on the basis of concrete cases; and, on the other, ensuring the revision of the Guidelines as the need arises. The Guidelines are still valid, after several successive partial reformulations, and are indeed the object of increasing recent attention, as a process of reviewing is ongoing. In addition to the Guidelines, the Declaration included decisions addressed to Governments that dealt with several specific aspects of TNC treatment: national treatment; problems of incentives and disincentives; and conflicting requirements imposed on TNCs. Taken together, these instruments provided important elements of a framework on both the conduct and the treatment of TNCs in the OECD area.

Parallel efforts were undertaken within the framework of the United Nations system. The most comprehensive instrument of this kind was the United Nations draft Code of Conduct on Transnational Corporations (box 4). After lengthy negotiations, from the late-1970s to the mid-1980s, and despite agreement over the contents of many of its provisions, a number of important points were left open (especially as regards host country obligations), and the instrument was never adopted, even in non-binding form. Although the United Nations draft Code of Conduct and the OECD Guidelines resembled one another in significant respects, the former's scope was considerably broader.

Box 4. United Nations draft Code of Conduct on Transnational Corporations [Structure of the 1983 version]

PREAMBLE AND OBJECTIVES

DEFINITIONS AND SCOPE OF APPLICATION

ACTIVITIES OF TRANSNATIONAL CORPORATIONS

A. General and political
- Respect of national sovereignty and observance of domestic laws, regulations and administrative practices
- Adherence to economic goals and development objectives, policies and priorities
- Review and renegotiation of contracts
- Adherence to socio-cultural objectives and values
- Respect for human rights and fundamental freedoms
- Non-collaboration by transnational corporations with racist minority regimes in southern Africa
- Non-interference in internal political affairs
- Non-interference in intergovernmental relations
- Abstention from corrupt practices

B. Economic, financial and social
- Ownership and control
- Balance of payments and financing
- Transfer pricing
- Taxation
- Competition and restrictive business practices
- Transfer of technology
- Consumer protection
- Environmental protection

C. Disclosure of information

TREATMENT OF TRANSNATIONAL CORPORATIONS

A. General treatment of transnational corporations by the countries in which they operate
B. Nationalization and compensation
C. Jurisdiction

INTERGOVERNMENTAL CO-OPERATION

IMPLEMENTATION OF THE CODE OF CONDUCT

A. Action at the national level
B. International institutional machinery
C. Review procedure

Source: UNCTAD, 1996a, pp. 161-180.

Other codes of conduct, dealing with specific issues, were also negotiated, with varying results: the International Labour Organization's (ILO) Governing Body adopted in 1977 a Tripartite Declaration of Principles concerning Multinational Enterprises and Social Policy. The United Nations General Assembly adopted in 1980 a Set of Multilaterally Agreed Equitable Rules and Principles for the Control of Restrictive Business Practices, negotiated under the auspices of UNCTAD. On the other hand, long negotiations over an international Code of Conduct on Transfer of Technology within the framework of UNCTAD did not lead to adoption of a final agreed instrument. However, a number of other similar instruments, dealing with limited aspects of TNC activity, were adopted; for instance, the International Code of Marketing of Breast-milk Substitutes of the World Health Organization (WHO) and the United Nations guidelines for consumer protection.

The negotiations over international codes of conduct, whether ultimately successful or not, were instrumental in defining the areas of common understanding over the proper conduct of TNCs and in clarifying the standards for their treatment. While the proposed or adopted texts were largely concerned with reaffirming the competence of host States to determine and enforce national policies, they also sought to formulate international rules that went beyond merely requiring compliance with local laws and policies and themselves specified the appropriate kinds of conduct. Thus, the idea that international rules were appropriate for dealing with FDI and with important international actors, such as TNCs, acquired greater currency and acceptance, even though there remained considerable controversy concerning the actual substance of such rules.

D. The past two decades

When describing trends, an impression of uniformity, simplicity or clarity can be misleading. The general climate surrounding FDI started to change in the 1980s and is still fluid. It is now more favourable to FDI; but it still consists of many instruments and norms at several levels, differing from one another in many respects. Neither the past nor the present legal and policy situation concerning FDI is simple, universal and univocal. It is only by keeping this caveat in mind that one can correctly understand the current situation and its antecedents.

A series of national and international developments has led to a radical reversal of the policy trends prevailing.[7] To begin with, the international economy has changed. The industries in which TNCs are active are not the same as those of 20 years ago, and related attitudes have changed accordingly. As already noted, in the first decades after the Second World War, most discussions on FDI dealt, expressly or by implication, with the exploitation of petroleum and other natural resources. In recent years, while investment in natural resources has remained important, concern has shifted to investments in manufacturing, services and high technology. The very perception of the investment process has changed, reflecting current realities of the world economy. As the Uruguay Round negotiations have made evident, the *problématique* of FDI and technology transfer has become more closely linked to that of international trade, in the sense that they are both increasingly perceived as intertwined modalities of operation in the international production process. Some of these changes are reflected in varying manners in the more recent IIAs, but a more definite comprehensive picture of the process is only now beginning to appear.

The international political environment has also changed radically. The bargaining position of developing countries is now weaker, and their ability to determine the agenda of international economic relations decreased considerably. By the end of the 1970s, the developed countries had fully recovered from the "oil shock" and had regained their self-assurance and their willingness to pursue their perceptions and interests. On the other hand, the onset of the debt crisis in the developing countries, including in several of the oil-producing ones, helped to make these countries less assertive. The debt crisis brought about a relative scarcity of indirect investment and made FDI more desirable: not only was it relatively more easily available but it also did not burden the country as much with debt, and brought additional contributions to the host economy, in terms of know-how, technology, skills, and access to markets. Host countries thus became more interested in attracting foreign investors. Besides, in most developing countries, the process of gaining control over natural resources had considerably advanced since the immediate post-war period and was no longer a matter of first priority; interest shifted to the need for investment in other sectors and to the competition for it. Finally, the emphasis on the need to control FDI was further affected by a spreading perception that, despite marked successes in a few cases, the foreign investment control policies of host countries had often been ineffective.

Other important developments played a role. On an international political level, the relative cohesion of the third world decreased considerably, while the gradual collapse of the socialist bloc and the end of the cold war helped to strengthen market-oriented attitudes and forces and deprived developing countries of a bargaining tool. The international economic environment was drastically altered by the growth of TNCs and increasing global integration. In the national policies of many developed countries, where the need for direct government intervention in the economy was for long widely accepted, market-oriented approaches gained political momentum. The hegemony of these views soon spread to many developing countries as well, directly affecting their national economic policies.

All these developments had a significant impact on national laws and policies regarding inward FDI. The past two decades have been a time of investment liberalization, promotion and protection: of the 1,885 national FDI policy changes identified for the period 1991-2003, 94 per cent went in the direction of creating a more favourable climate for FDI (table 2). The screening requirements and other entry regulations imposed earlier have been considerably softened or eliminated. Restrictions on the operations of foreign affiliates have weakened considerably; investors are increasingly allowed freely to transfer their profits and capital out of the host country. The incidence of property takings has greatly decreased. And acceptance of international arbitration for resolving conflicts between investors and host Governments is expanding. Host countries now seek to attract foreign investment, by offering strict guarantees, both national and international, against measures seriously damaging the investors' interests.

Equally important is the change in the tone and direction of legal discourse. Emphasis is no longer laid on the international principles concerning national jurisdiction and its limits or the customary international law on the treatment of foreign property and foreign firms. Debate among policy makers is now centred on the most efficient ways of attracting foreign investment and technology and deriving benefits from it so as to enhance a country's economic growth. At the same time, the role of international law rules and processes in investment matters is increasingly accepted, even though the substance of pertinent rules is itself still changing.

Table 2. National regulatory changes, 1991-2003

Item	1991	1995	1998	1999	2000	2001	2002	2003
Number of countries that introduced changes in their investment regimes	35	64	60	63	69	71	70	82
Number of regulatory changes	82	112	145	140	150	208	248	244
of which:								
More favourable to FDI [a]	80	106	136	131	147	194	236	220
Less favourable to FDI [b]	2	6	9	9	3	14	12	24

Source: UNCTAD, 2004a, p. 8.

[a] Including liberalizing changes or changes aimed at strengthening market functioning, as well as increased incentives.

[b] Including changes aimed at increasing control as well as reducing incentives.

Recent policy changes at the national level, however, have not yet been extensively reflected in general multilateral instruments. The 1985 World Bank-sponsored Convention Establishing the Multilateral Investment Guarantee Agency (MIGA) heralded a period of increased interest in FDI. Yet, the most important multilateral instruments expressing the new trends are those of the 1994 Uruguay Round agreements, which address only in part topics directly or indirectly related to investment, especially the General Agreement on Trade in Services (GATS), the Agreement on Trade-Related Aspects of Intellectual Property Rights (TRIPS), and the Agreement on Trade-Related Investment Measures (TRIMs). Such trends have also found some expression in non-binding texts. The 1992 Guidelines on the Treatment of Foreign Direct Investment prepared within the framework of the World Bank are of particular relevance.

To understand fully the effects of current trends, one has to look at instruments at other levels, primarily regional and interregional, as well as bilateral. At the regional level, liberalization trends are particularly apparent in instruments reflecting the numerous efforts (of varying degrees of intensity and success) at economic integration. A particularly telling case is that of the 1991 amendments in the Andean countries' instruments on foreign investment and transfer of technology that replaced earlier, more restrictive, regulations. Equally relevant are the provisions of the association agreements concluded after 1989 by the European Community with countries of Central and Eastern Europe, as well as those of successive Lomé Conventions (and their successor) between the European Community and a large group of African, Caribbean and Pacific States.

Other economic integration instruments are also important. It is indeed significant that many, although not all, of the several recent free trade agreements do not limit themselves to trade issues only but also address FDI and related topics. The North American Free Trade Agreement (NAFTA) (1992) between Canada, Mexico and the United States may cover three States only, but their size and overall importance, as well as the process of liberalization the agreement has set in motion, make it particularly important. The two 1994 Protocols of the MERCOSUR countries specifically address FDI issues from countries inside and outside the regional economic integration arrangement.

Beyond regional integration efforts, similar processes are at work. The 1994 Asia-Pacific Economic Cooperation (APEC) Non-Binding Investment Principles and the Pacific Basin Charter on International Investments reflect in significant manner the prevailing trends. In October 1998, the members of the Association of South-East Asian Nations (ASEAN) concluded the Framework Agreement on the ASEAN Investment Area with a view to creating a more liberal and transparent investment environment in the area (ASEAN, 1998). Efforts in similar directions are under way in other regions (UNCTAD, 1999a, pp. 121-126).

In a different context, the Energy Charter Treaty, adopted by 50 countries, including most OECD members, countries of Central and Eastern Europe and members of the Commonwealth of Independent States, is limited to the energy sector but contains important provisions on investment liberalization and protection (Waelde, 1996a).

Developments at the OECD have been particularly interesting. The scope of the Liberalisation Codes was gradually expanded. Thus, in 1984, inward direct investment was redefined to cover the rights of establishment, while over the years most member countries lifted the reservations and exceptions on which they had initially insisted. More recently, the fate of the negotiations on a multilateral agreement on investment (MAI) is characteristic both of the current hegemonic position of investment liberalization and protection policies and of the remaining uncertainties, ambiguities and ambivalence. The negotiations, aimed at a text that would promote both the liberalization of investment regulations and the protection of foreign investors, proceeded at first at a fast pace, but then, just when they appeared to be nearing their conclusion, unexpected resistance emerged and the effort was discontinued (see the respective chapter in volume III). The possibility that an agreement on the same topic might be negotiated in a different forum, at the worldwide level, remains open, yet such a text is likely to differ in important respects from the MAI draft (in part precisely because of the failure of the previous effort). The OECD negotiations have however contributed to an important learning process, whose significance was enhanced by the character and intensity of the reactions caused by the draft text.

BITs have continued to be negotiated in increasing numbers, so that by the end of 2003 more than 2,332 such treaties had been concluded, about 85 per cent of them after 1990 (figure 2). In the beginning, the initiative for their conclusion was taken by the major capital-exporting developed countries, and most of these countries are now at the centre of extensive networks of BITs with developing countries or economies in transition. In recent years, however, a considerable number of such treaties has also been concluded by smaller capital-exporting countries, by countries with economies in transition and between developing countries. At the end of 2003, approximately 48 per cent of the total BITs involved developing or transition economies only (figure 3). While the treaties are by no means identical in their scope and language, they are by and large fairly similar in their import and provide important partial elements of the existing legal framework (UNCTAD, 1998a). Finally, the number of double taxation treaties has also risen, to reach 2,316 at the end of 2003 (UNCTAD, 2004a, p. 6).

Figure 3. BITs concluded in 2003, by country group
(Cumulative)

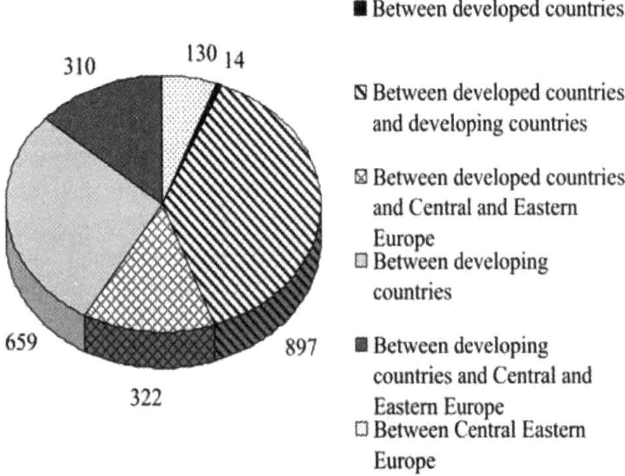

Source: UNCTAD, database on BITs.

Section II Methods and Instruments in Use

As the preceding historical overview has indicated, the international legal framework for FDI consists of a wide variety of national and international rules and principles, differing in form, strength and coverage. The present section attempts a summary listing and review of the methods and instruments in use, seeking briefly to identify the characteristics, possibilities and constraints applicable in each case.

The entire structure rests on the twin foundations of customary international law, on the one hand, and national laws and regulations, on the other. For its concrete substantive content, however, it relies primarily on international agreements as well as on other international legal instruments[8] and on other methods and materials. This review, therefore, first looks at the background for the rules and instruments involved, namely, national laws and regulations and customary international law; then examines the types of international instruments used -- multilateral, plurilateral, regional and bilateral agreements as well as several kinds of "soft law" prescriptions -- and concludes with a glimpse of other materials of immediate relevance, such as the case law of international tribunals, private business instruments and practices and the contributions of scholars and commentators.

A. National laws and regulations

National laws and policies are of paramount importance for FDI, the most concrete and detailed part of its legal framework (Rubin and Wallace, 1994; Juillard, 1994; Muchlinski, 1999). Policy trends concerning the treatment of FDI often make their appearance first at the national level, before spreading into many countries. Of particular importance in this respect are the laws dealing expressly and specifically with FDI. Such foreign investment laws or "codes" have often sought in the past to regulate and attract FDI, on the one hand focusing on conditions for the admission of foreign affiliates and regulation of their operation and on the other seeking to promote foreign investment through tax incentives or special treatment. Recent concerns over countries' competitiveness for FDI have led both to the proliferation of laws establishing specific regimes for FDI (table 3) and to their extensive

Table 3. Countries and territories with special FDI regimes,[a] 1998

Developed countries	Africa	Asia and the Pacific	Latin America and the Caribbean	Central and Eastern Europe [b]
Greece (1953)	Central African Republic (1963)	Kuwait (1965)	Brazil (1962)	Hungary (1988)
Turkey (1954, 1995)[c]	Kenya (1964)	Republic of Korea (1966)	Chile (1974)	Slovenia (1988)
Australia (1975)	Seychelles (1967, 1994)[c]	Pakistan (1976)	Argentina (1976)	Albania (1991)
Canada (1985)	Lesotho (1969)	Cook Islands (1977)	Barbados (1981)	Belarus (1991)
New Zealand (1985)	Liberia (1973)	Tonga (1978)	Panama (1983)	Croatia (1991)
Israel (1990)	Comoros (1982, 1992)[c]	Maldives (1979)	El Salvador (1988)	Estonia (1991)
Spain (1992)	Morocco (1983, 1995)[c]	Saudi Arabia (1979)	Bahamas (1990)	Latvia (1991)
Finland (1993)	Democratic Republic of Congo (1986)	Bangladesh (1980)	Bolivia (1990)	Poland (1991)
Ireland (1994)	Rwanda (1987)	Bahrain (1984)	Trinidad and Tobago (1990)	Romania (1991)
Portugal (1995)	Senegal (1987)	Samoa (1984)	Colombia (1991)	Russian Federation (1991)
France (1996)	Somalia (1987)	Solomon Islands (1984)	Nicaragua (1991)	Slovakia (1991)
	Botswana (1988)	Qatar (1985)	Peru (1991)	Bulgaria (1992)
	Gambia, The (1988)	Viet Nam (1987)	Honduras (1992)	Czech Republic (1992)
	Gabon (1989)	Myanmar (1988)	Paraguay (1992)	Republic of Moldova (1992)
	Mauritania (1989)	Iran, Islamic Republic of (1990)	Venezuela (1992)	Ukraine (1992)
	Niger (1989)	Sri Lanka (1990)	Ecuador (1993)	The former Yugoslav Republic of Macedonia (1993)
	Togo (1989)	Taiwan Province of China (1990)	Mexico (1993)	Lithuania (1995)
	Zimbabwe (1989)	Tuvalu (1990)	Cuba (1995)	
	Benin (1990)	Iraq (1991)	Domini can Republic (1995)	
	Mali (1991)	Thailand (1991)		
	Uganda (1991)	Yemen (1991)		
	Burkina Faso (1992)	Azerbaijan (1992)		
	Congo (1992)	Democratic People's Republic of Korea (1992)		
	Malawi (1992)	Nepal (1992)		
	Namibia (1992)	Papua New Guinea (1992)		
	Algeria (1993)	Mongolia (1993)		
	Cape Verde (1993)	Turkmenistan (1993)		
	Mauritius (1993)	Armenia (1994)		
	Mozambique (1993)	Cambodia (1994)		
	Sierra Leone (1993)	Indonesia (1994, 1995)c		
	Tunisia (1993)	Lao People's Democratic Republic (1994)		
	Zambia (1993)	Malaysia (1994)		
	Angola (1994)	Oman (1994)		
	Djibouti (1994)	Afghanistan (1995)		
	Eritrea (1994)	Bangladesh (1995)		
	Ghana (1994)	China (1995)		
	Côte d'Ivoire (1995)	Georgia (1995)		
	Guinea (1995)	Jordan (1995)		
	Nigeria (1995)	Palestinian territory (1995)		
	Libyan Arab Jamahiriya (1996)	Kazakhstan (1997)		
	Madagascar (1996)	Kyrgyzstan (1997)		
	Egypt (1997)	Micronesia, Federated States of (1997)		
	Ethiopia (1997)	Uzbekistan (1998)		
	United Republic of Tanzania (1997)			

Source: UNCTAD, 1998b, p. 56.

[a] Refers to a law or decree dealing specifically with FDI. This table does not cover provisions contained in laws or regulations that do not deal specifically with FDI, but are relevant to FDI.

[b] Includes developing Europe.

[c] The country has more than one set of legislation dealing with FDI.

Note: the year in which the prevailing legislation was adopted is indicated in parenthesis. Economies are listed according to the chronological order of their adoption of FDI legislation.

liberalization, in terms of entry and other conditions (see below).

While the laws specifically addressing FDI are of great importance for foreign investors and appear to influence their decisions, a country's entire legal system is directly relevant, as well. A country's commercial law, its property law, the laws concerning companies or labour, even civil procedure or criminal law, and of course the laws concerning the judicial system or the civil service, are also important. These laws create the legal environment for the operation of foreign firms and establish directly applicable sets of rules and reflect prevalent policy trends. While there is, naturally, great variety in national laws, because of differences in traditions, approaches and politics, there are also extensive similarities among legal systems, as far as FDI is concerned, reaching the point of uniformity on particular topics. At the same time, the legal system of each particular country, being limited in its territorial scope, can deal effectively only with a fraction of policies and operations of TNCs. The latter generally have a much wider geographical scope and are in a position to avoid some national prescriptions and regulation.

A last point of particular significance is that the legal concepts and categories used in national as well as international law are fashioned by national law -- what a "corporation" is or what the conditions are for the validity of a contract, is determined by national legal rules, not international ones. In fact, international rules and concepts operate in constant reference and interaction with national ones. While the number and importance of international norms keep increasing, their interplay with national ones remains at the heart of the matter. Much of the international legal regulation on FDI consists of rules that refer to national rules and principles and, in particular, determine the limits of permissible (or agreed) State action. Policy trends concerning FDI are thus manifested in national as well as international laws. National law and policies remain constantly in the visible background of the international legal framework for FDI.

B. Customary international law

To understand the ways in which the pertinent international legal rules are developed and applied, one must start from customary public international law, as crystallized at the end of the nineteenth and the beginning of the twentieth century. The rules and principles of customary international law constitute the indispensable background for any consideration of international legal rules and instruments. Depending on their form and substance, international instruments may give effect to, specify or supplement customary law, they may replace or derogate from it, and they may help create new rules. From the perspective of international law, even national legislation may be understood as being founded on customary law principles, on what they allow or forbid.

As already noted, classical international law approaches FDI issues in terms of two fundamental international law principles, the synergy and conflict between which account for much of international economic law.

- On the one hand, the principle of territorial sovereignty, a foundation of modern international law, asserts that each State exercises full and exclusive jurisdiction over persons and events in its territory. From the viewpoint of international law, it is from this principle that flows the power of the State to admit or exclude aliens (whether physical persons or companies) from its territory, to regulate the operation of all economic actors, and to take the property of private persons in pursuit of public purposes.
- On the other hand, the principle of nationality recognizes that each State has an interest in the proper treatment of its nationals and their property abroad (i.e. by and within other States) and may, through the exercise of diplomatic protection, invoke the rules concerning the responsibility of States for injuries to aliens and their property in violation of international law (Lillich, 1983; Sornarajah, 1994).

The importance of customary rules and principles at the foundation of all international law cannot be gainsaid; yet their practical effectiveness, the possibility of their day-to-day use, is constrained by a number of factors: they are often not specific enough, their exact contents are not clear and definite, and they normally may be invoked only at the State level, thus requiring the mediation of the State of the investor's nationality. At the same time, no international norm can be understood, nor its effects defined, without express or implied reference to its customary international law background. And in some domains, such as those involving the treatment of aliens, they may still be directly relevant in a great number of cases.

C. International agreements

Modern international economic law is largely based on international agreements — bilateral, regional, plurilateral and multilateral. They are the most effective means for developing and applying international norms, with respect to FDI as in other areas. On the one hand, their contents reflect the common, agreed positions of more than one State; on the other, they are legally binding, and States are under a duty to conform to their provisions.

With respect to FDI, no comprehensive global international convention dealing with FDI exists, and various efforts in this direction, in the past as well as more recently, have met with no success. However, several multilateral instruments of less comprehensive scope are directly relevant. In addition, regional agreements have increasingly dealt with FDI, sometimes pioneering in expressing international trends in the field. Moreover, the expanding BIT network has developed principles directly concerned with the treatment and protection of FDI.

1. Multilateral agreements

As already noted, an effort to create a comprehensive instrument, although on a non-binding basis, was undertaken in the 1970s and early 1980s. The instrument in question, the United Nations draft Code of Conduct on TNCs, would have addressed many of the concerns of home and host countries, while reflecting, of course, the policies and positions of the period. Several declaratory texts of that period reflected similar concerns (see below).

Of the relevant multilateral agreements in existence, some deal with broader issues that are important for FDI, as in the case of the Articles of Agreement of the International Monetary Fund, the GATT, or even the international conventions concerning intellectual property, within the framework of the World Intellectual Property Organization (WIPO) or the World Trade Organization (WTO). The pertinent international organizations constitute in fact the sole existing institutional structure at the worldwide level that is directly or indirectly relevant to FDI.

Other multilateral agreements, although not dealing with the FDI process in its entirety, address important aspects of it. Thus, the Convention on the Settlement of Investment Disputes between States and Nationals of Other States (1965), concluded under the auspices of the World Bank and administered by it, provides a comprehensive framework for the settlement of disputes. It is complemented by other agencies dealing in particular with international commercial arbitration. The agreement creating the MIGA (1986), also under World Bank auspices, serves to enhance legal security for FDI and supplements existing national and regional investment guarantee operations.

Some of the WTO agreements concluded within the framework of the Uruguay Round are also closely related to FDI. The GATS covers several investment situations; perhaps more important, it provides an important model for the regulation of FDI matters. The TRIMs deals with one particular kind of national measure relating to FDI and provides a forum for the study and exchange of views on performance requirements and related measures. As previously noted, the TRIPs also covers several FDI-related issues, in parallel with existing conventions on intellectual property matters.

Multilateral agreements, especially those of worldwide scope, are the closest equivalent to "legislation" that exists in international law. They make possible the formulation and application of "universal" rules, agreed by and applicable to all States, or a large majority of them. Such agreements are often endowed with institutional machinery for their application and with provisions for their review and development. On the other hand, the necessity to find common ground among a large number of States often makes their provisions either very general or riddled with possible special cases. And the very difficulty of achieving agreement on topics such as FDI, where the approaches and policies of States differ, accounts for the lack of comprehensive instruments of this type.

2. Regional and plurilateral agreements

Regional and/or plurilateral international agreements are agreements in which only a limited number of countries participate and which are often not open to the participation of all countries.[9] They are of course binding on the participating countries alone and applicable only to them. Such instruments are increasingly important in FDI matters.

Regional economic integration agreements are a significant subcategory. They often involve a higher than usual degree of unity and cooperation among their members, sometimes marked by the presence of "supranational" institutions, and it is therefore difficult to draw general conclusions from their provisions. The case of the European Community, now the European Union, is probably the most telling; the extensive liberalization of capital movements, the effective elimination of discriminatory measures and the adoption of common rules among its members has had far-reaching effects on FDI among member countries and an important impact on investment in and from third countries. Investment in developing countries has been affected by the successive agreements concluded between the European Union/ European Community and African, Caribbean and Pacific countries (the Lomé -- and successor -- Conventions), although the pertinent bilateral and multilateral arrangements foreseen in the Conventions have been slow in their realization.

Other regional integration arrangements involve "shallower" integration, but still affect in important ways FDI regulation. NAFTA is a significant illustration of a regional agreement which is not limited to developed countries only and may indeed be extended to other countries. It is pertinent to note that, although NAFTA is formally only a "free trade zone" -- and not a common market or an economic union like the European Community/ European Union -- the agreement covers FDI. Its provisions on the subject have already significantly influenced other arrangements. It may in fact be considered as characteristic of a recent trend for free trade agreements to include FDI in their scope.

The recently negotiated Framework Agreement on the ASEAN Investment Area, on the other hand, is focused on FDI alone. It seeks to promote investment in the area through the cooperation of the countries in the region in the liberalization of investment regulations, the provision of national treatment to all investors from the countries involved, increased transparency and an interstate dispute-settlement system.

Particularly important, on the broadly regional level, are a number of other agreements, such as the two OECD Liberalisation Codes, covering Capital Movements and Current Invisible Operations, respectively. They have shown a remarkable capacity for growth. Their coverage now extends to most facets of inward FDI. The recent effort to negotiate a multilateral agreement on investment (MAI), in one sense constituted an ambitious departure from earlier approaches which were limited, both in geographical and in substantive terms.

An interesting recent example of an "interregional" agreement that covers major areas of FDI is the Energy Charter Treaty, signed in late 1994 and recently entered into effect. Contracting parties are the European Union and its member States, other developed OECD member countries, and the countries of Central and Eastern Europe and the Commonwealth of Independent States. The agreement covers only a particular economic sector, albeit a very important one. Its investment provisions are fairly elaborate and are to be supplemented by a second agreement covering the issues of investment admission.

Where all the member States of a regional integration agreement are developing countries, their provisions concerning inward FDI and the operation of foreign affiliates may follow patterns similar to those of national investment laws. That has been, for instance, the case of the Andean Pact, whose decisions on the treatment of FDI from the early 1970s to the mid-1990s have followed the general trends outlined earlier, from restrictions and limitations on FDI to increasing liberalization.

Regional and plurilateral instruments have some of the characteristics of multilateral ones: the agreement of many countries is needed for their negotiation and conclusion, they often have important institutional structures and they generally provide for their continuing growth and development. At the same time, the number of countries involved is smaller and they tend to be relatively homogeneous; the adoption of instruments that serve common interests in fairly specific fashion is more feasible. With respect to FDI, regional and plurilateral agreements have helped to change pre-existing structures of law and policy and to create important habits and patterns of expectations on a broader transnational level, even though not a universal one. As a result in recent years, regional agreements have often been the harbingers of significant new trends in matters of investment law and regulation.

3. Bilateral investment treaties

BITs are a principal element of the current framework for FDI (UNCTAD, 1998a, with extensive bibliography). More than 2,300 bilateral treaties have been concluded since the early 1960s, most of them in the decade of the 1990s. Their principal focus has been from the very start on investment protection, in the wider context of policies that favour and promote FDI: the protection of investments against nationalization or expropriation and assurances on the free transfer of funds and provision for dispute-settlement mechanisms between investors and host States. BITs also cover a number of other areas, in particular, non-discrimination in the treatment, and in some cases, the entry, of foreign-controlled enterprises, subrogation in the case of insurance payment by the capital-exporting country's investment guarantee agency, and other topics. An important characteristic of the new generation of BITs is a considerable uniformity in the broad principles underlying the agreements, coupled with numerous variations in the specific formulations employed (box 5).

Box 5. Similarities and differences between BITs

Similarities:

- The definition of investment is broad and open-ended so that it can accommodate new forms of foreign investment; it includes tangible and intangible assets and generally applies to existing as well as new investments;
- The entry and establishment of investment is encouraged, although it is typically subject to national laws and regulations (most BITs do not grant a right of establishment);
- Investment promotion is weak and is based mainly on the creation of a favourable investment climate for investment through the conclusion of a BIT;
- Most treaties provide for fair and equitable treatment, often qualified by more specific standards, such as those prohibiting arbitrary or discriminatory measures or prescribing a duty to observe commitments concerning investment;
- Most treaties specify that when various agreements apply to an investment, the most favourable provisions amongst them apply;
- Most treaties now grant national treatment, the principle also being often subject to qualifications (to take into account the different characteristics between national and foreign firms) and exceptions (relating mainly to specific industries or economic activities, or to policy measures such as incentives and taxation);
- A guarantee of MFN treatment, subject to some standardized exceptions, is virtually universal;
- Virtually all BITs subject the right of the host country to expropriate to the condition that it should be for a public purpose, non-discriminatory, in accordance with due process and accompanied by compensation, while the standards for determining compensation are often described in terms that could result in similar outcomes;
- A guarantee of the free transfer of payments related to an investment is common to virtually all BITs, although it is often qualified by exceptions applicable to periods when foreign currency reserves are at low levels;
- A State-to-State dispute-settlement provision is also virtually universal;
- An investor-to-State dispute-settlement provision has become a standard practice, with a growing number of BITs providing the investor with a choice of mechanisms.

In addition, some BITs include one or several of the following:

- A requirement that the host country should ensure that investors have access to information on national laws;

/...

Box 5 (concluded)

- A prohibition on the imposition of performance requirements, such as local content, export conditions and employment requirements, as a condition for the entry or operation of an investment;
- A commitment to permit or facilitate the entry and sojourn of foreign personnel in connection with the establishment and operation of an investment;
- A guarantee of national and MFN treatment on entry and establishment.

There are also a number of issues that are generally not addressed in BITs but are nevertheless relevant for investment relations. These include:

- Obligations regarding progressive liberalization;
- The treatment of foreign investment during privatization;
- Control of restrictive business practices;
- Private management practices that restrain investment and trade;
- Consumer protection;
- Environmental protection;
- Taxation of foreign affiliates;
- Avoidance of illicit payments;
- Protection against violations of intellectual property rights;
- Labour standards;
- Provisions concerning the transfer of technology;
- Specific commitments by home countries to promote investments;
- Social responsibilities of foreign investors in host countries;
- Obligations of subnational authorities.

Source: UNCTAD, 1998a, pp. 137-139.

As elements of the international legal framework for FDI, BITs have been useful because they have developed a large number of variations on the main provisions of IIAs -- especially those related to the protection of investments, of course, but also those referring to the ways in which national investment procedures may be taken into account. Although the treaties remain quite standardized, they are able to reflect in their provisions the differing positions and approaches of the many countries which have concluded such agreements. The corpus of BITs may thus be perceived as a valuable pool of possible provisions for IIAs (Kline and Ludema, 1997).

BITs were initially addressed exclusively to relations between home and host, developed and developing, countries. Yet, they have shown over the years a remarkable capability for diversification in participation, moving to other patterns, such as agreements between developing countries, or with countries with economies in transition or even with the few remaining socialist countries. Thus, while lacking the institutional structures and emphasis on review and development of multilateral and regional instruments, BITs appear capable of adapting to special circumstances. They have been successfully utilized, for instance, in the past decade throughout the process of transition of Central and East European countries towards a market-type economy. The recent increase in the number of BITs between developing countries suggests that they may also be useful in dealing with some of the problems in such relationships.

There is very little known on the use that countries and investors have made of BITs. But are being invoked in an increasing number of international arbitrations (documented in UNCTAD, 2004c), and presumably in diplomatic correspondence and investor demands. Their most significant function appears to be that of providing signals of an attitude favouring FDI. Their very proliferation has made them standard features of the investment climate for any country interested in attracting FDI.

D. Soft law

In addition to rules found in customary law and international agreements, legal prescriptions of other kinds, of varying normative intensity and general applicability, form part of the international legal framework for FDI and are relevant for present purposes. Of particular interest among them are the category of standards that have become known by the term "soft law". These standards are not always legal in the traditional sense, in that they are not formally binding on States or individuals, but they may still possess considerable legal and political authority, to the extent that they often represent widely held expectations that affect in a variety of ways the actual behaviour of economic and political actors. It is possible to distinguish two major types of such standards.

The first type comprises standards based on international instruments that have been adopted by States in non-legally-binding form, such as resolutions of the General Assembly of the United Nations or formal declarations of States. Important illustrations of such standards directly relevant to FDI are those found in the General Assembly resolutions relating to a New International Economic Order (e.g. the Charter of Economic Rights and Duties of States) or to the "international codes of conduct" negotiated in the 1970s and 1980s, whether eventually adopted by resolution of the General Assembly or never agreed upon and remaining in draft form. At the regional level, the instruments related to the 1976 OECD Declaration on International Investment and Multinational Enterprises have been of special importance, in particular the Guidelines for Multinational Enterprises, interest in which was recently revived.

An interesting recent case of such a non-binding set of standards is the document entitled "Guidelines for the Treatment of Foreign Direct Investment", which was prepared by the legal services of the World Bank and MIGA, on the basis of a thorough study of recent practice (World Bank, 1992). The Guidelines were submitted to the IMF/World Bank Development Committee, which "called them to the attention of member countries" (World Bank, 1992, vol. II, p. 6). This instrument represents an effort to formulate "a set of *guidelines* embodying commendable approaches which would not be legally binding as such but which could greatly influence the development of international law in this area" (World Bank, 1992, vol. II, p. 5). They are addressed to all States (not only to developing countries) and were expected to be "both acceptable in view of recent trends, and likely to enhance the prospects of investment flows to developing countries" (World Bank, 1992, vol. II, p. 12). The soft law character of these prescriptions is made clear in the accompanying report, which stresses that the guidelines are not intended to codify international law principles and "are clearly not intended to constitute part of World Bank loan conditionality", while also expressing the expectation that, through the consistent future practice of States, the guidelines might "positively influence the development of customary international law" (ibid).

A second major type of soft law prescriptions are those found in formally binding legal documents, such as international agreements, in provisions couched in language that precludes an implication of strict obligation or right. Typical illustrations of such language are references to "best efforts" or to "endeavouring" to act in a certain manner.

Closely related to such soft law norms (although not quite part of this class of prescriptions) are voluntary instruments prepared by international non-governmental associations, whether from business (see below, under subsection F) or from other social partners (labour union associations, environmental, non-governmental organizations, etc.). While of course they do not reflect the positions of Governments, such associations are increasingly influential in their proposals for international norms and practices.

The exact legal status of soft law has long been a matter of controversy. To the extent that such standards represent widely shared expectations, they may, through repeated invocation and appropriate utilization, move to the status of a binding and enforceable rule. It is with this possibility in mind that soft law has sometimes been called "green law". Even apart, however, from an eventual elevation to the status of binding rules, standards of this sort may have other significant, albeit probably partial, legal effects: they may serve to confer increased legitimacy on actions and rules that conform to them, thus impeding their treatment as illegal, ensuring their eventual legal validity, or creating a basis for estoppel. They may also play an "educational" role, suggesting to Governments possible approaches acceptable to all concerned. Such effects are enhanced where an institutional implementation mechanism exists, even if it is based on persuasion rather than strict enforcement. A notable case in this respect is that of the role of the OECD Committee on International Investment and Multinational Enterprises (CIME) in the implementation of the Guidelines for Multinational Enterprises.

E. The case law of international tribunals

Relevant principles and rules may also be found in the norms applied by international tribunals, particularly arbitral ones, when deciding disputes relating to FDI. Transnational arbitration may thus not only provide the indispensable procedures for dispute settlement but may also, through the corpus of its awards, gradually fill in the gaps in the conceptual framework on FDI. While limited by the facts (and law) of each case and formally binding only on the parties to the specific arbitration, such decisions have contributed significantly to the development of the legal framework for FDI in the last four decades, though not at times without controversy. The extensive use of arbitration for settling disputes related to FDI obviously confers increasing importance on this class of rules.

F. Private business practices

Another category of standards of considerable importance are the rules and standardized instruments developed by professional or other associations and private business groups (e.g. the International Chamber of Commerce). In fields where powerful private actors are at work, private law-making has always been important. Through model clauses and instruments, patterns of private practices are developed and legitimized and the expectations of companies (and States) are crystallized. Such private sets of rules may even eventually be formally adopted at the national or international level and be incorporated in international agreements.

Individual enterprises, especially some of the larger and more powerful TNCs, have sometimes adopted "corporate codes of conduct" which spell out broader standards of social responsibility, as they relate to their operations (UNCTAD, 1999a, chapter XII). While the phenomenon is not new, it has recently acquired particular strength and support, in response to concerns involving human rights, the protection of the environment, or core labour standards, and to related pressures by non-governmental organizations. While sometimes, especially in the past, such corporate codes were mere exercises in public relations, they are increasingly becoming more significant instruments that affect the substance of corporate action

G. The contribution of scholars

Finally, the contribution of private persons and groups, scholars and learned societies should not be ignored -- and not only because the Statute of the International Court of Justice, in its famous article 38, provides, under subsection (d), that "the teachings of the most highly qualified publicists of the various nations" are a subsidiary means for the determination of rules of international law (ICJ, 1989a, p. 77). The writings of scholars and commentators do not, of course, provide authoritative rules; but they help to construct the conceptual framework and to crystallize approaches and expectations that may eventually find expression in formal binding texts.

Section III
Key Substantive Issues

At this stage in the evolution of the international legal framework for FDI, no description of its substantive contents can be exhaustive and all-encompassing. The situation is fluid. A number of trends are at work with respect to each particular topic or issue, and they are not all equally strong or in the same phase of their evolution. It is therefore futile to seek to construct a definitive catalogue of topics and issues for discussion.

Comprehensive classifications of issues -- or, for the purpose of this chapter, of provisions in IIAs -- can only be tentative. The various categories of measures and policies often overlap and cannot sometimes be clearly distinguished one from another. As a result, although a number of classifications and categories are in general use, there is as yet no general agreement on the matter.

A useful listing has to be so structured as to capture the interrelationships among issues, provisions and trends. A possible central criterion for the classification of key issues and provisions is their relationship to the interests of the parties involved: which issues serve the interests of, or are promoted by, investors and their countries of origin, which are defended by host countries, and so forth. It is, however, not clear that such a criterion would be particularly helpful: one is dealing here with key issues in actual international agreements (or other instruments), that is to say, with provisions agreed to by the parties involved. It follows that such issues relate, by definition, to interests that have been accepted as common, albeit, obviously, with differences in degree and in approach, since investors may be more interested in certain provisions and host countries in others, while the preferred substance of such provisions may also, from the point of view of each party, differ to a degree from the one agreed upon.

Another classification, prevalent in the recent practice of IIA negotiations, focuses on what is apparently a temporal dimension of investment, looking at issues in terms of their dealing with problems and situations that occur before or after an actual investment is made. Obviously, "pre-investment" issues concern measures that address prospective investors, foreign firms which have not yet invested in the host country concerned, have not entered it or been admitted into it. "Post-investment" issues, on the other hand, concern the situation and treatment of investments that have already been made.

The distinction reflects the differential treatment of these issues in classical international law: the principle of territorial sovereignty gives States the power to admit or exclude aliens, including foreign firms, from their territory as well as full jurisdiction over existing investments. While, however, the exercise of that jurisdiction has been traditionally subject to qualifications -- for instance, by reference to so-called "acquired rights" of foreigners or by virtue of the rules of State responsibility for the treatment of aliens -- State powers over admission have been far less circumscribed. It is true that much of modern international law concerning foreign investment consists of interpretations of and qualifications to the principle of territorial sovereignty, whether by national law or through international agreements. Yet, it remains true that, even today, there are fewer limitations on a State's right to exclude investment (or aliens in general) than on its jurisdiction over investors already established (admitted) in its territory.

The distinction therefore retains its validity. For the purposes of this chapter, however, it is of limited usefulness because the issues and provisions under review are unequally divided between the two categories. Problems of admission and establishment are but a relatively small part of the *problématique* arising in connection with FDI, much of which either refers to post-investment alone or covers both pre- and post-investment situations.

A more appropriate criterion is that of the object and purpose of the provisions in question, or of what each category of provisions seeks to accomplish. In seeking to classify provisions in this manner, existing policy trends and tendencies provide the controlling tests. It is thus possible to distinguish today two principal categories of key issues, each of which covers a variety of sub-issues closely (and sometimes, not so closely) linked to one another:

- A first class of issues may be linked to the process of liberalization, a process which, in its application to FDI, involves the gradual decrease or elimination of measures and restrictions on the admission and operations of firms, especially foreign ones, the application of positive standards of treatment with a view towards the elimination of discrimination against foreign enterprises, and the implementation of measures and policies seeking to promote the proper functioning of markets (UNCTAD, 1994, ch. VII).
- A second category covers provisions that concern the protection of foreign investments after they have been made against Government measures damaging to them.

Another class of provisions and approaches, of a different character, must also be examined. It cuts across, as it were, the two former categories, and serves as a possible corrective to them. It covers provisions and approaches which, by importing into the operation of IIAs the necessary flexibility, seek to ensure and enhance the development of the host countries concerned.

After a brief discussion of the preliminary question of definitions in IIAs, the rest of this section will then address the two classes of key issues enumerated. This involves, in effect, going over the "key issues" already listed (table 1), which form the subject of these volumes.[10] The last category, flexibility, will be briefly considered in the next section.

A. Definitions

In legal instruments, definitions are not neutral and objective descriptions of concepts; they form part of an instrument's normative content. They determine the object to which an instrument's rules apply and thereby interact intimately with the scope and purpose of the instrument. Particular terms may be given a technical meaning, which may or may not coincide with their "usual" or "generally accepted" meaning. The meaning of a term, as found in a definition in a particular instrument, may be specific to that instrument, and may or may not be easily transferable to other instruments and contexts.

The way in which a term is defined in an international instrument, whether by a formal definition or through the manner in which it is used, affects significantly the substance of the legal rules involved. Moreover, like all provisions in an instrument, those on definitions interact with other provisions. The meaning of a term may change, because of the way in which another term is defined or because of the formulation of a particular rule. Thus, the definition of "investment" may determine the exact scope of a provision concerning expropriation; at the same time, the exact formulation of a provision on expropriation may in fact supplement or amend the formal definition of "investment".

The definition of the key term "investment" will be briefly discussed here, as an illustration of the kinds of problems that arise. With respect to the definition of that term, earlier instruments dealing with FDI fall in two broad categories:

- Instruments that concern the cross-border movement of capital and resources usually define investment in narrow terms, distinguishing FDI from other types of investment (e.g. portfolio investment) and insisting on an investor's control over the enterprise as a necessary element of the concept of FDI. Such instruments thus tend to stress the differences between various types of investment of capital. A classical definition of this type is found in Annex A of the OECD Code of Liberalisation of Capital Movements.
- Instruments mainly directed at the protection of FDI usually define investment in a broad and comprehensive manner. They cover not only the capital (or the resources) that have crossed borders with a view to the acquisition of control over an enterprise, but also most other kinds of assets of the enterprise or of the investor -- property and property rights of various kinds; non-equity investment, including several types of loans and portfolio transactions; and other contractual rights, sometimes including rights created by administrative action of a host State (licences, permits, etc.). Such a definition is found, for instance, in BITs, as well as in the World Bank-sponsored Convention on the creation of MIGA.

The rationale for these differing approaches is evident. Capital movement-oriented instruments look at investment before it is made, whether with a view to its regulation and control (as was the case in past decades), or with a view to removing obstacles to its realization (as in the current context of liberalization). Since the package that constitutes an investment consists of resources of many kinds, the policy context, and therefore the legal treatment, of each type may differ; it would not do therefore to define investment in broad terms covering all types of resources.

Protection-oriented instruments, on the other hand, seek to safeguard the interests of the investors (or, in broader context, to promote FDI by safeguarding the investors' interests). For the purposes of protection, investment is understood as something that is already there (or that will be there, by the time protection becomes necessary). The older terminology, which referred to "acquired rights" or to "foreign property" (see, for example the 1967 OECD draft Convention on the Protection of Foreign Property), makes the context clear, as does the more recent usage of "assets" as the key term. From such a perspective, the exact character of the particular assets is not by itself important, since protection (mainly against extraordinary Government action damaging to them) is to be extended to them after their acquisition by the investor, when they already form part of the investor's patrimony. Definitions tend therefore to be broad, in order to cover as many as possible of the investor's assets.

The two types of definitions are not inconsistent. They simply serve different purposes. In fact, they overlap, since the broader, protection-oriented, definition normally contains all the elements of the narrower one, along with additional elements. Use of a single definition in a multi-purpose instrument assumes that the same policies apply to all the investment transactions and activities involved, in particular, both to the act of investing and to the treatment of assets already acquired. Recent practice in regional and multilateral agreements that are intended both to liberalize investment regulation and to protect investments appears to favour broader definitions -- witness the definitions found in NAFTA, the MERCOSUR Protocols, the Energy Charter Treaty and especially the draft MAI. This practice extends the scope of liberalization, since obstacles and discriminatory measures are removed with respect to a greater variety of investments and investment operations.

B. Liberalization

As already noted, the process of liberalization of FDI laws and policies may be understood as consisting of three principal elements: (a) the removal of restrictive, and thereby market-distorting, Government measures; (b) the application of certain positive standards of treatment, primarily directed at the elimination of discrimination against foreign investors; and (c) measures intended to ensure the proper operation of markets (figure 4).

These types of measures are closely interconnected. But it is useful for analytical purposes to keep them distinct. Restrictions and standards of treatment may apply to different phases or different aspects of an investment: its entry and establishment, its ownership or its operations after entry. They were and are established by national law. They are reflected in international instruments chiefly to the extent that international rules may seek to restrict or even prohibit certain kinds of national measures. A necessary background element may be added, namely, the presence of a general legal, administrative and even political framework. To the extent that this element is reflected in international instruments on FDI, it may take the form of recognizing certain types of international duties of investors and the promotion of national and international measures to ensure the proper functioning of the market.

To understand the process of liberalization concerning FDI, it is necessary to view current developments against the background of earlier trends. As already noted, in the early post-war decades, extensive restrictions were imposed on foreign affiliates, with a view to protecting the

Figure 4. The liberalization of FDI policies

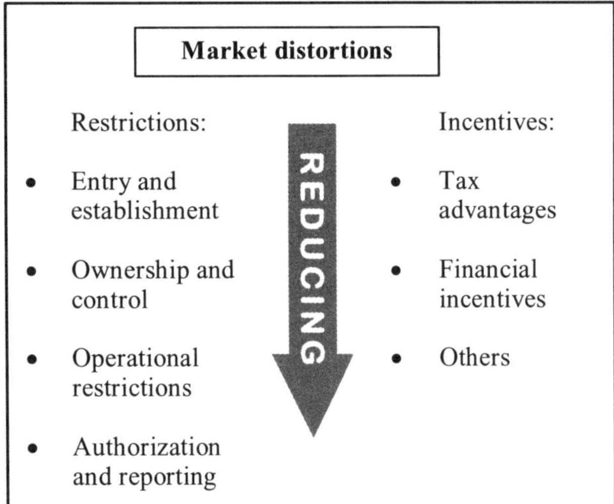

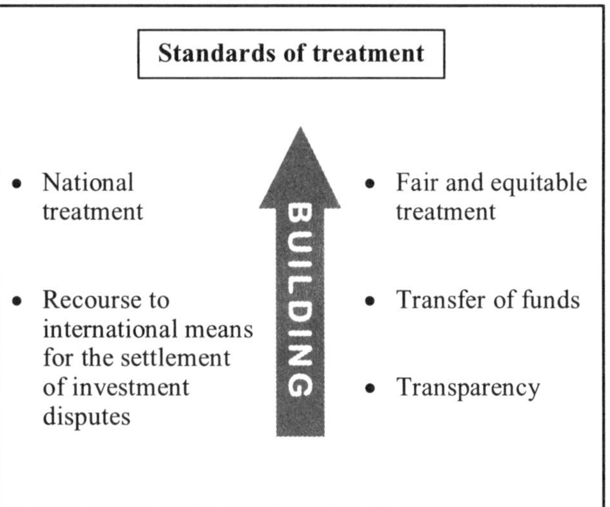

Market supervision

- Competition policy (including, international M&As)
- Monopoly regulation
- Prudential supervision
- Disclosure of information

Source: UNCTAD, 1998b, p. 94.

national economy from excessive foreign influence or domination and supporting local firms against powerful foreign competitors. Current directions of national and international FDI regulation may reflect a reconsideration of the need for such measures but also of the form they are to take. Not only is the reality of the dangers against which they are directed contested, but there are doubts, based on the experience from their application, as to the possibilities for effective administration of restrictive measures, and there is also an awareness of their impact on a country's position in the competition for FDI. Moreover, as later discussion will show, in no case is it a matter of all or nothing; like all policies, liberalization is a matter of degree, phasing and manner of implementation.

Investment measures may be directed at both domestic and foreign investment. In many instances, however, they are directed specifically at foreign investment. In that case, the relaxation or elimination of investment measures and restrictions directed at FDI may be brought about through adoption of general standards of nondiscriminatory treatment. The application of general standards as the principal method for the decrease or elimination of restrictive measures is indeed an important, and relatively novel, feature of current trends in IIAs.

1. Standards of treatment

The most common standards of treatment in use in IIAs are the "most-favoured-nation" (MFN) standard, the national treatment standard and the standard of "fair and equitable" treatment. The first two are known as relative (or contingent) standards, because they do not define expressly the contents of the treatment they accord but establish it by reference to an existing legal regime, that of other aliens in the one case and that of host State nationals in the other. The legal regime to which reference is made changes over time, and the changes apply to the foreign beneficiaries of MFN or national treatment as well. The last standard is qualified as "absolute" (or non-contingent), because it is supposed itself to establish, through its formulation, its unchanging contents.

While the distinction between the two kinds of standards is not in fact all that clear and rigid, it does point to an important characteristic of the two. They are meant to ensure, not uniformity of treatment at the international level, but nondiscrimination, as between foreign investors of differing origins -- from different (foreign) countries -- in the case of the MFN standard, and as between foreign and domestic investors, in the case of the national treatment standard.

The usual formal definitions of these two standards refer, not to equal or identical treatment, but to "treatment no less favourable" than that accorded to the "most-favoured" third nation, in the one case, and to the nationals (and products) of the host country, in the other. The clear implication of the formula is that privileged treatment, discrimination in favour of the foreign investor, is allowed, even though, with few exceptions, equality of treatment is accorded in practice. There have been some cases where actual equality of treatment is provided for.

The precise interpretation of the two relative standards, when applied to concrete circumstances, raises a number of problems. Since they are, by definition, comparative in character, their actual content depends on the extent to which the legal situation of other aliens or nationals can be determined with any degree of clarity. In United States practice, the standard is said to be applicable "in like situations", a formula that sounds reasonable but is criticized as introducing new complications.

When providing for the application of treatment standards, IIAs allow for a number of exceptions or qualifications. The most frequent among the express exceptions refer to matters relating to public order and health and national security; the latter exception may be interpreted so as to cover a wide number of topics. In a number of cases, particular industries or types of business activities may be listed where these standards (especially that of national treatment) may not apply. In recent practice, exceptions, particularly to national treatment, may be provided for in a number of ways. The practice of attaching to the main instrument extensive detailed "negative lists", often by each country involved, has been developed both in BITs and in some plurilateral or multilateral agreements. It is also possible to provide for "positive lists", that is to say, for listing the cases where the country concerned accords the relevant general standard of treatment.

There is a recent trend towards utilization of both the MFN and national treatment standards, "whichever is more favourable", with respect to post-investment treatment. Who judges what is or is not more favourable, on the basis of which criteria and as to what feature of the investment or its treatment, is by no means clear.

The two standards are increasingly accepted in the current practice concerning foreign investment. More precisely, the MFN standard appears by and large generally accepted in current pre-and post-investment practice with few specific exceptions; discrimination as between firms from different countries is not common. The national treatment standard, for its part, is increasingly but by no means universally accepted; many host countries still wish to retain the ability to favour their own domestic firms when needed, not only with respect to the admission and establishment of investments, but also in some cases to the treatment of investments after their admission.

In earlier treaty practice, a number of absolute or noncontingent standards were used (e.g. treatment "according to international law"). Some of them are still in use (box 6). However, the 1967 OECD draft Convention on the Protection of Foreign Property introduced the standard of "fair and equitable treatment". Initially proposed in a draft for an investment convention (Abs and Shawcross, 1960), this standard has made its fortune since the 1960s in BITs practice. Although its precise purport is not quite clear, since its meaning is not defined in the pertinent instruments, it is gradually acquiring a more specific content through diplomatic and arbitral practice. Since it is an absolute standard, its contents do not vary according to local law and policy, and its comprehensive character has found favour among investors and capital-exporting countries.

Box 6. Noncontingent standards of treatment: the example of the Energy Charter Treaty

Article 10
PROMOTION, PROTECTION AND TREATMENT OF INVESTMENTS

(1) Each Contracting Party shall, in accordance with the provisions of this Treaty, encourage and create stable, equitable, favourable and transparent conditions for Investors of other Contracting Parties to Make Investments in its Area. Such conditions shall include a commitment to accord at all times to Investments of Investors of other Contracting Parties fair and equitable treatment. Such Investments shall also enjoy the most constant protection and security and no Contracting Party shall in any way impair by unreasonable or discriminatory measures their management, maintenance, use, enjoyment or disposal. In no case shall such Investments be accorded treatment less favourable than that required by international law, including treaty obligations. Each Contracting Party shall observe any obligations it has entered into with an Investor or an Investment of an Investor of any Contracting Party.

Source: UNCTAD, 1996a, p. 555.

2. Entry and establishment

Measures concerning FDI involve in many instances the exercise of controls over the admission of investments. Such controls may extend over a very broad spectrum: from prohibition to selective admission to mere registration. Total prohibition of FDI was always very rare and is no longer to be found anywhere nowadays. Certain key industries may be closed to foreign investment, or investment in them may be allowed subject to conditions (e.g. foreign investors may only have minority participation).

The screening of investments before admission was once very common, nearly universal. The prevailing pattern, with numerous variations, was fairly settled. Prospective investors had to apply to the host country's authorities for permission to invest; the latter would allow an investment only when it met the policy criteria set out in the relevant laws and regulations, including possible conditions relating to the structure of ownership (e.g. participation of local investors) or to the nature of a firm's operations (e.g. employment of local personnel, utilization of local raw materials and supplies, emphasis on exports).

Today, screening is to be found in far fewer, although still numerous, cases. Where it exists, it tends to be less strict and demanding. As noted, restrictions relating to the protection of national security, sometimes very broadly defined, are still common. In countries where exchange controls are in effect, the registration or authorization of foreign investment on entry is often a precondition for allowing later transfer of profits or capital outside the host country.

Restrictions and other requirements were and are established by national law. They are not imposed by international instruments, although some regional economic agreements provided for such a possibility. Thus, Decision 24 of the Commission of the Cartagena Agreement (1970) allowed (and in some cases required) member States to take specified types of measures with a view towards controlling the entry and operations of foreign investors. Decision 24 was amended in 1988 and eventually replaced by Decision 291 of 1991, which removed many of the restrictive features of the earlier provisions.

Despite the extensive changes in policies in the past decade, recent surveys of investment admission requirements in national law show that, while there is a definite trend towards their elimination, controls and restrictions on entry of widely varying import are still in effect in many countries. In most cases, they involve limitations on entry into particular sectors or industries, or the direct or indirect application of screening.

Since entry restrictions often apply only to foreign investment, their removal may be brought about, as already noted, by the application of non-discriminatory standards of treatment, especially national treatment, even though, at first blush, the position of foreign investors seeking admission is not formally comparable to that of domestic investors (since the latter are already in the host country). Most BITs recommend a favourable approach to FDI and the removal of entry restrictions, but provide that investments are to be admitted in accordance with local laws and regulations. The position of the World Bank's Legal Framework for the Treatment of Foreign Investment is essentially similar, accepting the host countries' right to regulate entry, yet recommending "open admission, possibly subject to a restricted list of investments (which are either prohibited or require screening and licensing)" (World Bank, 1992, p. 37). The APEC Non-Binding Investment Principles provide for MFN treatment as far as admission of investments is concerned.

A number of international instruments, however, including some bilateral agreements -- those that adopt the United States approach -- provide for national and MFN treatment in matters of entry and establishment, that is to say, for removal of all discrimination in matters of admission. It is nevertheless common, to allow notification of "negative lists" of the industries in which the rule of nondiscrimination does not apply.

As already noted, this "negative list" approach has found favour in recent multilateral or regional IIAs. It is, for instance, largely reflected in NAFTA. Most recently, it has been adopted with regard to pre-investment treatment in the draft Supplementary Treaty to the Energy Charter Treaty. The main Treaty, concluded in 1994, provides that participating States will accord national and MFN treatment, whichever is most favourable, to existing energy investments of other Parties, but will merely "endeavour" to accord such treatment as far as admission is concerned (Art. 10 (2)). This was intended to be a provisional arrangement. On the basis of an express provision in the treaty, negotiations for a supplementary treaty started immediately upon the main Treaty's conclusion, with a view to providing (in binding terms) for the grant of the same treatment to the admission of energy investments. The negotiations that followed led in December 1997 to a draft text which provides that national and MFN treatment will be accorded in the pre-investment phase, subject to the exemption of duly notified negative lists of non-conforming measures. As of October 1999, however, the Energy Charter Conference had not proceeded to adopt the draft.

The draft MAI negotiated in the OECD also adopted the "negative list" approach to commitments regarding the national treatment of foreign investments. The sheer bulk of the pertinent listing has indeed been cited as one of the problems that led to the abandonment of the negotiations.

It is, however, possible to provide for exceptions and qualifications on the basis of a "positive" approach, where States "open" particular industries and operations to FDI, usually in exchange for similar action by other States. This pattern, which moves along the lines of the exchange of "concessions" in trade negotiations, is found, for instance, in the GATS.

Regional arrangements, whether for the purpose of economic integration or other forms of closer economic cooperation, have often provided for special legal regimes regarding admission, as well as post-admission treatment, for enterprises from participating countries. Such efforts have multiplied in recent years, although the degree of their success or even of their reality, in terms of effective and extensive application, varies widely.

The Andean Pact countries were the first to create (in 1971) a subregional type of corporation, the "multinational enterprise". These are duly registered companies owned predominantly by nationals of participating countries (with limits on the participation of extraregional investors). Such enterprises are to be accorded special treatment, in most cases national treatment, in each participating State. Similar entities, with extensive variations as to their specific legal status and treatment, have also been created in the framework of other economic integration or cooperation efforts: "multinational companies", in the Central African Customs and Economic Union; "community enterprises", in the Economic Community of the Great Lakes Countries in Central Africa; "ASEAN industrial joint ventures", in the ASEAN framework; "CARICOM enterprises", in the framework of the Caribbean Common Market; and "multinational industrial enterprises", in the Preferential Trade Area for Eastern and Southern African States. It is not clear whether and how far this device has been successful. In the Andean countries, very few such "multinational enterprises" were established in the first two decades of the relevant Decision's effect, and it was extensively amended in the early 1990s. In the European Community, proposals for the creation of a "European company" with a special status in Community law have been debated for a long time, but no agreement has been reached.

Investors from countries participating in economic cooperation or integration arrangements are frequently accorded national treatment as to admission and operation in the absence of a requirement for a common corporate form. This has been the case in the European Community, by virtue of the founding treaty's provisions on establishment. Provisions for free admission of investments are found in other regionally oriented agreements, such as the Unified Agreement for the Investment of Arab Capital in the Arab States, the Agreement on Promotion, Protection and Guarantee of Investments among Member States of the Organisation of the Islamic Conference, and NAFTA.

3. Treatment after admission

Foreign affiliates already admitted in a country are subject to that country's jurisdiction and operate under its legal system. As a general rule, subject to specific exceptions, they are not entitled to special treatment. The main problems of international relevance that may arise in this respect (apart from expropriation and similar measures) concern the possibility of restrictive and/or discriminatory national measures affecting their operations.

The rules on post-establishment treatment have been considerably liberalized in recent years. As already noted, the MFN standard is by now generally accepted in this context, while the national treatment standard has gained considerable strength, although it certainly is not universally accepted. The application of both standards is provided in several recent regional instruments, such as NAFTA and the Energy Charter Treaty, and in a number of important "soft law" texts, such as the World Bank-sponsored Legal Framework for the Treatment of Foreign Investment and the APEC Non-Binding Investment Principles.

Treatment after admission obviously involves many possible topics. Some of the older multilateral instruments had sought to deal with all or most of the relevant topics. This was eminently the case with the draft United Nations Code of Conduct on Transnational Corporations. Most recent instruments, however, address only a limited range of issues.

Many facets of post-admission treatment fall within distinct and well-established broader domains of international action. Accordingly, they are often regulated by general instruments - multilateral and regional conventions, networks of bilateral treaties or decisions of international organizations -- that deal with the relevant domain as a whole, specific FDI matters being regulated incidentally along with other topics. This is the case, for instance, with taxation issues, which are of principal importance to investors, but which constitute a separate, large and highly technical field, regulated at the international level mainly through bilateral agreements. The United Nations Model Double Taxation Convention between Developed and Developing Countries and the OECD Model Tax Convention on Income and Capital provide model texts for such agreements that have been widely utilized. A related text that points to another direction of action is the Caribbean Common Market's Agreement on the Harmonisation of Fiscal Incentives to Industry.

Some specific issues of this kind are of major importance to investments or assume special forms in connection with them, so that they are dealt with both in general agreements and in special, FDI-related, instruments. Thus, while many of the legal issues relating to transfer of technology are governed, apart from national legislation, by multilateral conventions on intellectual property, related matters are often found in instruments concerning FDI. Current definitions of FDI in international instruments, for instance, often cover the contractual aspects of technology transfer, such as licensing of patents, trademarks and other kinds of intellectual property rights, even when they are not associated with the acquisition of control over an enterprise. In the 1970s, in response to the growth of international technology flows and an awareness of the role of technology in the development process, there was an effort to prepare an international code of conduct that would establish universally acceptable norms and standards for transfer of technology transactions. After lengthy negotiations, in the United Nations Conference on an International Code of Conduct on Transfer of Technology in the framework of UNCTAD, no consensus was reached. The topic has come up again in recent years, although with a different focus and emphasis. Intellectual property issues were dealt with in the agreement on TRIPS, in the WTO framework, and transfer of technology issues were briefly addressed in the 1994 Energy Charter Treaty.

Beginning in the 1960s, and increasingly in the decades that followed, in order to enhance the local economy's benefits from FDI, host countries sought to impose on foreign investors, usually as conditions for admission or for the grant of special incentives, requirements concerning certain aspects of their operations, such as local content and export performance. By replacing stricter and more rigid regulations, such "performance requirements" contributed for a time to the liberalization of FDI admission, at the cost of creating trade distortions. Since the mid-1980s, however, their effects on trade have led to demands for their removal or limitation. The United States took the lead in including clauses to that effect in bilateral investment agreements, and by now other countries have followed suit. At the multilateral level, the Uruguay Round agreement on TRIMs ("trade-related investment measures", another name for performance requirements), which bans certain categories of performance requirements, is of particular importance. Developing country arguments that performance requirements were necessary to counter possible restrictive practices of TNCs and to enhance the beneficial effects of FDI (Puri and Brusick, 1989; Fennell and Tyler, 1993; UNCTC and UNCTAD, 1991; Puri and Bondad, 1990) did not carry the day at the Uruguay Round, although the issue is still a matter of concern to many developing countries and considerable controversy persists.

4. Measures to ensure the proper operation of markets

Another important dimension in the legal regulation of FDI and TNCs has become apparent in recent decades. The liberalization process at work seeks to bring about a situation in which national, regional and world markets function efficiently and where the impact of Government measures that adversely affect or distort their functioning is minimized. In an increasingly integrated world economy, however, the proper functioning of the market depends not only on the control of Government measures that seek to regulate, or otherwise directly influence, the conduct of foreign investors, but also on the presence of a broader national and international legal framework protecting the market from public or private actions and policies that distort its operation (UNCTAD, 1997).

Regional and to a lesser extent multilateral instruments already embody rules and mechanisms to that effect, although the general picture is still mixed and no comprehensive regulatory framework has emerged. One difficulty in establishing such a framework, apart from obvious policy differences between States, is that international law and international instruments generally do not directly address investors. While they may impose on States duties (or recognize rights and competencies) that concern investors, to their benefit or to their detriment, they normally do not deal directly with TNCs or their affiliates, expressly recognizing rights to or imposing obligations on them. This pattern is beginning to change, just as the international law status of individuals, on which it is modelled, is changing. The development of international legal norms for the protection of human rights and for the suppression of international crimes and terrorism is increasingly bringing individuals within the ambit of international law as to rights as well as duties established by international law. There is obviously no clear and ready-made analogy between business activities, however harmful to the operation of markets, and the extreme kinds of conduct such recent developments address. Still, it is important to note that it can no longer be assumed with any certainty that international law norms cannot reach individuals and cannot regulate private conduct.

In the particular context of FDI, a number of international standards may be emerging which relate and may be directly applicable to the conduct of TNCs and their affiliates. The legal mechanisms by which such standards may become operative are complicated and at this moment still uncertain. This is even more so the case when it is taken into account that TNCs usually lack legal personality in national and even more in international law. The most convenient avenue for lending effectiveness to such standards and rules remains the traditional one of having recourse to national action through the recognition of national competence over related activities or the undertaking by States of specific international obligations to act on particular matters.

In a number of areas, however, the contents of international standards for TNC activities are becoming increasingly clear and definite. An important domain in which international standards appear to be developing is that of competition and restrictive business practices. International concern in this area dates back to the first post-war years. Repeated efforts have been made since then, although for a long time with very limited success. The only comprehensive related instrument is the Set of Multilaterally Agreed Equitable Principles and Rules for the Control of Restrictive Business Practices, negotiated in the framework of UNCTAD and adopted by the United Nations General Assembly in 1980. The issue was also extensively debated in UNCTAD, in the context of the negotiations over the draft International Code of Conduct on Transfer of Technology. Recently, the matter has come again to the foreground during the Uruguay Round negotiations, in the context of the agreements on TRIPS and TRIMs. The former Agreement addresses, among other things, the relation between restrictive business practices and transfer of technology. And as already noted, during the negotiations of the latter Agreement, developing countries placed great emphasis on the need to counter restrictive business practices by TNCs. The resulting Agreement provides that, at the first review of related issues, the possibility of adding provisions on "competition policy" shall be considered. A significant amount of work on the topic had been undertaken since then in the framework of the pertinent WTO Working Group.

The protection of the environment is probably the domain in which the process of international regulation is today most active. Relevant provisions are found in many recent instruments. In some cases, most of them only indirectly related to FDI, as in the case of maritime pollution, legally-binding rules have been adopted. In most of the cases that are more directly related to FDI, either the instruments themselves are not legally binding, or, when they are, the formulation of the relevant provisions tends to be relatively "soft". Among texts of the former type, one may cite the UNCTC Criteria for Sustainable Development Management: Towards Environmentally Sustainable Development, and the relevant provisions of the draft United Nations Code of Conduct on TNCs. An illustration of the latter case are the provisions on protection of the environment in the Energy Charter Treaty. At the regional level, the pertinent chapter of the OECD Guidelines for Multinational Enterprises, under renewed consideration at the end of 1999, is of particular significance. On specific issues, the series of OECD recommendations on the avoidance of transborder pollution is of immediate relevance.

Similar standards have been proposed in other areas of FDI-related activity. The codes of conduct adopted in the 1970s or early 1980s contain numerous pertinent provisions. Labour and employment issues are dealt with in the ILO's Tripartite Declaration of Principles concerning Multinational Enterprises and Social Policy and more recently in the ILO Declaration on Fundamental Principles and Rights at Work (ILO, 1998). The relevant chapters in the OECD Guidelines should acquired increased significance in view of the renewed attention being paid to that instrument. Protection of consumers is the topic of several instruments, such as the WHO International Code of Marketing of Breast-milk Substitutes and the United Nations guidelines for consumer protection. Protection of privacy and regulation of transborder data flows have also been dealt with by a Council of Europe Convention and by important OECD instruments. Other issues closely related to FDI are dealt with chiefly through networks of bilateral agreements; this is particularly the case with taxation problems and the related issue of transfer pricing.

The issue of bribery and illicit payments has recently received considerable attention. The topic had already been addressed earlier, at a time when efforts were made to draft international codes of conduct. In the past few years, however, several proposed international agreements have dealt with that issue, notably, the 1996 Inter-American Convention against Corruption (OAS, 1996a), the 1997 OECD draft Convention on Combating Bribery of Foreign Public Officials in International Business Transactions (OECD, 1996a) (which follows in the footsteps of an earlier Recommendation on the same topic), and the Council of Europe's 1999 draft Criminal Law Convention on Corruption (CoE, 1999). A number of other recent instruments have dealt with the same topic, in particular, two United Nations General Assembly resolutions in successive years, namely, resolution 51/191 (1996), United Nations Declaration against Corruption and Bribery in International Commercial Transactions (UNGA, 1997), and resolution 52/87, on International Cooperation against Corruption and Bribery in International Commercial Transactions (UNGA, 1998), as well as the International Chamber of Commerce's recently updated Rules of Conduct to Combat Extortion and Bribery.

It is clear that international standards relating to TNC conduct have by no means reached the stage of legal perfection that would render them capable of being effectively invoked by States (and others, whether non-governmental organizations or individuals) in their relations with TNCs and their affiliates. It is, however, significant that at the moment this is an area of active concern in international forums. Apart from providing models for national legislation, whose international legitimacy is thus ensured in advance, such standards may also be contributing the creation of a general climate on their various subject matters, a climate that TNCs are increasingly taking into account in assuming the burden of socially responsible action in conducting their operations.

C. Investment protection

The general heading of "investment protection" covers international rules and principles designed to protect the interests of foreign investors against host Government actions unduly detrimental to their interests. The norms in question have their roots in customary law, but in recent years they have found expression in numerous treaty provisions.

Protection was a topic of particular importance in the decades after the Second World War, when established investments, especially in natural resources, were affected by Government takings, in the context of either large-scale socio political reforms or recent decolonization. The wide spread use of exchange controls, in most countries, including for a long time most developed ones, created another major issue, less emotional perhaps but of great practical importance -- that of the "repatriation of benefits and capital", as it was called at the time (nowadays covered by the broader term of "transfer of funds"). And a far-ranging spirit of mistrust towards foreign investment in host countries gave rise to fears that few neutral decision makers could be found in the courts and administrative agencies of these countries. By and large, these same topics, albeit with significant variations in intensity, are still on the agenda of international action concerning foreign investment.

It is obvious that whatever a Government does may affect, positively or negatively, the interests of the enterprises operating in its territory, foreign or, for that matter, domestic. Even routine regulatory action, such as zoning regulation or the issuance of construction permits and operation licences, can affect the profitability of an enterprise and may even sometimes lead to its closing down. The impact can be more serious where regulations for the protection of public health, the protection of the environment or other such core governmental responsibilities are concerned. An enterprise, whether domestic or foreign, functions under the laws in effect in the host country. One may construe the foreign investors' demands for national treatment in precisely these terms: they seek to be able to operate under the laws in force, with no discrimination or differential treatment. It would be unreasonable to expect that foreign enterprises would be protected against any and all measures that, in one way or another, may be detrimental to their interests.

It is thus necessary to try to determine more clearly the kinds of measures against which protection might be sought. At first blush, they would have to be those that cause "undue" damage -- measures, that is to say, that either contravene accepted international norms or infringe on the legitimate expectations of investors. Given the diversity of situations and regimes in the world, it is necessary to explore in more specific terms the types of action that may be involved.

The Government measures against which protection may be sought may thus be seen as falling into three broad categories:

- First and foremost, measures, such as property takings and abrogations of contracts, that cause major disruptions to, or even terminate, an investor's operations in the host country, contrary to what could be legitimately expected or foreseen at the time of entry.
- Secondly, other measures, possibly less catastrophic but still seriously detrimental to an investor's interests, such as discriminatory taxation, disregard of intellectual property rights, or arbitrary refusal of licences.
- A third category would cover measures which, although not necessarily unfair or even unpredictable, affect foreign investors in a disproportionate manner, compared to domestic enterprises, so that pertinent assurances are considered necessary.

There is no clear borderline between these types of measures. Distinctions between them are chiefly based on the scale of the impact of the measures, on the intent behind the measures, even on what may normally be expected. Thus, the terms of "creeping", "indirect" or "constructive" expropriation, or "regulatory takings", are sometimes applied to measures that are not qualified expressly as expropriations or property takings, but whose intended impact is ruinous for the investor.

It is evident that the entire category of investment protection issues is a fluid one and depends largely upon the state of the broader international legal framework for FDI. To the extent that this framework evolves -- that restrictions are eliminated, for instance, or positive general standards applied -- the need for measures of protection will presumably diminish. The scope of investment protection may thus be understood as changing, in that the number of such issues decreases, as other international norms concerning investment are expanding. At the very least, problems will no longer be perceived as relating to investment protection but rather as concerning possible infringements of general standards of treatment.

Conceptually, in fact, these are issues that may be best understood as coming under the rubric of "treatment". It is not easy to specify what exactly serves to differentiate them from other treatment issues, apart from the fact that "investment protection" is an established class of issues in international law and practice. In many instances, the differentiating factor may be the intent behind the measures, especially where discrimination against aliens is present. In more objective terms, situations of vital importance to investors may be involved, which relate to their status as aliens and to the fact that they are not, at least initially, members of the political community of the host country or that they may continue to have close links outside the country (e.g. the foreign firms' profit centre may be located outside the host country, so that the application of "normal" exchange controls may be particularly detrimental to it).

One last point may help further to clarify matters. A number of possible assurances to investors, for example concerning special tax incentives or guarantees as to the immutability of the legal regime under which the investment was undertaken, are generally the subject of contractual or quasi-contractual arrangements between investor and host State. Such specific assurances are generally not covered by clauses in broader international instruments, save to the extent that the latter frequently seek to ensure that all promises to investors should be carried out in good faith.

1. Takings of property

The principal measures against which investors seek protection are expropriations, nationalizations and other major cases of deprivation of property and infringement of property rights of investors. As already noted, the first post-war decades saw many instances of large-scale action of this kind, the consequences of sociopolitical change, in Western and Eastern Europe, and of decolonization and resulting efforts to assert control over their natural resources, in other continents. Both the historical context and the ideological motivations have today changed. Although the not-so-distant past has left some mistrust and apprehension in its wake, the actual likelihood of large-scale action of this sort is today rather unlikely. However, because of political problems or of real or perceived failures in the application of laws or the administration of justice, the possibility of arbitrary measures against individual investors, has not totally disappeared.

In the classical international law of State responsibility for injuries to aliens, a sharp distinction was made between measures affecting the property of aliens and those dealing with their rights from contracts with the State. The distinction reflected in part doctrinal classifications (sometimes found in national constitutional law) which resulted in increased legal protection for property rights as compared to contractual ones. It was also based, however, on the perception that aliens entering into contracts with foreign Governments were cognizant of the risks and could not therefore complain as to any sovereign action affecting their interests. In the Latin American international law tradition, State contracts were generally subject to local jurisdiction, whether by an express clause inserted in the contract itself (the so-called "Calvo clause") or by express constitutional provision (Shea, 1955). The distinction was of considerable practical significance, since the most important activities of interest to foreign investors were the exploitation of natural resources and the operation of public utility enterprises, both of which were generally based on contracts of concession with the Government. In the decades after the Second World War, the importance of State contracts for foreign investors was enhanced by the practice of according special tax treatment or other rights by means of "investment conventions" or other special instruments, often deemed to be of a contractual character.

The international law of "State contracts", as it came to be called, went through several phases and an extensive case law of arbitral awards developed (Fatouros, 1962; Kuusi, 1979; Sacerdoti, 1972; Paasivirta, 1990). On the one hand, the contractual (or "quasi-contractual") character of administrative acts governing a State's relations with foreign private persons was put in doubt, and their administrative character emphasized. On the other hand, for many international jurists, the actual importance of such arrangements for the host State and even for the world economy brought them increasingly closer to the status of international (i.e.

intergovernmental) agreements and outside the exclusive jurisdiction of the State involved. Yet, the consequences of such "internationalization" were by no means clear. For some writers (and arbitrators), "internationalization" meant that the strict international law rules governing treaty obligations were applicable. For others, to the contrary, a politically informed approach was necessary, whose reasoning went along the more flexible lines of "administrative contracts" in national law (especially, French administrative law). By and large, however, the trend has been to treat aliens' rights derived from State contracts in manners approximating those of property rights.

Relevant international law norms, concerning both deprivation of foreign property and abrogation of State contracts, have been the object of considerable debate in the decades since the end of the Second World War. In practice, most of the debate centred on the requirement of compensation and the modalities of its assessment and payment. Developed countries have insisted that, for such actions to be internationally lawful, they have to meet the requirements established in classical international law: the measures have to be taken in the public interest, they should not be discriminatory, and they should be accompanied by full compensation. Developing countries, while frequently allowing that appropriate compensation should normally be paid, have asserted that any conditions or prerequisites for property takings within a country's territory are to be determined by that country's own laws and are subject to the exclusive jurisdiction of its courts.

The controversies just outlined are mirrored in several of the earlier international instruments. A successful effort at reaching a compromise, in a specific context, was the 1962 United Nations General Assembly resolution 1803(XVII), on permanent sovereignty over natural wealth and resources (box 2). The developed countries' positions are reflected in such texts as the 1967 OECD draft Convention, while the positions of developing countries in the 1970s may be seen in the General Assembly resolutions associated with a New International Economic Order. The problems of investment protection were a major point of difference in the negotiations on the United Nations draft Code of Conduct on Transnational Corporations.

The current situation is not totally clear, although, once again, certain trends are unmistakable. The most important change in the attitudes of both Governments and investors has been one in perspective. To begin with, the dichotomy between home and host countries characteristic of earlier discussions has been overtaken by changes in the structure of the world economy. An increasing number of countries now see themselves on both sides of that divide. Partly as a result, concern has shifted from dealing with past situations to establishing rules for the future. Host countries appear to be increasingly inclined to provide assurances of fair treatment to future investors, including undertakings against expropriation, promises of full compensation and acceptance of dispute-settlement procedures, both because they consider it useful for attracting FDI and because they do not consider it probable that they would wish to take such measures in the foreseeable future. The positions that thus appear to crystallize in several recent texts are closer to those that were in the past supported by the capital-exporting countries. In fact, for several decades now, host countries have accepted many of these positions in BITs, while generally resisting their incorporation into regional and multilateral instruments. It is chiefly in this last respect that their attitudes appear to be evolving. As a result, strong provisions on the subject are found in such recent instruments as NAFTA, the Energy Charter Treaty and the World Bank Guidelines on the Treatment of Foreign Direct Investment.

The formulation of pertinent provisions in international instruments raises issues related to the problems of definition already discussed. Efforts to expand the scope of the notion of expropriation or "taking", by covering "indirect" measures, so that so-called "regulatory takings" are covered, raise the possibility of excessively limiting generally accepted regulatory powers of the host State. Recent debate over the MAI brought such concerns to the fore. One suggested way of coping with the issue is to include in IIAs declaratory provisions on preserving the State's regulatory powers. Yet, the actual value of such general statements will become clearer only when such texts are applied and are interpreted by arbitral or other tribunals. In the past, indeed, such issues were sometimes dealt with when fixing the amount of compensation to be awarded, for instance, by taking into account not only the extent of an investor's injury but also the State's benefit or enrichment from the measures (or lack thereof).

In the wake of provisions on property takings in regional and multilateral instruments, provisions may also be found that concern protection against injuries caused by civil war or internal disorder. These provisions, however, assure investors not of indemnification in all cases, but of non-discrimination in the award of compensation. That is to say, contrary to the usual run of expropriation provisions, foreign firms in such cases are to be compensated only when domestic firms in similar situations are.

2. Other issues of investment protection

Provisions on other possible measures detrimental to the investors' interests are found in international instruments specifically directed at investment protection, particularly BITs. Since they cover a variety of possible situations, they are usually less specific and concrete than the provisions on protection against expropriation and they are closely related to the provisions on the general treatment of investors. Thus, the general nondiscrimination standards may be invoked to protect against discriminatory treatment in matters of taxation. In addition, absolute standards, preeminently that of "fair and equitable treatment", are utilized.

The case of the Energy Charter Treaty is characteristic. The first paragraph in the article dealing with investment provides a series of norms and (essentially non-contingent) standards regarding the appropriate treatment of investments (before and after admission) (box 6). According to that provision, parties shall "accord at all times to investments ... fair and equitable treatment" and treatment no less favourable than "that required by international law"; investments "shall enjoy the most constant protection"; and no party "shall in any way impair by unreasonable or discriminatory measures their management, maintenance, use, enjoyment or disposal". Subsequent paragraphs address other issues, such as nondiscrimination.

Finally, an important aspect of investment protection is the availability, at both the national and international levels, of investment insurance against non-commercial risks, which cover measures relating to several protection issues. National programmes to that effect have been operating for several decades in most capital-exporting countries. On the international level, the adoption in 1985 of the convention establishing MIGA, under the auspices of the World Bank, made possible the provision of insurance to investments that might not have been fully eligible under national programmes. The Agency has also undertaken a useful role in promoting the development of a favourable legal climate for foreign investments.

At the regional level as well, several international agreements have established investment guarantee agencies, as in the case of the Convention Establishing the Inter-Arab Investment Guarantee Corporation, and the Articles of Agreement of the Islamic Corporation for the Insurance of Investment and Export Credit. BITs, as well as several regional and multilateral instruments, supplement these schemes by providing for the possibility of subrogation of the guarantee agencies to the investors' rights.

3. Transfer of funds and related issues

A major category of investment protection provisions consists of measures that seek to address concerns that are specific to foreign investors, because, for instance, their investment crosses national borders, their base of operations and profit centres are in another country, their managerial personnel is often foreign, etc. The main such provisions are those concerning the transfer of funds (profits, capital, royalties and other types of payments) by the investor outside the host country and the possibility of employing foreign managerial or specialized personnel without restrictions.

These matters fall within the broad area of the regulation of movement of capital and payments, on the one hand, and persons, on the other. Many of the former issues are covered by the Articles of Agreement of the International Monetary Fund and its decisions and acts. Among OECD members, the Liberalisation Codes provide for the removal of restrictions not only on capital movements but also on current payments, including transfer of profits from investments.

Given the presence of exchange controls and restrictions in many host countries, instruments specifically concerned with investment frequently address this issue. In many cases, indeed, provisions on transfer of funds go beyond the mere assurance that foreign investors will be free to buy foreign exchange; where exchange restrictions are in effect, foreign investors may be guaranteed that foreign exchange will be made available to them or that they will have priority access to it. In national legislation on FDI, provisions were common, and still persist in a number of cases, whereby investors were guaranteed the right to transfer abroad, under specified conditions, their profits (or a percentage thereof) and, usually under more restrictive terms, the capital invested.

In the first post-war decades, when exchange controls were still widely prevalent, international instruments, even among developed countries, tended to avoid strong provisions on fund transfers. The pertinent recommendation in the OECD 1967 draft Convention is characteristically weak. Recent instruments tend to be stronger, although this is true of few multilateral instruments; one important example is that of the World Bank Guidelines on the Treatment of Foreign Direct Investment. Such provisions are more common on the regional level, as, for instance, in Decision 291 of the Andean Pact and in several regional instruments. Provisions allowing the free transfer of funds are also found in the APEC Non-Binding Investment Principles, in the Energy Charter Treaty and in BITs. In several cases, the provisions are subject to an exception when the host country faces major balance-of-payments problems.

4. Settlement of disputes

The complex operations of a modern enterprise give rise to a host of legal problems that may lead to disputes. Proper legal planning combined with good management may succeed in resolving most of them before they reach the point where they become legal disputes. Still, it is to be expected that, since problems will arise, some of them will not be resolved through negotiations or other friendly arrangements. With respect to the operations of a foreign affiliate in a host country -- and depending on the parties concerned -- three classes of possible disputes may be distinguished: disputes between the investor and another private party; interstate (or State-to-State) disputes; and disputes between a host State and an investor.

Disputes between private parties. These are normally left to be resolved through recourse to the host country judicial system or to arbitration between the parties ("commercial arbitration"). The presence of a properly functioning national system of administration of justice is a central element of a country's investment climate. It is also a necessary part of the general legal framework that is indispensable for effective liberalization. International instruments can encourage the growth of such institutions but they cannot establish them. In the past, capital-exporting countries had sometimes sought to ensure that the option of private commercial arbitration would be available to investors, but such proposals are no longer common, at least at a governmental level.

Classical international law has generally not been directly concerned with disputes between private parties, save in exceptional cases, where some failure on the part of the State organs might be detected and the rules of the law of State responsibility can be invoked. IIAs and other international instruments have addressed this issue with a view towards facilitating the execution of eventual arbitral awards, something that in many countries had initially met with procedural and jurisdictional obstacles. This is the task that the New York Convention on the Recognition and Enforcement of Foreign Arbitral Awards has performed with considerable success.

Arbitration procedures and mechanisms that can be voluntarily used by private investors in such disputes (as well as in disputes between States and investors) have been established by various intergovernmental and non-governmental instruments. The United Nations Commission on International Trade Law (UNCITRAL) rules of arbitration and the International Chamber of Commerce rules and institutional mechanisms are prime illustrations of successful such efforts.

State-to-State arbitration. State-to-State arbitration or adjudication is, of course, a major possibility in traditional public international law. Older instruments as well as the relatively recent Rules of Arbitration prepared by the International Law Commission provide for relevant procedures. Many IIAs provide that, with respect to any dispute concerning the interpretation or application of the instrument itself and usually after the failure of diplomatic or other efforts at resolving the dispute, recourse may be had to interstate arbitration (or adjudication before the International Court of Justice). Such provisions are of direct relevance to the topic at hand because they also would normally cover the possibility of espousal of an investor's claim by his home State, on the basis of the rules on diplomatic protection and the law of State responsibility. It is precisely in order to avoid elevating an investment dispute to an interstate problem that provision for investor-to-State arbitration is made in many investment-related international instruments.

Investor-to-State disputes. The disputes between an investor and a host State are the ones where the search for a dispute-settlement method has been most active in recent years. In the past, such disputes either were resolved by the host country's national courts or resulted in an interstate dispute, through espousal of the private claim by the State of the investor's nationality. In several instances, on the basis of international agreements between the host State and the State of the investor's nationality, concluded after the dispute had arisen, such disputes came before special (arbitral) tribunals (sometimes called "mixed claims commissions"). A major recent instance is the operation of the Iran-United States Claims Tribunal. Such an approach may be appropriate where a considerable number of disputes have accumulated or where the disputes have arisen in special contexts.

Investor-to-State disputes are normally subject to the jurisdiction of the host State's courts. To the extent, for instance, that foreign investors have been accorded national treatment, they are entitled to seek redress before the local courts. In most instances this remains an option open to the investors, and many States insist that, with respect to at least some issues (e.g. taxation or constitutional questions), foreign investors should remain subject to local jurisdiction.

Investors, and their States of nationality, have insisted, however, that alternative means of dispute settlement are preferable and help better to protect investments, because of a number of possible considerations: the mistrust towards foreign investment prevalent in many host countries, combined with the high political importance of some of the disputes, which gives rise to fears that no neutral national decision makers can be found; the lack of judicial expertise in modern financial and other issues in some developing countries; and a desire for speedier resolution of possible conflicts. All these arguments militate in favour of a recourse to special dispute-settlement procedures, on the basis of existing international commercial arbitration mechanisms. Providing for some form of arbitration before a dispute has arisen helps moreover to avoid elevating a future dispute to the intergovernmental, political, level.

One major instrument to that effect is the Convention on the Settlement of Investment Disputes between States and Nationals of Other States, concluded in 1965 (Broches, 1972). It was proposed by and negotiated under the auspices of the World Bank and is administered by the International Centre for Settlement of Investment Disputes, which operates in the framework of the World Bank. A permanent machinery and binding procedures for arbitration (and conciliation) of investment disputes has thus been established. In addition, Permanent Court of Arbitration has issued a set of optional Rules for such disputes (not necessarily restricted to investment). Other instruments and institutions that deal in the main with disputes between private persons are also available for disputes between investors and States. This is the case with the rules and institutional machinery of the International Chamber of Commerce and with the UNCITRAL Rules, which were applied before the Iran-United States Claims Tribunal.

Most recent IIAs contain provisions on dispute settlement. Among recent regional and interregional instruments, NAFTA, the Energy Charter Treaty and the draft MAI cover in lengthy provisions the possibilities of State-to-State and investor-to-State arbitration. Similar clauses are found in the numerous BITs that have been concluded in the past four decades.

The practice that has prevailed is to allow a choice of procedures, often after unsuccessful recourse to negotiations or conciliation procedures. The adjudication procedures range usually from the local courts and tribunals to any of several arbitration institutions or sets of rules, such as those named above, at the choice of the party that has recourse to them -- that is to say, usually the foreign investor.

Interesting problems of legal sociology arise out of the operation of such a diffuse and decentralized system of dispute settlement, which are outside the scope of this paper (Dezaley and Garth, 1996). One important facet, however, should be mentioned. Dispute-settlement procedures of any kind have two basic functions. One is to settle in a fair and mutually acceptable manner the particular dispute that has arisen. The other is to contribute to the eventual development of a body of rules on the topics involved. Many national and international bodies of law have developed through the case law of individual courts. While the first function is predominant from the point of view of any individual investor, the second becomes increasingly important when one deals with a broader framework of rules and procedures that covers a large number of possible investment relationships. In the current practices (and debates) concerning investment-related dispute settlement, the first function is taken fully into account. It may be, however, that more attention should be paid to the manner in which the second function is served by the methods today prevalent.

Section IV
The Development Dimension of IIAs and the Need for Flexibility

In considering current trends concerning IIAs, it is important to pay particular attention to their impact on development. Developing countries seek FDI in order to promote their economic development; this is their paramount objective. To that end, by participating in IIAs and through national legislation, they have sought to establish a legal framework that would reduce obstacles to FDI, strengthen positive standards of treatment and ensure the proper functioning of markets, while also assuring foreign investors of a high level of protection for their investments. A question that must be examined, then, at the end of this brief study of IIAs, is the manner and extent to which participation in IIAs may indeed assist developing countries in their efforts to advance their economic development.

To begin with, it is by now generally accepted that host countries can derive considerable benefits from increased FDI (UNCTAD, 1999a; see also the chapter on FDI and development in volume III). Developing country Governments participate in IIAs because they believe that, on balance, these instruments help them attract FDI and benefit from it. At the same time, IIAs, like all international agreements, limit to a certain extent the freedom of action of the States party to them, and thereby limit the policy options available to decision makers for pursuing development objectives. A question arises, therefore, as to whether and how far developing countries participating in IIAs can maintain a certain policy space to promote their development by influencing, through direct or indirect measures, the amount and kinds of FDI that they receive and the conduct of the foreign firms involved. National Governments, after all, remain responsible for the welfare of their people in this, as in other, domains.

Thus, when concluding IIAs, developing countries face a basic challenge: how to link the goal of creating an appropriate stable, predictable and transparent FDI policy framework that enables firms to advance their corporate objectives on the one hand, with that of retaining a margin of freedom necessary to pursue their national development objectives, on the other. These objectives are by no means contradictory. A concept that can help link them is "flexibility", which, for present purposes, can be defined as the ability of IIAs to adapt to the particular conditions prevailing in developing countries and to the realities of the economic asymmetries between these countries and developed countries (see chapter 2).

A discussion of flexibility in IIAs can be approached from four main angles:[11]

- **Objectives**. IIAs often address development concerns by including in their text, usually in the preamble, declaratory statements referring to the promotion of development as a main objective of the agreement, or to specific ways by which to contribute to development objectives, or a generally worded recognition of the special needs of developing and/ or least developed country parties requiring flexibility in the operation of the obligations under the agreement. There are many variations of such language, and it is hard to generalize regarding its actual role and importance. Preambles and similar declarations normally do not directly create rights and obligations for the parties to the instrument, but they are relevant to its interpretation. In fact, the texts of preambles are often the result of hard bargaining. To the extent that such language reflects the will of the participating countries, it helps to reaffirm the acceptance of development as a central purpose of current international arrangements. The specific language used in each case and its relationship to the rest of the instrument is, of course, important. The pertinent language may be less significant if it is merely a declaration of intentions, while it may have greater impact when it is so formulated (or so located in the instrument) as to permit its utilization, in negotiations, in court, or in arbitration, so as in turn to make development a test for the interpretation or application of other provisions or otherwise to vary their effect.
- **Overall structure.** Promotion of development can also be manifested in the very structure of IIAs. For example, an agreement may expressly (or, in certain cases, by clear implication) distinguish between developed and developing participating countries, by establishing, for instance, separate categories, the members of which do not have exactly the same rights and duties. There may also be general clauses allowing for special and differential (in fact, more favourable) treatment of developing countries.

The most common device aimed at promoting the development of developing countries in IIAs is the inclusion of various kinds of exceptions and special clauses, essentially granting developing countries a certain freedom to waive or postpone the application of particular provisions of the instrument, with a view to taking action to promote their development. Such exceptions take a great variety of forms: they may be general (e.g. for the protection of national security) or sectoral (e.g. the so-called "cultural exception"), they may set a timelimit (so-called "transitional provisions") or they may be country-specific. It is also possible to allow the gradual expansion of commitments on the basis of a positive listing of industries or activities, as opposed to a listing of exceptions. The compilation of the latter is by no means easy, since it involves a thorough command of the actual effects of national measures, an accurate prediction of future interpretations of particular provisions of the IIA involved and a full understanding of future needs and policy decisions.

- **Substantive provisions.** A balance of rights and obligations can also find expression in the substantive content of an IIA -- beginning with the choices countries make about the issues they wish to include in an IIA, and those they wish to keep outside the scope of an agreement -- and in the formulation of its substantive provisions, through ways that allow countries to retain some flexibility regarding the commitments they made, keeping also in mind the various interactions between issues and provisions. The range of approaches and permutations that can be used in formulating substantive provisions in IIAs is broad. Of course, flexibility might need to be approached in different ways for each individual substantive issue depending on its characteristics and developmental effects. For example, the type of approaches to flexibility that can be useful in a development context regarding the admission and establishment of FDI might not be relevant to post-establishment national and MFN treatment provisions, or to expropriation, labour or environmental standards. There are no general prescriptions on the matter. The choice of approach depends on the conditions prevailing in each country and the particular development strategies pursued by each Government.

  Furthermore, it is self-evident that, for the purposes of assessing its impact on development, it is the entire instrument that counts and not particular facets or provisions.

- **Modalities of application.** Flexibility for development can also be exercised during the application stage of an IIA. The manner in which an IIA is interpreted, and the way in which it is to be made effective, determine whether its objectives, structure and substantive provisions produce the desired developmental effects. The degree of flexibility allowed for the interpretation and application of an IIA depends to a large extent on the legal character of an agreement and the formulation of individual provisions. Legally binding agreements, even if they do not provide for implementation mechanisms, impose on the States signatories a legal obligation under international law to comply with their provisions. How far such an obligation actually limits the subsequent freedom of action of the States concerned largely depends on the language of the agreement or the type of obligations imposed. Voluntary instruments, on the other hand, are not legally enforceable but can have an influence on the development of national and international law.

  The institutional arrangements involved in the application of IIAs are crucial in the context of development. Action at the national level is fundamental to give effect to the provisions of an IIA. In fact, the adoption of an IIA, whether as an international agreement or as a formally non-binding instrument, is bound to have an impact on the national policies of the adopting States. The impact, of course, would be stronger and more immediate in the case of the former. In that case, in giving effect to an IIA its provisions may require some kind of incorporation into national law. At the international level, the development outcome of an IIA is intimately related to the intergovernmental institutional machinery for follow-up and monitoring its application. There are various mechanisms that can be involved, ranging from simple reporting requirements (which nevertheless can be a significant inducement to act in compliance) and advisory and consultative functions (aimed at resolving questions arising out of the continuing application of an IIA), to complaint and clarification mechanisms (aimed at facilitating application of non-binding instruments under procedures of a non-adjudicatory nature) and various international methods of settlement of disputes (which may allow more or less freedom to the parties to accept proposed ways for resolution of the dispute). In addition, an agreement might eventually need partial or extensive revisions. This is a fundamental facet of the entire process of the elaboration of an IIA, which is to be understood neither as a preliminary document, nor as a final definitive formulation of rules and procedures. Instead, it may rather be seen as part of a continuing process of interaction, review and adjustment to changing realities and to new perceptions of problems and possibilities.

  An important final consideration is the difficulties that many developing countries may experience in trying to apply an IIA, due to lack of adequate skills and resources. These constraints may prevent them from putting in place appropriate mechanisms and institutions to give effect to an IIA. To address such difficulties, IIAs can make special arrangements for technical and financial assistance. In addition, to ensure that the development goals of an IIA are fully realized, it may be desirable for developed countries parties to undertake promotional measures to encourage FDI flows to developing countries.

In conclusion, these are some of the techniques that can be used, combined in a multitude of manners, in the construction of an investment instrument to provide for a certain flexibility in the interest of development. Whatever the combination of elements, the point is that IIAs can be constructed in a manner that ensures an overall balance of rights and obligations for all actors involved, so that all parties can derive benefits from it. Nevertheless, it must be recognized that, like all international agreements, IIAs typically contain obligations that, by their very nature, reduce to some extent the autonomy of the participating countries. At the same time, such agreements need to recognize important differences in the characteristics of the parties involved, in particular the economic asymmetries and levels of development between developing and developed countries. More specifically, if IIAs do not allow developing countries to pursue their fundamental objective of advancing their development -- indeed make a positive contribution to this objective --they run the risk of being of little or no interest to them. This underlines the importance of designing, from the outset, IIAs in a manner that allows their parties a certain degree of flexibility in pursuing their development objectives. To find the proper balance between obligations and flexibility -- a balance that leaves sufficient space for development-oriented national policies -- is indeed a difficult challenge faced by negotiators of IIAs. This is particularly important as international investment treaty-making activity at all levels has indeed intensified in recent years.

Concluding Observations

In the past four decades, national and international legal policies and rules concerning FDI have repeatedly changed. FDI itself has also changed, in its form, its magnitude and its context. It is now generally agreed that many facets of the legal regulation of FDI are a matter of international concern.

In the national laws and policies relating to FDI, the trends towards liberalization and increased protection have gathered strength during the past 15 years, and at a faster pace in the 1990s.

Entry controls and restrictions have been relaxed and in many cases dismantled. Nondiscriminatory treatment after admission is becoming the rule rather than the exception. Guarantees of non-expropriation and of the free transfer of funds are increasingly given. These trends are gradually spreading to the international level. Guarantees of protection are predominant at bilateral level while, along with liberalization measures, they are expanding at the regional level and have begun approaching the multilateral, worldwide level.

The study of existing regional and multilateral instruments, however, raises a number of difficult questions. The international legal framework for FDI is fluid, chiefly because, despite recent developments, there is no established, clear policy consensus on the subject and its many facets. As a result, there is no comprehensive global instrument. Existing multilateral instruments are partial and fragmentary. Regional and bilateral agreements have in the recent past taken the lead in adapting legal rules to new conditions. But it is not self-evident that the approaches (and even the technical language) appropriate at the regional, and even less, at the bilateral, level are possible and proper at the worldwide level. While the trends in effect appear, in their general lines, reasonably definite, the actual situation in international law and policy with respect to investment lacks coherence and clarity, and the exact relationship among legal actions and measures at the various levels is unclear, since many developments in question are relatively recent and little actual practice and even less case law, judicial or arbitral, has had the chance to crystallize.

It is in this context that the present volumes have been prepared. They not only cover most of the important issues that may arise in discussions about IIAs, but also seeks to provide balanced analyses that can shed more light on those issues. To that end, each chapter develops a range of policy options that could facilitate the formation of consensus on the various facets of investment frameworks.

Notes

1 For notable recent efforts to discuss particular aspects of this legal framework, see Juillard, 1994; Sornarajah, 1994; and Sacerdoti, 1997.

2 Unless otherwise noted, the agreements and other instruments mentioned in this chapter are reproduced in UNCTAD, 1996a and 2000.

3 The literature on the subject of this chapter -- especially certain aspects such as nationalization -- is vast. The chapter refrains from referring to this literature. Instead, the reader is referred to the bibliography in volume III.

4 For a discussion of the determinants of FDI, see UNCTAD, 1998b.

5 There is considerable literature on this topic; see, e.g., Muchlinski, 1999; Sauvant and Aranda, 1994; and Fatouros, 1994.

6 See, for instance, UN-ECOSOC, 1956 and 1957.

7 Developments in national and international law and policy in the 1990s have been reported over the years in the successive *World Investment Reports;* see UNCTC, 1991; UN/DESD/TCMD, 1992; UNCTAD, 1993, 1994, 1995, 1996b, 1997, 1998b, 1999a, 2003, 2004a.

8 The use of the more comprehensive term "international instrument" is meant to reflect the variety of form and effect of the international acts and documents involved, whose diversity is enhanced by their varying substantive scope and their differing policy orientations. Moreover, while the term "international agreements" refers, of course, to legally binding treaties between or among States, the term "international instruments" includes, in addition to agreements, other international texts with no legally binding force, such as recommendations, declarations and agreements not in effect.

9 The relevant international law terminology is not very clear or fully consistent. In United Nations language, in particular, the term "regional" does not necessarily have a geographical connotation; it covers essentially multilateral arrangements which are not, in fact or in prospect, worldwide. The recent introduction of the terms "plurilateral" and "interregional" has further complicated the terminology. On the other hand, the geographical connotation is preserved in the case of "regional integration agreements".

10 References to individual chapters seem redundant in this context, except when specific points at issue are involved. Since the volumes, moreover, contain a bibliography, bibliographical references in this section have been kept to a minimum.

11 For a detailed discussion, see chapter 2.

Annex 1. Main international instruments[a] dealing with FDI, 1948-2003

Year[b]	*Title*	*Setting*	*Level*	*Form*	*Status*
1948	Havana Charter for an International Trade Organization	International Conference on Trade and Employment	Multilateral	Binding	Not ratified
1948	Draft Statutes of the Arbitral Tribunal for Foreign Investment and of the Foreign Investments Court	International Law Association	Non-governmental	Non-binding	Not adopted
1949	International Code of Fair Treatment for Foreign Investments	International Chamber of Commerce	Non-governmental	Non-binding	Adopted
1957	Treaty Establishing the European Economic Community	European Economic Community	Regional	Binding	Adopted
1957	Agreement on Arab Economic Unity	Council of Arab Economic Unity	Regional	Binding	Adopted
1958	Convention on the Recognition and Enforcement of Foreign Arbitral Awards	United Nations	Multilateral	Binding	Adopted
1959	Draft Convention on Investments Abroad	Abs-Shawcross Draft Convention	Non-Governmental	Non-binding	Not adopted
1961	Code of Liberalisation of Capital Movements	OECD	Regional	Binding	Adopted
1961	Code of Liberalisation of Current Invisible Operations	OECD	Regional	Binding	Adopted
1962	United Nations General Assembly Resolution 1803 (XVII): Permanent Sovereignty over Natural Resources	United Nations	Multilateral	Non-binding	Adopted
1963	Model Tax Convention on Income and on Capital	OECD	Regional	Model	Adopted
1965	Common Convention on Investments in the States of the Customs and Economic Union of Central Africa	Customs and Economic Union of Central Africa	Regional	Binding	Adopted
1965	Convention on the Settlement of Investment Disputes between States and Nationals of Other States	World Bank	Multilateral	Binding	Adopted
1967	Revised Recommendation of the Council Concerning Co-operation Between Member Countries on Anticompetitive Practices Affecting International Trade	OECD	Regional	Non-binding	Adopted
1967	Draft Convention on the Protection of Foreign Property	OECD	Regional	Non-binding	Not adopted
1969	Agreement on Andean Sub-regional Integration	Andean Common Market	Regional	Binding	Adopted
1969	Agreement Establishing an Association between the European Economic Community and the Malagasy States	European Community-Malagasy States	Inter-regional	Binding	Adopted
1969	Agreement Establishing an Association between the European Economic Community and the United Republic of Tanzania, the Republic of Uganda and the Republic of Kenya	European Community-Tanzania, Uganda and Kenya	Inter-regional	Binding	Adopted
1970	Agreement on Investment and Free Movement of Arab Capital among Arab Countries	Arab Economic Unity	Regional	Binding	Adopted
1970	Decision No. 24 of the Commission of the Cartagena Agreement: Common Regulations Governing Foreign Capital Movement, Trade Marks, Patents, Licences and Royalties	Andean Common Market	Regional	Binding	Superseded
1971	Convention Establishing the Inter-Arab Investment Guarantee Corporation	Inter-Arab Investment Guarantee Corporation	Regional	Binding	Adopted
1972	Joint Convention on the Freedom of Movement of Persons and the Right of Establishment in the Central African	Central African Customs and Economic Union	Regional	Binding	Adopted
1972	Guidelines for International Investment	International Chamber of Commerce	Non-Governmental	Non-binding	Adopted
1973	Treaty Establishing the Caribbean Community	Caribbean Community	Regional	Binding	Adopted
1974	United Nations General Assembly Resolution 3201 (S-VI): Declaration on the Establishment of a New International Economic Order and United Nations General Assembly Resolution 3202 (S-VI): Programme of Action on the Establishment of a New International Economic Order	United Nations	Multilateral	Non-binding	Adopted

Year[b]	*Title*	*Setting*	*Level*	*Form*	*Status*
1974	United Nations General Assembly Resolution 3281 (XXIX): Charter of Economic Rights and Duties of States	United Nations	Multilateral	Non-binding	Adopted
1975	The Multinational Companies Code in the UDEAC	Customs and Economic Union of Central Africa	Regional	Binding	Adopted
1975	Charter of Trade Union Demands for the Legislative Control of Multinational Companies	International Confederation of Free Trade Unions	Non-Governmental	Non-binding	Adopted
1975	International Chamber of Commerce Rules of Conciliation and Arbitration	International Chamber of Commerce	Non-Governmental	Non-binding	Adopted
1976	Declaration on International Investment and Multinational Enterprises	OECD	Regional	Binding/ non- binding[c]	Adopted
1976	Arbitration Rules of the United Nations Commission on International Trade Law	United Nations	Multilateral	Model	Adopted
1976	Agreement between the Government of the United States of America and the Government of the Federal Republic of Germany Relating to Mutual Cooperation Regarding Restrictive Business Practices	Germany-United States	Bilateral	Binding	Adopted
1977	ILO Tripartite Declaration of Principles Concerning Multinational Enterprises and Social Policy	International Labour Organization	Multilateral	Non-binding	Adopted
1977	International Chamber of Commerce Recommendations to Combat Extortion and Bribery in Business transactions	International Chamber of Commerce	Non-Governmental	Non-binding	Adopted
1979	Draft International Agreement on Illicit Payments	United Nations	Multilateral	Binding	Not adopted
1979	United Nations Model Double Taxation Convention between Developed and Developing Countries	United Nations	Multilateral	Model	Adopted
1980	Cooperation Agreement between the European Community and Indonesia, Malaysia, the Philippines, Singapore and Thailand member countries of the Association of South-East Asian Nations	ASEAN-EC	Inter-regional	Binding	Adopted
1980	The Set of Multilaterally Agreed Equitable Principles and Rules for the Control of Restrictive Business Practices	United Nations	Multilateral	Non-binding	Adopted
1980	Guidelines Governing the Protection of Privacy and Transborder Flows of Personal Data	OECD	Regional	Non-binding	Adopted
1980	Unified Agreement for the Investment of Arab Capital in the Arab States	League of Arab States	Regional	Binding	Adopted
1980	Treaty Establishing the Latin American Integration Association (LAIA)	LAIA	Regional	Binding	Adopted
1981	International Code of Marketing of Breast- milk Substitutes	World Health Organization	Multilateral	Non-binding	Adopted
1981	Convention for the Protection of Individuals with Regard to Automatic Processing of Personal Data	Council of Europe	Regional	Binding	Adopted
1981	Agreement on Promotion, Protection and Guarantee of Investments among Member States of the Organisation of the Islamic Conference	Islamic Conference	Regional	Binding	Adopted
1981	Treaty for the Establishment of the Preferential Trade Area for Eastern and Southern African States	Preferential Trade Area for Eastern and Southern African States	Regional	Binding	Adopted
1982	Community Investment Code of the Economic Community of the Great Lakes Countries (CEPGL)	CEPGL	Regional	Binding	Adopted
1983	Draft United Nations Code of Conduct on Transnational Corporations	United Nations	Multilateral	Non-binding	Not adopted
1983	Treaty for the Establishment of the Economic Community of Central African States	Economic Community of Central and African States	Regional	Binding	Adopted
1985	Draft International Code of Conduct on the Transfer of Technology	United Nations	Multilateral	Non-binding	Not adopted
1985	United Nations General Assembly Resolution 39/248: Guidelines for Consumer Protection	United Nations	Multilateral	Non-binding	Adopted
1985	Convention Establishing the Multilateral Investment Guarantee Agency	World Bank	Multilateral	Binding	Adopted
1985	Declaration on Transborder Data Flows	OECD	Regional	Non-binding	Adopted
1987	Agreement for the Establishment of a Regime for CARICOM Enterprises	Caribbean Common Market	Regional	Binding	Adopted
1987	Revised Basic Agreement on ASEAN Industrial Joint Ventures	ASEAN	Regional	Binding	Adopted

Year[b]	Title	Setting	Level	Form	Status
1987	An Agreement Among the Governments of Brunei Darussalam, the Republic of Indonesia, Malaysia, the Republic of the Philippines, the Republic of Singapore and the Kingdom of Thailand for the Promotion and Protection of Investments	ASEAN	Regional	Binding	Adopted
1989	Fourth ACP-EEC Convention of Lomé	African, Caribbean and Pacific countries-European Commnuity	Inter-regional	Binding	Adopted
1989	Cooperation Agreement between the European Economic Community, of the one part, and the countries parties to the Charter of the Cooperation Council for the Arab States of the Gulf (the State of the United Arab Emirates, the State of Bahrain, the Kingdom of Saudi Arabia, the Sultanate of Oman, the State of Qatar and the State of Kuwait) of the other part	Arab States of the Gulf-European Community	Inter-regional	Binding	Adopted
1990	Criteria for Sustainable Development Management: Towards Environmentally Sustainable Development	United Nations	Multilateral	Non-binding	Adopted
1990	Charter on a Regime of Multinational Industrial Enterprises (MIEs) in the Preferential Trade Area for Eastern and Southern African States	Preferential Trade Area for Eastern and Southern African States	Regional	Binding	Adopted
1984 1990	Protocol A/P1/11/84 Relating to Community Enterprises and Supplementary Protocol A/Sp.2/5/90 on the Implementation of the Third Phase (Right of Establishment) of the Protocol on Free Movement of Persons, Right of Residence and Establishment	ECOWAS	Regional	Binding	Adopted
1991	Treaty Establishing the African Economic Community	African Economic Community	Regional	Binding	Adopted
1991	Decision 285 of the Commission of the Cartagena Agreement: Rules and Regulations for Preventing or Correcting Distortions in Competition Caused by Practices that Restrict Free Trade Competition	Andean Community	Regional	Binding	Adopted
1991	Decision 291 of the Commission of the Cartagena Agreement: Common Code for the Treatment of Foreign Capital and on Trademarks, Patents, Licenses and Royalties	Andean Community	Regional	Binding	Adopted
1991	Decision 292 of the Commission of the Cartagena Agreement: Uniform Code on Andean Multinational Enterprises	Andean Community	Regional	Binding	Adopted
1991	The Business Charter for Sustainable Development: Principles for Environmental Management	International Chamber of Commerce	Non-Governmental	Non-binding	Adopted
1992	Agreement on the European Economic Area	EC-EFTA	Regional	Binding	Adopted
1992	Guidelines on the Treatment of Foreign Direct Investment	World Bank	Multilateral	Non-binding	Adopted
1992	Articles of Agreement of the Islamic Corporation for the Insurance of Investment and Export Credit	Islamic Conference	Regional	Binding	Adopted
1992	North American Free Trade Agreement	Canada, Mexico and the United States	Regional	Binding	Adopted
1992	The CERES Principles	CERES	Non-Governmental	Non-binding	Adopted
1993	Framework Cooperation Agreement between the European Economic Community and the Republics of Costa Rica, El Salvador, Guatemala, Honduras, Nicaragua and Panama	EC-Costa Rica, El Salvador, Guatemala, Honduras, Nicaragua and Panama	Inter-regional	Binding	Adopted
1993	Permanent Court of Arbitration Optional Rules for Arbitrating Disputes between Two Parties of which only One is a State	Permanent Court of Arbitration	Multilateral	Binding	Adopted
1993	Revised Treaty of the Economic Community of West African States (ECOWAS)	ECOWAS	Regional	Binding	Adopted
1993	Framework Agreement for Cooperation between the European Economic Community and the Cartagena Agreement and its Member Countries, namely the Republic of Bolivia, the Republic of Colombia, the Republic of Ecuador, the Republic of Peru and the Republic of Venezuela	EC-Andean Community	Inter-regional	Binding	Adopted
1993	Treaty Establishing the Common Market for Eastern and Southern Africa	Common Market for Eastern and Southern Africa	Regional	Binding	Adopted

Year[b]	Title	Setting	Level	Form	Status
1994	Free Trade Agreement between Azerbaijan, Armenia, Belarus, Georgia, Moldova, Kazakhstan, the Russian Federation, Ukraine, Uzbekistan, Tajikistan and the Kyrgyz Republic	Azerbaijan, Armenia, Belarus, Georgia, Moldova, Kazakhstan, the Russian Federation, Ukraine, Uzbekistan, Tajikistan and the Kyrgyz Republic	Regional	Binding	Adopted
1994	Free Trade Agreement between the United Mexican States and the Republic of Bolivia	Mexico Bolivia	Bilateral	Binding	Adopted
1994	Free Trade Agreement between Mexico and Costa Rica	Mexico-Costa Rica	Bilateral	Binding	Adopted
1994	Treaty on Free Trade between the Republic of Colombia, the Republic of Venezuela and the United Mexican States	Colombia, Venezuela, Mexico	Regional	Binding	Adopted
1994	Marrakesh Agreement Establishing the World Trade Organization. Annex 1A: Agreement on Trade-Related Investment Measures (1994)	World Trade Organization	Multilateral	Binding	Adopted
1994	Marrakesh Agreement Establishing the World Trade Organization. Annex 1B: General Agreement on Trade in Services	World Trade Organization	Multilateral	Binding	Adopted
1994	Marrakesh Agreement Establishing the World Trade Organization. Annex 1C: Agreement on Trade-Related Aspects of Intellectual Property Rights (1994)	World Trade Organization	Multilateral	Binding	Adopted
1994	Protocol of Colonia for the Reciprocal Promotion and Protection of Investments in the MERCOSUR	MERCOSUR	Regional	Binding	Adopted
1994	Protocol on Promotion and Protection of Investments from States not Parties to MERCOSUR	MERCOSUR	Regional	Binding	Adopted
1994	Agreement Among the Governments of the Member States of the Caribbean Community for the Avoidance of Double Taxation and the Prevention of Fiscal Evasion With Respect to Taxes on Income, Profits or Gains and Capital Gains and for the Encouragement of Regional Trade and Investment	Caribbean Community	Regional	Binding	Adopted
1994	Recommendation of the OECD Council on Bribery in International Business Transactions	OECD	Regional	Non-binding	Adopted
1994	Free Trade Agreement of the Group of Three	Colombia, Mexico and Venezuela	Regional	Binding	Adopted
1994	APEC Non-Binding Investment Principles	APEC	Regional	Non-binding	Adopted
1994	Trade and Investment Agreement between the Government of Australia and the Government of the United Mexican States	Australia-Mexico	Bilateral	Binding	Adopted
1994	Energy Charter Treaty	European Energy Charter Organisation	Regional	Binding	Adopted
1995	Interregional Framework Cooperation Agreement between the European Community and its Member States, of the one part, and the Southern Common Market and its Party States, of the other part	EC-MERCOSUR	Inter-regional	Binding	Adopted
1995	ASEAN Framework Agreement on Services	ASEAN	Regional	Binding	Adopted
1995	Consumer Charter for Global Business	Consumers International	Non-Governmental	Non-binding	Adopted
1995	Pacific Basin Charter on International Investments	Pacific Basin Economic Council	Non-Governmental	Non-binding	Adopted
1995	Agreement between the Government of the United States of America and the Government of Canada regarding the Application of Their Competition and Deceptive Marketing Practice Laws	Canada-United States	Bilateral	Binding	Adopted
1995	Osaka Action Agenda on Implementation of the Bogor Declaration	APEC	Regional	Non-binding	Adopted
1996	Protocol to amend the 1987 Agreement among ASEAN Member Countries for the Promotion and Protection of Investments	ASEAN	Regional	Binding	Adopted
1996	Protocol on the Protection of Competition of MERCOSUR	MERCOSUR	Regional	Binding	Adopted
1996	Inter-American Convention Against Corruption	Organization of American States	Regional	Binding	Adopted
1996	Acuerdo de Complementación Económica MERCOSUR-Chile	Chile-MERCOSUR	Regional	Binding	Adopted
1996	Resolution 51/191. United Nations Declaration Against Corruption and Bribery in International Commercial Transactions	United Nations General Assembly	Multilateral	Non-binding	Adopted
1997	Free Trade Agreement between Mexico and Nicaragua	Mexico-Nicaragua	Bilateral	Binding	Adopted

Year[b]	*Title*	*Setting*	*Level*	*Form*	*Status*
1997	Fourth Protocol to the General Agreement on Trade in Services (on Basic Telecommunications Services)	WTO	Multilateral	Binding	Adopted
1997	Fifth Protocol to the General Agreement on Trade in Services (on Financial Services)	WTO	Multilateral	Binding	Adopted
1997	Protocol Amending the Treaty Establishing the Caribbean Community. Protocol II: Establishment, Services, Capital	Caribbean Community	Regional	Binding	Adopted
1997	Draft NGO Charter on Transnational Corporations	People's Action Network to Monitor Japanese TNCs	Non-Governmental	Non-binding	Not adopted
1997	United Nations General Assembly Resolution 52/87 on International Cooperation against Corruption and Bribery in International Commercial Transactions	United Nations General Assembly	Multilateral	Non-binding	Adopted
1997	Resolution (97) 24 on the Twenty Guiding Principles for the Fight Against Corruption	Council of Europe	Regional	Non-binding	Adopted
1997	OECD Convention on Combating Bribery of Foreign Public Officials in International Business Transactions	OECD	Regional	Binding	Adopted
1991 1998	Agreement between the Government of the United States of America and the Commission of the European Communities Regarding the Application of their Competition Laws and Agreement between the European Communities and the Government of the United States of America on the Application of Positive Comity Principles in the Enforcement of their Competition Laws	European Community-United States	Bilateral	Binding	Adopted
1998	Agreement Establishing the Free Trade Area between the Caribbean Community and the Dominican Republic	Caribbean Community-Dominican Republic	Regional	Binding	Adopted
1998	Free Trade Agreement between Chile and Mexico	Chile-Mexico	Bilateral	Binding	Adopted
1998	DECISION 439 of the Andean Community: General Framework of Principles and Rules and for Liberalizing the Trade in Services in the Andean Community	Andean Community	Regional	Binding	Adopted
1998	DECISION 40 of the Andean Community: Approval of the Agreement Among Member Countries to Avoid Double Taxation and of the Standard Agreement for Executing Agreements on Double Taxation between Member Countries and Other States Outside the Subregion	Andean Community	Regional	Binding	Adopted
1998	Protocol Amending the Treaty Establishing the Caribbean Community. Protocol III: Industrial Policy.	Caribbean Community	Regional	Binding	Adopted
1998	Framework Agreement on the ASEAN Investment Area	ASEAN	Regional	Binding	Adopted
1998	Trade and Investment Cooperation Arrangement between Canada and MERCOSUR	Canada and MERCOSUR	Regional	Binding	Adopted
1998	Memorandum of Understanding on Trade and Investment between the Governments Canada, Costa Rica, El Salvador, Guatemala, Honduras and Nicaragua	Canada and Central American countries	Regional	Non-binding	Adopted
1998	OECD Council Recommendation on Counteracting Harmful Tax Competition	OECD	Regional	Non-binding	Adopted
1998	OECD Council Recommendation Concerning Effective Action Against Hard Core Cartels	OECD	Regional	Non-binding	Adopted
1998	Draft Multilateral Agreement on Investment	OECD	Regional	Binding	Not adopted
1998	ILO Declaration on Fundamental Principles and Rights at Work	International Labour Office	Multilateral	Non-binding	Adopted
1998	Draft International Agreement on Investment	Consumer Unity & Trust Society	Non-Governmental	Non-binding	Not adopted
1998	Towards a Citizens' MAI: an Alternative Approach to Developing a Global Investment Treaty Based on Citizen's Rights and Democratic Control	Council of Canadians	Non-Governmental	Non-binding	Adopted
1999	Resolution of the European Parliament on European Union Standards for European Enterprises Operating in Developing Countries: towards a European Code of Conduct	European Parliament	Regional	Non-binding	Adopted
1999	Criminal Law Convention on Corruption	Council of Europe	Regional	Binding	Adopted
1999	OECD Principles of Corporate Governance	OECD	Regional	Non-binding	Approved
1999	Model Clauses for Use in Contracts Involving Transborder Data Flows	International Chamber of Commerce	Model	Non-binding	Adopted
1999	Core Standards	World Development Movement	Non-Governmental	Non-binding	Not-adopted

Year[b]	*Title*	*Setting*	*Level*	*Form*	*Status*
1999	Rules and Recommendations on Extortion and Bribery in International Business Transactions (1999 Revised Version)	International Chamber of Commerce	Non-Governmental	Non-binding	Adopted
1999	Agreement on Customs Union and Single Economic Area between the Kyrgyz Republic, the Russian Federation, the Republic of Belarus, the Republic of Kazakhstan and the Republic of Tajikistan	Kyrgyz Republic, the Russian Federation, the Republic of Belarus, the Republic of Kazakhstan and the Republic of Tajikistan	Regional	Binding	Adopted
1999	Civil Law Convention on Corruption	Council of Europe	Regional	Binding	Adopted
1999	The Treaty Establishing the East African Community	East African Community	Regional	Binding	Adopted
1982 1999	Agreement between the Government of the United States of America and the Government of Australia Relating to Cooperation on Antitrust Matters and Agreement between the Government of the United States of America and the Government of Australia on Mutual Antitrust Enforcement Assistance	Australia-United States	Bilateral	Binding	Adopted
1999	Agreement between the Government of the United States of America and the Government of the Federative Republic of Brazil Regarding Cooperation Between Their Competition Authorities in the Enforcement of Their Competition Laws	Brazil-United States	Bilateral	Binding	Adopted
1999	Agreement between the European Communities and the Government of Canada Regarding the Application of their Competition Laws	Canada-Eurpean Union	Bilateral	Binding	Adopted
1999	Agreement between the Government of the United States of America and the Government of Japan Concerning Cooperation on Anticompetitive Activities	Japan-United States	Bilateral	Binding	Adopted
1999	Free Trade Agreement between the Governments of Central America and the Government of the Republic of Chile	Chile-Central American countries	Regional	Binding	Adopted
1999	Short-Term Measures to Enhance Asean Investment Climate	ASEAN	Regional	Binding	Adopted
2000	Free Trade Agreement between Mexico, El Salvador, Guatemala and Honduras	The Northern Triangle	Regional	Binding	Adopted
2000	Revised OECD Declaration on International Investment and Multilateral Enterprises (including the Revised Guidelines for Multinational Enterprises and commentaries)	OECD	Regional	Binding/ non-binding[c]	Adopted
2000	Revised United Nations Model Taxation Convention between Developed and Developing Countries	United Nations	Multilateral	Model	Adopted
2000	Agreement between New Zealand and Singapore on Closer Economic Partnership	New Zealand-Singapore	Bilateral	Binding	Adopted
2000	Protocol VIII of the Caribbean Community: Competition Policy, Consumer Protection, Dumping and Subsidies Amending the Treaty of Chaguaramas	Caribbean Community	Regional	Binding	Adopted
2000	Revised Partnership Agreement between the Members of the African, Caribbean and Pacific Group of States of the One Part, and the European Community and Its Member States, of The Other Part	African, Caribbean and the Pacific-European community	Regional	Binding	Adopted
2001	European Convention on the Legal Protection of Services Based on, or Consisting of, Conditional Access	Council of Europe	Regional	Binding	Adopted
2001	Additional Protocol to the Convention for the Protection of Individuals with Regard to Automatic Processing of Personal Data Regarding Supervisory Authorities and Transborder Data Flows	Council of Europe	Regional	Binding	Adopted
2001	Convention Establishing the European Free Trade Association (Amendment)	EFTA	Regional	Binding	Adopted
2001	Protocol to Amend the Framework Agreement on the ASEAN Investment Area	ASEAN	Regional	Binding	Adopted
2001	Revised Treaty of Chaguaramas Establishing the Caribbean Community Including the CARICOM Single Market and Economy	Caribbean Community	Regional	Binding	Adopted
2001	Free Trade Agreement between the Government of Canada and the Government of the Republic of Costa Rica	Canada-Costa Rica	Bilateral	Binding	Adopted
2002	Agreement between Japan and The Republic of Singapore for a New-Age Economic Partnership (JSEPA)	Japan- Singapore	Bilateral	Binding	Adopted
2002	Free Trade Agreement between the Central America and Panama	Panama-Central American countries	Regional	Binding	Adopted

Year[b]	Title	Setting	Level	Form	Status
2002	Treaty on Investment and trade in Services between Costa Rica, El Salvador, Guatemala, Honduras and Nicaragua	Costa Rica, El Salvador, Guatemala, Honduras and Nicaragua	Regional	Binding	Adopted
2002	ASEAN-China Framework Agreement on Comprehensive Economic Cooperation	ASEAN-China	Bilateral	Binding	Adopted
2003	Free Trade Agreement between the Government of the Republic of Chile and the Government of the Republic of Korea	Chile-Korea	Bilateral	Binding	Adopted
2003	Singapore-Australia Free Trade Agreement (SAFTA)	Singapore-Australia	Bilateral	Binding	Adopted

Source: UNCTAD, 2004a, annex table. The instruments listed here are reproduced in whole or in part in UNCTAD, *International Investment Instruments: A Compendium,* vols. I, II, III, IV, V, VI, VII, VIII, IX, X and XI (United Nations publication, Sales Nos. E.96.II.A.9.10.11, E.00.II.D.13. 14, E.01.II.D.34, E.02.II.D.14, E.02.II.D.15, E.02.II.D.16, E.02.II.D. 21 and forthcoming).

[a] Bilateral treaties for the promotion and protection of investment (BITs) and for the avoidance of double taxation (DTTs) are not included in this table. For a list of BITs, as of 1 January 2000, see *Bilateral Investment Treaties, 1959-1999* (UNCTAD/DITE/IIA/2), available on the Internet: www.unctad.org/en/pub/poiteiiad2.en.htm. The most recent list of BITs and DTTs (as of 1 January 2004) is available on the Internet: www.unctad.org/iia. The list of bilateral association, partnership and cooperation agreements signed by the European Community and/or the European Free Trade Association and third countries, and including investment provisions, is available in annex table 3).

[b] Dates given relate to original adoption. Subsequent revisions of instruments are not included, unless explicitly stated.

[c] The OECD Declaration on International Investment and Multinational Enterprises is a political undertaking supported by legally binding Decisions of the Council. The Guidelines on Multinational Enterprises are non-binding standards.

Annex table 2. Selected bilateral, regional and inter-regional agreements containing FDI provisions concluded or under negotiation, 2003-2004 [a]

Year	Title	Setting	Level	Status
Developing countries				
Africa				
2003	ECOWAS Energy Protocol	Benin, Burkina Faso, Cape Verde, Cote d'Ivoire, Gambia, Ghana, Guinea, Guinea-Bissau, Liberia, Mali, Niger, Nigeria, Senegal, Sierra Leone, Togo	Regional	Signed
2004	CEMAC-European Union Economic Partnership Agreement	CEMAC (Central African Economic and Monetary Community - Cameroon, Gabon, Chad, Equatorial Guinea, Central African Republic, Congo)-European Community	Inter-regional	Under negotiation
2004	Economic Partnership Agreement between ECOWAS and the European Union	ECOWAS (Economic Community of West African States-Benin, Burkina Faso, Côte d'Ivoire, Gambia, Ghana, Guinea, Liberia, Mali, Niger, Senegal, Sierra Leone and Togo)-European Community	Inter-regional	Under negotiation
2004	Egypt-Singapore Free Trade Agreement	Egypt-Singapore	Bilateral	Under negotiation
2004	Economic Partnership between ESA and the European Union	ESA (Eastern and Southern Africa - Burundi, Comoros, Democratic Republic of the Congo, Djibouti, Eritrea, Ethiopia, Kenya, Madagascar, Malawi, Mauritius, Rwanda, Seychelles, Sudan, United Republic of Tanzania, Uganda, Zambia, Zimbabwe)-European Community	Inter-regional	Under negotiation
2004	Free Trade Agreement between SACU and the United States	SACU (Southern African Customs Union - Botswana, Lesotho, Namibia, South Africa, Swaziland)-United States	Bilateral	Under negotiation
2004	SADC-European Union Economic Partnership Agreement	SADC (Southern African Development Community-Angola, Botswana, Democratic Republic of the Congo, Lesotho, Malawi, Mauritius, Mozambique, Namibia, South Africa, Swaziland, United Republic of Tanzania, Zambia, Zimbabwe)-European Community	Inter-regional	Under negotiation
Asia and the Pacific				
2003	Framework for Comprehensive Economic Partnership Between the Association of Southeast Asian Nations and Japan	ASEAN - Japan	Bilateral	Signed
2003	Chile-Republic of Korea Free Trade Agreement	Chile – Republic of Korea	Bilateral	Signed
2003	Mainland China and Hong Kong Closer Economic Partnership Arrangement	China-Hong Kong (China)	Bilateral	Signed
2003	Mainland and Macao (China) Closer Economic Partnership Arrangement	China-Macao (China)	Bilateral	Signed
2003	Framework Agreement on Comprehensive Economic Cooperation Between the Republic of India and the Association of South East Asian Nations	India-ASEAN	Bilateral	Signed
2003	Framework Agreement for Establishing Free Trade Area Between the Republic of India and the Kingdom of Thailand	India-Thailand	Bilateral	Signed
2003	Singapore-Australia Free Trade Agreement	Singapore-Australia	Bilateral	Signed
2004	Bahrain-United States Free Trade Agreement	Bahrain-United States	Bilateral	Signed
2004	Framework Agreement on the BIMST-EC Free Trade Area [b]	Bhutan, India, Myanmar, Nepal, Sri Lanka, Thailand	Regional	Signed
2004	Singapore-Jordan Free Trade Agreement	Singapore-Jordan	Bilateral	Signed
2004	Framework Agreement on South Asian Free Trade Area	SAARC (South Asian Association for Regional Cooperation-Bangladesh, Bhutan, India, Maldives, Nepal, Pakistan, Sri Lanka)	Regional	Signed
2004	ASEAN-Republic of Korea	ASEAN-Republic of Korea	Bilateral	Under consultation
2004	ASEAN - Closer Economic Relations (CER) countries	ASEAN-Australia-New Zealand	Inter-regional	Under negotiation
2004	Bahrain-Singapore Free Trade Agreement	Bahrain-Singapore	Bilateral	Under negotiation

Year	Title	Setting	Level	Status
2004	India-Singapore Comprehensive Economic Cooperation Agreement	India-Singapore	Bilateral	Under negotiation
2004	Free Trade Agreement between India and the Gulf Cooperation Council countries (GCC)	India- GCC (Bahrain, Kuwait, Oman, Qatar, Saudi Arabia, United Arab Emirates)	Bilateral	Under negotiation
2004	Comprehensive Economic Cooperation Agreement between India and China	India-China	Bilateral	Under discussion
2004	Comprehensive Economic Cooperation Agreement between India and Mauritius	India-Mauritius	Bilateral	Under discussion
2004	Republic of Korea-Singapore Free Trade Agreement	Republic of Korea-Singapore	Bilateral	Under negotiation
2004	SAARC agreement on the promotion and protection of investment	SAARC member States	Regional	Under negotiation
2004	Sri Lanka-Singapore Comprehensive Economic Partnership Agreement	Sri Lanka-Singapore	Bilateral	Under negotiation
2004	Thailand-United States Free Trade Agreement	Thailand-United States	Bilateral	Under negotiation
Latin America and the Caribbean				
2003	Free Trade Agreement Between the Government of the Republic of Uruguay and the Government of the United Statesof Mexico	Uruguay-Mexico	Bilateral	Signed
2004	Central American Free Trade Agreement	Central America (Costa Rica, El Salvador, Honduras, Guatemala, plus Dominican Republic)-United States	Bilateral	Signed
2004	Agreement Between the Caribbean Community (CARICOM), Acting on Behalf of the Governments of Antigua and Barbuda, Barbados, Belize, Dominica, Grenada, Guyana, Jamaica, St. Kitts and Nevis, Saint Lucia, St. Vincent and the Grenadines, Suriname and Trinidad and Tobago and the Government of the Republic of Costa Rica	CARICOM-Costa Rica	Bilateral	Signed
2004	Free Trade Agreement between Andean Community – Mercosur	Mercosur (Argentina, Brazil, Paraguay, Uruguay)- Andean countries (Bolivia, Colombia, Ecuador and Peru)	Inter-regional	Signed
2004	Free Trade Agreement of the Americas	All countries of the Western Hemisphere, except Cuba	Regional	Under negotiation
2004	Andean countries-United States Free Trade Agreement	Andean countries-United States	Bilateral	Under negotiation
2004	Brazil-Russian Federation	Brazil-Russian Federation	Bilateral	Under negotiation
2004	CARICOM-EFTA	CARICOM- EFTA (Iceland, Liechtenstein, Norway, Switzerland)	Inter-regional	Under negotiation
2004	CARICOM-European Union Agreement	CARICOM-European Community	Inter-regional	Under negotiation
2004	Costa Rica-Panama Free Trade Agreement	Costa Rica-Panama	Bilateral	Under negotiation
2004	Mexico – Singapore Free Trade Agreement	Mexico – Singapore	Bilateral	Under negotiation
2004	Peru-Thailand Free Trade Agreement	Peru-Thailand	Bilateral	Under negotiation
Developed countries				
2003	Australia-China Trade and Economic Framework Agreement	Australia-China	Bilateral	Signed
2003	Association Agreement Between the European Union and the Syrian Arab Republic	European Community - Syrian Arab Republic	Bilateral	Concluded
2003	Free Trade Agreement between the Government of the United States of America and the Government of the Republic of Chile	United States-Chile	Bilateral	Signed
2003	Agreement between the Government of the United States of America and the Government of Pakistan Concerning the Development of Trade and Investment Relations	United States-Pakistan	Bilateral	Signed
2003	Agreement between the Government of the United States of America and the Government of the Kingdom of Saudi Arabia Concerning the Development of Trade and Investment Relations	United States-Saudi Arabia	Bilateral	Signed
2003	United States - Singapore Free Trade Agreement	United States-Singapore	Bilateral	Signed
2003	Political Dialogue and Cooperation Agreement Between the European Community and Its Member States of the One Part, and the Andean Community and Its Member Countries (Bolivia, Colombia, Ecuador, Peru And Venezuela), of the Other Part	European Community-Andean countries	Inter-regional	Concluded

Year	*Title*	*Setting*	*Level*	*Status*
2004	Australia-Thailand Free Trade Agreement	Australia-Thailand	Bilateral	Signed
2004	Agreement between the Government of the United States of America and the Government of the State of Qatar Concerning the Development of Trade and Investment Relations	United States- Qatar	Bilateral	Signed
2004	Agreement between the Government of the United States of America and the Government of the United Arab Emirates Concerning the Development of Trade and Investment Relations	United States- United Arab Emirates	Bilateral	Signed
2004	United States - Australia Free Trade Agreement	United States-Australia	Bilateral	Signed
2004	Agreement between the United States and Central Asian Countries Signed Concerning Regional Trade and Investment Framework	United States-Kazakhstan, Kyrgyzstan, Tajikistan, Turkmenistan, and Uzbekistan		Bilateral
2004	Agreement between the Government of the United States of America and the Government of the State of Kuwait Concerning the Development of Trade and Investment Relations	United States-Kuwait	Bilateral	Signed
2004	Malaysia-United States Trade and Investment Framework Agreement	United States-Malaysia	Bilateral	Signed
2004	United States-Morocco Free Trade Agreement	United States-Morocco	Bilateral	Signed
2004	Agreement between the Government of the United States of America and the Government of the Republic of Yemen Concerning the Development of Trade and Investment Relations	United States-Yemen	Bilateral	Signed
2004	Japan-Chile Free Trade Agreement	Japan-Chile	Bilateral	Under consideration
2004	Japan-Philippines Economic Partnership Agreement	Japan-Philippines	Bilateral	Under consideration
2004	Japan-Thailand Economic Partnership Agreement	Japan-Thailand	Bilateral	Under consultation
2004	Canada-Andean countries Free Trade Agreement	Canada-Andean countries	Bilateral	Under discussion
2004	Canada-CARICOM Free Trade Agreement	Canada-CARICOM	Bilateral	Under consideration
2004	Canada-Central America Free Trade Agreement	Canada-Central America (Costa Rica, El Salvador, Guatemala, Honduras)	Bilateral	Under negotiation
2004	Agreement between Canada-Dominican Republic	Canada-Dominican Republic	Bilateral	Under consideration
2004	Canada-European Free Trade Association (EFTA) Free Trade Agreement	Canada-EFTA	Bilateral	Under negotiation
2004	Canada-Singapore Free Trade Agreement	Canada-Singapore	Bilateral	Under negotiation
2004	EFTA and SACU Free Trade Agreement	EFTA-SACU	Bilateral	Under negotiation
2004	European Union–MERCOSUR	European Community-Mercosur	Inter-regional	Under negotiation
2004	Japan- Republic of Korea Free Trade Agreement	Japan- Korea	Bilateral	Under negotiation
2004	Pacific Three Free Trade Agreement	New Zealand-Chile-Singapore	Pluraliteral	Under negotiation
2004	United States-Uruguay Free Trade Agreement	United States-Uruguay	Bilateral	Under negotiation

Source: UNCTAD. 2004a, annex table.

a Excluding BITs and DTTs.

b BIMST-EC comprises Bangladesh, India, Myanmar, Sri Lanka and Thailand. Bhutan and Nepal joined in February 2004. In the same month, the members of the association, except Bangladesh, signed the Framework Agreement.

Note: Every instrument is mentioned only once. The listing is made on the basis of the first regional/country partner name mentioned in the official or current (in the case of "under negotiation") title of the agreements. For example, in the agreement between the United States and Pakistan, the United States is mentioned first. Thus, this agreement is listed under "Developed countries", and not under Asia and the Pacific.

Annex table 3. Bilateral association, cooperation, framework and partnership agreements signed by the European Community, by the European Free Trade Association, by the United States and by Canada with third countries, including investment-related provisions, as of April 2003

Country/territory/group of countries	Date of signature	Date of entry into force
European Community and its member States		
Malta	5 December 1970	1 April 1971
Jordan	18 January 1977	1 January 1979
Syrian Arab Republic	18 January 1977	1 January 1978
China	21 May 1985	1 October 1985
Pakistan	23 July 1985	1 May 1986
Argentina	2 April 1990	...
Uruguay	4 November 1991	1 January 1994
Hungary	16 December 1991	1 February 1994
Poland	19 September 1989a	
Poland	16 December 1991	1 February 1994
San Marino	16 December 1991	Not yet in force
Albania	11 May 1992	1 December 1992
Mongolia	16 June 1992	1 March 1993
Brazil	26 June 1992	1 November 1995
Macao	5 June 1992	Not yet in force
Romania	22 October 1990[a]	...
Romania	1 February 1993	1 February 1995
Czechoslovakia	16 December 1991[a]	...
Czech Republic	4 October 1993	1 February 1995
Bulgaria	8 May 1990[a]	...
Bulgaria	8 March 1993	1 February 1995
Czechoslovakia	16 December 1991[a]	...
Czech Republic	4 October 1993	1 February 1993
Slovakia	4 October 1993	1 February 1993
India	23 June 1981[a]	...
India	20 December 1993	1 August 1994
Ukraine	14 June 1994	1 March 1998
Soviet Union	8 December 1989[a]	
Russian Federation	24 June 1994	1 December 1997
Sri Lanka	2 July 1975[a]	
Sri Lanka	18 July 1994	2nd trimester 1995
Republic of Moldova	28 November 1994	1 July 1998
Kazakhstan	23 January 1995	1 July 1999
Kyrgyzstan	9 February 1995	1 July 1999
Belarus	6 March 1995	Not yet in force
Turkey	12 September 1963[a]	1 December 1964
Turkey	6 March 1995	Not yet in force
Latvia	11 May 1992[a]	1 February 1993
Latvia	12 June 1995	1 February 1998
Lithuania	11 May 1992[a]	1 February 1993
Lithuania	12 June 1995	1 February 1998
Estonia	11 May 1992[a]	1 March 1993
Estonia	12 June 1995	1 February 1998
Tunisia	25 April 1976[a]	1 November 1978
Tunisia	17 July 1995	1 March 1998
Viet Nam	17 July 1995	1 June 1996
Israel	11 May 1975	1 July 1975
Israel	20 November 1995	... June 2000
Nepal	20 November 1995	1 June 1996
Morocco	27 April 1976	1 November 1978
Morocco	26 February 1996	...
Armenia	22 April 1996	1 July 1999
Azerbaijan	22 April 1996	1 July 1999
Georgia	22 April 1996	1 July 1999
Slovenia	5 April 1993	1 September 1993
Slovenia	10 June 1996	1 February 1999
Chile	21 June 1996	1 February 1999
Uzbekistan	21 June 1996	Not yet in force
Republic of Korea	28 October 1996	...
Cambodia	29 April 1997	1 November 1999
Palestine Authority	24 February 1997	1 July 1997
Lao People's Democratic Republic	29 April 1997	1 December 1997
Macedonia, The Former Yugoslav Republic of	29 April 1997	1 January 1998
Yemen		25 November 1997
Turkmenistan	25 May 1998	Not yet in force
South Afirca	11 October 1999	Not yet in force
Bangladesh	22 May 2000	...
Mexico	26 April 1991	1 November 1991
Mexico	8 December 1997	1 January 2000
Mexico	27 February 2001	1 March 2001
Egypt	18 January 1977	1 January 1979
Egypt	30 April 2001	...

Country/territory/group of countries	Date of signature	Date of entry into force
Croatia	29 October 2001	...
Algeria	26 April 1976	1 January 1978
Algeria	22 April 2002	...
Lebanon	3 May 1977	1 November 1978
Lebanon	17 June 2002	...
Lebanond	17 June 2002	...
Chile	18 November 2002	...
European Free Trade Association and its member States		
Turkey	10 December 1991	1 April 1992
Israel	17 September 1992	1 January 1992
Poland	10 December 1992	1 September 1993
Romania	10 December 1992	1 May 1993
Bulgaria	29 March 1993	1 July 1993
Hungary	29 March 1993	1 October 1993
Czech Republic	20 March 1992	1 July 1992c
Slovak Republic	20 March 1992	1 July 1992 c
Slovenia	13 June 1995	1 September 1998
Estonia	7 December 1995	1 October 1997
Latvia	7 December 1995	1 June 1996
Lithuania	7 December 1995	1 January 1997
Morocco	19 June 1997	1 December 1999
Palestine Authority	30 November 1998	1 July 1999
Macedonia, The Former Yugoslav Republic of	19 June 2000	1 January 2001
Mexico	27 November 2000	...
Croatia	21 June 2001	...
Jordan	21 June 2001	...
Singapore	26 June 2002	...
United States		
Morocco	March 16 1995	...
Israel	22 April 1985	1 September 1985
Philippines	11 June 1905	...
Taiwan Province of China	19 September 1994	...
Indonesia	18 June 1905	...
Central America	20 March 1998	...
Andean Community	30 October 1998	...
Egypt	1 July 1999	1 July 1999
Egyptb	1 July 1999	1 July 1999
Ghana	26 February 1999	26 February 1999
South Africa	18 February 1999	18 February 1999
Turkey	29 September 1999	11 February 2000
Jordan	24 October 2000	24 October 2000
Nigeria	16 February 2000	16 February 2000
Viet Nam	13 July 2000	...
Algeria	13 July 2001	...
COMESA	1 October 2001	...
West African Economic and Monetary Union	24 April 2002	...
Bahrain	18 July 2002	...
Sri Lanka	25 July 2002	...
Brunei Darussalam	16 December 2002	...
Thailand	23 October 2002	...
Singapore	24 June 1905	...
Tunisia	2 October 2002	
Chile	19 May 1998	...
Chile	11 December 2002	...
Canada		
ASEAN	28 July 1993	...
Ukraine	24 October 1994	...
Australia	15 November 1995	...
Chile	5 December 1996	5 July 1997
Norway	3 December 1997	...
Switzerland	9 December 1997	...
Iceland	24 March 1998	...
MERCOSUR	16 June 1998	...
South Africa	24 September 1998	...
Andean Community	31 May 1999	...
Costa Rica	23 April 2001	1 November 2002

Source: UNCTAD, 2004a, annex table.
Key: ... Information not available.

a No longer in force.
b Investment Incentive Agreement between the Government of the United States and the Government of the Arab Republic of Egypt.
c Signed with former CSFR 20 on March 1992. Protocols of the succession of the Czech Republic and the Slovak Republic were signed and entered into force on 19 April 1993 simultaneously.
d Interim Agreement on Trade and Trade-related Matters between the European Community, of the One Part, and the Republic of Lebanon, of the Other Part

Chapter 2. International Investment Agreements: Flexibility for Development *

Executive summary

Developing countries seek foreign direct investment (FDI) in order to promote their economic development. This is their paramount objective. To that end, they have sought to establish — through national legislation and international instruments — a legal framework aimed at reducing obstacles to FDI, while providing foreign investors with high standards of treatment and legal protection for their investments and increasingly putting in place mechanisms to assure the proper functioning of markets.

Developing countries participate in international investment agreements (IIAs) — whether at bilateral, regional, interregional or multilateral levels — because they believe that, on balance, these instruments help them to attract FDI and to benefit from it. At the same time, IIAs, like most international agreements, limit to a certain extent the policy options available to governments to pursue their development objectives through FDI. A question arises, therefore, how, nevertheless, IIAs can allow developing countries a certain policy space to promote their development. This is all the more important since the principal responsibility for the design and implementation of development objectives and policies remains in the hands of the individual countries' governments.

Thus, when concluding IIAs, developing countries face a basic challenge: how to achieve the goal of creating an appropriate stable, predictable and transparent FDI policy framework that enables firms to advance their corporate objectives, while, at the same time, retaining a margin of freedom necessary to pursue their particular national development objectives.

A concept that can help link these objectives is "flexibility" which, for present purposes, can be defined as the ability of IIAs to be adapted to the particular conditions prevailing in developing countries and to the realities of the economic asymmetries between these countries and developed countries.

Flexibility can be approached from four main angles: the objectives of IIAs, their overall structure and modes of participation, their substantive provisions and their application.

Objectives. IIAs often address development concerns by including in their text, usually in their preamble, declaratory statements referring to the promotion of development as a main objective of the agreement, or to specific ways by which the agreement is to contribute to development objectives, or a generally worded recognition of the needs of developing and/or least developed country parties requiring flexibility in the operation of the obligations under the agreement. There are many variations in such language, and it is difficult to generalize its actual role and importance. Preambles and similar declarations normally do not directly create rights and obligations for the parties to an instrument, but they are relevant to its interpretation. In fact, the texts of preambles are often the result of hard bargaining. To the extent that such language reflects the will of the participating countries, it helps to reaffirm the acceptance of development as a central purpose of IIAs. The specific language used in each case and its relationship to the rest of the instrument is, of course, important.

Overall structure and modes of participation: special and differential treatment. Promotion of development can also be manifested in the structure of IIAs. Central to this is the application of special principles and rules for developing countries which have as their common characteristic that these countries assume less

* The present chapter is based on a 2000 manuscript prepared by Victoria Aranda, with contributions from Boubacar Hassane, Patrick Juillard, Abraham Negash and Assad Omer. The final version reflects comments received from Marise Cremona, A.V. Ganesan, Donald M. Goldberg, Patrick Robinson and M. Sornarajah. Comments were also provided by Jean-Luc Le Bideau, Susan Borkowski, Rainer Geiger, Murray Gibbs, Joachim Karl, Mark Koulen, Miguel Rodriguez Mendoza, Magda Shahin, Marinus Sikkel, Dilip Sinha and Kenneth Vandevelde. The chapter benefitted also from the papers submitted and comments made by experts during the various expert meetings, and from comments made by delegations during the deliberations of the Commission on Invesment, Technology and Related Financial Issues.

onerous obligations — either permanently or temporarily — on a non-reciprocal basis. This approach is reflected in the principle of "special and differential treatment" for developing countries (or categories among them). Broadly speaking, this principle encompasses such aspects as granting lower levels of obligations for developing countries; asymmetrically phased implementation timetables; best endeavour commitments; exceptions from commitments in certain areas; flexibility in the application of, and adherence to, disciplines under prescribed circumstances; and technical assistance and training. A key issue in dealing with the principle of special and differential treatment is whether a broad spectrum of flexibility should be given to the beneficiaries, or whether well defined criteria should be established. One way of applying the principle of special and differential treatment in the structure of an agreement is to distinguish between developed and developing countries by establishing, for instance, separate categories of countries, the members of which do not have the same rights and duties. Beyond that, international practice has evolved a number of methods to allow countries that wish to participate in an agreement to do so in ways that take into account their individual situations. Although the methods in question may be used, in principle, by any country, they can be particularly relevant as a means of addressing development concerns. The principal methods can be grouped into two main approaches. The first approach is to allow for different stages and degrees of participation in an IIA, by, for example, allowing countries to accede to an agreement at different times and in different ways; or permitting countries that are not ready to become full members of an IIA to be associated with it or to cooperate on matters of mutual interest. The second approach to structural flexibility is to allow the inclusion of various kinds of exceptions, reservations, derogations, waivers or transitional arrangements. Exceptions take a great variety of forms: they may be general (e.g. for the protection of national security), subject specific (e.g. the so-called "cultural exception"), or they may be country specific. A subset of this approach is the use of "positive" and "negative" lists. Finally, an investment framework can be built consisting of several instruments that can be negotiated over time and combine a variety of approaches.

By using these or other methods, IIAs can be constructed in a manner that ensures an overall balance of rights and obligations for all actors involved, so that all parties derive benefits from it.

Substantive provisions. The substantive content of an IIA is particularly important in reflecting development concerns and an overall balance of rights and obligations. This begins with the choices countries make about the issues they wish to include in an IIA, and those they wish to keep outside the scope of an agreement. (The range of relevant issues is reflected in the topics covered in the individual chapters of these volumes.) It continues with the formulation of the substantive provisions, through ways that allow countries to address the issues in a manner beneficial to them and, when need arises, to retain some flexibility regarding the commitments they made, keeping also in mind the various interactions between issues and provisions. The range of approaches and permutations that can be used in formulating substantive provisions in IIAs is broad. Of course, flexibility might need to be approached in different ways for each individual substantive issue, depending on its characteristics and development effects. For example, the type of approach to flexibility that can be useful in a development context regarding admission and establishment of foreign affiliates might not be relevant to post-establishment national and MFN treatment provisions, or to expropriation, labour or environmental standards. There are no general prescriptions on this matter. The choice of approach depends on the conditions prevailing in each country and the particular development strategies pursued by each government.

Application. Flexibility for development can also be exercised during the application stage of an IIA. The manner in which an IIA is interpreted, and the way in which it is to be made effective determine whether its objectives, structure and substantive provisions produce, in the end, the desired developmental effects. The degree of flexibility for the interpretation and application of an IIA depends to a large extent on the legal character of an agreement and the formulation of individual provisions. Legally-binding agreements, even if they do not provide for implementation mechanisms, impose on the States signatories a legal obligation under international law to comply with their provisions. How far such an obligation will actually limit the subsequent freedom of action of the States concerned largely depends on the language of the agreement or the type of obligations imposed. Voluntary instruments, on the other hand, are not legally enforceable but can have an influence on the development of national and international law. One way of mitigating some of the most rigorous implications of concluding a legally-binding investment agreement is to include one or several "soft" obligations among its binding provisions.

Many IIA provisions require some kind of action at the national level in order to produce their effects. Where explicit provisions requiring specific national action are absent, each State would be free to decide the particular manner in which it may implement an agreement's provisions. Variations in normative intensity and specificity of language regarding the effects of IIAs on national systems provide possibilities for developing countries to advance their development interests. At the regional and multilateral levels, the effectiveness of an IIA is intimately related to the intergovernmental institutional machinery for following up and monitoring its application, including through built-in agendas. There are various mechanisms that can be created, ranging from simple reporting requirements (which nevertheless can be a significant inducement to act in compliance), to advisory and consultative functions (aimed at resolving questions arising out of the continuing application of an IIA), to complaint and clarification mechanisms (aimed at facilitating application of non-binding instruments under procedures of a non adjudicatory nature), to various international methods of settlement of disputes which may allow more or less freedom to the parties to accept proposed ways for the resolution of the dispute. Finally, an agreement might eventually need partial or extensive revisions. This is a fundamental facet of the entire process of the elaboration of an IIA, which is to be understood as a continuing process of interaction, review and adjustment to changing realities and to new perceptions of problems and possibilities.

In fulfilling its various functions, an international institutional machinery can play several major development roles. It is therefore of critical importance for developing countries to make the best use of the means provided by the relevant institutional arrangements for follow up, including the review of built-in agendas, to ensure that the development objectives are given full effect. An important consideration in this respect are the difficulties that many developing countries experience in participating fully and effectively in these arrangements due to lack of adequate skills and resources. To address such difficulties, IIAs can make special provision for technical and financial assistance. In addition, to ensure that the development goals of an IIA are fully realized, it may be desirable that developed countries commit themselves to undertake promotional measures to encourage FDI flows to developing countries.

In conclusion, it needs to be re-emphasized that IIAs, like all international agreements, typically contain obligations that, by their very nature, reduce to some extent the autonomy of the participating countries. At the same time, such agreements need to recognize important differences in the characteristics of the parties involved, in particular the economic asymmetries and levels of development between developing and developed countries. If IIAs do not allow developing countries to pursue their fundamental objective of advancing their development — indeed make a positive contribution to this objective — they run the risk of being of little or no interest to them. This underlines the importance of designing, from the outset, IIAs in a manner that allows their parties a certain degree of flexibility in pursuing their development objectives. To find the proper balance between obligations and flexibility — a balance that leaves sufficient space for development-oriented national policies — is indeed a difficult challenge faced by negotiators of IIAs. This is particularly important as treaty-making activity in this area at all levels has intensified in recent years.

Introduction

During the 1990s, the number of international agreements dealing with foreign investment increased dramatically at the bilateral, regional and interregional levels. As the new millennium begins, negotiating activity in this area continues to be intense. Many of these instruments and negotiations involve countries at different levels of development. Indeed, the full participation of developing countries in IIAs is important, given that these countries are increasingly becoming destinations and even, slowly, important sources of FDI. While developing countries acknowledge the value of FDI for their economic growth and development, they are equally keen that IIAs in which they participate strike a balance between the interests of foreign investors and the national development objectives of host countries. In particular, they consider that development needs and concerns should be built into IIAs, to enable developing countries to pursue their development policies according to their own needs and conditions.

The present chapter deals with this question and examines ways in which IIAs can provide for flexibility with a view towards promoting development, while encouraging FDI and providing stability and predictability in investment relations. The chapter first discusses briefly the meaning and purpose of flexibility in the interest of development in the context of IIAs (section I) and then looks at how existing IIAs have provided for flexibility from four main angles: the objectives of an agreement (section II), its overall structure and modes of participation (section III), its substantive provisions (section IV) and its application (section V). The chapter reflects discussions during the three expert meetings convened by the Commission on Investment, Technology and Related Financial Issues during 1997-1999, dealing with existing IIAs and their development dimensions.[1] As recommended by the third expert meeting, it revises and expands the Note submitted by the UNCTAD secretariat to the Expert Meeting entitled "International investment agreements: concepts allowing for a certain flexibility in the interest of development" (UNCTAD, 1999b).[2]

Part One: Flexibility

I. Flexibility in the Interest of Development

Development is a fundamental objective of developing countries and has generally been accepted as a goal of the international community as a whole.[3] Crucially, this involves the attainment of sufficient levels of economic growth to allow for a progressive improvement in the material standard of living of the populations of these countries. However, it also encompasses wider social objectives for which wealth creation is only a starting point. Thus, not only economic but social, political and cultural issues are involved in the process of development, a factor which development-oriented policies on FDI need to take into account (UNCTAD, 1999a).

Today, most developing countries seek to attract FDI as part of their development strategies.[4] Although economic factors are the principal determinants of FDI flows (figure I.1), an appropriate enabling policy and normative framework has a role to play (UNCTAD, 1998b, ch. IV). Virtually all countries have sought to establish such a framework through the liberalisation of relevant FDI laws and regulations. They have done so by reducing obstacles to FDI (e.g. facilitating entry and operations), strengthening the standards of treatment of foreign affiliates by host countries (e.g. by providing national treatment) and by seeking to ensure the proper functioning of the market (especially through competition policies) (figure I.2). While most liberalisation measures have been taken unilaterally by host countries, some have also been enshrined in IIAs, especially bilateral investment treaties (BITs) and regional agreements.[5] Governments conclude such agreements because they believe that, on balance, they help them to attract FDI and to benefit from it. At the same time, IIAs, by their very nature, limit to a certain extent the freedom of action of the parties involved. Governments seek, therefore, to tailor such agreements in a manner that allows them the policy space they need to advance their paramount objective of *national* development (Corrales, 1999).

Transnational corporations (TNCs), for their part, seek to advance their paramount corporate objectives of competitiveness and profitability. They do that, by definition, in an *international* context. In a globalizing world economy, this means increasingly that TNCs need to acquire a portfolio of locational assets to obtain access to markets and resources (UNCTAD, 1995). An enabling FDI framework is therefore important for them, especially one that is stable, predictable and transparent, and one that is guaranteed to remain so through international agreement.

Seeking to advance *national* development and *international* corporate competitiveness are not mutually exclusive objectives. On the contrary: "generally speaking, an investor-friendly agreement will be development-friendly also" (Ganesan, 1998, p. 8). But the overlap is not complete. Indeed, it is the task of national policies to see to it that the benefits of FDI are maximised while its costs are minimized (UNCTAD, 1999a). Ideally, this task should be further helped by IIAs — or, at a minimum, it should not be hindered by them.[6]

This poses a challenge: namely, how to link, when concluding IIAs, the quest for an appropriate policy space that government require to pursue their national development objectives with the quest for an appropriate stable, predictable and transparent FDI policy framework through which firms seek to advance their corporate competitiveness objectives. This challenge is all the more important as the number of IIAs at all levels is growing rapidly (UNCTAD, 1999a ch. IV, and 2000). It is further complicated by the fact

Figure I.1. Host country determinants of FDI

Host country determinants
I. Policy framework for FDI • economic, political and social stability • rules regarding entry and operations • standards of treatment of foreign affiliates • policies on functioning and structure of markets (especially competition and M&A policies) • international agreements on FDI • privatization policy • trade policy (tariffs and NTBs) and coherence of FDI and trade policies • tax policy
II. Economic determinants
III. Business facilitation • investment promotion (including image-building and investment-generating activities and investment-facilitation services) • investment incentives • hassle costs (related to corruption, administrative efficiency, etc.) • social amenities (bilingual schools, quality of life, etc.) • after-investment services

Type of FDI classified by motives of TNCs	Principal economic determinants in host countries
A. Market-seeking	• market size and per capita income • market growth • access to regional and global markets • country-specific consumer preferences • structure of markets
B. Resource/ asset-seeking	• raw materials • low-cost unskilled labour • skilled labour • technological, innovatory and other created assets (e.g. brand names), including as embodied in individuals, firms and clusters • physical infrastructure (ports, roads, power, telecommunication)
C. Efficiency-seeking	• cost of resources and assets listed under B, adjusted for productivity for labour resources • other input costs, e.g. transport and communication costs to/from and within host economy and costs of other intermediate products • membership of a regional integration agreement conducive to the establishment of regional corporate networks

Source: UNCTAD, 1998b, table IV.1, p. 91.

that, while countries parties to IIAs are often at widely differing levels of economic and technological development and differ from one another in many other important respects (economic asymmetry), they are usually formally equal (legal symmetry). As it is generally recognized that IIAs need to take into account the interests and concerns of all participating countries (UNCTAD, 1996b), the economic asymmetries require special attention to ensure that the application of an agreement does not increase these asymmetries, but positively contributes to the aim of development.[7]

A concept that can help link these two objectives is "flexibility". "Flexibility" is a broad concept. It denotes an instrument's ability to serve, and to be adapted to, several differing uses and functions. The flexibility considered here relates to a particular set of objectives, those that concern the promotion of the development of developing countries parties to IIAs, without losing sight of the need for stability, predictability and transparency for investors.[8] More specifically, the function of flexibility is to adapt IIAs to the particular conditions prevailing in developing countries and to the realities of the economic asymmetries between these countries and developed countries, which act as the home to most TNCs.[9] This is particularly challenging in view of the fact that developing countries are a heterogeneous group. Their approach to utilising FDI for their development varies therefore widely. Consequently, the flexibility built into IIAs may not be equally relevant to each party; this depends on the conditions prevailing in each country and the particular development strategies pursued by each government.

In fact, whatever flexibility there is in an IIA may not be used by each country in the same manner. Nonetheless, from the point of view of developing countries, IIAs need to be designed, from the start, with development considerations in mind. At the same time, a distinction needs to be made between flexibility in the interest of development on the one hand, and arbitrariness, or excessive discretion, in dealing with foreign investors, on the other hand. In short, in order to be viable, IIAs need to strike a balance between the interests of all concerned. The question is not so much whether IIAs should provide for flexibility,

Figure I.2. The process of liberalization of FDI policies

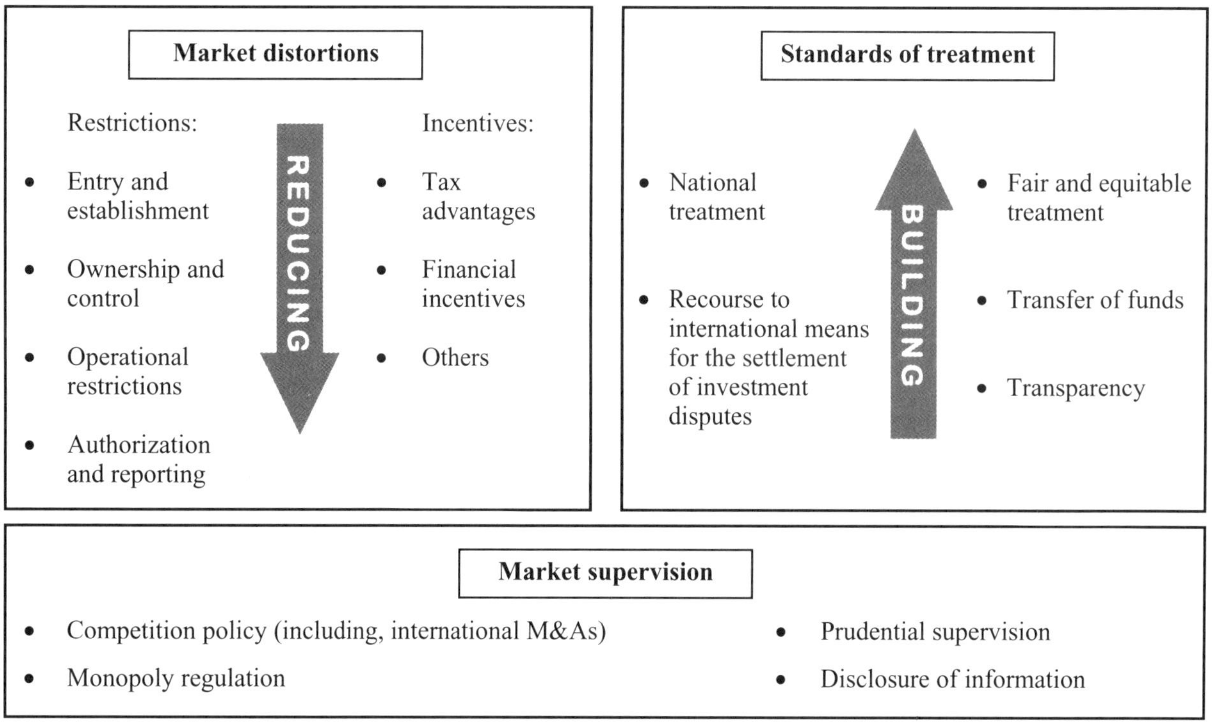

Market distortions

REDUCING

Restrictions:

- Entry and establishment
- Ownership and control
- Operational restrictions
- Authorization and reporting

Incentives:

- Tax advantages
- Financial incentives
- Others

Standards of treatment

BUILDING

- National treatment
- Recourse to international means for the settlement of investment disputes
- Fair and equitable treatment
- Transfer of funds
- Transparency

Market supervision

- Competition policy (including, international M&As)
- Monopoly regulation
- Prudential supervision
- Disclosure of information

Source: UNCTAD, 1998b, box IV.2, p. 94-97.

but rather what degree of flexibility would be consistent with the aims and functions of such agreements. In other words, there is a need to balance flexibility and commitments, in order to arrive at a realistic level of flexibility and commitment from each contracting party according to its state of development.

A matter of functional significance, therefore, is the identification of features of IIAs that can provide for flexibility in these agreements in the interest of development while, at the same time, allowing the agreements to serve other objectives, in particular stability, predictability and transparency. Ways and means in which flexibility with respect to development concerns can be given effect in IIAs are examined in Part Two.

Part Two: Approaches to Flexibility

The manner in which flexibility in the interest of development is approached in an IIA depends to a large extent on the characteristics of the agreement (including whether it is bilateral, regional or multilateral), its purpose, the composition of its members and the negotiating strategies pursued by the parties. These strategies are typically influenced by broader economic or political considerations prevailing at a particular time. Despite growing convergence, IIAs negotiations are seldom identical; each agreement is the outcome of a series of decisions and trade-offs that are made in particular contexts. Thus, flexibility can be considered, in principle, from many different perspectives. For analytical purposes, this part identifies four main categories of approaches, and the discussion is structured accordingly. But other classifications are also possible. In reality, moreover, there is considerable overlap between categories and approaches.

Flexibility in IIAs may be approached from four different angles:

- **Objectives.** IIAs may include preambular statements or general principles referring broadly to development as an overall objective, outlining specific development objectives or introducing the concept of flexibility.
- **Overall structure and modes of participation.** An agreement's structure can give effect to development considerations by designing the instrument accordingly and granting, where appropriate, special and differential treatment to developing countries, e.g. by spelling out different rights and obligations for developing countries, by distinguishing explicitly between categories of participants, by allowing different stages or degrees of participation for individual countries, by allowing parties to limit the substance of their obligations or to assume

gradually certain obligations, or by concluding separate related instruments.

- **Substantive provisions**. Development concerns can be reflected in the substantive content of an agreement, notably in the types of issues that are included in an IIA, in how these issues are dealt with, and in the extent to which they reflect a balance of rights and obligations for all actors concerned.
- **Application**. The mechanisms by which an agreement is put into operation can also provide a basis for promoting development objectives, as these can allow varying degrees of flexibility for interpreting an IIA or adapting it to changing needs and conditions. They can also facilitate compliance and help developing countries benefit from it, especially through promotional measures and provision of technical assistance.

Examples from existing IIAs[10] and other international economic agreements in respect of each of these approaches are examined below. They are intended to be indicative rather than exhaustive. In drawing from examples of other instruments, however, attention needs to be given to the subject matter, general purpose and underlying philosophy of the agreement in determining the utility of adopting its approach.

II. Objectives

Many IIAs have incorporated the objective of development in their basic aims, purposes or principles. This has been expressed in a wide variety of ways either in preambular statements or in declaratory clauses articulating general principles. These may refer to development as an overall objective or principle of the agreement or may identify specific development dimensions and objectives, including the concept of flexibility.

According to the Vienna Convention on the Law of Treaties (United Nations, 1969, article 31 (2)), the preamble is part of a treaty for the purpose of interpretation. It is the repository of the general aims and purposes of the agreement and offers a summary of the grounds upon which it is concluded. Thus, while preambles and similar declarations normally do not directly create rights and obligations for the parties to an instrument, they are relevant for the interpretation of its provisions. In fact, the texts of preambles are often the result of hard bargaining. Therefore, to the extent that preambles reflect the will of the participating countries, they reaffirm development as a central purpose of international arrangements. Moreover, as preambles are an important aid to the interpretation of specific provisions, an express reference to development in the preamble is a factor that would contribute to their interpretation so as to further development goals.

Numerous examples of preambular statements that mention development goals and principles can be found among IIAs, both in agreements concluded between developed and developing countries and agreements among developing countries. There are many variations in the language they use, and it is hard to generalise regarding their actual role and importance. The specific language in each case and its relationship to the rest of the instrument is, of course, important. This chapter provides some examples of declaratory statements addressing development which, for presentation purposes, can be grouped in a few main categories as follows:

- A generally worded recognition of the special needs of developing and/or least developed country parties requiring flexibility in the operation of obligations under the agreement, especially as regards the content of national laws and regulations and/or the investment regime, though in some cases there is no reference to national laws and regulations (box II.1).
- An expression of a more specific way to contribute to economic development through, for example, progressive liberalization or certain standards of treatment in investment matters which is seen to contribute to development (box II.2).

IIAs may also include general clauses containing declaratory language referring to development as part of their overriding objectives and principles. These may elaborate upon themes in the preamble or they may be the first indicators of development concerns in an agreement, although this would be uncommon. The question remains, however, to what extent and under what conditions they could be applied to all commitments undertaken in an agreement. In order to measure the degree of flexibility for the parties concerned, it may be necessary to look at these general clauses in the context of other more specific provisions of the particular agreement. The Fourth ACP-EEC Convention of Lomé, for example, states numerous development objectives in the opening provisions: the promotion of economic, cultural and social development of the African, Caribbean and Pacific (ACP) States; a more just and balanced international economic order (article 1); the right of ACP States to determine

Box II.1. Preambles that recognize the need for flexibility for developing/least developed countries

Preamble of the General Agreement on Trade in Services
"*Recognizing* the right of Members to regulate, and to introduce new regulations, on the supply of services within their territories in order to meet national policy objectives and, given asymmetries existing with respect to the degree of development of services regulations in different countries, the particular need of developing countries to exercise this right; ..."

Preamble of the Agreement on Trade-Related Aspects of International Property Rights
"*Recognizing* also the special needs of the least-developed country Members in respect of maximum flexibility in the domestic implementation of laws and regulations in order to enable them to create a sound and viable technological base; ..."

Preamble of the Asia Pacific Cooperation (APEC) Non-Binding Investment Principles
"Acknowledging the diversity in the level and pace of development of member economies as may be reflected in their investment regimes, and committed to ongoing efforts towards the improvement and further liberalisation of their investment regimes; ..."

Preamble of the Treaty Establishing the Latin American Integration Association
"AWARE that it is necessary to ensure a special treatment for countries at a relatively less advanced stage of economic development; ..."

Preamble of the Treaty for the Establishment of the Economic Community of Central African States
"*Conscious* of the different levels of development in the countries of the subregions, more particularly of the situation in countries which are land-locked or semi-land-locked, islands and/or belong to the category of the least advanced countries; ..."

Preamble of the United Nations Convention on the Law of the Sea[a]
"*Bearing in mind* that the achievement of these goals will contribute to the realization of a just and equitable international economic order which takes into account the interests and needs of mankind as a whole and, in particular, the special interests and needs of developing countries, whether coastal or land-locked; ..."

[a] United Nations, 1983.

their development principles and strategies in all sovereignty (article 3); respect for human rights as part of the development goal (article 5); and special treatment for the least developed ACP countries (article 8). The Treaty Establishing the Latin American Integration Association spells out a number of development- related principles, including the principle of flexibility (box II.3). Read together, these principles appear to seek to establish a balance between the objectives of economic integration and growth coupled with the need for flexible and individual responses to the development needs of the parties to the agreement. It is noteworthy that these countries are differentiated by their level of development and that more freedom is given to the least developed countries signatories to the Treaty. Another example of an agreement that spells out broad development principles which inform the overall approach and philosophy of the agreement include the Agreement on Andean Subregional Integration.

Box II.2. Preambles that include specific development objectives

Preamble of the Agreement on Trade-Related Investment Measures
"*Desiring* to promote the expansion and progressive liberalisation of world trade and to facilitate investment across international frontiers so as to increase the economic growth of all trading partners, particularly developing country Members, while ensuring free competition, ..."

Preamble of the BIT between Argentina and the Netherlands (1992)
"*Recognizing* that agreement upon the treatment to be accorded to such investments will stimulate the flow of capital and technology and the economic development of the Contracting Parties and that fair and equitable treatment of investments is desirable, ..."

Preamble of the Set of Multilaterally Agreed Equitable Principles and Rules for the Control of Restrictive Business Practices
"*Recognizing* that restrictive business practices can adversely affect international trade, particularly that of developing countries, and the economic development of these countries, ..."

The interpretation of an IIA as favouring development can be strengthened if mention is made of the "right to development", either in the preamble or as a general principle of the instrument. Many observers (Alston, 1979; Asante, 1979; Haquani, 1979; Umbricht, 1979; Zacklin, 1979) agree that this right is grounded in customary international law. This can be done by recalling the relevant instruments, such as, for example, the United Nations Declaration on the Right to Development annexed to the General Assembly Resolution 41/128 of 1986 (United Nations, 1986a), in particular, articles 3 (3) and 4 (1) (box II.4).

Box II.3. Development principles in the Treaty Establishing the Latin American Integration Association

Article 3

"In the implementation of the present Treaty and the evolution towards its final objective, member countries shall bear in mind the following principles: (a) Pluralism, sustained by the will of member countries to integrate themselves, over and above the diversity which might exist in political and economic matters in the region; (b) Convergence, meaning progressive multilateralization of partial scope agreements by means of periodical negotiations between member countries, with a view to establishing the Latin American common market; (c) Flexibility, characterized by the capacity to allow the conclusion of partial scope agreements, ruled in a form consistent with the progressive attainment of their convergence and the strengthening of integration ties; (d) Differential treatment, as determined in each case, both in regional and partial scope mechanisms, on the basis of three categories of countries, which will be set up taking into account their economic-structural characteristics. Such treatments shall be applied in a determined scale to intermediate developed countries, and in a more favourable manner to countries at a relatively less advanced stage of economic development; and (e) Multiple, to make possible various forms of agreements between member countries, following the objectives and duties of the integration process, using all instruments capable of activating and expanding markets at regional level. "

Box II.4. Reference to the right to development: The United Nations Declaration on the Right to Development

Article 3

"3. States have the duty to co-operate with each other in ensuring development and eliminating obstacles to development. States should realize their rights and fulfil their duties in such a manner as to promote a new international economic order based on sovereign equality, interdependence, mutual interest and co-operation among all States, as well as to encourage the observance and realization of human rights. "

Article 4

"1. States have the duty to take steps, individually and collectively, to formulate international development policies with a view to facilitating the full realization of the right to development. "

Source: United Nations, 1986a.

It can also be helpful to recall in the preamble or in a general clause of an IIA instruments that address development issues relevant for foreign investment relations. This is done, with respect to labour rights, in the International Labour Organization (ILO) Tripartite Declaration of Principles Concerning Multinational Enterprises and Social Policy which, under the heading dedicated to general policies, refers to the need to respect the Universal Declaration of Human Rights (United Nations, 1948) the corresponding International Covenants adopted by the General Assembly of the United Nations and the relevant ILO Conventions. With respect to environmental protection, the preamble of the Energy Charter Treaty recalls the United Nations Framework Convention on Climate Change (United Nations, 1992a), the Convention on Long-Range Transboundary Air Pollution (United Nations, 1979) and its protocols, and other international environmental agreements with energy-related aspects.

Finally, although not specifically mentioned in article 31 (1) of the Vienna Convention, the title of an agreement is also part of its context and, therefore, a reflection of the agreement's objective and purpose. Consequently, an express reference to "development" not only in the preamble of an IIA, but also in its title could further strengthen a development-oriented interpretation.[11] An example of a United Nations instrument with an express reference in its title to development is the United Nations Declaration on Environment and Development (UNDED) (United Nations, 1992b).

III. Overall Structure and Modes of Participation: Special and Differential Treatment

The objectives of an agreement can inform its substance not only through the specific language of particular provisions but also through the overall design of the agreement, i.e. its structure. If an agreement seeks to serve development, this needs to be reflected in the agreement's very structure. This is all the more important because international agreements, as noted before, are generally based on reciprocity and legal symmetry, that is, the rights and obligations of the parties are generally the same — they are "mirror images" of each other. Where the parties are at different levels of development, however, formal symmetry can obscure an underlying economic asymmetry. International practice in the past half-century has sought to take account of that asymmetry by developing a number of ways in which differences in the level of development among parties can be taken into account. Although the approaches and methods discussed below may be used by any country or group of countries for a variety of reasons, they can be particularly relevant as a means of addressing development concerns.

A. Special and differential treatment: the principle

Central in this respect is the development of special principles and rules applicable to developing countries (or certain categories of developing countries). In other words, the condition of being a developing country can be invoked to vary the exact content of the rights and obligations of developing countries parties to an international agreement, on a non-reciprocal basis. This approach is reflected notably in the principle of "special and differential treatment" according to which one category of countries — developing countries (or categories of countries such as least developed countries or smaller developing economies) — assumes less onerous obligations (either permanently or temporarily), on a non-reciprocal basis. It was developed — originally mainly in the area of international trade — to give legal expression to the special needs and concerns of developing countries and/or least developed countries in international economic agreements (box III.1). Broadly speaking, it involves such issues as lower levels of obligations for developing countries, asymmetrically phased implementation timetables; exceptions from commitments in certain areas; flexibility in the application of, and adherence to, disciplines under prescribed circumstances; and technical assistance and training (Bernal, 1998).

The extension of the application of the principle of special and differential treatment to various aspects of international economic relations was further recognized in articles 18 and 19 of the Charter of Economic Rights and Duties of States (1974). In relation to domestic industries or firms of developing countries, the principle was included in the Set of Multilaterally Agreed Equitable Principles and Rules for the Control of Restrictive Business Practices; a subsection of the Set was devoted to this principle (box III.2). In the negotiations of the Draft United Nations Code of Conduct on Transnational Corporations, an attempt by some negotiators to legitimize special and differential treatment for domestic firms was reflected in a proposed formulation, in brackets, according to which exceptions to the principle of national treatment for foreign investors could be justified on the basis of development policies of

Box III.1. The principle of special and differential treatment for developing countries: background and evolution in the context of the multilateral trading system

The principle of special and differential treatment was first formulated in the context of inter-State trade relations as a result of coordinated efforts by developing countries to correct the perceived inequalities of the international trading system by introducing preferential treatment in their favour across the spectrum of international economic relations. The principle found expression in a succession of articles and instruments associated with the multilateral trading system created by GATT, notably article XVIII of GATT, "Governmental Assistance to Economic Development" (WTO, 1995) (which enabled developing countries to maintain a certain flexibility in their tariff structure in order to develop their industrial base, and to apply quantitative restrictions for balance-of-payments reasons), and Part IV of GATT, adopted in 1964 (in which, among other things, the developed countries parties declared that they "do not expect reciprocity for commitments made by them in trade negotiations to reduce or remove tariffs and other barriers to the trade of less-developed contracting parties" (GATT, Part IV, article XXXVI, p. 8 (WTO, 1995, p. 534)). The Generalized System of Preferences (GSP) accorded by developed countries to developing countries in international trade -- introduced at the UNCTAD II Conference in New Delhi, 1968 was a further manifestation of the principle. (The GSP was covered by a GATT waiver, not Part IV.) At the regional level, preferential treatment for developing countries was also embodied in the provisions of the First ACP-EEC Lomé Convention regulating non-reciprocal trade preferences granted by the European Union (European Commission, 1975).

During the Tokyo Round, the "Decision on Differential and More Favourable Treatment, Reciprocity and Fuller Participation of Developing Countries" (usually described as the "Enabling Clause") reconfirmed[a] the principle of non-reciprocity (GATT, 1986a). The Punta del Este Declaration launching the Uruguay Round of Multilateral Trade Negotiations contained four clauses (out of seven) dealing with developing countries. Three of these confirmed that developing countries would be accorded special and differential treatment, and the fourth affirmed that developing countries would participate more fully in the framework of rights and obligations as their economies developed (GATT, 1986b). The Uruguay Round agreements provided for special and differential treatment mainly in the form of time-limited derogations, greater flexibility with regard to certain obligations and "best endeavours" clauses. The time limits for such derogations would be phased out in the early 2000s. Only in the Agreement on Subsidies and Countervailing Measures is special and differential treatment linked to economic criteria.

Source: UNCTAD.

[a] This instrument pertains primarily to the Generalized System of Preferences, non-tariff measures in the context of GATT instruments, regional and global arrangements among developing countries and special treatment for least developed countries.

Box III.2. Extension of special and differential treatment to firms from developing countries

The Set of Multilaterally Agreed Equitable Principles and Rules for the Control of Restrictive Business Practices

Section C.7

"In order to ensure the equitable application of the Set of Principles and Rules, States, particularly developed countries, should take into account in their control of restrictive business practices the development, financial and trade needs of developing countries, in particular the least developed countries, for the purposes especially of developing countries in:

(a) Promoting the establishment or development of domestic industries and the economic development of other sectors of the economy, and
(b) Encouraging their economic development through regional or global arrangements among developing countries. "

Fourth ACP-EEC Convention of Lomé
Part III. The instruments of ACP-EU cooperation
Title IV
General provisions for the least-developed, landlocked and island ACP States

Article 328

"Special attention shall be paid to the least-developed, landlocked and island ACP States and the specific needs and problems of each of these three groups of countries in order to enable them to take full advantage of the opportunities offered by the Convention, so as to step up their respective rates of development. "

Article 329

"The least-developed ACP countries shall be accorded special treatment in order to enable them to overcome the serious economic and social difficulties hindering their development, so as to step up their rates of development. "

developing countries ("development clause") (see also under section III.B.3.a). The Fourth ACP-EEC Convention of Lomé — which includes provisions on investment — differentiates in Title IV of Part III among the developing contracting States by providing for special and differential treatment for the least developed, landlocked and island ACP States (box III.2), and identifies the articles of the Convention that contain provisions pursuant to this principle.

A recent expression of the principle of special and differential treatment is found in the General Agreement on Trade in Services (GATS). Among the main general obligations of the GATS is the principle of "increasing participation of developing countries", spelled out in article IV. Among other things, it calls on countries to give priority to the liberalisation of access in the modes of supply and service industries of export interest to developing countries (box III.3). Apart from that article, the overall structure of GATS seeks to serve the needs and capacities of developing countries. Thus market access and national treatment in GATS are negotiated concessions that allow for tradeoffs and obtaining reciprocal benefits (see below section B.4 and chapter IV.B.2). In addition, GATS article XIX.2 provides for flexibility for developing countries for opening fewer industries, liberalizing fewer types of transactions, progressively extending market access in line with their development situation and, when making access to their markets available to foreign suppliers, attaching to such access conditions (e.g. transfer of technology, training) aimed at achieving the objectives referred to in article IV (box III.3). The GATS provisions dealing with special and differential treatment for developing countries are, of course, directly relevant to FDI (under the heading "commercial presence") in the area of services as FDI is one of the four modes of supply of services identified in GATS.

A key issue in dealing with special and differential treatment is whether a broad spectrum of flexibility should be given to the beneficiaries, or whether well defined criteria should be established. A broad spectrum of flexibility grants wider discretionary authority to governments and, therefore, reduces predictability. The establishment of well defined criteria, on the other hand, is often complex and may not always cover new developments that are unforseen and may justify the application of the principle.

A special variant of the principle of special and differential treatment relates not to countries but to companies. The concept of "small and medium-sized enterprises"[12] has been broadly invoked by both developing and developed countries to allow for special and differential treatment for enterprises falling within certain parameters. Such treatment typically involves exempting the relevant firms from certain obligations (notably in the area of competition law and policy) and qualifying for special incentives. In the context of liberalization and globalization the concept of "small and medium-sized enterprises" can be further refined and focused on the ability of enterprises to compete in global markets, thus measuring "small and medium-sized enterprises" in terms of global standards.

One feature of concepts such as "least developed countries", "smaller economies" or "small and medium-sized enterprises" is that they rely on concrete economic criteria. Given that developing countries are a rather heterogeneous group with significant differences in levels of development and economic and social strategies, such concepts can provide an identifiable common characteristic.

Box III.3. Increasing participation of developing countries in world trade
General Agreement on Trade in Services

Article IV
Increasing Participation of Developing Countries

"1. The increasing participation of developing country Members in world trade shall be facilitated through negotiated specific commitments by different Members pursuant to Parts III and IV of this Agreement, relating to:

(a) the strengthening of their domestic services capacity and its efficiency and competitiveness, *inter alia* through access to technology on a commercial basis;
(b) the improvement of their access to distribution channels and information networks; and
(c) the liberalisation of market access in sectors and modes of supply of export interest to them.

2. Developed country Members, and to the extent possible other Members, shall establish contact points within two years from the date of entry into force of the WTO Agreement to facilitate the access of developing country Members' service suppliers to information, related to their respective markets, concerning:

(a) commercial and technical aspects of the supply of services;
(b) registration, recognition and obtaining of professional qualifications; and
(c) the availability of services technology.

3. Special priority shall be given to the least-developed country Members in the implementation of paragraphs 1 and 2. Particular account shall be taken of the serious difficulty of least-developed countries in accepting negotiated specific commitments in view of special economic situation and their development, trade and financial needs."

Article XIX
Negotiations of Specific Commitments

"2. The process of liberalization shall take place with due respect for national policy objectives and the level of development of individual Members, both overall and in individual sectors. There shall be appropriate flexibility for individual developing country Members for opening fewer sectors, liberalizing fewer types of transactions, progressively extending market access in line with their development situation and, when making access to their markets available to foreign service suppliers, attaching to such access conditions aimed at achieving the objectives referred to in Article IV. "

* * *

Except for earlier attempts to extend to IIAs the principle of special and differential treatment for developing countries, and in particular for the GATS, by and large, most of the new generation of IIAs do not state the principle as such. Instead, they have used a number of component concepts as the basis for effectively granting special and differential treatment, especially by distinguishing between categories of countries, determining stages and degrees of participation, using methods by which one or more countries can select, modify or postpone certain treaty obligations, and concluding several instruments combining different approaches. While some of these concepts may well be applicable to all countries, they can also be limited, in their applicability, to developing countries (or certain categories of developing countries) only.

B. Applying the principle

1. Distinguishing between categories of countries

One way of applying the principle of special and differential treatment in order to structure an IIA is to distinguish between developing and developed countries overall. While IIAs generally do not distinguish, in their overall structure, between these categories of countries, important exceptions exist. Thus, the Convention Establishing the Multilateral Investment Guarantee Agency (MIGA) is based on an overall distinction between developed and developing countries. More specifically, MIGA covers investments made in the territory of developing member countries only (listed in schedule A of the Convention). Another important exception in this respect are the four Lomé conventions which were signed between a group of developed countries (the members of the European Community) on the one hand, and a group of developing countries (African, Pacific and Caribbean countries) on the other hand (European Commission, 1975; 1979; 1985; 1990). This pattern is also found in other development cooperation agreements -- intended to help developing countries in their development efforts -- where the distinction between developed and developing countries is often an essential part of their structure, reflecting their objectives.[13]

A variation of this approach is to identify specific groups of developing countries. Most common is to single out least developed countries. An example is the Fourth ACP-EEC Convention of Lomé, which dedicates a title (Title IV) to general provisions for the least-developed, landlocked and island ACP States (cited in box III.2 above). Another possibility is to single out "small economies". This has been discussed in the negotiations of a Free Trade Area of the Americas where a Consultative Committee has been created to keep under review the concerns and interests of the smaller economies and bring these to the attention of the negotiating groups (OAS, 1998). The concept of "smaller economies" seeks to recognize that countries whose land area, population, GDP or other similar criteria have special concerns and interests that may call for different treatment in the application of international disciplines.

Finally, even though most BITs do not make a structural distinction between developed and developing country parties overall, they may do so indirectly when some of their provisions apply only to relationships between developed and developing countries. Such a de facto differentiation does not always or necessarily involve the favourable treatment of the developing country party to the treaty, but in some instances it may. An instance of this is the provisions found in BITs concerning subrogation by the home country to claims for payments made on the basis of the issuance of investment guarantees by that country (or by a State-sponsored agency) which are normally available only for investment in developing countries (box III.4).

Box III.4. Subrogation clause in BITs
BIT between Georgia and United Kingdom (1995)

Article 10
Subrogation

"(1) If one Contracting Party or its designated Agency ("the first Contracting Party") makes a payment under an indemnity given in respect of an investment in the territory of the other Contracting Party ("the second Contracting Party"), the second Contracting Party shall recognize:

(a) the assignment to the first Contracting Party by law or by legal transaction of all the rights and claims of the party indemnified, and
(b) that the first Contracting Party is entitled to exercise such rights and enforce such claims by virtue of subrogation, to the same extent as the party indemnified.

(2) The first Contracting Party shall be entitled in all circumstances to the same treatment in respect of

(a) the rights and claims acquired by it by virtue of the assignment, and
(b) any payments received in pursuance of those rights and claims, as the party indemnified was entitled to receive by virtue of this Agreement in respect of the investment concerned and its related returns.

(3) Any payments received in non-convertible currency by the first Contracting Party in pursuance of the rights and claims acquired shall be freely available to the first Contracting Party for the purpose of meeting any expenditure incurred in the territory of the second Contracting Party. "

2. Stages and degrees of participation

Some flexibility may result from provisions relating to entry into force of an international agreement. While the provisions of an agreement normally enter into force immediately after the necessary number of parties have expressed their consent to be bound by that agreement, it may well be, however, that all prospective parties do not accede to the agreement at the same time or in the same way. This can be done through a number of techniques.

Accession. This method can be used to extend an agreement to countries that have not been associated with the original negotiation for any of a number of reasons, including because they had not reached some of the minimum requirements needed for membership. For many agreements, accession is automatic, without the need for adjustment or further approval of earlier parties.

In other cases, the original signatories would extend an offer of a negotiated accession to non-members. Typically, the offer would provide that the new members accept the obligations resulting from the original agreement, under reserve of the "adjustments" to the original treaty which can be mutually agreed upon at the time the new members enter the accession treaty. The "adjustment" technique would enable them to join the agreement under conditions that reflect their economic situation. This technique has been used in order to work out the successive enlargements of membership in especially the GATT/WTO, but also as regards the Energy Charter Treaty, the OECD and ASEAN. Thus, for example, the protocols of accession to WTO by individual countries usually contain specific schedules of concessions and commitments undertaken by the acceding country that may be implemented in stages, as specified in the schedules (box III.5).

Association. Countries that are not ready to become full members of an agreement may still be associated with it and thus obtain certain special benefits not available to third countries. An association agreement typically involves mutual rights and obligations between the members of the agreement on the one hand, and the associated country, on the other hand. The nature and level of commitments however tend to be different — usualy less strict — from those applying between the countries having full membership status. Where the associated country or countries are developing countries or countries with economies in transition, the association agreement tends to include provisions of a nonreciprocal nature that take into account their "developing" or "transitional" status. Examples of this approach can be found in the association agreements concluded between the European Union members and individual non-member countries, such as Tunisia (box III.6), and between the members of European Free Trade Association and individual third countries.

Box III.5. Accession
Protocols of accession to WTO

The following text was included in the Protocol of Accession of Mongolia to WTO, after paragraph 2: "Mongolia will notify the Secretariat annually of the implementation of the phased commitments with definitive dates referred to in paragraphs 10, 13, 20, 21, 23, 24, 29, 35, 42, 44, 45, 46, 48, 51, 59 and 60 of the Working Party Report, and will identify any delays in implementation together with the reasons therefore" (WTO, 1999, p. 66).

The following texts were included in the Protocols of Accession to WTO of Bulgaria, Panama, Kyrgyz Republic and Latvia:
"4. ... [name of country] ... may maintain a measure inconsistent with paragraph 1 of Article II of GATS provided that such measure is recorded in the List of Article II Exemptions annexed to this Protocol and meets the conditions of the Annex to the GATS on Article II Exemptions " (WTO, 1999, p. 66).

Box III.6. Association
Euro-Mediterranean Agreement Establishing an Association between the European Communities and their Member States, of the one part, and the Republic of Tunisia, of the other part

Article 1
"1. An association is hereby established between the Community and its Member States, of the one part, and Tunisia, of the other part.

2. The aims of this Agreement are to:...
--establish the conditions for the gradual liberalisation of trade in goods, services and capital, ..."

Chapter I. Current payments and movement of capital
Article 34
"1. With regard to transactions on the capital account of balance of payments, the Community and Tunisia shall ensure, from the entry into force of this Agreement, that capital relating to direct investments in Tunisia in companies formed in accordance with current laws can move freely and that the yield from such investments and any profit stemming therefrom can be liquidated and repatriated.
2. The Parties shall consult each other with a view to facilitating, and fully liberalizing when the time is right, the movement of capital between the Community and Tunisia. "

Gradual integration. Some association agreements are intended to serve as an intermediate step towards full membership; in that case they tend to include a number of transitional provisions aimed at preparing the way towards accession. The association or partnership agreements between the European Community countries and a number of Central and Eastern European countries reflect this approach (box III.7).

Box III.7. Gradual integration
Europe Agreement Establishing an Association between the European Communities and their Member States, of the one part, and the Republic of Latvia, of the other part

Article 1[a]
"1. An association is hereby established between the Community andits Member States, of the one part, and Latvia, of the other part.
2. The objectives of this association are:
-- To provide an appropriate framework for the gradual integration of Latvia into the European Union. Latvia shall work towards fulfilling the necessary requirements in this respect. "

Chapter II. Establishment
Article 44
"3. Latvia shall, during the transitional period referred to in paragraph 2(i) not adopt any measures or actions which introduce discrimination as regards the establishment and operations of Community companies and nationals in its territory in comparison to its own companies and nationals.

4. The Association Council shall during the transitional period referred to in paragraph 2(i) examine regularly the possibility of accelerating the granting of national treatment in the sectors referred to in Annex XV. Amendments may be made to this Annex by decision of the Association Council.

Following the expiration of the transitional period referred to in Article 3, the Association Council may exceptionally, upon request of Latvia, and if the necessity arises, decide to prolong the duration of exclusion of certain areas or matters listed in Annex XV for a limited period of time."

[a] European Communities, 1998.

Cooperation. It is also possible for the full members of an agreement to enter into a separate agreement with third countries or with the members of another group of countries, with a view towards cooperating in a number of areas of mutual interest. Cooperation agreements tend to be framework instruments spelling out broad programmatic provisions with few, if any, specific binding substantive rules. In the case of cooperation agreements involving a group of developed countries, on the one hand, and one or many developing countries, on the other hand, these agreements tend to include provisions aimed at helping the developing country or countries in their development efforts. In some cases, cooperation agreements are a first step towards developing closer economic links. Examples of these agreements include the European Union cooperation agreements signed with a number of non-member countries and regional groups (box III.8).

Box III.8. Cooperation
Framework Agreement for Cooperation between the European Economic Community and the Cartagena Agreement and its Member Countries, namely, the Republic of Bolivia, the Republic of Colombia, the Republic of Ecuador, the Republic of Peru and the Repubilc of Venezuela

Article 9 (1)
Investment

"1. The Contracting Parties agree:
--to promote, so far as their powers, rules and regulations and policies permit, an increase in mutually beneficial investment,
--to improve the climate for such investment by seeking agreements on investment promotion and protection between the Community's Member States and the Andean Pact countries based on the principles of non-discrimination and reciprocity. "

3. Structural flexibility for one or many participating countries: degrees and methods

International practice has evolved a number of methods to allow a degree of flexibility so that countries that wish to participate in an agreement may be able to do so in ways that take account of their individual situations. Some of these methods have been codified in the Vienna Convention on the Law of Treaties (United Nations, 1969).

a. "Ratione materiae": flexibility to limit the substance of treaty obligations

A number of well known methods exist in international treaty law and practice that allow treaties to limit the *substance* of treaty obligations with respect to one or a number of parties (*ratione materiae*). There are, of course, limits to the capacity of the parties to exempt one or several of them from the operation of a treaty. The exemption should not be so broad as to defeat the object and purpose of the treaty (see below). Still, methods such as those outlined below can be used to choose "à la carte" on the treaty menu.

Selecting binding provisions. All provisions of international agreements are normally binding upon the parties thereto, unless the agreement provides otherwise. The European Social Charter (Council of Europe, 1965), which was drafted within the framework of the Council of Europe, sets up a mechanism that enables the parties to select the provisions of the Charter that will be binding upon them. Part I of the Charter lists the 19 "rights and principles" that the parties should try to respect. Part II sets out, paragraph by paragraph, these rights and principles. Part III allows the parties to select the provisions that will be binding for each of them, it being understood that these provisions may not be less than 10 numbered articles, or 45 numbered paragraphs. This allows a modulation of the international commitments and, therefore, allows for flexibility. It may be worthwhile examining to what extent this approach could be used in IIAs.

Protocols are agreements that, generally, include additional understandings reached before or after signature of a treaty. They have the same legal force and value as the treaty provisions themselves and may serve a variety of purposes.[14] One such purpose is to exempt one or several of the parties from the operation of certain treaty provisions, or to vary their effect on these parties. The Protocol of the BIT between Indonesia and Switzerland is one example (box III.9). Yet another example is in the Protocol annexed to the Maastricht Treaty relating to the acquisition of real estate by non-residents in Denmark, under which the parties agreed that Denmark, notwithstanding the provisions of the treaty relating to the free movement of capital, may still impose restrictions on the acquisition of secondary residences by non-residents in Denmark (European Union, 1997).

Reservations.[15] According to the Vienna Convention on the Law of Treaties, reservations are unilateral statements a State makes when it signs, ratifies or accedes an agreement "whereby it purports to exclude or modify the legal effect of certain provisions of a treaty in their application to that State" (Vienna Convention, article 2 (1) (d) (United Nations, 1969)). The Convention also provides in article 19 that a State may formulate a reservation to a treaty unless it is prohibited by the treaty, or the treaty allows for certain reservations only (not including the reservation made), or, as noted, the reservation is incompatible with the objective and purpose of the treaty. At the same time, and in line with United Nations practice, the filing of reservations upon accession to existing multilateral agreements is normally subject to the scrutiny of the contracting parties to determine whether the reservation filed meets the Vienna

Convention criteria (i.e. is not incompatible with the object and purpose of the treaty). This represents one major possibility of control over the contents of reservations.

Box III.9. Protocols exempting one or several of the parties from the operation of certain treaty provisions BIT between Indonesia and Switzerland (1974) Protocol

"At the time of signing the Agreement concerning the Encouragement and the Reciprocal Protection of Investments concluded between the Swiss Confederation and the Republic of Indonesia, the undersigned Plenipotentiaries have, in addition, agreed on the following provisions which shall be regarded as an integral part of the said Agreement:

1. Notwithstanding the provisions of article 4, paragraph 3 of the present Agreement, it is understood by both of the Contracting Parties that the application of restrictive legislations concerning the acquisition of landed property by aliens is not contrary to the provisions of the present Agreement.
2. In derogation of the national treatment provided for in article 4, paragraph 3, of the present Agreement, the government of the Republic of Indonesia in view of the present stage of development of the Indonesian national economy reserves its position with regard to national treatment of Swiss investments in the territory of the Republic of Indonesia as follows:

Certain provisions such as article 4, 6 and 14 of the Domestic Investment Law (Law No. 6 of 1968) as amended by law No. 12 of 1970 still contain additional advantages to Indonesian domestic investment as compared to foreign investments in Indonesia under the foreign investment law (law No. 1 of 1967) as amended by law No. 11 of 1970. When, pursuant to present or subsequent legislation the Indonesian Government extends additional advantages to Indonesian investors, the Indonesian Government shall, in order to ensure fair and equitable treatment, grant identical or compensating facilities to investments by companies and nationals of the Swiss Confederation in similar economic activities.

Equivalent treatment may be applied in the Swiss Confederation to investments by nationals or companies of the Republic of Indonesia. "

Canada - Chile Free Trade Agreement Annex G-09.1

"1. For the purpose of preserving the stability of its currency, Chile reserves the right:

(a) to maintain existing requirements that transfers from Chile of proceeds from the sale of all or any part of an investment of an investor of Canada or from the partial or complete liquidation of the investment may not take place until a period not to exceed
    (i) in the case of an investment made pursuant to Law 18.657 Foreign Capital Investment Fund Law ("Ley 18.657, Ley Sobre Fondo de Inversiones de Capitales Extranjeros"), five years has elapsed from the date of transfer to Chile, or
    (ii) subject to subparagraph (c)
    (iii) in all other cases, one year has elapsed from the date of transfer to Chile; ..."

Some agreements however, explicitly prohibit the making of reservations, or prohibit reservations subject to certain exceptions. An example is the United Nations Convention on the Law of the Sea (United Nations, 1983) which prohibits reservations unless they are expressly permitted by other articles of the Convention. Otherwise, certain types of reservations made by one party may not be accepted by the other parties. Article 72 of the TRIPS Agreement, for example, prohibits the making of reservations without the consent of the other parties. A similar provision is to be found in the Agreement on Technical Barriers to Trade (article 15 (WTO, 1995), the Agreement on the Implementation of Article VII of the GATT 1994 (article 21) (WTO, 1995), the Agreement on the Implementation of Article VI of the GATT 1994 (article 18 (2)) (WTO, 1995) and the Agreement on Subsidies and Countervailing Measures (article 32 (2)) (WTO, 1995). The regime for acceptance of reservations, as set out in article 20 of the Vienna Convention is fairly complex. Conversely, some multilateral agreements expressly authorise certain reservations. An example is the New York Convention on the Recognition and Enforcement of Foreign Arbitration Awards (box III.10). Reservations tend to rest upon reciprocity -- i.e. when a country makes a reservation, other countries can invoke the same reservation against the reserving party -- although some international agreements permit the making of reservations even though they are not based on reciprocity.[16]

More generally, treaty law would not prevent States from negotiating IIAs that would permit issuance of reservations with respect to a number of its provisions in the interest of development, or from limiting the filing of these reservations to one specific category of parties. To the extent that a reservation seeks to modify the legal effect of certain provisions in an IIA, it can in principle offer some flexibility. The general trend however seems to be to set stringent conditions for reservations in IIAs.

Exceptions are provisions in agreements relating to situations in which a particular principle does not apply, or applies only in part. Thus, they qualify *ab initio* the extent of the obligations undertaken by countries participating in an international agreement. They seem to be favoured over reservations as far as international economic agreements are concerned (Juillard, 1994). IIAs contain three kinds of exceptions:

- **General exceptions** typically relate to public health, order, morals, and national security.

Such exceptions are present in a number of IIAs (box III.11), but they are not necessarily related to development. They limit the operations of an agreement because of considerations of the highest public character. The drafters of the 1992 World Bank Guidelines, for instance, sought to insert in the guideline on admission a clause to the effect that States might refuse admission to foreign investments that they thought would not be conducive to economic development (Shihata, 1993, p. 403); this clause, however, did not appear in the final version of the Guidelines. "Essential national economic interests" was one of the considerations proposed by some negotiators for a draft general exception clause on national treatment included in brackets in the Draft United Nations Code of Conduct on Transnational Corporations. It read: "consistent with [national constitutional systems and] national needs to [protect essential/national economic interests,] maintain public order and to protect national security" (UNCTAD, 1996a, p. 173).

Box III.10. Reservations
Convention on the Recognition and Enforcement of Foreign Arbitral Awards[a]

Mozambique
"Reservation:
The Republic of Mozambique reserves itself the right to enforce the provisions of the said Convention on the base of reciprocity, where the arbitral awards have been pronounced in the territory of another Contracting State."

The Philippines
"Upon signature:
Reservation
The Philippines delegation signs *ad referendum* this Convention with the reservation that it does so on the basis of reciprocity."

United Nations Convention on Contracts for the International Sale of Goods[b]

Finland
"*Reservation made upon signature and confirmed upon ratification*:
Finland will not be bound by Part II of the Convention.

Upon ratification
With reference to Article 94, in respect of Sweden in accordance with paragraph (1) and otherwise in accordance with paragraph (2) the Convention will not apply to contracts of sale where the parties have their places of business in Finland, Sweden, Denmark, Iceland or Norway."

International Convention on the Harmonization of Frontier Controls of Goods[c]

Russian Federation
Reservation
"*Regarding article 20, paragraphs 2 to 7:*
The Union of Soviet Socialist Republics does not consider itself bound by article 20, paragraphs 2 to 7, of the International Convention on the Harmonization of Frontier Controls of Goods concerning the settlement of disputes. "

[a] United Nations, 1959, pp. 11 and 12.
[b] United Nations, 1980a, p.3.
[c] United Nations, 1982, p.3.

Box III.11. General exceptions
General Agreement on Trade in Services

Article XIV
General Exceptions
"Subject to the requirement that such measures are not applied in a manner which would constitute a means of arbitrary or unjustifiable discrimination between countries where like conditions prevail, or a disguised restriction on trade in services, nothing in this Agreement shall be construed to prevent the adoption or enforcement by any member of measures:
(a) necessary to protect public morals or to maintain public order;...
(b) necessary to protect human, animal or plant life or health;
(c) necessary to secure compliance with laws or regulations which are not inconsistent with the provisions of this Agreement including those relating to:
   (i) the prevention of deceptive and fraudulent practices or to deal with the effects of a default on services contracts;
   (ii) the protection of the privacy of individuals in relation to the processing and dissemination of personal data and the protection of confidentiality of individual records and accounts;
   (iii) safety;"

OECD Code of Liberalisation of Capital Movements

Article 3
Public Order and Security
"The provisions of this Code shall not prevent a Member from taking action which it considers necessary for:
i) the maintenance of public order or the protection of public health, morals and safety;
ii) the protection of its essential security interests;
iii) the fulfilment of its obligations relating to international peace and security."

BIT between Bolivia and Peru (1993)

Article 3 (5)
"Nothing in this Treaty shall prevent a Contracting Party from adopting measures, if not discriminatory, for reasons of internal and external national security, public or moral order."

- **Subject-specific exceptions** are those that exempt specific matters from the application of individual provisions. For example, national treatment and most-favoured-nation (MFN) treatment clauses may contain exceptions in relation to intellectual property, benefits arising from membership in a regional economic integration scheme, and taxation provisions (box III.12).

Box III.12. Subject-specific exceptions

BIT between Chile and Malaysia (1992)

Article 3
Most favoured nation

"1. Investments by nationals or companies of either Contracting State on the territory of the other Contracting State shall ... not be subject to a treatment less favourable than that accorded to investments by nationals or companies of third States. ...

3. The provision in this Treaty relating to treatment no less favourable than that accorded to investments of third States shall not be interpreted to oblige a Contracting party to extend to investors of the other Contracting Party the benefits of any treatment, preference or privilege by virtue of:

(a) any customs union, free trade area, common market or monetary union, or any similar international convention or other forms of regional cooperation, present or future, of which any of the Contracting Parties might become a party; or the adoption of an agreement designed to achieve the formation or expansion of such union or area within a reasonable time; or

(b) any international convention or agreement related totally or principally to taxation, or any national legislation related totally or partially to taxation."

- **Country-specific exceptions** identify industries and measures that can be exempted from the operation of an IIA by allowing each individual party to list the specific industries or measures for which it claims exceptions. An example of this approach is article 7 of the Framework Agreement on the ASEAN Investment Area (box III.13) and article 1108 of NAFTA (cited in box III.18 below).

Derogations and waivers. In addition to exceptions, which qualify an agreement from the outset, international agreements can also provide for derogations. Their role is to allow countries that find conformity with certain treaty obligations particularly onerous, to ask the appropriate body established by the instrument to free them, temporarily or permanently, from some of their obligations. This course of action may also be taken when new situations arise, which are not fully provided for in the original agreement, but which are similar enough to exceptions or qualifications already provided for to make insistence on fulfilment of formal obligations inequitable. Examples of derogations and waivers include article 7 of the OECD Code of Liberalisation of Capital Movements (box III.14), the transitional arrangements provided for under Article 32 of the Energy Charter Treaty and, in the context of WTO, the decision to allow countries members of the Fourth ACP-EEC Convention of Lomé of 9 December 1994 to derogate from Article 1 (1) of GATT (GATT, 1994) (box III.14).[17] Derogations assume a legally-binding

Box III.13. Country-specific exceptions Framework Agreement on the ASEAN Investment Area Opening up of Industries and National Treatment

Article 7

"1. Subject to the provisions of this Article, each Member State shall:

(a) open immediately all its industries for investments by ASEAN investors;

(b) accord immediately to ASEAN investors and their investments, in respect of all industries and measures affecting investment including but not limited to the admission, establishment, acquisition, expansion, management, operation and disposition of investments, treatment no less favourable than that it accords to its own like investors and investments ("national treatment").

2. Each Member State shall submit a Temporary Exclusion List and a Sensitive List, if any, within 6 months after the date of the signing of this Agreement, of any industries or measures affecting investments (referred to in paragraph 1 above) with regard to which it is unable to open up or to accord national treatment to ASEAN investors. These lists shall form an annex to this Agreement. In the event that a Member State, for justifiable reasons, is unable to provide any list within the stipulated period, it may seek an extension from the AIA Council.

3. The Temporary Exclusion List shall be reviewed every 2 years and shall be progressively phased out by 2010 by all Member States except the Socialist Republic of Vietnam, the Lao People's Democratic Republic and the Union of Myanmar. The Socialist Republic of Vietnam shall progressively phase out the Temporary Exclusion List by 2013 and the Lao People's Democratic Republic and the Union of Myanmar shall progressively phase out their Temporary Exclusion Lists by 2015.

4. The Sensitive List shall be reviewed by 1 January 2003 and at such subsequent periodic intervals as may be decided by the AIA council."

instrument. Clearly, nonbinding instruments or instruments formulated in such manner as not to limit the options of participating countries do not need derogations.

Box III.14. Derogations
OECD Code of Liberalisation of Capital Movements

Article 7
Clauses of derogation

"a. If is economic and financial situation justifies such a course, a Member need not take the whole of the measures of liberalisation provided for in Article 2(a).
b. If any measures of liberalisation taken or maintained in accordance with the provisions of Article 2(a) result in serious economic and financial disturbance in the Member State concerned, that Member may withdraw those measures. ... "

WTO Decision of 9 December 1994 regarding the Fourth ACP-EEC Convention of Lomé

"The Contracting parties, acting pursuant to the provisions of paragraph 5 of Article XXV of the General Agreement,

Decide that:

1. Subject to the terms and conditions set out there under, the provisions of paragraph 1 of Article 1 of the General Agreement shall be waived, until 29 February 2,000, to the extent necessary to permit the European Communities to provide preferential treatment for products originating in ACP States as required by the relevant provisions of the Fourth Lomé Convention, without being required to extent the same preferential treatment to like products of any other contracting party."

Safeguards or "escape clauses" are provisions included in an agreement that allow parties to take action otherwise not permitted by an instrument, in order to cope with unforeseen events arising after the adoption of the instrument. As in the case of reservations, they involve, in the first place, unilateral action by the country concerned. In later phases, however, in order to enter into effect, they require prior notification and/or approval from the competent organ. Moreover, the relevant provisions normally set definite limits in terms of time and substantive measures to the action to be taken through invocation of safeguards. The most common situations contemplated in safeguard clauses in IIAs relate to balance-of-payments crises or emergency economicsituations. The Framework Agreement on the ASEAN Investment Area contains such clauses (box III.15). Other examples include article 7 of the OECD Code of Liberalisation of Current Invisible Operations and article XII of GATS.

Box III.15. Safeguards
Framework Agreement on the ASEAN Investment Area

Article 14
Emergency Safeguard Measures

"1. If, as a result of the implementation of the liberalisation programme under this Agreement, a Member State suffers or is threatened with any serious injury and threat, the Member State may take emergency safeguard measures to the extent and for such period as may be necessary to prevent or to remedy such injury. The measures taken shall be provisional and without discrimination.
2. Where emergency safeguard measures are taken pursuant to this Article, notice of such measure shall be given to the AIA Council within 14 days from the date such measures are taken.
3. The AIA Council shall determine the definition of serious injury and threat of serious injury and the procedures of instituting emergency safeguards measures pursuant to this Article."

Article 15
Measures to Safeguard the Balance of Payments

"1. In the event of serious balance of payments and external financial difficulties or threat thereof, a Member State may adopt or maintain restrictions on investments on which it has undertaken specific commitments, including on payments or transfers for transactions related to such commitments. It is recognised that particular pressures on the balance of payments of a Member State in the process of economic development or economic transition may necessitate the use of restrictions to ensure, inter alia, the maintenance of a level of financial reserves adequate for the implementation of its programme of economic development or economic transition.
2. Where measures to safeguard balance of payments are taken pursuant to this Article notice of such measures shall be given to the AIA Council within 14 days from the date such measures are taken.
3. The measures referred to in paragraph (1):
(a) shall not discriminate among Member States;
(b) shall be consistent with the Articles of Agreement of the International Monetary Fund;
(c) shall avoid unnecessary damage to the commercial, economic and financial interests of any other Member State;
(d) shall not exceed those necessary to deal with the circumstances described in paragraph 1; and
(e) shall be temporary and be phased out progressively as the situation specified in paragraph 1 improves.

4. The Member States adopting the balance of payments measures shall commence consultations with the AIA Council and other Member States within 90 days from the date of notification in order to review the balance of payment measures adopted by it. "

5. The AIA Council shall determine the rules applicable to the procedures under this Article. "

b. "Ratione temporis": flexibility in relation to the timing of assuming obligations under an agreement

Transitional arrangements. Temporal (phasing) provisions can be used to grant to developing countries (or certain categories of them) an extra period of time so as to enable them to get ready to assume fully and entirely their international obligations. Thus, transitional arrangements do not create rights of a permanent character. Rather, they are an acknowledgment that developing countries may not always be in a position to act in the same manner as developed countries. The TRIMs and TRIPS Agreements provide examples of such transition arrangements (box III.16). The BIT between Poland and the United States is another example. It provides for a transitional period within which Poland was to gradually assume certain obligations, such as free convertibility of its currency. Other examples of agreements outside the investment field that grant longer transitional periods for compliance to developing countries (expressly linked to an understanding that differential and more favourable treatment for developing country members was to be an integral part of the agreement) are article 15 of the WTO Agreement on Agriculture (WTO, 1995) (box III.16), the WTO Agreement on the Application of Sanitary and Phytosanitary Measures (WTO, 1995) (box III.16) and the United Nations Framework Convention on Climate Change (United Nations, 1992b) and its Kyoto Protocol (United Nations, 1997) (see box V.10 below).

4. The use of "positive" and "negative" lists

Another basic approach to provide for structural flexibility, and one that is not confined to developing countries alone, involves the use of "positive" and "negative" lists. The former kind of lists enumerate those industries or measures in respect of which obligations are to be undertaken; the latter kind of lists enumerate those industries or measures to which obligations do not apply. Thus, in the negative list approach there is a general obligation from which a country can "opt-out". In the positive list approach, there is no general obligation, but a country may assume it, i.e. "opt-in". In other words, in the first case, a country is bound by an obligation unless it acts; in the second case, a country is not bound unless it acts. (See also under "Admission", chapter IV.B, for a further elaboration of the application of positive and negative lists in the context of clauses on admission and establishment of FDI.)

An example of a *positive list* can be found in GATS, where no party is compelled to permit market access or national treatment; rather it has the right, under articles XVI and XVII, to list in its schedule those service industries in which it is willing to make such commitments (box III.17). This approach reflects the fact that the commitments are negotiated on the basis of reciprocity, which can be provided in other service modes of supply or in access for trade in goods. By following this approach, GATS encourages the increased participation of developing countries in trade in services by facilitating their efforts to liberalize their service industries as they are able to obtain reciprocal commitments in other areas of negotiations.

In addition, as noted above in this chapter (section III. A), GATS article XIX.2 grants additional flexibility for developing countries in the context of setting out their positive lists, for opening only a few industries, liberalizing fewer types of transactions, progressively extending market access in line with their development situation and, when making access to their markets available to foreign suppliers, attaching to such access conditions (e.g. transfer of technology, training) aimed at achieving the objectives referred to in Article IV.

An example of a *negative list* can be found in NAFTA, where parties accept a set of principles and then negotiate sectoral exceptions (box III.18). This approach may result in a long list of reservations submitted by the parties. Negative lists can be adopted on a "stand still" basis -- i.e. non-conforming measures or exceptions are allowed to be maintained, as are any amendments thereto (provided these do not increase the restrictive nature of the measures) -- or they can be subject to "roll back" provisions, calling for progressive liberalization. Examples of the first approach are found in some BITs. Typical examples of the latter approach are the OECD Liberalisation Codes and the Framework Agreement on the ASEAN Investment Area.

It should be noted that these two approaches are not mutually exclusive. An agreement could contain both approaches. GATS, for example, also has a negative listing for limitations on market access and national treatment with respect to those sectors and subsectors included in the schedule (box III.17).[18] One could also imagine other combinations. For example, the

Box III.16. Phasing the implementation of specific commitments Agreement on Trade-Related Investment Measures

Article 5
Notification and Transitional Arrangements

"1. Members, within 90 days of the date of entry into force of the WTO Agreement, shall notify the Council for Trade in Goods of all TRIMs they are applying that are not in conformity with the provisions of this Agreement. Such TRIMs of general or specific application shall be notified, along with their principal features. ...

2. Each Member shall eliminate all TRIMs which are notified under paragraph 1 within two years of the date of entry into force of the WTO Agreement in the case of a developed country Member, within five years in the case of a developing country Member, and within seven years in the case of a least–developed country Member.

3. On request, the Council for Trade in Goods may extend the transition period for the elimination of TRIMs notified under paragraph 1 for a developing country Member, including a least developed country Member, which demonstrates particular difficulties in implementing the provisions of this Agreement. In considering such a request, the Council for Trade in Goods shall take into account the individual development, financial and trade needs of the Member in question.

4. During the transition period, a Member shall not modify the terms of any TRIM which it notifies under paragraph 1 from those prevailing at the date of entry into force of the WTO Agreement so as to increase the degree of inconsistency with the provisions of Article 2. TRIMs introduced less than 180 days before the date of entry into force of the WTO Agreement shall not benefit from the transitional arrangements provided in paragraph 2.

5. Notwithstanding the provisions of Article 2, a Member, in order not to disadvantage established enterprises which are subject to a TRIM notified under paragraph 1, may apply during the transition period the same TRIM to a new investment (i) where the products of such investment are like products to those of the established enterprises, and (ii) where necessary to avoid distorting the conditions of competition between the new investment and the established enterprises. Any TRIM so applied to a new investment shall be notified to the Council for Trade in Goods. The terms of such a TRIM shall be equivalent in their competitive effect to those applicable to the established enterprises, and it shall be terminated at the same time."

Agreement on Trade-Related Aspects of Intellectual Property Rights

Article 65
Transitional Arrangements

"1. Subject to the provisions of paragraphs 2, 3 and 4, no Member shall be obliged to apply the provisions of this Agreement before the expiry of a general period of one year following the date of entry into force of the WTO Agreement.

2. A developing country Member is entitled to delay for a further period of four years the date of application, as defined in paragraph 1, of the provisions of this Agreement other than Articles 3, 4 and 5.

3. Any other Member which is in the process of transformation from a centrally-planned into a market, free-enterprise economy and which is undertaking structural reform of its intellectual property system and facing special problems in the preparation and implementation of intellectual property laws and regulations, may also benefit from a period of delay as foreseen in paragraph 2.

4. To the extent that a developing country Member is obliged by this Agreement to extend product patent protection to areas of technology not so protectable in its territory on the general date of application of this Agreement for that Member, as defined in paragraph 2, it may delay the application of the provisions on product patents of Section 5 of Part II to such areas of technology for an additional period of five years.

5. A Member availing itself of a transitional period under paragraphs 1, 2, 3 or 4 shall ensure that any changes in its laws, regulations and practice made during that period do not result in a lesser degree of consistency with the provisions of this Agreement."

WTO Agreement on Agriculture[a]

Article 15
Special and Differential Treatment

"1. In keeping with the recognition that differential and more favourable treatment for developing country Members is an integral part of the negotiation, special and differential treatment in respect of commitments shall be provided as set out in the relevant provisions of this Agreement and embodied in the Schedules of concessions and commitments.

2.Developing country Members shall have the flexibility to implement reduction commitments over a period of up to 10 years. Least-developed country Members shall not be required to undertake reduction commitments."

WTO Agreement on the Application of Sanitary and Phytosanitary Measures[a]

Article 10
Special and Differential Treatment

"1. In the preparation and application of sanitary or phytosanitary measures, Members shall take account of the special needs of developing country Members, and in particular of the least-developed country Members.

2. Where the appropriate level of sanitary or phytosanitary protection allows scope for the phased introduction of new sanitary orphytosanitary measures, longer time-frames for compliance should be accorded on products of interest to developing country Members so as to maintain opportunities for their exports.

3. With a view to ensuring that developing country Members are able to comply with the provisions of this Agreement, the Committee is enabled to grant to such countries, upon request, specified, time-limited exceptions in whole or in part from obligations under this Agreement, taking into account their financial, trade and development needs.

4. Members should encourage and facilitate the active participation of developing country Members in the relevant international organizations."

[a] WTO, 1995.

negative list approach could apply to one part of a given principle (e.g. national treatment in the post establishment phase) while the positive list approach applies to another part of the same principle (e.g. national treatment in the pre-establish phase). Or developing countries are allowed to use the positive list approach while developed countries are required to use the negative list approach.

Box III.17. Use of positive lists
General Agreement on Trade in Services

Article XX
Schedules of Specific Commitments

"1. Each Member shall set out in a schedule the specific commitments it undertakes under Part III of this Agreement. With respect to sectors where such commitments are undertaken, each Schedule shall specify:

(a) terms, limitations and conditions on market access;
(b) conditions and qualifications on national treatment;
(c) undertakings relating to additional commitments;
(d) where appropriate the time-frame for implementation of such commitments; and
(e) the date of entry into force of such commitments.

....

3. Schedules of specific commitments shall be annexed to this Agreement and shall form an integral part thereof."

Specific Commitments
Article XVI
Market Access

"1. With respect to market access through the modes of supply identified in Article 1, each Member shall accord services and service suppliers of any other Member treatment no less favourable than that provided for under the terms, limitations and conditions agreed and specified in its Schedule. ...

2. In sectors where market-access commitments are undertaken, the measures which a Member shall not maintain or adopt either on the basis of a regional subdivision or on the basis of its entire territory, unless otherwise specified in its Schedule, are defined as:

(a) limitations on the number of service suppliers whether in the form of numerical quotas, monopolies, exclusive service suppliers or the requirements of an economic needs test;
(b) limitations on the total value of service transactions or assets in the form of numerical quotas or the requirement of an economic needs test;
(c) limitations on the total number of service operations or on the total quantity of service output expressed in terms of designated numerical units in the form of quotas or the requirement of an economic needs test; ...
(d) limitations on the total number of natural persons that may be employed in a particular service sector or that a service supplier may employ and who are necessary for, and directly related to the supply of a specific service in the form of numerical quotas or the requirement of an economic needs test;
(e) measures which restrict or require specific types of legal entity or joint venture through which a service supplier may supply a service; and
(f) limitations on the participation of foreign capital in terms of maximum percentage limit on foreign share holding or the total value of individual or aggregate foreign investment."

Box III.18. Use of negative lists
North America Free Trade Agreement

Article 1108
Reservations and Exceptions

"1. Articles 1102, 1103, 1106 and 1107 do not apply to:

(a) any existing non-conforming measure that is maintained by
    (i) a Party at the federal level, as set out in its Schedule to Annex I or III,
    (ii) a state or province, for two years after the date of entry into force of this Agreement, and thereafter as set out by a Party in its Schedule to Annex I in accordance with paragraph 2, or
    (iii) a local government;
(b) the continuation or prompt renewal of any non-conforming measure referred to in subparagraph (a); or
(c) an amendment to any non-conforming measure referred to in subparagraph (a) to the extent that the amendment does not decrease the conformity of the measure, as it existed immediately before the amendment, with Articles 1102, 1103, 1106 and 1107.

2. Each Party may set out in its Schedule to Annex I, within two years of the date of entry into force of this Agreement, any existing non-conforming measure maintained by a state or province, not including a local government.

3. Articles 1102, 1103, 1106 and 1107 do not apply to any measure that a Party adopts or maintains with respect to sectors, subsectors or activities, as set out in its Schedule to Annex II.

4. No Party may, under any measure adopted after the date of entry into force of this Agreement and covered by its Schedule to Annex II, require an investor of another Party, by reason of its nationality, to sell or otherwise dispose of an investment existing at the time the measure becomes effective.

...

6. Article 1103 does not apply to treatment accorded by a Party pursuant to agreements, or with respect to sectors, set out in its Schedule to Annex IV."

Whatever approach is used, the overriding concern for a country is to identify those industries and/or activities that ought to be included/excluded in light of its particular situation and its comparative advantage. Thus, an understanding of the particular situations and comparative advantages of domestic industries is a crucial element in how a developing country will approach the listing of negative exceptions or positive commitments.

What may be potentially problematic in this context is the "information asymmetry" that a developing country might experience in that it may not have the informational resources, or access to such resources held by others, to be able to make a full and informed judgement as to the nature, scale and scope of its comparative advantages. Furthermore, the selection of exclusions from a positive list might be influenced by local interests seeking to shield themselves from international competition. Similarly, foreign investors might seek the liberalization of sectors at the cost of local competitors. Thus, the process of selecting negative or positive lists is one that assumes adequate information and a balance of special interests and lobbies, so that a proper and objective choice can be made by a given developing country. Where this is not the case, inappropriate exclusions from, or inclusions in, the liberalization process may occur.

5. Concluding several separate instruments

The discussion of possible structural approaches so far has assumed an IIA as a single instrument. It is possible however to construct an overall investment framework consisting of several instruments combining various approaches. One possibility is to conclude two or more instruments with differing binding force. This is the method used in, for example, the 1976 OECD Declaration on International Investment and Multinational Enterprises. The Declaration (which itself is not legally-binding) encompasses decisions on National Treatment, Incentives and Disincentives and Conflicting Requirements that impose certain obligations on OECD member Governments, and Guidelines for Multinational Enterprises that are recommendations by the OECD member countries as regards the behaviour of TNCs.

The logic for combining legally-binding and voluntary instruments may respond to the technical characteristics of an agreement, such as the different types of addressees involved (i.e. governments and foreign investors), but can also be a way of allowing certain groups of countries more flexible commitments on account of their development needs. It is also conceivable that the legal form of these instruments may evolve over time. Thus, a nonbinding instrument may evolve into a more binding one. The proposed OECD Multilateral Agreement on Investment (MAI), for example, was intended to strengthen the binding character of some existing OECD investment instruments, such as the national treatment instrument. Conversely, an agreement imposing strict obligations may be chosen as a point of departure which may be supplemented by more flexible additions or specifications later. This is the case of, for example, the North American Agreement on Environmental Cooperation (Canada, Mexico and the United States, 1993a) and the North American Agreement on Labor Cooperation (Canada, Mexico and the United States, 1993b) which were adopted as side agreements to NAFTA. While NAFTA imposes high standards for the liberalization and treatment of investment, the two side agreements require the parties to cooperate on environment and labour matters, but recognize the right of each country to establish their own levels of domestic environmental protection and their own domestic labour standards. Similarly, in the MAI negotiations there appeared to have been a general understanding among negotiators that the OECD Guidelines for Multinational Enterprises would be annexed to the binding MAI text, but without losing their voluntary character.

The scope of the contents of an IIA may also be a consideration. For example, a comprehensive investment instrument may deal with broad principles at the outset, and move progressively towards developing detailed provisions in additional instruments later. This approach has been followed in, for example, GATS where the agreement contemplates the conclusion of individual supplementary agreements dealing with specific services industries that follow the main principles stipulated in the framework agreement. Alternatively, it may cover only certain areas and move progressively into other supplementary agreements to cover presumably more controversial areas. A case in point is the above mentioned NAFTA side agreements on Environmental Cooperation and on Labor Cooperation. The characteristics of the parties may be another. Regional integration groups sometimes sign separate agreements aimed at governing investment relations with each other and with third parties, respectively, with, typically, the provisions affecting investment relations with third countries not being as advanced as those applying among the members of the group. This is the approach followed in, for example, the MERCOSUR Protocol on Protection and Promotion of Investments within the Countries members of MERCOSUR (Intrazone) and the Protocol on Protection and Promotion of Investments from States not Parties of MERCOSUR. These two agreements deal with the same issues and resemble one another in most respects, except for a few issues such as admission of investment where the latter is more restrictive in terms of the host countries' flexibility to allow or deny FDI entry. This method can be used to conclude separate side agreements with countries or groups of countries at different levels of development, each providing for different degrees of commitment and flexibility.

A variation of this approach is to postpone the negotiation of additional elements of an agreement or the strengthening of the existing agreement or certain provisions in it. This can be done to facilitate the conclusion of an IIA when it becomes obvious that the majority of the parties are not ready to agree to certain provisions, or can only accept "soft" obligations, at least for the time being. A case in point is the Energy Charter Treaty as regards the extension of investment protection standards to the pre-establishment phase (box III.19). Consideration to adding possible new elements to an IIA is usually given as part of its review process, after some years of experience with its application (see below under chapter V.A). In some cases, however, the possibility of adding new elements is already contemplated in the original agreement, so that the matter is included for consideration in a "built-in" agenda. Thus, some agreements include from the outset a provision giving some indication of the type of issues a complementary agreement might address. Such a provision would commit the parties at least to look at the matter over time. Article 9 of the TRIMs agreement offers an example of the "built-in agenda" approach (box III.19).

Box III.19. Postponing negotiation of additional elements of an agreement
Energy Charter Treaty

Article 10
Promotion, protection and treatment of investments
"(4) A supplementary treaty shall, subject to conditions to be laid down therein, oblige each party thereto to accord to Investors of other parties, as regards the Making of Investments in its Area, the Treatment described in paragraph (3). That treaty shall be open for signature by the states and Regional Economic Integration Organizations which have signed or acceded to this Treaty. Negotiations towards the supplementary treaty shall commence no later than 1 January 1995, with a view to concluding it by 1 January 1998."

Agreement on Trade-Related Investment Measures

Article 9
"Not later than five years after the date of entry into force of the WTO Agreement, the Council for Trade in Goods shall review the operation of the Agreement and, as appropriate, propose to the Ministerial Conference amendments to its text. In the course of this review, the Council for Trade in Goods shall consider whether the Agreement should be complemented with provisions on investment policy and competition policy."

* * *

The preceding discussion suggests that there are many elements involved in the construction of an IIA. These elements can be combined in a multitude of ways, and different variations can be added. Whatever the combination of elements, IIAs need to be constructed in a manner that ensures an overall balance of rights and obligations for all actors involved, so that all parties can derive benefits from it. In the context of IIAs, this issue may also include consideration of the question of the responsibilities of TNCs in their host countries with respect to development.

Of course, to achieve an overall balance of rights and obligations in an IIA, such balance needs also to find expression in the substantive content of the agreement and the formulation of its substantive provisions, keeping in mind the interactions among them. How this can be achieved is the topic of the next section.

IV. Substantive Provisions

The contents of IIAs are the concrete means by which concepts such as flexibility are given effect. When concluding an IIA, countries make choices about the issues they wish to include and those they wish to keep outside the scope of an agreement, to deal with them in specialized agreements (e.g. on double taxation), as a matter of national law and policy, or not at all. Even when they decide to include certain issues in an IIA, countries may wish to retain some flexibility regarding the commitments they make. They may therefore use formulations that allow them some discretion to pursue their national policies while keeping in line with the broad principles of an agreement. Development concerns can also determine the extent to which the contents of an IIA reflect a balance of rights and obligations for all actors concerned.

IIAs -- especially multilateral and regional instruments -often differ when it comes to the kind of substantive provisions they contain and the manner in which these are addressed. An important matter for countries to decide is thus what issues to include in a particular agreement they choose to negotiate and how to define rights and responsibilities as to the issues they decide to include. This section does not address the first question -- what issues to include; the list of issues appearing in IIAs is indeed quite long. Rather, it illustrates, for a selected number of issues and in no particular order, how these issues have been dealt with in existing IIAs. In doing so, the section draws on the other chapters in these volumes.

There is little point in attempting to list all the various permutations that have been, or can be, used in formulating substantive provisions in IIAs, as the outcome depends on a process of negotiation in the light of specific circumstances. The range of permutations can be gleaned from the various alternative formulations reviewed below. In fact, the approaches indicated below are merely analytical constructs whose principal purpose is to indicate broad -- including hypothetical -- approaches to a given subject.

A. Scope and definition of investment[19]

The purpose of definitions in legal instruments is to determine the object to which an instrument's rules apply and the scope of these rules' applicability. Hence, they form part of the normative content of the instrument. The scope of application of an IIA depends on the definition of certain terms, principally "investment". This definition determines which investments are covered by its provisions or are excluded from the coverage of the agreement. The main approaches to the definition of investment are outlined below.

1. A broad definition

The most common trend in recent IIAs is to have a broad, inclusive definition of "investment" which may or may not be subject to limitations (box IV.1). A broad definition has implications for the development policy of the States parties to an agreement. The developmental concern can be stated quite simply: treaty coverage of all assets included within the definition may not be consistent with a State's development policy at every period in the life of an agreement.

A broad definition of "investment" may also be open-ended. This is the approach followed in BITs, as illustrated in, for example, the BIT between Ecuador and the United Kingdom (box IV.2). Reasons for this approach are that first, as a technical matter, it may be difficult to draft a more precise definition that would cover all the assets that parties wish to be covered by an agreement. Second, because the concept of investment has evolved over time and because many investment agreements are intended to last for many years, those who draft them appear to seek, as a matter of policy, to utilize language that can extend an agreement to new forms of investment as they emerge, without renegotiation of the agreement. Both of these considerations are particularly important in agreements that are intended to facilitate international investment flows.

Box IV.1. A broad and open-ended definition of investment
BIT between Ecuador and the United Kingdom (1994)

Article 1
Definitions

"For the purposes of this Agreement:

(a) investment means every kind of asset and in particular, though not exclusively, includes:
   (i) movable and immovable property and any other property rights such as mortgages, liens or pledges;
   (ii) shares, stock and debentures of companies or interests in the property of such companies;
   (iii) claims to money or to any performance under contract having a financial value;
   (iv) intellectual property rights and goodwill;
   (v) business concessions conferred by law or under contract, including concessions to search for, cultivate, extract or exploit natural resources. "

A broad open-ended definition, at the same time, may be undesirable for countries that are concerned about certain effects of foreign investment. The danger of an open-ended definition is that it may commit a host country to permitting, promoting or protecting forms of investment that it had not contemplated at the time it entered into an agreement and might not have agreed to include within the scope of the agreement had the issue arisen explicitly. There are several ways to limit the scope of the definition, as discussed below.

2. A narrower definition

A number of agreements have narrowed the definition of investment, although there are advantages and disadvantages to any particular way of narrowing the definition. Taking each type of narrower definition in turn, the following development implications may be envisaged:

- A number of IIAs exclude portfolio investment from the definition of investment because it may be regarded as less desirable than FDI, given that it generally does not bring with it technology transfer, training or other benefits

Box IV.2. Excluding portfolio (or some types of portfolio) investment

Framework Agreement on the ASEAN Investment Area

Article 2
Coverage

"This Agreement shall cover all direct investments other than -

a. portfolio investments; and
b. matters relating to investments covered by other ASEAN Agreements, such as the ASEAN Framework Agreement on Services."

Free Trade Agreement between Canada and the United States

Chapter Sixteen
Investment
Article 1611: Definitions

"For purposes of this Chapter, not including Annex 1607.3: investment means:

a) the establishment of a new business enterprise, or
b) the acquisition of a business enterprise;
c) as carried on, the new business enterprise so established or the business enterprise so acquired, and controlled by the investor who has made the investment; and
d) the share or other investment interest in such business enterprise owned by the investor provided that such business enterprise continues to be controlled by such investor."

BIT between Denmark and Lithuania (1992)

Article 1

"The term "investment" shall mean (1). Every kind of asset connected with economic activities acquired for the purpose of establishing lasting economic relations between an investor and an enterprise ..."

BIT between Germany and Israel (1976)

Article 1

"For the purpose of this Treaty

(1) (a) The term "investment" shall mean, as the context may require, either
(i) investment in an enterprise involving active participation therein and the acquisition of assets ancillary thereto;"

OECD Code of Liberalisation of Capital Movements

Annex A
List A
I. Direct investment

"Investment for the purpose of establishing lasting economic relations with an undertaking such as, in particular, investments which give the possibility of exercising an effective influence on the management thereof:

A. In the country concerned by non-residents by means of:

1. Creation or extension of a wholly-owned enterprise, subsidiary or branch, acquisition or full ownership of an existing enterprise;
2. Participation in a new or existing enterprise;
3. A loan of five years or longer.

B. Abroad by residents by means of:

1. Creation or extension of a wholly-owned enterprise, subsidiary or branch, acquisition of full ownership of an existing enterprise;
2. Participation in a new or existing enterprise;
3. A loan of five years or longer."

WTO General Agreement on Trade in Services

Article XXVIII
Definitions

"For the purpose of this Agreement:

(d) a "commercial presence" means any type of business or professional establishment, including through
(i) the constitution, acquisition, or maintenance of a juridical person, or
(ii) the creation or maintenance of a branch or a representative office, within the territory of a Member for the purpose of supplying a service. ..."

North American Free Trade Agreement (NAFTA)

Chapter Eleven
Investment
Section C - Definitions
Article 1139: Definitions

"For the purpose of this Chapter:

Investment means:

(a) an enterprise;
(b) an equity security of an enterprise;
(c) a debt security of an enterprise
(i) where the enterprise is an affiliate of the investor, or
(ii) where the original maturity of the debt security is as least three years, but does not include a debt security, regardless of original maturity, of a state enterprise;
(d) a loan to an enterprise
(i) where the enterprise is an affiliate of the investor, or
(ii) where the original maturity of the loan is at least three years, but does not include a loan, regardless of original maturity, to a state enterprise;
(e) an interest in an enterprise that entitles the owner to share in income or profits of the enterprise;
(f) an interest in an enterprise that entitles the owner to share in the assets of that enterprise on dissolution, other than a debt security or a loan excluded from subparagraph (c) or (d);
(g) real estate or other property, tangible or intangible, acquired in the expectation or used for the purpose of economic benefit or other business purposes; and
(h) interests arising from the commitment of capital or other resources in the territory of a Party to economic activity in such territory, such as under
(i) contracts involving the presence of an investor's property in the territory of the Party, including turnkey or construction contracts, or concessions, or
(ii) contracts where remuneration depends substantially on the production, revenues or profits of an enterprise;

/...

Box IV.2 (concluded)

but investment does not mean,
(i) claims to money that arise solely from
  (i) commercial contracts for the sale of goods or services by a national or enterprise in the territory of a Party to an enterprise in the territory of another Party, or
  (ii) the extension of credit in connection with a commercial transaction, such as trade financing, other than a loan covered by subparagraph (d); or
(j) any other claims to money, that do not involve the kinds of interests set out in subparagraphs (a) through (h);..."

associated with FDI. Further, portfolio investment can be easily withdrawn, thus creating the potential for capital volatility in the event of economic turbulence. Examples of this approach include the Framework Agreement on the ASEAN Investment Area, the Free Trade Agreement between Canada and the United States, the BIT between Denmark and Lithuania, the BIT between Germany and Israel and the WTO General Agreement on Trade in Services in relation to the definition of "commercial presence" (box IV.3). The OECD Code of Liberalisation of Capital Movements differentiates between portfolio transactions and direct investment and includes each of these types of transactions in separate subheadings of the liberalization lists. NAFTA includes portfolio investment in its definition of investment but excludes certain types of debt securities and loans and also seeks to exclude ordinary commercial contracts (box IV.2).

- Some IIAs exclude assets of less than a certain value, perhaps because these investments are considered too small to justify the costs of treaty coverage or perhaps because of a desire to reserve to domestic investors those parts of the economy in which small investments are likely to be made. Examples of this approach are the Framework Agreement on the ASEAN Investment Area and article 15 of the Community Investment Code of the Economic Community of the Great Lakes Countries (box IV.3). However, the exclusion of small investments could discourage small and medium-sized investors that some developing Countries may seek to attract, at least during certain stages of the development process. In such cases a size limitation may not be useful.
- Other IIAs exclude investments established prior to entry into force of the agreement, or another instrument (i.e. a law of the host country) in order to avoid bestowing a windfall on the investor. An example of this approach is article 9 of the BIT between Germany and Sri Lanka (box IV.4). Such an exclusion could be interpreted as calling into question the parties' commitment to investment promotion or protection and in exceptional cases could provide a permanent competitive advantage to investors who invest after the conclusion of the agreement.
- Investment agreements may limit the parts of the economy to which the agreement applies. This is the approach to definition taken by the Energy Charter Treaty (box IV.5) and GATS. It can be envisaged that other sector-specific agreements could adopt a similar approach to definitional issues.

Box IV.3. Narrowing the definition according to the size of the investment

Framework Agreement on the ASEAN Investment Area
Article 1
Definition

"For the purpose of this Agreement:
" ASEAN investor" means
i. a national of a Member State; or
ii. any juridical person of a Member State,

making an investment in another Member State, the effective ASEAN equity of which taken cumulative with all other ASEAN equities fulfills at least the minimum percentage required to meet the national equity requirements of domestic laws and published national policies, if any, of the host country in respect of that investment."

Community Investment Code of the Economic Community of the Great Lakes Countries (CEPGL)
Section I: Conditions for authorization
Article 15

"Any joint enterprise or Community enterprise conducting or wishing to conduct operations in the territory of a CEPGL member State either in order to rationalize its production methods or for purpose of modernization or extension may qualify for a decision authorising inclusion under a preferential regime if it meets the criteria provided for in article 2.

The minimum volume of investments is set at one million United States dollars or the equivalent."

Box IV.4. Limitations on time of establishment BIT between Germany and Sri Lanka (1963)

Article 9

"The present Treaty shall apply to all investments made on or after November 8, 1963, by nationals or companies of either Contracting Party in the territory of the other Contracting Party consistent with the latter's legislation."

Box IV.5. Limiting the definition of investment to certain parts of the economy
Energy Charter Treaty
Article 1
DEFINITIONS

"As used in this Treaty:
(6) (in fine) An "Investment" refers to any investment associated with an Economic Activity in the Energy Sector and to investments or classes of investments designated by a Contracting Party in its Area as "Charter efficiency projects" and so notified to the Secretariat."

3. A broad definition subject to the right to screen and conditional entry

Another alternative is to adopt a broad definition of "investment", but reserve the right to screen or place conditions on the establishment of individual investments. In this way, the host country does not exclude any category of investment a priori, but can exclude any specific investment. This approach has been adopted in a number of BITs and in the ASEAN Agreement for the Promotion and Protection of Investments which was superseded in 1998 by the Framework Agreement on the ASEAN Investment Area (box IV.6). It ensures that only those investments that have been approved by the host country are entitled to protection under the agreement. Moreover, such screening usually includes a review of the development implications of the investment. Consequently, approval of the investment signifies, in principle, conformity to the host country's development goals.

4. A broad definition with limiting substantive provisions

A further alternative is to adopt a broad definition of investment, but limit the scope of the substantive provisions. For example, if the concern about portfolio investment is that it may be withdrawn quickly, an investment agreement might define "investment" to include portfolio investment, but the currency-transfers provision would apply only if an investment has been established for some minimum period of time, such as one year. This approach has been followed in the BIT between Chile and the Czech Republic (box IV.7). Such a limitation is directed at the volatility of the investment, which may be one particular concern regarding portfolio investment. By addressing concerns generally in the operative provisions, this approach eliminates some of the burden on the investment screening agency to take account of every concern on a case-by-case basis. It also avoids the problem of an "all-or-nothing" approach. Thus, some investments may be admitted, but with only limited rights under an agreement.

Box IV.6. Broad definition of investment subject to the right to screen entry
China model BIT

Article 1
"For the purposes of this Agreement,
1. The term "investment" means every kind of asset invested by investors of one Contracting Party in accordance with the laws and regulations of the other Contracting Party in the territory of the latter, ..."

ASEAN Agreement for the Promotion and Protection of Investments
Article 1
Definition

"For the purpose of this Agreement:
3. The term "investment" shall mean every kind of asset and in particular shall include, through not exclusively:

(a) movable and immovable property and any other property rights such as mortgages, liens and pledges;
(b) shares, stocks and debentures of companies or interests in the property of such companies;
(c) claims to money or to any performance under contract having a financial value;
(d) intellectual property rights and goodwill;
(e) business concessions conferred by law or under contract, including concessions to search for, cultivate, extract, or exploit natural resources."

Article II
Applicability or scope

"1. This Agreement shall apply only to investments brought into, derived from or directly connected with investments brought into the territory of any Contracting Party by nationals or companies of any other Contracting Party and which are specifically approved in writing and registered by the host country and upon such conditions as it deems fit for the purposes of this Agreement. "

This approach places a heavy burden on the negotiators of an agreement to consider the potential ramifications of each type of investment and to incorporate language in the agreement during negotiations to protect the host country's ability to execute its development policy.

5. A mixed approach

It is also possible for the parties to adopt a mixture of, for example, broad and narrow definitions or asset-based and transaction-based definitions in relation to the different purposes of an investment agreement. Thus, while some countries may wish to define "investment" to include not every kind of asset, but only the specific categories included in a list, those same countries may wish to define "investment" more broadly in an agreement that regulates foreign investment, such as an agreement on transfer pricing. Generally speaking, the liberalization of investment flows is one of the aspects of investment agreements that has most concerned many developing countries. One possibility in this respect is to use a broad asset-based definition for the purpose of protecting investments, and a narrower asset-based or transaction-based definition for cross-border investment liberalization agreements.

* * *

Box IV.7. Broad definition of investment with limiting substantive provisions
BIT between Chile and the Czech Republic (1995)

Article 1 Definitions
"(2) The term "investment" shall comprise every kind of asset invested ... "
Article 5
"(4) Capital can only be transferred one year after it has entered the territory of the Contracting Party unless its legislation provides for a more favourable treatment."

The development implications of a broad definition of "investment" in an investment agreement are substantial. Although developmental concerns can be addressed in part by narrowing the definition of "investment", that is not necessarily the only approach in every case. Depending upon the nature of the operative provisions of an agreement and the purpose(s) of the parties in concluding the agreement, these developmental concerns in particular cases may be addressed alternatively through reservations of the right to exclude investments or by limiting the applicability of specific operative provisions. It is important to remember in this context that the ultimate effect of an investment agreement results from the interaction of the definition provisions with the operative provisions. There should be sufficient flexibility in the definition to ensure the achievement of developmental objectives.

B. Admission and establishment[20]

The effects of FDI on a host country's economy, in particular its growth and development prospects, are of special interest to developing countries (UNCTAD, 1999a). Concerns in this respect have sometimes led to controls over admission and establishment. Various considerations have figured in host government limitations on admission and establishment: infant industry considerations, defence capabilities, employment effects, technology transfer, and environmental and cultural effects. Host government policies in this respect emerge from the specific mix of political and economic circumstances characterizing particular countries. They tend to reflect the policy approaches, or a combination of them, outlined below.

1. State discretion/investment control

This approach is often preferred by countries that are uncertain about the benefits that may flow from a liberalized policy on entry and establishment. It is followed in the majority of BITs and in a number of other IIAs (box IV.8). Arguments in favour of such an approach include the possibility that foreign investors engage in business activities that are not desirable (such as uncompetitive mergers and acquisitions or restrictive practices), requiring a degree of pre-entry control to assess the overall costs and benefits to the host economy of a proposed investment and to impose specific limitations on such practices. The retention of screening procedures may not deter inward FDI, though it may create an unfavourable image for the host country. At the same time, the use of screening may offer a "once-and-for-all" determination of the right to enter the host State and the added attraction of possible protection against competitive investment by rival firms. Preferences for screening and restrictions over entry differ according to the industry or activity involved. Thus host countries may prefer to protect infant industries and domestic producers deemed not strong enough to compete with foreign firms. Such restrictions may only be removed where effective competition with foreign investors becomes possible — or, indeed, necessary — to ensure the development of the indigenous industry, as was the case, for example, in the liberalization of foreign entry conditions to the Brazilian informatics industry. Land and natural resources may also be subject to screening controls and ownership restrictions to protect what is considered to be part of the natural wealth and resources of the host country. Ownership and establishment restrictions may be more prevalent in certain services industries (e.g. financial services) than in manufacturing, owing to the pivotal role these industries play in the national economy and thus the consequent need for effective prudential supervision. Liberalization in this area has thus proceeded at a slower pace. They are prime candidates for an "opt in" approach as described above. It is also conceivable that restrictions over foreign ownership of infrastructure in a host country are motivated by a desire to regulate a natural monopoly in the public interest. Another justification for controls over foreign entry and establishment is the protection of small and medium-sized enterprises. Finally, controls over foreign access to cultural industries may be justified to protect the cultural heritage of the host country. However, technological change — including the rise of satellite and digital broadcasting and the widespread use of the Internet — has thrown into doubt the ability of States to apply effective national controls in this area.

Box IV.8. Admission clauses with complete State discretion/ investment control
BIT between Estonia and Switzerland (1992)

Article 2 (1)

"Each Contracting Party shall in its territory promote as far as possible the investments by investors of the other Contracting Party and admit such investments in accordance with its laws and regulations."

MERCOSUR Protocol on the Promotion and Protection of Investments from non-member States of MERCOSUR

Articulo 2

B. Promoción de inversiones

"1. Cada Estado Parte promoverá en su territorio las inversiones de inversores de Terceros Estados, y admitirá dichas inversiones conforme a sus leyes y reglamentaciones."

Agreement on the Promotion, Protection and Guarantee of Investment among Member States of the Organization of the Islamic Conference

Article 2

"The contracting parties shall permit the transfer of capitals among them and its utilization therein in the fields permitted for investment in accordance with their laws."

2. Selective liberalization

A less restrictive approach is to allow for selective liberalization of entry and establishment in specific activities or industries. This approach is exemplified in GATS, articles XVI.1, XIX.1 (box IV.9), XX, XVI.2 (box III.17) and XIX.2 (box III.3). It offers the advantage of making liberalization commitments more sensitive to the real locational advantages of a host country, permitting the country more control over the process of negotiating liberalization measures, given the "stepped" approach to this goal that such a policy entails through the establishment of a positive list of industries in which FDI is allowed. This approach may be useful for developing countries that have concerns about full liberalization, but would not be opposed to such a policy in activities where they are able to compete on more or less equal terms with foreign investors. It also offers a way of allowing a host country to enhance its future development and competitiveness through the introduction of investment that can stimulate the production of more complex goods and services. To the extent that this approach, too, involves an element of loss of sovereignty, it is a gradual and controlled loss, offset by the prospects of future economic development.

Box IV.9. Selective liberalization
WTO General Agreement on Trade in Services (GATS)

Article XVI

Market Access

"1. With respect to market access through the modes of supply identified in Article I, each Member shall accord services and service suppliers of any other Member treatment no less favourable than that provided for under the terms, limitations and conditions agreed and specified in its Schedule. ..."

Progressive liberalization

Article XIX

Negotiation of specific commitments

"1. In pursuance of the objectives of this Agreement, Members shall enter into successive rounds of negotiations ... with a view to achieving a progressive higher level of liberalization. Such negotiations shall be directed to the reduction or elimination of the adverse effects on trade in services of measures as a means of providing effective market access. This process shall take place with a view to promoting the interests of all participants on a mutually advantageous basis and to securing an overall balance of rights and obligations."

The circumstances in which a host country may be willing to liberalize a specific activity will echo the explanations given above as to why a specific host country may wish to restrict entry and establishment. Thus, different industries or activities may be more or less amenable to liberalization; and liberalization in manufacturing and services may be easier than in natural resources, though even in manufacturing and service industries, national interest may dictate a selective approach.

3. Regional programmes

This approach is a variant of the economic integration model favoured by regional integration groups, applied to a specific policy that seeks to set up a supranational form of business organization aimed at encouraging intraregional economic activity. As such, it offers a vehicle for regional economic development. It has been pursued by a number of regional groups such as for example the Common Market for Eastern and Southern Africa (COMESA) (box IV.10). Other agreements that have followed a similar path are the Revised Treaty of the Economic Community of West African States (ECOWAS) and the Revised Basic Agreement on ASEAN Industrial Joint Ventures. However, the practical results of such a policy may prove to be mixed. It assumes that regional capital exists and sufficient technical and managerial skills exist in the region to be able to perform economic functions without investment from outside the region. This policy may ignore the fact that technology and capital are unevenly spread both within and across regions. On the other hand, such a policy may be useful as a means of breaking down structural barriers to intraregional integration where sufficient resources exist within the region to make such enterprises viable.

Box IV.10. Encouraging the establishment of regional multinational enterprises
Treaty Establishing the Common Market for Eastern and Southern Africa

Article 101
Multinational Industrial Enterprises

"(1) The Member States shall promote and encourage the establishment of multinational industrial enterprises in accordance with the laws in force in the Member States in which such enterprises shall be established, having due regard to the economic conditions and priorities of the particular Member States concerned."

4. Mutual national treatment

This approach involves a greater commitment to full liberalization than do those discussed above, though it requires a joint commitment to this process by the States participating in a regional economic integration organization. Consequently, liberalization may proceed between States that see a common interest in regional integration, but which are not necessarily committed to full multilateral liberalization. A major issue in this case is whether the effect of such a commitment is to enhance intraregional investment (and trade) without creating a diversion away from trade with non-members. Importantly, regional integration can offer a larger geographical area within which globally competitive industries can be established. The most significant and influential example of this approach are the Treaty Establishing the European Community (box IV.11).

Box IV.11. Mutual national treatment on entry and establishment

Treaty Establishing the European Community
Right of establishment

Article 43

"Within the framework of the provisions set out below, restrictions on the freedom of establishment of nationals of a Member State in the territory of another Member State shall be abolished by progressive stages in the course of the transitional period. Such progressive abolition shall also apply to restrictions on setting up of agencies, branches or subsidiaries by nationals of any Member State established in the territory of any member State.

Freedom of establishment shall include the right to take up and pursue activities as self-employed persons and to set up and manage undertakings ..., under the conditions laid down for its own nationals by the law of the country where such establishment is effected ...."

Source: European Union, 1997.

5. National and MFN treatment with negative list of exceptions

This is the approach preferred by firms and countries that are supportive of liberalization, as it offers the best access to markets, resources and opportunities. It allows investment decisions to be determined on the basis of commercial considerations, by reducing entry controls that create barriers to the integration of production across borders, a strategy increasingly pursued by TNCs (UNCTAD, 1993). Examples of this approach include the BITs signed by the United States and Canada, NAFTA, the MERCOSUR

Protocol on Investments from other MERCOSUR Member Countries, the Framework Agreement on the ASEAN Investment Area and the Asia-Pacific Economic Cooperation (APEC) Non-Binding Investment Principles (box IV.12).

Box IV.12. National treatment and MFN with negative list of exceptions
BIT between Canada and Trinidad and Tobago (1995)

Article II

"(3) Each Contracting Party shall permit establishment of a new business enterprise or acquisition of an existing business enterprise or a share of such enterprise by investors or prospective investors of the other Contracting Party on a basis no less favourable than that which, in like circumstances, it permits such acquisition or establishment by: (a) its own investors or prospective investors; or (b) investors or prospective investors of any third state."

North American Free Trade Agreement (NAFTA)

Chapter Eleven

Investment

Section A - Investment

Article 1102: National Treatment

"1. Each Party shall accord to investors of another Party treatment no less favorable than that it accords, in like circumstances, to its own investors with respect to the establishment, acquisition, expansion, management, conduct, operation, and sale or other disposition of investments.

2. Each Party shall accord to investments of investors of another Party treatment no less favorable than that it accords, in like circumstances, to investments of its own investors with respect to the establishment, acquisition, expansion, management, conduct, operation, and sale or other disposition of investments.

3. The treatment accorded by a Party under paragraphs 1 and 2 means, with respect to a state or province, treatment no less favorable than the most favorable treatment accorded, in like circumstances, by that state or province to investors, and to investments of investors, of the Party of which it forms a part.

4. For greater certainty, no Party may:

(a) impose on an investor of another Party a requirement that a minimum level of equity in an enterprise in the territory of the Party be held by its nationals, other than nominal qualifying shares for directors or incorporators of corporations; or

(b) require an investor of another Party, by reason of its nationality, to sell or otherwise dispose of an investment in the territory of the Party."

Article 1103: Most-Favored-Nation Treatment

"1. Each Party shall accord to investors of another Party treatment no less favorable than that its accords, in like circumstances, to investors of any other Party or of a non-Party with respect to the establishment, acquisition, expansion, management, conduct, operation, and sale or other disposition of investments.

2. Each Party shall accord to investments of investors of another Party treatment no less favorable than that its accords, in like circumstances, to investments of investors of any other Party or of a non-Party with

/...

Box IV.12 (continued)

respect to the establishment, acquisition, expansion, management, conduct, operation, and sale or other disposition of investments."

Article 1104: Standard of Treatment

"Each Party shall accord to investors of another Party and to investments of investors of another Party the better of the treatment required by Articles 1102 and 1103."

Article 1108: Reservations and Exceptions

"1. Articles 1102, 1103, 1106 and 1107 do not apply to:

(a) any existing non-conforming measure that is maintained by

(i) a Party at the federal level, as set out in its Schedule to Annex I or III,

(ii) a state or province, for two years after the date of entry into force of this Agreement, and thereafter as set out by a Party in its Schedule to Annex I in accordance with paragraph 2, or

(iii) a local government;

(b) the continuation or prompt renewal of any non-conforming measure referred to in subparagraph (a); or

(c) an amendment to any non-conforming measure referred to in subparagraph (a) to the extent that the amendment does not decrease the conformity of the measure, as it existed immediately before the amendment, with Articles 1102, 1103, 1106 and 1107.

2. Each Party may set out in its Schedule to Annex I, within two years of the date of entry into force of this Agreement, any existing non-conforming measure maintained by a state or province, not including a local government.

3. Articles 1102, 1103, 1106 and 1107 do not apply to any measure that a Party adopts or maintains with respect to sectors, subsectors or activities, as set out in its Schedule to Annex II.

4. No Party may, under any measure adopted after the date of entry into force of this Agreement and covered by its Schedule to Annex II, require an investor of another Party, by reason of its nationality, to sell or otherwise dispose of an investment existing at the time the measure becomes effective.

5. Articles 1102 and 1103 do not apply to any measure that is an exception to, or derogation from, the obligations under Article 1703 (Intellectual Property - National Treatment) as specifically provided for in that article.

6. Article 1103 does not apply to treatment accorded by a Party pursuant to agreements, or with respect to sectors, set out in its Schedule to Annex IV.

7. Articles 1102, 1103 and 1107 do not apply to:

(a) procurement by a Party or a state enterprise; or

(b) subsidies or grants provided by a Party or a state enterprise, including government-supported loans, guarantees and insurance."

/...

Box IV.12 (continued)

Protocolo de Colonia Para la Promoción y Protección Reciproca de Inversiones en el MERCOSUR (Intrazona)

Artículo 2

Promoción y Admisión

"Cada Parte Contratante promeverá las inversiones de inversores de las otras Partes Contractantes y las admitirá en su territorio de manera no menos favorable que a las inversiones de sus proprios inversores o que a las inversiones realizadas por inversores de terceros Estados, sin perjuicio del derecho de cada Parte a mantener transitoriamente exceptiones limitadas que correspondan a alguno de los sectores que figuran en el Anexo del presente Protocolo."

Framework Agreement on the ASEAN Investment Area

Article 7

"Opening up of Industries and National Treatment

1. Subject to the provisions of this Article, each Member State shall:
   (a) open immediately to ASEAN investors and their investments by ASEAN investors;
   (b) accord immediately to ASEAN investors and their investments in respect of all industries and measures affecting investment including but not limited to the admission, establishment, acquisition, expansion, management, operation and disposition of investments, treatment no less favourable than that it accords to its own like investors and investments ("national treatment").

2. Each Member State Shall submit a Temporary Exclusion List and a Sensitive List, if any, within 6 months after the date of the signing of this Agreement, of any industries or measures affecting investments (referred to in paragraph 1 above) with regard to which it is unable to open up or to accord national treatment to ASEAN investors. These lists shall form an annex to this Agreement. In the event that a Member State, for justifiable reasons, is unable to provide any list within the stipulated period, it may seek an extension from the AIA Council.

3. The Temporary Exclusion List shall be reviewed every 2 years and shall be progressively phased out by 2010 by all Member States except the Socialist Republic of Vietnam, the Lao People's Democratic Republic and the Union of Myanmar. The Socialist Republic of Vietnam shall progressively phase out their Temporary Exclusion list by 2013 and the Lao People's Democratic Republic and the Union of Myanmar shall progressively phase out their temporary exclusion Lists by 2015.

4. The Sensitive List shall be reviewed by 1 January 2003 and at such subsequent periodic intervals as may be decided by the AIA council.

However, the extension of the national treatment/MFN model to the pre-entry stage is not without its problems. This was illustrated in the negotiations leading up to the Energy Charter Treaty. The principal advocates of such an approach sought to incorporate national treatment into the pre-establishment phase so that the Treaty would reflect a standard of protection similar to that of article II of the 1994 United States model BIT. All delegations prepared negative lists for the purpose of negotiations on the pre-establishment stage, but countries in transition requested a grace period in which to finalize national legislation. As a result, a compromise position was reached whereby the contracting parties would "endeavour" to accord national treatment at the pre-investment phase and would negotiate a supplementary treaty on the issue (Energy Charter Treaty, article 10 (2)-(4)). While agreement has been reached on this supplementary treaty along the national treatment/MFN model with negative lists of existing legislation and the process of privatization, the Charter Conference has not yet adopted the text.

The fact that the national treatment/MFN model allows for negative lists of excepted industries or activities is significant, since it makes clear that this approach recognizes that certain strategic industries may be beyond the reach of liberalization measures. However, it must be noted that such lists are difficult to negotiate and compile and may result in a lengthy and complex final text, as NAFTA exemplifies. In countries in which competition is a desired policy goal, such reservations may be of special importance in relation to infant industries that may not be able to withstand the vagaries of open international competition, or as a means of protecting natural resources against foreign ownership. On the other hand, care needs to be taken that such measures are not used to protect inefficient domestic monopolies against competition that may encourage a more efficient use of resources and improvements in consumer welfare.

6. A mixed approach

This approach combines elements of more than one of the five basic approaches. The economic effects of a mixed approach would be to offer specialized alternatives that may be more compatible with the mix of locational advantages enjoyed by particular host countries. The following combinations are examples:

The *State discretion/investment control* approach can be coupled with selective *liberalization* and/or *regional programmes* to produce a policy of investment screening with sectoral liberalization and/or regional industrial development programmes. The *State discretion/investment control* approach can also be coupled with *mutual national treatment* so long as the former is restricted to investments originating in States that are not members of the relevant regional economic integration organization. However *State discretion/ investment control* is incompatible with *mutual national treatment* as regards investments originating in other member States of a regional economic integration grouping. This mixed approach would suit a host State that is opposed to full multilateral liberalization on national treatment/MFN principles but which sees benefits in gradual regional integration. Such combinations are exemplified by the Arab regional agreements, and the earlier ASEAN agreements mentioned above.

Mutual national treatment may be coupled with *selective liberalization* and/or *regional programmes* to produce a policy of mutual national treatment coupled with sectoral "opt-in" policies for gradual liberalization vis-à-vis non-members of a regional economic integration grouping and/or regional industrial development programmes. This mixed approach is useful to a host country that wishes to achieve full regional liberalization with its neighbours as a long-term goal but which may want to control that process through gradual sectoral liberalization and which may perceive a need to enhance regional industrial integration through specific projects. The history of European Community market integration is an example of this approach.

National treatment and MFN with negative list of exceptions can be combined with *selective liberalization* to produce a policy of general national treatment and MFN, coupled with a negative list subject to "opt-in" sectoral liberalization at a future date. This approach would suit a host country that wants liberalization on the basis of national treatment/MFN principles, but prefers gradual liberalization in specific activities. NAFTA is a good example of this approach.

National treatment and MFN with negative list of exceptions and *State discretion/investment control* appear, at first sight, to be incompatible. However, the MERCOSUR agreements attempt a reconciliation by using the latter approach in relation to non-MERCOSUR investors, and the former for MERCOSUR-based investors. *Mutual national treatment* is difficult to combine with *national treatment and MFN with negative list of exceptions* except to the extent that special clauses are used. It is arguable that the Framework Agreement on the ASEAN Investment Area of 1998 attempts a combination of these two approaches by extending national treatment and MFN to ASEAN investors first and then extending national treatment to non-ASEAN investors by 2020. However, MFN is only extended to ASEAN-based investors. Thus a transitional phase approach is used from one option to another.

An important final consideration relates to the types of exceptions and reservations on admission and establishment provisions that may be appropriate for countries in order to pursue their development objectives. Reservations and exceptions to rights of entry and establishment provisions in investment agreements indeed offer a compromise option for host States that wish to make those rights compatible with their development priorities, so as to avoid having imposed on them blanket commitments to the granting of such rights. The consequences for national laws of having an agreement that protects rights of entry and establishment depend to a large extent on the nature of the derogations and reservations available under that regime. In particular, it has been noted that national security and public health/public policy concerns, including of countries that pursue national and MFN treatment, are frequently the subject of such measures. Furthermore, in relation to certain specific economic and social issues, States are likely to reserve some degree of flexibility, including the discretion to approve or disapprove privatization proposals; control of access on the grounds of prudential supervision in the financial services sector; controls over entry and establishment for environmental protection purposes; and restrictions on strategic industries or activities based on economic development considerations.

C. National treatment[21]

National treatment may be interpreted as formal equality of treatment between foreign and domestic enterprises. However, where countries at different levels of development are parties to an IIA, such formal equality may disregard important differences in the actual situation and capabilities of the enterprises on each side. In such a context, application of the national treatment standard may require more than formal equality, so that the development needs of a developing country party to an IIA are taken into account in the definition and application of the standard. These considerations have played a more or less important role in the various approaches that have been followed in IIAs, discussed below.

1. No national treatment provision

Some IIAs have not included the standard of national treatment among their provisions. The reason is to avoid granting equality of treatment between national and foreign investors. This approach has been followed by host countries that have strong reservations about limiting their freedom to offer preferential treatment to domestic firms for certain purposes or by home countries that feel that the treatment of national enterprises is not very favourable. It is the most restrictive in terms of investors' rights and the most respectful in terms of host country discretion. Agreements enshrining this approach include the ASEAN Agreement for the Protection and Promotion of Investments (box IV.13) and some early BITs signed by China, Norway and Sweden, but they are not frequent.

Box IV.13. IIAs that do not grant national treatment

ASEAN Agreement for the Protection and Promotion of Investments

ARTICLE IV
Treatment

"4). Any two or more of the Contracting Parties may negotiate to accord national treatment within the framework of this Agreement. Nothing herein shall entitle any other party to claim national treatment under the most-favoured-nation principle."

2. National treatment provision

There are a number of ways in which a national treatment clause can be granted. In each case some general exceptions may apply, in line with the common practice in many IIAs. The basic policy variations are outlined below.

a. Post-establishment national treatment

- **Limited post-establishment national treatment, strong host country control.** This approach preserves the strongest host country discretion while offering national treatment to foreign investments and/or investors at the post-entry stage. It has been used by host countries that wish to offer a degree of national treatment without limiting their regulatory powers too greatly. Its principal features include some or all of the following:
  - Application to post-establishment treatment only, thereby preserving the right to treat domestic and foreign investors differently at the point of entry, e.g. through screening laws and operational conditions on admission.
  - A development exception in the form of a development clause in the context of the declared development objectives of a host country. A development clause can be justified on the basis for example of the need to grant special and differential treatment to a developing country's domestic firms on account of their weaker competitive position vis-à-vis their foreign counterparts (see above section III). However, as a development clause is potentially quite wide in its scope of application, the wide discretion it reserves for a developing host country could be seen as creating uncertainty as to when and where national treatment actually applies and therefore would not be regarded favourably by foreign investors. Clear lists of excepted or included industries or activities may offer greater certainty.
  - Short of a general exception for development, provisions are made for a national treatment exception in respect of special incentives granted by a host country only to its nationals and companies, especially for the purpose of stimulating local enterprise development.
  - Exception of specific industries, activities and/or policy measures from the standard of national treatment.
  - The substantive test of national treatment is limited to:
    - -- the "same" circumstances, thereby avoiding wider comparisons based on "like" circumstances;
    - -- the "same" treatment, thereby avoiding the possibility of treatment more favourable to the foreign investor that can arise from the formulation "no less favourable".
  - An exception for political subdivisions and/or local government measures, as appropriate, reflecting the internal political organization of the host country.
  - Limitation to *de jure* national treatment only, thereby allowing for *de facto* differentiation in the treatment of foreign investors.[22]

- A stand-alone national treatment clause without reference to other standards such as MFN or fair and equitable treatment.

The principal development implication of this approach is its flexibility in terms of preserving host country discretion. Examples of instruments that have some or all of these features include the BIT between Denmark and Indonesia (article 3) — which does not refer to "treatment" but to the "imposition of conditions" thereby excluding from the application of the standard any benefits or advantages given to investments — (box IV.14), the Agreement on Investment and Free Movement of Arab Capital Among Arab Countries (article 4), the draft United Nations Code of Conduct on Transnational Corporations (1983 version), and the BIT between Indonesia and Switzerland (Protocol on article 3, paragraph 3) (cited in box III.8 above).

- **Full post-establishment national treatment**. This approach offers a higher standard of national treatment for the foreign investor and limits the discretion of the host country to treat national and foreign investors differently. Its principal features include some or all of the following:
  - Application to post-establishment treatment only.
  - A minimal number of exceptions based on specific industries or activities seen as vital to national economic policy, and/or that need protection to survive on the basis of infant industry concerns.
  - The substantive test of national treatment is extended to:
    - "like" circumstances, allowing for the application of national treatment to similar, though not necessarily identical, situations;
    - "no less favourable treatment", thereby allowing for better treatment of foreign investors;
    - nothing is said as to whether or not national treatment applies to specified activities or factual situations or circumstances.
  - No exception for political subdivisions and/or local government measures.
  - Application of national treatment *de jure* and *de facto*, thereby ensuring both formal and informal protection for foreign investors.
  - A national treatment clause that coexists with, or incorporates within its text, the better of several standards of treatment such as MFN or fair and equitable treatment.

Box IV.14. Limited post-establishment national treatment

BIT between Denmark and Indonesia (1968)

Article 3

"Neither Contracting Party shall in its territory impose on the activities of enterprises in which such approved investments are made by nationals or corporations of the other Contracting Party conditions which are less favourable than those imposed in its territory on activities in connection with any similar enterprises owned by nationals or corporations of the other Contracting Party or nationals or corporations of third countries."

The development implications of this approach are that a host country extends the application of post-entry national treatment disciplines to as wide a range of situations as possible. Examples of instruments that include some or all of the features outlined above include most recent BITs signed by the United Kingdom, France, Switzerland and Germany, the MERCOSUR Protocol on Third Countries Investors and the original text of the OECD National Treatment instrument (box IV.15).

The following approaches add national treatment at the *pre-establishment* phase to national treatment at the *post-establishment* stage as described above.

Box IV.15. Full post-establishment national treatment

OECD Declaration on International Investment and Multinational Enterprises

THE GOVERNMENTS OF OECD MEMBER COUNTRIES:

DECLARE:

"National Treatment

II. 1. That Member countries should, consistent with their needs to maintain public order, to protect their essential security interests and to fulfil commitments relating to international peace and security, accord to enterprises operating in their territories and owned or controlled directly or indirectly by nationals of another Member country (hereinafter referred to as "Foreign-Controlled Enterprises") treatment under their laws, regulations and administrative practices, consistent with international law no less favourable than that accorded in like situations to domestic enterprises (hereinafter referred to as "National Treatment"); ..."

b. Pre-establishment national treatment

- **Limited pre-establishment national treatment**. In this approach, national treatment extends to pre-establishment as well as post-establishment treatment, thereby limiting a host country's discretion as regards the entry of foreign investors. But the host country still retains some degree of control over the extent and pace of the liberalization of limitations and conditions of entry. This approach would be suitable for a host country that wishes to liberalize investment entry in its economy at a gradual pace. Its principal features may include one of the following two main variations:

- Use of an "opt-in", "bottom up" or "positive list" approach *à la* GATS, article XVII (box IV.16). No industry and/ or activity is made subject to national treatment at the pre-establishment phase until and unless it is specifically agreed upon by the host country.
- A "best endeavours" option such as that used in the APEC Non-Binding Investment Principles (box IV.16), so that developing countries are not legally bound to grant national treatment at the pre-establishment phase. In a variation of this approach, a best endeavours provision is coupled with a commitment to grant (or negotiate) legally binding national treatment at the pre-establishment phase at a later stage (as done in the Energy Charter Treaty (see above, box III.19 and below box V.1). This has the advantage of allowing a transitional period for developing countries before they become subject to national treatment disciplines. Its disadvantage is that it involves uncertainty before entry for foreign investors in the short to medium term, which could act as a disincentive; it may also encourage some investors to refrain from investing in order to await the new instrument.

- **Full pre-establishment national treatment**. Under this approach, a host country's commitment to grant national treatment on entry extends in principle to all foreign investors unless such investment is to take place in activities or industries specifically excluded by the host country in a treaty. This approach narrows considerably the discretion of a host country, since it can only use its prerogative to exclude specific activities from the operation of the standard at the time an agreement is completed.

  Such a policy choice limits to a considerable extent a host country's traditional right to control the entry of aliens into its territory. It may be of value where a host country government considers that a number of industries or activities can benefit from increased openness and from a more competitive market environment. At the same time, a host country may protect certain industries or activities by way of a "negative list", although this involves a difficult assessment as to which industries or activities need such special treatment. Failure to include an industry or activity may result in it being subjected to potentially damaging competition from foreign investors, especially where an IIA contains a standstill commitment on further restrictive policies. This would prevent a host country from including industries or activities in a "negative list" in the future.

As with the post-establishment approaches noted above, pre-establishment national treatment may be broader or narrower, depending on the wording of the principle and the use of various qualifications indicated earlier. Examples of this approach include the BITs signed by the United States (following the United States model, box IV.17) and Canada, as well as the MERCOSUR Protocol on Intra-MERCOSUR investments and NAFTA (see above box IV.12).

Box IV.16. Limited pre-establishment national treatment

General Agreement on Trade in Services

Article XVII

National Treatment

"1. In the sectors inscribed in its Schedule, and subject to any conditions and qualifications set out therein, each Member shall accord to services and services suppliers of any other Member, in respect of all measures affecting the supply of services, treatment no less favourable than that it accords to its own like services and service suppliers. ...

2. A Member may meet the requirement of paragraph 1 by according to services and service suppliers of any other Member, either formally identical treatment or formally different treatment to that it accords to its own like services and services suppliers.

3. Formally identical or formally different treatment shall be considered to be less favourable if it modifies the conditions of competition in favour of services or service suppliers of the Member compared to like services or service suppliers of any other Member.

APEC Non-Binding Investment Principles

National Treatment

"With exceptions as provided for in domestic laws, regulations and policies, member economies will accord to foreign investors in relation to the establishment, expansion, operation and protection of their investments, treatment no less favourable than that accorded in like situations, to domestic investors."

Box IV.17. Full pre-establishment national treatment

The United States model BIT (1994 version)

Article II

"1. With respect to the establishment, acquisition, expansion, management, conduct, operation and sale or other disposition of covered investments, each Party shall accord treatment no less favorable than that it accords, in like situations, to investments in its territory of its own nationals or companies (hereinafter "national treatment") or to investments in its territory of nationals or companies of a third country (hereinafter "national and most favored nation treatment"), which ever is most favourable (hereinafter "national and most favoured nation treatment"). Each Party shall ensure that its State enterprises, in the provision of their goods and services, accord national and most favored nation treatment to covered investments.

2. (a) A Party may adopt or maintain exceptions to the obligations of paragraph 1 in the sectors or with respect to the matters specified in the Annex to this Treaty. In adopting such an exception, a Party may not require the divestment, in whole or in part, of covered investments existing at the time the exception becomes effective."

3. A mixed approach

Various combinations of the elements of post- and pre-establishment national treatment are available to produce a compromise between the various possibilities outlined above. For example, different permutations of the substantive test of differential treatment could be devised, resulting in wider or narrower application of national treatment. Other matters open to variation from the above options include the distinction between *de jure* and *de facto* differential treatment; the degree of interaction between national treatment and MFN and fair and equitable treatment; and the extent to which subnational entities are subjected to national treatment disciplines.

D. MFN treatment[23]

The MFN standard means that a host country must extend to investors from one foreign country the same or no less favourable treatment than it accords to investors from any other foreign country. IIAs have dealt with MFN treatment in a variety of ways, reflecting varying investment strategies that are briefly outlined below.

1. Extending MFN to pre-entry treatment or limiting it to post-entry treatment

The first set of issues concerns whether to limit MFN to post-entry treatment only or to extend the standard to both pre-entry and post-entry treatment. It suffices to note here that the issue depends much, to begin with, on whether a country differentiates between pre-entry and post-entry treatment in general. Examples of IIAs that grant pre-entry and post-entry MFN include NAFTA Article 1103, and the APEC Non-Binding Investment Principles. Examples of IIAs that grant MFN only after entry and establishment include most BITs and the Energy Charter Treaty, article 10 (7).

2. Treating investors from different countries in different ways

Countries that apply liberal policies vis-à-vis foreign investors assume that foreign investment is a means for increasing domestic competitiveness. The MFN standard is typically an inherent part of their development policies, since an open-door policy means that no restrictions on, or discrimination between, foreign investors are in effect. In fact, countries are often less willing to grant national treatment than MFN for developmental reasons. In other words, they often reserve the right to discriminate in favour of domestic investors without reserving the right to discriminate in favour of only certain foreign investors. Thus, while a number of IIAs do not guarantee national treatment to investments, virtually every IIA requires that investment covered by the agreement should receive MFN treatment.

On the other hand, it may be argued that an exception to MFN based on the nationality of foreign investors is consistent with the strategy of a host country that has made the judgement that the best way to pursue the economic development of the country is to establish and maintain special economic relations with one or several specific other countries, which are selected as strategic partners. The countries concerned thus grant market access or other special privileges only to investors from these countries. Such a strategy assumes that one or several countries with strategic advantages over other potential partners can be identified (and that granting the same conditions to investors from other countries could undermine this strategic partnership). The host country thus aligns its own pattern of comparative advantages and its stage of development to the comparative advantages of the partner.

What is not clear is why obtaining the desired investment from one set of investors is more desirable than obtaining them from another set of investors, as long as the underlying development objectives are being served. Rather, it would appear that strategies of this type are normally based on a distinction between foreign and domestic investors and not on a distinction among foreign investors.[24]

3. The use of exceptions

As has been suggested above, it would seem that in most cases host countries can pursue their development strategies without having to discriminate among investors from different foreign countries. In other words, the standard of MFN treatment does not seem to involve, in principle, significant potential negative implications for development. However, as these countries become more integrated into the global economy, they may need, in some cases, to make use of MFN-specific exceptions, even though these may not necessarily be inspired by development considerations.

In particular, a number of reciprocal subject-specific exceptions appear to be broadly accepted (box IV.18). For example, when a country develops a network of bilateral double taxation agreements, it may find it appropriate not to grant MFN treatment to third countries in this respect. Mutual recognition arrangements are another area that could be undermined by a unilateral extension of the benefits of an arrangement to third countries. Finally, countries may increasingly seek recourse to MFN exceptions through regional economic integration organization (REIO) clauses.[25]

Beyond these specific exceptions, many IIAs contain general exceptions based on public policy and national security; they are not targeted at MFN *per se*, but they can indirectly limit its application. The protocol to Germany's model BIT contains a typical reservation (box IV.19). Other examples of general exceptions applying to MFN treatment can be found in GATS (article XIV and bis), the OECD Code of Liberalisation of Capital Movements (articles 2 and 3), the Energy Charter Treaty (article 24 (c), 24 (2) (b) (1) and 24 (3), and NAFTA, article 2102.

Box IV.18. MFN treatment exceptions in respect of specific matters agreed beforehand by all contracting parties BIT between Chile and Malaysia (1992)

Article 3

"Most favoured nation

1. Investments by nationals or companies of either Contracting Stateon the territory of the other Contracting State shall ... not be subjected to a treatment less favourable than that accorded to investments by nationals or companies of third States.

...

3. The provision in this Treaty relating to treatment no less favourable than that accorded to investments of third States shall not be interpreted to oblige a Contracting Party to extend to investors of the other Contracting Party the benefits of any treatment, preference or privilege by virtue of:

(a) any customs union, free trade area, common market or monetary union, or similar international convention or other forms of regional cooperation, present or future, of which any of the Contracting Parties might become a party; or the adoption of an agreement designed to achieve the formation or expansion of such union or areas within a reasonable time; or

(b) any international convention or agreement related totally or principally to taxation, or any national legislation relate totally or partially to taxation.

BIT between Armenia and the United States (1992)

Article II (1)

Each Party shall permit and treat investment, and activities associated therewith, on a basis no less favorable than that accorded in like situations to investment or associated activities of its own nationals and companies, or of nationals or companies of any third country, whichever is the most favorable, subject to the right of each Party to make or maintain exceptions falling within one of the sectors or matters listed in the Annex to this Treaty. Each Party agrees to notify the other Party before or on the date of entry into force of this Treaty of all such laws and regulations of which it is aware concerning the sectors or matters listed in the Annex. Moreover, each Party agrees to notify the other of any future exception with respect to the sectors or matters listed in the Annex, and to limit such exceptions to a minimum. Any future exception by either Party shall not apply to investment existing in that sector or matter at the time the exception becomes effective. The treatment accorded pursuant to any exceptions shall unless specified otherwise in the Annex, be no less favorable than that accorded in like situations to investments and associated activities of nationals or companies of any third country."

* * *

MFN treatment is at the heart of multilateralism and is a core principle in IIAs. At the same time, IIAs allow for flexibility for countries to pursue their policies, both in relation to the question of the treatment of foreign investment before and after entry, and through exceptions and reservations to the MFN standard. Whether or not a country actually wants to utilize any of these exceptions needs to be evaluated by it, in the context of its specific conditions. Exceptions to MFN would only exceptionally be justified for development purposes.

Box IV.19. General exceptions to MFN treatment based on public policy or national security

BIT model by Germany
Article 3
"(1) Neither Contracting Party shall subject investments in its territory owned or controlled by nationals or companies of the other Contracting Party to treatment less favourable than that it accords to investments of ... any third State.
..."

Protocol
"(3) Ad Article 3
(a) .... Measures that have to be taken for reasons of public security and order, public health or morality shall not be deemed "treatment less favourable" within the meaning of Article 3."

E. Fair and equitable treatment[26]

The fair and equitable standard plays a significant role in IIAs. In addition to filling gaps and providing a context for the interpretation of specific provisions, it seeks to provide a means for resolving problems not only by reference to strict legal rules but on the basis of equity, taking into account the surrounding circumstances of each individual case. The main basic approaches to this standard are outlined below.

1. No reference to fair and equitable treatment

States may opt not to incorporate the fair and equitable standard in their investment relations. Where this is done, the standard is not likely to be implied in the relevant investment instrument, so that, in effect, the foreign investor will not have the benefits contemplated by this standard. Its absence from a treaty may prompt investor concerns about the nature of protection to be offered by a host State. Fair and equitable treatment is not mentioned in the BITs between Egypt and Japan and between Italy and Romania and, more generally, in early BITs signed by Pakistan, Rwanda, Saudi Arabia and Singapore. Nor is the clause mentioned in the models recommended by the Asian African Legal Consultative Committee (AALCC). At the multilateral level, no reference is made to the standard in, for example, GATS and TRIPS. However, most treaties that omit reference to fair and equitable treatment provide alternative standards of treatment, usually the national treatment and MFN treatment standards. Where this is done, such standards provide some degree of contingent protection to foreign investors; principles of customary international law will also apply.

2. The hortatory approach

Under this approach States may include a clause exhorting the observance of fair and equitable treatment for foreign investors and their investments. It is doubtful that this approach gives rise to any special economic implications. This is so because, by definition, the hortatory approach does not create a binding obligation on host States to grant investors fair and equitable treatment. Rather, it indicates that fairness and equity are desirable in investment relations, but, without more, it leaves host States with a substantial degree of flexibility as to how they will treat foreign investors. In some circumstances, however, the hortatory approach reflects the starting point in a negotiating process in which fair and equitable treatment may be included in binding form in a subsequent investment agreement. This is exemplified by the Havana Charter (box IV.20), which indicated that it would be desirable for States to enter into treaties making provision for the fair and equitable standard.

Box IV.20. The hortatory approach to fair and equitable treatment

Havana Charter for an International Trade Organization
Chapter III
Economic development and reconstruction
Article 11
"Means of Promoting Economic Development and Reconstruction

2. The Organization may, in such collaboration with other intergovernmental organizations as may be appropriate:
(a) make recommendations for and promote bilateral or multilateral agreements on measures designed:
  (i) to assure just and equitable treatment for the enterprise, skills, capital, arts and technology brought from one Member country to another."

3. Reference to "fair and equitable" treatment, "just and equitable" treatment or "equitable" treatment

The terms "fair and equitable" treatment, "just and equitable" treatment and "equitable" treatment appear to be equivalent and, though different in formulation, prompt the same degree of protection for investors. In each case, they mean that the host State is required, as a matter of law, to accord fair treatment to the foreign investor. This approach creates a legal environment in which aliens may undertake capital investments with some degree of confidence that they will not be subject to arbitrary or capricious treatment. The investor may also derive confidence from the simple fact that the host country has found no reason to resist offering fair and equitable treatment in practice. The BIT between the Netherlands and the Philippines offers a fairly common example of the fair and equitable standard (box IV.21).

Box IV.21. Reference to fair and equitable treatment

BIT between the Netherlands and the Philippines (1985)

Article 3

"2. Investments of nationals of either Contracting Party shall, in their entry, operation, management, maintenance, use, enjoyment or disposal, be accorded fair and equitable treatment and shall enjoy full protection and security in the territory of the other Contracting Party."

4. Reference to "fair and equitable treatment" and related standards

Where the fair and equitable standard is combined with other standards such as the MFN and national treatment standards, it probably is seen as strongest by investors, compared with situations in which only one type of these standards is granted. This is in fact the most common approach followed in IIAs, including NAFTA, the MERCOSUR Protocols and the majority of BITs, as exemplified in the model BITs prepared by Chile (box IV.22). There is reason to believe that investors will have more confidence in the host country than in situations in which only one type of these standards is granted.

Box IV.22. Reference to fair and equitable treatment and related standards

Model BIT prepared by the Government of the Republic of Chile

Article 4

Treatment of investments

"(1) Each Contracting Party shall extend fair and equitable treatment to investments made by investors of the other Contracting Party on its territory and shall ensure that the exercise of the right thus recognized shall not be hindered in practice.

(2) A Contracting Party shall accord investments of the investors of one Contracting Party in its territory a treatment which is no less favourable than that accorded to investments made by its own investors or by investors of any third country, whichever is the most favourable."

5. Reference to "fair and equitable treatment" in combination with the international minimum standard

There have been different views on the relationship between fair and equitable treatment and the international minimum standard. While both standards seem to overlap significantly, fair and equitable treatment is not automatically assumed to incorporate the international minimum standard. Some countries have specifically reinforced the fair and equitable standard with formulations such as "full protection and security" which may imply the international minimum standard. Examples of this approach include the BIT between Mexico and Switzerland (box IV.23).

Box IV.23. Reference to fair and equitable treatment incombination with the international minimum standard

BIT between Mexico and Switzerland (1995)

Article 4

Protection and Treatment

"(1) Investments by investors of each Party shall at all times be accorded fair and equitable treatment and shall enjoy full protection and security in the territory of the other Party in accordance with international law. Neither Party shall in any way impair by discriminatory measures the management, maintenance, use, enjoyment or disposal of investments in its territory of investors of the other Party."

* * *

In deciding the type of substantive provisions an IIA should contain to serve development objectives fully, the parties need to take into account the various and sometimes complex interactions between individual provisions. These interactions can be instrumental for achieving a balance of rights and obligations, not only within individual provisions, but also between *all* provisions of an agreement, or between separate agreements, and for *all* parties concerned.

V. Application

The parties to an IIA may be required to take a number of concrete actions to give effect to the agreement and comply with specific provisions. These tend to be taken over time through a variety of mechanisms and interactions at the national and international levels. They can have a significant influence on the development effects of an agreement. The types of mechanisms used may depend on the characteristics of the agreement, including whether it is a stand-alone agreement (like a BIT) or a part of a larger body of commitments. Application is, of course, crucial in the context of development as the effectiveness of international economic rules "depends on satisfying the interests of all parties involved, either because compliance is beneficial, or because noncompliance is damaging. .... An effective instrument is one that has a significant impact, in the direction desired, on the behaviour of those with whom it is concerned. Consequently, it is the ultimate outcome that will determine whether ...[an international investment instrument] is or is not effective" (UNCTC, 1978, p. 3).

The developmental outcome of an IIA is intimately related in particular to the arrangements the parties make for a follow-up and monitoring of its application after the agreement has entered into force. It is through such arrangements — which, in turn, often depend on the legal character of the instrument — that it can ultimately be tested whether an IIA is performing its development functions well. In order to facilitate application and reap the benefits of such agreements it may also be necessary to put in place special promotional and technical assistance measures.

A. Legal character, mechanisms and effects[27]

The manner in which an IIA is interpreted, and the way in which it is to be made effective, ultimately determine whether its objectives, structure and substantive provisions produce the desired developmental effects. The degree of flexibility allowed for the interpretation and application of an IIA depends to a large extent on the legal character of the agreement, the formulation of individual provisions and the institutional machinery involved in its application. IIAs are intrinsically intended to have certain effects, both at the national and international levels, even when they do not provide for follow-up mechanisms specific to them. This section discusses first variations in the binding character of IIAs, and then looks at the levels at which the application of an agreement can take place, and the institutional arrangements that may be involved.

1. Normative intensity of instruments and provisions

IIAs may be adopted as legally binding agreements (i.e. treaties and conventions) or as voluntary or non-legally-enforceable instruments. The latter can, in turn, take different forms, such as resolutions, declarations, recommendations and guidelines.

Legally-binding agreements impose on the States signatories a legal obligation under international law to comply with their provisions. How far such an obligation will actually limit the subsequent freedom of action of the States concerned will largely depend on the language of the agreement and the type of obligations imposed. Legally-binding or mandatory instruments usually contain obligations that are enforceable in national and international courts of law, and they may involve penalties or sanctions. Most bilateral and regional instruments dealing with investment, and an increasing number of multilateral instruments, have been adopted as legally-binding instruments.

Voluntary instruments, on the other hand, are not legally enforceable. For that reason, their provisions need not be couched in precise legal formulations. Still, they can have an influence on the development of national and international investment rules.[28] A considerable number of such investment instruments exist, adopted mainly during the 1970s and 1980s in international fora such as the OECD and the United Nations and its agencies. Examples are the Set of Multilaterally Agreed Equitable Rules and Principles for the Control of Restrictive Business Practices, the United Nations Guidelines for Consumer Protection and the ILO Tripartite Declaration of Principles Concerning Multinational Enterprises and Social Policy. More recent examples of comprehensive non-binding investment instruments are the APEC Non-Binding Investment Principles and the World Bank Guidelines on the Treatment of Foreign Direct Investment.

Intermediate degrees of binding force. Within the set limits outlined above, it is possible to perceive varying degrees of binding force among investment instruments, depending, for example, on the form the instrument takes and the level at which it is adopted. Thus, in a number of international organizations, a *decision* of the intergovernmental policy making body is considered a formal act which is normally binding on the governments of the countries members. Such is the case of, for example, the OECD Third Revised Decision on National Treatment adopted by the OECD Council.[29] A solemn *declaration,* not in the form of a binding treaty adopted by sovereign States, or a formal *resolution* of an organ of an international organization, may spell out principles that the parties declare to be appropriate or desirable. Obviously, States are free to comply with these recommendations. Beyond that, however, States may feel compelled not to act inconsistently with instruments that they have formally accepted. The circumstances of adoption of an instrument also influence the degree of effective respect it will receive. In the case of United Nations General Assembly resolutions, for example, such elements as a unanimous vote in favour, supporting statements of States during the pertinent debates, and the actual language of the resolutions, can be important in determining their real impact (UNCTC, 1978). Thus, the General Assembly resolution 1803 (XVII) on "Permanent sovereignty over natural resources" adopted by unanimous vote in 1962 enjoyed a wide measure of support from both developed and developing countries. Whereas ten years later, when the General Assembly adopted the Charter of Economic Rights and Duties of States (Resolution 3281 (XXIX), a number of developed countries abstained. In short, international instruments, whether mandatory or voluntary, need to rely on good faith, peer pressure and the political will of the signatories to be effective.

Variations in binding force within individual instruments are often expressed with terms such as "shall" or "should". Thus, when the term "shall" is used in a non-binding instrument the implication would be that the signatories expect a stronger level of commitment to comply than when the recommendation is expressed with the word "should".

Including soft obligations among binding provisions. One way of mitigating some of the most rigorous implications of concluding a legally-binding investment agreement is to include one or several "soft" obligations among binding provisions, for the benefit of all or some parties. For example, IIAs may include a binding obligation to "endeavour" to act in a certain manner, or to "seek as far as possible" to avoid certain measures, or to "give sympathetic consideration" to the needs or aspirations of other parties or "to consult with the other parties". In the Energy Charter Treaty the difference in language between paragraphs 1 and 2 of article 10 is used to impose a softer obligation with respect to national and MFN treatment for foreign investment at the pre-establishment phase (box V.1). By avoiding rigorously binding obligations, this method eases the way for countries that may wish to sign an IIA but would find it difficult to commit themselves fully to certain specific disciplines.

Finally, as legal obligations and recommendations can be expressed in a wide variety of ways, a key element for the interpretation and application of provisions is the degree of specificity of their language. The more specific the language, the more restricted the choices open to the parties. The more general the language, the larger the margin of freedom allowed. A provision may directly impose an obligation or make a recommendation concerning a particular action (e.g. to open up a particular industry or to refrain from imposing a performance requirement). Alternatively, it may be directed at a desirable outcome or result, thereby indirectly permitting or encouraging any action that brings about that result. This is the case, for example, where broad standards of treatment are mentioned using such formulations as "appropriate", "reasonable" or "fair".

2. Levels of application

a. National level

Many IIA provisions require some kind of action at the national level in order to be made effective. This is so independently of whether or not an IIA provides for application or follow-up mechanisms specific to it. Thus, the types of actions discussed under this subheading may well be taken in the absence of any international institutional machinery, as in the case of BITs. The very fact of the adoption of an IIA, whether as an

Box V.1. Including soft obligations among binding provisions

Energy Charter Treaty
Article 10
PROMOTION, PROTECTION AND TREATMENT OF INVESTMENTS

"(1) Each Contracting Party shall, in accordance with the provisions of this Treaty, encourage and create stable, equitable, favourable and transparent conditions for Investors of other Contracting Parties to Make Investments in its Area. Such conditions shall include a commitment to accord at all times to Investments of Investors of other Contracting Parties fair and equitable treatment. Such Investments shall also enjoy the most constant protection and security and no Contracting Party shall in any way impair by unreasonable or discriminatory measures their management, maintenance, use, enjoyment or disposal. In no case shall such Investments be accorded treatment less favourable than that required by international law, including treaty obligations. Each Contracting Party shall observe any obligations it has entered into with an Investor or an Investment of an Investor of any other Contracting Party.

(2) Each Contracting Party shall endeavour to accord to Investors of the other Contracting Parties, as regards the Making of Investments in its Area, the Treatment described in paragraph (3).

(3) For the purposes of this Article, "Treatment" means treatment accorded by a Contracting Party which is no less favourable than that which it accords to its own Investors or to Investors of any other Contracting Party or any third state, whichever is the most favourable."

BIT between the United States and Zaire (now Democratic Republic of the Congo) (1984)
Article II

"7. Within the context of its national economic policies and goals, each Party shall endeavor to avoid imposing on the investments of nationals or companies of the other party conditions which require the export of goods produced or the purchase of goods or services locally. This provision shall not preclude the right of either Contracting Party to impose restrictions on the importation of goods and services into their respective territories."

BIT between Malaysia and the United Arab Emirates (1991)
Article 2

"9. Contracting States shall seek as far as practicable to avoid performance requirements as a condition of establishment, expansion or maintenance of investment, which require or enforce commitments to export goods produced or services or services must be purchased locally must be purchased locally or which impose any other similar requirements."

international agreement or as a formally non-binding instrument, is bound to have an impact on the national policies of the adopting States. The impact, of course, would be stronger and more immediate in the case of the former. In that case, giving effect to an IIA often implies that its provisions are given formal recognition in the national system. The various legal techniques that are stipulated by individual constitutional systems for incorporating an international agreement into the national system are recalled here, as these will provide the legal parameters through which this objective can be obtained.

A major direct effect of an IIA, whether legally-binding or voluntary, would be that the States that have adopted it would not be able to challenge successfully an action by other States taken in accordance with provisions of the agreement on the grounds that it is inherently unlawful or improper. Obviously, problems might arise as to whether particular measures were or were not in accord with the agreement's principles. But the principles themselves would not be a viable subject of contention among the parties.

Where the relevant provisions call for the enactment of national legislation, whether expressly or by implication, the binding or non-binding character of the instrument makes, at first blush, a considerable difference. In the former case, specific legislative or administrative action would be required. Failure to take such action would be *prima facie* in breach of an international obligation. In some cases, further specification into detailed provisions would be needed, unless the agreement provides detailed treatment of the particular topic. The OECD Convention on Combating Bribery of Foreign Public Officials in International Business Transactions, article 1, is an example of a provision that requires the adoption of more specific national legislation to give it effect (box V.2).

The degree of specificity of the provisions calling for enactment of national legislation is of particular importance in this context. If they are phrased in broad terms, a greater margin of freedom of action is left to the States concerned. Thus, article 6 (2) of the Energy Charter Treaty dealing with competition leaves ample margin to the country to determine what type of laws might be adopted (box V.2).

Even in the case of a non-binding investment instrument, it seems reasonable to assume that the States adopting it would seek to give some effect to its principles in the national legal system. The International Code of Marketing of Breast-milk Substitutes, for example, though not legally binding, calls for the adoption of appropriate national legislation and other suitable measures (box V.2). In such cases, the principal ground for subsequent compliance is likely to be the continuing perception of common interest. Unless circumstances change radically, the common ground for compliance with an agreement is likely to continue to be valid for the parties involved.

Box V.2. Provisions calling for enactment of national legislation

OECD Convention on Combating Bribery of Foreign Public Officials in International Business Transactions

Article 1

The Offence of Bribery of Foreign Public Officials

"1. Each Party shall take such measures as may be necessary to establish that it is a criminal offence under its law for any person intentionally to offer, promise or give any undue pecuniary or other advantage, whether directly or through intermediaries, to a foreign public official, for that official or for a third party, in order that the official act or refrain from acting in relation to the performance of official duties, in order to obtain or retain business or other improper advantage in the conduct of international business."

The Energy Charter Treaty

Article 6

Competition

"(2) Each Contracting Party shall ensure that within its jurisdiction it has and enforces such laws as are necessary and appropriate to address unilateral and concerted anti-competitive conduct in an Economic Activity in the Energy Sector."

International Code of Marketing of Breast-milk Substitutes

Article 11

"11.1. Governments should take action to give effect to the principles and aim of this Code, as appropriate to their social and legislative framework, including the adoption of national legislation, regulations or other suitable measures ..."

Non-binding instruments can also have an educational effect at the national level, as they provide guidance on the expectations of the international community with respect to the behaviour of foreign investors and governments, which may be replicated in national practice.

Where explicit provisions requiring national action are absent from an IIA, each State is free to decide on the particular manner in which it implements the provisions of an IIA. This approach is exemplified by BITs. In fact, as a result of that — in addition to the lack of independent monitoring — little is known about how BIT provisions have been applied in practice, except in a few cases of serious disagreements where the treaty obligations have been enforced through proceedings in national courts and/ or international tribunals (which provide binding interpretations of the provisions under review) (UNCTAD, 1998a). The resulting legal and administrative activity of States however can be diverse, and possibly even contradictory, even though the likely outcome may be a move in the general direction of the instrument.

* * *

Seen from a development perspective, the main implication of the foregoing discussion is that, in the process of advancing their development interests, developing countries can take advantage of the possibilities offered by variations in normative intensity and specificity of language of IIAs regarding their effects on the parties' national systems. They can, for example, insist on hard-binding and explicit commitments to be enacted in national laws when it comes to matters of interest to them — for example, with respect to commitments by developed countries to undertake promotional measures to encourage FDI flows to developing countries — while selecting softer, more general and flexible approaches with respect to issues for which application at the national level is likely to raise policy difficulties. The application of provisions granting developing countries more favourable thresholds for complying with their obligations under IIAs is of particular relevance in this context.[30]

b. International level

(i) Intergovernmental cooperative action

Intergovernmental cooperation here relates to the types of measures taken by individual States, either unilaterally or on the basis of inter-State arrangements, in the absence of international institutional machinery for monitoring and follow up. These are measures and actions with a clear international dimension, but on the basis of the traditional international legal pattern of decentralized decision-making and action.

One reason for this type of action is that, as foreign investors operate in several or many host countries at the same time, no single country is in a position, by its own independent action, to acquire the information on the world-wide operations of TNCs which it may need for evaluating their operations within its territory, or to exercise jurisdiction over the TNC as a whole. Moreover, jurisdictional conflicts may arise when individual States seek to exercise jurisdiction over TNC activities partly involving their territory but also involving the territories of other States. Consequently, intergovernmental cooperation is often an essential tool to facilitate compliance with the provisions of IIAs. In particular, it can enhance the ability of developing countries to deal effectively with the full dimensions of TNC operations in the application of their development strategies through FDI, minimising possible negative effects of such operations and maximising their beneficial effects, while avoiding potential conflicts that can be disruptive of productive operations.

The principal types of measures that may be envisaged include the following:

- Exchange of information between governments concerning investors' operations and related governmental activity. This is the kind of cooperation sought in most bilateral cooperation agreements on competition (UNCTAD, 1997).
- Arrangements between the parties for reciprocal recognition and enforcement of final decisions and other such measures by national courts and administrative authorities. The United Nations Convention on the Recognition and Enforcement of Foreign Arbitration Awards provides such arrangements. IIAs — especially BITs — sometimes refer to the Convention's arrangements in connection with the settlement of investment disputes (UNCTAD, 1998a).
- Arrangements between governments for cooperation and reciprocal assistance with respect to measures of national authorities that do not amount to final decisions, particularly preliminary measures or orders concerning matters of evidence in connection with national proceedings for the application of an IIA. Some cooperation agreements (e.g. the Agreement between Australia and the United States on Mutual Antitrust Enforcement Assistance) provides for notification of competition investigations.
- Arrangements between governments for consultations whenever problems arise out of the implementation of an agreement. Increasingly, BITs provide for consultations among the parties as a means of resolving difficulties arising out of the application of the agreement, thus preventing formal disputes. In this respect, a measure of the success of a BIT lies as much in its ability to prevent a dispute as its ability to provide a basis for resolving it. In the kind of investment climate that a BIT is intended to promote, investors and their host country would normally seek to operate on the basis of cooperation rather than confrontation (UNCTAD, 1998a). That might be a reason why this approach is followed in BITs where broader political and economic considerations appear to play a significant role in the parties' relations.
- Direct cooperation between national authorities at the working level. An example of this approach is found in double taxation treaties (UNCTAD, 1998b).

In addition to providing essential tools for facilitating the application of development-related provisions in IIAs that impinge upon the transnational nature of FDI operations, the forms of intergovernmental cooperation being described can provide flexible approaches to deal with issues arising out of the application and interpretation of IIAs in as much as they contribute to facilitating dialogue between the parties and resolving potential difficulties.

(ii) Intergovernmental institutional machinery

An international institutional machinery for monitoring and follow up on the application of an IIA can play several major developmental roles. Thus, for example, it can:

- provide the tools for studying the provisions of an IIA from the perspective of their implications for the flexibility they give to pursue policies and strategies for economic development;
- provide the basis for governments to assess in a timely manner the implications of an agreement, or specific provisions thereof, for the development of developing countries in the light of concrete situations;
- facilitate compliance by clarifying the interpretation of provisions that are found to be unclear, and providing advice and technical assistance as to the most beneficial and least costly ways of achieving compliance in the light of specific development objectives;
- provide the mechanisms by which countries can seek relief from certain obligations under certain circumstances;
- enable developing countries to make periodic determinations on the state of implementation of provisions that are of particular interest to them, such as those relating to commitments to grant them special concessions;

- facilitate a continuing dialogue among the parties to find flexible solutions to problems; and
- move the process forward, including the implementation of in-built agendas for further negotiations and/or amendments to the agreement.

It is therefore of critical importance for developing countries to make the best of the international institutional machinery provided in an IIA to ensure that development objectives are given full effect (Youssef, 1999).

Many IIAs have set out institutional arrangements for their application, monitoring and/or follow-up in general, or have spelled out concrete procedures for dealing with specific matters. This is the case in the majority of regional and multilateral investment agreements, whether legally binding or not. The specific functions of an international machinery can vary considerably. An IIA may make provision for any or all of the functions discussed below.

Administrative, technical and monitoring functions. The actual scope of such functions ranges widely from coordination, documentation and depository functions to tasks involving extensive initiative and study, capable of having an impact on policies. The types of functions described here are typically entrusted to the secretariat of the international organizations that are charged with the administration of an IIA, such as, for example, WTO, UNCTAD, OECD, or the Energy Charter Secretariat. Secretariats often play a significant role as guardians of the institutional memory of the negotiation and application of IIAs, in coordinating the work of governments and providing technical, procedural and substantive backup to negotiations and follow up processes. These functions undertaken by an international secretariat can be especially useful for countries with limited resources and capabilities.

Reporting requirements. A simple monitoring procedure involves mainly reporting by contracting parties upon their practice in the observance of the provisions of the agreement. In some cases, reporting is meant to ensure transparency of existing national policy and practice. In other cases, the parties are requested to report on specific measures and/or changes introduced in national policies pursuant to the commitments made in an agreement. Where an investment instrument requires regular or ad hoc reporting on the part of the States parties on various aspects of the application of an instrument, this obligation can be seen as a significant inducement for States to act in compliance. Reporting requirements may be imposed not only by formally binding instruments, but also by instruments that otherwise lack a binding character. Reporting requirements relating to existing national practice are provided for in, for example, the TRIMs Agreement. Reporting requirements regarding changes in national policy and practice are found in article III.3 of the GATS, which requires each member to inform the Council for Trade in Services promptly, and at least annually, of the introduction of any new, or any changes to existing, laws regulations or administrative guidelines that significantly affect trade in services covered by the members' specific commitments under the Agreement.

Reporting requirements can be instrumental in facilitating a systematic flow of information on the manner in which certain commitments made by one group of countries to grant preferential treatment (e.g. non-reciprocal concessions to developing countries) are given effect, so as to allow developing countries continuously to monitor the situation (Youssef, 1999).

Consultative functions. Consultations on the application and interpretation of an instrument can provide useful and flexible means for dealing with problems and situations that have not yet crystallized into disputes. Consultations of this kind typically stress non-adversary procedures of inquiry and discussion. They may deal with general or specific issues submitted to the relevant body by any concerned party or — through appropriate screening procedures — by a non-State entity, such as a trade union or a TNC. Consultations are a central task of most monitoring and follow up mechanisms established by investment instruments, such as GATS, TRIMs and TRIPS in the WTO, the Liberalisation Codes, the National Treatment Instrument and the Guidelines for Multinational Enterprises in the OECD, the Tripartite Declaration on Multinational Enterprises and Social Policy in the ILO and the Framework Agreement on the ASEAN Investment Area.

An important development function of the consultation machinery can be to ensure coherence between the development objectives of an IIA and the actual implementation of its provisions.[31] Development objectives are by definition flexible and sometimes require adjustments to link the conceptual and practical levels effectively. In particular, the difficulties facing developing countries in complying with their obligations within transitional periods in various agreements can be examined in a flexible and practical manner, in order to evaluate the adequacy of these thresholds and whether they should be refined more or even reconsidered in the light of experience in implementing relevant agreements. Another function can be to interpret development-related provisions that are vague or ineffective or are expressed in "best endeavour" terms and perhaps give them a more precise and action oriented interpretation. This can be achieved through the establishment of guidelines, or the adoption of appropriate decisions by the relevant bodies. Measurable criteria for the evaluation of the implementation of development-related commitments can also be devised. In some cases, the implementation of certain provisions can be facilitated by developing model laws or clauses that countries may take into consideration when developing appropriate national legislation.

Complaint and clarification mechanisms. Some investment instruments of a voluntary nature include a rather unique mechanism for dealing with questions relating to the meaning of their provisions arising from an "actual situation". In the OECD, the mechanism in question is known as "clarifications". It was first developed as part of the follow-up arrangements for the application of the OECD Guidelines for Multinational Enterprises. The clarifications are intended to facilitate the application of the Guidelines by allowing governments of member countries, and the trade unions and business advisory committees (TUAC and BIAC) to submit specific questions arising in a concrete case. The clarifications are prepared by the Committee on International Investment and Multinational Enterprises — which is the body with authority to monitor the applicationof the Guidelines — under procedures of a non-adjudicatory nature. However, since the clarifications arise from "actual situations", they inevitably involve ascertainment of certain facts, though not resolution of matters of fact and law, the factual situation being treated as hypothetical. Although these interpretations are not legally binding, they have helped to adapt the Guidelines to changing situations.

The ILO Tripartite Declaration has adopted a similar procedure for examination of disputes concerning the application of the Tripartite Declaration. This procedure cannot be invoked for matters covered by the ILO Conventions or recommendations.

Most of the clarifications so far have related to employment issues at the instance of trade unions. However, they can be used for other purposes as well, including, notably, for defining and clarifying the social responsibilities of TNCs. Moreover, while the clarification mechanisms have been used in the context of voluntary instruments, they can also be utilized in the context of legally binding instruments as a means of avoiding more formal, rigid -- and costly -- procedures.

Settlement of disputes. Another category of functions are those related to the settlement of disputes arising out of the application and interpretation of an investment instrument. In this respect, a distinction needs to be made between disputes between States and disputes between States and foreign investors or other non-State entities. The question of settlement of disputes is not discussed in this chapter.[32] Only a few aspects of interest for the overall discussion on flexibility are briefly mentioned in the following paragraphs.

International methods of dispute settlement that involve a binding decision by a third party must be distinguished from those where the parties to a dispute retain the right to decide whether to accept proposed ways for the resolution of a dispute (i.e. procedures known as mediation, conciliation etc.). As to the latter, there is a certain overlap with the functions described in the context of some of the approaches discussed above, since non-adversarial procedures directed at an ultimate agreement between the parties are involved. It needs to be emphasized here that, in the case of inter-State disputes, for a matter to become a "dispute" in the legal sense of the term, either party concerned, or both, must decide to treat it as such. This is particularly true with respect to procedures involving decision by a third party. Conciliation and mediation are part of the follow up systems created by many IIAs, for example, BITs, GATS and NAFTA.

An IIA may include provisions on methods of dispute settlement involving a binding decision by a third party -- an arbitrator or arbitration tribunal. The relevant provision may establish a fully voluntary system of dispute settlement: whenever a dispute arises, the parties may agree to have recourse to arbitration or judicial procedures. In other words, the parties to a dispute would retain the right to decide whether to proceed to arbitration or judicial settlement. This is the system followed by BITs and most regional agreements, such as NAFTA. Alternatively, an IIA might provide for a compulsory system of dispute settlement by arbitration or judicial proceedings. This would require a binding provision in the agreement to the effect that, when a dispute arises concerning the application and interpretation of the instrument, it must be submitted to the applicable procedures of arbitration or judicial settlement. Article 8 of the TRIMs agreement, for example, stipulates that the dispute settlement system of the GATT, as elaborated and applied by the WTO Dispute Settlement Understanding, "shall apply to consultations and the settlement of disputes under this Agreement". Chapter IX of MIGA is another example of a compulsory system for the settlement of disputes between the Agency and its members.

Sanctions. An investment instrument, whether legally-binding or not, may include provisions for sanctions against parties that have been found to have seriously infringed the rules established by the instrument. However, if sanctions are provided for, several preconditions for their proper administration need to be met. For instance, the procedures to be established would need to protect the rights of all parties concerned, allow a right to a hearing and establish a reasonably impartial body to decide upon the facts and law. A reasonable gradation of sanctions may be appropriate to correspond to violations of differing weight.

Sanctions decided at the international level may be applied at the international or at the national level. Internationally-administered sanctions tend to include measures involving publicity, "blacklisting", or calls for denial of contracts or suspension of membership. An example of the last type of sanction is article 52 of MIGA, in relation to a failure to fulfil the membership obligations under the Convention. Sanctions administered by national authorities tend to be more diverse and often more effective. This type of sanction is provided by the OECD Convention on Combating Bribery of Foreign Officials in International Business Transactions which stipulates in article 3 that "the bribery of a foreign public official shall be punishable by effective, proportionate and dissuasive criminal penalties".

Policy making and revision of an instrument. Policy decisions and actions that may need to be taken through the follow up process range from resolving individual problems arising out of monitoring the application of an agreement, to imposing sanctions, to giving effect to built-in agendas (including follow up negotiations), to undertaking partial or extensive revisions of the instrument. Clearly, such functions can be discharged only by a political body composed of government representatives of the States parties to the agreement, or by subsidiary bodies with specific functions mandated and appointed by them. In other words, through this decision-making process the parties retain control over important systemic matters arising out of an agreement, including whether or not to depart from the original implementation plans.

Among the most important policy functions to be discharged by the relevant intergovernmental body are those related to the application of built-in agendas for further negotiations, and those concerning limited or substantial revisions of an instrument. Such functions, in turn, require full evaluation of the operation of the IIA provisions and of the implementation process, including, for example, the transition periods granted to developing countries for meeting certain obligations. In some cases, the agreements themselves foresee the possibility that the transition periods could be extended (e.g. in the case of the TRIMs Agreement and the Subsidies Code of WTO). The need for previous evaluation may be recognized in an agreement. This is the case in GATS which contains provisions that link progressive liberalization in the context of each round of negotiations to an assessment of trade in services in overall terms and on a sectoral basis with reference to the Agreement's objectives, including those set out in paragraph 1 of article IV. This means that future liberalization is related directly to the achievement of concrete benefits in terms of capacity building and export opportunities for developing countries (Shahin, 1999). In other agreements, experience with the operation and application of certain provisions may be such as to indicate that there could be considerable room for improvement. Thus the documentation of developing countries' experiences with the operation of provisions in IIAs can provide elements for specific proposals for improvements. These can be linked to concrete measures to be adopted by developed countries to give effect to their commitments towards developing countries (Youssef, 1999).

Finally, given the complexity of some of the issues involved in the elaboration of an IIA, the functioning of an instrument may need to be continually re-evaluated, with a view towards its revision. This is a fundamental matter in the process of preparation of an IIA which is to be understood neither as a preliminary document, nor as a final definitive formulation of rules and procedures. Instead, it may rather be seen as part of a continuing process of interaction, review and adjustment to changing realities and to new perceptions of problems and possibilities. Like any legal instrument, an IIA may be seen not as a body of rules but as a process of ongoing decision making.

To sum up, as IIAs, by their very nature, are intended to produce their effects over a (typically) long period of time, their implementation mechanisms need to be devised in such a way as to ensure that their effective aspects are enhanced and their ineffective ones can be changed through adequate revision procedures.

Combinations. Most IIAs that include an international institutional machinery for follow up combine some or all of the mechanisms discussed above. Thus, while a number of investment-related instruments provide for a simple reporting mechanism as a means of monitoring their application (e.g. some United Nations General Assembly resolutions containing recommendations or declarations), others combine simple reporting procedures with consultations and other informal means of conflict resolution based on peer pressure (e.g. the OECD Declaration on International Investment and Multinational Enterprises and the Liberalisation Codes), while still others include, in addition, an institutional system for the settlement of disputes (e.g. the WTO agreements). Emphasis on formality is not necessarily a guarantee for better results in terms of achieving the objectives of an IIA. As noted before, the effectiveness of any institutional mechanism depends ultimately on the political will of the parties to make it functional.

* * *

In considering appropriate mechanisms for the application of an IIA it needs to be borne in mind that a fundamental aim of IIAs is to promote growth and development. These are, by definition, flexible objectives. Therefore, care needs to be taken that the modalities of application are not so rigid as to prevent the very purpose of the agreement to be realized. In particular, legally-binding agreements require mechanisms that permit timely adaptation to the needs of developing countries. However, in this respect, many developing countries experience difficulties in trying to apply an international agreement due to lack of adequate skills and resources. This problem is addressed in the next section.

B. Promotional measures and technical assistance

Developing countries often face certain handicaps in meeting obligations under IIAs and deriving benefits from them. Financial, administrative and human resource constraints often prevent them from putting in place appropriate mechanisms and institutions to give full effect to the possibilities contained in such agreements and to participate fully in the machinery designed to monitor and follow-up on their implementation. To facilitate the realisation of development objectives and address the economic asymmetries between the parties, IIAs can include provisions spelling out measures that can be taken to enhance the developmental effects of such agreements. These measures are typically addressed to developed countries that are home countries, and they can be complemented with provisions for technical assistance through relevant international organizations. As home country measures are addressed in these volumes (chapter 22), these are dealt with here only in summary fashion.

* * *

The traditional approach to promoting investment and technology flows to developing countries involves a range of **unilateral home country measures**. Apart from liberalising the regulatory framework for outward FDI — the basis for FDI flows to developing countries — promotional home country measures can encourage investment by helping to overcome market failures and risks that sometimes inhibit outward FDI to developing countries, such as incomplete or inaccurate information about investment potential and investment risks. These measures can be grouped into several broad categories (UNCTAD, 1995):

- Information and technical assistance. Government agencies or government-owned special banks in virtually all developed countries offer information and technical assistance programmes, including some support for feasibility studies and sometimes start-up support for smaller or less experienced investors. Some home country agencies make available to developing countries information database on home country enterprises interested in investing abroad. Information is disseminated through publications, seminars, teleconferences, trade fairs, investment missions and hosting foreign delegations for prospective investment sits. Matchmaking activities represent more direct interventions that seek to link a particular investor with an identified opportunity.
- Direct financial support and fiscal incentives. Financial support is provided by about half of the OECD countries through some type of development finance institution. Fiscal

incentives generally do not differentiate in their application between FDI in developing or developed countries. However certain incentives may be offered in conjunction with regionally oriented development assistance programmes (see below).

- Investment insurance. National investment insurance exists in most developed countries to provide coverage for expropriation, war and repatriation risks. Some programmes are designed to cover FDI only in developing countries.

Unilateral home country measures to promote FDI to developing countries are generally part of national development assistance programmes which, at the same time, may be designed to promote the competitiveness of the home country's TNCs. Examples of home country agencies that undertake these measures include the United States' Overseas Private Investment Corporation (OPIC), Japan's JETRO, Finland's Finnfund, Denmark's IFU and Canada's Export Development Corporation.

Bilateral investment treaties can be a vehicle to encourage home country promotional measures. The BIT model A prepared by the Asian African Legal Consultative Committee (AALCC) provides an example of mandatory language for concrete measures: Article 2 (I) commits home country partners to "take steps to promote investments in the territory of the other Contracting Party and encourage its nationals, companies and State entities to make such investments through offer of appropriate incentives, wherever possible, which may include such modalities as tax concessions and investment guarantees". However, in the few cases in which the promotional provisions of BITs are directed explicitly at the home country partner, they use hortatory language. Article 2 (3) of the BIT between the Belgium-Luxembourg Economic Union and Cameroon (box V.3) is an example of a BIT that addresses specifically the home country in this respect. This clause, however, is unusual in BIT practice in that it acknowledges the asymmetrical nature of the relationship between a capital—exporting developed country and a developing country, for it does not impose a similar obligation on Cameroon to promote investment in the Belgium—Luxembourg Economic Union. Because few concrete actions in this regard are specified, any substantive follow-up to relevant provisions depends on the voluntary adoption of home country measures. There are, however, some BITs that specify concrete actions that one or the other contracting party should take to promote investment. This is done, for example, in the BIT between Malaysia and the United Arab Emirates (box V.4) which, among other things, stipulates consultations about investment opportunities.

Box V.3. Home country promotional measures in BITs

BIT between the Belgium-Luxembourg Economic Union and Cameroon (1980)

Article 2

"3. Aware of the importance of investments in the promotion of its policy of cooperation for development, the Belgium-Luxembourg Economic Union shall strive to adopt measures capable of spurring its commercial operations to join in the development effort of the United Republic of Cameroon in accordance with its priorities."

In the context of the mutuality of benefits promised by BITs, there is still room for the BIT partners to explore more specific home country promotional measures. For example, embodied in a "technical cooperation clause" such measures could include the dissemination of information to the partners' investment communities on business opportunities, sponsoring investment missions by the representatives of their companies and provision of advisory assistance on ways to encourage the transfer of technology. These and similar commitments from home countries can positively contribute to enhancing the development dimension of BITs.

Box V.4. Mutual investment promotion measures in BITs

BIT between Malaysia and the United Arab Emirates (1991)

Article 2

"(6) The Contracting Parties shall periodically consult between themselves concerning investment opportunities within the territory of each other in various sectors of the economy to determine where investments from one Contracting State into the other may be most beneficial in the interest of both Contracting States.

(7) To attain the objectives of the Agreement, the Contracting States shall encourage and facilitate the formation and establishment of the appropriate joint legal entities between the investors of the Contracting States to establish, develop and execute investment projects in different economic sectors in accordance with the laws and regulations of the host State."

Regional and interregional trade and investment arrangements with a development orientation often encompass commitments involving the adoption of home country promotional measures. For example, the Lomé Conventions reflected many of the development-oriented programmes adopted by countries of the European Community. The Fourth ACP-EEC Lomé Convention contains a number of provisions concerning investment promotion and investment financing that are meant to encourage private investment flows from the European Community to ACP States; the Convention also specifies measures that home countries should take at the national level in this respect (box V.5).

Box V.5. Home country promotional measures in interregional agreements

Fourth ACP-EEC Convention of Lomé
Article 259

"In order to encourage private investment flows and the development of enterprises, the ACP States and the Community, in cooperation with other interested bodies, shall within the framework of the Convention:

(a) support efforts aimed at promoting European private investment in the ACP States by organizing discussions between any interested ACP State and potential investors on the legal and financial framework that ACP States might offer to investors;
(b) encourage the flow of information on investment opportunities by organizing investment promotion meetings, providing periodic information on existing financial or other specialized institutions, their facilities and conditions and encouraging the establishment of focal points for such meetings;
(c) encourage the dissemination of information on the nature and availability of investment guarantees and insurance mechanisms to facilitate investment in ACP States;
(d) provide assistance to small and medium-sized enterprises in ACP States in designing and obtaining equity and loan financing on optimal terms and conditions;
(e) explore ways and means of overcoming or reducing the host-country risk for individual investment projects which could contribute to economic progress;
(f) provide assistance to ACP States in:
    (i) creating or strengthening the ACP States' capacity to improve the quality of feasibility studies and the preparation of projects in order that appropriate economic and financial conclusions might be drawn;
    (ii) producing integrated project management mechanisms covering the entire project development cycle within the framework of the development programme of the State."

Other association and cooperation agreements between the European Community and its country members, on the one hand, and third countries or groups of countries, on the other hand, tend to include some mutual promotional measures to encourage investment flows (box V.6 and III.8).

Box V.6. Mutual investment promotion measures in association and cooperation agreements

Partnership and Cooperation Agreement Between the European Communities and Their Member States and Ukraine
Article 54

"Investment promotion and protection

1. Bearing in mind the respective powers and competences of the Community and the Member States, cooperation shall aim to establish a favourable climate for investment, both domestic and foreign, especially through better conditions for investment protection, the transfer of capital and the exchange of information on investment opportunities.

2. The aims of this cooperation shall be in particular:

-- the conclusion, where appropriate, between the Member States and Ukraine, of agreements for the promotion and protection of investment;
-- the conclusion, where appropriate, between the Member States and Ukraine, of agreements to avoid double taxation;
-- the creation of favourable conditions for attracting investments into the Ukrainian economy;
-- to establish stable and adequate business laws and conditions; and
-- to exchange information on investment opportunities in the form of, inter alia, trade fairs, exhibitions, trade weeks and other events."

There are also action plans and programmes that, although non-legally-binding, are indicative of what can be done. The United States' Caribbean Basin Initiative represents a regional approach similar to that of the Lomé Conventions to an area of special development concern and includes United States policies that provide tax and trade incentives to encourage FDI in Caribbean Basin countries. The European Union measures to boost FDI in Asia set out in its policy document "Towards a new Asia strategy" are another example in this respect (box V.7).

Regional agreements also can provide for mutual promotional measures within the countries members of the regional group. The Framework Agreement on the ASEAN Investment Area, for example, provides (article 6) that, for the implementation of their obligations under the Agreement, the member countries shall jointly undertake to develop and implement, among others, Promotion and Awareness Programme which sets out detailed promotional measures to encourage investment flows within the Area (box V.8).

Box V.7. Non-binding action plans
Measures adopted in the context of the Asia-Invest Programme

The European Union's overall approach to Asia was set out in the document "Towards a new Asia strategy" adopted in 1994. The elaboration of this policy was the first step towards developing a consistent and comprehensive strategy regarding the region.

Among its main initiatives is the Asia-Invest Programme which establishes a number of new instruments to assist investment including the following:

- The Business Priming Fund. The principal types of activities supported are:
  -- market-place monitoring;
  -- language and business culture familiarization;
  -- technical assistance.
- The Asia Enterprise and Asia Partenariat
- The Asia Investment Facility. Activities include:
  -- research by country and by industrial sector;
  -- initial guidance for European Union companies seeking to invest in Asia;
  -- dissemination in Asia of information on investment opportunities in the European Union.
- The Asia-Invest Network. Activities include:
  -- the Asia-Invest antennae;
  -- the annual Asia-Invest conference;
  -- the Asia-Invest Membership Scheme;
  -- The Asia-Invest Inforoute.
- Asia-Invest Support Activities. Activities include:
  -- Asia Branch Network meetings;
  -- BC-Net/EIC/BRE support for Asia;
  -- Seminars, training and information materials;
  -- newsletters.
- European Community Investment Partners. It supports five facilities:
  -- Facility 1: identification of potential partners;
  -- Facility 2: feasibility-study loans;
  -- Facility 3: capital investment in companies or share-secured loans;
  -- Facility 4: management assistance and training loans;
  -- Facility 5: grants for privatization.
- European Investment Bank financing. One or more of the following criteria are used for project approval:
  -- joint ventures between Asia and European Union firms;
  -- projects with a high technology transfer from the European Union;
  -- projects fostering closer relations between Asia and Europe;
  -- projects involving environmental improvements;
  -- investments fostering regional integration.

Source: UNCTAD, 1998c and d.

Box V.8. Mutual investment promotion measures in regional agreements

Framework Agreement on the ASEAN Investment Area
Schedule II
Promotion and Awareness Programme

"In respect of the Promotion and Awareness Programme, Member States shall

1. Organise joint investment promotion activities e.g., seminars, workshops, inbound familiarisation tours for investors from capital exporting countries, joint promotion of specific projects with active business sector participation;
2. Conduct regular consultation among investment agencies of ASEAN on investment promotion matters;
3. Organise investment-related training programmes for officials of investment agencies of ASEAN;
4. Exchange lists of promoted sectors/industries where Member States could encourage investments from other Member States and initiate promotional activities; and
5. Examine possible ways by which the investment agencies of Member States can support the promotion efforts of other Member States."

Multilateral instruments present another opportunity to negotiate commitments for home country measures beneficial to development objectives. To begin with, MIGA has been established precisely to provide insurance to firms investing in developing countries. The TRIPS Agreement provides an example in the more specific area of transfer of technology. It calls upon developed contracting parties to provide incentives to their enterprises and institutions for the purpose of promoting and encouraging technology transfer to the least developed countries in order to enable them to create a sound and viable technological base (box V.9). In order to facilitate the implementation of the Agreement, it goes further in detailing technical cooperation (UNCTAD, 1996c). The Energy Charter Treaty also contains provisions encouraging the promotion of transfer of technology on non-commercial terms to assist in the effective implementation of the objectives of the agreement (box V.9). Home country measures are furthermore included among the provisions of article IV of GATS (box III.3). In particular, developed countries are required to establish contact points to facilitate the access of developing countries services suppliers to key information related to their respective markets. In addition, technical cooperation is to be made available under article XXV (box V.9).

Box V.9. Home country promotional measures in multilateral agreements

Agreement on Trade-Related Aspects of Intellectual Property

Article 66
Least-Developed Country members

"2. Developed country Members shall provide incentives to enterprises and institutions in their territories for the purpose of promoting and encouraging technology transfer to least-developed country Members in order to enable them to create a sound and viable technological base.

Article 67
Technical Cooperation

In order to facilitate the implementation of this Agreement, developed country Members shall provide, on request and on mutually agreed terms and conditions, technical and financial cooperation in favour of developing and least developed country Members. Such cooperation shall include assistance in the preparation of laws and regulations on the protection and enforcement of intellectual property rights as well as on the prevention of their abuse, and shall include support regarding the establishment or reinforcement of domestic offices and agencies relevant to these matters, including the training of personnel."

Energy Charter Treaty

Article 8
Transfer of Technology

"(1) The Contracting Parties agree to promote access to and transfer of energy technology on a commercial and non-discriminatory basis to assist effective trade in Energy Materials and Products and Investment and to implement the objectives of the Charter subject to their laws and regulations, and to the protection of Intellectual Property rights.

(2) Accordingly, to the extent necessary to give effect to paragraph (1) the Contracting Parties shall eliminate existing and create no new obstacles to the transfer of technology in the field of Energy Materials and Products and related equipment and services, subject to nonproliferation and other international obligations."

General Agreement on Trade in Services

Article XXV
Technical Cooperation

"1. Service suppliers of Members which are in need of such assistance shall have access to the services of contact points referred to in paragraph 2 of Article IV."

Finally, the recent United Nations Framework Convention on Climate Change and its Kyoto Protocol offers an example in the area of environment of a multilateral instrument that provides for flexibility for developing countries, not only in its objectives and preambular provisions, its structure and its substantive provisions, but, most notably, in its application. To assist developing countries in meeting their commitments and achieve sustainable development, the Convention provides for financial assistance and technology transfer, and establishes a Clean Development Mechanism that seeks to benefit both developed and developing countries (boxV.10).

Box V.10. "Flexibility mechanisms" for developing countries in the United Nations Framework Convention on Climate Change and its Kyoto Protocol

Objectives

Article 2 of the United Nations Framework Convention on Climate Change states that the objective of the agreement is "to achieve ... stabilization of greenhouse gas concentrations in the atmosphere at a level that would prevent dangerous anthropogenic interference with the climate system" and "to enable economic development to proceed in a sustainable manner".

Preamble and principles

Three key principles can be discerned:

(1) Common but differentiated responsibilities: parties to the Framework Convention have a common responsibility to protect the climate for present and future generations. Different countries, at different levels of economic development, are expected to fulfil their common responsibilities in different ways. Developing countries' emissions are expected to grow, albeit less rapidly than they would without the Framework Convention;

(2) Developing countries, particularly low-lying island and coastal States, States with semi-arid areas, areas subject to floods, drought or desertification, or fragile mountain ecosystems are especially vulnerable to the adverse effects of climate change and deserve special consideration;

(3) The parties should promote sustainable development, and measures to avert climate change should be appropriate for the specific conditions of each party and should be integrated into national development programmes.

Substantive provisions

The principles identified in the preamble and principles section of the Framework Convention are given full expression in its substantive provisions and those of its Kyoto Protocol. Some of these provisions remain to be fully negotiated, but are likely to contain flexible approaches.

Differentiated emission limitation and reduction commitments

The Framework Convention contains two categories of emission limitation or reduction commitments, the general commitments contained in article 4.1 whereby

/...

Box V.10 (concluded)

all parties must adopt measures to mitigate climate change and the specific commitments contained in article 4.2 (a) and (b), whereby the developed countries must aim to return their emissions to 1990 levels by 2000. The Kyoto Protocol goes further. It obligates Annex I Parties (developed countries) only to reduce their emissions by a specified amount during the period 2008-2012. Unlike the commitments in article 4.2 (a) and (b) these obligations are considered legally binding on Annex I Parties. Developing countries may choose, but are not required, to adopt similar commitments. Argentina and Kazakhstan indicated at the recent Conference of the Parties held in Buenos Aires in November 1998 that they will undertake voluntary commitments.

Financial assistance and technology transfer
A financial mechanism has been established to provide financial assistance to developing countries in meeting their obligations under the Framework Convention and Kyoto Protocol. The operating entity of the financial mechanism is the Global Environment Facility, which, under article 4.3 of the Convention, will pay the agreed full costs of developing country reporting requirements. It also pays the agreed full incremental cost of measures in developing countries to reduce emissions and or in other ways further the objectives of the Convention. The parties are still discussing the modalities for implementing the provisions of the Convention relating to the development and transfer of technologies.

Compliance and adaptation
In furtherance of principle 2, measures have been adopted to assist developing countries adapt to climate change. The Global Environment Facility funds studies to determine vulnerability and adaptation needs, and recently has been assigned the task of helping developing countries. The Clean Development Mechanism to be established under the Kyoto Protocol, discussed below, must apply a portion of its proceeds to meet the adaptation requirements of developing countries.

The Clean Development Mechanism and sustainable development
The Kyoto Protocol establishes a Clean Development Mechanism (CDM) to assist developed countries in meeting their emissions reduction commitments and developing countries in achieving sustainable development. Through the CDM, developed countries — or private companies in them — pay for projects in developing countries that will reduce emissions. The developed country investor gets some or all of the credit for the reductions, which it can apply against its own emissions or sell to another party. The project must enhance sustainable development in the host developing country. The parties are still discussing the CDM and the modalities for its operation. "

Source: United Nations, 1992a; and 1997.

* * *

Regional and multilateral instruments appear to provide the best opportunities for securing developed home country commitments to promote FDI flows to developing countries. Explicit and concrete undertakings are of course preferable to broad and hortatory goals. Consideration can also be given to initiatives that encourage FDI flows among developing countries which, simultaneously, would strengthen the international competitive capabilities of developing country TNCs. Home country promotional measures can also be complemented with technical assistance provided by relevant international organizations to enhance the capacity of developing countries to deal effectively with foreign investors. Such capacity, in terms of skill, information, negotiation and implementation abilities, is needed to ensure that the increased flexibility provided for in IIAs to implement their development policies and strategies is used to "deliver" all the benefits FDI can offer.

Summary and Conclusions

Developing countries seek FDI in order to promote their economic development. This is their paramount objective. To that end, they have sought to establish — through national legislation and international instruments — a legal framework aimed at reducing obstacles to FDI, while providing foreign investors with high standards of treatment and legal protection for their investments and increasingly putting in place mechanisms to assure the proper functioning of markets.

Developing countries participate in IIAs — whether at bilateral, regional, interregional or multilateral levels — because they believe that, on balance, these instruments help them to attract FDI and to benefit from it. At the same time, IIAs, like most international agreements, limit to a certain extent the policy options available to governments to pursue their development objectives through FDI. A question arises, therefore, how, nevertheless, IIAs can allow developing countries a certain policy space to promote their development. This is all the more important since the principal responsibility for the design and implementation of development objectives and policies remains in the hands of the individual countries' governments.

Thus, when concluding IIAs, developing countries face a basic challenge: how to achieve the goal of creating an appropriate stable, predictable and transparent FDI policy framework that enables firms to advance their corporate objectives, while, at the same time, retaining a margin of freedom necessary to pursue their particular national development objectives. A concept that can help link these objectives is "flexibility" which, for present purposes, can be defined as the ability of IIAs to be adapted to the particular conditions prevailing in developing countries and to the realities of the economic asymmetries between these countries and developed countries.

Flexibility can be approached from four main angles: the objectives of IIAs, their overall structure and modes of participation, their substantive provisions and their application.

Objectives. IIAs often address development concerns by including in their text, usually in their preamble, declaratory statements referring to the promotion of development as a main objective of the agreement, or to specific ways by which the agreement is to contribute to development objectives, or a generally worded recognition of the needs of developing and/or least developed country parties requiring flexibility in the operation of the obligations under the agreement. There are many variations in such language, and it is difficult to generalize its actual role and importance. Preambles and similar declarations normally do not directly create rights and obligations for the parties to an instrument, but they are relevant to its interpretation. In fact, the texts of preambles are often the result of hard bargaining. To the extent that such language reflects the will of the participating countries, it helps to reaffirm the acceptance of development as a central purpose of IIAs. The specific language used in each case and its relationship to the rest of the instrument is, of course, important.

Overall structure and modes of participation: special and differential treatment. Promotion of development can also be manifested in the structure of IIAs. Central to this is the application of special principles and rules for developing countries which have as their common characteristic that these countries assume less onerous obligations -- either permanently or temporarily -- on a non-reciprocal basis. This approach is reflected in the principle of "special and differential treatment" for developing countries (or categories among them). Broadly speaking, this principle encompasses such aspects as granting lower levels of obligations for developing countries; asymmetrically phased implementation timetables; best endeavour commitments; exceptions from commitments in certain areas; flexibility in the application of, and adherence to, disciplines under prescribed circumstances; and technical assistance and training. A key issue in dealing with the principle of special and differential treatment is whether a broad spectrum of flexibility should be given to the beneficiaries, or whether well defined criteria should be established. One way of applying the principle of special and differential treatment in the structure of an agreement is to distinguish between developed and developing countries by establishing, for instance, separate categories of countries, the members of which do not have the same rights and duties. Beyond that, international practice has evolved a number of methods to allow countries that wish to participate in an agreement to do so in ways that take into account their individual situations. Although the methods in question may be used, in principle, by any country, they can be particularly relevant as a means of addressing development concerns. The principal methods can be grouped into two main approaches. The first approach is to allow for different stages and degrees of participation in an IIA, by, for example, allowing countries to accede to an agreement at different times and in different ways; or permitting countries that are not ready to become full members of an IIA to be associated with it or to cooperate on matters of mutual interest. The second approach to structural flexibility is to allow the inclusion of various kinds of exceptions, reservations, derogations, waivers or transitional arrangements. Exceptions take a great variety of forms: they may be general (e.g. for the protection of national security), subject specific (e.g. the so-called "cultural exception"), or they may be country specific. A subset of this approach is the use of "positive" and "negative" lists. Finally, an investment framework can be built consisting of several instruments that can be negotiated over time and combine a variety of approaches.

By using these or other methods, IIAs can be constructed in a manner that ensures an overall balance of rights and obligations for all actors involved, so that all parties derive benefits from it.

Substantive provisions. The substantive content of an IIA is particularly important in reflecting development concerns and an overall balance of rights and obligations. This begins with the choices countries make about the issues they wish to include in an IIA, and those they wish to keep outside the scope of an agreement. (The range of relevant issues is reflected in the topics covered in the chapters in these volumes.) It continues with the formulation of the substantive provisions, through ways that allow countries to address the issues in a manner beneficial to them and, when need arises, to retain some flexibility regarding the commitments they made, keeping also in mind the various interactions between issues and provisions. The range of approaches and permutations that can be used in formulating substantive provisions in IIAs is broad. Of course, flexibility might need to be approached in different ways for each individual substantive issue, depending on its characteristics and development effects. For example, the type of approach to flexibility that can be useful in a development context regarding admission and establishment of foreign affiliates might not be relevant to post-establishment national and MFN treatment provisions, or to expropriation, labour or environmental standards. There are no general prescriptions on this matter. The choice of approach depends on the conditions prevailing in each country and the particular development strategies pursued by each government.

Application. Flexibility for development can also be exercised during the application stage of an IIA. The manner in which an IIA is interpreted, and the way in which it is to be made effective determine whether its objectives, structure and substantive provisions produce, in the end, the desired developmental effects. The degree of flexibility for the interpretation and application of an IIA depends to a large extent on the legal character of an agreement and the formulation of individual provisions. Legally-binding agreements, even if they do not provide for implementation mechanisms, impose on the States signatories a legal obligation under international law to comply with their provisions. How far such an obligation will actually limit the subsequent freedom of action of the States concerned largely depends on the language of the agreement or the type of obligations imposed. Voluntary instruments, on the other hand, are not legally enforceable but can have an influence on the development of national and international law. One way of mitigating some of the most rigorous implications of concluding a legally-binding investment agreement is to include one or several "soft" obligations among binding provisions.

Many IIA provisions require some kind of action at the national level in order to produce their effects. Where explicit provisions requiring specific national action are absent, each State would be free to decide the particular manner in which it may implement an agreement's provisions. Variations in normative intensity and specificity of language regarding the effects of IIAs on national systems provide possibilities for developing countries to advance their development interests. At the regional and multilateral levels, the effectiveness of an IIA is intimately related to the intergovernmental institutional machinery for follow up and monitoring its application, including through built-in agendas. There are various mechanisms that can be created, ranging from simple reporting requirements (which nevertheless can be a significant inducement to act in compliance), to advisory and consultative functions (aimed at resolving questions arising out of the continuing application of an IIA), to complaint and clarification mechanisms (aimed at facilitating application of non-binding instruments under procedures of a non adjudicatory nature), to various international methods of settlement of disputes which may allow more or less freedom to the parties to accept proposed ways for the resolution of the dispute. Finally, an agreement might eventually need partial or extensive revisions. This is a fundamental facet of the entire process of the elaboration of an IIA, which is to be understood as a continuing process of interaction, review and adjustment to changing realities and to new perceptions of problems and possibilities.

In fulfilling its various functions, an international institutional machinery can play several major development roles. It is therefore of critical importance for developing countries to make the best use of the means provided by the relevant institutional arrangements for follow up, including the review of built-in agendas, to ensure that the development objectives are given full effect. An important consideration in this respect are the difficulties that many developing countries experience in participating fully and effectively in these arrangements due to lack of adequate skills and resources. To address such difficulties, IIAs can make special arrangements for technical and financial assistance. In addition, to ensure that the development goals of an IIA are fully realized, it may be desirable that developed countries commit themselves to undertake promotional measures to encourage FDI flows to developing countries.

In conclusion, it needs to be re-emphasized that IIAs, like all international agreements, typically contain obligations that, by their very nature, reduce to some extent the autonomy of the participating countries. At the same time, such agreements need to recognize important differences in the characteristics of the parties involved, in particular the economic asymmetries and levels of development between developing and developed countries. If IIAs do not allow developing countries to pursue their fundamental objective of advancing their development — indeed make a positive contribution to this objective — they run the risk of being of little or no interest to them. This underlines the importance of designing, from the outset, IIAs in a manner that allows their parties a certain degree of flexibility in pursuing their development objectives. To find the proper balance between obligations and flexibility — a balance that leaves sufficient space for development-oriented national policies — is indeed a difficult challenge faced by negotiators of IIAs. This is particularly important as treaty-making activity in this area at all levels has intensified in recent years.

Notes

1 The first expert meeting, held from 28 to 30 May 1997, dealt with bilateral investment treaties and their development dimensions. The second expert meeting took place from 1 to 3 April 1998 and focused on regional and multilateral investment agreements, examining in particular the nature and implications of those agreements, the range of issues addressed by them and the extent to which the development dimension was taken into account. The third expert meeting, held from 24 to 26 March 1999, dealt with the question of flexibility in IIAs and looked into the ways in which flexibility with respect to development concerns has been given effect in existing agreements.

2 The Expert Meeting recommended that "the report submitted by the UNCTAD secretariat entitled "International investment agreements: concepts allowing for a certain flexibility in the interest of promoting growth and development" be revised in light of the discussions during the Expert Meeting and submitted to the next session of the Commission" (see "Agreed Conclusions", UNCTAD, 1999c, p. 2).

3 Regarding the right to development, see section II and box II.4 below.

4 For a discussion of the role of FDI in development, see UNCTAD, 1999 a and chapter 27 (in volume III).

5 For a collection of these agreements, see UNCTAD, 1996a and 2000.

6 Increasingly, outward investment is becoming part of the development strategies of developing countries. Thus, it is important that discussions on investment facilitation and promotion in the interest of development do not lose sight of the potential home country status of developing countries. This is not, however, the focus of this chapter. For a detailed discussion of developing country strategies on outward investment, see UNCTAD, 1995.

7 The legal symmetry/economic asymmetry situation is best illustrated by the older BITs which were usually intended to govern investment relations between a developed capital exporting country and a developing capital importing country. Although the developing country party enjoyed under the BIT reciprocal rights -- to national treatment etc. -- for the protection of its investors in the territory of the developed country partner, the reality was that, in practice, it would have little investment in that other State. Thus, the rights in a BIT which related to the capital exporting capacity of a party were, in so far as the developing treaty partner were concerned, effectively "paper rights", at any rate until the developing country's firms invested in the territory of its developed treaty partner. This is now beginning to happen as firms in a number of developing countries are becoming outward investors.

8 Developed countries also often seek flexibility in IIAs for their own reasons (e.g. to allow subnational authorities to implement their own policy measures on FDI, in accordance with their constitutional powers). Thus, while flexibility is primarily seen here in a development context, it may have other functions as well. Moreover, IIAs may need to introduce an element of flexibility simply because it is not possible for the parties to foresee all possible future developments that may affect the operation of their provisions.

9 It should be noted that all developed countries are also host countries and that (as observed earlier) an increasing number of developing countries are becoming home countries.

10 Unless otherwise indicated, the instruments referred to are contained in UNCTAD, 1996a and 2000; or in ICSID, 1972. The texts of theses instruments can also be found on UNCTAD's website at www.unctad.org/iia.

11 According to an author and IIAs' negotiator, should it ever come to the negotiation of a multilateral framework for investment, it "should become the Multilateral Agreement on Investment and Development — MAID —, an appropriate acronym, since the agreement should be servant both to investment and development" (Robinson, 1998, p. 88).

12 The notion is commonplace in the legislation of most developed countries.

13 A clear illustration is the case of the International Development Association (IDA), the World Bank affiliate which provides development credits to developing countries on favourable terms. Members of the IDA are classed in two main groups: Part I countries, which are donors of aid, and Part II countries, most of which are aid recipients.

14 Strictly speaking, a protocol need not be additional to an agreement; an agreement by itself may be called a "protocol".

15 The meaning of terms such as exceptions, derogations, reservations, waivers, etc. is not fixed, and may vary from agreement to agreement.

16 This would be the case of a number of treaties relating to human rights, including the European Convention of Human Rights (Council of Europe, 1950). The rationale here is that treaties on human rights do not reflect mutual concessions: they just express fundamental rights, the respect of which does not depend upon reciprocity. But these are not the only treaties which are not premised upon reciprocity.

17 This waiver gave rise to a trade dispute between the European Union and some Caribbean States on one hand, and the United States and some Latin American States on the other, concerning bananas (WTO, 1997). The case shows clearly the need for drafting waivers, derogations, etc. (many of which are intended to be of benefit for the developing

countries) with the outmost care and attention to details.

[18] The GATS also has a negative-list approach with regard to MFN (article 2).

[19] For an in-depth discussion of the topic of scope and definitions in IIAs, see chapter 3.

[20] For an in-depth discussion of the topic of admission of investments in IIAs, see chapter 4.

[21] For an in-depth discussion of national treatment in IIAs, see chapter 5.

[22] *De jure* treatment refers to treatment of foreign investors provided for in national laws and regulations. *De facto* treatment includes any measure or action that in fact works against national treatment, as in the case for example of licensing requirements for the conduct of a business activity which depend on the possession of qualifications by skilled personnel that can only be obtained in the host country.

[23] For an in-depth discussion of MFN treatment in IIAs, see chapter 6.

[24] In any case, an MFN exception on these grounds might cause "victim" countries to retaliate, in particular, by denying the host country MFN as well. As an increasing number of firms from a growing number of countries become foreign investors, such retaliation could have adverse economic consequences.

[25] As to the last of these cases, a question concerns the stage of integration at which an MFN exception may be justified. One approach is that an exception can be justified if integration within a region is qualitatively different from integration based only on the standard of non-discrimination (see chapter 6). The regional economic integration organization may therefore have to reach a stage in which member States have committed themselves to removing virtually all barriers to cross-border investment irrespective of whether these barriers are discriminatory or not. As long as the REIO members have only accepted the standard of non-discrimination amongst themselves, an MFN exception with regard to non-members may be more difficult to justify. For an in-depth discussion of the REIO clause in IIAs, see UNCTAD, forthcoming

[26] For an in-depth discussion of the topic of fair and equitable treatment in IIAs, see chapter 7.

[27] This section draws extensively on UNCTC, 1978.

[28] For a more detailed discussion on the role of voluntary instruments dealing with foreign investment, see, Blanpain (1979); Horn (1980); Rubin and Hufbauer (1984); Kline (1985); Sauvant and Aranda (1994); Fatouros (1994).

[29] The different degrees of binding force among OECD investment instruments can be illustrated by comparing the National Treatment instrument and the Guidelines for Multinational Enterprises.

[30] See, for example, Youssef (1999) for a discussion on the issue of the adequacy of the transitional periods in the TRIMs and TRIPS agreements; and Shahin (1999) for a discussion on the weakness in the implementation of provisions in GATS granting developing countries special and differential treatment.

[31] See Youssef (1999) for suggestions on how the implementation of many provisions granting special and differential treatment could be made more effective and meaningful to address development concerns. Some of these are outlined in this paragraph.

[32] The issue of settlement of investment disputes is discussed in chapters 11 and 12. For a documentation of the number of treaty-based investment disputes until November 2004, see UNCTAD, 2004c.

Chapter 3. Scope and Definition*

Executive summary

In furtherance of their economic development policies, most countries have entered into one or more investment agreements that in various ways liberalize, promote, protect or regulate international investment flows. Such agreements typically apply to investment in the territory of one country by investors of another country.

The scope of investment agreements is delimited primarily through definitions of key terms, such as "investment" and "investor". By themselves and in conjunction with the operative provisions, these definitions may play one or both of two critical functions in an agreement: they identify those assets to which the treaty applies; and they may determine the nature of the obligations created by the treaty. The terms "investment" and "investor" are the principal focus of this chapter. The discussion will consider both how these terms have been defined in existing investment agreements and how these definitional provisions interact with key operative provisions of investment agreements.

Investment agreements often define "investment" in a way that is both broad and open-ended. The broadest definitions embrace every kind of asset. They include in particular movable and immovable property, interests in companies (including both portfolio and direct investment), contractual rights (such as service agreements), intellectual property, and business concessions.

Each of these types of investment has different economic and development implications for home and host countries. The parties to an investment agreement thus may not wish to liberalize, promote, protect or regulate all investment flows in the same manner or to the same extent. For example, the economic development policies of treaty parties may call for excluding certain assets from coverage by a particular investment agreement or for treating certain assets differently under the agreement.

Many investment agreements have therefore narrowed the definition of investment in various ways in furtherance of the parties' economic policies, including development policies. For example, they often exclude from the definition investment not established in accordance with host country legislative requirements, which tend to reflect a country's development policy. They may exclude investment established prior to the entry into force of an investment agreement or the host country's foreign investment law, again because the investment may have been established outside the framework of the host country's development policy; certain types of investment, such as portfolio investment or short-term contracts (which may be regarded as less desirable than direct investment for the purposes of long-term economic development) or investments that do not meet certain minimum capital requirements or that are in certain industries of the economy. All of these limitations have appeared in at least some investment agreements, generally in furtherance of the economic development policies of some or all of the parties.

Alternatively, a host country seeking to exclude or regulate certain types of foreign investment may decide to impose conditions on the establishment of particular foreign investments or to exclude them from its territory entirely. Furthermore, a host country may prefer language limiting the applicability of specific provisions to certain types of investment.

Investment agreements usually define "investor" to include both natural persons and legal entities. Both are considered "investors" within the meaning of an agreement if they have the nationality of a particular State or are otherwise linked to that State, such as through domicile or residence. For legal entities, the criterion for determining nationality is usually based on the country of organization, the country of the seat or the country of ownership and/or control of the entity.

---

* The chapter is based on a 1999 manuscript prepared by Kenneth J. Vandevelde. The final version reflects comments received from Mark Koulen and Manfred Schekulin.

Introduction

This chapter analyses the scope and definitions of investment agreements. Investment agreements must specify not only their geographical and temporal coverage, but, most importantly, their subject-matter coverage. This is done primarily -- though, as this chapter will show, not exclusively -- through the provisions on definition, especially the definitions of the terms "investment" and "investor".

The terms "investment" and "investor" lend themselves to a significant variety of definitions, resulting in distinct drafting choices. In particular, this chapter identifies a range of alternatives from wide to narrow definitions and shows how these might affect, on the one hand, the extent of treaty coverage granted to foreign investors and, on the other, the degree of host State discretion in directing and implementing its foreign investment policy.

Of particular importance in this regard is an understanding of approaches to definitions. In the case of "investment" is the term defined by reference to types of assets that, in theory, could amount to an "investment", or does one also refer to the underlying transaction in which those assets are involved? In the case of the term "investor", is this term defined by reference to categories of legally recognized persons or on the basis of the transactions involved, regardless of the legal status of the person or entity undertaking that transaction?

The answers to such questions materially affect the actual role of the agreements. Indeed they guide the structure of the present chapter which, in section I, elaborates on these initial conceptual issues. Section II then provides a stocktaking and analytical background: it describes how these terms have been defined in existing international instruments and explains the rationales for various definitions. Section III analyses the interaction of these definitions with some of the other issues addressed by investment agreements. It is here that the interaction between the scope of the definitions used -- and the means by which other concepts further affect the operation of definitional terms -- is considered. Thereby the full range of concerns relevant to determining the subject-matter of an investment agreement is shown. Finally, the concluding section assesses the development implications behind the wider and narrower definition clauses identified in section.

Section I
Explanation of the Issue

A. Scope of international investment agreements

The scope of an international investment agreement[1] is delimited in at least three ways:[2]

- **By its geographical coverage.** The geographical scope of an investment agreement is determined, to begin with, by the number and identity of the States that are party to it. It is also determined by the territorial limits of the States concerned. The definition of the term "territory" is important in this respect and will be briefly addressed later.
- **By its temporal application.** To ascertain the exact temporal scope of an agreement, its date of entry into force with respect to each party and its duration has to be determined. Apart from such general international law questions, the temporal scope of an agreement raises two main issues: the first is whether the agreement applies to an investment established prior to its entry into force; this issue often is addressed in the definition of "investment" and will be discussed in connection with that term. The second issue is whether an agreement's provisions continue to apply to an investment subsequent to its formal termination. This issue generally is not addressed in provisions on definitions and will not be discussed here.[3]
- **By its subject matter.** The subject matter scope of an investment agreement is determined by the definition of two terms in particular: "investment" and "investor". These terms refer to major dimensions of the economic activities to which the provisions of an agreement apply. Accordingly, they play an important role in determining the normative content of an instrument. Typically, an international investment agreement applies only to certain types of investment. One important feature of such investment is that it must be "foreign", that is to say, investment by investors from one country in the territory of another. The definition of the term "investor" therefore supplements in an important manner the definition of "investment". This chapter

discusses these terms at length. The term "returns" is occasionally relevant to the subject-matter scope of specific provisions of some investment agreements and is discussed briefly.

In short, while there are at least three dimensions to the scope of an investment agreement, it is chiefly with respect to the subject matter of an instrument that definitions are important. The geographical and temporal scope are not usually determined by means of definitions, but through specific provisions (usually among the instrument's "final clauses"). This chapter addresses in the main the problems of definitions, and especially those of the terms "investment" and "investor", around which cluster most of the important questions.

It should be noted at this point that the terms "investment" and "investor" are not defined in every investment instrument; the discussion in this chapter does not presuppose that these terms should be defined in every case. Whether the instrument includes explicit definitions or not, however, its application requires that the parties use some working definition of these terms. Some appreciation of the meaning of the terms is thus essential to an understanding of the scope of any investment instrument.

B. Definitions of key terms

Definitions serve many purposes. In international agreements, they raise difficult policy issues and are often the subject of hard bargaining between the negotiating parties. Accordingly, they should be seen not as objective formulations of the meaning of terms, but as part of an agreement's normative content, since they determine the extent and the manner in which the other provisions are to be applied. Thus, the decision on a definition of terms will be made on a case-by-case basis, taking into account the purpose and circumstances of the negotiations at stake.

1. Investment

a. Historical context

There is no single, static conception of what constitutes foreign investment. Rather, the conception has changed over time as the nature of international economic relations has changed.

Prior to the middle of the nineteenth century, trans-frontier capital flows typically assumed the form of lending by European investors to borrowers in other European States (Kindleberger, 1993, pp. 208-224). The difficulties involved in travel and communication over long distances were a strong impediment to foreign direct investment (FDI).

In that period, foreign-owned property in a country often took the form of merchandise imported for sale to the domestic market or vessels that had shipped the merchandise. Foreign nationals -- more often than not, resident in the home countries -- might also hold bonds that had served to finance foreign manufacturing and transportation enterprises. In addition, foreign nationals residing abroad generally owned for their personal use and consumption a certain amount of personal and real property in the host country where they resided. International investment law was thus concerned principally with the protection of tangible property against seizure and the right of creditors to collect debts. Some countries negotiated treaties that protected foreign property, such as merchandise and vessels, against expropriation.[4]

In the late nineteenth century, improvements in transportation and communication facilitated the management of enterprises owned by foreign nationals, in natural resources, in public utilities or in large manufacturing plants. In all three cases, major capital investments as well as advanced technology were required, which were often not available to local entrepreneurs. At the same time, use of the corporate form of business organization became more widespread and securities markets emerged (Cameron, 1997, pp. 213-214, 308). The result was that a number of countries developed the economic and legal foundations necessary for the establishment of foreign-owned investment in companies.

Traditionally, investment in companies has been categorized as either direct or portfolio investment. An investment is considered direct when the investor's share of ownership is sufficient to allow control of the company, while investment that provides the investor with a return, but not control over the company, generally is considered portfolio investment.[5] Because an investor may be able to control a company with less than the majority of the stock, the degree of ownership required for investment to be regarded as direct may vary with the circumstances. In some instances, investment may be defined as direct if it is to be of lasting duration.

In the nineteenth century, because of the difficulties of controlling an enterprise from abroad, the dominant form of investment in foreign companies was portfolio investment, with the principal exceptions being in specific sectors (e.g. public utilities, natural resources). By the mid-twentieth century, however, with further improvements in transportation and communication, the stock of FDI exceeded the total amount of foreign portfolio investment. The protection of foreign investment in the form of equity stock in companies became an increasing concern of foreign investment law. Since much FDI was in the primary sector, concession agreements for natural resource extraction became a matter of importance in international investment law.[6]

In the late twentieth century, the forms of foreign investment have become more diverse. As technological innovations have spread around the world, the producers of technology have sought to protect their patents and copyrighted materials against infringement. The consolidation of business enterprises to form transnational corporations (TNCs) with global name recognition has given great value to certain trademarks that are associated with high quality and/or high demand goods. Thus, the regulation of intellectual property is a concern of growing importance to national and international law. Many developed economies that had concentrated their productive resources in the manufacturing sector in the nineteenth century began to shift a large portion of these resources to the services sector, and continuing improvements in communication and transportation made it feasible for service providers to render services to clients in foreign countries. As this suggests, changing circumstances create new ways of investment in foreign countries. In other words, there is an increasing array of foreign-owned assets that have economic value and thus may be regarded as foreign investment.

b. Impact on investment definitions

This brief foray into the history of the matter helps explain another aspect of the topic at hand, namely, the relatively recent emergence of the notion (and term) of "investment" in the language of international agreements and international legal practice in general. Customary international law and earlier international agreements did not generally utilize this notion. They relied instead on the notion of "foreign property", approaching in the same (or similar) manner cases of imported (and invested) capital and cases of property of long-resident foreign nationals, where no transfer of capital took place or the original transfer was lost in history.[7] As a result, the question of whether portfolio investment was an asset protected under traditional rules of customary international law has been an open question. The outcome of the Barcelona Traction case suggests that it might not have been protected (ICJ, 1970). One reason for this possibility is that the risk involved in some portfolio investments for the investor would not be as high as that involved in a direct investment, since the former investment could normally be pulled out of a host country more easily than the latter (Sornarajah, 1994). Similarly, traditionally, such intangible assets as intellectual property were not thought to be assets that came within the ambit of customary international legal protection (Sornarajah, 1994). Earlier instruments and practice are thus of little help in addressing the issue of the definition of "investment" today, although they may account in part for the emphasis on assets in such definitions that later discussion will show.

The important issue to be looked at in addressing the issue of definition, with a view towards establishing the subject matter scope of an agreement, is which of the many types of investment activities that are of value in the modern economy should be included within the definition of "investment". Because that definition will specify the economic activities to which the operative provisions of agreements apply, the terms of the definition are as important to the normative content of the agreement as the terms of the operative provisions and reflect the investment policies of the parties. An assessment of the economic implications of various alternative definitions of "investment" in the context of an agreement's operative provisions is therefore important.

A detailed analysis of possible definitions (and categories of definitions) of investment is undertaken in concrete context in the next section, where existing investment instruments are reviewed. At this point, it is necessary to point out that an "investment" may, in the language of the agreements, be itself a legal person. For instance, a corporation established in the host country by a foreign investor is, in effect, the foreign investor's "investment". Yet the foreign investor, if it is a parent company, is itself a corporation. Furthermore, should the corporation in the host state make its own investments -- as through acquisitions, joint ventures or the establishment of a local subsidiary -- it too becomes an "investor". Thus both "investors" and "investments" can in practice possess legal personality.

As will be seen later, moreover, different types of international investment flows have different economic implications. In implementing their economic and development policies, countries thus may wish to accept different rules concerning the treatment of different types of foreign investment. In other words, countries may be willing to assume certain obligations only with respect to foreign investment that has specified economic implications. Thus, the scope of the definition of "investment" generally will depend upon the purpose and the operative provisions of an investment agreement. For example, an investment agreement that deals with rules on the admission of investment may define "investment" differently from one that deals with post-admission treatment.

2. Investor

Investment agreements generally do not apply to all investment. Rather, they typically apply only to investment by investors who are connected with at least one of the other treaty partners through nationality or other links, according to the agreement's provisions. The definition of the term "investor" thus can be critical to determining the scope of an investment agreement.

Two general issues arise in defining the term "investor": what types of person or entity may be considered investors? And what are the criteria that determine that a person is covered by an agreement?

a. Entities considered "investors"

Two types of entity may be included within the definition of "investor": natural persons or individuals and artificial or legal persons, also referred to as legal or juridical entities. Sometimes, the term "investor" is not used. Instead, agreements refer to "nationals" and "companies", with the former defined to include natural persons and the latter defined to include a range of legal entities.

The category of natural persons requires no elaboration. The only issue that arises in determining whether a natural person is covered by an agreement concerns the qualifying links of the person with the State party to the agreement, such as nationality.

The category of legal entities, by contrast, can be defined to include or exclude a number of different types of entities. Entities may be excluded on the basis of their legal form, their purpose or their ownership. These, too, are discussed in more detail in the next section.

Differences in the legal form of an entity may be important to a host country in a variety of circumstances. The form of the entity determines, for example, which assets may be reached by creditors of the entity to satisfy debts and perhaps the extent to which the entity can be sued in its own name in the courts. A host country may wish to exclude from operating in its territory entities that, because of legal limitations on liability or susceptibility to suit, are insulated from financial responsibility for any injuries that they may cause.

b. Which investors are covered

The second important issue is establishing a link between the States party to an agreement and investors, sufficient to allow them to qualify for coverage under the agreement. The most common link is nationality; but other links, such as permanent residence, domicile, residence or combinations thereof are also in use. For natural persons, the criteria for determining nationality are found both in customary international law and, in the cases at hand, in the agreements involved. With respect to legal persons, the criteria by which nationality is established vary among countries. Among the criteria in use, the place of incorporation, the location of the company seat and the nationality of the controlling shareholders or owners are prominent.

In policy terms, the issue of establishing the nationality of an investor presents the question of the extent to which the parties to an agreement wish to link the legal coverage of the agreement with the economic ties between the parties and the covered investment. One country may be seeking to establish a generally favourable investment climate and may be prepared to extend treaty coverage to investments that have minimal economic ties with the other party, while another country may wish to extend treaty coverage only to investments with strong economic ties to the treaty parties.

Section II Stocktaking and Analysis

A. Investment

With respect to the definition of "investment", earlier instruments dealing with foreign investment fall in two broad categories:

- Those that concern the cross-border movement of capital and resources, whether in view of its control or of its liberalization. Such instruments usually define foreign investment in narrow terms, insisting on an investor's control over the enterprise as a necessary element of the concept. Such instruments may list the differences between various types of investment of capital, though they may not necessarily apply different rules to each type. A classic definition employing this methodology is the one found in Annex A of the OECD Code of Liberalisation of Capital Movements (box 1).

Box 1. Definition of "direct investment" in the OECD Code

"Investment for the purpose of establishing lasting economic relations with an undertaking such as, in particular, investments which give the possibility of exercising an effective influence on the management thereof:

A. In the country concerned by non-residents by means of:
   1. Creation or extension of a wholly-owned enterprise, subsidiary or branch, acquisition of full ownership or an existing enterprise;
   2. Participation in a new or existing enterprise;
   3. A loan of five years or longer.

B. Abroad by residents by means of:
   1. Creation or extension of a wholly-owned enterprise, subsidiary or branch, acquisition of full ownership of an existing enterprise;
   2. Participation in a new or existing enterprise;
   3. A loan of five years or longer."

Source: Code of Liberalisation of Capital Movements, Annex A, from UNCTAD, 1996a, volume II, p. 17.

- Instruments mainly directed at the protection of foreign investment. Definitions of investment in such instruments are generally broad and comprehensive. They cover not only the capital (or the resources) that has crossed borders with a view towards the creation of an enterprise or the acquisition of control over an existing one, but most other kinds of assets of the enterprise or of the investor, such as property and property rights of various kinds, non-equity investment, including several types of loans and portfolio transactions, as well as other contractual rights, including sometimes rights created by administrative action of a host State (licenses, permits, etc.). Such a definition is found, for instance, in the World Bank-sponsored Convention Establishing the Multilateral Investment Guarantee Agency and in BITs.

The rationale for these differing approaches is evident. Capital movement-oriented instruments address investment before it is made, whether with a view towards its control, as was the case in past decades, or with a view towards removing obstacles to its realization, in the current context of liberalization. The resources invested may be of several kinds -- funds, technology or other elements of the package that constitutes an investment. The policy context, and therefore the legal treatment, of each type of resource may differ from that of the others.

Protection-oriented instruments, on the other hand, seek to safeguard the interests of the investors (or, in broader context, to promote foreign investment by safeguarding the investors' interests). Investment is seen as something that already exists (or that will exist, by the time protection becomes necessary). The older terminology, which referred to "acquired rights" or to "foreign property" (see the 1967 OECD Draft Convention on the Protection of Foreign Property) makes the context clear. The exact character of the particular assets is not by itself important in this case, since protection is to be extended to assets after their acquisition by the investor, when they form part of the investor's patrimony.

Recent practice in international investment agreements that seek both to liberalize investment regulations and to protect foreign investment seems to move in the direction of broad definitions. The most common approach is to define "investment" so as to include certain assets (ICSID, 1998). In many cases, the definition is a broad one that includes all assets in the territory of one party owned by investors of another party. Some investment agreements limit the definition in various ways. They may exclude from the definition, for example, assets that were established prior to a certain date or that are in certain sectors of the economy. Another approach, exemplified by United States BITs is to limit the definition of investment to "every kind of investment owned or controlled directly or indirectly by [a] national or company" followed by an illustrative list of investments based on assets (UNCTAD, 1996a, vol. III, p. 196). A further variation is exemplified by the definition considered under the negotiations for a Multilateral Agreement on Investment (MAI) (OECD, 1998a). This was in terms of assets but at the same time it was recognised that there was a need for an interpretative note to clarify that "in order to qualify as an investment under the MAI, an asset must have the characteristics of an investment, such as the commitment of capital or other resources, the expectation of gain or profit, or the assumption of risk". These examples show that investment may need to be defined in terms that go beyond a range of assets though, as will be shown below, some agreements do just that.

One can make few, if any, generalizations about the circumstances under which any of the various limitations will be utilized. There are no consistent patterns, and the limitations do not necessarily appear in standard combinations. An investment agreement may contain a single limitation or multiple limitations in different combinations. Thus, while there is a fairly standard broad definition of "investment", there is not a typical narrow definition.

There are several reasons for the absence of consistent patterns in the way that the definition of "investment" is limited. As already noted, some agreements do not define the term, and where the parties seek to limit the scope of the agreement, they may seek to do so through its operative provisions, rather than the provisions on definitions. Further, individual countries may have special concerns that cause them to include limitations on the scope of an agreement that reflect their unique situation.

Nevertheless, investment policies differ among countries, and these differences are reflected in significant variations in the definitions of "investment" found in investment agreements. This section surveys those variations. It begins with the broad definition and then describes some of the ways in which this definition has been narrowed in specific instruments. Finally, it discusses some of the instances in which investment agreements have adopted an approach different from that found in typical investment promotion and protection agreements.

1. The broad asset-based definitions of investment

Many investment promotion and protection agreements concluded in recent years contain a broad definition of investment. A typical broad definition is that used in article 1(3) of the ASEAN Agreement for the Promotion and Protection of Investments[8] (box 2). This definition indicates the breadth of the term "investment" as used in many such texts. It states, initially, that investment includes "every kind of asset", suggesting that the term embraces everything of economic value, virtually without limitation.

Box 2. Example of a broad definition of investment

"The term 'investment' shall mean every kind of asset and in particular shall include though not exclusively:

a) movable and immovable property and any other property rights such as mortgages, liens and pledges;
b) shares, stocks and debentures of companies or interests in the property of such companies;
c) claims to money or to any performance under contract having a financial value;
d) intellectual property rights and goodwill;
e) business concessions conferred by law or under contract, including concessions to search for, cultivate, extract or exploit natural resources."

Source: ASEAN Agreement for the Promotion and Protection of Investments, article 1(3), from UNCTAD, 1996a, volume II, p. 294.

The general definition is followed by an illustrative list of five categories of investment. These five categories are expressly included within the definition of "investment", but the listing is not exhaustive. Accordingly, assets of "every kind" are included, even if they do not fall under the five categories. These categories are typical of those that appear in investment agreements with broad definitions of "investment":

- The first category comprises *movable and immovable property*. Thus, the definition explicitly includes merchandise and other tangible property of the sort that was protected by customary international law centuries ago. The reference to immovable property makes clear that land is included as well. Moreover, "investment" includes legal interests in property that are less than full ownership. This is indicated by the reference to "property rights such as mortgages, liens and pledges".
- The second category comprises various types of *interests in companies*. The language does not require that the investor's interest or participation in the company be a controlling one and, as the explicit reference to debentures shows, it covers debt as well as equity investment. The language in other words is broad enough to include portfolio as well as direct investment. Debt investment may include bonds issued by public agencies. This may occur, for example, if an investment agreement defines "company" to include public entities. Or, an agreement may explicitly include such bonds directly in the definition of "investment". For example, the Treaty Establishing the Common Market for Eastern and Southern Africa, in article 159.2 (c), defines "investment" to include "stocks, bonds, debentures, guarantees or other financial instruments of a company or a firm, government or other public authority or international organisation".
- The third category includes *claims to money and claims under a contract having a financial value*. This category suggests that "investment" includes not only property rights, but contractual rights as well. Thus, it provides an explicit textual basis for concluding that "investment" may embrace contractual rights for the performance of services, such as, for example, management agreements, contracts for accounting or other professional services, turnkey contracts, and insurance policies. Further, the language does not seem to require that the contracts be long-term contracts. As written, it does not appear to distinguish between transactions that might be regarded as trade in services and those that might be regarded as investment in services. The inclusion of contractual rights in the definition of "investment" raises a number of questions. The performance of a contract in a host country by a foreign entity may involve the creation of an investment and, as such, would be a natural element of a definition of investment. However, it is not so clear whether even in a broad definition of investment all contracts would be included, or a distinction needs to be made between a contract that constitutes trade (e.g., contracts for the sale of goods or services) and those in which an investor has allocated significant financial, technical and/or human resources (Canada, 1998).
- The fourth category comprises *intellectual property rights*. Such rights may include trademarks, trade secrets, patents and copyrights. In some investment agreements[9] the reference to intellectual property explicitly includes "technical processes" and "know-how", which suggests that investment can include at least some forms of valuable information that are not legally protected as traditional forms of intellectual property. This category also includes goodwill, an indication that the protected assets of a company may include not only its tangible property, but its reputation as well.
- The fifth category is *business concessions, including natural resource concessions*. This category suggests that investment may sometimes include privileges or rights granted to private parties by the government through special adminstrative or legislative action, in addition to more traditional forms of property that are generally acquired through transfer among private parties in accordance with property laws of general application. Indeed, the Energy Charter Treaty, in article 1 (6) (f), defines "investment" to include "any right conferred by law or contract or by virtue of any licenses and permits granted pursuant to law to undertake any Economic Activity in the Energy Sector".

These five categories are common to many investment agreements, although there are numerous variations in the precise language used to describe them. Such variations, however, may be of relatively small importance because the five categories are merely illustrative of the types of interests included within the term "investment". An interest that does not fall within any of the five categories is nevertheless an "investment" if it can be considered an "asset".

Nothing in this broad definition of investment requires that the asset be a monetary one. Some investment treaties state explicitly that it need not be. For example, article 15.3 of the Convention Establishing the Inter-Arab Investment Guarantee Corporation states that "[i]n appraising the eligibility of an investment for the purpose of insurance no distinction shall be made on account of the monetary or non-monetary form of the transaction".

The third category of investment (claims to money and to contract performance) in combination with the first (movable and immovable property) and the fourth (intellectual property rights) suggests that the definition of "investment" used in many investment agreements is quite different from the concept of "capital", as used by economists. Capital is commonly regarded as productive capacity. Yet, the first category indicates that investment may include mere inventory, i.e. finished products stored in a warehouse awaiting sale to consumers. The third category suggests that it may also include short-term services agreements that ordinarily would be considered current transactions. The fourth category indicates that investment includes technology assets, which economists often distinguish from capital and the other factors of production, land and labour.

Thus, the term "investment" as used in investment agreements is a legal term of art. It is given a certain scope in order to accomplish the economic and political purposes of the treaty parties. It is not necessarily synonymous with the word "investment" as used in other contexts, such as in national income accounting, or with other, related economic terms, such as "capital".

Finally, another approach to a broad definition is to define "investment" so as to include assets generally, without the lengthy enumeration of specific assets. For example, article 1.4 of the Agreement on Promotion, Protection and Guarantee of Investments Among Member States of the Organisation of the Islamic Conference defines "capital" as "[a]ll assets (including everything that can be evaluated in monetary terms) owned by a contracting party to this Agreement or by its nationals, whether a natural person or a corporate body and present in the territories of another contracting party whether these were transferred to or earned in it, and whether these be movable, immovable, in cash, in kind, tangible as well as everything pertaining to these capitals and investments by way of rights or claims and shall include the net profits accruing from such assets and the undivided shares and intangible rights". Like the broad definition discussed above, this definition also encompasses "all assets", but the illustrative listing of assets is not nearly as detailed.

One other question is whether the term "investment" covers *reinvestment*, that is to say, the investment of the proceeds of the initial investment. Those proceeds have presumably been earned in the host country and have not been imported from abroad, as may have been the initial capital (or part of it). To the extent that national or international rules on foreign investment seek to encourage the importation of foreign capital, in whatever form, the reinvestment of earnings may be seen from the host country's point of view as not qualifying. On the other hand, foreign investors, in making investment decisions, will take into account a host country's policies regarding treatment of all their assets and are likely to prefer that they be treated in the same manner, whether purchased initially by imported capital or financed through subsequent reinvestment.

Many BITs provide that reinvestment is covered to the same extent as the original investment. For example, article I (a) of the 1991 United Kingdom model BIT provides that "[a] change in the form in which assets are invested does not affect their character as investments ...". Because this language indicates that reinvestment is covered as "investments" it would seem that any limitations imposed on the scope of covered investment would also apply to reinvestment and that, if investment were covered only if made in accordance with host country law, then reinvestment similarly would be covered only on that condition as well.

To address such concerns, however, some investment treaties state explicitly that reinvestment is covered only if established in accordance with the conditions placed on the initial investment. For example, article 2 of the BIT between the Belgium-Luxembourg Economic Union and Cyprus provides that "[a]ny alteration of the form in which assets are invested shall not affect their classification as investment, provided that such alteration is not contrary to the approval, if any, granted in respect of the assets originally invested".

Reinvestment also may be eligible for benefits conferred by an investment treaty. For example, the Convention Establishing the Inter-Arab Investment Guarantee Corporation provides, in article 15.3, that "[r]einvestment of earnings accrued out a previous investment shall also be eligible for insurance".

2. Narrowing the asset-based definition

In view of the potential breadth of the term "investment", many investment agreements include various limitations on the scope of investment covered. This subsection analyses the more important among the many variations.

a. Limitation to permitted investment under host country laws

Certain investment agreements contain a specification that investment is covered only if made in accordance with the laws of the host country. For example, the model BIT used by the People's Republic of China, in article 1.1, provides that "[t]he term 'investment' means every kind of asset invested by investors of one Contracting Party in accordance with the laws and regulations of the other Contracting Party in the territory of the Latter ...". In agreements that apply this limitation, investment that was not established in accordance with the host country's laws and regulations would not fall within the definition of "investment" as used in the agreement.

An alternative approach is to include a separate provision stating that an agreement shall apply only to investment made in accordance with the laws and regulations of the host country or previously approved by host state officials. Thus, article II(1) of the ASEAN Agreement for the Promotion and Protection of Investments provides that "[t]his Agreement shall apply only to investments brought into, derived from or directly connected with investments brought into the territory of any Contracting Party by nationals or companies of any other Contracting Party and which are specifically approved in writing and registered by the host country and upon such conditions as it deems fit for the purposes of this Agreement".

Such a limitation in an investment agreement obviously is intended to induce foreign investors to ensure that all local laws and regulations are satisfied in the course of establishing an investment by denying treaty coverage to non-compliant investment. This will have the additional effect of ensuring that both foreign and domestic investors are required to observe the laws of the land, thereby ensuring a "level playing field". Moreover, on the assumption that the host country's investment laws will be written and applied to further its development policy, this limitation also is intended to ensure that investment is covered only if it is consistent with the host country's development policy, and other policies, such as immigration or internal security that impact on investment.

Some investment agreements that require that investment be established in accordance with host country law include a provision stating that investments are included within the definition of "investment" if later approved by the host country's government. For example, article 9 of the Egypt-Germany BIT provides that "[t]he present Agreement shall also apply to investments by nationals or companies of either Contracting Party, made prior to the entering into force of this Agreement and accepted in accordance with the respective prevailing legislation of either Contracting Party".

Particular attention to this feature of investments, whether strictly in terms of definitions or otherwise, is paid by agreements providing investment insurance or guarantees. For example, article 15.6 of the Convention Establishing the Inter-Arab Investment Guarantee Corporation provides that "[t]he conclusion of insurance contracts shall be subject to the condition that the investor shall have obtained the prior approval of the competent official authority in the host country for the making of the investment and for its insurance with the Corporation against the risks to be covered." And the Convention Establishing the Multilateral Investment Guarantee Agency, in Article 12 (d) on eligible investments, provides that "In guaranteeing an investment, the Agency shall satisfy itself as to: ... (ii) compliance of the investment with the host country's laws and regulations; (iii) consistency of the investment with the declared development objectives and priorities of the host country".

b. Limitations on time of establishment

A second limitation on the definition of "investment" is to exclude investment established prior to a certain date, such as the date on which an agreement is signed or enters into force. For example, article 9 of the Germany-Sri Lanka BIT provides that "[t]he present Treaty shall apply to all investments made on or after November 8, 1963, by nationals or companies of either Contracting Party in the territory of the other Contracting Party consistent with the latter's legislation".

Developing countries sometimes seek to exclude investment established prior to entry into force of an investment protection agreement. Mainly in cases where an agreement offers financial advantages, one theory is that covering such investment constitutes a windfall for the investor who established the investment without any promise or expectation of treaty coverage; some investment agreements may therefore exclude pre-existing investments from financial benefits made available by them.[10] Another reason for the reluctance to cover investments established prior to the entry into force of an agreement is legal certainty. This argument is especially used in situations in which a new agreement supersedes older treaty obligations, potentially giving an investor the right to choose between different international regimes; some investment agreements therefore cover all investments but exclude claims from arbitration if the events leading to these claims occurred before the entry into force of the agreement. On the other hand, exclusion of pre-existing investment creates the possibility that existing investors will oppose ratification of an agreement by their home State because it provides them no benefits and it may place them at a competitive disadvantage relative to investors who establish investments after entry into force of the agreement. More generally, excluding preexisting investment may undermine the credibility of a host country's promise to provide a favourable investment climate by implying that the host country is not committed to such a climate as a matter of principle.

Most bilateral investment agreements do not specifically exclude pre-existing investment. Some of them even state explicitly that they do apply to existing investment. For example, article 6 of the BIT between Estonia and Switzerland provides that "[t]he present Agreement shall also apply to investments in the territory of a Contracting Party made in accordance with its laws and regulations by investors of the other Contracting Party prior to the entry into force of this Agreement".

A few investment agreements exclude investment established prior to some other date, such as the date on which the host country's foreign investment law entered into force. For example, article 2 (3) of the BIT between Indonesia and the United Kingdom provides that "[t]he rights and obligations of both Contracting Parties with respect to investments made before 10 January 1967 shall be in no way affected by the provisions of this Agreement". This provision presumably was to exclude investment established prior to the entry into force of Indonesia's Foreign Capital Investment Law No. 1 of 1967.

c. Limitations on the nature of the investment

A third limitation is to exclude certain types of investment. Some investment agreements, for example, specify that they apply to foreign direct, as opposed to portfolio, investment. Thus, the BIT between Denmark and Poland provides, in article 1 (1) (b), that the term "investment" shall refer "to all investments in companies made for the purpose of establishing lasting economic relations between the investor and the company and giving the investor the possibility of exercising significant influence on the management of the company concerned." This limitation may be included in an agreement intended to facilitate international investment flows where the host country is seeking to attract foreign direct, but not necessarily foreign portfolio, investment or where a host country is concerned about the possible detrimental effects of applying treaty provisions to certain types of investment, such as portfolio investment.

In this context, other definitions of direct investment which do not appear in legally binding agreements need to be mentioned. Thus, the International Monetary Fund defines direct investment as reflecting "the objective of obtaining a lasting interest by a resident entity in one economy in an enterprise resident in another economy...[t]he lasting interest implies the existence of a long-term relationship between the direct investor and the enterprise and a significant degree of influence by the investor on the management of the enterprise" (IMF, 1993, p. 86); while the OECD benchmark definition "recommends that a direct investment enterprise be defined as an incorporated or unincorporated enterprise in which a foreign investor owns 10 per cent or more of the ordinary shares or voting power of an incorporated enterprise or the equivalent of an unincorporated enterprise" (OECD, 1996a, p. 8).

Alternatively, an investment agreement may include portfolio investment, but only if it is long term. In such a definition, the degree of influence the investor has over the investment may not be relevant, but the duration of the investment could be. For example, article 15 of the Convention Establishing the Inter-Arab Investment Guarantee Corporation defines the investments eligible for insurance by the corporation. It states

> "1. [i]nvestments eligible for insurance shall comprise all investments between the contracting countries whether they are direct investments (including enterprises and their branches or agencies, ownership of a part of capital and ownership of real estate) or portfolio investments (including ownership of shares, stocks and bonds). Eligible investments also comprise loans for a term exceeding three years as well as such shorter term loans as the Council may in exceptional cases decide to treat as eligible for insurance. 2. In identifying investments for the purpose of the preceding paragraph, the Corporation shall be assisted by the guidelines issued by the International Monetary Fund on the Definition of long term assets and liabilities in the context of the preparation of balance of payment statistics."

While short-term investments are not necessarily excluded, this definition indicates a clear preference for long-term investments, though it should be noted that this arises in the context of an investment guarantee agreement.

The North American Free Trade Agreement (NAFTA) includes portfolio investment in its definition of "investment", but excludes debt securities of, or loans to, a State enterprise. The NAFTA also seeks to exclude ordinary commercial contracts (box 3).

The exclusion of certain types of investment may be found in agreements that regulate, as well as in those that facilitate, international investment. A host country may be concerned that foreign controlled companies will operate in ways that are inconsistent with domestic policy. These concerns are minimized, however, where the foreign investor does not control the company, as in the case of portfolio investment. Thus, because host country concerns may focus on the problem of foreign control, an agreement regulating foreign investment often will be directed primarily at FDI.

Box 3. Scope of investment under NAFTA

"Investment means:

(a) an enterprise;
(b) an equity security of an enterprise;
(c) a debt security of an enterprise
  (i) where the enterprise is an affiliate of the investor, or
  (ii) where the original maturity of the debt security is at least three years, but does not include a debt security, regardless of original maturity, of a state enterprise;
(d) a loan to an enterprise
  (i) where the enterprise is an affiliate of the investor, or
  (ii) where the original maturity of the loan is at least three years, but does not include a loan, regardless of original maturity, to a state enterprise;
(e) an interest in an enterprise that entitles the owner to share in income or profits of the enterprise;
(f) an interest in an enterprise that entitles the owner to share in the assets of that enterprise on dissolution, other than a debt security or a loan excluded from subparagraph (c) or (d);
(g) real estate or other property, tangible or intangible, acquired in the expectation or used for the purpose of economic benefit or other business purposes; and
(h) interests arising from the commitment of capital or other resources in the territory of a Party to economic activity in such territory, such as under
  (i) contracts involving the presence of an investor's property in the territory of the Party, including turnkey or construction contracts, or concessions, or
  (ii) contracts where remuneration depends substantially on the production, revenues or profits of an enterprise;

but investment does not mean,

(i) claims to money that arise solely from
  (i) commercial contracts for the sale of goods or services by a national or enterprise in the territory of a Party to an enterprise in the territory of another Party, or
  (ii) the extension of credit in connection with a commercial transaction, such as trade financing, other than a loan covered by subparagraph (d); or
(j) any other claims to money, that do not involve the kinds of interests set out in subparagraphs (a) through (h);"

Source: NAFTA, article 1139(h), from UNCTAD, 1996a, volume II, pp. 93-94.

d. Limitation on the size of investments

A fourth limitation is to exclude investments based on their size. For example, article 15 of the Community Investment Code of the Economic Community of the Great Lakes Countries states that, for purposes of inclusion within certain provisions of the code, "[t]he minimum volume of investments is set at one million United States dollars or the equivalent". Such a limitation may be found in agreements seeking to promote foreign investment, where the parties are unwilling to provide certain benefits to foreign investment unless the investment is of such a magnitude that it will be likely to bring significant benefits to the host country. Many countries, however, seek foreign investment from small and medium-sized companies and thus limitations on the size of investment are not common in investment agreements.

e. Limitations on the sector of the economy

Finally, the term "investment" may be limited to investment only in certain sectors of the economy. For example, article 1 of the Energy Charter Treaty provides that "'investment' refers to any investment associated with an Economic Activity in the Energy Sector and to investments or classes of investments designated by a Contracting Party in its Area as "Charter efficiency projects" and so notified to the Secretariat". In this particular case, the agreement was intended to cover only the energy sector and all its provisions were limited to that sector. It cannot be excluded, however, that, particularly in an agreement that liberalizes or promotes international investment flows, a host country may wish to limit treaty coverage to investment in certain sectors of the economy. Such an approach is illustrated by the General Agreement on Trade in Services (GATS). Rather than narrowing the definition of investment it uses, the GATS, by Article XVI, allows signatory states to "opt-in" to sectoral commitments to the extent desired by the State concerned.

3. Other approaches: enterprise-based and transaction-based definitions

As the foregoing discussion indicates, a common approach is an "asset-based definition approach": a broad definition of investment that includes all assets, followed by an enumeration of specific assets covered. Some investment agreements then carve out exceptions.

One alternative approach is to focus on the "business enterprise" or the "controlling interests in a business enterprise". The Canada-United States Free Trade Agreement is an example.[11] The Agreement defines investment as including the establishment or acquisition of a business enterprise, as well as a share in a business enterprise which provides the investor control over the enterprise (Canada – United States, 1988). This type of definition is sometimes referred to as an "enterprise-based" definition. However, distinguishing it from the "asset-based" definition is not without difficulties.

While most asset-based definitions are usually broader than the enterprise-based definition because they include assets other than companies and the enterprise-based definition does not, a number of examples in this chapter indicate that some narrower asset-based definitions make the two approaches very similar. Two examples illustrate the difficulty in making the distinction. First, the broad, asset-based definition usually includes "companies", and it is not clear that a company is really different from a business. The term "business" is perhaps narrower than "companies" because it would seem limited to commercial enterprises. But as will be noted in the discussion of the definition of an "investor", some treaties with asset-based definitions of investment define companies to include only those established for a commercial purpose. Second, the Canada-United States agreement seems to limit investment to enterprises that are direct investment and thus excludes portfolio investment. But again, as has already been pointed out, the asset-based definition can also be narrowed, and sometimes is, by excluding various types of assets such as portfolio investment.

Another alternative to the asset-based approach is to omit the reference to assets generally and to include instead an enumeration of the transactions covered. An example of such a "transaction based" definition of investment is contained in the OECD Code of Liberalisation of Capital Movements. While the Code does not define the term "investment" or "capital" as such, it does contain in Annex A lists of capital movements to be liberalized. The list is quite lengthy and includes a wide variety of capital movements. Among those included is direct investment (box 1).

The transaction-based definition is conceptually different from the asset-based definition in some respects. The OECD Code by its nature applies to transactions, not assets. Because the Code has only one principal purpose --the liberalization of capital movements --its approach to investment necessarily considers only the transaction of establishing or liquidating an investment, not the protection of assets. This is where the important point of distinction between asset and transaction based definitions emerges. That point is that the definitions of investment should depend upon the purpose of an agreement and that, if the purpose is to liberalize investment, a country may want a different definition than if the purpose is to protect investment.

B. Investor

Investment agreements apply typically only to investment by investors who qualify for coverage. The definition of the term "investor" is thus as important in determining the scope of an agreement as that of "investment".

1. Entities considered investors

The definition of "investor" normally includes natural persons and artificial or legal persons (or juridical entities). As noted earlier, with respect to natural persons, the only issue that arises is that of determining the relevant link between the investor and the home State party to an agreement. Legal entities, by contrast, can be defined to include or exclude a number of different types of entity. Generally speaking, legal entities may be excluded because of their legal form, their purpose or their ownership.

a. Exclusions based on legal form

The exclusion of entities based on their legal form is rare. The model BIT used by the Swiss Confederation, for example, provides in article I (1) (b) that the term "investor" refers to "legal entities, including companies, corporations, business associations and other organisations ...". This language indicates that all legal entities, regardless of form, may be considered investors. Thus, the term "investors" may include, for example, partnerships as well as corporations.

Differences in the legal form of an entity, however, may be important to a host country in a variety of circumstances. The form of the entity determines, for example, which assets may be reached by creditors of the entity to satisfy debts and perhaps the extent to which the entity can be sued in its own name in the courts.

In many cases, of course, it is the investment and not the investor that is present in the host country, since the term "investment" includes the company or other entity created when the investor's capital is invested. Local businesses often have contracts with the investment, not the investor; damage to local property or to the environment is more likely to be the result of activity by the investment than by the investor. As this suggests, the legal form of the investment may be of much greater importance to the host country than the legal form of the investor. If the investment has limited liability, for example, then it may not matter what the investor does since creditors may have no recourse against the investor.

At the same time, the host country could find that restricting the legal form of the investors may have an adverse impact on its ability to attract certain types of investment. For example, small or medium-sized investors are often organized differently from large investors, making greater use of forms of business associations other than the corporation or *société anonyme*. And, certain types of investments are likely to be associated with certain types of investors. For example, professional service agreements often are associated with partnerships. Thus, a decision to discourage certain forms of investors ultimately may have the effect of discouraging certain types of investment. Perhaps for all these reasons, the term "investor" usually includes all legal entities, regardless of their form.

b. Exclusions based on purpose

Entities may be excluded because of their purpose. For example, an investment agreement may exclude non-commercial entities, such as educational, charitable or other entities not operated for profit. This is illustrated by article 13 (a) (iii) of the Convention Establishing the Multilateral Investment Guarantee Agency, which defines an eligible investor to include only those juridical entities that "operate[s] on a commercial basis".

In many cases, the State parties to an investment agreement may want to include non-profit entities in the definition of "investor". For example, the 1991 model BIT used by the Federal Republic of Germany, in article 1.4 (a), defines "companies" in respect of Germany to include "any juridical person as well as any commercial or other company or association with or without legal personality . . . irrespective of whether or not its activities are directed at profit". As an initial matter, the kinds of activities in which a nonprofit entity engages may produce desirable forms of investment, such as a research facility. Further, non-profit entities often acquire portfolio investment in commercial enterprises in order to earn revenue to support their charitable or educational activities. In that capacity, non-profit entities are likely to act in the same way as any other portfolio investor and their distinct status as non-profit entities would seem of little significance.

c. Exclusions based on ownership

Legal entities also may be excluded from the definition of "investor" because they are State-owned rather than private.[12] Some investment agreements, of course, make clear that State entities are included. Article 1.4 of the Unified Agreement for the Investment of Arab Capital in the Arab States, for example, provides that "Arab States and bodies corporate which are fully State-owned, whether directly or indirectly, shall likewise be regarded as Arab citizens". Similarly, article 13 (a) (iii) of the Convention Establishing the Multilateral Investment Guarantee Agency defines eligible investors to include a juridical person "whether or not it is privately owned...".

2. Establishing the link

a. Natural persons

Natural and artificial persons are considered "investors" within the meaning of an agreement only if they have the nationality of a particular State, generally another treaty partner or, in a number of cases, if they are linked to that State in another manner, such through permanent residence, domicile or residence. Under customary international law, a State may not be required to recognize the nationality of a person unless the person has a genuine link with the State of asserted nationality.[13] Most investment agreements do not require such a link, at least in the case of natural persons.

Rather, the common practice in investment agreements (as in more general international practice) is that a natural person possesses the nationality of a State if the law of that State so provides. For example, article I (1) of the ASEAN Agreement for the Promotion and Protection of Investments provides that "[t]he term 'nationals' shall be as defined in the respective Constitutions and laws of each of the Contracting Parties". This language clearly does not require that there be a genuine link between the person and the state of asserted nationality.

As noted certain investment agreements require some link beyond nationality. For example, the Germany-Israel BIT provides, in article 1 (3) (b), that the term "nationals" means, with respect to Israel, "Israeli nationals being permanent residents of the State of Israel". On the other hand, a concept like permanent residence can be used not only in addition to a nationality link but also as an alternative. The latter may be especially in the interest of high immigration countries in which a considerable proportion of the economically active population may not yet be full citizens. Such countries (e.g., Australia, Canada and the United States) regularly extend a special legal status to permanent residents. Other investment agreements allow a natural person to claim, for the purposes of the agreement, the nationality of a country or some other basis, such as residency or domicile in that country. For example, article 3.1 of the Treaty Establishing the Caribbean Community (CARICOM) Agreement on the Harmonisation of Fiscal Incentives to Industry defines "national" to mean "a person who is a citizen of any Member State and includes a person who has a connection with such a State of a kind which entitles him to be regarded as belonging to or, if it be so expressed, as being a native or resident of the State for the purpose of such laws thereof relating to immigration as are for the time being, in force". One question not explicitly addressed by most investment agreements is whether a natural person is a covered investor if he or she possesses the nationality of both the home and the host countries which are parties to the agreement. This issue is likely to arise in particular in an investment agreement that provides for the protection of foreign investment.

Under customary international law, a State could exercise diplomatic protection on behalf of one of its nationals with respect to a claim against another State, even if its national also possessed the nationality of the other State, provided that the dominant and effective nationality of the person was of the State exercising diplomatic protection.[14] This test, however, typically is not found in existing investment agreements, which, as noted, tend to be silent on the matter of dual nationality. One exception is the Convention Establishing the Multilateral Investment Guarantee Agency, article 13 (b), which provides that "[i]n case the investor has more than one nationality [...], the nationality of a member shall prevail over the nationality of a non-member and the nationality of the host country shall prevail over the nationality of any other member".

Article 17.3 of the Convention Establishing the Inter-Arab Investment Guarantee Corporation has similar language, but states even more explicitly in article 17.1 that "[i]n no event shall the investor be a natural person who is a national of the host country or a juridical person whose main seat is located in such country if its stocks and shares are substantially owned by this country or its nationals". Another agreement addressing dual nationality is the Unified Agreement for the Investment of Arab Capital in the Arab States, article 1.7 of which defines an "Arab investor" as "an Arab citizen who owns Arab capital which he invests in the territory of a State Party of which he is not a national".

The literal language of many agreements requires that the host country protect investment owned by nationals of the other party, and nothing explicitly states that this obligation lapses where the investors happen also to be nationals of the host country. A host country may argue that limitations on the rights of dual nationals are implied, but a country that does not wish to extend treaty coverage to investment owned by dual nationals would be well advised to insert explicit language to that effect in the agreement.

b. Legal entities

In the case of legal entities, most investment agreements use one of three different criteria for determining nationality: the country of *organization*, the country of the *seat* or the country of *ownership or control*. In many cases, they use some combination of these criteria. Other criteria are occasionally used as well.

An example of an agreement using the place of organization as the criterion of nationality is the Energy Charter Treaty, which in article 1 (7) (a) (ii) defines "investor" with respect to a Contracting Party to include "a company or other organization organized in accordance with the law applicable in that Contracting Party". The use of country of organization is consistent with the decision of the International Court of Justice in *Barcelona Traction* (ICJ, 1970).[15]

The advantage of using the country-of-organization test is ease of application, as there usually will not be any doubt concerning the country under whose law a company is organized. Further, the country-of-organization is not easily changed, meaning that the nationality of the investor usually will be permanent under this approach. Because an important purpose of some investment agreements is to attract investment by providing a stable investment regime and because changes in the nationality of an investor will result in the loss of treaty protection for investment owned by the investor, a definition of "investor" that stabilizes the nationality of the investor and thus the protection afforded to investment is particularly consistent with the purposes of investment agreements that seek to promote or protect foreign investment.

The disadvantage of using country-of-organization is that this test relies on a relatively insignificant link between the investor and the country of nationality. Under this test, a company may claim the nationality of a particular country even though no nationals of that country participate in the ownership or management of the company and even though the company engages in no activity in that country. In effect, the company could claim the benefits of nationality of a particular country, including protection under the treaties of that country, despite the fact that it conferred no economic benefit of any kind on that country.

This should perhaps be of concern principally to the home country, which finds itself protecting an investor that brings it no economic benefit. It may also be of concern to the host country, however. The effect of this test may be that the host country is extending protection to investment ultimately owned by persons who live in a country that extends no reciprocal benefits to the host country's own investors. Indeed, the country of ownership or control may not even have normal economic relations with the host country. For this reason, the model BIT used by the United States, which also uses country-of-organization as the test of nationality, permits the host country to refuse to extend treaty protection to investment owned by investors of the other party if the investors do not have substantial business activities in the territory of the other party or if the country of ultimate control does not have normal economic relations with the host country. For example, article XII of the April 1994 model treaty provides that:

> "Each Party reserves the right to deny to a company of the other Party the benefits of this Treaty if nationals of a third country own or control the company and
> (a) the denying Party does not maintain normal economic relations with the third country; or
> (b) the company has no substantial business activities in the territory of the Party under whose laws it is constituted or organized."

An example of a treaty using the company seat as the basis for attributing nationality is the 1991 German model BIT. That treaty defines "company" in article 1.4(a) to include in respect of Germany "any juridical person as well as any commercial or other company or association with or without legal personality having its seat in the territory of the Federal Republic of Germany ...".

The seat of a company may not be as easy to determine as the country of organization, but it does reflect a more significant economic relationship between the company and the country of nationality. Generally speaking, "seat of a company" connotes the place where effective management takes place. The seat is also likely to be relatively permanent as well.

The country-of-ownership or control may be the most difficult to ascertain and the least permanent, particularly in the case of companies whose stock is traded on major stock exchanges. Its principal benefit as a test is that it links coverage by an agreement with a genuine economic link. Perhaps for these reasons, the ownership or control test sometimes is used in conjunction with one of the other tests. Combining the criteria in this way lends a degree of certainty and permanence to the test of nationality, while also ensuring that treaty coverage and economic benefit are linked. For example, the Asian-African Legal Consultative Committee's (AALCC) model BIT includes the following definition of 'companies': "corporations, partnerships or associations incorporated, constituted or registered in a Contracting Party in accordance with its laws [and includes such entites in which nationals of a Contracting Party have substantial interest and majority shareholding]".[16] Including the bracketed language combines the country-of-organization text with the country-of-ownership or control. The United States model language previously quoted combines the country of organization as the criterion for nationality with that of ownership by allowing the host country in any specific case to deny treaty protection to an entity if the country of ownership test is not also met.

Alternatively, the ownership or control criterion may be used in conjunction with the country of the seat criterion. For example, article 17.1 of the Convention Establishing the Inter-Arab Investment Guarantee Corporation provides that "[t]o be accepted as a party to an insurance contract, the investor must either be a natural person, who is a national of a contracting country, or a juridical person whose stocks or shares are substantially owned by one or more of the contracting countries or by their nationals, and whose main seat is located in one of the countries". It should be noted that the Convention authorizes waiver of the company seat requirement for a juridical entity that is at least 50 per cent owned by nationals of the contracting countries.

Just as the ownership or control criterion may be used in conjunction with the country-of-organization or the country of the seat criterion, the latter two criteria may be used in conjunction with each other. For example, article I (2) of the ASEAN Agreement for the Promotion and Protection of Investments provides that "[t]he term "company" of a Contracting Party shall mean a corporation, partnership or other business association, incorporated or constituted under the laws in force in the territory of any Contracting Party wherein the place of effective management is situated".

Similarly, article 35.6 (a) of the Treaty Establishing the Caribbean Community provides that "a person shall be regarded as a national of a

Member State if such person [...] is a company or other legal person constituted in the Member State in conformity with the laws thereof and which that State regards as belonging to it, provided that such company or other legal person has been formed for gainful purposes and has its registered office and central administration, and carries on substantial activity, within the Common Market." Under this language, a legal entity must be organized under the laws of a country and have its seat in the territory of that country to be considered a national of that country.

The Convention Establishing the Multilateral Investment Guarantee Agency also combines the country-of-organization test with the country-of-the-seat test, but allows the use of the country-of-ownership test as an alternative. Article 13 (a) (ii) provides that a legal entity is an eligible investor under the agency's insurance programme provided that "such juridical person is incorporated and has its principal place of business in a member or the majority of its capital is owned by a member or members or nationals thereof, provided that such member is not the host country in any of the above cases".

The Charter on a Regime of Multinational Industrial Enterprises (MIES) in the Preferential Trade Area for Eastern and Southern African States requires that all three tests be met. Article 1 defines a "national" in pertinent part as "any legal person established under the laws of a Member State having its head office or seat in that Member State and having at least fifty one (51) per cent of its equity held by nationals or agencies of the government of that Member State ....".

As these various provisions have shown, although country-of-organization, country of the seat and country-of-ownership are the most common criteria, other criteria are occasionally used.

The Treaty Establishing the Caribbean Community, for example, requires that the legal entity carry on "substantial activity" in the country of nationality. The United States model BIT, although requiring only that a legal entity be organized in the country of nationality, allows the host country to deny treaty protection if the country of ownership is one with which the host country does not maintain normal economic relations.

Finally, it should be noted that a significant number of internationally active enterprises can be excluded from the scope of an investment agreement through the cumulative use of the various above-mentioned criteria. This is a matter of greater importance to bilateral rather than multilateral agreements, because the latter tend to allow for a "cumulation of nationality" among countries party to the agreement.

C. Own or control

One other issue that arises in determining the scope of an investment agreement is the nature of the relationship that must exist between an investment and the investor for the investment to be covered. Typically, investment agreements apply to investment "of" or "by" a covered investor. The obvious inference is that the investment must be owned or controlled by the investor.

Only a few investment agreements define the terms "own" or "control". A relevant definition is found in the GATS (box 4). This definition attempts to describe ownership or control in quantitative terms, such as 50 per cent of the equity interest or the ability to name a majority of directors. Where ownership or control is described in quantitative terms, it is typical to require at least 50 per cent ownership or majority control.

Box 4. GATS definition of control

The GATS defines a juridical person as follows:

"(n) a juridical person is:
(i) "owned" by persons of a Member if more than 50 per cent of the equity interest in it is beneficially owned by persons of that Member;
(ii) "controlled" by persons of a Member if such persons have the power to name a majority of its directors or otherwise to legally direct its actions;
(iii) "affiliated" with another person when it controls, or is controlled by, that other person; or when it and the other person are both controlled by the same person..."

Source: GATS, Article XXVIII(n), from UNCTAD, 1996a, volume I, pp. 309-310.

A similar approach is taken in the Agreement for the Establishment of a Regime for CARICOM Enterprises. Article 1.1 defines a "regionally-owned and controlled" company as one in which nationals of at least two member States "exercise management and control by beneficially owning shares carrying between them directly or indirectly:

(a) the right to exercise more than one-half of the voting power in that company; and

(b) the right to receive more than one-half of any dividends that might be paid by that company; and

(c) the right to receive more than one-half of any capital distribution in the event of the winding-up or of a reduction in share capital of that company; ...".

Article 6.1 of the proposed Statute for a European Company defines a "controlled undertaking" as any undertaking in which a natural or legal person:

"(a) has a majority of the shareholders' or members' voting rights; or

(b) has the right to appoint or remove a majority of the members of the administrative, management or supervisory board, and is at the same time a shareholder in, or member of, that undertaking; or

(c) is a shareholder or member and alone controls, pursuant to an agreement entered into with other shareholders or members of the undertaking, a majority of the shareholders' or members' voting rights."

An alternative approach is to describe ownership or control in *qualitative* terms. For example, the Protocol to the Egypt-United States BIT defines "control" as having "a substantial share of ownership rights and the ability to exercise decisive influence". Similar is the draft United Nations Code of Conduct on Transnational Corporations, which speaks of "significant influence".

Definitions of ownership or control in qualitative terms generally do not require majority or any specific quantum of ownership. This approach reflects the fact that effective control of a company often is exercised by shareholders who own less than half of the stock. By lowering the requirement to less than majority ownership, a treaty makes it easier for an investor to have the necessary relationship with an investment to bring the investment within the coverage of the treaty and thus broadens the scope of the treaty. Indeed, the International Monetary Fund, for the purpose of defining FDI, uses a lower threshold, namely, one that "owns 10 per cent or more of the ordinary shares or voting power (for an incorporated enterprise) or the equivalent (for an unincorporated enterprise)" (IMF, 1993, p. 86). Similarly, the OECD provides that "[a]n effective voice in the management, as evidenced by an ownership of at least 10 per cent, implies that the direct investor is able to influence or participate in the management of an enterprise; it does not require absolute control by the foreign investor" (OECD, 1996b, p. 8).

A specific problem that may arise is whether a company indirectly owned or controlled by another comes within the scope of an agreement. For example, where company "A" has a controlling interest in company "B" that has a controlling interest in company "C", does that make company "C" an investment controlled by company "A" as well as company "B"? This has particular repercussions where not every country in which the companies operate is a party to an agreement. Thus, to return to the example, should company "B" have the nationality of a country not party to the agreement, while companies "A" and "C" have the nationality of countries party to the agreement, can company "A" still claim the protection of the agreement despite the fact that its investment in "C" is channelled through "B", i.e. through a non-party? This is an issue that each agreement must address, especially given the proliferation of integrated international production systems established by TNCs.

D. Other terms

1. Territory

Investment generally is covered by an investment agreement only if it is in the territory of one of the State parties to the agreement. Some investment agreements define the term "territory". The most common definition is typified by article 1 (3) of the Chilean model BIT, which provides that "'territory' means in respect of each Contracting Party the territory under its sovereignty, including the exclusive economic zone and the continental shelf where that Contracting Party exercises, in conformity with international law, sovereign rights or jurisdiction."

The Energy Charter Treaty provides a similar, although lengthier, definition in Article 1, para. (10):

"'Area' means with respect to a state that is a Contracting Party:

(a) the territory under its sovereignty, it being understood that territory includes land, internal waters and the territorial sea; and

(b) subject to and in accordance with the international law of the sea: the sea, sea-bed and its subsoil with regard to which that Contracting Party exercises sovereign rights and jurisdiction."

As is evident, the purpose of the definition of "territory" generally is not to describe the land territory of the parties, but to indicate that "territory" includes maritime zones over which the host country exercises jurisdiction. The significance is that investments located within the host country's maritime jurisdiction, such as mineral exploration or extraction facilities, would be covered by the agreement.

Even where it is completely clear which geographical areas constitute the territory of a party, there may still be uncertainty concerning whether an investment is located in the territory of a party. Because "investment" includes many intangible rights, the location of a particular asset may be difficult to identify. For example, a service provider in one country may sign an agreement with a company headquartered in a second country to perform professional services for a branch of the company in a third country. The definition of "investment" may well include the rights derived from that contract, but it may be unclear which of the three countries should be considered the location of the "investment" of contractual rights. The texts of investment agreements, however, provide little assistance in resolving issues concerning the location of investments.

2. Transnational corporation or multinational enterprise

In some investment instruments, the object of the rights and duties created is not an individual investment, but a group of affiliated entities referred to collectively as a "transnational corporation" (TNC) or a "multinational enterprise" (Muchlinski, 1999, ch. 1, 3). Typically, the affiliation among these entities involves ownership or direction of some entities by another (box 5).

Box 5. Definitions of transnational corporations and enterprises

A. The draft United Nations Code of Conduct on Transnational Corporations (para. 1) has defined "transnational corporations" to mean:

> "an enterprise, comprising entities in two or more countries, regardless of the legal form and fields of activities of these entities, which operates under a system of decision-making, permitting coherent policies and a common strategy through one or more decision-making centres, in which the entities are so linked, by ownership or otherwise, that one or more of them may be able to exercise a significant influence over the activities of others, and, in particular, to share knowledge, resources and responsibilities with the others" (UNCTAD, 1996, volume I, p. 162).

B. The Set of Multilaterally Agreed Equitable Principles and Rules for the Control of Restrictive Business Practices adopted by the United Nations General Assembly on 5 December 1980 provides that the term "enterprises" means:

> "firms, partnerships, corporations, companies, other associations, natural or juridical persons, or any combination thereof, irrespective of the mode of creation or control or ownership, private or State, which are engaged in commercial activities, and includes their branches, subsidiaries, affiliates, or other entities directly or indirectly controlled by them" (UNCTAD, 1996, volume I, p. 136).

C. The OECD Guidelines for Multinational Enterprises (para. 8) describe a multinational enterprise as:

> "These usually comprise companies or other entities whose ownership is private, state or mixed, established in different countries and so linked that one or more of them may be able to exercise a significant influence over the activities of others and, in particular, to share knowledge and resources with others. The degrees of autonomy of each entity in relation to the others varies widely from one multinational enterprise to another, depending on the nature of the links between such entities and the fields of activity concerned" (UNCTAD, 1996a, volume II, p. 186).

Definitions of "transnational corporation", "multinational enterprise", or like terms generally must address two issues: the types of entity that may be included; and the nature of the affiliation that must exist among the entities. As the three definitions in box 5 demonstrate, the tendency is to include a wide range of entities. The focus of the definition thus is on the nature of the affiliation that must exist among the entities, which, as noted above, typically is one of interfirm ownership or control. Indeed, it is the fact of several entities controlled in a coordinated fashion by another foreign entity that gives rise to the special concerns that instruments using these definitions are intended to address. Such instruments are often regulatory and multilateral in nature and they seek, through coordination among governments of different

States, to obtain a measure of control over enterprises that involve coordinated entities in the territories of different States.

Because the affiliation is typically one of ownership or control, the definition of these terms becomes of considerable importance for understanding the definitions of "transnational corporation" or "multinational enterprise". The terms "own" or "control" are of importance in other contexts as well. They typically characterize the relationship that must exist between an investment in one country and an investor of another country for the investment to fall within an investment agreement. The definition of these terms is discussed in the next subsection.

Before the discussion proceeds to the definition of "own" or "control", however, the concept of the TNC or multinational enterprise as used here must be distinguished from two related, but different, concepts. The first is the concept of a regional enterprise. A regional enterprise, in broad generic terms, is an entity that generally is owned or controlled by two or more persons that possess the nationality of countries in the region. Several investment agreements confer special privileges such as tax concessions on such regional enterprises, generally as part of a strategy of promoting regional economic integration. For example, the Charter on a Regime of Multinational Industrial Enterprises (MIEs) in the Preferential Trade Area for Eastern and Southern African States provides for the designation of companies as MIEs if they meet several conditions, including capital contributions from nationals of two or more member states accounting for at least 51 per cent of the capital. MIEs enjoy a number of benefits, including access to foreign currency, tax concessions and infrastructural support.

TNCs often have been perceived as presenting a challenge to the sovereignty of the host country, while the regional enterprise generally is perceived as presenting an opportunity for regional development. Thus, while TNCs are typically the subject of a regulatory investment instrument, the regional enterprise is typically the subject of an investment promotion agreement.

The second concept from which the notion of a TNC as used here must be distinguished is that of a strategic alliance (Dunning and Narula, 1996, pp. 16-18). This concept refers to firms of different nationalities that operate in a coordinated fashion, but without ties of ownership or control among them. Firms that are not linked by common ownership or control may form strategic alliances for a number of reasons, such as to gain access to markets or to create reliable forward and backward linkages. Investment agreements generally do not address strategic alliances as a distinct phenonemon, except perhaps insofar as they may raise issues of competition policy (UNCTAD, 1995, 1997).

3. Returns

Many investment agreements include definitions of the term "returns", that is to say, essentially the earnings from an investment. While returns are typically included in provisions dealing with the transfer of funds, whether "returns" are or are not covered by an agreement makes considerable difference in terms of the extent of the guarantee of free transfer of funds accorded the investor, of the protection against expropriation or other action, or of their coverage for the purpose of the settlement of investment disputes.

The elements of the term "returns" often mirror the elements of the term "investment". "Investment" includes shares in a company, and thus "returns" includes dividends. Because "investment" includes debt, "returns" includes interest payments. Because "investment" includes intellectual property, "returns" includes royalties. And because "investment" includes contracts, such as professional or management service agreements, "returns" includes fees.

E. Summary

To summarize, the principal models of clauses identified in this section are as follows:

Regarding investment

1. A broad, inclusive definition which may simply include every kind of asset and/or contain an illustrative list of categories of investment based on types of asset.
2. A similar model but where the illustrative list is based on types of transaction.
3. A narrow definition which may either:
   - contain a broad definition of investment and then narrow its scope through various limitations; or which
   - has no general definition of investment, but rather specifies the classes of

investment, whether by asset or transaction that are covered by the agreement.

Regarding investor

1. This will normally include
   - natural persons, defined by an effective link, usually that of nationality, with a State contracting party to the agreement
   - legal persons possessing such an effective link with a State contracting party.
2. Certain exclusions may be introduced into the agreement based on either
   - legal form of the entity
   - the purpose of the entity
   - the nature of ownership.
3. The crucial drafting issue is to determine which links are to count as effective links for the purpose of the agreement.

Regarding ownership and control

1. Some agreements may introduce a clause defining the control of an investment by an investor.
2. This will usually involve a reference to a prescribed level of ownership from which control can be surmised and/or a definition of functional control. These concepts are derived from widely used general principles of company law.

Other terms

1. The investment must be on the "territory" of a contracting party, though some treaties refer to an "area" as in regional agreements.
2. Some investment agreements refer to "transnational corporations" or "multinational enterprises" as the relevant entity for the purposes of defining the subject-matter of the agreement.
3. Some agreements extend their coverage to reinvestment and returns from investment.

Section III
Interaction with other Issues and Concepts

Definitions are of great significance to the operation of the provisions of an investment agreement. Such provisions may address a broad array of issues (table 1). This section highlights the issues for which the terms "investment" and "investor" may be of special significance, and it describes the implications of particular definitions of "investment" and "investor" for these issues. The discussion here, however, is not meant to suggest that additional issues are not or should not be included in an investment agreement.

As an initial matter, the breadth of the definition raises a number of potential concerns entirely apart from developmental considerations. For example, the inclusion of contractual claims within the meaning of "investment" could convert government regulatory action affecting the validity of private contracts into an expropriation. The inclusion of trade-related transactions within the meaning of "investment" could result in the submission of a broad range of matters to the special investor-to-state dispute settlement mechanisms created by investment agreements. In short, the interaction of a broad definition of "investment" within the operative provisions of an agreement could result in the application of treaty rules and procedures to a great range of transactions unrelated to FDI.

Table 1. Interaction across issues and concepts

	Concepts in this chapter	
Issue	Investment	Investor
Admission and establishment	++	+
Competition	+	+
Dispute settlement (investor-State)	++	++
Dispute settlement (State-State)	+	+
Employment	+	0
Environment	0	0
Fair and equitable treatment	++	++
Home country measures	+	+
Host country operational measures	+	+
Illicit payments	0	0
Incentives	++	++
Investment-related trade measures	0	0
Most-favoured-nation treatment	++	++
National treatment	++	++
Social responsibility	0	0
State contracts	+	+
Taking of property	++	0
Taxation	0	0
Transfer of funds	++	+
Transfer of technology	+	0
Transfer pricing	0	0
Transparency	0	0

Source: UNCTAD.
Key: 0 = negligible or no interaction.
+ = moderate interaction.
++= extensive interaction.

Further, as investment agreements move beyond the traditional concerns of investment promotion and protection agreements, the broad definition of "investment" could raise other issues. For example, the inclusion of competition policy within the coverage of an investment agreement would require careful consideration of how the competition rules interact with a definition of investment that includes exclusive, potentially anticompetitive rights, such as intellectual property rights and concessions.

This is not to say, however, that broad definitions coupled with broad substantive provisions are necessarily problematic. Ultimately, the scope of the agreement is established by the interaction between all its provisions. In order to achieve a specific policy goal, parties to an agreement can choose, for example, between:

(i) narrowing a definition; or
(ii) narrowing one or more substantive provisions; or
(iii) allowing general and/or sectoral exceptions from treaty obligations; or
(iv) any combination of these approaches.

Thus not only narrow definitions or broad definitions, or narrow or wide substantive clauses, are the solutions available in determining the scope of the agreement. The choice is considerable in these matters.

Turning to interactions with other issues covered in these volumes:

- **Admission and establishment**. The term "investment" is important to provisions on admission and establishment of investment because it describes the types of activity by foreign investors that the host country must allow (to the extent required by the provision). Where "investment" includes all assets, this provision potentially opens the host country's economy to virtually every form of economic activity. For example, the typical broad definition of "investment" combined with an unqualified right of establishment would grant to foreign investors in principle the right to acquire land and mineral resource rights and form companies or other legal entities to engage in every kind of activity, commercial or otherwise, in which such entities may engage. Further, inclusion of contract rights within the meaning of "investment" would suggest that the right to establish investment might include the right of covered investors (typically entities from the home country) to enter into contracts which generate property interests or assets in the territory of the host country.

  Host country concerns about admission of foreign investment in many cases are industry specific, i.e. the host country may not want foreign investment in some activities of the economy, while not objecting to it in others. To the extent that objections to foreign investment in particular activities are expected to endure over the long term, the host country could qualify the definition of "investment" to include only assets in certain industries or activities of the economy. For example, the Energy Charter Treaty is an agreement applicable only to the energy sector while the GATS only applies to services. Similarly, article III.1 of the BIT between the Belgium-Luxembourg Economic Union and Egypt provides that "[t]he term 'investments' shall comprise every direct or indirect contribution of capital and any other kinds of assets, invested or reinvested in enterprises in the field of agriculture, industry, mining, forestry, communications and tourism."

- **Incentives.** Many investment agreements contain a commitment on the part of the host country to encourage inward foreign investment. Often, because the obligation to permit the establishment of foreign investment is subject to local law, the commitment to promote inward investment places few, if any, specific commitments on the host country. The function of such a provision thus is to reflect the host country's policy of encouraging the establishment of foreign investment, even if the host country has reserved the right to prohibit foreign investment in particular cases.

  As has been noted,[17] some investment agreements promote foreign investment by affording special benefits to certain foreign investments, particularly those that are owned or controlled by regional investors. For example, article 4 of the Agreement on Promotion, Protection and Guarantee of Investments Among Member States of the Organization of the Islamic Conference provides that "[t]he contracting parties will endeavor to offer various incentives and facilities for attracting capital and encourage its investment in their territories such as commercial, customs, financial, tax and currency incentives, especially during the early years of the investment projects, in accordance with the laws, regulations and priorities of the host state".

The term "investment" in these agreements determines the range of entities entitled to special incentives.

- **National treatment and most-favoured-nation treatment**. Investment agreements commonly require the host country to provide investment by investors of the other party with treatment no less favourable than that afforded investment of the host country (national treatment) or investment of any third country (MFN treatment). These provisions are intended to eliminate discrimination among investments based on the nationality of the investor.

  The terms "investment" and "investor" obviously are important in that they describe those activities that are the beneficiary of the host country's obligation not to discriminate. The terms play a special role in the non-discrimination provisions, however, because they also determine the content of the obligation created by those provisions. The obligation is to treat covered investment as favourably as investment of host-country and third-country investors. Thus, the terms "investment" and "investor" establish the standard against which the treatment of covered investment is to be measured. For example, the term "investor" may include governmental entities. If so, then the national treatment provision may require that foreign private investment be treated as favourably as host-country public enterprises, not merely private enterprises, assuming that there is sufficient "likeness" of the circumstances of the enterprises concerned.

- **General treatment: "fair and equitable treatment" or "full protection and security".** Many investment agreements contain provisions that specify general standards of treatment that the host country must afford to foreign investment. Such provisions may require "fair and equitable treatment" or "full protection and security". The obligation to provide "full protection and security" requires the host country to exercise reasonable care to protect covered investment. Unlike most investment treaty provisions, this provision requires a host country to protect investment against injurious action by private parties as well as by the State. This provision originally found its principal application in situations involving damage to real or tangible personal property. Because destruction of private property is generally a criminal offence, the question presented by this provision involved the extent of the host country's duty to provide police or fire protection to prevent the damage or at least to apprehend the wrongdoers following commission of a crime. As the term "investment" has expanded to include a broader variety of intangible forms of property, the range of protection that an investor may argue is required by the obligation of full protection and security has potentially expanded. For example, where "investment" includes intellectual property, an investor may contend that the obligation to exercise reasonable care to protect intellectual property against private infringement may require making available some form of remedy against those who infringe copyrights or patents.

- **Taking of property.** Many investment agreements impose restrictions on the right of the host country to expropriate investment, including in particular an obligation to pay compensation for expropriated investment. The term "investment" indicates the types of interests for which a host country must pay compensation in the event of an expropriation. This is important for two reasons.

  First, the interest must be defined before there can be a determination whether the interest has been expropriated. As has been noted, many investment agreements define "investment" to include partial or fragmentary interests. Thus, an expropriation may occur even though the investor had only a partial interest in the asset, as long as the investor's interest has been taken or substantially impaired. For example, the holder of mineral rights in land may claim that a prohibition on mineral exploration constitutes an expropriation of the mineral rights because the investor's entire investment has been rendered worthless. In short, the same act may or may not constitute an expropriation, depending upon how the investment is defined.

Second, the definition of "investment" determines the elements of the expropriated entity that are compensable. For example, many investment agreements define "investment" broadly enough to include debt as well as equity interests. Thus, expropriation of a company could give rise to an obligation to compensate not only the owners of the company, but its creditors as well. Similarly, where the definition of "investment" includes concessions or administrative permits and licenses, action to abrogate such administrative acts may constitute compensable expropriation.

- **Funds transfer.** Many investment agreements guarantee to investors covered the right to free transfer of payments related to an investment. Thus, the term "investor" is of special importance in indicating the identity of those who are entitled to access to foreign currency. The term "investment" indicates the range of activities for which investors may obtain convertible currency. For example, if "investment" includes insurance policies, then the currency-transfer provision in many investment agreements would grant to the owner of the investment, i.e., the insurance company, the right to obtain foreign currency for purposes of repatriating the insurance premiums paid by the insured entity in the host country.

  Some investment agreements list the payments that are covered. For example, the model BITs prepared by the AALCC provide for transfer of the investment and "returns", with the latter term defined in article 1(e) to include "profits, interests, capital gains, dividends, royalties or fees".

  As this indicates, as a general matter, the broader the term "investment", the greater the host country's potential obligation to provide convertible currency. Of equal importance, however, is the breadth of the term "returns". Repatriation of the returns is a far more common occurrence than repatriation of the liquidated investment and thus on a day to day basis the obligation to permit free transfer of returns may impose a much greater burden on a host country with small foreign currency reserves than the obligation to permit free transfer of the investment itself.

- **Dispute settlement.** Investment agreements frequently include provisions on two different types of dispute-settlement mechanisms, namely, mechanisms and procedures for the settlement of disputes between the parties to the agreement and for the settlement of disputes between an investor and a host country.

  The former provision typically does not use the term "investment" or "investor". It usually provides for arbitration of disputes concerning the interpretation or application of the agreement. Thus, those two terms are usually of importance only to the latter type of provision. However, other relevant terms such as "national" can be of importance to State-to-State dispute-settlement provisions.

  The investor-to-State dispute-settlement provision typically provides for submission to binding, third-party arbitration of disputes "concerning an investment".[18] The term "investment" thus is critical to determining the jurisdiction of the arbitral tribunal. For example, to the extent that the term investment is defined broadly enough to include trade-related assets, the possibility exists that an investor-to-State arbitration provision could be invoked for trade disputes.

  Investment agreements usually provide that arbitration provisions may be invoked by the investor. Thus, the term "investor" or, in some agreements, the terms "national" and "company", are critical to determining who may invoke the investor-to-state arbitration provision.

  With respect to investors who are natural persons, the most important issue that arises is perhaps whether dual nationals may submit disputes with the host country to arbitration. As was noted above, many investment agreements ascribe to natural persons the nationality of either party if such persons are nationals under that party's law. Nothing precludes a person from having the nationality of both parties. Further, nothing in the typical investor-to-State dispute provision explicitly prohibits a national of one party, who happens also to be national of the other party, from submitting to arbitration a dispute with the other party. A State that wishes to preclude dual nationals from invoking the investor-to-State dispute provision should include clear language to that effect.

The issue of nationality also may be important with respect to investors that are legal entities. In the case of an investment agreement that uses the country-of-organization test for nationality, nationals of the host country may organize a company under the laws of a treaty partner and thereby create a legal entity that would have the legal capacity to submit an investment dispute with the host country to arbitration. In other words, the country-of-organization test creates the possibility that a host country will be involved in arbitration with an entity that is organized under the laws of another country, but wholly owned by host country nationals. The same possibility arises in the case of an investment treaty that ascribes nationality based on the country of the seat, although the possibility is somewhat more remote because the host country's nationals must establish a headquarters in the other country, a much more difficult task than merely forming a legal entity there. The possibility becomes even more remote where an investment agreement ascribes nationality based on the country-of-ownership. Even then, however, the possibility is not totally eliminated, because nationals of the host country could be minority stockholders in the company that is considered the investor. The fact that the controlling interest is held by nationals of the treaty partner would permit the company to submit a dispute with the host country to arbitration, but nationals of the host country still would be among the ultimate beneficiaries of an arbitral award.

Conclusion: Economic and Development Implications and Policy Options

The way in which the term "investment" is defined should be determined by the purpose of an investment agreement. As has been seen, investment agreements may have any combination of four purposes. First, they may protect investment, as in the case of a provision that provides for compensation for expropriation. Second, they may liberalize investment flows, as in the case of a provision that grants to an investor the right of establishment. Third, they may promote investment, as in the case of a provision that facilitates investment insurance. Or, fourth, they may regulate investment, as in the case of a provision that prohibits corrupt practices.

In section II, a number of model clauses for defining the terms "investor", "investment" and other related terms were considered. The most common trend is to have a broad, inclusive definition, which may or may not be subject to limitations. In the case of the term "investment" such a definition could be asset (or enterprise) or transaction based. In the case of the term "investor" the most important element is the link whereby the entity concerned is entitled to enjoy access to the subject-matter of an agreement. Usually, but not always, this is a link of nationality. Such a link could be especially complex in the context of a TNC with affiliates in many countries and a widespread, global, shareholding structure (UNCTAD, 1993, ch. VIII). Other links such as residence or control through ownership and/or functional capacity become significant.

A. Investment

- **Option 1: adopting a broad definition.** A broad and open-ended definition of "investment" has implications for the development policy of the State parties to an agreement. The developmental concern can be stated quite simply: treaty coverage of all assets included within the definition may not be consistent with a State's development policy at every period in the life of an agreement.

  The broad definition of "investment" can be flexible and open ended. There are at least two reasons for this approach. First, as a technical matter, it may be difficult to draft a more precise definition that would cover all the assets that parties wish to be covered by an agreement. Second, because the concept of investment has evolved over time and because many investment agreements are intended to endure for many years, those who draft them appear to seek, as a matter of policy, to utilize language that can extend an agreement to new forms of investment as they emerge, without renegotiation of the agreement. Both of these considerations are particularly important in agreements that are intended to facilitate international investment flows.

The broad, open-ended definition, at the same time, may be undesirable for countries that are concerned about certain effects of foreign investment. The danger of an open-ended definition is that it may commit a host country to permitting, promoting or protecting forms of investment that the host country did not contemplate at the time it entered into an agreement and would not have agreed to include within the scope of the agreement had the issue arisen explicitly. There are several ways to limit the scope of the definition, discussed below as options 2 to 4.

- **Option 2: adopting a narrower definition of investment.** The first alternative is to adopt a narrower definition of investment. As noted in section II, a number of agreements have done so, although there are advantages and disadvantages to any particular narrowing of the definition. Taking each type of narrower definition in turn, the following development implications may be envisaged:
  - A number of agreements exclude portfolio investment because it may be regarded as less desirable than FDI, given that it generally does not bring with it technology transfer, training or other benefits associated with FDI. Further, portfolio investment is easily withdrawn, thus creating the potential for capital volatility in the event of economic turbulence. In addition, portfolio investment is less easily monitored than direct investment, giving rise to concerns that it may be used as a mechanism for money laundering.

    On the other hand, inclusion of portfolio investment can make a positive contribution to development. It is a potential source of capital and foreign exchange. Some investors may not wish to control an investment or even have any kind of equity position in the investment. Further, given that one traditional concern about FDI was that it permitted domestic assets to fall under the control of foreign nationals, there may be sound reasons of national interest to encourage portfolio rather than direct investment in certain enterprises.
  - Some investment agreements exclude assets of less than a certain value, perhaps because these investments are considered too small to justify the costs of treaty coverage or perhaps because of a desire to reserve to domestic investors those parts of the economy in which small investments are likely to be made. However, the exclusion of small investments could discourage small and medium-sized investors that some developing countries may be seeking to attract, at least during certain stages of the development process (UNCTAD, 1998b). In such cases a size limitation may not be useful.
  - Other investment agreements exclude investments established prior to entry into force of an agreement, in order to avoid bestowing a windfall on the investor. Such an exclusion could be interpreted as calling into question the parties' commitment to investment promotion or protection and in exceptional cases could provide a permanent competitive advantage to investors who invest after the conclusion of the agreement.
  - Investment agreements may limit the parts of the economy to which the agreement applies. As noted in section II, this is the approach to definition taken by the Energy Charter Treaty. It can be envisaged that other sector-specific agreements could adopt a similar approach to definitional issues.

  The above analysis suggests that countries need to consider carefully the consequences of including or excluding certain types of investment in the definition of "investment". Critical considerations include the purpose(s) of the investment agreement and the precise nature of the operative provisions to which the definition is applied.
- **Option 3: adopting a broad definition subject to right to screen and conditional entry.** A second alternative is to adopt a broad definition of "investment", but reserve the right to screen or place conditions on the establishment of individual investments. In this way, the host country does not exclude any category of investment a priori, but can exclude any specific investment. This approach is adopted in many investment

agreements. It ensures that only those investments that have been approved by the host country are entitled to protection under the investment agreement. Moreover, such screening will usually include a review of the development implications of the investment. Consequently, approval of the investment signifies, in principle, conformity to the host country's development goals.

- **Option 4: adopting a broad definition with limiting substantive provisions.** A third alternative is to adopt a broad definition of investment, but limit the scope of the substantive provisions. For example, if the concern about portfolio investment is that it may be withdrawn quickly, an investment agreement might define "investment" to include portfolio investment, but the currency-transfers provision would apply to investment only if an investment has been established for some minimum period of time, such as one year. Such a limitation would be directed at the volatility of the investment, which may be one particular concern regarding portfolio investment. Similarly, if the concern is that the expropriation provision may lead to claims that ordinary regulatory action is expropriatory and requires compensation, the expropriation provision could be modified to exclude ordinary regulatory action.

  By addressing concerns generally in the operative provisions, this approach eliminates some of the burden on the investment screening agency to take account of every concern on a case-by-case basis. It also avoids the problem of an "all-or-nothing" approach. Thus, some investments may be admitted, but with only limited rights under an agreement.

  This approach places a heavy burden on the negotiators of an agreement to consider the potential ramifications of each type of investment and to incorporate language in the agreement during negotiations to protect the host country's ability to execute its development policy.

- **Option 5:** adopting a hybrid approach. One other option is to adopt a hybrid mixture of, for example, broad and narrow definitions or asset-based and transaction-based definitions in relation to the different purposes of an investment agreement. Thus, while some countries may wish to define "investment" to include not every kind of asset, but only the specific categories included in a list, those same countries may wish to define "investment" more broadly in an agreement that regulates foreign investment, such as an agreement on transfer pricing. Generally speaking also, the liberalization of investment flows is one of the aspects of investment agreements that has most concerned many developing countries. One option in this respect is to use a broad asset-based definition for the purpose of protecting investments, and a narrower asset-based or transaction-based definition for cross-border investment liberalization agreements.

B. Investor

The definitional options in this area are, perhaps, less difficult to describe. In essence, the central issue is the choice of links with one or more contracting parties whereby natural and legal persons become integrated into the scheme of an investment agreement.

Natural persons. Usually a nationality link is sufficient as long as the contracting party's internal law recognizes the individual to be a national. There do not appear to be significant development implications stemming from this matter. Where a natural person possesses dual or multiple nationality, then an effective link criterion could be inserted into the clause. Most bilateral treaties do not follow this option. On the other hand, the insertion of other connecting factors may ensure that an effective link can be proved on the facts. Examples include residence or domicile in the country of nationality. The main development implication of such a variation is to ensure that only persons with a significant involvement in the economy and society of the home country could claim the protection of an investment agreement in the host country. "Free-riding" on the basis of the nationality provisions of an agreement is minimized.

Legal persons. Two issues need to be addressed: first the range of legal persons covered and, secondly, the links between the legal person and a contracting party to an investment agreement. As to the first issue, one option is to have all legal persons covered. This gives maximum flexibility to investors as to the choice of the legal vehicle through which to invest in a host country. The development implications of such a "free choice of means" would centre on whether the regulatory objectives of internal law can be achieved regardless of the legal form that an investor adopts. That, in turn, depends on the nature and context of internal laws and regulations. The other option is to narrow the range of legal persons covered. This might be done where the host country has a strict regime as to the legal form that a foreign investment is permitted to take.

As to the second issue, a strict linkage based on nationality may be adopted. Such a linkage is very common in investment agreements but may be difficult to apply in practice, as was discussed in relation to the definition of "transnational corporation" or "multinational enterprise". Alternatively, a wider provision could concentrate not on the formal nationality of the legal person but its effective nationality as exemplified by the nationality of the controlling interest. Such a formulation would be favoured by investors, especially as it would ensure that foreign affiliates incorporated in a host country can benefit from an agreement. However, these may in any case be protected as "investments of the investor". As with natural persons, the major problem to be borne in mind is not to adopt a linkage provision that would permit legal persons from non-contracting states to benefit from the legal protection of the agreement on a "free rider" basis.

C. Summary

The development implications of a broad definition of "investment" in an investment agreement are substantial. Although developmental concerns can be addressed in part by narrowing the definition of "investment", that is not necessarily the only approach in every case. Depending upon the nature of the operative provisions of an agreement and the purpose(s) of the parties in concluding the agreement, these developmental concerns in particular cases may be addressed alternatively through reservations of the right to exclude investments or by limiting the applicability of specific operative provisions. It is important to remember in this context that the ultimate effect of an investment agreement results from the interaction of the definition provisions with the operative provisions. There should be sufficient flexibility in the definition to ensure the achievement of developmental objectives.

Notes

1 The term "agreement" generally denotes a binding international instrument. The term "treaty" usually has the same meaning, although in a somewhat more formal context. In what follows the two terms are used interchangeably. The term "instrument", on the other hand, covers all kinds of agreements as well as non-binding documents, such as declarations of principles or guidelines. A study of the definition of investment should take account of binding and non-binding instruments alike. After all, any international investment framework, in whatever exact form or at what level, is negotiated in the context of the entire body of existing and emerging norms of international investment law.
Unless otherwise noted, all instruments cited herein may be found in UNCTAD, 1996a. All bilateral investment treaties (BITs) between specific countries cited herein may be found in ICSID (1972 -) and on the UNCTAD website (at www.unctad.org/iia).

2 For a detailed analysis of the scope and definitions of international investment agreements, see UNCTAD, 1998a; Parra, 1995; UNCTC, 1990a; Sornarajah, 1994.

3 Many BITs provide that investment will be protected for some period of time, often 10 years, following termination of the treaty. This issue has also been addressed in some regional investment instruments.

4 See, e.g. Article 10, General Convention of Peace, Amity, Navigation and Commerce, United States-Colombia, 3 October 1824 (*United States Treaty Series*, No. 52).

5 The distinction between direct and portfolio investment is not a sharp one. In many companies, no one investor owns a majority of the stock, and effective control rests in the hands of an investor who owns a significant minority of the stock. Thus, a quantity of stock that would constitute portfolio investment in one corporation could constitute direct investment in another. In other words, there is no single quantum of investment that in every case accurately establishes the distinction between direct and portfolio investment. Accordingly, economists often adopt an admittedly arbitrary standard for distinguishing between direct and portfolio

investment. For example, ownership of corporate stock sometimes is considered direct investment if the investor owns 10 per cent or more of the outstanding stock.

6 Investment in companies also is often categorized as either debt or equity investment. A debt investment, which typically is in the form of a bond issued by the company, generally consists of a right to a monetary payment (interest) over some fixed period of time. Equity investment, which typically is in the form of stock in the company, includes a right not only to payment of a monetary return (dividend) for an indefinite period of time, but also a right to participate in the control of the company and a claim on the liquidation value of the company. Debt investment generally is considered portfolio investment, although the terms of the debt obligation may be so restrictive that they give the creditor a very substantial measure of control over the operation of the company. Equity investment may be direct or portfolio investment.

7 See, e.g., Petroleum Development Limited v. Sheikh of Abu Dhabi (ILR, 1951); Sapphire International Petroleum Limited v. National Iranian Oil Company (ILR, 1967); Ruler of Qatar v. International Marine Oil Company Limited (ILR, 1953); Saudi Arabia v. Arabian American Oil Company (ARAMCO) (ILR, 1963).

8 Formerly known as An Agreement Among the Governments of Brunei Darussalam, the Republic of Indonesia, Malaysia, the Republic of the Philippines, the Republic of Singapore and the Kingdom of Thailand for the Promotion and Protection of Investments. The agreement was amended in 1996 and its name changed (see http://www.asean.or.id/economic/agrfin96.htm).

9 See, e.g. the United Kingdom 1991 model BIT, article I (a) (iv).

10 For example, article 15.4 of the Convention Establishing the Inter-Arab Investment Guarantee Corporation provides that investment insurance "shall not be made available except for new transactions commencing after the conclusion of insurance contracts with the exception of operations for which the Corporation has agreed to issue re-insurance".

11 The Canada-United States Agreement is no longer of much importance because of the subsequent entry into force of the NAFTA -- an asset-based definition treaty.

12 The question whether State-owned or controlled enterprises are covered by an investment agreement has to be treated differently from the question whether States parties to the agreement themselves can act as investors. Usually, State enterprises are covered even if not explicitly stated while States themselves tend not to be unless this is expressly provided for.

13 See, e.g. Nottebohm Case (Liechtenstein v. Guatemala), (ICJ, 1955).

14 See, e.g. Esphahanian v. Bank Tejarat, *Iran-U.S. Claims Tribunal Reports* (1983).

15 In that case, Belgium sought to exercise diplomatic protection on behalf of a company, the majority of the stock in which was owned by Belgians, but which was organized, under the law of Canada. The International Court of Justice held that only Canada, the State of the company's nationality, could bring suit for compensation for the injury suffered by the company.

16 The brackets appear in the original AALCC text.

17 See the discussion above of regional enterprises.

18 See, e.g. article 8 (1) of the June 1991 United Kingdom model BIT.

Chapter 4. Admission and Establishment*

Executive summary

This chapter analyses the legal and policy options surrounding the admission and establishment of foreign direct investment (FDI) by transnational corporations (TNCs) into host countries. This topic raises questions that are central to international investment agreements in general. In particular, the degree of control or openness that a host country might adopt in relation to the admission of FDI is a central issue. The purpose of this chapter is to describe and assess the kinds of policy options that have emerged from the process of FDI growth and host country responses thereto in national laws and, more importantly, in bilateral, regional, plurilateral and multilateral investment agreements.

A discussion of the inter-relationship between the issue of admission and establishment and other concepts covered in this series shows that the extent to which rights of entry and establishment are accorded to investors in an agreement is affected particularly by such matters as: the definition of investment; the relationship between rights of entry and establishment and the nature of post-entry treatment; the transparency of regulatory controls; exceptions and derogations to treaty-based rights of entry and establishment; dispute settlement as it relates to host country rights to control entry and establishment; and investment incentives as an aspect of entry and establishment decisions.

The economic and development implications of different policy options depend on a number of variables concerning the nature and location advantages of a host country, the motives for, and nature of, the foreign investment a host country attracts, and the bargaining relationship between a particular investor and the host country. The mix of such variables in a given situation is likely to shape the approach that policy makers take when formulating and implementing policies regarding admission and establishment.

Introduction

States have traditionally reserved to themselves absolute rights, recognised in international law, to control the admission and establishment of aliens, including foreign investors, on their territory. However, in today's world economy, the issue of more open policies regarding the entry and establishment of foreign investors is receiving increased attention. This may be based on a variety of concepts and standards, including adapted and evolved versions of non-discrimination standards commonly met in international trade treaties, notably national treatment (NT) and most-favoured-nation treatment (MFN).

However, while there is some pressure on States to liberalize conditions of entry and establishment for foreign investment, actual practice has moved in a variety of directions. At the national level, while policies offering greater market access are on the increase, national laws reveal continuing State control and discretion over entry and establishment, even in more "open-door" economies. At the international level, although market access provisions in investment agreements are common, they do *not* uniformly display provisions that offer foreign investors completely unrestricted or full rights of entry and establishment.

Country approaches to entry and establishment may be seen as falling into five major categories or models:

- the "investment control" model, which preserves full State control over entry and establishment;
- the "selective liberalization" model, which offers limited rights of entry and establishment, i.e. only in industries that are included in a "positive list" by the agreement of the contracting States;
- the "regional industrialization programme" model, which offers full rights of entry and establishment based on national treatment for

---

* The chapter is based on a 1999 manuscript prepared by Peter T. Muchlinski. The final version reflects comments received from Padma Mallampally.

investors from member countries of a regional economic integration organisation only for the purposes of furthering such a programme;

- the "mutual national treatment" model, which offers full rights of entry and establishment based on national treatment for all natural and legal persons engaged in cross-border business activity from member countries of a regional economic integration organization;
- the "combined national treatment/most-favoured-nation treatment" (NT/MFN) model, which offers full rights of entry and establishment based on the better of NT or MFN, subject only to reserved "negative" lists of industries to which such rights do not apply.

In practice, the first model is most widely used, albeit in a wide variety of forms, while the last model is increasingly favoured by States seeking to establish a liberal regime for entry and establishment in an international framework for investment.

The models suggest the following policy options:

- **Option 1:** To accept complete State discretion through the investment control model, thereby preserving the general power to screen proposed investments.
- **Option 2:** To liberalize cautiously through the adoption of the selective liberalization model, opening up one or more industries at a time.
- **Option 3:** To follow the regional industrial programme model and encourage the establishment of regional multinational enterprises, thereby setting up a supranational form of business organization aimed at encouraging intraregional economic development.
- **Option 4:** To grant full liberalization of entry and establishment on the basis of mutual national treatment, thereby allowing such rights to exist between States that see a common interest in regional integration, but which are not necessarily committed to full multilateral liberalization.
- **Option 5:** To follow the full NT/MFN model and open up entry and establishment for investors from the contracting States on the basis of the better of these two standards, subject only to a "negative list" of reserved activities, industries or applicable policies. The existence of a negative list of excepted industries emphasizes that certain strategic industries may be beyond the reach of liberalization measures.
- **Option 6:** To follow a mix of models bearing in mind that some of the options appear to be incompatible or difficult to combine. The economic effect of these hybrid options would be to offer more specialized alternatives that may be more compatible with the mix of location advantages enjoyed by particular host countries.

All of these options focus narrowly on the question of admission and establishment; they do not address the extent to which States subsequently pursue policies aimed at, for instance, increasing the benefits associated with FDI and minimizing any negative effects.

Section I
Explanation of the Issue

The issue underlying this chapter is best introduced by making reference to the State's sovereign right, under customary international law, to control the entry and establishment of aliens within its territory.[1] Such entry is a matter of domestic jurisdiction arising out of the State's exclusive control over its territory (Brownlie, 1998, p. 522). Accordingly, a host State has a very wide margin of discretion when deciding on whether and under what conditions to permit the entry of foreign investors (Wallace, 1983, pp. 84-85).[2]

The regulation of entry and establishment of TNCs has taken the form of controls or restrictions over the admission and establishment of foreign investors including the acquisition of interests in local businesses (box 1), and limitations on foreign ownership and control (box 2). Such measures may consist of absolute restrictions or limits on foreign presence, or may involve discretionary authorization, registration and reporting requirements (UNCTAD, 1996b, pp. 174-177). Measures short of exclusion may also affect the conditions of entry for foreign investors. Examples include performance requirements such as local content rules, technology transfer requirements, local employment quotas, or export requirements. Equally, incentive regimes materially affect the conditions under which an investment is made (UNCTAD, 1996b, pp. 178-181). The effects of the various measures have been considered in detail in a number of recent studies (UNCTC and UNCTAD, 1991; Shihata, 1994; Muchlinski, 1999; UNCTAD, 1996c), and some of them are the subject of separate chapters in these volumes.

Box 1. Measures relating to admission and establishment

1. Controls over access to the host country economy

- Absolute ban on all forms of FDI (e.g. controls in some former centrally-planned economies prior to the transition process).
- Closing certain sectors, industries or activities to FDI for economic, strategic or other public policy reasons.
- Quantitative restrictions on the number of foreign companies admitted in specific sectors, industries or activities for economic, strategic or other public policy reasons.
- Investment must take a certain legal form (e.g. incorporation in accordance with local company law requirements).
- Compulsory joint ventures either with State participation or with local private investors.
- General screening/authorization of all investment proposals; screening of designated industries or activities; screening based on foreign ownership and control limits in local companies.
- Restrictions on certain forms of entry (e.g. mergers and acquisitions may not be allowed, or must meet certain additional requirements).
- Investment not allowed in certain zones or regions within a country.
- Admission to privatization bids restricted, or conditional on additional guarantees, for foreign investors.
- Exchange control requirements.

2. Conditional entry into the host country economy

General conditions:

- Conditional entry upon investment meeting certain development or other criteria (e.g. environmental responsibility; benefit to national economy) based on outcome of screening evaluation procedures.
- Investors required to comply with requirements related to national security, policy, customs, public morals as conditions of entry.

Conditions based on capital requirements:

- Minimum capital requirements.
- Subsequent additional investment or reinvestment requirements.
- Restrictions on import of capital goods needed to set up investment (e.g. machinery, software) possibly combined with local sourcing requirements.
- Investors required to deposit certain guarantees (e.g. for financial institutions).

Other conditions:

- Special requirements for non-equity forms of investment (e.g. BOT agreements, licensing of foreign technology).
- Investors to obtain licences required by activity or industry specific regulations.
- Admission fees (taxes) and incorporation fees (taxes).
- Other performance requirements (e.g . local content rules, employment quotas, export requirements).

Sources: UNCTAD, 1996b, p. 176; Muchlinski, 1995, ch. 6.

Box 2. Measures relating to ownership and control

1. Controls over ownership

- Restrictions on foreign ownership (e.g. no more than 50 per cent foreign-owned capital allowed).
- Mandatory transfers of ownership to local firms usually over a period of time (fade-out requirements).
- Nationality restrictions on the ownership of the company or shares thereof.

2. Controls based on limitation of shareholder powers

- Restrictions on the type of shares or bonds held by foreign investors (e.g. shares with non-voting rights).
- Restrictions on the free transfer of shares or other proprietary rights over the company held by foreign investors (e.g. shares cannot be transferred without permission).
- Restrictions on foreign shareholders rights (e.g. on payment of dividends, reimbursement of capital upon liquidation, on voting rights, denial of information disclosure on certain aspects of the running of the investment).

3. Controls based on governmental intervention in the running of the investment

- Government reserves the right to appoint one or more members of the board of directors.
- Restrictions on the nationality of directors, or limitations on the number of expatriates in top managerial positions.
- Government reserves the right to veto certain decisions, or requires that important board decisions be unanimous.
- "Golden" shares to be held by the host Government allowing it, for example, to intervene if the foreign investor captures more than a certain percentage of the investment.
- Government must be consulted before adopting certain decisions.

4. Other types of restriction

- Management restrictions on foreign-controlled monopolies or upon privatization of public companies.
- Restrictions on land or immovable property ownership and transfers thereof.
- Restrictions on industrial or intellectual property ownership or insufficient ownership protection.
- Restrictions on the use of long-term (five years or more) foreign loans (e.g. bonds).

Source: UNCTAD, 1996b, p. 177.

A few words of explanation regarding the measures listed in boxes 1 and 2 are appropriate here:

- The measures listed vary in the degree of restriction involved. The most restrictive policies involve prohibitions on foreign investment, either in the economy as a whole -- a practice not currently followed -- or in certain activities or industries, a practice widely used even in the most "open-door" economies to protect strategic industries from foreign domination. By contrast, limiting the percentage of foreign shareholding in local companies and/or the requirement to form a joint venture with a local partner would not prohibit FDI in the sector concerned, but would place limits on its participation in that activity.

- The use by host countries of screening procedures suggests the desirability of FDI but the scrutiny of individual projects ensures their economic and social utility to the host country. This approach may result in the stipulation of performance or other requirements (to the extent permitted under international agreements) deemed necessary to ensure such utility. Hence it is useful to distinguish between prohibitions and restrictions over entry itself and the conditions that may be placed on entry that is in principle permissible.
- Specialized regulatory regimes may be developed to meet the characteristics of particular types of FDI, leading to specific conditions being set according to the activity or industry involved, or to the development of new forms of FDI such as the build-operate-transfer (BOT) system.
- Even in an open-door environment, host countries may wish to maintain a certain control over the investor or the investment. Hence, various techniques for the supervision of FDI have been developed, including limits on foreign shareholding with reserved shares or special voting rights for the host Government or local private investors to ensure local control over important management decisions, registration requirements and disclosure and reporting rules. These powers are not normally incompatible with rights of entry and establishment, but co-exist with such rights.

The underlying rationale for granting rights of establishment for foreign investors is to allow the efficient allocation of productive resources across countries through the operation of market forces by avoiding policy-induced barriers to the international flow of investment. In this sense it can be said that rights of establishment attempt to avoid discriminating between foreign and domestic investors and/or investors from different home countries.

In contrast, host countries have sought to control the entry and establishment of foreign investors as a means of preserving national economic policy goals, national security, public health and safety, public morals and serving other important issues of public policy (Dunning, 1993, ch. 20; Muchlinski, 1995, ch. 6). Such controls represent an expression of sovereignty and of economic self-determination, whereby Governments judge FDI in the light of the developmental priorities of their countries rather than on the basis of the perceived interests of foreign investors.

The State's right to control entry and establishment may be contrasted with increasing pressures for market access and rights of establishment arising out of the process of globalization. Given the absolute nature of the State's right to control the entry and establishment of aliens, there is no compulsion in law upon a prospective host State to grant such rights to foreign investors. On the other hand, countries that seek to encourage FDI may restrict their wide area of discretion both through unilateral liberalization of entry and establishment conditions in national laws and through international agreements, by the inclusion of a clause embodying rights of entry and establishment for foreign investors.

At the outset it should be stressed that these rights are treaty-based rights and not rights based in customary international law. Indeed, they operate as exceptions to the general customary law principle that recognizes the right of States to admit or exclude aliens from the territory of the State. Examples of such provisions will be analysed in section II below, where it will be shown that such provisions may vary widely in the extent to which they offer rights of admission and establishment, emphasizing the State's continuing control over the granting of such rights.

Prior to that it is necessary to explain some conceptual issues inherent in rights of admission and establishment (UNCTC, 1990a). These rights need to be distinguished. Rights of admission deal with the right of entry or presence while rights of establishment deal with the type of presence that may be permitted. The right of admission may be temporary or permanent. Temporary admission may be sufficient where a foreign enterprise seeks a short-term presence for the purposes of a discrete transaction, but would be insufficient for the purposes of a more regular business association with the host country. Should the host Government wish to encourage that association, a permanent right of market access may be granted. This would allow the enterprise to do business in the host country, but would not necessarily include a right to set up a permanent business presence. Market access rights may be sufficient where a foreign enterprise is primarily involved in regular cross-border trade in goods or services, or where business is carried out by way of electronic transactions, obviating the need for a permanent presence in the host country.

On the other hand, where some form of permanent business presence is preferred, a right of establishment ensures that a foreign investor, whether a natural or legal person, has the right to enter the host country and set up an office, agency, branch or subsidiary (as the case may be), possibly subject to limitations justified on grounds of national security, public health and safety or other public policy grounds (UNCTC, 1990b, pp. 192-195). Thus, the right to establishment entails not only a right to carry out business transactions in the host country but also the right to set up a permanent business presence there. It is therefore of most value to investors who seek to set up a long-term investment in a host country.[3]

Rights of establishment can be articulated through a variety of concepts and standards. In particular, issues concerning the avoidance of discrimination as between foreign and domestic investors and/or investors from different home countries have arisen. The former type of discrimination may be addressed by granting NT upon entry, while the latter can be addressed by granting MFN:

- National treatment can be defined as treatment no less favourable than that accorded to nationals engaged in the same line of business as the foreign investor. This standard is of particular relevance in the post-entry treatment of foreign investors (OECD, 1993). However, as will be shown in section II below, it has also been used as a means of granting rights of entry and establishment on the basis of mutual rights granted to States participating in a treaty regime granting such rights.
- Most-favoured-nation treatment can be defined as treatment no less favourable than that accorded to other foreign investors in the same line of business. The MFN standard ensures that any more favourable terms of investment granted to investors from one home country are automatically extended to investors from another home country.

These standards may be used separately or in combination with one another, whichever offers the higher standard of protection (see, for example, the United States model bilateral investment treaty (BIT), 1994, article II (1), in UNCTAD, 1996a, vol. III, p. 197); they are discussed in more detail in separate chapters of these volumes. Other concepts and standards, such as an expansive definition of market access encompassing all forms of market presence, may also be adapted and developed to articulate a right to establishment for foreign investors. Moreover, in the case of highly integrated groups of countries, the possibility of evoking the notion of an absolute right of establishment, or even a right to invest, for foreign investors within the group cannot be excluded a priori.

Finally, it must be stressed that the granting of a right to establishment is only one approach among many to the issue under discussion. As the next section will show, actual practice has developed not only models for the liberalization of entry and establishment but also models for the preservation of the State's sovereign right to control such matters. In this respect the grant of full rights of entry and establishment can be seen as the most open-door policy choice among the various options.

Section II
Stocktaking and Analysis

A. National legal approaches

In recent UNCTAD surveys regarding the direction and nature of liberalization of FDI entry and establishment, a number of findings have emerged (UNCTAD, 1994; 1995; 1996b; 1997; 1998b).[4] Traditionally, controls of FDI upon entry have centred on one or more of the following types of restrictions: prohibitions of FDI in specific activities or industries; foreign ownership limits in specific activities or industries; and screening procedures based on specified economic and social criteria.[5] Reforms have taken place through reductions in the number of activities/industries closed to FDI, usually by revising the lists of such activities/industries in negative lists which specify those activities/industries that are closed, leaving all other areas open to FDI;[6] reduction or removal of foreign ownership and control limits in previously controlled activities/industries; and the liberalization or removal of screening procedures. In this last area there has been a general move from substantive screening for the evaluation of investment projects towards more streamlined procedures such as registration requirements. The process of privatization has also increased the number of activities now open to FDI, though such processes may involve elaborate approval procedures for privatization bids from potential investors. However, it would be wrong to see liberalization of entry and establishment as a uniform process. Numerous controls remain, reflecting the different approaches taken by

Governments to economic and social policy in the field of FDI. Moreover, as liberalization proceeds, more and more countries are introducing screening and review procedures for international mergers and acquisitions (M&As) to ensure that the removal of policy obstacles to FDI is not replaced by anti-competitive private practices (UNCTAD, 1997).

B. Recent international agreements

Entry and establishment provisions can be found in BITs (UNCTAD, 1998a), regional and plurilateral instruments as well as multilateral agreements dealing with investment. The present chapter identifies five models or approaches in this area (see the Introduction above). Each represents a point along a continuum -- from complete State control over entry and establishment at one extreme, to entry and establishment rights subject to limited exceptions at the other extreme.

- **The investment control model.** This model is followed in most BITs, although some exceptions exist, notably the BITs signed by the United States and, more recently, Canada. It recognises the restrictions and controls on the admission of FDI stipulated by the laws and regulations of the host country. Indeed, this model does not offer positive rights of entry and establishment, leaving the matter to national discretion. Such an approach is also favoured by certain regional instruments.
- **The selective liberalization model**. This approach offers selective liberalization by way of an agreed "opt-in" on the part of the host State, resulting in a "positive list" of industries in which rights of entry and establishment may be enjoyed. Such rights may be subject to restrictions that the host State is permitted by the agreement to maintain. In addition, signatory States may make commitments to undertake further negotiations over liberalization in specific industries at an agreed future date.
- **The regional industrialization programme model**. Certain regional groups have experimented with supranational investment programmes. These involve regimes for the encouragement of intraregional investment, including the setting up of regional enterprises with capital from more than one member country. Such regimes may or may not specify rights of entry and establishment. Nonetheless, such regimes have such rights implicit in their policies, as they endeavour to encourage cross-border investment by way of regionally integrated enterprises and projects.
- **The mutual national treatment model**. This arises out of the practice of certain regional economic integration organizations where rights of entry and establishment are offered only to investors located in member States, who either possess the nationality of such a State and/or are resident for business purposes in a member State. The aim is to establish a common regime for entry and admission for investors from member States. MFN treatment for investors from non-member States is not normally available. This model differs from the previous model in that a right of establishment is generally available and is not dependent on the adoption, by investors, of a particular form of industrial programme or joint enterprise.
- **The combined national treatment/most-favoured-nation treatment model**. This is exemplified by United States BIT practice. The United States model BIT stipulates NT and MFN, whichever is the more favourable to foreign investors from the States parties, at pre-entry (as well as post-entry) stages of investment. The aim is to widen entry and establishment rights as far as possible, thereby enabling investors from States signatories to obtain the same rights of access as the most favoured third country investor. However, MFN treatment for investors from third countries is normally not available. Exceptions to these rights are also part of the understanding, but these must be specified and included in country-specific schedules annexed to the treaty, creating a negative list of protected activities or industries.

Each approach is illustrated below by examples from bilateral, regional, plurilateral and multilateral treaty practice. It should be stressed that each model is an ideal type which is often modified in practice through negotiation to achieve a balance of interests between the parties involved regarding the extent of liberalization and the extent of control required.

1. The investment control model

BITs are the most frequent international investment agreements. With some notable exceptions, as a matter of law, they do not accord positive rights of entry and establishment to foreign investors from the other contracting party. Such treaties have, in general, expressly preserved the host State's discretion through a clause encouraging the contracting parties to promote favourable investment conditions between themselves but leaving the precise conditions of entry and establishment to the laws and regulations of each party (Dolzer and Stevens, 1995, pp. 50-57; UNCTAD, 1998a).[7]

Turning to regional agreements displaying the use of this approach:

- The Agreement on Investment and Free Movement of Arab Capital among Arab Countries of 1970, reasserts, in article 3, each signatory's sovereignty over its own resources and its right to determine the procedures, terms and limits that govern Arab investment. However, by articles 4 and 5, all such investments are accorded NT and MFN once admitted (UNCTAD, 1996a, vol. II, pp. 122, 124).
- Controlled rights of entry and establishment can be found in the Unified Agreement for the Investment of Arab Capital in the Arab States of 1980 (UNCTAD, 1996a, vol. II, especially articles 2 and 5, pp. 213, 214).
- This approach is also followed in article 2 of the Agreement on Promotion, Protection and Guarantee of Investments among Member States of the Organisation of the Islamic Conference of 1981 (UNCTAD, 1996a, vol. II, p. 241).
- The 1987 version of the Association of South-East Asian Nations (ASEAN) Agreement for the Promotion and Protection of Investments follows the general practice in BITs and applies only to "investment brought into, derived from or directly connected with investments brought into the territory of any Contracting Party by nationals or companies of any other Contracting Party and which are specifically approved in writing and registered by the host country and upon such conditions as it deems fit for the purposes of this agreement" (article II, in UNCTAD, 1996a, vol. II, p. 294). Amendments made in 1996 introduced provisions on the simplification of investment procedures, approval processes and increased transparency of investment laws and regulations. However, the Framework Agreement on the ASEAN Investment Area (1998) offers a radical departure from this model.[8] It displays elements of a mutual national treatment model and, after a period of transition, a combined NT/MFN model. These elements will be considered further below.
- In the framework of the Southern Common Market (MERCOSUR), each member State agrees to promote investments of investors from non-member States in accordance with its laws and regulations (Decision 11/94 of the Council of MERCOSUR of 5 August 1994; in UNCTAD, 1996a, vol. II, p. 527). This commitment is subject to each State making best efforts to ensure that all relevant licences and administrative procedures are properly executed once an investment has been admitted (UNCTAD, 1996a, vol. II, p. 529).
- The first and most extensive inter-State investor screening regime was Decision 24 of the Agreement on Andean Subregional Integration (ANCOM).[9]
- In Africa, the Common Convention on Investments in the States of the Customs and Economic Union of Central Africa (UDEAC) of 1965 sets up a common system of investment screening for undertakings from the member countries that leads to preferential treatment in accordance with the agreement for any approved activity listed in the Preferential Schedules in Part II thereof (see UDEAC Treaty, articles 614, in UNCTAD, 1996a, vol. II, pp. 90-92). An approved undertaking may be the subject of an "establishment convention" which grants to it certain guarantees and imposes certain obligations (UDEAC Treaty, chapter IV, in UNCTAD, 1996a, vol. II, pp. 96-97).
- The World Bank Guidelines on the Treatment of Foreign Direct Investment accept the investment control model used in the majority of BITs (UNCTAD, 1996a, vol. I, p. 247). Thus Guideline II affirms that each State maintains the right to make regulations to govern the admission of foreign investments. Furthermore, States may, exceptionally, refuse entry on the grounds of national security, or because an industry is reserved to a State's nationals on account of the State's economic development objectives or the strict exigencies of its national interest. Restrictions applicable to national investment on account of public policy, public health and environmental protection can equally apply to foreign investment.

Today, the investment control model is the most widely used. The number of BITs that have followed this approach and the wide geographical distribution of regional agreements applying the investment control approach show a broad acceptance of its underlying rationale by many States, namely, that FDI is welcome but remains subject to host State regulation at the point of entry. The adoption of this model in preference to more liberal models in the World Bank Guidelines is also significant in view of the fact that the Guidelines were drawn up to express general trends in international treaty practice in the field of FDI promotion and protection.

2. The selective liberalization model

This approach is illustrated by the General Agreement on Trade in Services (GATS): a right of establishment exists where a member of GATS makes specific commitments on market access under article XVI. This provides that, in industries for which a member undertakes market access commitments, that member is prohibited from imposing certain listed limitations on the supply of services, unless it expressly specifies that it retains such limitations. These limitations include measures that would affect access through, *inter alia*, FDI. Thus, in the absence of an express reservation, the member cannot restrict or require, for example, specific forms of legal entity or joint venture through which a service could be provided, nor impose limits for the participation of foreign capital drawn up in terms of limits on maximum foreign shareholding or total value of individual or aggregate foreign investment (article XVI (2) (e)-(f)).

The wording of article XVI makes clear that the receiving State has considerable discretion in determining the extent of its market access commitments, and that it may expressly reserve powers to limit the mode of supply; there is no general obligation to remove all barriers concerning the entry and establishment of service providing firms. Each member of GATS is obliged to do no more than set out the specific market access commitments that it is prepared to undertake in a schedule drawn up in accordance with article XX of the GATS. Thereafter, members shall enter into subsequent rounds of negotiations with a view to achieving progressively higher levels of liberalization (article XIX(1)).

This model is useful where States do not wish to liberalize across the board but wish to follow controlled and industry-specific liberalization in exchange for equivalent action by other States, where, after negotiation, it appears useful to do so.

3. The regional industrialization programme model

The oldest example of this approach is offered by ANCOM: the Cartagena Agreement (concluded in 1969, codified in Decision 236 of the Commission of the Agreement, UNCTAD, 1996a, vol. III, p. 27), provides for the progressive integration of the economies of the member countries. This is to be done, *inter alia*, through "industrial programmes and other means of industrial integration" (article 3), which include industrial integration programmes aiming at the participation of at least four member countries, and which may involve the location of plants in countries of the subregion (article 34). Thus, while not including an express provision on the right of establishment, such a right is implicit in the very mechanisms of the industrial policy behind the Cartagena Agreement. Along similar lines, the creation of "Andean Multinational Enterprises" has been provided for since 1971 (see Decision 292 (1991), UNCTAD, 1996a, vol. II, p. 475). These are corporations established in a member country by investors from two or more member countries, which are accorded rights of entry on the basis of national treatment in all member countries.

Other agreements have followed a similar path:

- An industrial integration model has been adopted by the Treaty Establishing the Common Market for Eastern and Southern Africa (COMESA Treaty, article 101, in UNCTAD, 1996a, vol. III, p. 103; Protocol on Co-operation in the field of Industrial Development, article 4, in UNCTAD, 1996a, vol. III, p. 111).
- The revised Treaty of the Economic Community of West African States (ECOWAS) also provides for a policy on intra-regional cross-border joint ventures (article 3(2)(c) and (d)(f) ECOWAS Revised Treaty, 1993, ECOWAS, 1996).
- ASEAN uses this approach for intraregional investors in the Revised Basic Agreement on ASEAN Industrial Joint Ventures of 1987 (UNCTAD, 1996a, vol. II, p. 281) and in the ASEAN Framework Agreement on Enhancing ASEAN Economic Cooperation (ASEAN, 1992) which, in article 6, encourages cooperation and exchanges among the ASEAN private sectors. The ASEAN Industrial Cooperation Scheme (AICO) of 1996, which

replaces the Basic Agreement on Industrial Joint Ventures, and the 1988 Memorandum of Understanding on the Brand-to-Brand Complementation Scheme, offers a preferential regime for products produced or used in cooperative arrangements involving companies from different ASEAN countries. To qualify, companies must be incorporated and operating in any ASEAN country, have a minimum of 30 per cent national equity and undertake resource sharing, industrial complementation or industrial cooperation activities (WTO, 1998, p. 30).

More generally, this approach is typical of regional economic integration groups, and is not often used outside such contexts. It is arguable, however, that treaties creating public international corporations offer a variant in that a special purpose transnational commercial regime is set up between two or more States, and that the resulting legal entity has rights of establishment within the several founding States (Muchlinski, 1995, pp. 79-80).

4. The mutual national treatment model

The most significant and influential examples of this approach are to be found in the Treaty Establishing the European Community (EC) and in the Code of Liberalisation of Capital Movements and the Code of Liberalisation of Current Invisible Operations of the OECD:

- The EC Treaty ensures that restrictions on the freedom of establishment, or the freedom to supply services, are removed for natural and legal persons possessing the nationality of a member State (EC Treaty, articles 52-66; UNCTAD, 1996a, vol. III, pp.9-14; European Commission, 1997b; Wyatt and Dashwood, 1993, ch.10; Muchlinski, 1999, pp. 245-247). These rights can be enjoyed by a company formed in accordance with the law of a member State and having its registered office, central administration or principal place of business within the EC. This is wide enough to cover the EC-based affiliates of non-EC parent companies. However, the EC Treaty does not guarantee these rights to companies that have no legally recognized EC presence. The above-mentioned rights are subject to exceptions, in accordance with article 56 of the EC Treaty, which allows differential treatment of foreign nationals on grounds of public policy, public security or public health. Such exceptions, however, are construed strictly.
- This approach is followed in the agreements concluded between the European Union and associated Central and East European States (WTO, 1998, p. 9). However, the Partnership and Co-operation Agreements between the European Union and the States of the Commonwealth of Independent States limit rights of establishment to the setting up of subsidiaries or branches and do not extend to self-employed persons (WTO, 1998, p. 10).
- The two OECD Liberalisation Codes (UNCTAD, 1996a, vol. II, p. 3 and p. 31, respectively)[10] contain a duty to abolish any national restrictions upon the transfers and transactions to which the codes apply. This is reinforced by a positive duty to grant any authorization required for the conclusion or execution of the transactions or transfers covered, and by a duty of non-discrimination in the application of liberalization measures to investors from other member States. The Codes permit members to lodge reservations in relation to matters on which full liberalization cannot be immediately achieved.[11] Furthermore, a member is not prevented from taking action that it considers necessary for: "(i) the maintenance of public order or the protection of public health, morals and safety; (ii) the protection of essential security interests; (iii) the fulfilment of its obligations relating to international peace and security". Members can also take measures required to prevent evasion of their laws or regulations. Moreover, where the economic and financial situation of a member justifies such a course, the member need not take all the measures of liberalization provided for in the Codes. Similarly, where the member has taken such liberalization measures, it may derogate from those measures where these result in serious economic and financial disturbance or where there exists a seriously deteriorating balance-of-payments situation.
- In 1984 the OECD Code of Liberalisation of Capital Movements was extended to include rights of establishment. Thus annex A states: "The authorities of Members shall not maintain or introduce: Regulations or practices applying to the granting of licences, concessions, or similar authorisations, including conditions or requirements attaching to such authorisations and affecting the operations of enterprises, that raise special barriers or limitations with respect to non-resident (as compared to resident) investors,

and that have the intent or the effect of preventing or significantly impeding inward direct investment by nonresidents."

This definition of the right of establishment is wide enough to cover most policies that restrict, or make conditional, access to non-resident investors, subject to the above-mentioned public policy exemptions to the Code.

This model has also been adopted by several regional organizations established by developing countries:

- Rights of establishment are specifically mentioned in Article 35 of the Treaty Establishing the Caribbean Community (CARICOM); (see UNCTAD, 1996a, vol. III, pp. 44-45). This provision was amended by a protocol adopted in July 1997 which prohibits new restrictions on rights of establishment of nationals of other member States and obliges member States to remove existing restrictions in accordance with the programme to be determined by the Council of Trade and Economic Development, which will set the procedures and timetables for their removal and will specify activities which are exempt from rights of establishment (WTO, 1998, pp. 10-11).
- Similar provisions appear in the Treaty for the Establishment of the Economic Community of Central African States (ECCAS) (article 40, ECCAS Treaty, in UNCTAD, 1996a, vol. III, p. 65), and the 1972 Joint Convention on the Freedom of Movement of Persons and the Right of Establishment in the Central African Customs and Economic Union (Part III, in UNCTAD, 1996a, vol. II, pp. 157-159).
- The Community Investment Code of the Economic Community of the Great Lakes Countries (CEPGL) of 1987 also contains provisions for rights of entry and establishment (CEPGL article 6, in UNCTAD, 1996a, vol. II, p. 254). However, these are preceded by a detailed regime for what are termed "joint enterprises" and "Community enterprises" (CEPGL articles 2-5, in UNCTAD, 1996a, vol. II, pp. 252-254). Such classes of enterprise are subject to an authorisation process, without which they will not benefit from various advantages offered under the Code (CEPGL Articles 14-42, in UNCTAD, 1996a, vol. II, pp. 256-263). Thus, this agreement also displays aspects of the regional industrialization programme and the investment control models.
- Certain economic cooperation agreements in Africa make commitments to offer rights of establishment to investors from signatory States at a future date through the conclusion of additional protocols. These include the COMESA Treaty (article 164), and the 1991 Treaty Establishing the African Economic Community (article 43) (WTO, 1998, p. 11).
- The ECOWAS Revised Treaty of 1993, in articles 3 (2) and 55, commits member States to the removal of obstacles to the right of establishment within five years of the creation of a customs union between member States (ECOWAS, 1996, p. 660).
- The Framework Agreement on the ASEAN Investment Area (1998) contains a commitment to national treatment for ASEAN investors by 2010, subject to the exceptions provided for under the Agreement (article 4 (6)).

This model is, like the previous model, peculiar to regional economic integration groups, based as it is on preferential rights of entry and establishment for investors from other member States. The two models should be kept distinct, however, because the former deals with specific industrial integration programmes, including the setting up of regional multinational enterprises/joint ventures, while the present model offers general rights of entry and establishment to all investors from other member States. Particular agreements may, of course, combine more than one model. The European Union/Commonwealth of Independent States agreements are distinct in that they are limited for the present to corporate investors, displaying the characteristics of a transitional regime aimed at eventual full mutual national treatment along the lines of the European agreements with Central and East European States.

5. The combined national treatment and most-favoured-nation treatment model

This model has its origins in United States BIT practice. The United States model BIT states in article II (1):

> "With respect to the establishment, acquisition, expansion, management, conduct, operation and sale or other disposition of covered investments, each Party shall accord treatment no less favorable than that it accords, in like situations, to investments in its territory of its own nationals or companies (hereinafter "national treatment"), or to investments in its territory of nationals or companies of a third country (hereinafter "most favored nation treatment"),

whichever is most favorable (hereinafter "national and most favored nation treatment")" (United States model BIT 1994, in UNCTAD, 1996a, vol. III, p. 197; and UNCTAD, 1998a).

This provision makes entry into the host State subject to the NT/ MFN principle and, to that extent, the host State accepts to limit its sovereign power to regulate the entry of foreign investors. However, this general commitment is made subject to the right of each party to adopt or maintain exceptions falling within one of the activities or matters listed in an annex to the BIT (United States model BIT, 1994, article II (2)).[12] In addition, under article VI performance requirements must not be imposed as a condition for the establishment, expansion or maintenance of investments.

The most significant example of the NT/MFN model is the North American Free Trade Agreement (NAFTA) (UNCTAD, 1996a, vol. III, pp. 73-77):[13]

- Article 1102 of NAFTA grants NT to investors and investments of another contracting party with respect to "the establishment, acquisition, expansion, management, conduct, operation, and sale or other disposition of investments."
- Article 1103 extends the MFN principle to investors and investments of another contracting party on the same terms as article 1102.
- Under article 1104, investors and investment from another contracting party are entitled to the better of national or MFN treatment.
- Article 1106 prohibits the imposition of performance requirements in connection with, *inter alia*, the establishment or acquisition of an investment in the host State contracting party.
- Article 1108 permits reservations and exceptions to be made to the above-mentioned Articles for any existing non-conforming measures. These are to be placed in each party's schedule to the Agreement.

Other agreements contain similar provisions:

- The 1994 Treaty on Free Trade between Colombia, Mexico and Venezuela (Article 17-03) accords NT and MFN treatment to investors of another party and their investments subject, *inter alia,* to the right of each party to impose special formalities in connection with the establishment of an investment and to impose information requirements.[14]
- In MERCOSUR, investments of investors from other MERCOSUR member States are to be admitted on the basis of treatment no less favourable than that accorded to domestic investors or investors from third States, subject to the right of each member State to maintain exceptional limitations for a transitional period, which must be detailed in an annex to the Protocol. (Decision 11/93 of the Council of MERCOSUR of 17 January 1994; UNCTAD, 1996a, vol. II, p. 513 and p. 520, for listed exceptions.)
- The Asia-Pacific Economic Cooperation (APEC) Non-Binding Investment Principles are reminiscent of the United States model BIT as they advocate rights of establishment based both on the MFN and NT principles (UNCTAD, 1996a, vol. II, p. 536). However, the APEC instrument is not legally binding, and its provisions represent "best efforts" only. Also, the NT provision is more restrictive than in the United States model BIT in that it makes non-discrimination subject to domestic law exceptions (Sornarajah, 1995a).
- The Framework Agreement on the ASEAN Investment Area of 1998 extends NT to all investors, not only ASEAN investors, by 2020 subject to exceptions provided for under the Agreement (article 4 (b), 7). Furthermore, all industries are opened for investment to ASEAN investors by 2010, and to all investors by 2020, subject to exceptions provided for in the Agreement (article 4 (c), 7). However, the MFN principle extends only to investors and investments from other member States (Articles 8 and 9). This makes clear that investors and investments from non-member States cannot benefit from measures aimed at investors and investments from member States.

The combined NT/MFN model is not as widespread as the investor control model; it is followed in the draft text of the Multilateral Agreement on Investment (MAI).[15]

Section III
Interaction with other Issues and Concepts

The meaning and scope of admission and entry provisions can be significantly affected by their interaction with other issues addressed in international investment agreements (table 1). In particular, the actual extent of regulation should be viewed from at least two perspectives:

(i) the extent to which treaty-based rights of entry and establishment are enhanced and/or limited by other provisions in an investment agreement; and

(ii) the degree to which the treaty provisions concerned actually affect the operation of the internal laws of the host country.

In relation to these issues, the following matters are of special importance:

- **Definition of investments.** The definition of investment in an instrument that limits the powers of the host State to control, restrict or impose conditions on the entry of FDI (i.e. that grants entry and establishment rights to foreign investors) may bear on the scope of the host country limitations. A broad definition that covers a wide variety of categories of investment (e.g. one which covers both direct and portfolio investment) would limit more extensively a State's powers (Dolzer and Stevens, 1995, pp. 26-31; Energy Charter Treaty, 1994, article 1(6), in UNCTAD, 1996a, vol. II, pp. 548-549). A more restrictive definition would have the effect of covering a smaller range of operations and transactions over which the powers of the host State are limited by an agreement, thereby allowing greater discretion to the host State with respect to categories of investment not covered.
- **Exceptions and derogations.** No existing investment agreement offers absolute and unconditional rights of entry and establishment. The range of exceptions and derogations has already been indicated earlier, where it was shown that most investment instruments accept legitimate exceptions to such rights on the basis of national security, public health and public policy concerns and for specific activities or industries. Equally, temporary reservations for balance-of-payments and exchange-rate protection have been accepted in agreements at all levels. Furthermore, there is always the possibility of a contracting State to "opt out" by making reservations to provisions that it feels go beyond what it is willing to accept as a restriction on its sovereign power to exclude aliens. Finally, a complicating problem involves sub-national entities in that States may be unable to guarantee compliance with entry and establishment provisions on the part of these authorities, should the national constitution require their consent to such limitations on their sovereignty and such consent is not forthcoming. Thus exceptions for sub-national authorities may be included in a liberalization measure.
- **Incentives.** A further issue related to entry and establishment rights is that of investment incentives (UNCTAD, 1996c). In some instances, the administration of incentives by a host country duplicates the investment control model, in that a set of specific criteria is applied by a government service, although with a view to according the promised incentives, rather than approving the admission or establishment of an investment. As a result, problems and disputes concerning the granting of incentives may often be quite similar to those relating to admission and establishment.

Table 1. Interaction across issues and concepts

Issue	Admission and establishment
Competition	+
Dispute settlement (investor-State)	++
Dispute settlement (State-State)	+
Employment	+
Environment	+
Fair and equitable treatment	+
Home country measures	+
Host country operational measures	+
Illicit payments	+
Incentives	++
Investment-related trade measures	+
Most-favoured-nation treatment	++
National treatment	++
Scope and definition	++
Social responsibility	++
State contracts	+
Taking of property	+
Taxation	+
Transfer of funds	+
Transfer of technology	+
Transfer pricing	+
Transparency	++

Source: UNCTAD.

Key: 0 = negligible or no interaction.
\+ = moderate interaction.
++ = extensive interaction.

- **Post-entry national treatment and most-favoured-nation treatment.** The application of NT and MFN treatment standards to the post-entry treatment of foreign investors ensures that the original decision to admit an investor is not rendered commercially ineffective by subjecting the investor to discriminatory practices prejudicial to its business interests. In the absence of such treatment it is arguable that rights of entry and establishment can become worthless. Such problems may arise as a result of "hidden screening", namely the control of inward investment through procedures applied by host authorities as part of their internal regulatory order. Specialized authorization and licensing procedures for specific operations related to the investment (e.g. purchasing of land) that are separate from the original entry decision may be of special concern. Indeed, such restrictions can exist even in an open-door environment. In this connection, it is useful to have all decisions on entry and establishment centralized in a single screening agency (Wint, 1993).
- **Social responsibility.** Interactions between admission and establishment issues and wider issues of social responsibility can be considerable. In particular, it is at the point of entry that a host country may require certain commitments from a foreign investor. For example, some countries may require a particular legal form to be taken by the foreign investment, such as an incorporated company or a joint venture with local interests, which has as its purpose the furtherance of the host country's policy on corporate governance and accountability. Another example may be the imposition of an obligation to provide for consultation with workers through a workers' council. Furthermore, social responsibility goals could be achieved through the imposition of appropriate performance requirements at the point of entry.
- **Transparency.** The extent to which the regulatory environment in a host country is transparent will materially affect the capacity of foreign investors to gauge the degree of regulatory control and restrictions to which they will be subject. This concept is mentioned in the 1994 United States model BIT (article II (5), UNCTAD, 1996a, vol. III, p. 198), but not in other model treaties, though it may be implicit in the concept of "fair and equitable treatment". On the other hand, the concept is frequently found in plurilateral and multilateral investment agreements (Energy Charter Treaty, article 20, in UNCTAD, 1996a, vol. II, p. 562; GATS, article III, in UNCTAD, 1996a, vol. I, p. 289). The practical effect of such a clause is hard to determine, as the obligation it entails may be easily discharged through, for example, the promulgation of relevant laws and regulations in the official bulletin and the regular updating of investment promotion literature. Whether it would be effective in dealing with "hidden screening" is more open to question. In any case, clear treaty entry and establishment language would help to ensure that investors know in advance where State control over such matters remains.
- **Dispute settlement.** Dispute-settlement provisions can enhance rights of entry and establishment by offering effective means for raising claims to investors who feel that a host contracting State has not acted in accordance with its treaty obligations with respect to entry and establishment. However, with respect to agreements in which investors do not have enforceable rights in pre-investment situations, host-country disputes would concern issues arising in later stages of an investment. Therefore, disputes over admission and establishment are likely to involve allegations about State conduct inconsistent with the State's treaty commitments or with its own laws and regulations concerning entry of FDI.

Conclusion: Economic and Development Implications and Policy Options

The effects of FDI on a host country's economy, in particular its growth and development prospects, are of special interest to developing countries (UNCTAD, 1995, 1997, and UN/DESD/TCMD, 1992; see also chapter 27 in volume III). Concerns in this respect have sometimes led to controls over admission and establishment -- for example, under foreign exchange regulations. Several other, strategic and socio-economic considerations have also regularly figured in host government limitations on admission and establishment; these include defence capabilities, employment effects, technology transfer, and environmental and cultural effects. Host government policies in this respect emerge from the specific mix of political and economic circumstances characterizing particular countries. However, they tend to reflect the following policy options (discussed above), or a combination of them:

(1) To accept complete State discretion through the investment control model;
(2) To liberalize cautiously through the adoption of the "opt-in" approach of the selective liberalization model;
(3) To follow the regional industrial programme model and encourage the establishment of regional multinational enterprises;
(4) To follow the mutual national treatment model and only allow full liberalization in the framework of a regional economic integration organization;
(5) To follow the full NT/MFN model and further open up entry and establishment, subject only to a negative list of reserved activities/industries;
(6) To follow a mix of models bearing in mind that some of the options appear to be inconsistent or difficult to combine.

A. Option 1: State discretion/investment control

This approach is often preferred by countries that are uncertain about the benefits that may flow from a liberalized policy on entry and establishment. Arguments in favour of such an approach include the possibility that foreign investors engage in business activities that are not desirable -- such as uncompetitive mergers and acquisitions or restrictive practices --requiring a degree of pre-entry control to assess the overall costs and benefits to the host economy of a proposed investment and to impose specific limitations on such practiccs. The retention of screening procedures may not deter inward FDI, though it may create an unfavourable image for the host country.[16] Moreover, the use of screening may offer a "once-and-for-all" determination of the right to enter the host State and the added attraction of possible protection against competitive investment by rival firms.

Preferences for screening and restrictions over entry differ according to the industry or activity involved (Conklin and Lecraw, 1997). Thus host countries may prefer to protect infant industries and domestic producers deemed not strong enough to compete with foreign firms. Such restrictions may only be removed where effective competition with foreign investors becomes possible -- or, indeed, necessary -- to ensure the further development of the indigenous industry, as was the case, for example, in the liberalization of foreign entry conditions to the Brazilian informatics industry. Land and natural resources may be subject to screening controls and ownership restrictions to protect what is considered to be part of the natural wealth and resources of the host country. Ownership and establishment restrictions may be more prevalent in certain services industries (e.g. financial services) than in manufacturing owing to the pivotal role these industries play in the national economy and thus the consequent need for effective prudential supervision. Liberalization in this area has thus proceeded at a slower pace. They are prime candidates for an "opt-in" approach as described under option 2 below. It is also conceivable that restrictions over foreign ownership of infrastructure in a host country are motivated by a desire to regulate a natural monopoly in the public interest. Another justification for controls over foreign entry and establishment is the protection of small and medium-sized enterprises. Finally, controls over foreign access to cultural industries may be justified to protect the cultural heritage of the host country. However, technological change -- including the rise of satellite and digital broadcasting and the widespread use of the Internet -- has thrown into doubt the ability of States to apply effective national controls in this area (Conklin and Lecraw, 1997, p. 18).

B. Option 2: Selective liberalization

A less restrictive option -- to allow for selective liberalization of entry and establishment in specific activities or industries -- may have the advantage of making liberalization commitments more sensitive to the real locational advantages of a host country, and to permit the country more control over the process of negotiating liberalization measures, given the "stepped" approach to this goal that such a policy entails through the establishment of a positive list of industries in which FDI is allowed. It may be useful for developing countries that fear full liberalization, but would not be opposed to such a policy in activities where they are able to compete on more or less equal terms with foreign investors. It may also be an option which would allow a host country to enhance its future development and competitiveness through the introduction of investment that can stimulate the production of more complex goods and services. To the extent that this option, too, involves an element of loss of sovereignty, it is a gradual and controlled loss offset by the prospects of future economic development.

The circumstances in which a host country may be willing to liberalize a specific activity will echo the explanations given above as to why a specific host country may wish to restrict entry and establishment. Thus, different industries or activities may be more or less amenable to liberalization; liberalization in manufacturing and services may be easier than in natural resources (Conklin and Lecraw, 1997), though even in manufacturing and service industries, national interest may dictate protection.

Finally, it should be noted that the preamble and a number of provisions of the GATS relating to developing countries stress the right of countries to regulate the supply of services within their territories in order to meet national policy objectives. Equally, article IV (1) encourages the negotiation of specific commitments by different members relating to the strengthening of the domestic services capacity of developing countries, their efficiency and competitiveness through, *inter alia:* access to technology on a commercial basis; the improvement of developing country access to distribution channels and information networks; and the liberalization of market access in sectors and modes of supply of export interest to developing countries. Furthermore, developed country members are encouraged, under article IV (2), to establish contact points designed to facilitate service suppliers from developing countries in obtaining relevant commercial and technological information. Thus, GATS does not subject developing countries to immediate liberalization and, in addition, offers certain general commitments to ensure that service suppliers from developing countries can compete in international markets.[17] However, these commitments do not impose positive duties to open up markets for such suppliers.

C. Option 3: Regional programmes

This approach is a variant of the economic integration model favoured by regional integration groups, applied to a specific policy which seeks to set up a supranational form of business organization aimed at encouraging intraregional economic activity. As such, it offers a vehicle for regional economic development. However, the practical results of such a policy may prove to be mixed. It assumes that local regional capital exists and possesses sufficient technical and managerial skills to be able to perform economic functions without investment from outside the region. This policy may ignore the fact that technology and capital are unevenly spread both within and across regions. On the other hand, such a policy can be useful as a means of breaking down structural barriers to intraregional integration where sufficient resources exist within the region to make such enterprises viable.

D. Option 4: Mutual national treatment

This approach involves a greater commitment to full liberalization than do those discussed above, though it requires a joint commitment to this process by the States participating in a regional economic integration organization. Consequently, liberalization may proceed between States that see a common interest in regional integration, but which are not necessarily committed to full multilateral liberalization. One major issue in this case is whether the effect of such a commitment is to enhance intraregional investment (and trade) without creating a diversion away from trade with non-members. Importantly, regional integration can offer a larger geographical area within which globally competitive industries can be established.

E. Option 5: National and MFN treatment with negative list of exceptions

This is the approach preferred by firms and countries that are supportive of liberalization, as it offers the best access to markets, resources and opportunities. It allows investment decisions to be determined on the basis of commercial considerations, by reducing entry controls that create barriers to the integration of production across borders, a strategy increasingly pursued by TNCs (UNCTAD, 1993a).

However, the extension of the NT/MFN model to the pre-entry stage is not without its problems. This was vividly illustrated in the negotiations leading up to the Energy Charter Treaty (Dore, 1996, pp. 143-153; Konoplyanik, 1996; Waelde, 1996b, p. 277). The principal advocates of such an approach sought to incorporate national treatment into the pre-investment phase so that the Treaty would reflect a standard of protection similar to that of article II of the 1994 United States model BIT. All delegations prepared negative lists for the purpose of negotiations on the pre-investment stage, but countries in transition requested a grace period in which to finalize national legislation. As a result, a compromise position was reached whereby the contracting parties would "endeavour" to accord national treatment at the pre-investment phase and would negotiate a supplementary treaty on the issue (Energy Charter Treaty, article 10 (2)-(4) in UNCTAD, 1996a, vol. II, p. 555). While agreement has been reached on this supplementary treaty along the NT/MFN model with negative lists of existing legislation and the process of privatization, the Charter conference has not yet adopted the text (UNCTAD, 1998b).

The fact that the NT/MFN model allows for negative lists of excepted industries or activities is significant, since it makes clear that this approach recognizes that certain strategic industries may be beyond the reach of liberalization measures. However, it must be emphasized that such lists are difficult to negotiate and compile and may result in a lengthy and complex final text, as NAFTA exemplifies. In countries in which competition is a desired policy goal, such reservations may be of special importance in relation to infant industries that may not be able to withstand the vagaries of open international competition, or as a means of protecting natural resources against uncontrolled foreign ownership. On the other hand, care needs to be taken that such measures are not used to protect inefficient domestic monopolies against competition that may encourage a more efficient use of resources and improvements in consumer welfare.

F. Option 6: Hybrid

This approach combines elements of more than one of the five basic models. The economic effects of these hybrid options would be to offer more specialized alternatives that may be more compatible with the mix of locational advantages enjoyed by particular host countries. The following combinations are examples:

- Option 1 can be coupled with option 2 and/or 3 to produce a policy of investment screening with sectoral liberalization and/or regional industrial development programmes. Option 1 can also be coupled with option 4 so long as option 1 is restricted to investments originating in States that are not members of the relevant regional economic integration organization. Option 1 is incompatible with option 4 as regards investments originating in other member States of a regional economic integration grouping. This hybrid approach would suit a host State that is opposed to full multilateral liberalization on NT/MFN principles but which sees benefits in gradual regional integration. Such combinations are exemplified by the Arab regional agreements, and the earlier ASEAN agreements mentioned in section II.
- Option 4 may be coupled with options 2 and/or 3 to produce a policy of mutual national treatment coupled with sectoral "opt-in" policies for gradual liberalization vis-à-vis non-members of a regional economic integration grouping and/or regional industrial development programmes. This hybrid approach is useful to a host country that wishes to achieve full regional liberalization with its neighbours as a long-term goal but which may want to control that process through gradual sectoral liberalization and which may perceive a need to enhance regional industrial integration through specific projects. The history of European Community market integration is an example of this approach.
- Option 5 can be combined with option 2 to produce a policy of general NT and MFN, coupled with a negative list subject to "opt-in" sectoral liberalization at a future date. This approach would suit a host country that wants liberalization on the basis of NT/MFN principles, but prefers gradual liberalization in specific activities. NAFTA is a good example of this approach. Option 3 is not used outside a regional economic integration context and is unlikely to be combined with option 5.[18] Option 5 and option 1 appear, at first sight, to be incompatible. However, the MERCOSUR agreements attempt a reconciliation by using option 1 in relation to non-MERCOSUR investors, and option 5 for MERCOSUR-based investors. Option 4 would be difficult to combine with option 5 except to the extent that special clauses are used (Karl, 1996). It is arguable that the Framework Agreement on the ASEAN Investment Area of 1998 attempts a combination of options 4 and 5 by extending NT and MFN to ASEAN investors first and then extending NT to non-ASEAN investors by 2020. However, MFN is only extended to ASEAN-based investors. Thus a transitional phase approach is used from one option to another.

An important final consideration relates to the types of exceptions and reservations on admission and establishment provisions that may be appropriate for countries in order to pursue their development objectives. Reservations and exceptions to rights of entry and establishment provisions in investment agreements indeed offer a compromise option for host States that wish to make those rights compatible with their development priorities, so as to avoid having imposed on them blanket commitments to the granting of such rights. The consequences for national laws of having an agreement that protects rights of entry and establishment depend to a large extent on the nature of the derogations and reservations available under that regime. In particular, it has been noted that national security and public health/public policy concerns, including of countries that pursue option 5, are frequently the subject of such measures. Furthermore, in relation to certain specific economic and social issues, States are likely to reserve some degree of flexibility, including: the discretion to approve or disapprove privatization proposals;[19] control of access on the grounds of prudential supervision in the financial services sector; controls over entry and establishment for environmental protection purposes; and restrictions on strategic industries or activities based on economic development considerations.

Notes

1 For a detailed analysis of the concepts and principles of customary international law applying to foreign investment, see Fatouros (1994).

2 This is stressed in the Organisation for Economic Co-operation and Development (OECD) draft Convention on the Protection of Foreign Property of 1962, which states in article 1 (b): "The provisions of this Convention shall not affect the right of any Party to allow or prohibit the acquisition of property or the investment of capital within its territory by nationals of another Party" (UNCTAD, 1996a, vol. II, p. 114).
Unless otherwise noted, all instruments cited herein may be found in UNCTAD (1996a).

3 For a detailed analysis of the various degrees of market presence in the area of services, see UNCTAD and the World Bank (1994).

4 See also Muchlinski, 1999, chapters 6 and 7; and WTO, 1996a, pp. 33-34.

5 On national regulatory frameworks for foreign investment see Rubin and Wallace (1994).

6 For instance, Nigeria Investment Promotion Commission Decree, 1995, sections 18 and 32; Ghana Investment Promotion Centre Act, 1994, section 18 and Schedule (ICSID, 1995, updated looseleaf, vol. III). Bulgaria Law on Business Activity by Foreign Nationals and Protection of Foreign Investment, 1992, article 5 (3), (ICSID, 1992, updated looseleaf, vol. I); Kazakhstan Law on Foreign Investment, 1991, article 9 (ICSID, 1994, updated looseleaf, vol. IV).

7 Typical of this type of provision is article 2(1) of the Barbados-United Kingdom BIT of 1993: "Each Contracting Party shall encourage and create favourable conditions for nationals and companies of the other Contracting Party to invest capital in its territory, and, subject to its right to exercise powers conferred by its laws, shall admit such capital." Similar provisions can be found in model treaties; see, e.g., article 3, Chilean model BIT 1994; article 2, Chinese model BIT; article 2, French model BIT; article 2, German model BIT 1991; article 3, Swiss model BIT; and article 3, African-Asian Legal Consultative Committee model 1985 (UNCTAD, 1996a, vol. III; UNCTAD 1998a).

8 http://www.asean.or.id/economic/aem/30/frm_aia.htm.

9 This was repealed and replaced by subsequent decisions of ANCOM. The current position is contained in Decision 291 of 21 March 1991 which effectively abandoned a common ANCOM policy on FDI regulation. Decision 291 devolves this question to the level of the member countries' national laws, taking the issue out of ANCOM jurisdiction.

10 The codes are regularly updated by Decisions of the OECD Council to reflect changes in the positions of members. The updated codes are periodically republished. (For background to the codes, see OECD, 1995; Muchlinski, 1995, pp. 248-250.)

11 These reservations are set out in annex B to each Code. They offer a good periodic indicator of how far liberalization has actually progressed among the OECD members.

12 See further Pattison, 1983, pp. 318-319, for a discussion of the United States-Egypt BIT in this respect.

13 See further Eden, 1996, and Gestrin and Rugman, 1994, 1996. See also the Canada-Chile Free Trade Agreement, 5 December 1996, chapter G, Articles G01 to G-08, for similar provisions (Canada and Chile, 1997).

14 http://www.sice.oas.org/Trade/G3_E/G3E_TOC. stm.

15 http://www.oecd.org/daf/cmis/mai/negtext.htm.

16 See, for example, Kudrle, 1995, on Canada, and South Centre, 1997, pp. 6064, on East Asia.

17 The OECD recommends the liberalization of services in developing countries as a positive stimulus to development (OECD, 1989).

18 Indeed, a multilateral regional integration programme is a contradiction in terms. However, multilateral industrial development programmes are not inconceivable and could take the form of a public international corporation or an intergovernmental agency of which the Multilateral Investment Guarantee Agency (MIGA) may be an example (see Muchlinski, 1995, pp. 79-80, 515-519).

19 There may be differences between States over the extent to which they may seek to guard this discretion (see Muchlinski, 1996; and de Castro and Uhlenbruck, 1997).

Chapter 5. National Treatment*

Executive summary

The national treatment standard is perhaps the single most important standard of treatment enshrined in international investment agreements (IIAs). At the same time, it is perhaps the most difficult standard to achieve, as it touches upon economically (and politically) sensitive issues. In fact, no single country has so far seen itself in a position to grant national treatment without qualifications, especially when it comes to the establishment of an investment.

National treatment can be defined as a principle whereby a host country extends to foreign investors treatment that is at least as favourable as the treatment that it accords to national investors in like circumstances. In this way the national treatment standard seeks to ensure a degree of competitive equality between national and foreign investors. This raises difficult questions concerning the factual situations in which national treatment applies and the precise standard of comparison by which the treatment of national and foreign investors is to be compared.

National treatment typically extends to the post-entry treatment of foreign investors. However, some bilateral investment treaties (BITs) and other IIAs also extend the standard to pre-entry situations. This has raised the question of the proper limits of national treatment, in that such an extension is normally accompanied by a "negative list" of excepted areas of investment activity to which national treatment does not apply, or a "positive list" of areas of investment activity to which national treatment is granted. In addition, several types of general exceptions to national treatment exist concerning public health, safety and morals, and national security, although these may not be present in all agreements, particularly not in BITs.

National treatment interacts with several other investment issues and concepts. Most notably there are strong interactions with the issues of admission and establishment, the most-favoured-nation (MFN) standard, host country operational measures and investor-State dispute settlement. National treatment raises some of the most significant development issues in the field of foreign direct investment (FDI). It stipulates formal equality between foreign and national investors. However, in practice national investors, especially those that could be identified as "infant industries" or "infant entrepreneurs", may be in an economically disadvantageous position by comparison with foreign investors, who may be economically powerful transnational corporations (TNCs). Such "economic asymmetry" may require a degree of flexibility in the treatment of national investors, especially in developing countries, for instance through the granting of exceptions to national treatment.

Introduction

The national treatment standard is one of the main general standards that is used in international practice to secure a certain level of treatment for FDI in host countries. Other general standards include principally, fair and equitable treatment (chapter 7) and MFN treatment (chapter 6). National treatment is a contingent standard based on the treatment given to other investors. Thus, while MFN seeks to grant foreign investors treatment comparable to other foreign investors operating in the host country, national treatment seeks to grant treatment comparable to domestic investors operating in the host country.

For many countries, the standard of national treatment serves to eliminate distortions in competition and thus is seen to enhance the efficient operation of the economies involved. An extension of this argument points to the ongoing internationalization of investment and production and concludes that access to foreign markets under non-discriminatory conditions is necessary for the effective functioning of an increasingly integrated world economy. On the other hand, there may be no substitute for the promotion by host countries of domestic industries to ensure economic development and, in a world marked by stark inequalities in economic power, technical capabilities and financial strength, a certain

---

* The chapter is based on a 1999 manuscript prepared by Peter T. Muchlinski. Victoria Aranda was responsible for the substantive supervision of this chapter. The final version reflects comments received from Joachim Karl, Mark Koulen, Hamid Mamdouh and Marinus Sikkel.

differentiation between national and non-national firms may be necessary precisely in order to bring about a degree of operative equality.

As will be discussed further in section I, national treatment is a relative standard whose content depends on the underlying state of treatment for domestic and foreign investors alike. It is also a standard that has its origins primarily in trade treaties, though, as noted below, the term has also been used in a quite different context, namely in relation to the customary international law standards for the treatment of aliens and their property. A certain degree of adaptation of the standard to the characteristics of investment is therefore required so that it may be used in an effective way in IIAs.

In the context of foreign investment relations, until relatively recently, national treatment was seen to be relevant almost exclusively to the treatment accorded to foreign investors after they had entered a host country. However, some more recent IIAs particularly the BITs entered into by Canada and the United States (apart from the Friendship Commerce and Navigation (FCN) treaties of the United States), have extended national treatment to the pre-entry stage so as to ensure market access for foreign investors on terms equal to those enjoyed by national investors. As national treatment traditionally applied in most BITs only to the post-establishment phase of an investment, and there was little question that the pre-establishment phase was left to the sovereign right of States in terms of deciding on admission of an investment (chapter 4), the extension of national treatment from the post- to the pre-investment phase is a "revolution"[1] for many countries. This has made the discussions about the type and extent of exceptions to national treatment that may be required in order to retain a measure of host country discretion in investment matters all the more important. In particular, as will be considered in sections I and II below, there may be a choice between granting a general right to national treatment subject to a "negative list" of excepted industries and areas to which national treatment does not apply, and proceeding on the basis of a "positive list" where no *a priori* general right to national treatment is granted and national treatment extends only to those industries and areas specifically included in the positive list. The development implications of these alternatives are discussed in the concluding section.

The substantive test of differential treatment takes up much of the discussion in section II. Here there are a significant number of alternatives. Thus, the factual area to which national treatment applies may be limited only to the "same" or "identical" situations, or it may be delimited by reference to a list of economic activities, or by reference to "like" or "similar" cases or circumstances. Some agreements are silent on this issue, leaving it up to the parties to determine on a case-by-case basis whether national treatment applies to a particular situation. Once the factual area of application has been determined, the next question is that of comparing the treatment offered to national and foreign investors. This may require that the treatment be the "same as" or "as favourable as" that accorded to national investors, or that it be "no less favourable", the latter offering the possibility not only of equal treatment but also of better treatment for foreign investors where this is deemed appropriate.

Given the significance of national treatment for development, some countries may find it hard to give up their power to treat foreign and domestic investors differently. Thus, in certain rare cases IIAs are silent on national treatment. However, in the majority of recent IIAs national treatment is present. As will be shown particularly in section II and the concluding section, the inclusion of national treatment may be done in such a way as to preserve a high level of host country authority or in a way that ensures a high standard of treatment for foreign investors. Alternatively, a hybrid approach may be taken. Through the judicious use of qualifications and exceptions to national treatment, a balance can be struck between host country authority and the treatment of investors. In particular, the development needs of a developing country may require such flexibility in an agreement. How this can be achieved will be discussed in the concluding section.

Section I
Explanation of the Issue

A. The nature and origins of the national treatment standard

One of the principal characteristics of the national treatment standard is its relativity. Given that the standard invites a comparison in the treatment accorded to foreign and domestic investors, this makes a determination of its content dependent on the treatment offered by a host country to domestic investors and not on some *a priori* absolute principles of treatment.

In international law, the national treatment standard has been invoked in two different contexts. In one context, the standard represents one of the competing international law doctrines for the treatment of the person and property of aliens which has come to be known as the "Calvo doctrine". Under this doctrine, which was supported especially by Latin American countries, aliens and their property are entitled only to the same treatment accorded to nationals of the host country under its national laws. In contrast with this doctrine, the doctrine of State responsibility for injuries to aliens and their property, which historically has been supported by developed countries, asserts that customary international law establishes a minimum international standard of treatment to which aliens are entitled, allowing for treatment more favourable than that accorded to nationals where this falls below the international minimum standard.[2]

In treaty practice, national treatment has its origins in trade agreements. The first treaties to apply a concept of non-differentiation between foreign and local traders can be traced back to the practices of the Hanseatic League in the twelfth and thirteenth centuries (VerLoren van Themaat, 1981, pp. 16 ff). More recently, United States FCN treaties included a clause offering national treatment (Jackson, 1997, p. 397). Equally, national treatment has been a long-standing standard in patent and copyright conventions. Article 2 of the Paris Convention for the Protection of Industrial Property (1883) sanctions the principle that nationals of the member countries "shall have the same protection" as nationals of the host member country in which protection for intellectual property right is sought (United Nations, 1972, p. 313).

In trade matters, national treatment of imported products with respect to internal measures is one of the basic principles of the multilateral trading system created by the General Agreement on Tariffs and Trade (GATT). At least as originally negotiated in 1947, the primary focus of the GATT was on the control and liberalization of border measures restricting international trade in goods. A fundamental principle in this respect is that, as a general rule, any border measures designed to give a competitive advantage to domestic products should take the form of customs tariffs imposed at the border, and that the level of such customs tariffs should be a matter for negotiation and binding in national schedules. Within this scheme of things, article III of the GATT ("National Treatment on Internal Taxation and Regulation") plays a critical role since, as its paragraph 1 makes clear, it is designed to ensure that "internal" measures are not applied to imported or domestic products so as to afford protection to domestic production. It thus serves the purpose of ensuring that internal measures are not used to nullify or impair the effect of tariff concessions and other multilateral rules applicable to border measures. The role of the national treatment principle of GATT article III must therefore be understood in light of the distinction between border measures and internal measures.

In relation to FDI, national treatment involves an economic aim not dissimilar to that which has motivated its adoption in trade agreements: foreign and domestic investors should be subject to the same competitive conditions on the host country market, and therefore no government measure should unduly favour domestic investors.[3] However, because the distinction made in the field of trade in goods between border measures and internal measures has no meaningful equivalent in the field of investment, national treatment clauses in IIAs differ in scope and purpose from the national treatment principle of GATT article III. In particular, a key question arising in regard to the scope of application of national treatment in investment agreements is whether the principle applies to all phases of an investment, i.e. whether it applies only to the treatment of foreign investment after its entry, or whether it also applies to the entry of foreign investment.

Initially, the standard was thought not to be pertinent to entry issues, on the ground that countries have a sovereign right, well established in international law (chapter 4), to control the entry of aliens. In addition, a foreign investor, being "outside" the host country, was not in a similar or comparable position to the domestic investor, so that national treatment was not seen to make sense. Yet the extension of national treatment to the pre-entry phase, starting with United States FCN treaties, and, more recently, in United States and Canadian BITs[4] and the North American Free Trade Agreement (NAFTA)[5], may begin to change the approach to this issue. (See further chapter 4.)

The scope of national treatment in the investment field goes well beyond its use in trade agreements. In particular, the reference to "products" in article III of the GATT is inadequate for investment agreements in that it restricts national treatment to trade in goods. The activities of foreign investors in their host countries encompass a wide array of operations, including international trade in products, trade in components, know-how and technology, local production and distribution, the raising of finance capital and the provision of services, not to mention the range of transactions involved in the creation and administration of a business enterprise. Hence wider categories of economic transactions may be subjected to national treatment disciplines under investment agreements than under trade agreements.

The principal beneficiaries of national treatment are "investors" and "investments". The scope and definitions of these terms are the subject of a separate chapter in these volumes and will not be discussed in detail here (chapter 3). In the context of a national treatment provision, the question of whether the beneficiaries of the standard are foreign investors only or include also foreign investments can have important practical implications.

B. Principal issues

Principal issues arising from the application of the national treatment standard in IIAs to be discussed in greater detail later in this chapter include the following:

1. Scope and application

The question of the scope of application of the national treatment standard involves two separate issues: first, at what stage of the investment process does national treatment apply; secondly, what is the meaning of national treatment where States have subnational authorities exercising constitutional powers to make investment policy?

The first issue involves consideration of whether national treatment applies to both the pre- and post-entry stages of the investment process or whether the national treatment standard applies only to investments that have already been admitted to a host country.

As to the second issue, there is little doubt that under international law the host country Government has the duty (irrespective of the pecularities of its constitutional system) to ensure the observance of national treatment commitments (as well as other international commitments) by all its subnational authorities, unless it is otherwise agreed. However, questions arise where subnational entities enjoy constitutional powers that may affect the treatment of a foreign investor. A question that may arise in this respect is: what category of national investors constitutes the criterion for comparison with foreign investors for the purpose of national treatment -- local subnational investors or other national investors? Further issues arise in relation to non-governmental self-regulatory organizations that undertake regulatory functions in many industries. Should such bodies be subject to national treatment disciplines and, if so, how?

2. The substantive content of the national treatment standard

This issue involves two closely related questions: first, what are the factual situations in which national treatment applies? Second, in what manner, and to what extent, is the treatment of foreign investors assimilated to that of nationals? The first issue defines the limits of factual comparison, while the second issue deals with the techniques of comparison, the application of which is limited to the factual situations identified in answering the first question.

3. The relationship between national treatment and other general standards of treatment

National treatment may co-exist in an IIA with other standards of treatment, notably MFN and fair and equitable treatment. This raises the technical question of how the relevant clauses relate to one another. National treatment may be stated in a "stand alone" provision or it may be combined with other general standards of treatment. It is common practice in IIAs to combine national treatment with MFN (less commonly with fair and equitable treatment) in one clause (see chapters 6 and 7). The main effect of such combinations is to emphasize the close interaction between the various standards of treatment. This may be supplemented by a further clause which entitles the foreign investor to the better of national treatment or MFN, whichever is more advantageous (and, in some cases, may result in treatment for foreign investors that is better than national treatment and therefore discriminates against local investors). Thus, for example, if a foreign investor received better treatment under an MFN clause than under a national treatment standard, the former would apply. This may be the case in situations in which some foreign investors already enjoy preferential treatment in a host country vis-à-vis national firms regarding, for example, incentives.

4. "De jure" and "de facto" treatment

A question that arises is whether national treatment covers not only *de jure* treatment, that is, treatment of foreign investors provided for in national laws and regulations, but also *de facto* treatment, as where a measure in fact works against national treatment. One example may be licensing requirements for the conduct of a certain business activity which depend on the possession of qualifications by skilled personnel that can only be obtained in the host country. Although this measure may be justifiable on policy grounds, as where health and safety issues are involved, it would require a foreign investor to ensure that its own personnel have the relevant national qualifications, requiring additional time and cost to be incurred before the investor can begin to operate.

5. Exceptions to national treatment

The use of exceptions enables host countries to exclude certain types of enterprises, activities or industries from the operation of national treatment. These may consist of:

- **General exceptions** based on reasons of public health, order and morals, and national security. Such exceptions are present in most regional and multilateral investment agreements, and also in a number of BITs.
- **Subject-specific exceptions** which exempt specific issues from national treatment, such as intellectual property, taxation provisions in bilateral tax treaties, prudential measures in financial services or temporary macroeconomic safeguards.
- **Country-specific exceptions** whereby a contracting party reserves the right to differentiate between domestic and foreign investors under its laws and regulations -- in particular, those related to specific industries or activities -- for reasons of national economic and social policy.

The number and scope of exceptions determines the practical effect of national treatment under an investment agreement.

Another issue related to the question of exceptions is whether the standard is based on reciprocity of treatment between the home and host countries of an investor. Some provisions have made national treatment conditional upon the reciprocal granting of national treatment to investors of all contracting parties to an IIA, while others retain a non-reciprocal commitment to the standard

Section II
Stocktaking and Analysis

As noted in section I, in treaty practice the national treatment standard has been widely used in trade agreements. More recently, the standard has been extended to the sphere of FDI through its adoption in bilateral, regional, plurilateral and multilateral investment-related instruments. It has also been reflected in national laws. Developed countries generally include the principle of national treatment in their constitutions or basic laws (UNCTAD, 1994, p. 303). Equally, according to a World Bank survey of some 51 investment codes adopted by developing countries, the overwhelming majority of these countries have adopted provisions that aim at avoiding differences in treatment between foreign and local investors. Many of those countries have favoured a definition of national treatment which excludes the possibility of granting more favourable treatment to FDI, through the use of a test of treatment similar or equal to that given to local investors (World Bank, 1992).

Existing IIAs have taken at least three major policy approaches towards national treatment, which are discussed next.

A. An agreement does not mention national treatment

Some agreements that otherwise provide standards of treatment for foreign investors do not grant national treatment. This (unusual) approach is exemplified by the Assocation of South-East Asian Nations (ASEAN) Agreement for the Protection and Promotion of Investments and the early BITs signed by China, Norway and Sweden. Article 2 of China's BIT with Sweden spells out the general standards of treatment granted to foreign investors as follows:

> "(1) Each Contracting State shall at all times ensure fair and equitable treatment to the investments by investors of the other Contracting State.
>
> (2) Investments by investors of either Contracting State in the territory of the other Contracting State shall not be subjected to a treatment less favourable than that accorded to investments by investors of third States.

(3) Notwithstanding the provisions of paragraph (2) of this Article, a Contracting State, which has concluded with one or more other States an agreement regarding the formation of a customs union or free-trade area, shall be free to grant a more favourable treatment to investments by investors of the State or States, which are also parties to the said agreement, or by investors of some of these States. A Contracting State shall also be free to grant a more favourable treatment to investments by investors of other States, if this is stipulated under bilateral agreements concluded with such States before the date of the signature of this Agreement."

The omission of the national treatment standard may be explained in certain cases on the ground that the host country does not wish to extend preferential treatment enjoyed by its domestic enterprises to foreign enterprises. On the other hand, the reasons for not including the standard may be very specific to the situation in question. In some cases, for example, granting national treatment has been complicated by the provision of price subsidies for national State enterprises for utilities such as water and electricity. In situations where many firms remain State-owned it is difficult to grant the same price subsidies to foreign investors (and perhaps also to national private investors). Finally, home countries might not have found it worthwhile to insist on the granting of national treatment standard in host countries where the conditions available to national firms were below a certain minimum. Over the years China has changed its policy towards national treatment and has agreed to grant it in certain treaties.[6]

B. An agreement goes beyond a general national treatment clause and involves a more specific non-discrimination regime

Here national treatment is present in the content of substantive rules rather than in any single statement of the standard. It may be a fundamental part of the legal order created by the regime. The legal order of the European Union is the main example of this approach. National treatment plays a significant role in the Community legal order, particularly as regards entry and establishment (chapter 4). In addition, European Union law applies a wider concept of non-discrimination between nationals of member States to specific policy areas, thereby helping to harmonize national standards and to develop an integrated single market for trade and investment (box 1).

Box 1. Measures adopted by the European Union aimed at abolishing discrimination between nationals of different member States[a]

- general prohibition against discrimination on the grounds of nationality (article 12);
- free movement of goods (articles 28-29);
- state monopolies (article 31);
- free movement of workers (article 39 (2));
- entry and establishment (articles 43-48);
- freedom to provide services (articles 49-55);
- free movement of capital (articles 56-60);
- social security (Regulation 1408/71 article 3(1));
- competition (article 81(1) (d), 82 (c));
- state aids (articles 87-88);
- discriminatory taxation (articles 90-91).

[a] References are to the Treaty of Rome as amended by the Treaty of Amsterdam (which entered into force on 1 May 1999) (EU, 1997), unless otherwise stated.

C. An agreement contains a general national treatment clause

At the outset, it should be pointed out that national treatment provisions follow a standard general pattern. However, considerable scope for variation arises in the context of that pattern, each variant having significant implications for the process of economic development.

The first question that arises is whether it is the investment, the investor or both that are to receive national treatment. National treatment clauses typically address this question although their approaches vary considerably. In some BITs it is the investment that is entitled to national treatment. Others refer to "enterprises and the activities of enterprises".[7] These formulations would seem to exclude "investors" in the enterprise from national treatment in such matters as, for example, taxation. To guard against such results, an increasing number of IIAs include separate provisions granting the investor and the investment national treatment. Examples of this approach include the the BIT between Jamaica and the United Kingdom (article 3), NAFTA (article 1102 (1) and (2)) and the Asian-African Legal Consultative Committee (AALCC) model BITs A and B (article 5 Draft A and B, UNCTAD, 1996a, vol. III, pp. 119, 130).[8] In some contexts, on the other hand, the term "investment" could be interpreted as covering "investors" because of the inextricable linkage between the investment and the investor.

1. Scope of application

a. Extent of coverage of the investment process

As noted in section I, a national treatment clause can apply either to the pre- and post-entry stage or to the post entry stage only. The post-entry model is at present much more common. However, some recent IIAs have extended national treatment to the pre-entry stage through a combined pre- and post-entry clause. Finally, the operation of national treatment in the General Agreement on Trade in Services (GATS) offers a unique hybrid approach which requires separate consideration.

(i) The post-entry model

This model is typified by IIAs that restrict the operation of the treaty to investments from other contracting parties that are admitted in accordance with the laws and regulations of the host contracting party (chapter 4). This is followed with a provision that accords national treatment to investments so admitted. For example, the BIT between Germany and Namibia stipulates in article 2 that each contracting party shall promote as far as possible investments by nationals or companies of the other contracting party and "admit such investments in accordance with its legislation". Then, in article 3, the national treatment standard is introduced. This provision is divided into four paragraphs. Article 3 (1) states:

> "Neither Contracting Party shall subject investments in its territory owned or controlled by nationals or companies of the other Contracting Party to treatment less favourable than it accords to investments of its own nationals or companies or to investments of nationals or companies of any third State."

Article 3 (2) repeats the same basic phraseology but substitutes "investments" with a reference to "nationals or companies of the other Contracting Party" and accords to them national treatment "as regards their activity in connection with investments in its territory". This approach is followed closely in other BITs signed by European countries.[9]

The National Treatment Decision contained in the OECD Declaration on International Investment and Multinational Enterprises of 1976 makes clear in paragraph II (4) that "this Declaration does not deal with the right of Member countries to regulate the entry of foreign investment or the conditions of establishment of foreign enterprises" (UNCTAD, 1996a, vol. II, p. 184). Under the OECD regime, matters of entry and establishment are the concern of the OECD Code of Liberalisation of Capital Movements in which the right of establishment was introduced in 1984 (chapter 4). Taken together, the Code of Liberalisation of Capital Movements and the National Treatment instrument cover both pre- and post-entry treatment of investment. In order to ensure consistency between these two instruments, the Committee on Capital Movements and Invisible Transactions, the body responsible for the administration of the Codes, and the Committee on International Investment and Multinational Enterprises, the body responsible for the administration and review of the Declaration, cooperate over the interrelationship between the two instruments. According to the 1991 review of the Declaration, measures affecting investment by "direct branches" (branches whose parent company is a nonresident) are covered by the Capital Movements Code, while those of "indirect branches" (branches whose parent company is an established subsidiary of a non-resident) continue to be covered by the National Treatment instrument (OECD, 1992, p. 34). It should be noted that the OECD National Treatment instrument contains no legal obligation, but it is subject to a legally binding system of notification and examination of member countries' exceptions to national treatment. (This is briefly described below under the subheading on exceptions.) In sum, the OECD approach to national treatment has evolved over the years from its original post-entry model to a system that covers both entry and post-entry activities.

Other instruments that have followed the post-entry national treatment model include:

- Many BITs signed between developing countries.[10]
- The Energy Charter Treaty, article 10 (7), extends national treatment to the operations of foreign investments/investors after they enter the host country:

> "Each Contracting Party shall accord to Investments in its Area of Investors of other Contracting Parties, and their related activities including management, maintenance, use, enjoyment or disposal, treatment no less favourable than that which it accords to Investments of its own Investors or of the Investors of any other Contracting Party or any third state and their

related activities including management, maintenance, use, enjoyment or disposal, whichever is the most favourable" (UNCTAD, 1996a, vol. II, p. 556).

As regards the making of investments, contracting parties are only required to "endeavour to accord" national treatment. But the Agreement provides for subsequent negotiation and conclusion of a "supplementary treaty" that will "oblige" parties to accord national and MFN treatment (article 10 (2)-(4), UNCTAD, 1996a, p. 555).

- In the framework of MERCOSUR, investments of investors from non-member States, in contrast to investments of investors from member States, do not enjoy pre-entry national treatment. They are entitled to national treatment only after entry (Decision 11/94, UNCTAD, 1996a, vol. II, p. 530).

(ii) The pre- and post-entry model

The pre- and post-entry approach has its origins in United States treaty practice. Clauses to this effect were present in United States FCN treaties, and have been continued in the BITs signed by the United States and, more recently, by Canada. The United States model BIT (1994) states, in article II (1):

> "With respect to the establishment, acquisition, expansion, management, conduct, operation and sale or other disposition of covered investments, each Party shall accord treatment no less favorable than that it accords, in like situations, to investments in its territory of its own nationals or companies (hereinafter "national treatment") or to investments in its territory of nationals or companies of a third country (hereinafter "most favored nation treatment"), whichever is most favorable (hereinafter "national and most favored nation treatment") ..." (UNCTAD, 1996a, vol. III, p. 197).

This provision makes entry to the host State subject to the national (and MFN) treatment standard in addition to post-entry treatment. This general commitment is typically made subject to the right of each party to adopt or maintain exceptions falling within one of the sectors or matters listed in the annex to the BIT (United States model BIT, 1994, article II (2)).[11]

At the regional level -- apart from the OECD instruments and the ECT (which appears to represent a transition from post-to pre-establishment coverage) -- a significant example of the pre-and post-entry national treatment model is the NAFTA.[12] Article 1102 of the NAFTA grants national treatment to investors and investments of another contracting party with respect to "the establishment, acquisition, expansion, management, conduct, operation, and sale or other disposition of investments" (UNCTAD, 1996a, vol. III, p. 74).

Other agreements follow a similar approach:

- The Asia Pacific Economic Cooperation (APEC) Non-Binding Investment Principles extend the national treatment standard to "the establishment, expansion, operation and protection..." of investments by foreign investors (UNCTAD, 1996a, vol. II, p. 536). However, the APEC instrument is non-binding and represents only a "best efforts" commitment.
- The 1994 Treaty on Free Trade between Colombia, Mexico and Venezuela (article 17-03) accords national treatment (and MFN) to investors of another party and their investments (subject *inter alia* to the right of each party to impose special formalities in connection with the establishment of an investment and to impose information requirements)(http:www.sice.oas.org/Trade/G3_E/ G3E_TOC.stm).
- In MERCOSUR, investments of investors from other MERCOSUR member States are to be admitted on the basis of treatment no less favourable than that accorded to domestic investors or investors from third States, subject to the right of each member State to maintain exceptional limitations for a transitional period, which must be detailed in an annex to the Protocol (Decision 11/93 of the Council of MERCOSUR of 17 January 1994, in UNCTAD, 1996a, vol. II. pp. 513 and 520 for listed exceptions).
- The Framework Agreement on the ASEAN Investment Area adopted in 1998 accords national treatment "immediately to ASEAN investors and their investments, in respect of all industries and measures affecting investment including but not limited to the admission, establishment, acquisition, expansion, management, operation and disposition of investments" (article 7.1 (b)), subject to exceptions provided for under the Agreement (see below). Furthermore, article 4 states that the ASEAN Investment Area will be an area where "national treatment is

extended to ASEAN investors by 2010, and to all investors by 2020" (article 4 (b)).[13]

As noted, the pre- and post-entry approach is not as widespread in terms of numbers of investment agreements as the post-entry model. This approach was followed in the draft text of the Multilateral Agreement on Investment (MAI) (OECD, 1998a, p. 13). Apart from the United States BITs, the other examples deal not only with investment but also with wider trading arrangements.

(iii) The GATS hybrid model

The GATS is based on the principle of "progressive liberalization". Accordingly, the obligation of national treatment expressed in article XVII of the GATS is not a general obligation applicable to trade in servies in all sectors and by all members, but a specific commitment that applies only in sectors inscribed in a member's schedule, and its application is to be gradually extended to other sectors through successive rounds of negotiations. Furthermore, if a member decides to include a sector in its schedule, it still retains the possibility of deciding the level of national treatment it proposes to grant in that sector by listing specific limitations it wishes to maintain. Those limitations could actually be specific discriminatory measures that are inconsistent with the national treatment standard. However, by scheduling them, a member would maintain the legal right to continue to apply them.

The national treatment obligation in article XVII of the GATS requires each member to extend to services and service suppliers of other members treatment no less favourable than that it extends to like services and service suppliers of national origin.[14] Paragraph 1 of that article states:

"1. In sectors inscribed in its Schedule, and subject to any conditions and qualifications set out therein, each Member shall accord to services and service suppliers of any other Member, in respect of all measures affecting the supply of services, treatment no less favourable than that it accords to its own like services and service suppliers."

This may be achieved by according formally identical or formally different treatment. In other words, a national treatment commitment under the GATS would prohibit any form of discrimination whether *de jure* or *de facto*. Paragraphs 2 and 3 of article XVII state:

"2. A Member may meet the requirement of paragraph 1 by according to services and service suppliers of any other Member, either formally identical treatment or formally different treatment to that it accords to its own like services and service suppliers.

3. Formally identical or formally different treatment shall be considered to be less favourable if it modifies the conditions of competition in favour of services or service suppliers of the Member compared to like services or service suppliers of any other Member."

This is meant to ensure that the national treatment obligation provides foreign service suppliers with equal opportunities to compete in a domestic market. This provision is quite far-reaching in the sense that it would cover anything that "modifies conditions of competition" in favour of foreign service suppliers (who under mode 3 would be foreign investors).

As stated earlier, the national treatment obligation of the GATS applies to "all measures affecting the supply of services". Moreover, measures by members are defined in article 1 of the GATS as measures taken by central, regional or local governments and authorities and by non-governmental bodies in the exercise of powers delegated by all government authorities. According to article XVII of the GATS, furthermore, national treatment is to be granted to service suppliers as well as services of any other member.

b. The meaning of national treatment in relation to subnational authorities

It is clear that national treatment obligations apply to the host country Government and governmental bodies. Also, as a matter of the law of treaties, a treaty applies to the entire territory of a party unless a different intention appears from the treaty or is otherwise established. However, it is not always so clear in practice what national treatment means in relation to the political subdivisions of a State. This problem (which is also relevant to other clauses in IIAs) can become significant where a subnational authority has a constitutional power to make investment policy. Such power may be used to grant preferential treatment to local, as opposed to out-of-sub-division investors, as, for example, where a host subnational authority is seeking to encourage the growth of local small and medium-sized firms. A question that arises is whether a subnational authority has to extend such preferential treatment to foreign inward investors on the basis of the national treatment standard, regardless of how it treats national investors from outside the sub-division.

The question has been answered in the provisions of some IIAs, such as United States BITs which, following the United States model BIT (article XV) (UNCTAD, 1996a, vol. III, p. 204) state that the obligations of the treaty will apply to the political sub-divisions of the parties.[15] The United States model BIT specifies further that, in the case of a United States state, territory or possession national treatment means "treatment no less favorable than the treatment accorded thereby, in like situations, to investments from nationals of the United States of America resident in, and companies legally constituted under the laws and regulations of, other States, Territories or possessions of the United States of America" (article XV, (1) (b)). According to this provision, it appears that a foreign investor is to be treated by a United States subnational authority as if it were an investor from another United States subnational authority for the purpose of compliance with national treatment disciplines. Thus, if the host subnational state offers preferential treatment to local investors and does not extend such treatment to out-of-state investors, the foreign investor cannot invoke national treatment to obtain similar preferences. All that the foreign investor can do is require treatment no less favourable than that accorded to out-of-state United States investors. Although the United States model is ambiguous on the issue, it may be presumed that the comparable treatment should be with the best treated out-of-state United States investor, otherwise the treatment would be "less favourable".

This issue is made clearer in NAFTA article 1102 (3) which states that the treatment involved should be "no less favorable than the most favourable treatment accorded, in like circumstances, by that state or province to investors, and to investments of investors, of the Party of which it forms a part." This formulation can allow for differential treatment as between different out-of-sub-division investors of the host country. What it would not allow, however, is for the foreign investor to receive the worst treatment offered to out-of-sub-division investors. In the light of the words, "the most favourable treatment accorded" the foreign investor must be given the best available treatment offered to such local investors.[16]

The OECD National Treatment instrument specifically refers to the problem of subnational entities. By paragraph 3 thereof, "Member countries will endeavour to ensure that their territorial sub-divisions apply national treatment". This provision applies to "states, provinces, cantons, municipalities, regions and communities, but not to national government lands, and it covers areas of legislation in which powers of states are not subordinated to those of the national government" (OECD, 1993, pp. 26-27). The phrasing of the provision suggests that in some cases a member Government may not be in a position to "ensure" that territorial subdivisions apply national treatment. The OECD applies the following criteria to determine whether the treatment of a foreign investor by a territorial sub-division constitutes an exception to national treatment that must be notified to the OECD (OECD, 1993, p. 27):

- An exception exists where all domestic enterprises, both in-state and out-of-state, are given the same treatment, and the foreign investor is given less favourable treatment than these domestic enterprises.
- Where there are differences in the treatment of in-state and out-of-state domestic enterprises, differential treatment of out-of-state foreign-controlled enterprises by the territorial subdivision in question need not, in itself, constitute an exception to national treatment. In such cases the measures in question should be examined pragmatically, taking into account the extent to which the foreign-controlled and domestic enterprises concerned are placed in the same circumstances. Such measures are to be reported to the OECD in the interests of transparency.
- In determining whether a measure constitutes an exception, it is important to identify whether the discrimination implied by a measure is actually motivated, at least in part, by the fact that the enterprises affected are under foreign control. Here difficulties as to what is "foreign" may be encountered as enterprises from outside the territorial sub-division, both domestic and foreign-controlled, may be treated as "foreign" to that jurisdiction.

Turning to non-governmental associations or regulatory bodies, the OECD National Treatment instrument covers, in principle, measures of regulatory bodies only if they are attributable to Governments. However, there is an exception with regard to banking and finance. Here, all associations and regulatory bodies are covered, whether or not there is government involvement. In a similar vein, the MAI negotiating text made membership of self-regulatory bodies and associations in the field of financial services subject to national treatment (OECD, 1998a, p. 83).

2. The substantive content of the national treatment standard

The substantive content of the national treatment standard involves, in particular, an analysis of the following two issues: the factual situation in which the standard applies and the definition of the standard itself.

a. Factual situations in which national treatment applies

Some IIAs qualify the definition of the national treatment standard by specifying the factual situations in which the standard applies. The following alternatives present themselves:

(i) The "same" or "identical" circumstances

The most restrictive formulation would be to limit national treatment to the "same" or "identical" circumstances. This would offer a narrow scope to national treatment as the incidence of an "identical" situation may be hard to show. Such a formulation was proposed during the drafting of article 49 of the 1983 text of the United Nations draft Code of Conduct on Transnational Corporations (UNCTC, 1990b, p. 200).

Earlier BITs signed by the United Kingdom referred to the "same circumstances". For example, the 1982 BIT between Belize and the United Kingdom, article 3 (1), provides that "Neither Contracting Party shall... subject investments or returns of nationals or companies of the other Contracting Party to treatment less favourable than that which it accords in the same circumstances to investments or returns of its own nationals" (Dolzer and Stevens, 1995, p. 63). The more recent practice of the United Kingdom is not to qualify the national treatment standard.

(ii) The economic activities and/or industries to which national treatment applies

Some IIAs specify the economic activities or industries to which national treatment applies. Such an approach has the effect of narrowing the scope of national treatment to those areas of activity expressly mentioned in the agreement (box 2). It is another example of an approach which is used by host countries to preserve a degree of flexibility to act by narrowing the scope of national treatment. This is also the effect sought by the GATS provisions already mentioned above. National treatment is expected to apply only to those sectors to which commitments have been made.

Box 2. Examples of functional delineations of national treatment

Agreements delineating the functional scope of national treatment include:

The *Common Convention on Investments in the States of the Customs and Economic Union of Central Africa*, article 3, offers a functional list of cases to which the same conditions should apply as between undertakings whose capital derives from other countries and undertakings in the member countries of the Union (UNCTAD, 1996, vol. II, p. 89).

The *Agreement for the Establishment of a Regime for CARICOM Enterprises* (of 1987), article 12 (4), extends national treatment for CARICOM enterprises to specific functions comprising licences and permissions necessary for the proper conduct of affairs, the purchase or use of goods and services, access to credit, and protection by quantitative restrictions or other forms of protection against imports from third countries (UNCTAD, 1996, vol. II, p. 277).

The BIT between Denmark and Indonesia (article 3) refers not to "treatment" but to the "imposition of conditions". This language suggests that the host country is not obliged to give national treatment with respect to benefits and advantages.

Decision 292 of the Commission of the Cartagena Agreement, article 9, offers national treatment for Andean multinational enterprises with respect to preferences and for the acquisition of public sector goods and services (UNCTAD, 1996a, vol. II, p. 477).

Such functional delineation of national treatment can also arise as a result of the specialized nature of an agreement. (See also section III, interactions between the scope and definitions and the national treatment provisions.) This is the case in, for example, the GATS which limits its functional scope to services, thought this is in itself a vast area of commercial activity. Other agreements in which the functional scope of national treatment is similarly circumscribed include, in relation to the energy industries, the Energy Charter Treaty; in relation to intellectual property rights, the TRIPS Agreement (article 3); and, in relation to specific operational measures, the TRIMs Agreement. Some specialized agreements further specify their functional delineation in the formulation of the national treatment clause. Thus, for example, under article

XVII, GATS specifies that "each Member shall accord to *services and service suppliers* of any other Member, in respect of *all measures affecting the supply of services*, treatment no less favourable than that it accords to its own like *services and service suppliers*" (emphasis added).[17]

The ILO Tripartite Declaration of Principles Concerning Multinational Enterprises and Social Policy uses a standard similar to that of national treatment where it provides that wages, benefits and conditions of work and standards of industrial relations to be observed by TNCs should be not less favourable than those observed by comparable employers in the country concerned (UNCTAD, 1996a, vol. I, pp. 96-97). However, it must be made clear that the ILO Declaration uses a comparison between standards observed by TNCs and comparable domestic employers to determine the minimum obligations of TNCs. Thus, it could be said that where TNCs observe only the same standards as domestic employers, and these fall below the minimum standards required by the ILO Declaration, TNCs should observe the higher standards of the Declaration.

Another approach that has been used is to have an open-ended but indicative list of activities to which the national treatment standard applies (box 3). For example, the Energy Charter Treaty, article 10 (7), specifies that national treatment applies to investments of investors of other contracting parties and "their related activities, including management, maintenance, use, enjoyment or disposal..." (UNCTAD, 1996a, vol. II, p. 556). Thus, while it is an agreement aimed at the energy sector only, this formulation makes it clear that it encompasses all types of activities associated with the operation of an energy investment.[18]

Listing specific activities to which national treatment applies -- even if the lists are only indicative and not closed lists -- serve the purpose of providing guidance as to which types of activities the parties intended to cover under a national treatment provision and which were not to be so covered. Given the potentially broad range of activities to which national treatment may apply, such lists, whose coverage may vary considerably from instrument to instrument (box 3), respond to a concern that, otherwise, open-ended national treatment clauses (or national treatment clauses that are silent about the types of activities covered) may result in extending national treatment to aspects that were never intended by the parties.

It may be asked whether such wide wording results in "overkill" in that it may be difficult in practice to see the difference between words such as "management", "use", "enjoyment" or "maintenance".

Box 3. Examples of national treatment clauses covering a broad range of investment activities

The *World Bank Guidelines on the Treatment of Foreign Direct Investment* (1992) offer a functional list of areas to which national treatment applies. Thus, Guideline III (3) (a) states:

> "With respect to the protection and security of their person, property rights and interests, and to the granting of permits, import and export licenses and the authorization to employ, and the issuance of the necessary entry and stay visas to their foreign personnel and other legal matters relevant to the treatment of foreign investors.....such treatment will, subject to the requirement of fair and equitable treatment mentioned above, be as favourable as that accorded by the State to national investors in similar circumstances..." (UNCTAD, 1996a, vol. I, pp. 249-250).

NAFTA article 1102 (1) lists "the establishment, acquisition, expansion, management, conduct, operation and sale or other disposition of investments.." as being subject to national treatment (UNCTAD, 1996a, vol. III, p. 74).

The draft MAI uses the following formulation: "establishment, acquisition, expansion, operation, management, maintenance, use, enjoyment and sale or other disposition of investments" (OECD, 1998a, p. 13). This formulation was considered by several delegations to be a comprehensive one whose terms were intended to cover all activities of investors and their investments for both the pre- and post-establishment phases. Other delegations favoured a closed list of investment activities covered by national treatment. Others objected to this approach on the grounds that, while such a list had the advantage of certainty, it could omit elements that were of importance to the investor (OECD, 1998a, p. 11).

The Framework Agreement on the ASEAN Investment Area, as noted above, offers an interesting variant of this approach. By article 7 (1) (b), national treatment is accorded immediately to ASEAN investors and their investments in respect of all industries and measures affecting investment, "including but not limited to the admission, establishment, acquisition, expansion, management, operation and disposition of investments" (ASEAN, 1998). This approach makes clear that the list is only illustrative and not exhaustive as to cases in which national treatment applies.

(iii) "Like situations", "similar situations" or "like circumstances"

Qualifications such as "like situations", "similar situations" and "like circumstances" may be seen as synonymous and therefore can be discussed together. They may be less restrictive of national treatment in that they may apply to any activity or sector that is not subject to exceptions. What is a "like" situation or circumstance is a matter that needs to be determined in the light of the facts of the case. This assumes that clear comparisons of business situations are possible, and that agreement can be reached on what is a "like" circumstance. This may not be easy in practice, as the experience of GATT/WTO Dispute Panels has shown (Mattoo, 1997). It is implicit in the use of this term that the host country will assess cases in good faith and in full consideration of all relevant facts. According to an OECD report, among the most important matters to be considered are "whether the two enterprises are in the same sector; the impact of policy objectives of the host country in particular fields; and the motivation behind the measure involved" (OECD, 1985, pp. 16-17). A key issue in such cases is to "ascertain whether the discrimination is motivated, at least in part, by the fact that the enterprises concerned are under foreign control" (OECD, 1993, p. 22).

The "like situations" formulation is found in, for example, United States BITs, following the United States model BIT (article II (1), UNCTAD, 1996a, vol. III, p. 197) and in the OECD National Treatment instrument (UNCTAD, 1996a, vol. II, p. 184). The "like circumstances" formulation is found in NAFTA (article 1102 (1), (2), UNCTAD, 1996a, vol. III, p. 74) and in the Canada-Chile Free Trade Agreement (article G-02 (1) (2), Canada-Chile, 1997). The World Bank Guidelines on the Treatment of Foreign Investment use "in similar circumstances" (UNCTAD, 1996a, vol. I, p. 250). These are general phrases which allow considerable scope for determining what is "like" from the context surrounding an investor and an investment.

A variation of this approach is found in the Framework Agreement on the ASEAN Investment Area, which, after listing the functions to which national treatment applies, specifies that the treatment concerned will be that which the host country accords "to its own like investors and investments" (article 7 (1) (b), ASEAN, 1998). Here the comparison shifts from the general context of the investment to the nature and characteristics of investors and investments, a more exacting comparison.

The inclusion of the phrase "in like circumstances" was debated during the MAI negotiations, and no agreement was reached on its inclusion. Some delegations thought that national treatment implicitly provides the comparative context for determining whether a measure unduly treats foreign investments differently and that the inclusion of the words was unnecessary and open to abuse. Other delegations thought that the comparative context should be indicated, following the practice of the OECD National Treatment instrument, NAFTA and some BITs (OECD, 1998a, p. 11).[19]

(iv) No factual comparisons

A significant number of IIAs contain a description of the national treatment standard but are silent on whether national treatment applies to specified activities or like situations or circumstances. Here a simple reference is made to investors and/ or investments, usually in separate paragraphs, followed by a description of the standard of treatment required. Such an approach is seen in, for example, the Chilean, French, German, Swiss and United Kingdom model BITs, though the last retains a functional delimitation formula in relation to the treatment of investors. This approach offers the widest scope for comparison as, in principle, any matter that is relevant to determining whether the foreign investor is being given national treatment can be considered. The test will be an easier one for the investor than under formulations requiring proof of like situations, circumstances and/or functional contexts.

b. Definition of the standard

IIAs have defined the standard of national treatment in two main ways. One way requires a strict standard of equality of treatment between national and foreign investors. The other offers the possibility of granting more favourable treatment to foreign investors.

(i) "Same" or "as favourable as" treatment[20]

This formulation suggests that the treatment offered to foreign investors is no better than that received by national investors. In effect it excludes the possibility of the foreign investor claiming preferential treatment as a matter of treaty obligation on the part of the host country. However, there is nothing in this formulation to prevent a host country from treating foreign investors in a preferential way, should it so choose. National investors may challenge such preferential treatment. They may have rights under the host country law to challenge such treatment, for example, under national constitutional provisions against discrimination. In addition, the IIA might itself be incorporated into national law. This may have the effect of extending protection to national investors as well, although much depends on the actual wording of the agreement and the extent to which national laws give rights to domestic investors in such cases.

Examples of such an approach include:

- The Agreement on Investment and Free Movement of Arab Capital Among Arab Countries states in article 4 that "[m]ember states undertake to treat Arab investments in all areas designated thereto, without discrimination and on equal footing with indigenous investments" (UNCTAD, 1996a, vol. II, p. 122). The Unified Agreement for the Investment of Arab Capital in the Arab States requires that "the capital of the Arab investor shall, without discrimination, be treated in the same manner as capital owned by the citizens of that State" (article 6, UNCTAD, 1996a, vol. II, p. 214).[21]
- The Common Convention on Investments in the States of the Customs and Economic Union of Central Africa, article 3, states that "[u]ndertakings whose capital derives from other countries, shall be able to acquire rights of any kind deemed necessary for the exercise of their activities: real property and industrial rights, concessions, official authorisations and permits, participations in government contracts under the same conditions as undertakings in the member countries of the Union" (UNCTAD, 1996a, vol. II, p. 89).
- The Joint Convention on the Freedom of Movement of Persons and the Right of Establishment in the Central African Customs and Economic Union (CACEU), article 3, provides that, "Nationals of CACEU member States travelling, staying or establishing themselves in the territory of another member State shall enjoy the same rights and freedoms as the nationals thereof, except for political rights, " which are defined as "(a) the individual rights and guarantees; (b) the personal and public freedoms" (UNCTAD, 1996a, vol. II, p. 156).
- The Community Investment Code of the Economic Community of the Great Lakes Countries (article 9) also uses a reference to the "same conditions as enterprises of the host country" (UNCTAD, 1996a, vol. II, p. 255).
- Decision 291of the Commission of the Cartagena Agreement (ANCOM) (1991) article 2, provides that "Foreign investors shall have the same rights and obligations as national investors, except as otherwise provided in the legislation of each member country" (UNCTAD, 1996a, vol. II, p. 450). Decision 24, which preceded Decision 291, was more blunt: "Member countries may not accord to foreign investors treatment more favourable than to national investors." Thus the ANCOM position has shifted from an outright prohibition of preferential treatment for foreign investors to one of leaving to member countries the discretion whether or not to accord to those investors the same, less favourable or more favourable treatment than to national investors.
- The World Bank Guidelines on the Treatment of Foreign Direct Investment require treatment that is "as favourable as that accorded by the State to national investors in similar circumstances" (UNCTAD, 1996a, vol. I, p. 250).
- The draft United Nations Code of Conduct on Transnational Corporations, in its 1983 version, included two alternative formulations in brackets. The first one was "the treatment" and the second formulation was "treatment no less favourable" than that accorded to domestic enterprises (UNCTAD, 1996a, vol. I, p. 173).

(ii) "No less favourable" treatment

This formulation, which is the most commonly used in IIAs, offers treatment which will usually result in treatment as favourable as that received by national investors of a host country. However, it leaves open the possibility of subjecting host country actions to review in accordance with standards of treatment that may be in practice more favourable for foreign, as compared to national, investors. This may occur where standards of treatment accorded to national investors who are in situations comparable to those of foreign investors fall below international minimum standards. Again any consequential discrimination suffered by national investors would be beyond the scope of an IIA, though it may be subject to the same remedies under national law for national investors as mentioned in relation to the issue of "same" or "as favourable as" treatment, with the rider that the possibility of more favourable treatment for foreign investors is implied in the "no less favourable" formulation.

The principal example of this approach is the OECD National Treatment instrument contained in the OECD Declaration on International Investment and Multinational Enterprises of 1976 (UNCTAD, 1996, vol. II, p. 184; Muchlinski, 1995, pp. 583-587). According to the Declaration:

> ".. Member countries should, consistent with their needs to maintain public order, to protect their essential security interests and to fulfil commitments relating to international peace and security, accord to enterprises operating in their territories and owned or controlled directly or indirectly by nationals of another Member country (hereinafter referred to as "Foreign-Controlled Enterprises") treatment under their laws, regulations and administrative practices, consistent with international law and no less favourable than that accorded in like situations to domestic enterprises (hereinafter referred to as "National Treatment")."

The meaning and effect of the OECD National Treatment instrument has been regularly reviewed by the Committee on International Investment and Multinational Enterprises under powers granted to it by article 4 (a) of the Third Revised Council Decision on National Treatment (OECD, 1994). This has resulted in the Committee issuing guidelines for the interpretation of the principle as described in the Declaration (OECD, 1985, 1992, 1993). Furthermore, as part of its monitoring functions, the Committee has undertaken periodic surveys of member country measures that constitute exceptions to the "national treatment" principle, based upon its clarifications of the 1976 Declaration.

Thus, in OECD practice, according to the Committee's reports on national treatment, the phrase in the Declaration "treatment no less favourable than that accorded to domestic enterprises" has the following implications (OECD, 1985, 1993):

- An exception to national treatment is not created by the existence of a public monopoly which results in discriminatory measures against foreign affiliates.
- If a foreign affiliate already established in a member country receives less favourable treatment, this can constitute an exception to national treatment if it also falls within the other criteria for determining such an exception; on the other hand, if the foreign affiliate receives treatment at least as favourable as that given to domestic enterprises, there can be no case of an exception to national treatment.
- In cases where domestic enterprises do not all receive the same treatment, where a foreign affiliate already established in a member country is treated less favourably than the least well treated domestic enterprise, this can constitute an exception to national treatment; if it receives treatment equivalent to that given to the best treated domestic enterprise there can be no question of an exception to national treatment. In cases where a foreign affiliate receives treatment at least as favourable as the least well treated domestic enterprise but less favourable than the best treated enterprise, it is not certain that this constitutes an exception to national treatment.
- Each such case should be reviewed on its facts, taking account of individual national characteristics and the degree to which the foreign and domestic enterprises are placed in comparable circumstances.
- The reference to international law ensures that international minimum standards of treatment for aliens and their property, recognized by the member countries of the OECD, form part of the substantive test of treatment. This allows for the preferential treatment of foreign investors where national treatment falls below such international standards.

The "no less favourable treatment" standard is the most common formulation in treaty practice. It was also included in the MAI negotiating text (OECD, 1998a, p. 13). There was discussion as to whether the "same" or "comparable" treatment should be used, but the majority of delegates considered that this would unacceptably weaken the standard of treatment from the investor's viewpoint (OECD, 1998a, p. 10). Other agreements that use the "no less favourable treatment" formulation are listed in box 4.

Box 4. Other agreements using the "no less favourable" formulation

- The AALCC draft model BITs, article 5, models A and B; Chilean model BIT, article 4 (2); French model BIT, article 4; German model BIT, article 3 (1) (2); Dutch model BIT, article 3(2) (Netherlands, 1997); Portuguese model BIT, article 3 (2); Swiss model BIT, article 4 (2) (3); United Kingdom model BIT, article 3 (1) (2); United States model BIT, article II (1), and the majority of BITs that follow these models.
- NAFTA, article 1102; Canada-Chile Free Trade Agreement, article G02 (Canada-Chile, 1997).
- CARICOM Agreement for the Establishment of a Regime for CARICOM Enterprises, article 12 (4) (a) (b) (c) (g).
- MERCOSUR Decision 11/93, article 3 (Protocol on Intrazonal Investors), and Decision 11/94 Section C (2) (Protocol on Extrazonal Investors).
- Energy Charter Treaty, article 10 (7).
- Framework Agreement on the ASEAN Investment Area, article 7 (1) (b) (ASEAN, 1998).
- GATS, article XVII (1); TRIPS Agreement, article 3 (1).

3. "De jure" and "de facto" national treatment

As noted in section I, national treatment is primarily concerned with provisions in the national laws and regulations of host countries which specifically address the treatment of foreign investors. However, foreign investors may find themselves in disadvantageous situations vis-à-vis local investors as a result of regulations or practices that, although not discriminatory against them *per se*, nevertheless have a detrimental effect on their ability to operate in practice, precisely because of their being "foreign". A few IIAs have explicitly addressed this issue. An example of a provision that expressly deals with *de facto* as well as *de jure* treatment is article XVII of the GATS which states, in paragraphs 2 and 3:

> " 2. A Member may meet the requirement of paragraph 1 by according to services and service suppliers of any other Member, either formally identical treatment or formally different treatment to that it accords to its own like services and service providers.
> 3. Formally identical or formally different treatment shall be considered to be less favourable if it modifies the conditions of competition in favour of services or service suppliers of the Member compared to like services or service suppliers of any other Member" (UNCTAD, 1996a, vol. I, p. 302).

These provisions are of special significance in relation to financial services or insurance, where it is often the case that identical treatment cannot be granted to branches and other unincorporated entities of foreign controlled enterprises in view of the need to maintain prudential measures or because of legal/technical differences. In such cases, differences of treatment between domestic and foreign controlled enterprises may be justifiable provided that the difference in treatment is no greater than strictly necessary to meet prudential requirements and that *de facto* the competitive opportunities on the market for foreign investors are not unfavourably affected. This approach is often referred to as "equivalent treatment" (OECD, 1993, pp. 22-23).

4. "Stand alone" national treatment provision or national treatment combined with other general standards of treatment

The standard of national treatment is often combined in IIAs with other standards of treatment. The basic alternatives are described below.

a. "Stand alone" national treatment provision

In certain cases national treatment is the only general standard of treatment that an instrument seeks to grant. The OECD National Treatment instrument focuses on this standard and requires that member countries "consider applying 'National Treatment' in respect of countries other than Member countries" (paragraph 2, UNCTAD, 1996a, vol. II, p. 184). Similarly, perhaps, the TRIMs Agreement addresses performance requirements by reference only to national treatment under GATT article III and to prohibitions on quantitative restrictions under GATT article XI (UNCTAD, 1996a, vol. I, p. 280).

b. Separate national treatment provision followed by other general standards of treatment clauses

In other cases, the national treatment provision is found in a separate clause from those that relate to other general standards of treatment such as MFN and/or fair and equitable treatment.[22]

Some agreements with separate national treatment and MFN treatment clauses specify also that each contracting party shall accord to investors of the other contracting party or parties the better of national or MFN treatment. NAFTA articles 1102, 1103 and 1104 take such an approach (UNCTAD, 1996a, vol. III, p. 74).

c. Combined national and MFN treatment provision

The various general standards of treatment are often included in the same provision of an agreement, though there are variations in drafting. This practice is followed mainly in BITs and in the MAI negotiating text. Three basic models can be identified:

- Some agreements provide for national and MFN treatment in a combined provision without specifying whether one or the other standard should apply in case of conflict between the two. Examples are the German model BIT, article 3 (UNCTAD, 1996a, vol. III, p. 169); the Portuguese model BIT, article 3 (2), which combines national and MFN and fair and equitable treatment (UNCTAD, 1998a, p. 268); and the United Kingdom model BIT, article 3 (UNCTAD, 1996a, vol. III, p. 187).
- Other agreements specify that the standard which is the "more favourable" to the foreign investor and/or investment, as the case may be, applies: examples include the Swiss model BIT, article 4 (2) (UNCTAD, 1996a, vol. III, p. 179); the French model BIT, article 4 *"si celui-ci est plus avantageux"* (UNCTAD, 1996a, vol. III, p. 161); the Netherlands model BIT, article 3 (2); and the MAI negotiating text, part III, "Treatment of Investors" (OECD, 1998a, p. 13).
- The third model provides that the standard that is the "most favourable" to the foreign investor and/or investment, as the case may be, applies; examples include the Chilean model BIT, article 4 (2) (UNCTAD, 1996a, vol. III, p. 145); the United States model BIT, article II (1) (UNCTAD, 1996a, vol. III, p. 197); and the Energy Charter Treaty, article 10 (7) (UNCTAD, 1996a, vol. II, p. 556).

The effects of these variations revolve around the level to which the investor/investment is to be treated vis-à-vis other classes of investors. The first model, by not specifying which standard applies, leaves it to the host country to determine whether to compare the treatment accorded to a foreign investor with domestic or other foreign investors, regardless of which offers better protection. The second and third models differ in that they expressly require the better of national or MFN treatment to apply.

5. Exceptions

The number and scope of exceptions determine the practical effect of national treatment under an investment agreement. The most common approach is to have a wide formulation of the national treatment standard, as described above, followed by exceptions reflecting each contracting party's needs in terms of protecting essential interests. An "opt-out" approach is the more common model, though, as noted above in relation to GATS, an "opt-in" approach is also an option. Exceptions are more frequent where the pre-entry stage is covered. For developing countries, moreover, the question arises whether their special circumstances require special attention through a "development exception". Finally, the question of monitoring of exceptions has arisen in practice.

a. Classification of exceptions

Exceptions to national treatment can be divided into four main categories:

- **General exceptions**. As noted in section I, general exceptions are typically based on public health, order and morals, and national security. Such exceptions are present in many IIAs (and they often appear in a separate provision and apply to all provisions in the agreement, not only to national treatment), as exemplified in the following examples:
  - The OECD National Treatment instrument permits distinctions of treatment for foreign affiliates consistent with the need to maintain public order, the protection of essential security interests and the fulfilment of commitments to maintain international peace and security. The interpretation of these exceptions in concrete situations is left to the member countries, although the need was recognized to apply them with caution, bearing in mind the objectives of the National Treatment instrument; in other words, they should not be used as a general escape clause from the commitments under

this instrument (OECD, 1985, p. 16; OECD, 1993, p. 27).

- NAFTA contains a general national security exception in article 2102 which applies to investment matters. However, as regards exceptions to national treatment, the main approach is to use subject-specific and industry-specific exceptions, discussed below. A similar approach is taken in the Canada-Chile Free Trade Agreement (article O-02, Canada-Chile, 1997).
- The Energy Charter Treaty contains in article 24 a general exception for the adoption or enforcement of measures necessary to protect human, animal or plant life or health, to the acquisition or distribution of energy materials and products in conditions of short supply, and measures designed to benefit investors who are aboriginal people or socially or economically disadvantaged groups provided that such measures do not constitute a disguised restriction on economic activity in the energy sector or arbitrary or unjustifiable discrimination between contracting parties or investors. The provision goes on to cover protection of essential national security interests (UNCTAD, 1996a, vol.II, pp. 566-568).
- The MAI negotiating text contains general exceptions for essential security interests (OECD, 1998a, p. 77).
- GATS, article XIV, provides for exceptions based on the protection of public order and health, while article XIV bis provides for exceptions based on essential security interests (UNCTAD, 1996a, vol. I, pp. 299-300).

- **Subject-specific exceptions.** Subject-specific exceptions concern, in particular, the exclusion from national (and MFN) treatment commitments relating to, for example:
  - taxation (see, for example, BIT between the Republic of Korea and Mongolia article 7 (b); MAI, article VIII (OECD, 1998a))
  - intellectual property rights guaranteed under international intellectual property conventions (United States model BIT, article, II (2) (b), UNCTAD, 1998a, p. 289);
  - prudential measures in financial services (BITs signed by Canada; MAI, (OECD, 1998a)); -temporary macroeconomic safeguards (MAI (OECD, 1998a)); -incentives (BIT between Jamaica and the United Kingdom, article 3; NAFTA, article 1108.7 (a)); -public procurement (NAFTA, article 1108.7 (b)); -special formalities in connection with establishment (e.g. information, registration) (NAFTA; United States BITs);
  - cultural industries exception (NAFTA, annex 2106); (Muchlinski, 1995, pp. 241, 269).

- **Industry-specific exceptions**. A party may reserve the right to treat domestic and foreign investors in certain types of activities or industries differently under its laws and regulations for reasons of national economic and social policy. This practice appears to have its origins in the United States FCN treaties, and has been followed in the United States BITs, NAFTA, the Canada-Chile Free Trade Agreement and the MAI negotiating text, among others. The most common method of doing so is to "opt out" of the general national treatment obligation, typically by way of an annex of reserved industries and activities which fall outside the scope of the national treatment obligation and in which differential treatment is possible. Under NAFTA, Annex II, each contracting party is allowed to make reservations with respect to specific industries in which the party may adopt more restrictive measures. Exceptions have been made that preserve existing federal measures listed in Annex I to the Agreement. These include, *inter alia*, Mexico's primary energy sector and railroads, United States airlines and radio communications and Canada's cultural industries. Another example of the same approach is provided by the BITs signed by the United States. Thus, for example, the treaty between Grenada and the United States designates in an annex the industries with respect to which each party reserves the right to deny national treatment. The list of industries with respect to Grenada consists of the following: air transportation, government grants, government insurance and loan programmes, ownership of real estate, and use of land and natural resources. The list with respect to the United States is considerably broader and consists of: air transportation, ocean and coastal shipping, banking, insurance, government grants, government insurance and loan programmes, energy and power production, custom house brokers, ownership of real state, ownership and operation of broadcast or common carrier radio and television stations, ownership of shares of the Communications Satellite Corporation, the provision of common carrier telephone and telegraph services, the provision of submarine cable services, and use of land and national resources.[23]

- **Reciprocal national treatment clauses**. In some IIAs the granting of national treatment is contingent upon a reciprocal commitment from the other parties to the same effect. In 1985, the OECD concluded that, where the provision of equal treatment for a foreign affiliate by a host country was conditional on similar treatment being extended to enterprises from the host country in the home country, that constituted an exception to national treatment if it resulted in the foreign affiliate being treated less favourably than similar domestic enterprises (OECD, 1985). In 1993, the OECD declared that reciprocity measures were incompatible with a multilateral approach to liberalization and should be progressively removed (OECD, 1993).

b. *Exceptions based on development considerations*

As noted in the introduction, the standard of national treatment is an important principle for foreign investors, but it may raise difficulties for many host countries, since such treatment may make it difficult to foster the growth of domestic enterprises. This is especially the case for developing countries, since their national enterprises may be particularly vulnerable, especially vis-à-vis large TNCs. Indeed, host Governments sometimes have special policies and programmes that grant advantages and privileges to domestic enterprises in order to stimulate their growth and competitiveness. If a national treatment clause in an IIA obliges a host country to grant the same privileges and benefits to foreign investors, the host Government would in effect be strengthening the ability of foreign investors to compete with local business (UNCTAD, 1998a).

To address this issue, developing countries have at times sought to qualify or limit the application of national treatment in their negotiations through the introduction of a "development clause", in the form of a "development exception", to the general principle of national treatment. Such a "development clause" -- which also reflects the principle that developing countries, by virtue of their weaker economic position and their development needs, should receive special and differential treatment[24] -- serves the purpose of allowing for policy flexibility while maintaining the commitment to the basic principle. For these countries the need to maintain a certain amount of flexibility in the interest of promoting their growth and development is indeed an overriding concern, including when it comes to the application of the national treatment standard.

The industry-specific exceptions discussed above may be based on economic and social development considerations. In other cases, "best efforts" have served the same purpose in, for example, the APEC Non-Binding Investment Principles and in the case of the Energy Charter Treaty for the pre-establishment phase (see above).[25]

It is in this context that, during the negotiations on the draft United Nations Code of Conduct on Transnational Corporations (which was not adopted), a development exception was discussed in relation to national treatment. In particular the developing countries felt that, if the national treatment standard were applied without qualifications, it could prove to be costly to their development efforts in view of the unequal competitive position of domestic enterprises as compared to many TNCs. Accordingly, these countries argued that the national treatment standard should be qualified by a "development clause" which would accord national treatment to TNCs only when the characteristics of those two types of enterprises were the same and the circumstances under which they operated were also similar to those of domestic enterprises (United Nations Commission on Transnational Corporations, 1984, paragraph 27; Asante, 1989, p. 31). Developed countries, for their part, favoured a formulation that was flexible enough to allow preferential treatment for TNCs if the host country should deem this appropriate. The developing countries' views on that point were that, while the question of granting preferential treatment for TNCs was indeed within the sovereign discretion of individual countries, it should not be made a general international standard. Instead, developing countries insisted on the need to allow for preferential treatment to domestic enterprises on account of their development needs. Developed countries indicated that a "development clause" that was too broad and open-ended could undermine the basis of the entire principle.

The "development clause" that came out of these discussions was "without prejudice to measures specified in legislation relating to the declared development objectives of developing countries". More specifically, the last (1990) draft of the Code before negotiations were discontinued, proposed by the Chairperson of the reconvened special session of the Commission on Transnational Corporations, contained the following provision:[26]

> " 50. Subject to national requirements for maintaining public order and protecting national security and consistent with national constitutions and basic laws, and without prejudice to measures specified in legislation relating to the declared development objectives of the developing countries, entities of transnational corporations should be entitled to treatment no less favourable than that accorded to domestic enterprises in similar circumstances" (UN-ECOSOC, 1990, p. 15).

This formulation sought to make national treatment subject to legally specified development measures. It therefore requires a positive legal basis for different treatment by way of an exception to national treatment.

Development considerations of this kind have figured in certain national treatment clauses of BITs, though such a practice appears to have become less common in recent years. For example, Protocol 2 of the BIT between Indonesia and Switzerland allows derogation from national treatment of Swiss investors "in view of the present stage of development of the Indonesian national economy". However, Indonesia would grant "identical or compensating facilities to investments and nationals of the Swiss Confederation in similar economic activities" (UNCTAD, 1998a, p. 64). Similarly, Germany has accepted certain exceptions to national treatment provided these are undertaken for development purposes only, for example the development of small-scale industries, and that the measures do not substantially impair investments from a German investor (UNCTAD, 1998a, p. 64). Jamaica, too, has sought in its BITs to reconcile its growth and development concerns with the needs of foreign investors in reference to the granting of incentives.[27] A recent example of a development clause can be found in the BIT between Italy and Morocco, which provides:

> "Investors of the two Contracting Parties shall not be entitled to national treatment in terms of benefiting from aid, grants, loans, insurance and guarantees accorded by the Government of one of the Contracting Parties exclusively to its own nationals or enterprises within the framework of activities carried out under national development programmes."

c. *Monitoring*

Regional and multilateral investment agreements sometimes provide for a mechanism to follow up on the implementation of the agreement in question and, in particular, to ensure transparency of exceptions and/or to administer the gradual abolition of exceptions or time-derogations to the application of the national treatment. Perhaps the most tested mechanism in this respect is the OECD Committee on International Investment and Multinational Enterprises (CIME). It has undertaken periodic surveys of member country measures that constitute exceptions to the "national treatment" principle, based upon its clarifying interpretations of the 1976 Declaration. The Committee has considered the application of national treatment in five main areas: investment by established foreign affiliates, official aids and subsidies, tax obligations, government purchasing and public contracts, and access to local bank credits and the capital market. These are the principal areas in which the OECD member States have passed laws and regulations providing for different treatment for foreign affiliates.[28] Under the 1991 Review of the OECD Declaration, the application of national treatment to the privatization of enterprises previously under public ownership was taken up. The Committee considered that access to the areas newly opened up by such a policy should be on a non-discriminatory basis between private domestic and foreign affiliates already established in the country in question. Any restrictions applying to foreign affiliates should be reported as exceptions to national treatment (OECD, 1992, p. 27).

In order to assist the Committee in its work, the Third Revised Council Decision on National Treatment introduced a new requirement that member countries should notify to the Committee all measures constituting exceptions to the principle of national treatment. Thereupon the Committee is empowered to examine the notification. Furthermore, a member country may refer another member country to the Committee where the former considers itself to have been prejudiced by the introduction of measures by the latter. The Committee is also available as a forum for consultations, on the invitation of a member country, on any matter related to the implementation of the Declaration (OECD, 1994; Muchlinski, 1995, p. 584).

The TRIMs Agreement provides another example of a follow up mechanism in relation to the implementation of the Agreement. Pursuant to article 7 of the Agreement, a Committee on Trade-Related Investment Measures was established with a view to carrying out the responsibilities assigned to it by the WTO Council for Trade in Goods and to afford members the opportunity to consult on any matters relating to the operation and implementation of the TRIMs Agreement (article 7, 2). More specifically, the Committee is entrusted with the task of monitoring the operation and implementation of the Agreement and reporting thereon annually to the Council for Trade in Goods (article 7, 3). Moreover, according to article 8, the provisions of article XXII and article XXIII of GATT 1994, as elaborated by the Dispute Settlement Understanding, also apply to consultations and settlement of disputes under the TRIMS Agreement.

Monitoring mechanisms have often served to resolve implementation difficulties, as they provide a vehicle to explore flexible options.

Section III Interaction with other Issues and Concepts

National treatment has the potential to interact with all other provisions of an IIA (table 1). Indeed, the United Kingdom model BIT, in article 3 (3), expressly states that, " [f]or the avoidance of doubt it is confirmed that the treatment provided for in paragraphs (1) and (2) above [national and MFN treatment] shall apply to Articles 1 to 11 of this Agreement" (UNCTAD, 1998a, p. 281). This affirms the applicability of, *inter alia,* national treatment to all substantive provisions for the United Kingdom model BIT.

The following interactions, in particular, should be highlighted:

- **Scope and definition.** Given that the definitions of terms such as "investment" and "investor" determine the types of transactions, assets and activities to which the substantive provisions of an agreement apply, these terms interact strongly with national treatment in that they specify the beneficiaries of the standard on the basis of the subject matter of the agreement. In principle, the principal beneficiaries of national treatment are "investors" and "investments". Thus, national treatment can apply to those assets and/or transactions and/ or entities that are specified in the definition provision. For example, if the definition of "investment" does not include portfolio investment, the national treatment standard does not apply to this type of investment. With respect to the definition of "investor", an important issue here is the definition of the nationality of firms, since this would determine which enterprises are entitled to national treatment under a particular agreement. It is also a matter of practical importance to differentiate whether a foreign affiliate is entitled to national treatment under the provisions of an international agreement, or its treatment derives from its status as a "national firm" under the host country laws on nationality.

Table 1. Interaction across issues and concepts

Issue	National treatment
Admission and establishment	++
Competition	++
Dispute settlement (investor-State)	++
Dispute settlement (State-State)	0
Employment	++
Environment	0
Fair and equitable treatment	++
Home country measures	0
Host country operational measures	++
Illicit payments	+
Incentives	++
Investment-related trade measures	+
Most-favoured-nation treatment	++
Scope and definition	++
Social responsibility	++
State contracts	+
Taking of property	++
Taxation	++
Transfer of funds	+
Transfer of technology	+
Transfer pricing	0
Transparency	++

Source: UNCTAD.
Key: 0 = negligible or no interaction.
+ = moderate interaction.
++ = extensive interaction.

- **Admission and establishment.** As noted in section II, there is a strong interaction between the provision on national treatment and those dealing with admission and establishment of investments where an agreement extends national treatment protection to the pre-entry phase of the investment process. In such cases, national treatment operates to ensure that treatment of prospective foreign investors with respect to admission conditions, requirements and promotional measures is based on national treatment, as defined in the applicable IIA.

- **Incentives.** Where national treatment extends to incentives, the standard interacts closely with the incentive provisions as it seeks to ensure that incentives are available to foreign investors on terms equal to, or no less favourable than, those enjoyed by domestic investors of the host country. However, where preferential treatment is sought regarding eligibility for incentives for domestic investors, then exceptions to national treatment may be required. Equally, where special incentives are available to foreign investors only, national treatment has no role to play, although the MFN standard may be invoked to ensure no differences of treatment as between different foreign investors.
- **MFN treatment.** The interactions between national treatment and MFN are extensive and have been partly discussed in section II. For the purposes of this chapter, it may be noted that national treatment alone might be insufficient to exclude possible differences of treatment accorded to foreign investors from different home countries. Thus, where certain foreign investors are granted preferential treatment, MFN ensures that such treatment extends to other foreign investors, unless they are expressly excluded from MFN by way of an exception in the applicable IIA. Furthermore, it should also be noted that exceptions to MFN are less frequent than to national treatment, as it may be easier for host countries to treat foreign investors from various countries equally than to treat foreign and domestic investors equally. Finally, where national treatment is accorded only to certain classes of foreign investors, as may be the case for investors from other member countries of a regional economic integration organization (REIO), MFN may have to be specifically excepted so as to avoid "free rider" problems; otherwise foreign investors from non-member countries might demand national treatment without assuming the mutual obligations associated with REIO membership. This would be the case particularly in relation to regional economic agreements that extend national treatment to the pre-entry stage (Karl, 1996).
- In essence, the effect of an MFN provision in an IIA on a national treatment provision in another IIA is to raise all other country signatories of the first IIA to the standard of national treatment guarantee in the second IIA. Thus, while some IIAs do not explicitly include a promise of national treatment, parties may still be obligated to provide national treatment by virtue of the MFN provision. Occasionally, a country has included a guarantee of national treatment in an earlier IIA that it does not wish to extend to any other country through an MFN treatment clause. The interaction of MFN and national treatment provisions is therefore of special importance and requires careful wording.
- **Fair and equitable treatment.** National treatment and fair and equitable treatment often co-exist in an investment agreement. Fair and equitable treatment and national treatment complement each other in various ways, with the former providing a broad objective test to resolve doubtful situations regarding eligibility for national treatment.
- **Taxation.** Significant interactions occur in this field in that most tax treaties apply national treatment to the taxation of foreign investors operating in the host country (UNCTAD, 1998b, p. 87). On the other hand, as noted in section II, IIAs often exclude taxation from the operation of national treatment.
- **Employment.** As noted in section II, a standard similar to that of national treatment is used in the ILO Tripartite Declaration on Multinational Enterprises and Social Policy as one of the standards for determining the legitimacy of TNC practices in relation to terms and conditions of employment and industrial relations. In this respect, TNCs which observe the same standards as domestic employers in the same industry would have fulfilled only the minimum requirements under this voluntary code. However, national treatment is used here in a very specific manner. It is not the treatment of investors that is governed by the standard; rather it is used (here, and in the following paragraph) to specify their obligations.
- **Social responsibility.** As foreign investors are granted rights similar to those of domestic investors (national treatment), they may also be bound by similar obligations. As with employment issues, so also wider issues of the

social responsibility of TNCs can be made subject to national standards. Thus, a TNC may be seen as acting in accordance with its obligations to observe certain social policies in the host country if it operates in the same manner as domestic enterprises in the same industry or sector. However, for reasons of policy, the host country may require different standards of responsibility from domestic and foreign enterprises, for example where more onerous social responsibilities are imposed on the latter.

- **Host country operational measures.** National treatment has close interactions with the issue of host country operational measures since operational conditions that apply to foreign investors and not to domestic investors are, in principle, inconsistent with the national treatment standard.
- **Taking of property.** IIAs typically recognize the international-law-based right of a host State to expropriate foreign property within its territory, provided that such expropriation meets certain requirements, including that it does not discriminate between foreign and local investors. A provision of national treatment would seem to reinforce the obligation of the host country not to discriminate between local and foreign investors on matters of expropriation. Moreover, for the purposes of compensation, a distinction is usually made between an expropriation of foreign-owned property and loss caused by armed conflict. In the former case, the standard of compensation usually relates to the full market value of the expropriated assets at the date of expropriation. In the latter case, most BITs provide that compensation for this kind of loss should be given to the foreign investor on the basis of the MFN standard, though some agreements refer to national treatment (UNCTAD, 1998a, p. 73). This issue has led to disputes before ICSID between investors and host countries as to the precise nature of the latter's obligations (ICSID, 1990, 1997).
- **Transparency.** A vital aspect of national treatment is to ensure that foreign investors are fully informed of the laws, regulations and administrative practices that apply to their operations. Such matters may be better known to domestic investors. It is implicit in the national treatment standard that such information imbalances be eliminated. Equally, transparency may require that exceptions to national treatment are clearly reported so that foreign investors are aware of them. This practice is followed, for example, under the OECD National Treatment instrument (OECD, 1993) and in the TRIMs Agreement (Article 6, UNCTAD, 1996a, vol. I, p. 281).
- **Dispute settlement (investor-State).** National treatment interacts with dispute settlement issues in that it requires that a foreign investor be given access to national dispute settlement mechanisms on at least the same terms as national investors. However, where international means of investor-to-State dispute settlement are available, the principle of national treatment does not apply since such facilities are generally not available to national investors. Investor-to-State dispute settlement mechanisms may therefore be considered an exception to national treatment in favour of foreign investors.

The important interactions between the national treatment provision and many other provisions underscore the significance that the principle has in international investment relations. In drawing up IIAs, therefore, special attention needs to be given to this standard.

Conclusion: Economic and Development Implications and Policy Options

National treatment may be interpreted as formal equality of treatment between foreign and domestic enterprises. Indeed, such a perception may be reinforced in an IIA, given the formal equality or "legal symmetry" of the parties. However, where countries at different levels of development are parties to an IIA, such formal equality may disregard important differences in the actual situation and capabilities of the enterprises on each side. The formal "legal symmetry" of their legal situation may be accompanied by actual "economic asymmetry " (UNCTAD, 1999b).[29] In such a context, application of the national treatment standard may require more than formal equality, so that the development needs of a developing country party to an IIA are taken into account in the definition and application of the standard.

While there is no doubt that national treatment is an important principle for foreign investors, its actual implementation may cause difficulties for host developing countries. In particular, there is a risk that economically strong foreign firms may impede or distort the development of domestic enterprises in a host country. Effective competition regulations may counter anti-competitive behaviour of TNCs (UNCTAD, 1997). However, such regulations cannot deal with effects arising from the mere presence of powerful firms with better access to finance, technology, skills and markets. This may call for special policies to help domestic firms, bearing in mind the spillover effects that TNCs can have in respect to the development of local suppliers and the upgrading of domestic competitors (see chapter 27 in volume III). There is thus a trade-off between offering national treatment as a means of increasing FDI inflows, and circumscribing national treatment as a means of promoting local enterprise development. How this trade-off is made depends on the conditions, levels of development and objectives of each host country.

The discretion of central and local governmental agencies to pursue development strategies may be unnecessarily curtailed by the fear that differential treatment of domestic firms could jeopardize the national treatment principle. As a result, otherwise useful policies and programmes might never be attempted, and existing development schemes favouring local firms and other bodies abandoned (Nurick, 1998; World Development Movement, 1998).

At the same time, strategies for enhancing the development dimension in respect of national treatment need to be woven into the liberalization process that many host countries have undertaken. Thus, there is no point in simply proposing a strategy in respect of national treatment, for example exceptions to national treatment to protect and promote certain domestic industries, without going through the exercise of testing their effectiveness in the broader context of liberalization. In a real sense, the liberalization phenomenon has become the principal touchstone of the efficacy of strategies to enhance the development dimension in respect of national treatment or indeed in respect of any other aspect of an investment regime. But of course it assumes greater significance in respect of national treatment by reason of the predominant position that that standard has among others, not only in economic and political terms but also in psychological terms, that is, the effect on national psyche.

In light of the above, a measure of balance and flexibility may be appropriate to ensure that formal equality of treatment does not become the basis for *de facto* better treatment for foreign investors, while at the same time ensuring that foreign investors are treated equally in like situations. In order to achieve this, a number of options arise, discussed below.

A. Option 1: no national treatment provision

As noted in section II, one option is to conclude IIAs that do not provide for national treatment. The purpose of this option is to avoid equality of treatment between national and foreign investors for a host country with strong reservations about limiting its freedom to offer preferential treatment to domestic firms for certain purposes. This approach is the most restrictive in terms of investors' rights and the most respectful in terms of host country discretion. Agreements enshrining this approach are not frequent.

B. Option 2: national treatment provision

There are a number of ways in which a national treatment clause can be granted. In each case the general exceptions mentioned in section II apply, in line with the common practice in many IIAs. However, before outlining those ways, some general questions on the national treatment standard must be raised because, in a real sense, the kernel of the question lies in the efficient and transparent use and application of exceptions to national treatment. In this, national treatment is quite different from MFN, where fewer exceptions are likely.

Do exceptions to national treatment promote economic development and growth for developing countries? This should be assessed in the context of current pressures towards liberalization. In particular, where national treatment is granted at the pre-entry stage, this could prove threatening to national investors if it were to be an unqualified standard. Thus, national treatment in the establishment of an investment is seldom, if ever, granted without exceptions thereto. These usually relate to infant industries that need special treatment if they are to develop, or to other such cases.

Secondly, do exceptions to national treatment operate as a disincentive for inward investment? This question needs to be analysed on a case-by-case basis, in the context of other FDI determinants (UNCTAD, 1998b). In every case, caution and fairness must be exercised to avoid unnecessary exceptions that serve only to protect inefficient firms or industries, and that may signal an unwelcoming investment climate to foreign investors. In any event, the use of exceptions would need to meet transparency standards.

Thirdly, should exceptions be phased so that they operate only for a transitional period? This has the advantage of giving a period of grace to a developing country. During this period, the country can ensure the conditions compatible with granting national treatment in the future. However, even a transitional period may not be enough if development targets have not been attained by the end of the period. Thus, positive measures (e.g. technical assistance) might be required to achieve this objective. However, time limits may not be appropriate for all exceptions, e.g. those involving national security or the continuing importance of particular industries.

Fourthly, should exceptions be structured on the basis of the GATS type "opt-in" or "positive list" approach or the NAFTA type "opt-out" or "negative list" approach? The former may be preferable where gradual liberalization is sought. By contrast, the "opt-out" approach may have certain disadvantages: this approach may curtail the ability of a host country to distinguish between domestic and foreign investments as it may be difficult to identify with precision all the industries and activities to which national treatment should not apply.

Against this background the basic policy variations are as follows:

1. Post-establishment national treatment

- **Option 2.a: limited post-establishment national treatment with strong host country authority.** This option preserves the strongest host country discretion while offering national treatment to foreign investments and/or investors at the post-entry stage. It could be used by host countries that may wish to offer a degree of national treatment without limiting their regulatory powers too greatly. Its principal features include some or all of the following:

- Application to post-establishment treatment only, thereby preserving the right to treat domestic and foreign investors differently at the point of entry, e.g. through screening laws and operational conditions on admission (see further chapter 7).
- A development exception in the form of a development clause in the context of the declared development objectives of a host country. It may be arguable that, in view of the factual test of "same circumstances" (or even "like situations" or "like circumstances"), a development exception may not be needed, as the situation for foreign and domestic firms in developing countries may not be comparable. However, this may not be an adequate safeguard, as it could equally be argued that, if both types of firms compete in the same market, then preferential treatment for a domestic firm could be construed as an exception to national treatment. Therefore, to ensure that a developing host country has the discretion to assist its emerging firms, an express exception may be the surest way of proceeding in the context of an IIA. As a development clause is potentially quite wide in its scope of application, the wide discretion it reserves for a developing host country could be seen as creating uncertainty as to when and where national treatment actually applies and therefore would not be regarded favourably by foreign investors. Clear lists of excepted or included industries or activities offer greater certainty.

  Short of a general exception for development, provision can be made for a national treatment exception in respect of special incentives granted by a host country only to its nationals and companies, especially for the purpose of stimulating local enterprise development.
- Exception of specific industries, activities and/or policy measures from the standard of national treatment.
- The substantive test of national treatment is limited to:
  - the "same" circumstances, thereby avoiding wider comparisons based on "like" circumstances;
  - the "same treatment", thereby avoiding the possibility of treatment more favourable to the foreign investor that

can arise from the formulation "no less favourable".

- An exception for political subdivisions and/or local government measures, as appropriate, reflecting the internal political organization of the host country.
- Limitation to *de jure* national treatment only, thereby allowing for *de facto* differentiation in the treatment of foreign investors.
- A stand alone national treatment clause without reference to other standards such as MFN or fair and equitable treatment.

The principal development implication of this approach is its flexibility in terms of preserving host country discretion. On the other hand, this approach may be perceived by foreign investors as not offering adequate levels of protection against differential treatment -- in principle, as well as when it comes to the administration of a provision with extensive discretion.

- **Option 2.b: full post-establishment national treatment.** This option offers a higher standard of national treatment for the foreign investor and limits the discretion of the host country to treat national and foreign investors differently. Its principal features include some or all of the following:
  - Application to post-establishment treatment only.
  - A minimal number of exceptions based on specific industries or activities seen as vital to national economic policy, and/or that need protection to survive on the basis of infant industry concerns.
  - The substantive test of national treatment is extended to:
    - "like" circumstances, allowing for the application of national treatment to similar, though not necessarily identical, situations;
    - "no less favourable treatment", thereby allowing for better treatment of foreign investors;
    - nothing is said as to whether or not national treatment applies to specified activities or factual situations or circumstances.
  - No exception for political subdivisions and/or local government measures.
  - Application of national treatment *de jure* and *de facto*, thereby ensuring both formal and informal protection for foreign investors.
  - A national treatment clause that coexists with, or incorporates within its text, the better of several standards of treatment such as MFN or fair and equitable treatment.

The development implications of this approach are that a host country extends the application of post-entry national treatment disciplines to as wide a range of situations as possible.

The following options add national treatment at the pre-establishment phase to national treatment at the post-establishment stage as described above.

2. Pre-establishment national treatment

- **Option 2c: limited pre-establishment national treatment.** In this option, national treatment extends to pre-establishment as well as post-establishment treatment, thereby limiting a host country's discretion as regards the entry of foreign investors. But the host country still retains some degree of control over the extent and pace of the liberalization of limitations and conditions of entry. (For further discussion, see UNCTAD, 1999c.) It would be an option for a host country that wishes to liberalize investment entry in its economy at a gradual pace. Its principal features may include one of the following two main variations:
  - Use of an "opt-in" or "positive list" approach *à la* GATS. No industry and/or activity is made subject to national treatment at the pre-establishment phase until and unless it is specifically agreed upon by the host country.
  - A "best endeavours" option such as that used in the APEC Non-Binding Investment Principles so that developing countries are not legally bound to grant national treatment at the pre-establishment phase. In a variation of this option, a best endeavours provision could be coupled with a commitment to grant (or negotiate) legally binding national treatment at the pre-establishment phase at a later stage (as done in the Energy Charter Treaty). This has the advantage of allowing a transitional period for developing countries before they become subject to national treatment disciplines. Its disadvantage is that it involves uncertainty before entry for foreign investors in the short to medium term, which could act as a disincentive; it

may also encourage some investors to refrain from investing in order to await the new instrument.

- **Option 2d**: full pre-establishment national treatment. Under this option, a host country's commitment to grant national treatment on entry extends in principle to all foreign investors unless such investment is to take place in activities or industries specifically excluded by the host country in a treaty. This option narrows considerably the discretion of a host country, since it can only use its prerogative to exclude specific activities from the operation of the standard at the time an agreement is completed.

Such a policy choice limits to a considerable extent a host country's traditional right to control the entry of aliens into its territory. It may be of value where a host country Government considers that a number of industries or activities can benefit from increased openness and from a more competitive market environment. At the same time, a host country may protect certain industries or activities by way of a "negative list", although this involves a difficult assessment as to which industries or activities need such special treatment. Failure to include an industry or activity may result in it being subjected to potentially damaging competition from foreign investors, especially where an IIA contains a standstill commitment on further restrictive policies. This would prevent a host country from including industries or activities in a "negative list" in the future.

As with the post-establishment options noted above, pre-establishment national treatment may be broader or narrower, depending on the wording of the principle and the use of various qualifications indicated earlier.

3. Combinations

- **Option 2e: hybrid.** This option involves various combinations of the elements of post and pre-establishment national treatment to produce a compromise between the various possibilities outlined above. For example, different permutations of the substantive test of differential treatment could also be devised, resulting in wider or narrower application of national treatment. Other matters open to variation from the above options include *de jure* and *de facto* differential treatment; the degree of interaction between national treatment and MFN and fair and equitable treatment; and the extent to which subnational entities are subjected to national treatment disciplines.

There is little point in attempting to list all the various permutations under this heading, as the outcome depends on a process of negotiation in the light of specific circumstances. The range of permutations can be gleaned from the various alternative formulations reviewed in section II above. In fact, the options indicated above are merely analytical constructs whose principal purpose is to indicate broad -- but hypothetical -- approaches to the subject.

* * *

Notes

1 To quote Patrick Juillard, at a lecture on "Measures relating to the entry and establishment of investments", UNCTAD/WTO, Third Seminar on Investment, Trade and Economic Development, Evian-les-Bains, 21-22 April 1999.

2 For a detailed analysis of the concepts and principles of customary international law applying to foreign investment, see UNCTC, 1990a; Fatouros, 1994, and UNCTAD, 1998a.

3 However, the rationale for the granting of national treatment varies, depending on the economic sectors and the subject matter involved. Thus, in a certain sense, the assimilation of aliens and nationals may be seen as forming part of international protection and the promotion of human rights, as far as basic standards of treatment of the person and property are concerned (e.g. protection against arbitrary government action, guarantees of human rights). This rationale may or may not extend beyond the treatment of the person to touch upon property rights and the rights of legal persons (UNCTC, 1990a).

4 Unless otherwise noted, the texts of the BITs mentioned in this study may be found in the collection of BITs maintained by the International Centre for Settlement of Investment Disputes (ICSID) (ICSID, 1972-) and at www.unctad.org/iia.

5 Unless otherwise noted, all instruments cited herein may be found in UNCTAD, 1996a.

6 In fact, until the 1990s, China did not agree to incorporate the national treatment standard in BITs as a matter of principle, although it was granted in the BITs between China and Germany (article 3 (IV)) and China and the United Kingdom (article 3) (Denza and Brooks, 1987). Since the early

1990s, as China pursued its economic reforms and continued to open up to the outside world -- with a view towards attracting more FDI -- it began to provide national treatment in BITs, but with certain qualifications. The most important qualification is that national treatment shall be limited by national laws and regulations; such qualification appears in, for example, the BIT between China and Morocco (article 3 (1)). In some recent BITs concluded by China (e.g. the BIT between China and the Republic of Korea (article 3 (2)), the national treatment standard appears without qualifications. In 1996, the State Council of the Government of China declared its policy of according foreign investors full national treatment on a gradual basis.

7 See, for example, the BIT between Denmark and Indonesia. The draft United Nations Code of Conduct on Transnational Corporations refers to "entities of transnational corporations" (UNCTAD, 1996a).

8 The AALCC prepared three draft model BITs intended to provide possible negotiating texts for consideration by the countries of the region. Model A is a draft BIT patterned on the agreements entered into between some of the countries of the region with industrialized States, with certain changes and improvements particularly on the matter of promotion of investments. Model B reflects an agreement whose provisions are somewhat more restrictive in the matter of the protection of investment and contemplates a degree of flexibility in regard to admission and protection of investment. Model C reflects an agreement on the pattern of Model A but applicable to specific classes of investment only, as determined by the host State.

9 See for example the BIT between Jamaica and the United Kingdom (article 3).

10 For example, the BITs between Egypt and Jamaica, Argentina and Morocco, Niger and Tunisia.

11 See further Pattison (1983, pp. 318-319) for a discussion of the Egypt-United States BIT in this respect (it should be noted that the Egypt-United States BIT was renegotiated in recent years).

12 See further Eden (1996); and Gestrin and Rugman (1994, 1996). See also the Canada-Chile Free Trade Agreement (5 December 1996, Chapter G, articles G-01 to G-08) for similar provisions (Canada and Chile, 1997).

13 However, MFN treatment is limited to investors and investments from other member States, so as to ensure that investors and investments from non-member States cannot benefit from measures aimed only at investors and investments from member States (ASEAN, 1998).

14 The GATS applies to trade in services, defined in article I as the supply of services through any of four modes: cross-border trade, consumption abroad, commercial presence and presence of natural persons. The third mode of supply (commercial presence) is the one that mostly concerns investment policies and regulations. It involves the supply of a service through the establishment of an entity (which may or may not have juridical personality, e.g. a subsidiary or a branch). This section focuses mainly on how national treatment applies to mode 3 of the GATS.

15 See, for example, the BITs signed by the United States with Costa Rica, Armenia and Argentina.

16 See also Raby, 1990, pp. 410-411, on the similar provision, article 1604, of the Canada-United States Free Trade Agreement.

17 As noted earlier, the term "affecting" has been interpreted to bring within the scope of GATS any measure that affects, whether directly or indirectly, the supply of a service. This would include not only investment-related measures but also all other aspects of domestic regulation that affect the operations of a service supplying entity. For example, in the case of an accounting firm, a national treatment obligation would cover all measures relating to the establishment of the firm (the investment) as well as all other regulations affecting its operations (e.g. qualification requirements, licensing requirements, technical standards for accounting).

18 The same functional formulation is used in the United Kingdom model BIT, article 3 (2), in relation to the protection of investors (UNCTAD, 1996a, vol. III, p. 187).

19 t has been argued that inclusion of the phrase "in like circumstances" in the MAI was especially relevant in order to ensure that the national treatment standard would not interfere with a party's ability to take measures for environmental purposes.

20 The use of the word "same" or the term "as favourable as" may be seen as synonymous in practice.

21 However, preferential treatment for Arab investors vis-à-vis other foreign investors is possible at the discretion of the host country on the grounds specified in article 16 of the Agreement (UNCTAD, 1996a, vol. II, p. 217).

22 Examples of separate national treatment provisions followed by other general standards of treatment clauses are: NAFTA, articles 1102-1103; Canada-Chile Free Trade Agreement, articles G-02-G-03; TRIPS Agreement, articles 3-4; GATS, articles II, XVII; and AALCC model BITs, articles 4-5.

23 The list of national treatment and MFN treatment exceptions may differ considerably. For example, in the annex to the BIT between Jamaica and the United States, the United States identifies 17 exceptions to MFN and Jamaica identifies four. With respect to national treatment, the United States identifies 13 exceptions and Jamaica only one.

24 This principle has been recognized, for example, in the Set of Multilaterally Agreed Equitable Principles and Rules for the Control of Restrictive Business Practices.

25 The ECT however provided for future conclusion of a supplementary agreement that would accord

national treatment during the pre-establishment phase on a binding basis. (See the discussion above.)

26 That text of the draft Code of Conduct was submitted by the Chairperson of the reconvened special session of the Commission on Transnational Corporations to the President of the Economic and Social Council. In his letter to the President, the Chairperson indicated *inter alia* that the text of the draft Code represented an effort to facilitate compromise while preserving the texts already agreed *ad referendum*, and added that "the Bureau considers that the work of the reconvened special session of the Commission on Transnational Corporations has been concluded and it is the Chairperson's impression that the text annexed will receive the support of the overwhelming majority of countries from all regions" (UN-ECOSOC, 1990, p. 1).

27 See the 1990 Jamaica-Switzerland BIT, art. 3; and the 1991 Jamaica-Netherlands BIT, art. 3(6). A similar approach is contained in the BIT between Denmark and Indonesia (article 3).

28 The Committee has also considered the area of nationality requirements for example the requirement that a certain number of members of the board of a company must possess the nationality of the host State (OECD, 1985, pp. 20-34; OECD, 1993, pp. 28-47).

29 Economic asymmetry is illustrated by BITs in which one developing country partner will in practice operate only as a capital-importing country, so that its rights under the treaty as a home country may not mean much in reality.

Chapter 6. Most-Favoured-Nation Treatment*

Executive summary

The most-favoured-nation treatment (MFN) standard is a core element of international investment agreements. It means that a host country treats investors from one foreign country no less favourably than investors from any other foreign country. The MFN standard gives investors a guarantee against certain forms of discrimination by host countries, and it is crucial for the establishment of equality of competitive opportunities between investors from different foreign countries.

The MFN standard may also have implications for host countries′ room for manoeuvre in respect of future investment agreements, because it can create a so-called "free rider" situation in that the MFN standard commits a host country to extend unilaterally to its treaty partners any additional rights that it grants to third countries in future agreements. Furthermore, as the globalization of investment activities makes corporate nationality more difficult to use as a ground for distinguishing between companies, it may become equally more difficult to identify the nation that actually benefits from MFN.

While the MFN standard has for decades been a common feature of bilateral investment treaties (BITs), efforts have been undertaken in recent years to translate this standard in a multilateral framework.[1] Moreover, some recent agreements extend the MFN standard to both the pre- and post-establishment phases. On the other hand, there are several exceptions to the MFN standard which could be general exceptions (e.g. for national security reasons), exceptions based on reciprocity considerations (for example in the area of taxation and intellectual property) and individual country-specific exceptions. The annex provides a diagram of MFN clauses with illustrations of the extension of the MFN standard, its beneficiaries, scope and exceptions.

The MFN standard interacts with various other investment issues and concepts addressed in these volumes, in particular the so-called international minimum standard and the standard of national treatment (NT). While MFN is generally more than the minimum standard required under customary international law, it does not go so far as to put the foreign investor on an equal footing with domestic investors in the host country.

Although international investment agreements allow for exceptions from MFN, it seems that contracting parties have hitherto not used this freedom to discriminate among foreign investors from different countries beyond those policy areas where differential treatment is explicitly recognized (for instance, taxation, intellectual property or mutual recognition). However, the possibility of using exceptions to MFN introduces an element of flexibility in taking account of development objectives where this may be appropriate.

Introduction

One of the core provisions of international investment agreements concerns MFN. Indeed, that standard is at the heart of multilateralism. The MFN standard means that a host country must extend to investors from one foreign country treatment no less favourable than it accords to investors from any other foreign country in like cases. In other words, the MFN standard seeks to prevent discrimination against investors from foreign countries on grounds of their nationality. At the same time, the MFN standard sets certain limits upon host countries with regard to their present and future investment policies by prohibiting them from favouring investors of one particular foreign nation over those of another foreign country.

MFN applies both in the trade and the investment fields. However, contrary to trade, where the MFN standard only applies to measures at the border, there are many more possibilities to discriminate against foreign investment. This chapter,

* The chapter is based on a 1999 manuscript prepared by Joachim Karl. The final version reflects comments received from Mark Koulen and Hamid Mamdouh.

while taking stock of existing agreements, examines the fields in which there have been departures from MFN. Countries have followed very similar approaches with regard to these exceptions, although there are also a few substantial differences. It then examines potential interactive effects of the MFN standard with other investment-related issues. These include, *inter alia*, host country operational measures, the principle of national treatment and trade policy measures. In each case, the question is how the MFN standard in investment matters affects these other concepts or policy areas. Finally, the chapter assesses the economic and development implications of the MFN standard. It concludes that the MFN principle is itself flexible in the sense that it allows in-built exceptions that could accommodate development concerns of host countries.

Section I
Explanation of the Issue

A. Definition and scope

The MFN standard means that a host country must extend to investors from one foreign country the same treatment it accords to investors from any other foreign country in like cases. It potentially applies to all kinds of investment activities, such as the operation, maintenance, use, sale or liquidation of an investment. With regard to the admission and establishment of an investment, international MFN commitments are less frequent, although there is a certain movement towards an extension of the rule in this direction (see section II below). This comprehensive coverage ensures that investors are protected even if the investment-related activities change or expand during the lifetime of their investments. Moreover, the standard can be invoked with regard to any investment-related legislation.

In principle, one can distinguish several types of MFN clauses. They can be either unilateral or reciprocal, conditional or unconditional, limited (by territory, time, or substantive scope) or unlimited. The MFN standard (with exceptions) usually applies in the areas of trade, investment, foreign exchange, intellectual property, diplomatic immunities, and the recognition of foreign judicial awards.

As far as investment matters are concerned, MFN clauses show the same basic structure. They are usually reciprocal (which means that all contracting parties are bound by it), unconditional and apply to all investment-related matters. However, this does not mean that these clauses use identical language. Most agreements refer to "treatment no less favourable" when defining the MFN standard (for instance, the General Agreement on Trade in Services (GATS), article II, and the Energy Charter Treaty, article 10, paragraph 7). The North American Free Trade Agreement (NAFTA), while using the same terminology, includes the qualification that such treatment applies only "in like circumstances" (article 1103).

Many investment agreements entitle both foreign investors and their investments to MFN. This is so, for example, in the case of NAFTA (article 1103), and the BITs concluded by Germany, Switzerland and the United Kingdom (UNCTAD, 1998a). By contrast, the Energy Charter Treaty (article 10, paragraph 7) and the BITs of the United States only grant MFN to the *investment*. Still another approach has been followed in the French model treaty, which gives MFN to the investors with regard to their investments.

There is no evidence that, by using different wording, the parties to these various agreements intended to give the MFN clauses a different scope. Whatever the specific terminology used, it does not change the basic thrust of MFN, namely its non-discriminating character among foreign investors investing in a particular host country.

There are also variations concerning the investment activities covered by the MFN standard. In general, the coverage is broad (see chapter 3). NAFTA uses the terms "establishment, acquisition, expansion, management, conduct, operation, and sale or other disposition of investments" (article 1103). The Energy Charter Treaty covers all investment-related activities, "including management, maintenance, use, enjoyment, or disposal" (article 10, paragraph 7). The French model treaty refers to "activities in connection with an investment". The GATS applies MFN in respect of "any measure covered by this Agreement" (article II). Once again, irrespective of the concrete wording, the aim is to cover all possible investment operations.

However, not all treatment given by a host country to foreign investors falls under the scope of the MFN provision. In order to be covered by the MFN clause, the treatment has to be the *general* treatment *usually* provided to investors from a given foreign country. Therefore, if a host country granted special privileges or incentives to an individual investor in an investment contract between it and the host country (so-called "one-off" deals), there would be no obligation under the MFN clause to treat other foreign investors equally. The reason is that a host country cannot be *obliged to* enter into an individual investment contract. Freedom of contract prevails over the MFN standard. Only if this individual behaviour became general practice in the host country – for example, if an incentive is granted under a general subsidy programme – would the MFN provision apply. It may be difficult to decide at what point an individual practice, which has been repeated in several cases, becomes general treatment. The relevance of MFN in this particular instance is that all foreign investors should be treated equally for purposes of being potential candidates for the special privilege or incentive which in practice could only be granted to one individual investor.

Furthermore, the MFN standard does not mean that foreign investors have to be treated *equally* irrespective of their concrete activity in a given host country. Different treatment is justified vis-à-vis investors from different foreign countries if they are in different objective situations. The model BIT of the United States, as well as NAFTA, contain an explicit provision in this respect, according to which MFN applies only to investors and investments that are "in like situations" (United States model BIT) or "in like circumstances" (NAFTA)[2]. Thus, the MFN standard does not necessarily impede host countries from according different treatment in different sectors of economic activity, or to differentiate between enterprises of different size. It would therefore not violate the MFN standard *per se* for a host country to grant subsidies only to investments in, say, high-technology industries, while excluding foreign investment in other areas. Likewise, the MFN clause would not give a big foreign investor the right to claim government assistance under a programme that was designed only for small and medium-sized enterprises. However, such different treatment could still amount to *de facto* discrimination. This would be the case if the only purpose of the differentiation were to exclude investors of a particular nationality from the benefits of the programme.

The MFN standard is not without exceptions. While the degree and extent of these exceptions vary considerably in individual treaties, they can be traced back to some general considerations: exceptions are needed because the scope of the MFN standard is very broad. It potentially covers all industries and all possible investment activities. It therefore applies to such different issues as social and labour matters, taxation and environmental protection. In fact, many of these policy areas are governed by a reciprocity of intellectual property rights, or arrangements in the field of labour mobility and the harmonization and recognition of professional services. Reciprocity is also the rule for agriculture and for maritime, air and road transportation -- all industries in which foreign investment may occur. As a result, in all these areas, an unqualified commitment to MFN usually does not exist, as discussed further in section II below.

While the MFN standard applies in both the trade and investment fields, its sphere of operation differs in each area. In trade, the standard only applies to measures at the border, in particular to tariffs. In relation to investment, the MFN standard has usually applied to the treatment of investors *after* entry, though, as noted above, some agreements also extend its operation to the pre-entry stage. Despite their distinct spheres of operation, given the close interrelationship between trade and investment in the operations of transnational corporations (TNCs), the combined effect of trade-related and investment-related MFN is to offer freedom for TNCs to choose the precise mode of operation in a host country on an equal basis with their competitors. Thus, in relation to investment already made in a host country, discriminatory treatment may be prejudicial to existing investors, given the "sunk costs" already incurred in setting up an investment, and the more beneficial situation that other competing foreign investors enjoy on the same market. At the point of entry, both trade and investment-related MFN seek to avoid preferential access to the host State which could prove damaging to the excluded companies through the denial of commercial opportunities in the host State, which may not always be easily mitigated by trading and/or investing elsewhere.

B. MFN treatment and equality of competitive opportunities

Foreign investors seek sufficient assurance that there will not be adverse discrimination which puts them at a competitive disadvantage. Such discrimination includes situations in which competitors from other foreign countries receive more favourable treatment. The MFN standard thus helps to establish equality of competitive opportunities between investors from different foreign countries. It prevents competition between investors from being distorted by discrimination based on nationality considerations. The more foreign investors from various home countries play an important role in a host country, the more important the MFN standard becomes.

While a non-discrimination clause may already exist in the domestic legal system of a host country (for example as a principle of its constitution), this would often not be perceived as sufficient to give foreign investors the same degree of assurance as an obligation under international law. In the view of foreign investors, domestic law, including a domestic MFN provision, could be amended at any time by unilateral national action. Through an international commitment, investors could be confident that the host country cannot easily try to disguise discrimination among foreigners.

C. The "free rider" issue

Despite its importance for appropriate investment protection, MFN may at the same time limit countries' room for manoeuvre in respect of investment agreements they want to conclude in the future. This is so because the MFN standard obliges a contracting party to extend to its treaty partners any benefits that it grants to any other country in any future agreement dealing with investment. This can cause a so-called "free rider" situation: assume, for instance, that in an agreement between countries X and Z, X grants Z certain rights which it has not granted to country Y in an earlier agreement with an MFN clause; country Y can now claim the additional rights granted to Z. The original contractual balance between X and Y is thus upset, since the MFN clause has added additional obligations to country X, without imposing any other obligations on country Y.

To remedy this potential imbalance, certain countries initially construed the MFN clause as implying an obligation on the part of the country benefiting from its operation to renegotiate the initial agreement so as to redress the contractual balance between the two original parties. This was known as the "conditional" MFN clause, that is to say, the MFN treatment was granted on condition of strict and specific reciprocity. Other countries objected to this interpretation, arguing that it deprived the MFN clause of its automatic effect and thereby made it essentially inoperative. By the 1920s, the unconditional interpretation was generally accepted. To buttress the interpretation and counter the free rider argument, the reciprocity involved is now construed in a broader, more abstract sense: a country's promise of MFN treatment is given against a counter-promise to the same effect; it is the MFN treatment that is thus assured, while the actual specific treatment to be applied depends on the other treaty commitments of the parties. Of course, this is but an assumption, and it is inoperative if there is clear evidence that the parties intended their agreement to be governed by strict reciprocity.

The actual seriousness of the free rider problem varies from case to case. The issue may also take different forms in respect of bilateral and multilateral treaties. In the latter case, it may be less acceptable because of the potentially huge number of free riders involved. Furthermore, free riding would become less tolerable, the more the substantive obligations in the treaties concerned differ. In brief, the gravity of the free rider issue depends on the extent to which it creates asymmetrical situations.

One may ask whether the free rider issue has special relevance in the context of economic development. So far, the development strategies of many developing countries have been based on selective intervention. This means that these countries have favoured those foreign investors they considered able to make major contributions to their own economic development. A question, therefore, is whether an unconditional MFN commitment could undermine such a strategy -- an issue which is discussed further in the last section of this chapter.

D. The identity issue

The emergence of integrated international production systems makes the determination of corporate nationality more difficult (UNCTAD, 1993, pp. 188-190). A foreign affiliate is only entitled to MFN if it can show that its parent company is located in a country that is entitled to such a commitment. The issue of corporate nationality is not new. However, with the emergence of new forms of integrated production, and with management and decision-making possibly spread among several parts of a corporation, it becomes increasingly difficult to identify the nationality of the parent company. The relations among different units of a TNC no longer necessarily reflect the traditional pattern of subordination. Furthermore, if the units are incorporated and administered in different countries, especially if they are owned by shareholders of different nationalities or linked to one another by contractual arrangements, it may become difficult in practice to attribute nationality to a particular affiliate. The question of "who is us?" (Reich, 1991) may also arise with regard to how far back in the corporate chain it is appropriate to reach in order to determine an affiliate's nationality.

Furthermore, even if an investing company can be clearly identified, the owners of that company do not necessarily have the nationality of the country in which the investing company is located. This may result in a situation in which an investor indirectly benefits from an MFN obligation in a treaty that does not apply to it. If, for example, Volkswagen Mexico makes an investment in Colombia, it is both the Mexican investor and (indirectly) the German parent company that benefit from MFN obligations which may exist in favour of Volkswagen Mexico. Such situations may become more frequent as an increasing number of foreign-controlled companies become investors abroad, either because they were originally established as pure holding companies or because they function as bridgehead investments in the overall investment strategy of a TNC (UNCTAD, 1993, 1998b).

Section II Stocktaking and Analysis

A. The standard

MFN has traditionally been linked to trade agreements. The first example of an MFN clause was when King Henry V of England signed a treaty (Treaty for Mercantile Intercourse with Flanders on 17 August 1417) with Duke John of Burgundy in Amiens, according to which English vessels were granted the right to use the harbours of Flanders "in the same way as French, Dutch, Sealanders and Scots" (Kramer, 1989, p. 478). It was only in the seventeenth century that the point of reference for MFN was no longer a limited number of named countries, but any third state. An example is the treaty dated 16 August 1692 between Denmark and the Hanseatic League. The first "modern" trade treaty that included an unconditional MFN clause was the Cobden treaty dated 23 January 1860 between the United Kingdom and France. Later, in March 1929, the Council of the League of Nations adopted a model MFN clause in respect of tariffs. After the Second World War, the MFN standard was revived in the negotiation of the Havana Charter. Furthermore, the GATT 1947 contained the most classical unconditional MFN commitment in its article I (Kramer, 1989). With regard to *investment*, the development of MFN became common in the 1950s with the conclusion of international investment agreements, including BITs. The MFN standard was included in such treaties from the beginning, and the MFN standard is thus older than the parallel provision for "national treatment", which found its way into most BITs only at a later stage.

Although MFN clauses are characterized by a basic similarity in terms of structure and substantive coverage, they nevertheless differ in one important area, namely, whether they apply only at the post-entry stage or also at the pre-entry stage.

1. The post-entry model

The vast majority of BITs do not include binding provisions concerning the admission of foreign investment. This means that there is an obligation to apply MFN under these terms only *after* an investment has been made. With regard to the pre-establishment phase, contracting parties are usually encouraged to create favourable conditions for foreign investors and admit their investments in accordance with their domestic laws (see chapter 4). Other treaties restrict the MFN clause explicitly to post-entry investment only. This is exemplified by article 10 (7) of the Energy Charter Treaty:

> "Each Contracting Party shall accord to Investments in its Area of Investors of other Contracting Parties, and their related activities including management, maintenance, use, enjoyment or disposal, treatment no less favourable than that which it accords to Investments of its own Investors or of the Investors of any other Contracting Party or any third state and their related activities including management, maintenance, use, enjoyment or disposal, whichever is the most favourable."

However, the contracting parties can extend MFN to the pre-establishment stage according to a supplementary treaty (www.encharter.org).[3]

2. The pre- and post-entry model

By contrast to the first model, this model requires the application of the MFN standard in respect of both the establishment and subsequent treatment of investment. Most BITs of the United States and some recent treaties of Canada follow such an approach. Similarly, article 1103 of NAFTA contains the following clause:

"1. Each Party shall accord to investors of another Party treatment no less favorable than that it accords, in like circumstances, to investors of any other Party or of a non-Party with respect to the establishment, acquisition, expansion, management, conduct, operation, and sale or other disposition of investments.

2. Each Party shall accord to investments of investors of another Party treatment no less favorable than it accords, in like circumstances, to investments of investors of any other Party or of a non-Party with respect to the establishment, acquisition, expansion, management, conduct, operation, and sale or other disposition of investments."

Other similar pre- and post-entry clauses can be found in the Southern Common Market (MERCOSUR) Colonia Protocol (article 2) and in the Asia-Pacific Economic Cooperation (APEC) Non-Binding Investment Principles. This shows that, in the era of globalization, non-discriminatory treatment with regard to market access is becoming an increasingly important issue.

B. Exceptions

1. General exceptions

Investment agreements contain several types of exceptions of a general nature that are not specifically limited to MFN. Some of these general exceptions are discussed below.

a. Public order/health/morals

Most BITs allow contracting parties to derogate from the non-discrimination standard, if this is necessary for the maintenance of public order, public health or public morality (UNCTAD, 1998a). Nevertheless, it is hard to identify concrete cases where, for example, the maintenance of public order would actually require discriminating among foreign investors, although the case of a foreign investor being involved in systematic abuses of human rights might elicit such a response, especially if required by the resolution of an international organization.

On the other hand, a "public order" exception may be a substitute for a "national security" exception. For instance, the Treaty Establishing the European Community (article 56) refers to "public policy, security or health." In these cases, there may be a justification for discrimination based on nationality (see below the section on "national security").

The GATS (article XIV) also contains an exception clause concerning the protection of public morality and the maintenance of public order. In addition, an exception can also be made if this is necessary to protect human, animal or plant life or health, or to secure compliance with laws or regulations that are not inconsistent with GATS provisions, including those related to safety. Contrary to most bilateral agreements, the GATS exceptions relate to the agreement as a whole. However, such measures must not be applied in a manner which would constitute a means of arbitrary or unjustifiable discrimination between countries where like conditions prevail, or a disguised restriction on trade in services.

Likewise, the Organisation for Economic Co-operation and Development (OECD) Code on the Liberalisation of Capital Movements allows members to take any action they consider necessary for the maintenance of public order or the protection of public health, morality and safety (article 2).

Furthermore, the Energy Charter Treaty contains an exception clause in respect of the maintenance of public order and the protection of human, animal or plant life or health. With regard to public order, a contracting party is allowed to take any measure it considers necessary, except measures that would affect the treaty obligations concerning expropriation and losses due to war and civil disturbance (article 24, paragraph 3c). With regard to the protection of human, animal or plant life or health, a contracting party can take any measure, provided that it does not constitute a disguised restriction on economic activity in the energy sector, or arbitrary or unjustifiable discrimination between contracting parties or between investors or other interested persons of contracting parties (article 24, paragraph 2b(i)).

b. National security

Most BITs do not contain an exception for national security reasons. Nevertheless, it would seem that contracting parties could take at least any measure that the United Nations Security Council would authorize them to take. An explicit national security exception can be found in the GATS at article XIV bis(1):

"Nothing in this Agreement shall be construed:

......

(b) to prevent any Member from taking action which it considers necessary for the protection of its essential security interests:

(i) relating to the supply of services as carried out directly or indirectly for the purpose of provisioning a military establishment;

(ii) relating to fissionable and fusionable materials or the materials from which they are derived;

(iii) taken in time of war or other emergency in international relations; or

(c) to prevent any Member from taking any action in pursuance of its obligations under the United Nations Charter for the maintenance of international peace and security."

Accordingly, nothing in the GATS prevents a member from taking an action it considers necessary to protect its essential security interest or meet its obligations under the United Nations Charter for the maintenance of international peace and security. Likewise, article 3 of the OECD Code on the Liberalisation of Capital Movements allows members to take actions that they consider necessary for the protection of their essential security interests, or the fulfilment of their obligations relating to international peace and security. The Energy Charter Treaty has a similar provision (article 24, paragraph 3), but in this case, a member is not allowed to derogate from its obligations under the provisions on expropriation and protection from civil strife. NAFTA also includes a national security exception (article 2102).

These provisions give contracting parties broad discretion in deciding whether they want to invoke the exception clause or not (so-called "self-judging" clauses). In particular, it is not necessary for the party to be in an actual state of war. It would be sufficient for the party to consider its national security interests to be threatened.

2. Reciprocal subject-specific exceptions

A common element of many investment agreements is that they contain MFN exceptions based on reciprocity that are specifically focused on MFN provisions. The most frequent exceptions of this type are analysed in this section.

a. Taxation

All investment agreements dealing with taxation matters contain an MFN exception. This means that a contracting party is not obliged to extend to its treaty partners, via the MFN clause, any privilege or other advantage that it has granted to a third country and its investors under a bilateral agreement on the avoidance of double taxation. The reason is that, under the latter treaties, the contracting parties delimit their right to tax investors of the other contracting party. This means that the contracting parties partly renounce their right to tax investors located in their territories in order to avoid double taxation. This happens on a mutual basis. Each contracting party therefore waives its taxation rights only if the other contracting party undertakes the same commitment. Thus, a unilateral extension of the waiver vis-à-vis third countries via the MFN standard, including its financial implications, would not be acceptable. For example, the Chile - Malaysia BIT (article 3) provides:

> "The provision in this Treaty relating to treatment no less favourable than that accorded to investments of third States shall not be interpreted to oblige a Contracting Party to extend to investors of the other Contracting Party the benefits of any treatment, preference or privilege by virtue of:
>
> ...
>
> (b) any international convention or agreement related totallyor principally to taxation, or any national legislation related totally or partially to taxation" (UNCTAD, 1998a, p. 58).

b. Intellectual property

Most BITs apply the MFN clause fully with regard to intellectual property. However, where these treaties contain binding obligations only for the post-establishment phase, which is the case for BITs other than the United States and the more recent Canadian models, the MFN commitment only applies once the rights have been granted. The host country can therefore condition the acquisition of an intellectual property right on the fulfillment of certain requirements, including the requirement that its own investors receive a similar level of protection in the home country of the foreign investor.

In addition, some international conventions dealing with the protection of intellectual property rights, e.g. the Berne Convention (United Nations, 1980b) and the Rome Convention (United Nations, 1964), explicitly allow contracting parties to deviate from the MFN standard with regard to the acquisition and contents of certain intellectual property rights, namely copyrights. Under these conventions, the treatment accorded by one State to nationals of another member State is a function of the treatment accorded in that other country. The WTO-TRIPS Agreement (article 4 paragraph (b)) confirms this rule:

> "With regard to the protection of intellectual property, any advantage, favour, privilege or immunity granted by a Member to the nationals of any other country shall be accorded immediately and unconditionally to the nationals of all other Members. Exempted from this obligation are any advantage, favour, privilege or immunity accorded by a Member:
>
> ...
>
> (b) granted in accordance with the provisions of the Berne Convention (1971) or the Rome Convention authorizing that the treatment accorded be a function not of national treatment but of the treatment accorded in another country;" ...

A foreign investor may therefore acquire and use intellectual property rights covered by the Berne Convention and the Rome Convention in a particular host country only to the extent that investors from the latter country have the same rights in return (UNCTAD, 1996d).

Accordingly, recent regional investment agreements dealing with the pre-establishment phase include an MFN exception in this respect. Thus, NAFTA, article 1108, paragraph 5 stipulates:

> "Articles 1102 and 1103 do not apply to any measure that is an exception to, or derogation from, the obligations under Article 1703 (Intellectual Property - National Treatment) as specifically provided for in that Article."

And article 10, paragraph 10, of the Energy Charter Treaty provides:

> "Notwithstanding any other provision of this Article, the treatment described in paragraphs (3) and (7) shall not apply to the protection of Intellectual Property; instead, the treatment shall be as specified in the corresponding provisions of the applicable international agreements for the protection of Intellectual Property rights to which the respective Contracting Parties are parties."

However, as far as NAFTA is concerned, the MFN exception is not limited to a reciprocity requirement. It also allows for MFN exceptions in respect of intellectual property rights in general (article 1108, paragraph 5).

c. Regional economic integration

Investment agreements in which countries that are members of a regional economic integration organization (REIO) participate usually include a so-called REIO clause. Under this provision, REIO members are exempted from the obligation to grant MFN to nonmembers. The purpose of this provision is to allow members of a REIO to advance with their internal investment liberalization at a faster pace than that to which the non-members have agreed. For example, the Chile - Malaysia BIT (article 3) provides:

> "The provision in this Treaty relating to treatment no less favourable than that accorded to investments of third States shall not be interpreted to oblige a Contracting Party to extend to investors of the other Contracting Party the benefits of any treatment, preference or privilege by virtue of:
>
> (a) any customs union, free trade area, common market or monetary union, or any similar international convention or other forms of regional cooperation, present or future, of which any of the Contracting Parties might become a party;..." (UNCTAD, 1998a, p. 58).

Without such a clause, the MFN clause would oblige the REIO members unilaterally to grant investors from non-member countries all the privileges deriving from REIO membership.

Such an obligation could result in problematic situations for the following reasons (Karl, 1996):

- Investment liberalization in a REIO is usually based on the presence of common rules. All members undertake the same commitments. A non-member would benefit from all advantages of the internal liberalization without simultaneously being subject to the obligations deriving from the REIO membership and thus be a "free rider".
- The integration concept that applies in a REIO may differ substantially from the methods of investment liberalization generally used in international investment agreements. Under the latter agreements, investment liberalization is based on the standard of non-discrimination, that is, foreign investors must not be treated less favourably than domestic (or other foreign) investors. By contrast, investment liberalization in a REIO may also encompass the removal of

all existing unjustified investment barriers, irrespective of whether they are discriminatory or not (as in the European Union). Without an MFN exception, such far-reaching rights would have to be granted by the REIO to non-members on a unilateral basis.

- In a REIO, it may not be the individual member State that decides on a liberalization measure, but the REIO as a whole. For example, in the European Union the individual member state has transferred its competence for internal investment liberalization to the Union. An implicit extension of this competence towards the external relations of the REIO via an MFN clause would not be covered by the REIO constitution.
- Third countries may be outside the institutional framework of the REIO. They may not participate in the internal decision-making process which may result in investment liberalization. They are not bound by awards of a REIO court, such as the European Court of Justice. Nor do they contribute to the budget of the REIO.

On the other hand, REIO clauses do not usually result in a complete and unconditional waiver of MFN. The GATS, for instance, prohibits a REIO member, when adopting a new liberalization measure, from increasing the overall level of investment barriers vis-à-vis non-members (article V(4)). Furthermore, once a foreign investor is established in a member country, it can usually claim the same treatment as investors from REIO member States. It is considered to be a domestic enterprise. In this case, the REIO clause does not apply with regard to treaty provisions dealing with investment protection, in particular provisions concerning expropriations and dispute settlement. The practical effects of the REIO clause are therefore, in principle, limited to market access issues. It allows REIO members to restrict foreign investors from outside the region in industries that are open for intra-regional investment.

d. Mutual recognition

Mutual recognition arrangements are a common feature facilitating the cross-border provision of services, including through a commercial presence. In these agreements, the contracting parties recognize the legal requirements of the partner country concerning the provision of a particular service as equivalent to their own domestic requirements. Foreign investors can therefore offer their services in the host country without having to obtain domestic licences or permits there, provided that they possess the equivalent licences or permits from their home countries. The industries most frequently open to mutual recognition arrangements are professional services and financial services (banking, insurance).

Similarly, some international agreements, while not creating new substantive law provisions, considerably facilitate the acquisition of intellectual property rights by providing for harmonized application procedures. Among the most relevant ones are the treaties concerning international co-operation in the field of patent matters, the Washington Treaty (dated 19 June 1970 (United Nations, 1980c)), the European Patent Convention (dated 5 October 1973) and the Strasbourg Convention concerning the international classification of patents (dated 24 March 1971 (United Nations, 1980d)). As third countries would not be bound by these rules, they cannot claim that they unilaterally benefit from the harmonization they entail.

An unlimited MFN provision may imply that a party to a mutual recognition arrangement is obliged also to recognize the regulations relating to a particular service in a third country, although a recognition agreement does not exist in this respect. The third country would have to show that its domestic regulations are identical (or at least equivalent) to those of the country with which the recognition arrangement has been concluded. But, even then, doubt would remain as to whether the MFN provision could be successfully invoked.

Mutual recognition arrangements imply -- by definition -- a reciprocal commitment. This concept would be undermined by unilaterally extending the benefits of the recognition arrangement to third countries. Moreover, a condition for a recognition arrangement is that the parties have agreed upon certain common standards that an applicant has to fulfill in their countries before, for example, a licence or permission, can be granted. As third countries would not be obliged to adhere to these standards, a basic condition for applying the recognition arrangement to them would not be met.

Despite the considerable practical importance of mutual recognition only the GATS (article VII) contains an explicit provision dealing with recognition arrangements. However, it is not, as one might suppose, a mere MFN exception. Rather, it encourages countries that have entered into such agreements to negotiate similar treaties with other States. This means, on the one hand, that the GATS does not consider the MFN standard, as such, as being applicable to recognition arrangements. Otherwise, the provision encouraging negotiations on this subject would make little sense. On the other hand, the GATS does not simply allow for an MFN exception. It goes one step further by encouraging a gradual multilateralization of mutual recognition arrangements by subsequent rounds of bilateral negotiations (GATS, article VII, paragraph 2).

e. Other bilateral issues

There are a number of other investment-related issues that are usually addressed only on a bilateral basis, and thus do not lend themselves to a multilateralization via an MFN provision. Examples are bilateral transportation agreements (involving landing rights for vessels or aircraft) and fishing arrangements. They are all based on the concept of reciprocity.

Despite their relevance for investment matters, international investment agreements have not yet explicitly dealt with these issues. The reason may be that the link with investment activities is weak. In the context of negotiations in the OECD on a Multilateral Agreement on Investment (MAI) (OECD, 1998a), however, the possible need to make exceptions in this respect has been discussed.

3. Country-specific exceptions

Some treaties give contracting parties the right to make an MFN exception with regard to any measure, sector or activity, provided that the exception is listed in the country-specific schedule.

a. The GATS approach

Article II of the GATS states that, with respect to all measures covered by the Agreement, each member shall accord immediately and unconditionally to services and service suppliers of any other member treatment no less favourable than it accords to like services and service suppliers of any other country. According to paragraph 2, however, a member may maintain a measure inconsistent with paragraph 1, provided that such a measure is listed in, and meets the conditions of, the annex to the article. The annex states that the MFN exception should not apply for more than 10 years. Moreover, the exception is subject to revision in subsequent negotiating rounds. The GATS also includes a specific MFN exception for public procurement (article XIII). Furthermore, the application of MFN to the maritime transport sector has been suspended until the next round of negotiations (WTO, 1996b).[4]

The GATS therefore allows member countries to make any exception to MFN that they can negotiate. They do not have to show that there is an exceptional situation that merits exceptional measures such as a threat to national security or a danger to public health. Nor is the right to make an exception limited to certain categories of agreements. The only constraint is that exceptions need to be made at the time of the entering into force of the GATS. The exceptions also continue to be subject to negotiations in subsequent rounds. Member countries therefore know at least the extent to which exceptions exist when the agreement becomes effective, and they can be sure that no additional exceptions can be made in the future.

The explanation for this approach towards an MFN exception is that the scope of the GATS is very broad. It covers, in general, any measure of a member country affecting trade in services, including a service provided through "commercial presence", that is, FDI. Thus, the scope of the MFN provision is equally broad. Member countries may therefore not always be able to apply the clause to the fullest extent possible. Moreover, the GATS' focus is not on investment protection per se in the same way as the bilateral and regional agreements analysed above.

b. The NAFTA approach

NAFTA (article 1108, paragraph 1) allows for an exception similar to that found in the GATS. Accordingly, the MFN clause does not apply to non-conforming measures maintained at the level of the federal, state or local government. In addition, it permits member countries to adopt new non-conforming measures in the future. This is permitted with regard to those sectors, subsectors or activities which a country has set out in a specific schedule. This allows the country to take any kind of discriminatory measure in the future against foreign investors in the sectors or with regard to the activities so designated (article 1108, paragraph 3). The only limit is that, under no circumstances may a contracting party require an investor from another party, by reason of its nationality, to sell or otherwise dispose of an investment existing at the time the measure becomes effective (article 1108, paragraph 4).

Furthermore, NAFTA includes MFN exceptions with regard to public procurement and subsidies provided by a contracting party or a state enterprise, including government-supported loans, guarantees and insurance (article 1108, paragraph 7). In addition, there are MFN exceptions in connection with intellectual property rights and other international agreements that contracting parties have set out in their schedule (article 1108, paragraphs 5 and 6).

The NAFTA approach is based on the consideration that there may be a need to make an MFN exception for possible measures in the future which cannot be exactly foreseen at the moment. For instance, a contracting party may preserve its right to give certain subsidies only to domestically controlled enterprises, or to promote specific domestic economic activities.

Both the NAFTA and the GATS approach allow developing countries to make MFN exceptions for development purposes. Countries can identify those industries for which they would want to apply a policy of selective intervention and favour foreign investors of a particular nationality.

***

From the foregoing, the current state of practice regarding the use of the MFN standard in investment agreements can be summarized as follows:

- Most BITs offer the unconditional post-entry MFN standard.
- Some BITs, notably those of the United States and Canada, and some regional agreements offer a pre- and post-entry MFN standard. (During the MAI negotiations, it was also envisaged to have binding rules for both for the pre- and post-establishment phases.)
- There are various *possible* exceptions to the MFN standard. These can be classified as general exceptions based on public policy or national security; reciprocal subject-matter specific exceptions; and country-specific exceptions. Furthermore, there are a number of other treaty-specific discretionary exceptions which, in general, not only cover any existing discrimination but also permit future departures from MFN. These exceptions arise in respect of public procurement, government loans, subsidies, insurance agreements and intellectual property agreements.

Notwithstanding the necessarily extensive discussion of exceptions, it must be stressed that the majority of bilateral agreements contain very few exceptions to the MFN standard, even though most (if not all) BITs contain an exception for taxation; many also have an exception for REIOs. However, conditions and exceptions become more likely where more parties are added to an agreement.

Section III
Interaction with other Issues and Concepts

MFN interacts with nearly all investment-related issues discussed in this series. The key interactions are highlighted in table 1.

Table 1. Interaction across issues and concepts

Issue	MFN treatment
Admission and establishment	++
Competition	++
Dispute settlement (investor-State)	+
Dispute settlement (State-State)	+
Employment	+
Environment	+
Fair and equitable treatment	++
Home country measures	+
Host country operational measures	++
Illicit payments	+
Incentives	++
Investment-related trade measures	+
National treatment	++
Scope and definition	+
Social responsibility	+
State contracts	+
Taking of property	++
Taxation	+
Transfer of funds	+
Transfer of technology	+
Transfer pricing	+
Transparency	+

Source: UNCTAD.
Key: 0 = no interaction.
+ = moderate interaction.
++ = extensive interaction.

- **Admission and establishment**. Host countries can restrict or even prohibit FDI in certain industries. The main purpose of doing so is to promote indigenous capacities, especially a host country's technological development. Or, while being open to foreign investors, a host country can offer special incentives for investment in particular economic activities. The host country thereby seeks to attract those foreign investors and activities that are particularly conducive to the upgrading of the domestic economy and the deepening of its own technological infrastructure. In both alternatives, the question is whether these policies are influenced by MFN considerations.

Restrictions on the entry of foreign investment usually apply to particular industries or activities, not to the nationality of a particular foreign investor. To the extent that restrictions exist, they do not differentiate between investors from different home countries. As the purpose of these restrictions is to shield domestic enterprises from foreign competition in general, the entry barriers would have to apply to all foreign investors in order to be effective. Thus, market access is denied on a non-discriminatory basis. This entails an exception to NT, not to MFN.

- **Incentives**. Notwithstanding the general importance of the NT standard, there is one policy area in which MFN applies and NT does not necessarily do so. A host country may sometimes grant special investment incentives for foreign investors only. In cases where domestic investors cannot claim the same privileges, NT becomes irrelevant. On the other hand, the MFN standard does not give foreign investors full protection against possible discrimination in this field. The MFN clause would only apply to general incentive programmes designed for a particular industry as a whole. By contrast, the MFN standard would be of no avail with regard to so-called one-off deals in which a host country grants an incentive on an individual basis (see section I above).
- **National treatment**. There is a strong link between the MFN and the NT standard. The latter means that foreign investors must not be treated less favourably than domestic investors in a host country. MFN alone does not seem to be enough to exclude possible discrimination against foreign investors. It is therefore supplemented by NT in order to guarantee a more fully non-discriminatory legal environment. Otherwise, a host country could favour its domestic enterprises by ensuring them better treatment and a privileged place in the domestic market. In the extreme case, a host country could deny foreign investors all rights. As long as this happens on a non-discriminatory basis, it would not violate the MFN standard. It is the combination of the two standards, and the degree to which exceptions to both standards exist, that determines whether the legal situation in a host country is attractive to foreign investors or not.

It should be noted that exceptions to NT are more frequent than exceptions to MFN. This reflects the fact that countries find it more difficult to treat foreign and domestic investors equally than to provide for equal treatment among investors from different home countries. Furthermore, there may be special situations in which a privileged treatment of domestic enterprises can be justified (see below, Conclusion).

While MFN and NT are two distinct legal concepts, there may be situations in which the standards interfere with each other. If country X grants MFN to investors from country Y and NT to investors from country Z, it seems that investors from country Y could likewise claim NT via the MFN clause. However, the result would be different if country X has explicitly taken an exception to NT vis-à-vis country Y. In this case, MFN is not tantamount to NT.

Furthermore, a question may arise about which treatment prevails if a foreign investor can claim NT and MFN. Some investment agreements contain an explicit rule in this respect, entitling investors to the more favourable of the two standards of treatment. One example is the Energy Charter Treaty (article 10, paragraph 3). This becomes relevant in cases in which the two standards lead to different results. For instance, NT would mean that foreign investors could own up to 100 per cent of their affiliates in a host country, whereas they might have to respect ownership restrictions under MFN.

The above-mentioned rule raises a number of questions that -- it seems -- have not been dealt with so far in the international legal arena. First, it may be difficult to assess whether NT or MFN results in "better" treatment. For instance, with regard to dispute settlement, NT would mean that a foreign investor can sue a host government before its national courts -- like any domestic investor. MFN may allow a foreign investor to chose international arbitration. What kind of dispute settlement is more favourable? Furthermore, should one apply objective criteria for making this assessment, or is it a subjective judgment? In the latter case, should it be the opinion of the investor which matters or the host government which decides?

Moreover, one may ask whether the assessment needs to be made in respect of an individual case, or with regard to the issue in general. To revert to the above-mentioned example as regards dispute settlement, domestic law (the application of NT) may provide a foreign investor with a greater choice of judicial remedies than would be available under international arbitration. Could the investor nevertheless opt for the latter, because in the current situation the domestic courts of the host country do not function properly (for instance in a situation of political turmoil)?

Another issue is whether the "whichever-is-more-favourable" formula would allow investors to follow a "pick-and-choose" strategy. While NT might be better for them in respect of certain aspects of their investment activities, they may prefer MFN with regard to others (for instance in the exceptional case that MFN is better than NT -- so-called "reverse discrimination"). One may argue that foreign investors have to decide whether they want to be treated like a domestic enterprise (NT applies), or like a foreign company (MFN), and that, consequently, they should not be entitled to a "mixed" treatment. Still, the difficulty would remain how to assess whether -- all investment activities considered -- NT or MFN is more favourable. Moreover, the preference for one particular treatment may change over time as the legal framework for investment in a host country changes.

One might ask whether MFN alone would be sufficient in a host country where a given industry is dominated by foreign investors. In this case, NT would not be needed for governmental measures and programmes that apply to this industry only. However, NT would still be important for all laws and regulations of a general nature.

- **Fair and equitable treatment**. MFN and fair and equitable treatment may both be inserted into the same clause covering post-entry treatment of an investment. Although MFN and fair and equitable treatment may often lead to the same legal result, the two standards are not identical.
- **Competition**. The MFN standard needs to be understood in relation to competition laws, in particular antitrust rules (UNCTAD, 1997). In the absence of effective competition policy, the first foreign investor entering a host country may be able to acquire a monopolistic position. An MFN commitment would be of no help for subsequent competitors trying to break the monopoly. Likewise, MFN in the post-establishment phase could be undermined if the foreign investor is not protected against unfair competition from other foreign companies. Only competition laws can respond to these cases in order to restore a balance of competition between foreign investors operating on the host country market.
- **Host country operational measures.** As part of their individual development strategies, host countries sometimes impose upon foreign investors certain operational conditions, such as local content requirements or transfer of technology. Most BITs do not contain explicit provisions on this subject. However, such measures would be covered by the general MFN rule, because they relate to the "operation and maintenance" of an investment. A host country would therefore not be allowed to impose different requirements on foreign investors of different nationalities. This prohibition does not exist under the TRIMs Agreement, which imposes obligations on parties only in respect of the NT standard and quantitative restrictions.
- **Taking of property**. The importance of the MFN standard is underlined by the fact that it appears in other investment treaty provisions as well, in particular in rules on expropriation and protection from strife. The latter concept relates to losses that a foreign investor may suffer in a host country due to war or other armed conflict, a state of emergency, revolution, insurrection, civil disturbance or any other similar event. Any expropriation has to be non-discriminatory -- which includes MFN. With regard to protection from strife, a host country usually commits itself not to discriminate if it decides to pay compensation for the loss suffered; once again, the MFN standard applies.

In addition, there are two areas that are not covered separately in these volumes, but which nevertheless deserve mentioning as they bear on the consideration of MFN in international investment agreements:

- **Trade policy**. A major portion of international trade takes place among the various entities of TNCs. Furthermore, FDI can create new trade flows, and trade measures can influence FDI flows (see chapter 4 in volume III). With the growth of investment activities and the establishment of worldwide networks of integrated production, the interdependence between trade and investment policies is stronger than before (UNCTAD, 1996b). The entities of a

TNC are no longer quasi-autonomous, but tend to be closely interlinked by various production, trade and technology channels (UNCTAD, 1993).

The question arises as to whether an obligation to grant MFN in investment matters would automatically extend to trade as well. This may be the case because, as discussed before (section I), the MFN standard has a broad scope and covers, *inter alia*, the maintenance and use of an investment. One might argue that the trade relations of a TNC are part of these activities. Thus the MFN standard in respect of investment matters could prohibit a country from discriminating against foreign investors with regard to their trade activities. The conclusion of a preferential trade agreement with a particular country would, as such, not amount to discrimination, because any investor could, in principle, benefit from it. The assessment may be different if there is substantial intra-firm trade in competing TNCs. In this case, a parent company located in country X and its foreign affiliates would be unilaterally favoured. This could amount to *de facto* discrimination. However, to the extent that this preferential treatment is covered by an MFN exception under the WTO, this exception may also cover the investment-related MFN clause.

One might also pose the question the other way round and ask whether MFN in trade could be automatically extended to investment. This could be the case if investment could be considered as one possible means of doing trade. In general, trade and investment are regarded as two substantially different ways to supply a foreign market. However, as the example of the GATS shows, trade (in services) may include a commercial presence in the host country. If an international agreement contains such a broad definition of "trade", MFN in trade would therefore encompass investment as well.

- **International minimum standard**. Legal doctrine distinguishes the MFN standard from the so-called "international minimum standard" which is considered part of customary international law. The latter standard prohibits treatment that amounts "to an outrage, to bad faith, to wilful neglect of duty, or to an insufficiency of governmental action so far short of international standards that every reasonable and impartial man would readily recognize its insufficiency" (United States v. Mexico, 1926, pp. 61-62). Investment protection agreements usually refer to this standard by prohibiting any arbitrary or unreasonable action. Discrimination based on the nationality of an investor does not as such violate this standard. There may be valid reasons why a country would like to give preferential treatment to investors of a particular nationality. The MFN standard can therefore substantially improve the situation for foreign investors that would otherwise prevail under customary international law. It should also be remembered that, as a treaty-based standard, MFN ensures a binding obligation to which the disputed international minimum standards often do not apply.

* * *

The interaction between the MFN standard and other issues and concepts can therefore be summarized as follows:

- There are strong links between MFN and other investment-related concepts.
- The importance of the MFN standard is underlined by the fact that it applies to a broad range of issues, including investment incentives, trade and competition policies.
- The MFN standard alone is usually not sufficient to secure non-discriminatory treatment in the host country. It works, but if accompanied by the NT standard.

Conclusion: Economic and Development Implications and Policy Options

The above analysis has shown that the MFN standard, as such, is widely used and that, at the same time, exceptions and reservations to the standard exist. In determining the contents of an MFN clause, two sets of options arise:

- whether to limit MFN to post-entry treatment only or to extend the standard to both pre-entry and post-entry treatment;
- whether to make exceptions to the application of the standard in either case.

As regards the first issue, much depends, to begin with, on whether a country differentiates between pre-entry and post-entry treatment in general. The next question would be whether the prevailing circumstances or the national policies in effect involve treating investors from different countries in different ways. These matters are discussed further in chapter 4.

With regard to exceptions, three broad categories can be distinguished. The first includes general exceptions based on public policy or national security; these are not targeted at MFN per se but they can indirectly limit its application. The second allows MFN exceptions only in respect of a limited range of sectors or matters agreed beforehand by all contracting parties (especially, taxation, intellectual property, REIO, mutual recognition, transportation). The third approach gives more freedom to the parties and allows them, in principle, to make exceptions of their own choosing, provided that the exception is listed in country-specific schedules (e.g. with regard to subsidies).

A. Development strategies and MFN

In the past -- and in the present to a lesser extent -- national policies of developing countries concerning FDI have varied considerably. At opposite ends of the spectrum are open-door policies with no attempt at intervention either in the flow of international investment or in the behaviour of investors, and highly restrictive policies with prohibitions on foreign investment. It is not the purpose of the present analysis to assess which policy best promotes economic development. Rather, the question is whether MFN considerations play a particular role in the case of developing countries.

The countries that apply liberal policies vis-à-vis foreign investors assume presumably that foreign investment is a means for increasing local productivity and competitiveness. The MFN standard has been an inherent part of their development policies, since after all an open-door policy means that no restrictions on, or discrimination between, foreign investors are in effect that are based on the nationality of the investor.

On the other hand, there have also been strategies of selective intervention. Countries pursuing these strategies seek to steer foreign investors into those activities they consider particularly important for their economic development (Agosin and Prieto, 1993). There is evidence that such a policy can contribute to an acceleration and deepening of the process of industrial development in particular. This approach requires the identification of activities in which a country can reasonably expect to acquire a comparative advantage and the promotion of production in such areas.[5]

It may be argued that an exception to MFN based on the nationality of foreign investors would be consistent with the strategy of a host country that has made the judgement that the best way to pursue the economic development of the country is to establish and maintain special economic relations with one or several specific other countries, which would be selected as strategic partners. The countries concerned would thus grant market access or other special privileges only to investors from these countries. Such a strategy assumes that one or several countries with strategic advantages over other potential partners could be identified (and that granting the same conditions to investors from other countries would undermine this strategic partnership). The host country would align its own pattern of comparative advantages and its stage of development to the comparative advantages of the partner.

What is not clear is why obtaining the desired investment from one set of investors would be more desirable than obtaining them from another set of investors, as long as the underlying development objectives are being served. Rather, it would appear that strategies of this type are normally based on a distinction between foreign and domestic investors and *not* on a distinction among foreign investors.[6]

B. The use of exceptions

As has been suggested above, host countries can pursue their development strategies without discrimination among investors from different foreign countries. However, as they become more integrated into the global economy, they may, in some cases, need to make use of MFN-specific exceptions, even though these may not necessarily be inspired by development considerations.

In particular, a number of reciprocal subject-specific exceptions appear to be accepted. For example, the more a country develops a network of bilateral double taxation agreements, the more it may be faced with the issue of MFN exceptions in this respect. Mutual recognition arrangements are another area that would be undermined by a unilateral extension of benefits of an arrangement to third countries. Finally, countries may increasingly seek recourse to MFN exceptions through REIO clauses.[7]

* * *

In conclusion, it needs to be reaffirmed that the MFN standard is at the heart of multilateralism and is a core principle in international investment agreements. At the same time, the standard allows flexibility for countries to pursue their policies, both in relation to the question of the treatment of foreign investment before and after entry, and through exceptions and reservations to the MFN standard. But, thc fact that various ways to limit MFN have been discussed on the basis of an analysis of existing agreements is not meant to suggest that any of these ways are advocated. Rather, whether or not a country actually wants to utilize any of these exceptions needs to be evaluated by it, in the context of its specific conditions. Exceptions to MFN would only exceptionally be justified for development purposes.

Notes

1 Unless otherwise noted, all instruments cited herein may be found in UNCTAD, 1996a.

2 See article II, 1994 United States model BIT, and article 1103 of NAFTA.

3 The supplementary treaty had not been signed as of November 1998.

4 Decision adopted by the Council for Trade in Services on 28 June 1996.

5 It can be carried out either by way of controls over the entry of investors, where this can protect indigenous technological development, or by providing special incentives for foreign investment in activities in which foreign participation is seen as desirable. In the latter case, the purpose is to guide the resource allocation of foreign investors and to induce them to locate more complex functions in host countries than they would otherwise have done. Such a policy may in addition use certain performance requirements to try to advance economic development in certain respects.

6 In any case, an MFN exception on these grounds might cause "victim" countries to retaliate, in particular by denying the host country MFN as well. As an increasing number of firms from a growing number of countries become foreign investors, such retaliation could have adverse economic consequences.

7 As to the last of these cases, a question concerns the stage of integration at which an MFN exception may be justified. One approach is that an exception can be justified if integration within a region is *qualitatively* different from integration based only on the standard of non-discrimination (see section II). The REIO may therefore have to reach a stage in which member States have committed themselves to removing virtually all barriers to cross-border investment, irrespective of whether these barriers are discriminatory or not. As long as the REIO members have only accepted the standard of non-discrimination amongst themselves, an MFN exception with regard to non-members may be more difficult to justify. For an in-depth treatment of the REIO clause in international investment agreements, see UNCTAD, forthcoming.

Annex. Diagram of MFN clauses with illustrations

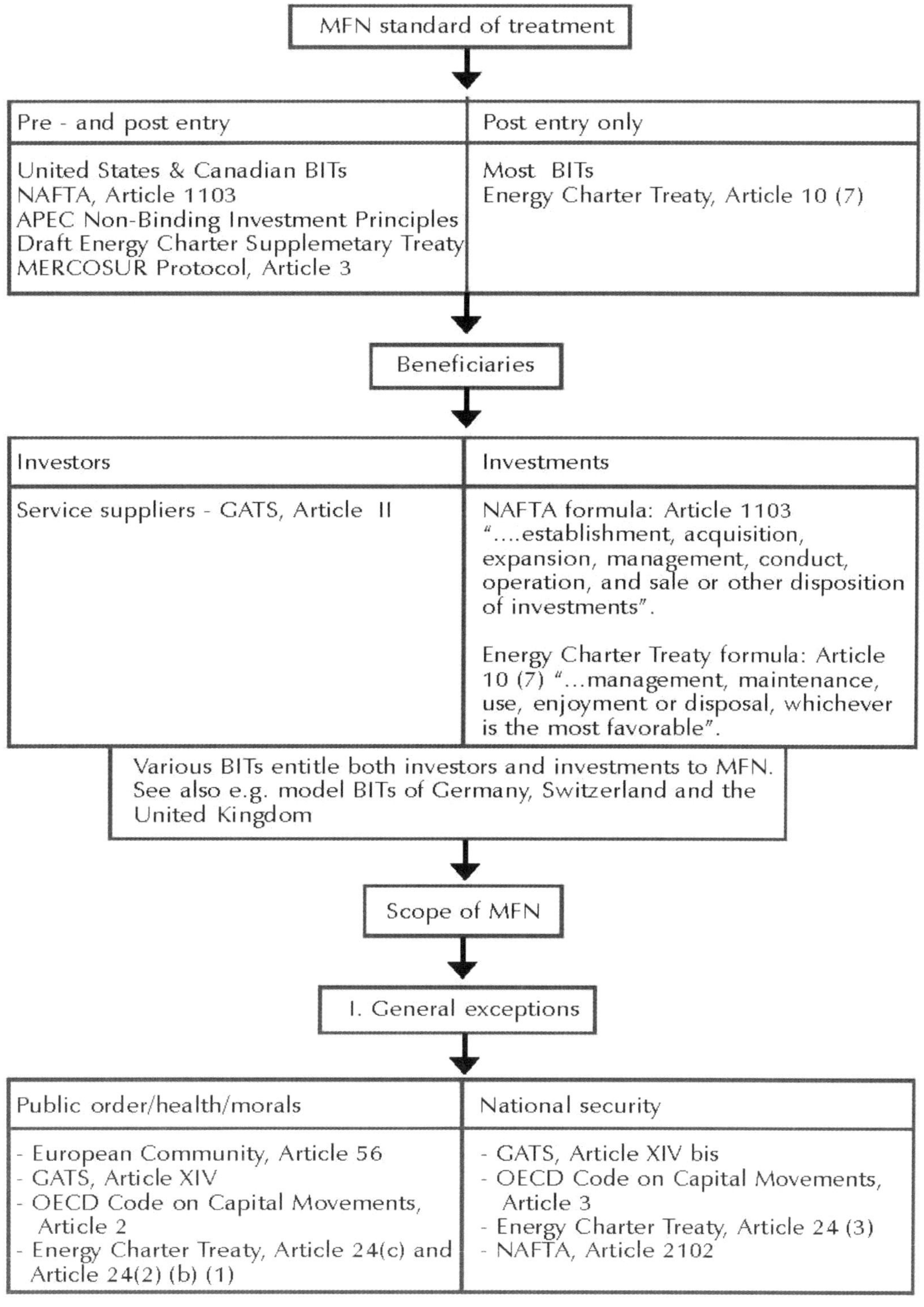

II. Reciprocal subject-specific MFN exceptions

Taxation	Intellectual property (IP)	REIO	Mutual recognition	Other bilateral issues
- Chile-Malaysia BIT, article 3: "shall not be interpreted to oblige a Contracting Party to extend to investors of the other Contracting Party the benefits of any treatment, preference or privilege by virtue of: (b) any international convention or agreement related totally or principally to taxation, or any national legislation related totally or partially to taxation."	- Berne Convention - Rome Convention - TRIPS Article 4(6) [Protection of Reciprocity Rule] - NAFTA Article 1108 (5) [not limited to protection of reciprocity but applies to IP rights in general]	- Chile-Malaysia BIT, article 3: "shall not be interpreted to oblige a Contracting Party to extend to investors of the other Contracting Party the benefits of any treatment, preference or privilege by virtue of: (a) any customs union, free trade area, common market or monetary union, or any similar international convention or other forms of regional cooperation, present or future, of which any of the Contracting Parties might become a party;..." - GATS, Article V	- Patents - GATS, Article VII	- Transport - Fisheries

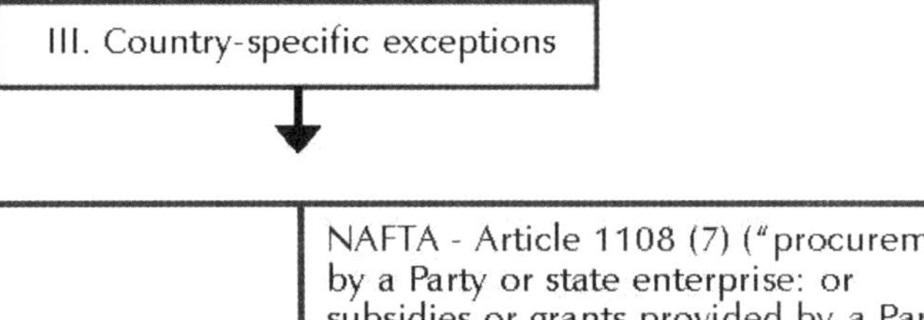

GATS - Articles II, XIII (public procurement)	NAFTA - Article 1108 (7) ("procurement by a Party or state enterprise: or subsidies or grants provided by a Party or a state enterprise, including government-supported loans, guarantees and insurance.")

Source: UNCTAD.

Chapter 7. Fair and Equitable Treatment*

Executive summary

In recent years, the concept of fair and equitable treatment has assumed prominence in investment relations between States. While the earliest proposals that made reference to this standard of treatment for investment are contained in various multilateral efforts in the period immediately following World War II, the bulk of the State practice incorporating the standard is to be found in bilateral investment treaties (BITs) which have become a central feature in international investment relations.

In essence, the fair and equitable standard provides a yardstick by which relations between foreign direct investors and Governments of capital-importing countries may be assessed. It also acts as a signal from capital-importing countries, for it indicates, at the very least, a State's willingness to accommodate foreign capital on terms that take into account the interests of the investor in fairness and equity. Furthermore, as most capital-importing countries have now entered into agreements that incorporate the standard, reluctance to accept this standard could prompt questions about the general attitude of a State to foreign investment.

At the same time, uncertainty concerning the precise meaning of the phrase "fair and equitable treatment" may, in fact, assume practical importance for States. The phrase carries at least two possible meanings. First it could be given its plain meaning, so that beneficiaries are entitled to fairness and equity as these terms are understood in non-technical terms. Secondly, it would mean that beneficiaries are assured treatment in keeping with the international minimum standard for investors. In practical terms, this uncertainty may influence the policy decisions of a host country that is willing to accept a treaty clause on fair and equitable treatment, but that is not prepared to offer the international minimum standard. This may be particularly the case where the host country believes that the international minimum standard implies that foreign investors could be entitled to more favourable treatment than local investors.

Although the concept of fair and equitable treatment now features prominently in international investment agreements, different formulations are used in connection with the standard. An examination of the relevant treaties suggests at least four approaches in practice, namely:

- An approach that omits reference to fair and equitable treatment.
- An approach in which it is recommended that States should offer investment fair and equitable treatment, but such treatment is not required as a matter of law (the hortatory approach).
- A legal requirement for States to accord investment "fair and equitable" treatment, "just and equitable" treatment, or "equitable" treatment.
- A legal requirement for States to accord investment fair and equitable treatment, together with other standards of treatment, such as most-favoured-nation (MFN) and national treatment.

These different approaches can serve as models for future practice though it should be noted that the approach that combines fair and equitable treatment with related standards of treatment has received most support in recent practice.

Because all States would, as a matter of course, seek to treat local and foreign enterprises fairly and equitably, the inclusion of a clause on the fair and equitable standard in investment agreements does not, generally speaking, raise complex issues, except that the precise meaning of the fair and equitable standard may vary in different contexts.

Introduction

The concept of fair and equitable treatment now occupies a position of prominence in investment relations between States. Together with other standards that have grown increasingly important in recent years, the fair and equitable treatment standard provides a useful yardstick for assessing relations between foreign direct investors and

* The chapter is based on a 1999 manuscript prepared by Stephen Vasciannie. The final version reflects comments received from Joachim Karl, Mark Koulen and Marinus Sikkel.

Governments of capital-importing countries. As a general proposition, the standard also acts as a signal from capital-importing countries: for, if a investment within its jurisdiction will be subject to treatment compatible with some of the main expectations of foreign investors.

The current prominence given to the idea of fair and equitable treatment in investment relations owes its origin primarily to BITs between developed and developing countries, as well as countries with economies in transition. Such BITs have become major instruments regulating the investment relations between foreign investors and host countries, and as such, they have exerted influence on State practice concerning investment relations. In the majority of these BITs, the parties concerned agree to grant each other fair and equitable treatment in investment matters, and contemplate that, if need be, an independent third party may be called upon to settle disputes concerning whether this standard has been violated.

Although the concept of fair and equitable treatment occurs most frequently in BITs of recent vintage, it has also had a place in multilateral efforts in the area of international investment law. For instance, in a provision that precedes most, if not all, references to the fair and equitable standard in investment law, the Havana Charter of 1948 contemplates that foreign investment should be assured just and equitable treatment.[1] Though the Havana Charter did not enter into force, its use of the term "just and equitable" has served as a precedent for subsequent efforts to reach agreement on treatment standards for foreign investment in international law. Thus, the Abs-Shawcross Draft Convention on Investments Abroad (Abs and Shawcross, 1960) and the Draft Convention on the Protection of Foreign Property (the OECD Draft Convention) proposed by the Organisation for Economic Co-operation and Development (OECD) in 1967 (OECD, 1967), two draft documents that generally reflect the perspective of capital-exporting countries, adopted the language of fair and equitable treatment in setting out basic protection for foreign investors. Likewise, the most recent multilateral draft treaty on investment issues prepared under the auspices of the OECD, the Multilateral Agreement on Investment (MAI) (OECD, 1998a), also contemplated that, with respect to investment protection, the basic standard should include fair and equitable treatment. As a preliminary observation, therefore, multilateral treaty efforts host country provides an assurance of fair and equitable treatment, it presumably wishes to indicate to the international community that among the capital-exporting countries share the tendency in favour of a fair and equitable treatment clause, which has become a common feature of BITs.

This is not to suggest, however, that only capital-exporting countries have supported fair and equitable treatment in their treaty practice. From a somewhat early stage in the United Nations efforts to formulate a Code of Conduct on Transnational Corporations, the concept was tentatively included in the main draft provisions on investment promotion and protection (UNCTC,1988a, pp. 241-242). The broad perception that most countries are prepared to guarantee fair and equitable treatment to foreign investors is further reinforced by investment provisions in various regional instruments. Among such instruments, the Fourth Convention of the African, Caribbean and Pacific group of States (ACP) and the European Economic Community (EEC) known as Lomé IV and the North American Free Trade Agreement (NAFTA) may be mentioned as treaties that now incorporate the standard.

Notwithstanding its currency in investment instruments, however, the fair and equitable standard still prompts a number of difficult questions in investment law. The precise meaning of the concept is sometimes open to enquiry, not least because the notions of "fairness" and "equity" do not automatically connote a clear set of legal prescriptions in some situations. Broadly speaking, most legal systems strive to achieve fairness and equity as a matter of course; however, when parties to a treaty agree, as a matter of law, that fair and equitable treatment must be granted to foreign investors, it may be presumed that the parties accept a common standard of treatment. One of the challenges in this area of the law is to identify the main elements of this common standard.

Questions also arise concerning the different policy options open to States that wish to include a fair and equitable treatment clause in an agreement. Having regard to the investment instruments published to date, States have made references not only to "fair and equitable" treatment, but also to "just and equitable" treatment and "equitable" treatment. In other cases, they have adopted language that recommends "fair and equitable treatment", but does not require it as a matter of law, and, in many instances, they have combined "fair and equitable treatment" with other standards. What are the implications of these apparently divergent approaches? To what extent do these implications vary according to the particular form of words used? And what is the significance of juxtaposing "fair and equitable" treatment alongside general treatment standards such as the most-favoured-nation and national treatment standards? This chapter addresses such questions.

Another important issue concerns the economic and development implications of the fair and equitable standard for host countries. As a matter of law, States are not obliged to allow foreign investments into their territory, but, especially in the prevailing liberal environment, most developing countries actively seek foreign investment as a means of encouraging growth and development. In this context, States have been willing to incorporate the fair and equitable standard in their investment agreements in the hope that this will enhance their reputation as countries hospitable to foreign capital. In practice, however, because the fair and equitable standard is often incorporated with other standards, and is often presented as only one element among several factors affecting investment decisions, it is difficult to identify the extent to which the fair and equitable guarantee, on its own, influences investor choices.

Section I Explanation of the Issue

A. History of the standard

1. Origins

The fair and equitable standard has been an important aspect of international investment law since the period immediately following the Second World War. Shortly after the war, in the course of efforts to establish an International Trade Organization in 1948, the standard was incorporated in Article 11(2) of the Havana Charter of 1948, as a desirable basis for the treatment of investments in foreign countries. Although the Charter did not enter into force, its reference to the fair and equitable standard served as a precedent in subsequent instruments concerned with international investment. So, for example, at the regional level, when the Ninth International Conference of American States (1948) adopted the Economic Agreement of Bogota, an agreement covering the provision of adequate safeguards for foreign investors, the parties concerned expressly contemplated fair and equitable treatment for foreign capital (Documents on American Foreign Relations, 1948).

Like the Havana Charter, however, the Economic Agreement of Bogota failed to come into effect owing to lack of support. But, this did not undermine the early treaty practice concerning the fair and equitable standard because, at the bilateral level, the United States and various other countries provided for this standard in a series of Friendship, Commerce and Navigation (FCN) treaties in the 1950s. More specifically, the United States FCN treaties with Belgium and Luxembourg, France, Greece, Ireland, Israel, Nicaragua and Pakistan contained the express assurance that foreign persons, properties, enterprises and other interests would receive "equitable" treatment, while other United States FCN treaties -- including those with Ethiopia, the Federal Republic of Germany, Oman and the Netherlands -- contemplated "fair and equitable" treatment for a similar set of items involved in the foreign investment process.

The approach taken in most United States FCN treaties in the 1950s was not fundamentally dissimilar from that incorporated in the next major development concerning the standard, namely, the Draft Convention on Investments Abroad, proposed in 1959 by a number of European business persons and lawyers under the leadership of Hermann Abs and Lord Shawcross. By virtue of its origins, and by its emphasis on investor protection, the Abs-Shawcross Draft was widely perceived as favouring the perspective of capital-exporting countries. To a certain degree, this observation is also applicable to the most influential of the early postwar drafts on investment, namely, the OECD Draft Convention. The Convention, first published in 1963 and revised in 1967, was actually approved by the Council of the OECD (with Turkey and Spain abstaining), but it was never opened for signature. As an unratified treaty, its importance rests mainly in the fact that, at a time when most developing countries -- and some developed countries too -- were very supportive of national controls over foreign direct investment, it placed emphasis on the protection of foreign investments. Given the economic and political influence represented by the OECD acting as a group, the draft agreement reflected the dominant trends and perspectives among capital-exporting countries in investment matters.

2. Recent usage

Since the early 1960s, BITs between capital-exporting and capital-importing countries have assumed increasing importance in regulating foreign investment issues. While some of the earlier BITs did not expressly refer to the standard, by the 1970s, this had changed substantially, so that the vast majority of BITs now place clear reliance on fair and equitable treatment. At the multilateral level, no comprehensive treaty on foreign investment incorporating the language of fair and equitable treatment exists. However, two major efforts in this direction since the formulation of the OECD Draft Convention should be mentioned. First, in the draft United Nations Code of Conduct on Transnational Corporations, it was contemplated that transnational corporations operating in foreign countries should receive fair and equitable treatment; while some issues concerning that standard remained outstanding in the draft United Nations Code – and bearing in mind the differences of opinion among capital-exporting and importing States concerning the draft – agreement on fair and equitable treatment, albeit in preliminary form, was a point of significance. Secondly, the MAI negotiated in the OECD placed emphasis on fairness in the treatment of investment. In addition to suggesting in the draft preamble that investment regimes should be fair, the proposed MAI contemplated both fair and equitable treatment as well as full and constant protection and security for investments.

Among regional treaties, Lomé IV and NAFTA are important treaties that also incorporate the fair and equitable standard. More particularly, Lomé IV, which entered into force for a 10-year period on 1 March 1990, is noteworthy in the present context because it reflects the perspective of a significant cross-section of both capital-exporting and capital-importing countries.

Reference should also be made to private sector initiatives designed to influence public policy on foreign investment. In this regard, the Abs-Shawcross Draft has already been mentioned. But other efforts -- such as the International Code of Fair Treatment for Foreign Investors, as approved by the International Chamber of Commerce (ICC) in 1949, and the ICC's Guidelines for International Investment -- should also be mentioned as documents that use the standard of fair and equitable treatment. More recently, the World Bank, through its 1992 Guidelines on Treatment of Foreign Direct Investment (the World Bank Guidelines), has also given support for fair and equitable treatment, and has sought to provide guidance on ways in which this standard maybe given specific application with respect to investment issues such as security of person and property rights, the granting of permits and licences and the repatriation of capital.

B. The meaning of fair and equitable treatment

At least two different views have been advanced as to the precise meaning of the term "fair and equitable treatment" in investment relations:

- the plain meaning approach; and
- equating fair and equitable treatment with the international minimum standard.

1. The plain meaning approach

In this approach, the term "fair and equitable treatment" is given its plain meaning: hence, where a foreign investor has an assurance of treatment under this standard, a straightforward assessment needs to be made as to whether a particular treatment meted out to that investor is both "fair" and "equitable".[2]

The plain meaning approach is consistent with accepted rules of interpretation in international law. Also, because there appear to be no judicial decisions on the precise meaning of the fair and equitable standard in particular situations, there may be a tendency to assume that the expression is so readily understood that it has not generated significant differences of opinion. This would suggest that States are agreed on the meaning of the term; in the absence of clear pronouncements to the contrary, this would also suggest that States are agreed that the term should be understood in its plain, or literal, sense.

Generally, however, the plain meaning approach is not without its difficulties. In the first place, the concepts "fair" and "equitable" are by themselves inherently subjective, and therefore lacking in precision. Consequently, if one relies only on the plain meaning of the words, it is conceivable that a given situation satisfies the standard of fair and equitable treatment in the perspective of a capital-importing country but fails to do so from the point of view of the foreign investor or the capital-exporting country. This is especially true in circumstances in which the parties involved have different legal traditions or approach the issue with different cultural assumptions (Walker, 1957-1958, p. 812).

Secondly, difficulties of interpretation may also arise from the fact that the concepts, "fair and equitable treatment", in their plain meaning, do not refer to an established body of law or to existing legal precedents. Instead, the plain meaning approach presumes that, in each case, the question will be whether a foreign investor has been treated fairly and equitably, without reference to any technical understanding of the meaning of "fair and equitable treatment" (Fatouros, 1962, p. 215). But this is problematic because, with there being no particular agreement as to the content of the term, the plain meaning approach could give rise to conflicting interpretations in practice.

On the other hand, although the plain meaning approach is vague in its application, this is not altogether disadvantageous. In some circumstances, both States and foreign investors may view lack of precision as a virtue, for it promotes flexibility in the investment process (Walker, 1957-1958, p. 812). Investment treaties and contracts are usually prepared in advance of the projects to which they are directly applicable; and, in most cases, the parties to these treaties and contracts cannot predict the range of possible occurrences that may affect the future relationship between a State and particular investors. Accordingly, States and investors may support the fair and equitable standard precisely because they believe it does not provide a detailed *a priori* solution to certain issues that could arise in the future.

This is not to suggest, however, that the plain meaning approach is devoid of content. In the first place, if a dispute arises, it is likely that the fair and equitable standard will be applied objectively: none of the agreements including the standard suggest that the interpretation of what is fair and equitable shall be as determined by the investor or the host country. Rather, provision is normally made for third party dispute settlement. In these circumstances, both sides may present their subjective views on the requirements of the fairness and equity standard in the particular case, but the third party is called upon to apply an objective standard.

In addition, some guidance on the plain meaning of fair and equitable treatment may be derived from international law in general. Specifically, although international law has had opportunities to incorporate concepts of equity from particular national legal systems, this has not been done. By extension, while maxims of equity from specific legal systems could add certainty to the concept of fair and equitable treatment, this approach should be avoided. At the same time, however, it is possible to identify certain forms of behaviour that appear to be contrary to fairness and equity in most legal systems and to extrapolate from this the type of State action that may be inconsistent with fair and equitable treatment, using the plain meaning approach. Thus, for instance, if a State acts fraudulently or in bad faith, or capriciously and wilfully discriminates against a foreign investor, or deprives an investor of acquired rights in a manner that leads to the unjust enrichment of the State, then there is at least a *prima facie* case for arguing that the fair and equitable standard has been violated.

2. International minimum standard

The second approach to the meaning of the concept suggests that fair and equitable treatment is synonymous with the international minimum standard in international law. This interpretation proceeds from the assumption that, under customary international law, foreign investors are entitled to a certain level of treatment, and that treatment which falls short of this level gives rise to liability on the part of the State. If, in fact, fair and equitable treatment is the same as the international minimum standard, then some of the difficulties of interpretation inherent in the plain meaning approach may be overcome, for there is a substantial body of jurisprudence and doctrine concerning the elements of the international minimum standard.

At the policy level, however, an approach that equates fair and equitable treatment with the international minimum standard is problematic in certain respects:

- If States and investors believe that the fair and equitable standard is entirely interchangeable with the international minimum standard, they could indicate this clearly in their investment instruments; but most investment instruments do not make an explicit link between the two standards. Therefore, it cannot readily be argued that most States and investors believe fair and equitable treatment is implicitly the same as the international minimum standard.
- Attempts to equate the two standards may be perceived as paying insufficient regard to the substantial debate in international law concerning the international minimum standard. More specifically, while the international minimum standard has strong support among developed countries, a number

of developing countries have traditionally held reservations as to whether this standard is a part of customary international law.

Against this background of uncertainty, it is difficult to assume that most countries have accepted that the international minimum standard should be applied to their investment treaties in instances in which they have not opted to incorporate that standard *express is verbis*.

3. "Equitable" vs. "fair and equitable" treatment

In most treaties and other instruments that provide for fair and equitable treatment for investments, the words "fair" and "equitable" are combined in the form of a reference to "fair and equitable treatment". This is particularly true with respect to recent investment instruments. So, for instance, the model BITs prepared by Chile, China, France, Germany, the United States, and the United Kingdom, as well as regional instruments such as NAFTA, the 1993 Treaty Establishing the Common Market for Eastern and Southern Africa (COMESA) and the 1994 Energy Charter Treaty, all use the phrase "fair and equitable treatment" apparently as part of a single concept.

This approach suggests that there is, in fact, a single standard, the fair and equitable standard, as distinct from two separate standards, one concerning fairness, and the other equity. Certain considerations support this perspective. First, the consistency with which States have linked the two terms in the format of "fair and equitable" treatment creates the impression that these States believe there is one standard. With respect to the OECD members, this interpretation is reinforced by the Notes and Comments to Article 1 of the OECD Draft Convention, which expressly assumed that there was only one standard. Secondly, if States wished to indicate that "fair and equitable" treatment actually referred to two separate standards, this option would be open to them. They could, for instance, set out the fairness standard in one treaty provision, and the equity standard in another; arguably, they have not done so precisely because they believe the phrase "fair and equitable treatment" connotes a single standard.

In some cases, however, treaties and other investment instruments contain references not to "fair and equitable" treatment, but to "equitable" treatment only. This applies, for instance, to some of the FCN treaties entered into by the United States and various other countries, including, for example, Greece, Ireland, Israel and Nicaragua. Having regard to the fact that other FCN treaties of the United States expressly contemplated" fair and equitable" treatment, this could prompt the view that the United States sought to make a legally significant distinction by using two different terms. This, however, does not seem to be the case. Given the similarity between the two terms in plain language, it is difficult to identify actions by a State towards foreign investors that would be "equitable" but not "fair", and vice versa. This approach also derives support from those who argue that the variation in the form of words in the United States FCN treaties "seems to be of no great importance"(Fatouros, 1962, p. 167). In fact it has been suggested that the phrase "fair and equitable treatment" used in recent United States BITs is the equivalent of the "equitable treatment" setout in various earlier FCN treaties (Vandevelde, 1988, p. 221).

C. The relationship with other treatment standards

In some of the post-war multilateral and regional instruments on investment, such as the OECD Draft Convention, the Bogota Agreement and the Abs-Shawcross Draft, the relevant treatment standards, while referring to fair and equitable treatment, do not include direct reference to the national or MFN treatment standards. This, however, is exceptional, for, in the vast majority of investment instruments, the standard of fair and equitable treatment is incorporated with both the MFN and national treatment standards, or with at least one of the latter standards. The more recent multilateral and regional efforts (including the MAI and the NAFTA investment provisions) conform to this general trend. At the same time, a study of approximately 335 BITs in force in the early 1990s found that no less than 183 combined the fair and equitable standard with the MFN and national treatment standards (Khalil, 1992, p. 355). The study also found that, as of the early 1990s, another 92 BITs combined fair and equitable treatment with the MFN standard, while 8 contained a combination of fair and equitable treatment and national treatment.

The frequency with which these standards are incorporated together in modern investment treaties raises the question of the relationship between fair and equitable treatment on the one hand, and national and MFN treatment on the other. In essence, fair and equitable treatment denotes a non-contingent or absolute standard. This means that the fair and equitable treatment standard applies to investments in a given situation without reference to standards that are applicable to other investments or entities; it may apply to other investments or entities, but its content does not vary according to how other investments or entities are treated (Walker, 1957-1958, p. 811). In contrast, both national and MFN treatment are contingent or relative standards. The actual content of a contingent standard is ascertained by reference, not to the contingent standard itself, but to an exterior state of law or fact. Thus, in the case of national treatment, in determining the content of the standard as it applies to foreign investment, reference must be made to the treatment of nationals of the country concerned; and, similarly, in determining the content of the MFN standard in any particular case, reference must be made to the treatment granted to investments from the "most favoured nation".

Therefore, where a capital-importing nation offers both fair and equitable treatment and combined national and MFN treatment, this provides foreign investors with both non-contingent and contingent forms of protection. From the perspective of the investor, the fair and equitable component provides a fixed reference point, a definite standard that will not vary according to external considerations, because its content turns on what is fair and reasonable in the circumstances. The fair and equitable standard will also prevent discrimination against the beneficiary of the standard, where discrimination would amount to unfairness or inequity in the circumstances. Simultaneously, national and MFN treatment, as contingent standards, protect each beneficiary of these standards by ensuring equality or non-discrimination for that beneficiary vis-à-vis other investments.

A foreign investor may conceivably believe that, even where protection by the national and MFN standards is offered, the level of protection is insufficient because the host State may provide inadequate protection to its nationals or to investors from the most favoured nation. In such cases, fair and equitable treatment helps to ensure that there is at least a minimum level of protection, derived from fairness and equity, for the investor concerned.

D. Principal drafting issues

1. The need for an express provision

Under customary international law, each State has the right to determine whether it will act as a host country to foreign investors and to specify the terms and conditions under which it will accept foreign investments in its territory (Brownlie, 1998, p. 522; see also chapter 4). This legal position, derived from the practice of States, acknowledges the exclusive control that each State has over its territory; it means that, whenever investors enter a foreign country, they do so subject to the discretion of the country concerned. It also means that, in many instances, the rules that govern foreign investment are set out in treaties concluded between capital-exporting countries and their capital-importing counterparts. In this general context, it is not surprising that most references to the fair and equitable standard in investment law are to be found in treaties and that, therefore, treaty law is the principal source for provisions on this standard and on related standards of treatment in international law.

Nevertheless, it is also possible, as a matter of theory, that the standard of fair and equitable treatment has become a part of customary international law. This possibility arises from the fact that, in some instances, where a treaty provision is norm-creating in character, this provision may pass into customary law once certain criteria are satisfied.[3] However, in the case of the fair and equitable standard, it is not likely that this has occurred in practice, essentially because States have not demonstrated any clear will to have the standard included in the body of customary international law.

This has practical results for the drafting of provisions concerning fair and equitable treatment in investment treaties. Specifically, if a host State enters into a treaty with a capital-exporting counterpart, and this treaty does not contain a reference to fair and equitable treatment, then it should not be assumed that the fair and equitable standard is applicable to the investments covered by that investment treaty; on the contrary, on the assumption that the standard has not passed into the body of customary international law, it is applicable in international law only in those cases in which the parties to a treaty make express provision for fair and equitable treatment. States wishing to ensure that their investment relations are governed by the fair and equitable standard would, therefore, need to include a provision on this issue in their investment treaties.

2. *Formulating the standard*

Where States have decided to incorporate the standard of fair and equitable treatment in an investment instrument, a number of possible formulations of the standard are open to them. With reference to the practice of States, the following models merit consideration:

- Model 1: no express reference to "fair and equitable" treatment;
- Model 2: the hortatory approach;
- Model 3: reference to "fair and equitable" treatment, "just and equitable" treatment or "equitable" treatment; and
- Model 4: reference to "fair and equitable" treatment together with related standards of treatment.

The content and implications of each of these models will be considered in greater detail in section II below. For the present purpose, however, certain general observations are appropriate. First, in the hortatory approach, no binding obligation is contemplated; under this approach, sometimes reflected in preambular statements in investment instruments, the parties acknowledge the importance of fairness in the investment process but refrain from expressly specifying a legal duty for the parties to act in accordance with the standard of fair and equitable treatment. Secondly, in some instances, the hortatory approach may be combined in the same instrument with a provision that gives rise to an obligation to provide fair and equitable treatment. In such instances, the hortatory reference to the need for fairness and equity provides the rationale for the operative provision which is binding on the relevant parties. Thirdly, where the fair and equitable standard is combined with other standards, such as full protection and security, or juxtaposed along with national treatment and/or MFN treatment, then the combined standard will connote more substantial protection for the investor than the equitable standard on its own.

In addition, it is open to conjecture whether a reference to "equitable" treatment or "just and equitable" treatment connotes weaker legal protection for investors than a reference to "fair and equitable" treatment. A reference to fairness and equity in conjunction must provide, at the very least, the same degree of protection as "equitable" treatment. However, given the similarity in meaning between fairness, on the one hand, and equity, on the other, in the context of investment relations, it is difficult to identify ways in which the conjunction of the two provides greater protection for investors in practice than the equitable standard on its own. Similarly, while the term "just and equitable" treatment occurs in some treaties, it is difficult to identify ways in which this formulation may be distinguished, in substance, from the fair and equitable standard.

Section II
Stocktaking and Analysis

A. Trends in the use of the standard

One of the underlying trends in the investment area has been the increasing use of the fair and equitable standard in treaty law in the post-war era. This trend reflects in part investor desire to have the safety net of fairness, in addition to assurances of national treatment and MFN treatment. To some extent, however, it also reflects the general movement towards greater liberalization that has come to characterize international economic relations since the end of the 1970s. This liberalization has been accompanied by greater legal safeguards for foreign investors, including assurances of fairness and equity.

But, even in the context of greater liberalization, the practice has not been universal, as a number of international instruments pertaining to investment do not incorporate the language of fair and equitable treatment in express terms. Some of these instruments reflect the context in which they were adopted. So, for instance, the Charter of Economic Rights and Duties of States, adopted 12 December 1974, which sought, *inter alia* , to assist in the establishment of "a new system of international economic relations based on equity, sovereign equality and interdependence of interests of developed and developing countries" does not address the issue of treatment standards in foreign investment. Admittedly, the Charter is not an investment instrument *per se*; however, because some of its terms itemize State rights in relation to investment, the absence of references to duties owed to investors demonstrates, implicitly, the absence of consensus between capital-exporting and -importing States on treatment issues during the period of deliberations concerning a New International Economic Order.

Other instruments that omit reference to the standard may reflect regional perspectives on investor-State relations. For example, for much of the post-war period, Latin American countries following the Calvo tradition were reluctant to enter into treaty arrangements that would result in the transfer of jurisdiction over foreign investment matters from domestic courts.[4] Consistent with this approach in favour of national control over foreign investment, certainly up to the early 1980s, these countries preferred to treat foreign investors in a way that would not be tantamount to discrimination against national investors.[5] As a contingent standard, national treatment may, in fact, amount to fair and equitable treatment, but the two standards are not necessarily the same.[6]

The increasing trend in favour of incorporating fair and equitable treatment in investment instruments is most pronounced with respect to BITs. Of some 335 BITs signed up to the early 1990s, only 28 did not expressly incorporate the standard (Khalil, 1992, p. 355). With the further explosion of BITs in the 1990s, to a total of 1,513 by the end of 1997 (UNCTAD, 1998b), the pattern has not changed, so that today BITs that omit reference to fair and equitable treatment constitute the exception rather than the rule.[7]

B. Models based on State practice

An examination of the practice in multilateral, regional and bilateral treaties, together with the practice in other investment instruments, reveals that the use of the concept of fair and equitable treatment does not convey the same legal result in each case. More particularly, because the context in which the term is used may vary from one text to another, the type of protection offered will not be constant. On the basis of the relevant practice, four distinctive models are the subject of analysis in this section.

1. No reference to fair and equitable treatment

Although the fair and equitable standard has been included in several draft multilateral instruments on investment and finds its place in the vast majority of bilateral agreements in this area, there are instances in which it has been omitted from investment arrangements among States. On the multilateral level, for example, no reference is made to the standard in the Agreement on Trade-Related Investment Measures, the General Agreement on Trade in Services and the Agreement on Trade-Related Aspects of Intellectual Property Rights, though these instruments expressly rely on the MFN and national treatment concepts. And, at the bilateral level, the 1978 agreement between Egypt and Japan, as well as the agreement between Italy and Romania, may be mentioned as instances, among others, in which the standard is not expressly incorporated in inter-State investment relations.

Where the formulation is not expressly included in an investment agreement, its presence cannot readily be implied. This is so because, as suggested in section I, the fair and equitable standard is generally not accepted as a part of customary international law. Accordingly, where an agreement omits reference to fair and equitable treatment, two possibilities arise concerning the standard of protection available to foreign investors covered by that agreement:

- Reliance may be placed, as a matter of priority, on the particular standard expressed in the agreement.
- Reliance may be placed on the standard of treatment for foreign investors available under customary international law. The precise formulation of the customary international law standard remains a matter of controversy, but most States now seem inclined to support the view that customary law guarantees an international minimum standard of due diligence in the protection of investors.

Finally, in their practice, States appear to have an "all-or-nothing" attitude to the fair and equitable standard. More particularly, international investment agreements do not incorporate the fair and equitable standard for some purposes but not for others; nor do they make provision for fair and equitable treatment and then subject the standard to a list of exceptions or derogations. This, of course, is in contrast to the approach taken in modern agreements with respect to the national treatment and MFN standards, both of which allow for more flexibility in application. It is suggested that the "all-or-nothing" approach to fair and equitable treatment derives from the nature of this standard. When a State offers fair and equitable treatment to foreign investors, it makes a general statement about its attitude to foreign investment. If it were to qualify this statement, by having it apply to some types of foreign investment but not others, this would raise the implication that in some matters, the State is prepared to be "unfair" or "less than fair", or that it is prepared to be "inequitable" in its attitude to some foreign investors. Simply put, this would be highly unattractive to foreign investors.

2. The hortatory approach

As a general rule, investors and capital-exporting countries wish the fair and equitable standard to act as a source of binding obligation, a type of safety net that ensures that basic standards of justice and fairness are granted to each investor. In some cases, however, the pertinent instruments that use the terminology of fairness and equity do not achieve this result.

A leading example in this regard is the Havana Charter of 1948, which as previously mentioned is a multilateral text prepared as the basis for establishment of an International Trade Organization. The post-war idea of establishing an international organization that would focus primarily on trade matters was proposed by the United States in its "Proposals for Expansion of World Trade and Employment" of 1945 (Nwogugu, 1965, p.137). Notwithstanding the focus on international trade, however, an important objective of the Charter, as eventually drafted, was to encourage economic development, especially in developing countries, and to foster "the international flow of capital for productive investment". Consequently, the Havana Charter contained a number of provisions concerning foreign investment and the relationship between the State and foreign investors.

Article 11(2) of the Havana Charter contained the main reference to treatment standards. It stated that the International Trade Organization would be authorized to:

> "(a) make recommendations for and promote bilateral or multilateral agreements on measures designed:
> (i) to assure just and equitable treatment for the enterprise, skills, capital, arts and technology brought from one Member country to another; ..." (UNCTAD, 1996a, vol. I, p. 4).

Among other things, the organization would be authorized to promote arrangements that facilitated "an equitable distribution of skills, arts, technology, materials and equipment", with due regard to the needs of all member States. Also, member States recognized the right of each State to determine the terms of admission of foreign investors on its territory, to give effect to "just terms" on ownership of investment, and to apply "other reasonable requirements" with respect to existing and future investments.

The reference in Article 11(2) to "just and equitable" treatment did not create a legal obligation on host countries vis-à-vis foreign investors. Instead, it merely authorized the International Trade Organization to recommend that this standard be included in future agreements. As such, Article 11(2) was simply an exhortation with respect to future activities.

Other instruments that adopt a non-binding approach to the standard include the Convention Establishing the Multilateral Investment Guarantee Agency (MIGA), the Guidelines for International Investment adopted by the Council of the International Chamber of Commerce in 1972, and the Pacific Basin Charter on International Investments, approved by the Pacific Basin Economic Council in 1995.

The MIGA Convention refers to fair and equitable treatment, but does not seek to create a direct obligation on States to provide such treatment to investors. Rather, it specifies in Article 12(d) that, in order to guarantee an investment, MIGA must satisfy itself that "fair and equitable treatment and legal protection for the investment" exist in the host country concerned. Thus, though the provision does not create liability on a host State where there has been a breach of the fair and equitable standard, it is designed to create a broad incentive for States to accord that standard of treatment.

The ICC Guidelines for International Investment consist of a substantial list of recommendations for investors, the investor's home country Government, and host country Governments. In the relevant provision, Section V, Article 3(a)(i), the ICC recommends that host country Governments should respect:

> "recognised principles of international law, reflected in many international treaties regarding the treatment of foreign property, concerning ... (f)air and equitable treatment of such property" (UNCTAD, 1996a, vol. III, p. 287).

Similarly, the Pacific Basin Charter shows deference for the principle of fairness, by noting as "basic principles" that domestic legislation affecting foreign investment should be "fair and reasonable among all types of investors" and that Government policies on investment should be applied "on a fair basis" (UNCTAD, 1996a, vol. III, p. 378 and 376) . The non-binding character of the ICC Guidelines and the Pacific Basin Charter does not suggest doubt on the part of the sponsors of either instrument about the place of the fair and equitable standard in investment relations. Rather, these provisions are worded in exhortatory language because the instruments in which they are placed were not designed in the format of binding treaties.

3. Reference to "fair and equitable treatment", "just and equitable" treatment or "equitable" treatment

In the preceding discussion, "fair and equitable treatment" has been regarded as the primary form of words used in investment treaties to ensure that notions of equity, fairness and justice are incorporated in investment instruments. This approach is based on the marked preference that States have demonstrated for this phrase in their practice. Among others, the phrase has been used in United States FCN treaties, the Abs-Shawcross Draft, the OECD Draft Convention, Lomé IV, the MAI, NAFTA, and the model BITs of a significant majority of capital-exporting States. Naturally, the precise context and usage of the phrase varies from one instrument to another, but, as a general matter, the pattern of usage demonstrates consistency in some respects.

In some cases, the fair and equitable standard is the only general treatment standard specified in an investment instrument without reference to contingent standards. Such cases include, for instance, the Abs-Shawcross draft and the OECD draft Convention. Article 1 of the Abs-Shawcross draft stipulates that:

> "Each Party shall at all times ensure fair and equitable treatment to the property of the nationals of the other Parties. Such property shall be accorded the most constant protection and security within the territories of the other Parties and the management, use, and enjoyment thereof shall not in any way be impaired by unreasonable or discriminatory measures" (Abs and Shawcross, 1960, p.116).

This provision clearly covered the idea that an investor, once established in a foreign country, would have a prescribed degree of protection. Noticeably, the Abs-Shawcross draft did not expressly provide for any contingent standards, though it did indicate that property to be accorded "fair and equitable treatment" should also be accorded "most constant protection and security" and non-discriminatory treatment. At the same time, the Abs-Shawcross draft, which was intended by its draftspersons to represent "fundamental principles of international law regarding the treatment of property, rights and interests of aliens" in the late 1950s, did not provide for a right of establishment for investors, an approach that distinguished it from the bilateral FCN treaties that prevailed during the same period.

The OECD draft Convention also exemplifies the approach relying on fair and equitable treatment without reference to contingent standards. Thus, in language that follows the Abs-Shawcross approach, the OECD sought to enshrine fair and equitable treatment, together with a reference to "most constant protection and security", in Article 1 of its draft Convention. For the avoidance of doubt, however, the OECD draft Convention also indicated that preferential treatment for investors from some States did not necessarily amount to discriminatory treatment under the law. Therefore, the Abs-Shawcross draft and the OECD draft Convention did not fully reflect all the primary interests that investors today may have in respect of foreign investment.

Also, in some instances in which both capital-exporting and capital-importing States reach agreement concerning investment treatment, the fair and equitable standard, without related contingent standards, is accepted by both sides. In particular, Article 258 of the Lomé IV Convention, while "recognizing the importance of private investment in the promotion of ... development cooperation" among ACP and EEC States, expressly mentions only the fair and equitable standard with respect to treatment of investors. As a similar provision was included in Article 240 of the Third ACP-EEC Convention, signed at Lomé on 8 December 1984, this implies, but does not necessarily prove, some degree of acceptance of the standard among capital-importing States (EC, 1985). The Association of South-East Asian Nations (ASEAN) Agreement for the Promotion and Protection of Investments (ASEAN Treaty), by providing fair and equitable reatment, without more, in Article IV, also gives credence to this point of view.

As noted in section I, a number of investment instruments rely on the terminology of "just and equitable treatment" or" equitable treatment", as distinct from "fair and equitable treatment", in providing legal protection for foreign investors. The first of these in the post-war period was the Economic Agreement of Bogota, Article 22 of which stated, in mandatory form, that:

> "... Foreign capital shall receive equitable treatment. The States therefore agree not to take unjustified, unreasonable or discriminatory measures that would impair the legally acquired rights or interests of nationals of other countries in the enterprises, capital, skills, arts or technology they have supplied..." (Documents on American Foreign Relations,1998, p. 521).

In addition, States would agree not to set up "unreasonable or unjustifiable impediments that would prevent other States from obtaining on equitable terms the capital, skills, and technology needed for their economic development" (Article 22). Though the Economic Agreement of Bogota did not enter into force, the provisions in Article 22 may still provide a useful model. It is noteworthy, for instance, that, in addition to the reference to equitable treatment, Article 22 also provides some guidance as to the substance of the equitable treatment standard: the structure of the article strongly suggests that, in the view of the draft persons, treatment will fall short of the standard if it is "unjustified, unreasonable or discriminatory" and it would affect legally acquired rights or interests of foreign investors.

But, though the form of words differs slightly from the "fair and equitable" formulation, the level of protection offered to foreign capital in the Bogota Agreement was, in effect, fair and equitable treatment. One explanation for the difference in formulation is the fact that, as an early instrument setting out the standard, the Bogota Agreement was drafted at a time when the particular formulation of "fair and equitable" treatment had yet to crystallize as the primary form of words to capture the standard under consideration. This historical background also furnishes an explanation for the reference to "just and equitable" treatment in the Havana Charter: as the concept developed in investment law, formulations such as "just and equitable" and "equitable" eventually became subsumed under the category of "fair and equitable" treatment.

In some cases, however, references to "just and equitable" treatment have occurred in regional and bilateral treaties, and in national legislation, of recent vintage. At the regional level, the member States of MERCOSUR have adopted this formulation in the Colonia Protocol on Reciprocal Promotion and Protection of Investments within MERCOSUR, signed in January 1994. Article 3 of this treaty expressly grants to investors from each MERCOSUR country "un tratamiento justo y equitativo". And, more generally, the Protocol on Promotion and Protection of Investments coming from States not Parties to MERCOSUR, signed in August 1994, extends the same treatment to investments of investors from third States (Article 2). Likewise, at the bilateral level, the French model BIT, and a number of BITs involving Switzerland, use the phrase "un traitement juste et équitable", in setting out the degree of protection contemplated for foreign investors. It would be misleading, however, to conclude that the countries involved in this practice wish to make a distinction of substance between "just and equitable" treatment, on the one hand, and "fair and equitable" treatment, on the other. On the contrary, as the phrases "un tratamien to justo y equitativo" and "un traitement juste et équitable" may readily be translated into English as "fair and equitable" treatment, the usage described in the MERCOSUR treaties and the French and Swiss BITs is tantamount to the fair and equitable standard.

The idea that "just and equitable treatment" is no more than another way of setting down the fair and equitable standard could be slightly bolstered by reference to investment legislation in Angola and Cape Verde. National legislation rarely makes express provision for fair and equitable treatment for foreign investment; nevertheless, in the case of these two countries, foreign investors are offered "just and equitable treatment".[8] It is suggested that Angola and Cape Verde, as developing countries wishing to attract foreign capital, have sought to incorporate the fair and equitable standard in their national legislation. That they have used alternative formulations without suggesting that they wish to depart from the majority practice gives marginal support to the view that countries regard phrases such as "just", "fair" and "equitable" as interchangeable in the context of investment protection.

One instrument that may raise some doubt about whether "equitable" treatment is equivalent to "fair and equitable treatment" is the draft United Nations Code of Conduct on Transnational Corporations. More specifically, Article 48 of the draft Code stated that:

> "Transnational corporations should receive [fair and] equitable [and non-discriminatory] treatment [under] [in accordance with] the laws, regulations and administrative practices of the countries in which they operate [as well as intergovernmental obligations to which the

Governments of these countries have freely subscribed] [consistent with their international obligations] [consistent with international law]" (UNCTAD, 1996a, vol. I, pp. 172-173).

Bearing in mind that brackets were inserted by participants in the Code negotiations to indicate language on which consensus had not been reached, it is evident that States had not reached agreement on whether to use the term "fair and equitable treatment" or the term "equitable treatment" up to 1986, the date for the provision quoted above. To some extent, this lack of agreement arose because some countries assumed that the use of the phrase "fair and equitable treatment" could possibly have introduced the international minimum standard of treatment into the provision on investment protection,[9] while reference to "equitable" treatment would not have done so. In the Code negotiations, however, this debate was inconclusive.

4. Reference to "fair and equitable" treatment with related standards

In terms of frequency, the leading trend with respect to treatment standards is for fair and equitable treatment to be combined with national and MFN treatment. A recent example in this regard is the MAI. The draft MAI, in its preamble, indicates that "fair, transparent and predictable investment regimes complement and benefit the world trading system". This emphasis on fairness is then given legal form in Article IV(1)(1.1), which specifies that:

> "Each Contracting Party shall accord to investments in its territory of investors of another Contracting Party fair and equitable treatment and full and constant protection and security. In no case shall a Contracting Party accord treatment less favourable than that required by international law" (OECD, 1998a, p. 57).

In separate clauses, the MAI also provides for national treatment and MFN standards, and contemplates that contracting parties shall not impair the operation, management, maintenance, use, enjoyment or disposal of investments in their territory by investors of another contracting party. Significantly, then, this approach combines fair and equitable treatment and full protection and security with the two main contingent standards in investment law, and provides even further assurance for investors by confirming that the treatment for investors shall not fall below the requirements of international law, and such treatment shall not impair particular investor activities. This approach represents the most extensive level of protection contemplated for investors in multilateral arrangements to date.

The NAFTA investment provisions, which attach considerable weight to the role of foreign private investment in fostering national development, also preserve the main safeguards sought by capital-exporting countries, including national and MFN treatment with respect to the acquisition, expansion, management and disposition of investments. In addition, Article 1105(1) of NAFTA, under the rubric "Minimum Standard of Treatment", stipulates that each State party shall accord to investments of other parties "treatment in accordance with international law, including fair and equitable treatment" -- a general approach that also finds favour in the Energy Charter Treaty (Article 10).

Recent bilateral treaty practice places emphasis on the comprehensive approach that incorporates various standards in addition to fair and equitable treatment. For instance, the model BIT of the United States, dated April 1994, stipulates that, subject to specified exceptions, in matters concerning the establishment, acquisition, expansion, management, conduct, operation and sale or other disposition of foreign investments, the host State shall accord national treatment or MFN treatment, whichever is more favourable (Article II(1)). This rule is then reinforced by Article II(3)(a), which stipulates that:

> "Each Party shall at all times accord to covered investments fair and equitable treatment and full protection and security, and shall in no case accord treatment less favorable than that required by international law" (UNCTAD, 1996a, vol. III, p. 198).

The approach in the 1994 United States model, which combines fair and equitable treatment with other standards, is broadly similar in substance, though not identical, to most United States treaties completed to date, including bilateral agreements with Panama, the Democratic Republic of Congo (then Zaire), Grenada, Cameroon, and Bangladesh. These treaties depart from the 1994 United States model in one particular respect, namely, they envisage that the treatment, in addition to being fair and equitable and no less favourable than international law, should also be "in accordance with applicable national laws". The 1994 model, by omitting this reference to national laws, makes the point that treatment entirely consistent with the laws of the host State may nonetheless fall short of the fair and equitable standard.

In most United States BITs, therefore, the fair and equitable standard is presented as one of a number of general standards applicable to foreign investment, and it is implied that all the standards are to be applied concurrently. At first glance, a slightly different approach appears to be taken in the model BIT prepared by the Federal Republic of Germany. Here, investments, nationals and companies of each contracting party are also offered both national and MFN treatment, as well as full protection and security. One distinguishing feature of the German approach, however, is that it sets the fair and equitable treatment standard apart, by stating that, while each Contracting Party shall promote investments and admit those investments in accordance with its legislation, the host State shall "in any case accord such investments fair and equitable treatment".

Though this form of words places emphasis on the applicability of the fair and equitable standard -- an approach that is also found in German treaties with Indonesia, Kenya, the Philippines, Sri Lanka (Ceylon, as it then was), Swaziland and Syria, among others -- it does not actually differ in substance from the United States approach. This is so because in each case investors are accorded a combination of national and MFN treatment, together with a general assurance of fairness and equity.

Two important questions that arise from the interaction between the fair and equitable standard and related standards are:

- Does the fair and equitable standard constitute an overriding obligation which includes other standards?
- Is the fair and equitable standard the same as the international minimum standard?

a. *Does the fair and equitable standard constitute an overriding obligation?*

Where the fair and equitable standard is applied with other standards, the question arises as to whether the fair and equitable standard sets out the general rule while the other standards amount to specific applications of the general rule. There is some support for this perspective in practice. In the United Kingdom model BIT, Article 2 (2) reads as follows:

> "Investments of nationals or companies of each Contracting Party shall at all times be accorded fair and equitable treatment and shall enjoy full protection and security in the territory of the other Contracting Party. Neither Contracting Party shall in any way impair by unreasonable or discriminatory measures the management, maintenance, use, enjoyment or disposal of investments in its territory of nationals or companies of the other Contracting Party. Each Contracting Party shall observe any obligation it may have entered into with regard to investments of nationals or investments of the other Contracting Party" (UNCTAD, 1996a, vol. III, p. 187).

If this paragraph is read as a whole, it could be suggested that the injunction against unreasonable or discriminatory measures is actually required by the standard of fair and equitable treatment. And, similarly, the idea of *pacta sunt servanda*, stated in the third sentence, may also be viewed as a part of the fair and equitable standard. This interpretation could also be applied to the United States prototype treaty prepared in 1984. This general approach has merit; by including non-discrimination, reasonableness and respect for contractual obligations as elements of the fair and equitable standard, it accords with the plain meaning of fairness and equity.

But the point may be taken further. On one reading of the United Kingdom BITs, the proposition that investments shall have fair and equitable treatment and full protection and security constitutes the "overriding obligation" concerning investment protection. And, it has been argued, this overriding obligation is wider than simply a prohibition on arbitrary, discriminatory or abusive treatment; it also embraces the MFN and national treatment standards, so that "it may well be that other provisions of the Agreements affording substantive protection are no more than examples or specific instances of this overriding duty" (Mann, 1990, p. 238).

Such an expansive perspective on the fair and equitable standard is broadly supported by the approach taken by the World Bank Guidelines, which stipulate, among other things, that "[e]ach State will extend to investments established in its territory by nationals of any other State fair and equitable treatment according to the standards recommended in these Guidelines" (Guideline III(2)). They then indicate, with greater specificity, the standards of treatment that are to be accorded to foreign investors in matters such as security of person and property rights, the granting of permits and licences, the transfer of incomes and profits, the repatriation of profits and so on. The approach suggested in the Guidelines is that, where treatment of a foreign investor falls short of any of the recommended standards, including the standard of national treatment, this amounts to a failure to satisfy the overarching requirement of fair and equitable treatment.

At the bilateral level, some treaties also imply acceptance of this perspective. For instance, Article 1 of the 1964 investment agreement between Belgium and Luxembourg on the one hand, and Tunisia on the other, reads as follows:

> "Each of the High Contracting Parties undertakes to assure on its territory fair and equitable treatment of investments ... of the other contracting party, and to take steps to ensure that the exercise of the right so recognized is not impeded by unjust or discriminatory measures.
>
> To that end, each of the contracting parties shall confer on these investments, ... at least the same security and protection that it grants to those of its own nationals or to the investments of nationals and companies of third states."

In other words, the national and MFN treatment contemplated in the second paragraph of this provision is granted expressly to ensure that fair and equitable treatment is not impeded. In practical terms, this is not much different from suggesting that fair and equitable treatment is the overriding duty, and the other standards are designed to ensure the fulfilment of this overriding duty.

The suggestion that fair and equitable treatment is perceived by States as a standard that encompasses other standards is also bolstered by instances in which reference is made to achieving the goal of ensuring equitable treatment in the preamble to a particular treaty. In this regard, consideration should be given to the 1948 FCN treaty between the United States and Italy (United Nations, 1951) and to the Agreement signed on 26 September 1951 supplementing this treaty (United Nations, 1961). The FCN treaty indicated in its preamble that it was "based in general upon the principles of national and most-favoured-nation treatment in the unconditional form...", and it reflected this approach in a number of operative provisions. It also incorporated the standards of "most constant protection and security" and "full protection and security required by international law". Subsequently, however, the Supplementary Agreement stipulated in its preamble that it sought to amplify "the principles of equitable treatment" set forth in the main treaty. In this context, the reference to principles of equitable treatment could be interpreted to mean that the national, MFN and other standards in the main treaty were simply particular forms of the overriding obligation to provide equitable treatment to investments.

Nevertheless, although some instances of practice support the notion that the fair and equitable treatment encompasses the other treatment standards in most investment instruments, this is the minority position. In most cases, fair and equitable treatment stands independently of the MFN and national treatment standards, and *vice versa*; following the plain meaning of the words, the general position is that, while the standards may overlap in particular instances, the national treatment and MFN standards will not always be a part of the fair and equitable standard. Accordingly, where a treaty makes provision for fair and equitable treatment, but does not expressly incorporate the national treatment standard, it cannot be assumed that the treaty automatically includes the national treatment standard. This approach would also be true with respect to the relationship between fair and equitable treatment and the MFN standard. Still with reference to plain meaning, however, if there is discrimination on arbitrary grounds, or if the investment has been subject to arbitrary or capricious treatment by the host State, the fair and equitable standard has been violated.

b. Is the fair and equitable standard the same as the international minimum standard?

As indicated in section I, another issue concerning the fair and equitable standard is whether it is tantamount to another standard or set of standards that form part of the international law on protection of nationals in foreign territory. On this issue a number of sources, derived mainly but not exclusively from traditional, capital-exporting perspectives, indicate that the fair and equitable standard is, in fact, equivalent to the international minimum standard, which a number of countries believe constitutes a part of customary law. In this regard, reference may be made especially to the OECD draft Convention which, though not ratified, highlights the view of OECD member

States on the point. More particularly, in the Notes and Comments to Article 1 of the OECD draft Convention, which provided for fair and equitable treatment, the Committee responsible for the draft indicated that the concept of fair and equitable treatment flowed from the "well-established general principle of international law that a State is bound to respect and protect the property of nationals of other States". The Committee added:

> "The phrase 'fair and equitable treatment', customary in relevant bilateral agreements, indicates the standard set by international law for the treatment due by each State with regard to the property of foreign nationals. The standard requires that ... protection afforded under the Convention shall be that generally accorded by the Party concerned to its own nationals, but, being set by international law, the standard may be more exacting where rules of national law or national administrative practices fall short of the requirements of international law. *The standard required conforms in effect to the 'minimum standard' which forms part of customary international law*" (emphasis added)(OECD, 1967, p. 120).[10]

However, in assessing the practice, there have been contrary conclusions on the relationship between fair and equitable treatment and the international minimum standard. It has been argued, for instance, that it is both pointless and misleading to equate the two concepts because fair and equitable treatment envisages conduct "which goes far beyond the minimum standard and afford[s] protection to a greater extent and according to a much more objective standard than any previously employed form of words" (Mann, 1990, p. 238). By this interpretation, therefore, in ascertaining the content of the fair and equitable standard, no other form of words is appropriate: for each dispute, the content of the standard is to be determined by inquiring whether "in all the circumstances the conduct in issue is fair and equitable or unfair and inequitable" (Mann, 1990, p. 238). In effect, this amounts to the application of the plain meaning of the words "fair and equitable" in each individual case, independently of other standards. In practice, too, it may mean giving considerable discretion to the tribunal entrusted with determining whether a breach of the standard has occurred, bearing in mind the subjectivity inherent in the notions of fairness and equity.

Some items of State practice also support the view that the fair and equitable standard does not necessarily amount to the international minimum standard. In a number of BITs involving the United States, and in its model BIT, the fair and equitable standard is combined with full protection and security, and this combined standard is reinforced by the rule that each party to the agreement "shall in no case accord treatment less favorable than that required by international law" (Article II(3)(a)). At the same time, however, the United States has consistently maintained that customary international law assures the international minimum standard for all foreign investments; it is therefore fair to assume that the reference to international law in Article II(3)(a) is an assurance that the international minimum standard shall form a safety net for all investments. This approach -- fair and equitable treatment with full protection and security on the one hand, and treatment no less favourable than that required by international law on the other -- suggests that the two sets of standards are not necessarily the same. To be sure, the reference to treatment no less than that required by international law could possibly be made *ex abundante cautela*, but its presence in most bilateral treaties involving the United States suggests that it is not perceived as verbiage.

Generally, therefore, the law on this point is characterized by some degree of contradiction and uncertainty. If the fair and equitable standard is the same as the international minimum standard which is traditionally supported by capital-exporting countries, then reference to fair and equitable treatment in investment instruments will incorporate by reference an established body of case law on the minimum standard for foreigners: States would fail to meet the minimum standard, and, by this reasoning, the fair and equitable standard, if their acts amounted to bad faith, wilful neglect, clear instances of unreasonableness or lack of due diligence.[11] On the other hand, the instances in which States have indicated or implied an equivalence between the fair and equitable standard and the international minimum standard appear to remain relatively sparse. Also, as noted above, bearing in mind that the international minimum standard has itself been an issue of controversy between developed and developing States for a considerable period, it is unlikely that all States would have accepted the idea that this standard is fully reflected in the fair and equitable standard without clear discussion.

These considerations point ultimately towards fair and equitable treatment not being synonymous with the international minimum standard. Both standards may overlap significantly with respect to issues such as arbitrary treatment, discrimination and unreasonableness, but the presence of a provision assuring fair and equitable treatment in an investment instrument does not automatically incorporate the international minimum standard for foreign investors. Where the fair and equitable standard is invoked, the central issue remains simply whether the actions in question are in all the circumstances fair and equitable or unfair and inequitable.

* * *

Overall, therefore, investment instruments prepared to date reveal a number of options for future consideration. Although the multilateral treaty practice has spanned a substantial portion of the post-war period, efforts to create a comprehensive treaty incorporating standards of treatment, including the fair and equitable standard, have met with mixed results. Nonetheless, the international efforts have helped to create a stock of approaches to fair and equitable treatment which, in some measure, influence State perspectives and practice. Partly because States have not adopted a multilateral investment treaty incorporating treatment standards, the bilateral practice, together with non-governmental efforts, has contributed substantially to the range of options concerning the standard. In some cases, the different options are similar in substance, so that in practice, for instance, where different treaties refer to "fair" treatment, "equitable" treatment or "fair and equitable" treatment, the same level of treatment may be contemplated for each case. In others, however, the different formulations reflect divergent perspectives on fair and equitable treatment. On occasion, the standard is designed as hortatory, while in other instances, it clearly has mandatory effect. In still other instances, the standard is designed to provide the only general measure of investor protection, while at other times, it is juxtaposed with other treatment standards in a variety of patterns.

Section III
Interaction with other Issues and Concepts

The fair and equitable treatment standard interacts withseveral other issues and concepts that arise in investment practice. A summary of the extent to which this interaction is likely to take place in practice is set out in table 1.

Table 1. Interaction across issues and concepts

Issue	Fair and equitable treatment
Admission and establishment	+
Competition	+
Dispute settlement (investor-State)	++
Dispute settlement (State-State)	++
Employment	+
Environment	+
Home country measures	+
Host country operational measures	+
Illicit payments	+
Incentives	++
Investment-related trade measures	+
Most-favoured-nation treatment	++
National treatment	++
Scope and definition	++
Social responsibility	+
State contracts	+
Taking of property	++
Taxation	+
Transfer of funds	++
Transfer of technology	+
Transfer pricing	+
Transparency	++

Source: UNCTAD.

Key: 0 = negligible or no interaction.
+ = moderate interaction.
++ = extensive interaction.

- **Scope and definition.** The definition of the beneficiaries of fair and equitable treatment has varied considerably in practice (see chapter 3). In the main multilateral and regional instruments on the point, beneficiaries have included, among others:
  - "foreign capital",
  - "the property of nationals of other contracting parties",
  - "transnational corporations",
  - "private investors", and
  - "investments of investors of another contracting party".

  This variety merits comment. In some cases, as in the reference to "transnational corporations" in the draft United Nations Code of Conduct on Transnational Corporations, the beneficiary is defined by the context of the instrument concerned. Also, some references, though using different formulations, appear quite similar. When, for instance, the OECD draft Convention refers to "the property of the nationals of other Parties" (Article 1), this is similar to the reference, in the MAI, to "investments...of investors of another Contracting Party" (Article IV(1)(1.1)). In either case, the treatment standard applies to the property, rights and interests held directly or indirectly by an investor. But the similarity is not complete; for instance, in the comparison between the OECD draft Convention and the MAI, fair and equitable treatment is safeguarded for both nationals and permanent residents in the latter draft treaty, while it is contemplated only for nationals in the former.

In all cases, the standard applies to protect beneficiaries within the host State. Sometimes this is set out in express terms, as in the MAI (Section IV, Article 1.1) and in NAFTA (Articles 1105 and 1101, read together), but in others it is implicit, both from the general foreign investment context of the instrument and from the form of words. Thus, for instance, where the Abs-Shawcross draft and the OECD draft Convention provide for fair and equitable treatment for foreign investments "at all times", this means, at least, that, unless otherwise stipulated, an investment must receive that treatment for its entire period in the host State. Similarly, where the Lomé IV Convention and the 1987 version of the ASEAN Treaty indicate that the treatment standard should be applied, respectively, to investors who, and investments which, comply with certain domestic legal preconditions, it is implicit that fair and equitable treatment within the territory of the host State is contemplated.

With reference to the scope of agreements, another point of difference among the various multilateral and regional instruments is whether fair and equitable treatment is owed only to investors or investments of States party to the instrument in question. More specifically, a significant majority of the multilateral and regional treaties and draft treaties clearly state that the host State is liable to investors of other Contracting Parties. In these cases, the host State will be liable to non-parties under customary international law and pursuant to general principles of law, but, if fair and equitable treatment is to be preferred, it does not arise as a treaty obligation.

Some instruments, however, appear to take a different approach, and could arguably give rise to an obligation for the host State to provide protection to all foreign investors. The Bogota Agreement provides an example in this category, for it simply asserted that "foreign capital shall receive equitable treatment", thus suggesting that the standard should be available to all foreign capital and not simply the capital held by nationals of State parties to the Bogota Agreement. In a similar vein, COMESA makes no distinction between private investors from States parties to COMESA and private investors generally in the relevant treatment provision. As a matter of interpretation, it is not entirely clear that fair and equitable treatment is meant to be offered to non-parties in either the Bogota or COMESA treaties, but this interpretation is possible.

- **Incentives**. Where a State offers incentives to some entities in an industry, the question arises as to whether a provision for fair and equitable treatment would require such incentives to be granted to foreign investors in that industry who are beneficiaries under the provision for fair and equitable treatment. The argument would be that, to deprive a foreign investor in this situation of the incentives would amount to discrimination, and would, therefore, amount to unfair or inequitable treatment. This would be particularly true where the incentives place those receiving them in an advantageous economic position vis-à-vis the beneficiaries under the fair and equitable provision. On the other hand, this approach may be difficult to apply in a case in which there are grounds to argue that the entities receiving incentives are not in the same industry as the beneficiaries under the fair and equitable provision, or where there are other grounds for distinguishing the recipients of incentives from the beneficiaries under the fair and equitable provision.

- **MFN treatment and national treatment**. Some aspects of the interaction between fair and equitable treatment with these other standards have already been considered. In essence, because fair and equitable treatment is an absolute standard, its precise delineation in each case does not depend on other levels of treatment granted by the host State concerned. In contrast, the actual contents of the MFN or the national treatment standard in any particular instance turn entirely on the actions of the host State vis-à-vis investors from third States or its own nationals.

  It has also been suggested that the MFN and national treatment standards are not simply specific examples of the type of treatment generally covered by a provision requiring fair and equitable treatment. This requires further comment. First, the two main contingent standards under consideration have had a well-established place in international commercial relations; thus, if States intend that the fair and equitable standard should automatically encompass MFN or national treatment, it is likely that their intention would need to be stated with considerable clarity. This has not been done. Secondly, although this may be a rare occurrence in practice, an assurance of fair and equitable treatment may produce a different result from the other standards. For example, in a specific case, the MFN standard may result in an investor receiving treatment from the host State that is significantly better than that required by fairness and equity. This may come about as a result of deliberate policy on the part of a host State, or it may be an indirect result arising from the operation of the MFN provision. In either event, what is required by fairness and equity will be respected, but the investor will receive even more favourable treatment.

Likewise, national treatment may, in some cases, differ significantly from fair and equitable treatment. An assurance of national treatment indicates that the host State will grant to the beneficiary treatment, which is "no less favourable than that it accords, in like situations, to investments in its territory of its own nationals or companies". In this sense, national treatment protects foreign investors from differential treatment in favour of domestic investors. But there is no reason to believe that this level of treatment will necessarily satisfy the standard of fair and equitable treatment, for, in some cases, host States treat domestic investors without regard to the elements of fairness and justice. In fact, the perception that national treatment is sometimes deficient from an investor viewpoint helps to explain why capital-exporting countries have sometimes insisted on the international minimum standard, in preference to the national standard which has traditionally been supported by a number of capital-importing countries.

Conversely, from an investor's standpoint, national treatment may also be superior to fair and equitable treatment in some instances. For example, where a host State wishes to promote domestic industries, it may adopt measures that treat local capital far more liberally than the requirements of fairness and equity dictate. The application of the national treatment standard in such cases could also place foreign investment beneficiaries in an advantageous position with respect to investments that are accorded only fair and equitable treatment.

Significantly, one effect of the growing network of BITs incorporating the MFN standard will be to generalize the applicability of the fair and equitable standard among States. In most instances in which a State has opted not to include an assurance of fair and equitable treatment in a BIT, it has provided for MFN treatment as an alternative treatment standard. Once this State enters into another treaty that grants fair and equitable treatment, then the MFN clause automatically extends fair and equitable treatment even to beneficiaries under the first treaty.

- **Taking of property**. In addition to the treatment provisions so far reviewed, many investment instruments also contain substantive provisions on matters pertaining to the taking or expropriation of foreign investments by a host State. This is especially, but not exclusively, true for BITs, many of which have been completed with concerns about expropriation under consideration. Most current BITs stipulate, as preconditions, that nationalization or expropriation, whether direct or indirect, must take place in the public interest, and must accord with principles of non-discrimination and the due process of law. They further stipulate in numerous instances that compensation for such taking shall be "prompt, adequate and effective", in accordance with the Hull formula.[12] Also, in some instances, the compensation formula expressly refers to equity, providing for effective and equitable compensation in conformity with international law.

While the dominant trend at the bilateral level is therefore in favour of the home country perspective on issues of expropriation, the situation is less definite with respect to multilateral efforts. Instruments such as the 1967 OECD draft Convention and the 1949 ICC Code of Fair Treatment reflect the basic perspectives of the developed countries. On the other hand, developing countries have traditionally maintained that expropriation issues must be settled in accordance with the municipal law of the host State, and the compensation standard may not necessarily amount to the full market value contemplated in the Hull formula.

In a treaty that accords "prompt, adequate and effective compensation" to investors, does an assurance of fair and equitable treatment add to the level of security on matters concerning expropriation? This question arises because, in the absence of language to the contrary, the fair and equitable standard seems to apply to expropriation as much as it does to other issues of treatment. In practice, however, where both fair and equitable treatment and particular provisions on expropriation are incorporated in an investment instrument, there is scope for the view that reference will be made primarily to the latter. This approach places emphasis on the particular provisions on expropriation because they are included in the investment instrument expressly and specifically to address expropriation issues. In the unlikely event that a treaty were to provide for fair and equitable treatment generally, but have no specific provision on compensation for a taking of property, then, where a taking has occurred, it would be open to the foreign investor affected to argue that the level of compensation should be fair and equitable in the circumstances. This approach would give some assurance to foreign investors, but it would be subject to the difficulties of interpretation concerning the precise meaning of fair and equitable treatment discussed in section I.

- **Funds transfer.** As in the case of taking of property, many investment agreements contain substantive provisions on matters pertaining to funds transfer. Thus, the specific safeguards for the investors are also complemented by the general duty on the part of the host State to provide fair and equitable treatment. In such case, it may be thought that the specific should prevail over the general, so that primary reference should be given to the particular provision in the investment instrument concerning free funds transfer. But this does not necessarily render the fair and equitable concept superfluous in the area of funds transfer. It is possible, for instance, that the provisions on funds transfer as drafted in a given instrument do not expressly give rise to liability on the part of the State in a particular set of circumstances. In such instances, fair and equitable treatment, as a general standard, would be applicable, and, assuming that the State action concerning the transfer of funds or payment for losses fell short of the requirements of fairness and equity, then liability would ensue.

One possible area of uncertainty concerning fund transfers deserves particular mention. Most BITs provide for the repatriation of investment-related funds. In some instances, however, as in the United Kingdom/Jamaica BIT, the right to free transfer is made subject to the host State's right in exceptional balance-of-payments difficulties "to exercise equitably and in good faith" currency restrictions conferred by its laws (Article 7(1)). What result should follow if a host State that is generally obliged to treat investors in accordance with the fair and equitable standard applies this free transfer exception inequitably? The exception also requires "bad faith" for liability to ensue, but the broader fair and equitable standard does not. The result is not clear, but, if it is assumed that the free transfer exception and the fair and equitable provision are to be read as complementary provisions, then arguably the investor will need to establish only the absence of fairness and equity in order to prevail (Mann, 1990, p. 240).

- **Transparency.** States have increasingly provided that host country actions on investment-related issues should be transparent. So, for example, the 1994 United States model BIT stipulates that each State party shall ensure that its "laws, regulations, administrative practices and procedures of general application, and adjudicatory decisions" concerning foreign investments are "promptly published or otherwise made publicly available" (Article II(5)). At the regional level, this approach has also been included in the Energy Charter Treaty.

The concept of transparency overlaps with fair and equitable treatment in at least two significant ways. First, transparency may be required, as a matter of course, by the concept of fair and equitable treatment. If laws, administrative decisions and other binding decisions are to be imposed upon a foreign investor by a host State, then fairness requires that the investor is informed about such decisions before they are imposed. This interpretation suggests that where an investment treaty does not expressly provide for transparency, but does for fair and equitable treatment, then transparency is implicitly included in the treaty. Secondly, where a foreign investor wishes to establish whether or not a particular State action is fair and equitable, as a practical matter, the investor will need to ascertain the pertinent rules concerning the State action; the degree of transparency in the regulatory environment will therefore affect the ability of the investor to assess whether or not fair and equitable treatment has been made available in any given case.

- **Dispute settlement.** Most multilateral, regional and bilateral instruments incorporate procedures for compulsory third party dispute settlement, even where, as in the case of the MAI, they also contemplate procedures for consultation and conciliation. In several instruments, a distinction is made between investor-State disputes and State-State disputes, but, usually, recourse to compulsory third party settlement is provided for in each case. Most investment instruments that incorporate the fair and equitable standard also make provision for third party dispute settlement. Third party dispute settlement provisions enhance the fair and equitable standard by allowing investors to have their claims about unfair or inequitable treatment considered by tribunals operating outside the control of the host State. Also, given that disputes about fairness may sometimes involve the different cultural and economic perspectives of the host State and the investor, the availability of third party dispute settlement serves to assure foreign investors that their views on fairness and equity in a particular situation will be given due consideration. However, although dispute settlement provisions enhance the standard, in practice there have been few instances in which investors have sought to have disputes about the meaning of fair and equitable treatment settled by third party tribunals.

Conclusion: Economic and Development Implications and Policy Options

Broadly speaking, an assurance of fair and equitable treatment in an investment instrument is meant to provide foreign investors with a minimum level of security. Accordingly, the standard is one of a number of measures designed to encourage the flow of investment capital across borders in a world that often lacks the degree of economic and political certainty desired by investors. Against this broad canvas, the main question to be considered in this section concerns the economic and development implications of including or not including a fair and equitable treatment standard in international investment agreements.

An important starting point is whether the absence of an express assurance of fair and equitable treatment in an investment treaty means that the standard is not available to investors from the parties to the treaty. This is, in fact, a question of law; for, if the fair and equitable standard has become a part of customary international law, then the standard will be available to investors in foreign countries even where there is no treaty obligation. However, as noted in section II, though this question is not clearly resolved, the stronger view appears to be that the fair and equitable standard is not a part of customary law. In practical terms, this means that, if a State is not bound by a treaty safeguarding the standard, it is not required to accord that standard to investors within its territory. If the conclusion had been that the standard is now a part of customary law, this would have rendered further enquiry into the economic and development implications of the standard largely superfluous, for most, if not all, States would be required to grant fair and equitable treatment, whether or not they consented to do so in an investment instrument.

A. The economic and development implications of incorporating the standard

There is a broad consensus that foreign direct investment, in general, can contribute to growth and development.[13] From a development perspective, this consensus has helped to stimulate the increasing efforts of developing countries to attract foreign direct investment from developed and developing countries and has prompted developing countries to provide assurances to investors as to the level of treatment they may anticipate upon entry. As noted before, these trends have manifested themselves in the rapid growth in the number of BITs concluded in the present decade; they are also reflected in host country efforts to liberalize their national legislation in ways designed to facilitate investment growth.

But, to what extent may the use of the fair and equitable standard contribute to the development process? In essence, if the standard contributes to development in any significant way, it is through its inclusion in BITs and in regional treaties. However, the precise nature of this contribution is a matter of speculation. This is so for a number of important reasons.

First, because the fair and equitable standard is included in BITs which themselves often include other treatment standards and cover issues other than fair and equitable treatment *simpliciter*, the impact that the standard has within a particular investment treaty may be largely indeterminate. The process of distinguishing the impact on investment flows arising from the standard would involve, among other things, an attempt to identify issues and problems for which fair and equitable treatment would be the only applicable standard. As is evident from the discussion above, however, fair and equitable treatment is often closely interwoven with the MFN and national treatment standards and, in numerous cases, it is at best a matter of judgement as to which of these standards will provide the solution to a given investment dispute. Accordingly, it may not be possible to specify how much value is to be attached to an assurance of fair and equitable treatment as distinct from the other standards of treatment. However, it is important to note that the fair and equitable treatment standard is an absolute standard, while national treatment and MFN are relative standards. The fair and equitable standard, therefore, remains particularly relevant where there are national treatment and MFN exceptions.

Furthermore, even assuming that some indication could be gathered of the relative contribution of the fair and equitable standard in international investment treaties, there are additional difficulties in assessing the overall contribution which such treaties themselves make in determining the flow of investment (UNCTC, 1988a, p. 14; UNCTAD, 1998b; UNCTAD, 1998a). The obvious point is that each investor, in determining the venue for investment, will have particular objectives. These objectives vary on a case-by-case basis; but, under the general heading of profit maximization, they include, among other things, the exploitation of natural resources in host States, access to created assets and market penetration (UNCTAD, 1998b). The general investment climate in prospective host countries may be influenced by an express assurance of fair and equitable treatment in some instances, but not in others. In this context of diverse, and sometimes subjective, considerations, it is again difficult to determine, with any degree of precision, the extent to which an assurance of fair and equitable treatment may influence investment decisions. Nevertheless, some broad observations on the value of the fair and equitable standard in assisting foreign capital flows may be appropriate. One of the key elements in an investment decision will be the degree of "country risk", a factor that will be weighed against other considerations. In determining country risk, an investor will take into account the efforts by the host country to address this factor; where a host State has made the effort, at least nominally, to safeguard fair and equitable treatment to investors, this provides a signal that the country intends to treat foreign investment fairly. The point may be made more forcefully when viewed from a negative perspective: if a prospective host State eschews the fair and equitable standard as a matter of policy, foreign investors would regard this as a negative factor in their assessment of the risks within the host economy. Given the preponderance of BITs that incorporate the standard, this risk factor may well assume some degree of importance because it might be presumed that the host State omitted the standard for reasons pertaining to future State intentions. Even countries that resisted entering into BITs until the beginning of the 1980s have abandoned their objections, and now accept the fair and equitable standard in such agreements. Therefore, in each case in which there is resistance to the provision by a host State, the capital-exporting counterpart will understandably wish to know what has motivated this resistance. If an answer satisfactory to the investor viewpoint is not forthcoming, this could undermine confidence in the prospective host country.

It should also be emphasized that, although there may be uncertainty about the precise role played by assurances of fair and equitable treatment in influencing investment flows, the net effect of the standard is likely to be positive. Countries whose foreign direct investment determinants are weak (UNCTAD, 1998b) may use the standard as a part of their investment promotion efforts. But this may be little more than a starting point; for, in the area of investment promotion, while the fair and equitable standard provides a standard sought by foreign investors, for most developing countries and countries with economies in transition, it is not sufficient, in itself, to attract foreign capital.

Finally, given that fair and equitable treatment may be a factor in engendering a positive investment climate, the question arises as to why a particular State may be reluctant to accord this standard to investors in practice. One may be inclined to presume, after all, that all States aspire to providing justice and fairness for both nationals and aliens, and that, therefore, the assurance of fair and equitable treatment for foreign investors would be entirely consistent with State objectives. This, together with the fact that foreign investors themselves have urged home countries to seek the standard in their treaties with host countries, may provide a case for the inclusion of the standard in investment instruments as a matter of course. And, indeed, the preponderance of references to the standard in modern BITs suggests that this perspective is increasingly pursued by States.

But the question remains as to whether there may be reasons for a State to resist the standard in its investment arrangements. Some States which, in the past, have been reluctant to rely generally on minimum international standards have based their position on the notion that the standard of treatment for foreign investors should be no more, or no less, than that offered to nationals. This approach, which takes its force from the Calvo doctrine, does not necessarily deny foreign investors the assurance that they will be treated fairly and equitably; rather, it simply proceeds on the basis that there should be one standard for all. In this context, some States may have feared that if they expressly singled out foreign investors for "fair and equitable treatment", they could have been accused of discriminating in favour of aliens and, thus, of undermining the principle of equal treatment for nationals and foreigners. This fear, however, may be countered by the suggestion that presumably States assure their own nationals fair and equitable treatment, so no discrimination occurs when the same assurance is given to foreigners.

On a related point, some States may be reluctant to offer fair and equitable treatment in their investment instruments because the implications of the standard are not always easy to anticipate. A capital-importing country may wish, for example, to provide a series of preferences and incentives to local investors in order to generate growth in its economy. The Government of that country may perceive these preferences and incentives as politically important, and may consider that it has the right to grant such preferential treatment to its nationals as part of its sovereign decision-making power. However, there is a possibility that some preferences and incentives may be regarded as incompatible with fair and equitable treatment for foreign investors. A foreign investor who is in competition with local investors in a particular industry may well be inclined to argue that certain incentives to local investors are discriminatory, and, therefore, unfair. Whether this argument would prevail as a matter of law is not really the point. The point is that, bearing this possibility in mind, a capital-importing country that wishes to pursue domestic preferences may be reluctant to grant fair and equitable treatment because some of its policies could be open to question as unfair or inequitable.

Conversely, foreign investors may support the fair and equitable standard as a means of ensuring that they are not placed at a disadvantage when a host country provides particular incentives for local investors. At the very least, the fair and equitable standard allows foreign investors in an industry with incentives for local investors to raise the argument that it would be unfair discrimination for foreign investors to be denied the same level of incentives. To be sure, where the national treatment standard is also available, it would also be open for foreign investors to argue that the incentives should be extended to foreigners on the basis of this standard alone. However, where provision has not been made for the national treatment standard, or where the national treatment standard is not applicable, foreign investors may rely on the fair and equitable standard as the basis for seeking the same level of incentives as local investors.

B. Policy options

The models of possible formulations of the fair and equitable treatment standard outlined in section II represent the main approaches to fair and equitable treatment based on the practice of States. To the extent that these models represent different approaches to the fair and equitable standard, they indicate different policy options.

- **Option 1: no reference to fair and equitable treatment**. States may opt not to incorporate the fair and equitable standard in their investment relations, in either hortatory or mandatory form. Where this is done, the standard is not likely to be implied in the relevant investment instrument, so that, in effect, the foreign investor will not have the benefits contemplated by the fair and equitable standard. However, most treaties that omit reference to fair and equitable treatment provide alternative standards of treatment, usually the national treatment standard or the MFN standard. Where this is done, such standards provide some degree of contingent protection to foreign investors; at the same time, a foreign investor will also be able to have customary international law applied to any investor-State dispute which may arise. The particular economic value of this level of protection cannot be fully assessed without regard to the standards included in lieu of fair and equitable treatment. Generally, however, as most BITs now provide expressly for fair and equitable treatment, its absence from such a treaty may prompt investor concerns about the nature of protection to be offered by a host State.

- **Option 2: the hortatory approach**. It is doubtful that the hortatory approach to fair and equitable treatment will give rise to any special economic implications. This is so because, by definition, the hortatory approach does not create a binding obligation on host States to grant investors fair and equitable treatment. Rather, it indicates that fairness and equity are desirable in investment relations, but, without more, it leaves host States with a substantial degree of flexibility as to how they will treat foreign investors. From an investor's perspective, therefore, hortatory language, without more, is really little different from a situation in which no mention is made of fair and equitable treatment: in either case, the particular treatment standard applicable to the investor will be the binding provision in the relevant treaty or national legislation, not fair and equitable treatment.

  In some circumstances, however, the hortatory approach reflects the starting point in a negotiating process in which fair and equitable treatment may be included in binding form in a subsequent investment agreement. This is exemplified by the Havana Charter, which indicated that it would be desirable for States to enter into treaties making provision for the fair and equitable standard. In such cases, States that accept the hortatory language are sending a signal that they are willing, in principle, to give a guarantee of fairness and equity to investors at a future date. This may not necessarily inspire investor confidence, but it provides the basis for further negotiations concerning the fair and equitable standard. And, again, in some circumstances, hortatory language in a convention may, in fact, serve as an incentive. For example, the Multilateral Investment Guarantee Agency will not guarantee an investment unless, among other things, fair and equitable treatment is available. In the current liberalized economic environment, this type of incentive may prove sufficient to prompt host States to grant fair and equitable treaty as a matter of law. In fact, the hortatory approach was more important when the standard was less well established than it is today.

- **Option 3: reference to "fair and equitable" treatment, "just and equitable" treatment or "equitable" treatment.** It has been suggested above that "fair and equitable" treatment, "just and equitable" treatment and "equitable" treatment appear to be equivalent terms and, though different in formulation, prompt the same degree of protection for investors. In each case, the host State is required, as a matter of law, to accord fair treatment to the foreign investor, and, in almost all instances, it will be left to an independent third party to determine whether the investor has been treated fairly. This model, as outlined in section II, creates a legal environment in which aliens may undertake capital investments with some degree of confidence that they will not be subject to arbitrary or capricious treatment. The investor may also derive confidence from the simple fact that the host country has found no reason to resist offering fair and equitable treatment in practice. However, as noted above, while the assurance of fairness and equity may help generally to enhance investor confidence in the host country, it is difficult, if not impossible, to quantify the extent to which the fair and equitable standard, without more, may contribute to increasing investment flows into particular economies.

- **Option 4: reference to "fair and equitable treatment" and related standards**. Where the fair and equitable standard is combined with other standards such as the MFN and national treatment standards, there is reason to believe that investors will have a more substantial degree of confidence in the host country than in situations where either option 2 or 3 is followed by the host country. In the typical case of option 4, the host country is indicating to the foreign investment community that it is prepared to offer most, if not all, the legal safeguards traditionally sought by investors; in return, the host State expects that, at the very least, the regulatory environment in the host will be perceived as "investor-friendly", and hopes that this will help to prompt capital investment. For this reason, in the open-door climate that prevails in most countries today, this approach has grown increasingly popular. Again, however, even with respect to option 4, which takes investor perspectives fully into account, it should be recalled that a guarantee of fair and equitable treatment in combination with other standards is really only one of a number of considerations that will enter into an investor's assessment of the host country as a venue for investment.

- **Option 5: reference to "fair and equitable treatment" in combination with the international minimum standard.** As pointed out in section II, there have been different conclusions on the relationship between fair and equitable treatment and the international minimum standard. While both standards seem to overlap significantly, fair and equitable treatment is not automatically assumed to incorporate the international minimum standard. Some States may, therefore, specifically reinforce the fair and equitable standard with formulations such as "full protection and security" which imply the international minimum standard.

In conclusion, therefore, although the fair and equitable standard is of more recent vintage than other standards such as the MFN and national treatment standards, it has become common in most modern investment agreements. Its place in such agreements is likely to remain secure essentially because it provides a guarantee that gives foreign investors some degree of security with respect to their investments, while, at the same time, it does not place a particularly heavy onus on States which, as a matter of course, seek to treat both local and foreign enterprises fairly and equitably. However, the concept is inherently vague, and as a result, foreign investors and capital-importing States may, in particular instances, have different expectations as to the level of protection provided by the standard. Nevertheless, this has not deterred States from relying on the standard and, in so doing, they have used different approaches to indicate their preferences. Thus, references to the standard are sometimes found in hortatory form, while in others, terms such as "fair and equitable", "just and equitable" and "equitable" treatment have assumed prominence. Where the fair and equitable standard is combined with the MFN and national treatment standards, this, in effect, provides the beneficiary of the combined treatment with substantial protection, for it ensures that there is no discrimination against that investor *vis-à-vis* other foreign nationals and local investors, even as it ensures a minimum level of treatment to the beneficiary, regardless of how other investors are treated. The dominant trend in recent practice is this combined level of protection. Making reference to the fair and equitable standard in combination with the international minimum standard is regarded by some States as even further reinforcement of protection; but it is a rare combination in practice.

Notes

1 Unless otherwise noted, all instruments cited herein may be found in UNCTAD (1996a). All BITs between specific countries cited herein may be found in ICSID (1972a) and at www.unctad.org/iia.

2 According to the dictionary definition, treatment is fair when it is "free from bias, fraud, or injustice; equitable, legitimate... not taking undue advantage; disposed to concede every reasonable claim" (The Oxford English Dictionary, 2nd ed. 1989); equitable treatment is that which is "characterized by equity or fairness... fair, just, reasonable" *(ibid)*.

3 See, for example, the "North Sea Continental Shelf Cases" (ICJ, 1969); Baxter, 1970, p. 27.

4 As used in the text, the "Calvo tradition" or the "Calvo doctrine" denotes the idea that foreign investors are, or ought to be, required to settle their foreign investment disputes exclusively in the courts of the host State. For a general overview, see, for instance, Jiménez de Aréchaga, 1968, pp. 590-593; O'Connell, 1970, pp. 1059-1066.

5 See, for example, Decision 24 of the Commission of the Cartagena Agreement, Article 50: "Member countries may not accord to foreign investors treatment more favourable than to national investors."

6 Latin American investment instruments that did not include reference to fair and equitable treatment included Decisions 24 and 291 of the Commission of the Cartagena Agreement, dated 1970 and 1991, respectively. In keeping, however, with the trend towards incorporating the fair and equitable standard, some Latin American countries, such as the members of MERCOSUR, provide for such treatment in their investment instruments (see, for example, the Colonia Protocol on Reciprocal Promotion and Protection of Investments within MERCOSUR, signed in January 1994).

7 In contrast to treaty practice, the standard of fair and equitable treatment has not assumed prominence in national investment codes. For instance, a 1991 study of national investment codes found that, while 31 countries offered the national treatment standard to foreign investors, 17 countries made no express provision for general standards of treatment, and only 3 countries -- Angola, Bangladesh and Viet Nam -- incorporated the fair and equitable standard into their legislation (Parra, 1992, p. 436).

8 Angola, Regulations of Law No. 13/88 of July 16, 1988 (Article 19); Cape Verde, Law No. 49/111/89 (1989) (Article 7) (ICSID, 1972b-).

9 For discussion, see, for example, Robinson (1985).

10 With similar effect, in 1979, the Swiss Foreign Office described the fair and equitable standard in the following terms: "On se réfère ainsi au principe classique de droits des gens selon lequel les Etats doivent mettre les étrangers se trouvant sur leur territoire et leurs biens au bénéfice du 'standard minimum' international c'est-à-dire leur accorder un minimum de droits personnels, procéduraux et économiques" (quoted by Mann, 1990, p. 238).

11 For case law on the meaning of the international minimum standard, see, for example, The Neer Claim (United States v. Mexico) (1926); Asian Agricultural Products Limited (AAPL) v. Sri Lanka (ICSID, 1990). For discussion, see also Vasciannie, 1992a.

12 The "Hull formula" denotes the standard of compensation supported by the major capital-exporting countries in cases concerning expropriation of foreign property. By this formula, named after former United States Secretary of State Cordell Hull, States are said to be in breach of international law if, upon expropriating foreign property, they fail to pay "prompt, adequate and effective" compensation to the foreign investor. For a brief summary and references concerning the formula, see, for instance, Vasciannie, 1992b, pp. 125-129.

13 See paragraph 36 of the "Partnership for Growth and Development", adopted by UNCTAD at its ninth session in 1996 (UNCTAD, 1996e).

Chapter 8. Taking of Property*

Executive summary

The taking of private assets by public authorities raises significant issues of international law, where such takings involve the assets of foreign private investors. This chapter examines the concept of "takings" in the context of international law and international investment agreements (IIAs). The focus of the analysis is twofold. First, different categories of takings are distinguished, addressing in particular the problem of the distinction between governmental measures that involve interference with the assets of foreign investors, yet do not require compensation, and those that do require compensation. Second, the requirements for a taking to be lawful are discussed, in particular the issue of the standard for compensation. The chapter highlights the challenges that remain when considering the takings clause in international investment agreements, and discusses policy options relative to defining a "taking" when drafting the clause. It also illustrates some drafting models.

The takings clause aims at protecting foreign investors by establishing standards for the manner in which host States might take or otherwise interfere with their property rights. That is to say, it limits the right of States to take property by imposing certain requirements. Under customary international law and typical international investment agreements, three principal requirements need to be satisfied before a taking can be considered to be lawful: it should be for a public purpose; it should not be discriminatory; and compensation should be paid. The first two requirements are generally accepted. As regards the third, it too is widely accepted in principle, but there is no universal agreement relating to the manner of assessment of the compensation due. The more recent bilateral investment treaties (BITs) use the formula that the compensation must be prompt, adequate and effective, but, alternative formulas, such as just compensation, are also used. An emerging trend in IIAs that deserves attention is the development of a fourth requirement, due process.

The issue of the formula for compensation aside, a threshold problem is how to provide for clear guidance on the type of governmental measures and their effects that would trigger the takings clause in an IIA. The measures that fit the classical category of takings are nationalizations (outright takings of all foreign property in all economic sectors, or on an industry-specific basis) and expropriations (takings that are property- or enterprise-specific).

Certain governmental measures may not involve an actual physical taking of property, but may still result in the effective loss of management, use or control, or a significant depreciation of the value, of the assets of a foreign investor. Such measures pose the problem of distinguishing between measures that trigger the takings clause and its requirement of payment of compensation, and those that involve interference with the property rights of foreign investors but would nevertheless be considered as not falling within the ambit of the takings clause. Typically, a measure that is a consequence of the violation of a regulation has been regarded as non-compensatory in many legal systems. A penal measure following the violation of a criminal statute cannot give rise to a compensatory taking. There is authority that a tax measure, if not excessive, also cannot amount to a taking. The same is true of violations of antitrust laws. In some jurisdictions, even interference with property rights in order to further environmental or planning decisions could be considered non-compensatory.

Drafting a provision that adequately addresses the issues of the protection of the foreign investor and the ability of a host State to govern its economy can pose a challenge. Although some IIAs have sought to list the regulatory measures the exercise of which will not amount to takings, the compilation of an exhaustive list is a difficult if not impossible task. Instead, the takings clause could be drafted to reflect the formulation of a certain relationship that can accommodate both the concerns of foreign investors and national policy makers. This chapter provides policy makers with a blend of policy options that could strike a balance

---

* The chapter is based on a 2000 manuscript prepared by M. Sornarajah. The final version reflects comments received from Joachim Karl, Nick Mabey and Marinus Sikkel.

between the level of investment protection, on the one hand, and the level of discretion retained by the host State in adopting measures that affect foreign investments, on the other hand.

Introduction

The taking of foreign property by a host country has constituted, at least in the past, one of the most important risks to foreign investment. As a foreign investor operates within the territory of a host country, the investor and its property are subject to the legislative and administrative control of the host country. The risk assessments that a foreign investor makes at the time of entry may not be accurate since internal policies relating to foreign investment are subject to change, as are the political and economic conditions in a host country. Changes could be brought about by several factors, such as a new Government, shifts in ideology, economic nationalism or monetary crises. Where these changes adversely affect foreign investment or require in the view of a host country a rearrangement of its economic structure, they may lead to the taking of the property of a foreign investor.

An understanding of the types of takings that could be effected and the legal and business precautions that could be taken against them are factors to be considered in making a foreign investment as well as in the shaping of international norms to regulate such interferences by host countries. So, too, a policy maker in a State that seeks to attract foreign investment must understand the implications of governmental interferences in foreign investment that amount to a taking and the extent of the international legal controls or restraints that exist in respect of them.

This chapter is an analysis of the law relating to takings of foreign property by host countries and of the clauses in IIAs seeking to provide protection against such takings. The chapter deals with the development of the law and considers both what possible protection against governmental interference can be given by international instruments and under what conditions and in which manner a State retains, under international law, the freedom to take action that may affect foreign property in the interests of its economic development.

The taking of property by Governments can result from legislative or administrative acts that transfer title and physical possession. Takings can also result from official acts that effectuate the loss of management, use or control, or a significant depreciation in the value, of assets. Generally speaking, the former can be classified as "direct takings" and the latter as "indirect takings". Direct takings are associated with measures that have given rise to the classical category of takings under international law. They include the outright takings of all foreign property in all economic sectors, takings on an industry-specific basis, or takings that are firm-specific. Usually, outright takings in all economic sectors or on an industry-specific basis have been labeled "nationalizations". Firm specific takings on the other hand have often been called "expropriations". Both nationalizations and expropriations involve the physical taking of property. In contrast, some measures short of physical takings may amount to takings in that they result in the effective loss of management, use or control, or a significant depreciation of the value, of the assets of a foreign investor (Christie, 1962; Weston,1975; Dolzer, 1986). Some particular types of such takings have been called" creeping expropriations",[1] while others may be termed "regulatory takings". All such takings may be considered "indirect takings".

The classifications of takings outlined above give an indication of how the terminology on takings is used in this chapter. But it needs to be pointed out that, despite the extensive legal and other literature on the topic in the past few decades, the terminology and to some extent the classification of takings of property is not fully clear, consistent or established. There are many reasons for this. To begin with, the terms (and concepts) in question have their origin in national law and practice and their "translation" in international law is sometimes problematic. In the second place, the actual practice of States evolves, partly in response to developments in the economy and in the forms that "property" takes, and partly because the ideologies and policies in effect change. Thirdly, the topic has a long history and has gone through several phases, during which the importance of the particular facets of the relevant problems varied considerably. What follows is a brief summary of some of the major phases.

In the twentieth century, the first major phase of taking of property of aliens by States which can be classified as "nationalizations" and had an impact on shaping international law on the subject of takings, began with the Russian and Mexican revolutions.[2] These takings were not accompanied by the payment of compensation and resulted in conflicts between the host countries and the home countries of the aliens whose property was taken. In response to the taking of United States property by Mexico, the Government of the United States did not contest Mexico's right to nationalize but argued that it was subject to certain international law standards, including the payment of "prompt, adequate and effective compensation" ("Hull formula").[3] The formula encapsulates the view that takings by a host country should conform to an external standard mandated by international law which would fully protect the investor's interests. This stance on takings has been maintained by the Government of the United States ever since as representing international law and has been generally espoused by other capital exporting countries. Developing countries, however, generally resisted this stance on the ground that such a high standard of compensation may deter national action in pursuance of objectives of restructuring their economies especially in cases of large-scale takings or where host countries are short of foreign exchange.

Another phase of takings followed the period of decolonization. Here, the newly independent States, seeking to wrest economic control from the nationals of the erstwhile colonial States, embarked on across-the-board nationalizations of foreign affiliates and their assets.[4] Their position was that only "appropriate compensation" needed to be paid for these takings of foreign property. This position came to be associated with the formulation of a series of resolutions in the General Assembly of the United Nations spelling out the doctrine of permanent sovereignty over natural resources[5] and the campaign for a New International Economic Order.[6] In this period, the discussion on takings was coloured by the objective of ending the economic control of former colonial powers. The General Assembly resolutions were intended to facilitate this objective.

Though outright nationalizations are still possible in situations of regime changes, this phase has generally passed. Likewise, nationalizations on an industry-wide basis are also a rare phenomenon.[7] This is not to say that such instances of takings may not reoccur.[8] In any event, interferences in specific industries that a State may want to reorganize for different reasons will continue to result in the direct takings of alien property. The United Kingdom and Canada have renegotiated contracts relating to natural resources investments when they turned out to be disadvantageous to them, indicating that governmental power will be utilized, both by developed and developing countries, in order to redraw disadvantageous contracts in important industries (Cameron, 1983; Mendes, 1981). Closely related to nationalization are large-scale take-overs of land by the State to distribute to the landless. This differs from nationalization proper in that the State does not retain the properties. Again, this is no longer a very important category in most countries but the issue has resurfaced in the recent past.

In the more usual situation, at least in recent times, direct takings are likely to be expropriations, that is, takings targeted at individual properties or enterprises. But -- perhaps even more importantly -- the focus on takings is increasingly turning to indirect takings. However, almost any governmental measure could be construed as an act of interference in the business of a foreign investor. The difficulty lies in distinguishing between regulatory measures that have to be compensated and measures that do not carry with them, under international law, the obligation to pay compensation.

This has become an increasingly grey area. The law will have to be developed to provide sufficient criteria for distinguishing between "tolerable"[9] regulatory takings that are not compensable and unjustified takings that are. Already, the issue has been raised that changes in ministerial and other policy having an effect of diminishing the profitability of investment should be considered as takings since the value of the investment is diminished as a result of these policy changes. An important case in point was that of a dispute between Canada and Ethyl Corporation of Virginia, United States (box 1).[10]

Box 1. Regulatory measures and depreciation in value: the Ethyl case

Canada's Manganese-based Fuels Additives Act came into force on 24 June 1997. Under the Act, the gasoline additive MMT was placed on a schedule which resulted in banning inter provincial trade and importation into Canada of MMT. Three legal challenges to the legislation were launched against the Government of Canada: an investor-State challenge under the North American Free Trade Agreement (NAFTA) Chapter Eleven by Ethyl Corporation; a constitutional challenge in the Ontario Court by Ethyl's Canadian affiliate (Ethyl Canada); and a dispute settlement panel was established under the Agreement on Internal Trade (AIT) at the request of Alberta (joined by three other provinces).

/...

Box 1 (concluded)

On 20 July 1998, the Government announced its decision to lift the trade restrictions on MMT by removing MMT from the schedule to the Act. This decision responded to the AIT Panel recommendations announced 19 July 1998, concerning the inconsistency of the Act with obligations under the AIT. The Government also dealt with the investor-State challenge launched by Ethyl Corporation and the constitutional challenge in the Ontario Court. Under the terms of settlement, the Government paid $13 million to Ethyl, representing reasonable and independently verified costs and lost profits in Canada. Ethyl dropped both claims.

At the time of settlement, the NAFTA case had not moved beyond a preliminary jurisdictional challenge initiated by the Government, and the merits of the claim had not yet been heard.

Studies in Canada and the United States are proceeding on the impact of MMT and other fuel additives on health and automotive tailpipe emissions. If subsequent federal government action is warranted, the Government would use the Canada Environmental Protection Act, based on further scientific analysis and full disclosure of data.

The case has raised concerns as to whether regulatory measures in the field of environment, public health and similar areas will be regarded as takings and that compensation could be claimed under the takings provision in treaties. The issue raised is whether acts such as Government interferences in areas like land use planning, health and zoning matters and similar areas could be construed as takings which are compensable under the takings provisions of IIAs.

Source: UNCTAD.

To a large extent, the debate here will track the constitutional debates within domestic legal systems on what amounts to a compensable taking and what amounts to a truly regulatory non-compensable taking.

Section I Explanation of the Issue

A. Categories of takings

From the discussion in the Introduction, a number of categories of takings can be identified. They include:

- **Outright nationalizations in all economic sectors.** These measures result in the termination of all foreign investment in a host country. They are usually motivated by policy considerations; the measures are intended to achieve complete State control of the economy and involve the takeover of all privately-owned means of production. [11]
- **Outright nationalizations on an industry-wide basis.** Here, a host country seeks to reorganize a particular industry, by taking over the private enterprises in the industry and creating a State monopoly. [12]
- **Large-scale taking of land by the State.** Usually the purpose for such takings is to redistribute land to the landless.
- **Specific takings.** In such cases, a foreign firm (such as a firm dominating a market or industry) or a specific lot of land (such as that necessary to build a road) is the target of the taking. The issue of legal significance is that no discrimination can usually be alleged in such a case (Amco v. Indonesia, 1992).
- **Creeping expropriation.** This may be defined as the slow and incremental encroachment on one or more of the ownership rights of a foreign investor that diminishes the value of its investment. The legal title to the property remains vested in the foreign investor but the investor's rights of use of the property are diminished as a result of the interference by the State (box 2). There is an accumulation of authority that assimilates creeping expropriation with the first three categories of takings (Zedalis, 1996; Paasivirta, 1990).

Box 2. Examples of creeping expropriation

- Forced divestment of shares of a company;
- interference in the right of management;
- appointment of managers;
- refusal of access to labour or raw materials;
- excessive or arbitrary taxation.

Source: UNCTAD.

- **Regulatory takings.** Regulatory takings are those takings of property that fall within the police powers of a State, or otherwise arise from State measures like those pertaining to the regulation of the environment, health, morals, culture or economy of a host country.

A taking by a host country destroys the ownership rights of an investor in its tangible or intangible assets. The first four categories of takings identified above clearly accomplish this, and the rules of international law apply to them, although there is still controversy as to the precise consequences. It is the last two categories of takings that present new and difficult legal issues.

B. Requirements for a lawful taking

A taking is lawful provided it satisfies certain conditions. To begin with, special limitations on a State's right to take property may be imposed by treaty. In customary international law, there is authority for a number of limitations or conditions that relate to:

- the requirement of a public purpose for the taking;
- the requirement that there should be no discrimination;
- the requirement that the taking should be accompanied by payment of compensation; and,
- the requirement of due process.

1. Public purpose

This requirement is not complicated. Usually, a host country's determination of what is in its public interest is accepted.[13] There is some indication that, where a taking is by way of reprisal against the act of a home State of a foreign national, it is considered illegal on the ground that it lacks public interest.[14]

2. Non-discrimination

Traditionally, the requirement relating to the absence of discrimination was directed particularly at the singling-out of aliens on the basis of national or ethnic origin. Where the taking, specific or general, is racially motivated, it is clearly violative of the *ius cogens* norm against racial discrimination and hence illegal (Sornarajah, 1994). In fact, the non-discrimination requirement would imply that measures that can be construed as expropriations be across-the-board. Progressively however, as the issue of regulatory takings becomes prominent, any taking that is pursuant to discriminatory or arbitrary action, or any action that is without legitimate justification, is considered to be contrary to the non-discrimination requirement, even absent any singling-out on the basis of nationality. This includes rohibition of discrimination with regard to due process and payment of compensation requirements. Moreover, the non-discrimination requirement demands that governmental measures, procedures and practices be non-discriminatory even in the treatment of members of the same group of aliens.

3. Compensation

The issue that is most likely to raise a dispute in the taking of alien property is the standard of compensation that is payable to a foreign investor. Historically, communist States, in keeping with the principle that there cannot be private ownership of property, took the view that no compensation is payable. This is not the current view taken by some communist States.[15] Capital exporting States have usually taken the position that the Hull standard of prompt, adequate and effective compensation should be met. This requires the payment of full market value as compensation, speedily and in convertible currency.[16] Some developing countries have taken the position that the payment of "appropriate compensation" would be sufficient. This is a vague standard, but the idea is that inability to pay immediate and full compensation should not deter a State which decides that it is necessary to take foreign property in the interest of economic development, from doing so. The standard of appropriate compensation contemplates that equitable principles should be the guide in the matter of assessing compensation rather than a hard and fast rule relating to market value. It implies a variable standard that permits consideration of past practices, the depletion of natural resources, possible lack of foreign exchange and other factors such as environmental damage.[17] Another variation used in investment agreements that do not adopt the Hull formula is an explicit reference to the book-value method of valuation. This may consist of either the net book value (depreciated assets value) or the updated book value, also referred to as the adjusted book value, taking inflation into account. Alternatively, the tax value of the assets could be referred to.[18] More generally, each of the competing formulas of compensation have acquired a certain symbolic value: the "Hull formula" suggests a fuller, more satisfactory to the investor type compensation, while the "appropriate compensation" formula suggests that additional concrete (historical or other) considerations may be taken into account which will result in a lower final payment.

The distinction between regulatory and other types of takings will cause concern in the future with regard to compensation.[19] The novel problem that has to be worked out is the extent to which regulatory actions by a State could be regarded as compensable takings. Clearly, a taking in response to criminal conduct by a foreign investor or in response to a violation of penal or other laws of a host country is legitimate and is not compensable as compensation will negate the punitive purpose behind such takings. This issue has been addressed in some international instruments.

For example, the first protocol of the European Convention on Human Rights specially states that punitive and tax measures are not to be regarded as violations of the right of property (Brownlie, 1992).[20] Perhaps, such punitive takings should be regarded as a separate category of takings. Punitive takings could be defined as responses to violations of laws by a foreign investor. In fact, they can be simply regarded as typical confiscations under criminal law.

But, the issue arises as to which non-punitive regulatory measures are to be treated like takings for which compensation is due. In many States, regulatory structures have been built up to harness the foreign investment to the economic objectives of a host country or to prevent harm to the economy, environment, health, morals or culture of the host country. An issue that could frequently arise in the future with regard to the response of international law to these non-punitive regulatory measures is the basis of assessment of compensation, if any.[21]

This can be an important issue if, for example, regulatory measures to protect the environment were to be included in the scope of treaty protection provisions against regulatory takings. Such provisions, it has been argued, would insure a foreign investor from the consequences of the environmental harm the foreign investment causes and hence remove all deterrence against the causing of such environmental harm. There is, also, the likelihood that Governments may be wary of challenges to the underlying scientific validity of their measures in case investors assert that there is no conclusive proof that there is danger from their production processes. Another objection is that whilst local business is subject to regulatory interferences in the environmental interest, foreign investment would be protected from such interferences. The argument is also made that, as a result of treaty protection against regulatory harm, a foreign investor may obtain greater protection in the international sphere than it would under the laws of its own home country.[22]

The issue also arises as to the conflict between IIAs containing protection against regulatory takings and conventions asserting environmental standards which form the basis of international environmental laws. A State effecting a regulatory taking may be conforming to the convention containing the environmental standard but may be contravening the IIA by not paying compensation. In that regard, IIAs have to be drafted taking into account possible conflicts with other international arrangements.

4. The due process requirement

In large-scale nationalizations in the past, countries often expressly denied judicial review of compensation. The requirement that the compensation due to a foreign investor should be assessed by an independent host country tribunal is now found in the takings provisions of many bilateral and some regional agreements. This requirement is usually satisfied by the legislation effecting the taking which will provide for the mechanism for the assessment of the compensation. Thus due process may be met by other kinds of regular administrative procedures other than courts of law. However, there remains some uncertainty as to the interpretation of the term "due process" in international law.[23]

Section II
Stocktaking and Analysis

This section of the chapter takes stock of the manner in which existing investment instruments have dealt with the main issues identified in section I. It first deals with what amounts to a taking. It then focuses on requirements for a taking to be lawful.

A. What amounts to a taking?

In the early instruments on foreign investment, the terms mostly used to describe takings were "nationalization" or "expropriation". Though the distinction between the two terms was not clearly made, they basically applied to the taking of property by the State through legislative or administrative measures. Modern BITs[24] started to widen the types of takings to include indirect takings so that any diminution in the value of property due to Government action would be caught up in the definition of takings. The treaty practice, however, still refers to "nationalization" or "expropriation" as the benchmark of takings and refers to indirect takings as "measures tantamount to nationalizations" or "measures having effect equivalent to nationalization or expropriation".[25] It indicates a reluctance to move away from the paradigm of the law that was developed in the context of direct takings, despite the fact that the legal form of takings has now undergone a change.

But, with the emphasis shifting to regulatory and other erosions of the rights of a foreign investor, a definition of takings that was not tied to the idea of nationalizations or expropriation had to be found. To be able to deal with the problem of indirect takings, BITs, while retaining the old notion of "nationalization" or" expropriation" increasingly sought to give a wider definition to those terms. For example, the Germany-Bangladesh BIT (1981) includes in its protocol, section 3, "the taking away or restricting of any property right which in itself or in conjunction with other rights constitutes an investment" (ICSID, 1981, p. 7). In some treaties, the prevention of "dispossession" was one primary aim of the treaty. Thus, the Belgium-Cyprus BIT (1991) in article 4 states :

> "Each Contracting Party undertakes not to adopt any measure of expropriation or nationalization or any other measure having the effect of directly or indirectly dispossessing the investors of the other Contracting arty of their investments..."(ICSID, 1991, p. 5).

The formulation in the Argentina-Sweden BIT (1991) provides an example of a technique that calls for the viewing of ownership of property as involving a bundle of rights so that the infringement of any one of the rights will amount to a taking.[26] Article 4 reads:

> "Neither of the Contracting Parties shall take any direct or indirect measure of nationalization or expropriation or any other measure having the same nature or the same effect..." (ICSID, 1991, p. 4).

It is not the physical invasion of property that characterizes nationalizations or expropriations that has assumed importance, but the erosion of rights associated with ownership by State interferences. So, methods have been developed to address this issue. The tendency in some cases has been to analogize the infringement of any right of ownership with nationalization or expropriation. This is the position adopted by the World Bank Guidelines on the Treatment of Foreign Direct Investment (1992) and the Energy Charter Treaty (1994), both of which seek to widen the definition of nationalizations or expropriations to include any measures producing effects akin to those of nationalization or expropriation. Article IV(1) of the World Bank Guidelines ties indirect takings to nationalizations or expropriations by referring to nationalizations or expropriations and then stating "or take measures which have similar effects". Similarly, article 13 (1) of the Energy Charter Treaty, reads:

> "Investments of Investors of a Contracting Party in the Area of any other Contracting Party shall not be nationalized, expropriated or subjected to a measure or measures having effect equivalent to nationalization or expropriation (hereinafter referred to as "Expropriation") except where ..." (UNCTAD, 1996a, vol. II, p. 558).

The alternative strategy is to give examples of the type of measures that could amount to takings so as to illustrate the width of the concept. Thus, for example, article 3 of the United States model BIT (1982)[27] refers to "any other measure or series of measures, direct or indirect, tantamount to expropriation (including the levying of taxation, the compulsory sale of all or part of an investment, or the impairment or deprivation of its management, control or economic value) ...". Canadian treaties have adopted yet another strategy to deal with specific regulatory interferences by addressing the issues as to circumstances in which these interferences could be regarded as takings (box 3).

The Organisation for Economic Co-operation and Development (OECD) draft Multilateral Agreement on Investment (MAI) also addresses the issue of indirect expropriation. Interestingly, it does so in two ways. First article IV(2) on expropriation states that " A Contracting Party shall not expropriate or nationalise directly or indirectly an investment ... of an investor of another Contracting Party...". It then continues "or take any measure or measures having equivalent effect..." (UNCTAD, 2000b). The reason for this double reference may well be the difference in BIT tradition between the OECD countries. Whereas some of them prefer the "directly or indirectly" approach, others are used to the "equivalent effect" approach. Since yet others are using the double reference, this may have resulted in a compromise combining both approaches.

At a much later stage during the MAI negotiations nongovernmental organizations and others, who first saw this text, feared that the double reference was meant to imply a broader definition of indirect expropriation than was used in most BITs so far. They specifically feared that this article, combined with the investor-State dispute settlement article, would have a negative effect on the ability of Governments to enact and implement new legislation in environmental and other fields.[28] The Ethyl case was used as an example to demonstrate this possibility.

Box 3. Examples of takings in Canadian IIAs

Tax measures. Tax measures could amount to a taking, particularly in circumstances where they are raised to siphon off profits that a foreign investor is seen as making. Canadian BITs specifically provide for situations regarding tax measures. They state that tax measures will not be affected by the provisions of the treaties; but that where there is a claim of excessive taxation, then the parties to the treaty will jointly determine whether the measure of taxation amounts to an expropriation. This is an innovative method of dealing with this situation. It is, however, unlikely that the State imposing the measure would accept that the measure amounts to an expropriation. In this case, a dispute would arise that under the terms of the treaty could be submitted to arbitral decision.

Compulsory licensing of technology. Canada has another innovation in its treaties relating to compulsory licensing of technology protected by patents and other forms of industrial property. Compulsory licensing is a regulatory measure that prevents a company from keeping unutilized patents. Potentially, where such licensing of technology belonging to a foreigner is ordered by a host country, there would be a taking of the intellectual property. The treaties state that such compulsory licensing requirements should be imposed only by courts or other competent tribunals, acknowledging that such infringements will not amount to takings protected by the treaty, provided some due process requirements have been satisfied.

Management control. Some Canadian treaties also specifically provide for the situation in which managers and directors are appointed by the State to impair the control of the company set up by a foreign investor.

Interferences in financial sectors. The Canadian treaties also exempt interferences in the financial services sector from the scope of the protection given in the treaties. Here again, there is a consciousness shown that regulatory interferences in certain areas should not be regarded as amounting to takings.

Source: UNCTAD, based on Canada-Barbados BIT, 1996; Canada-Venezuela BIT, 1996; Canada-Ecuador BIT, 1996.

In a reaction to these concerns, the MAI negotiators discussed several options to address the issue. They agreed on the objective of protecting Government regulators and their normal non-discriminatory work. They also agreed that this was a broader issue, not just relevant to environmental regulations. The solutions discussed included a general exception such as that of the General Agreement on Tariffs and Trade (GATT), article XX[29] and a clarification approach such as that of NAFTA, article 1114 (1).[30] This debate was not concluded before the negotiations came to a stop. However, in the Ministerial statement on the MAI of 28 April 1998, the ministers confirmed "that the MAI must be consistent with the sovereign responsibility of governments to conduct domestic policies. The MAI would establish mutually beneficial international rules which would not inhibit the normal non-discriminatory exercise of regulatory powers by governments and such exercise of regulatory powers will not amount to expropriation" (OECD, 1998b, p. 1).[31]

This text clearly covers not only environmental measures, but also all other sorts of regulatory measures taken by Governments. It does not contain a "carte blanche" for Government regulators, since it refers to "normal" exercise of regulatory powers. This is in line with the references to "arbitrary or unjustifiable discrimination or a disguised restriction on investment" in GATT, article XX and "otherwise consistent with this Chapter" in NAFTA, article 1114(1). Presumably, "normal" should be compared with words like "bona fide" and "commonly accepted". In the context of expropriation it refers to jurisprudence on what constitutes a compensable taking and what amounts to a truly regulatory non-compensable taking. Thus in the MAI context, while discussions on possible additions to the text were never finalized, it was felt necessary to issue a political declaration on the relation between regulation and expropriation.

The extent to which States will accept that regulatory measures could be covered by a takings provision remains uncertain. This is a concern that affects not only developing but also developed countries, some of which are among the largest recipients of foreign investment flows. Since developed countries have considerably more regulatory legislation in areas such as antitrust, corporate securities, environment and planning, they may show a greater reluctance in participating in treaties that transfer review of these matters to international tribunals.[32] The idea that State policies could be litigated or arbitrated before foreign courts or arbitration tribunals will cause unease to any State. It is for this reason that States may seek a narrower definition of taking or require that there are limiting criteria that would not make all regulatory interferences subject to the treaty provisions.[33]

B. Provisions on requirements for the legality of takings

IIAs recognize that it is lawful for a host country to take alien property provided four requirements are met. These four requirements (outlined below) are stated in almost all investment agreements, though terminology varies. There is considerable similarity among IIAs as to the provisions on public purpose and nondiscrimination. It is as to the requirement relating to the standard of compensation that there is variation. As for due process there remains, as indicated before, some uncertainty about the meaning of the term.

1. Public purpose

Almost all IIAs contain the requirement, in varying terminology, that there must be a public purpose for the taking. For example, NAFTA states, in article 1110 (1) (a):

> "No Party may directly or indirectly nationalize or expropriate an investment of an investor of another Party in its territory or take a measure tantamount to nationalization or expropriation of such an investment ("expropriation"), except:
>
> (a) for a public purpose ..." (UNCTAD, 1996a, vol. III, p. 79).

The BIT between the Netherlands and Sudan (1970) provides in article XI that:

> "The investments of nationals of either Contracting Party in the territory of the other Contracting Party shall not be expropriated except for the public benefit and against compensation" (UNCTAD, 1998a, p. 68).

The public purpose requirement is usually included in IIAs, despite the fact that, as already noted, a host country's determination that its taking was for a public purpose is seldom challenged. Yet, this requirement continues to be stated either because it is time hallowed or because of the still remaining view that a taking by way of a reprisal lacks a public purpose (BP v. Libya, 1973). Sometimes, this limitation is made clear, as in the United Kingdom-Costa Rica BIT (1982) which states that "the public purpose must be related to the internal needs" of the country (UNCTAD, 1998a, p. 68). The formulation clearly applies to takings by way of reprisals which are acts of external policy. But, this rule relating to takings by way of reprisals can be derived from customary law, without the aid of treaty provisions.

2. Non-discrimination

The non-discrimination requirement continues to have relevance with regard to takings, as it affects the legality of a taking, and therefore the quantum of compensation. Examples of the formulation of this requirement in IIAs are article 5 of the United Kingdom model BIT (1991) and article 1110(1)(b) of the NAFTA. Similarly, the Chinese model BIT (1994), article 4 states:

> "Neither Contracting Party shall expropriate, nationalize or take similar measures (hereinafter referred to as "expropriation") against investments of investors of the other Contracting Party in its territory, unless the following conditions are met:
>
> (a) for the public interests;
>
> (b) under domestic legal procedure;
>
> (c) without discrimination" (UNCTAD, 1996a, vol. III, p. 153).

In the Japan-China BIT (1988), article 5 (2) states:

> "Investments and returns of nationals and companies of either Contracting Party shall not be subjected to expropriation, nationalization or any other measures the effects of which would be similar to expropriation or nationalization, within the territory of the other Contracting Party unless such measures are taken for a public purpose, ... are not discriminatory, and ..."(UNCTAD, 1998a, p. 68).

Another similar formulation can be found in the Energy Charter Treaty, article 13 (1):

> "Investments of Investors of a Contracting Party in the Area of any Contracting Party shall not be nationalized, expropriated or subjected to a measure or measures having effect equivalent to nationalization or expropriation (hereinafter referred to as "Expropriation") except where such Expropriation is...... (b) not discriminatory ..." (UNCTAD, 1996a, vol. II, p. 558).

3. The standard of compensation

There is no uniformity in IIAs as to the standard of compensation that should apply upon a taking. A multiplicity of methods is employed in dealing with the matter, and much has depended on the bargaining strengths of the parties in the type of protection that is secured. Moreover, whatever the formulation of the standard of compensation, attention must be paid to the method of valuation of property that had been subject to a taking, which might be decisive on the issue.

The terminology preferred by some countries particularly developing ones is "appropriate compensation". The genesis of the term can be traced to a series of General Assembly resolutions associated with a New International Economic Order and Permanent Sovereignty over Natural Resources. In some cases, this standard has been construed to reflect the view that full compensation need not always follow upon expropriation, to provide the host country more flexibility in determining the compensation to be paid. There are treaties and other instruments that incorporate this view. For example, Model "B" of the Model Agreements on Promotion and Protection of Investments of the Asian-African Legal Consultative Committee (AALCC) provides in its first alternative formulation of article 7(i) that:

> "A Contracting Party may exercise its sovereign rights in the matter of nationalization or expropriation in respect of investments made... upon payment of appropriate compensation..." (UNCTAD, 1998a, p. 231).

The provision, in its first alternative in part (ii), defines appropriate compensation as "compensation calculated on the basis of recognized principles of valuation"(ibid., p. 232). Thus, there exists some flexibility for the host State to choose amongst different recognized principles of valuation.

The BIT between China and Thailand (1985) provides a variant of this formulation. Article 5 (1)(a) provides:

> "Only for the public interest and against compensation may either Contracting Party expropriate, nationalize or take similar measures.... Such compensation shall be equivalent to the appropriate value of expropriated investments...." (United Nations, 1986b, p. 56).

Again, the provision provides for a certain flexibility on the issue of the determination of the amount of compensation.

The alternative view which involves the use of the Hull formula has received recently increasing support. In particular, developing countries are prepared to deviate from standards that they have espoused collectively in the past as shown in the BITs they now conclude not only with developed countries but also with other developing countries (Guzman, 1998).[34] Of the treaties made in 1995, only one, the Netherlands-Oman treaty, uses the formula "just compensation" but it is followed by the requirement of market value being paid. Another formula refers to compensation without qualification but uses a method of valuation which will result in the payment of market value of the property taken. The Chinese model BIT, article 4(2), for example, states that "the compensation.....shall be equivalent to the value of the expropriated investments at the time when expropriation is proclaimed..." (UNCTAD, 1996a, vol. III, p. 153). The German model BIT in article 4 refers to compensation "equivalent to the value of the expropriated investment immediately before the date on which the actual or threatened expropriation, nationalization or comparable measure has become publicly known" (UNCTAD, 1996a vol. III, p. 169). The China-Japan BIT (1988) does not refer to market value but to restitution, that is restoration to the status quo ante. A further variation encountered in some BITs is a reference to the book-value method of valuation. This may involve either the net book value, also referred to as the depreciated assets value, or the updated book value, also referred to as the adjusted book value. One example of this approach can be found in the BIT between the Netherlands and Sudan (1970) where, by article XI, compensation shall represent the equivalent to the depreciated value of the investment (UNCTAD,1998a, p. 68).

It should be pointed out that the BITs practice of some individual countries does not show a uniform pattern. Thus, China, a prolific maker of such treaties, has used a variety of standards on compensation. Its treaty with Australia (1988) refers to the Hull standard but its treaty with France (1984) refers to appropriate compensation. Its treaties with Singapore (1985) and New Zealand (1988) simply mention compensation without any qualification. Negotiations with the United States on an investment treaty appeared to have failed because there could be no agreement, among other things, on the standard of compensation (Lin and Allison, 1994). Even Singapore, a State traditionally hospitable to foreign investment, lacks uniformity in this area. There are treaties that Singapore has made that refer to the Hull standard and those that refer to the alternative standard of "appropriate compensation" (Sornarajah, 1986a).

The regional instruments also seem to favour the payment of full compensation upon a taking. Thus, NAFTA and the Energy Charter Treaty both use the Hull formula. The NAFTA provisions are elaborate, refer to fair market value but are essentially a paraphrasing of the Hull standard (Levy, 1995) (box 4).

Box 4. The NAFTA provision on taking

"Article 1110: Expropriation and Compensation

1. No Party may directly or indirectly nationalize or expropriate an investment of an investor of another Party in its territory or take a measure tantamount to nationalization or expropriation of such an investment ("expropriation"), except:
   a) for a public purpose;
   b) on a non-discriminatory basis;
   c) in accordance with due process of law and Article 1105(1); and
   d) on payment of compensation in accordance with paragraphs 2 through 6.
2. Compensation shall be equivalent to the fair market value of the expropriated investment immediately before the expropriation took place ("date of expropriation"), and shall not reflect any change in value occurring because the intended expropriation had become known earlier. Valuation criteria shall include going concern value, asset value including declared tax value of tangible property, and other criteria, as appropriate, to determine fair market value.
3. Compensation shall be paid without delay and be fully realizable.
4. If payment is made in a G7 currency, compensation shall include interest at a commercially reasonable rate for that currency from the date of expropriation until the date of actual payment.
5. If a Party elects to pay in a currency other than a G7 currency, the amount paid on the date of payment, if converted into a G7 currency at the market rate of exchange prevailing on that date, shall be no less than if the amount of compensation owed on the date of expropriation had been converted into the G7 currency at the market rate of exchange prevailing on that date, and interest had accrued at a commercially reasonable rate for that G7 currency from the date of expropriation until the date of payment.
6. On payment, compensation shall be freely transferable as provided in Article 1109.
7. This Article does not apply to the issuance of compulsory licenses granted in relation to intellectual property rights, or to the revocation, limitation or creation of intellectual property rights, to the extent that such issuance, revocation, limitation or creation is consistent with Chapter Seventeen (Intellectual Property).
8. For purposes of this Article and for greater certainty, a nondiscriminatory measure of general application shall not be considered a measure tantamount to an expropriation of a debt security or loan covered by this Chapter solely on the ground that the measure imposes costs on the debtor that cause it to default on the debt."

Source: UNCTAD, 1996a, vol. III, pp. 79-80.

The Energy Charter Treaty uses the Hull standard directly.[35] Likewise, the APEC Non-Binding Investment Principles (1994) also adopted the Hull standard. The World Bank Guidelines specify "appropriate compensation", but go on to redefine the standard as no different from prompt, adequate and effective compensation. They state, in article IV (2):

> "Compensation for a specific investment taken by the State will, according to the details provided below, be deemed "appropriate" if it is adequate, effective and prompt" (UNCTAD, 1996a, vol. I, p. 252).

In line with the traditional position of capital exporting States, the MAI (chapter IV(2)) uses the Hull standard.

Overall, there is a trend in modern BITs towards the Hull standard of compensation. Though the traditional formula of "prompt, adequate and effective" compensation may not always be used, the treaties spell out the meaning of the formula in different, yet roughly equivalent ways. Thus, the Singapore-Mongolia BIT (1995) uses the words "effectively realizable" and "without unreasonable delay" and require that compensation shall be "the value immediately before the expropriation". The reference is to a standard no different from the Hull standard. The Hull standard is employed in BITs between developed and developing countries as well as in BITs between developing countries. While there are still modern BITs that use other formula such as "just compensation", even in such cases the treaties may spell out that the assets taken should be given a market value.[36]

4. Due process

The due process requirement is found in a variety of treaties, particularly those that the United States has concluded. The term "due process" itself is terminology that distinctly relates to United States law. In fact, it has no definite content except in United States law. Yet, it is employed in treaties entered into by other countries (for example, the Chile-Sweden BIT (1993)). However, the view that a taking must be reviewed by appropriate, usually judicial, bodies (especially in relation to the assessment of compensation) finds expression in the practice of a large number of States and is indeed found in many national constitutional provisions. For example, the United Kingdom model BIT (1991) states in article 5 (1):

> "... The national or company affected shall have a right, under the law of the Contracting Party making the expropriation, to prompt review, by a judicial or other independent authority of that

Party, of his or its case and of the valuation of his or its investment in accordance with the principles set out in this paragraph" (UNCTAD, 1996a, vol. III, p. 188).

Another example is the Chilean model agreement which in article 6 (3) provides that:

"The investor affected shall have a right to access, under the law of the Contracting Party making the expropriation, to the judicial authority of that Party, in order to review the amount of compensation and the legality of any such expropriation or comparable measure" (ibid., p. 146).

While bilateral investment dispute provisions do mention due process requirements, they usually seem to allude to the requirement only after a taking so that there could be a review of whether proper compensation standards were used in assessing the compensation. They do not face the issue of whether or not a foreign investor should be given an opportunity to show the regulatory authority the reason why measures proposed by it should not be taken against the investor. Indeed, this is a matter of the internal public law of the host State. Should proper procedural standards not be followed in such a case, then a different set of questions arises from those relating to the issue of expropriation, in particular, whether an investor has suffered a denial of justice for which no effective domestic remedy exists. That is an issue of State responsibility in general and not an issue related to expropriation as such.

Section III Interaction with other Issues and Concepts

The issue of taking of foreign property is central to the risk perceptions in foreign investment. Hence, the issue has relevance to a wide variety of other issues and concepts in the area of foreign investment.

- **Scope and definition**. Firstly, the issue of taking concerns the definition of foreign investment because the protected investment is defined in the scope and definitions provisions of IIAs. In the past, the concern was only with the physical property of a foreign investor. In modern times, the concern is not so much with the physical property but with the antecedent rights that are necessary for the enjoyment of these property rights as well as with incorporeal property such as patents, copyright and other rights connected with intellectual property and shares in companies which play a crucial role in international business. Most recent BITs include intellectual property within the definition of investment so that, if there are infringements of intellectual property rights by State interference, there would be a taking. So too, contractual rights and regulatory rights associated with the making of an investment are included within the definition of foreign investment in treaties. For example, a progressive enlargement of the categories of protected assets is reflected in the newer IIAs, a number of which have included within the definition of investment descriptions like "any right conferred by law or contract, and any licenses and permits pursuant to law" (United States-Sri Lanka 1991 BIT, article1) (ICSID, 1991, p. 2). This partly indicates concern on the part of developed countries with the newer problem of regulatory takings resulting from controls on foreign investment instituted by developing States.

Table 1. Interaction across issues and concepts

Issue	Taking of property
Admission and establishment	+
Competition	+
Dispute settlement (investor-State)	++
Dispute settlement (State-State)	++
Employment	+
Environment	++
Fair and equitable treatment	++
Home country measures	+
Host country operational meaures	0
Illicit payments	+
Incentives	0
Investment-related trade measures	+
Most-favoured-nation treatment	++
National treatment	
Scope and definition	++
Social responsibility	+
State contracts	++
Taxation	+
Transfer of funds	++
Transfer of technology	+
Transfer pricing	+
Transparency	+

Source: UNCTAD.

Key: 0 = negligible or no interaction.
+ = moderate interaction.
++ = extensive interaction.

But many developing countries continue to preserve the irregulatory structures. Thus, the Australia-Indonesian BIT (1992) applies only to investments made "in conformity with the laws, regulations and investment policies ... applicable from time to time" (ICSID, 1992, p. 2). This formula ensures that full play is given to the regulatory laws of a host country despite the treaty so that only foreign investment which conforms with legislation is entitled to the protection. In South-East Asian treaty practice, only "approved" investment is given treaty protection. This formula ensures that a State decides on an *ad hoc* basis whether a foreign investment is so desirable that it be given treaty protection.

- **Most-favoured-nation treatment.** The existence of a most-favoured-nation (MFN) treatment clause ensures that better standards of protection against taking flow through to the State that had negotiated a lower standard. Thus, a State which had agreed to appropriate compensation with another State may argue that it is entitled to the higher Hull standard, if the latter State had concluded a treaty agreeing to the Hull standard with a third State, provided there was an MFN clause in its treaty.
- **Fair and equitable treatment.** It has been suggested that the fair and equitable standard of treatment referred to in an IIA creates an obligation to pay full compensation upon a taking (Dolzer and Stevens, 1986). This is on the basis that fairness and equity require that a foreign investor be returned to its original position prior to the taking at least in monetary terms.
- **Environment.** The issue of takings also has relevance to environmental issues. Termination or lesser forms of interference may be necessary to ensure that a foreign investor does not do harm to the environment. Thus some IIAs like NAFTA have provisions that exclude environmental measures from the scope of treaty protection.[37] On the other hand, some IIAs may seem to include such measures and this may deter a State from intervening to protect the environment.[38]
- **State contracts.** Contracts are sometimes the basis on which firms enter a host country. The local partner may be the State or a State corporation. In the natural resources sphere, in particular, the making of agreements often involves a State corporation. Large projects in areas like telecommunications, transport, power-supply and other similar fields also often involve the making of contracts with the State or State agencies.

  The issue arises as to whether a breach of these contracts would amount to a taking. There are two opposing views on this question. One is that these contracts are, by their very nature, internationalized contracts. Quite apart from their nature, the inclusion of arbitration, choice of law and stabilization clauses in these contracts would indicate that the parties desired these contracts to be treated as internationalized contracts so that, when a State breaches these contracts, international responsibility would arise. The breach of a foreign investment agreement by State-induced measures (such as legislation or some regulatory action) would therefore be a taking that is compensable. This view finds support in several arbitral awards.[39] The other view is that a foreign investment contract of whatever kind is subject to the laws of a host country. The notion of permanent sovereignty over natural resources assures this result in the case of contracts in the resources sphere but the argument is equally applicable in the case of all other foreign investment contracts so that the breaches of these contracts can be remedied only in accordance with the laws of a host country. So where it is claimed that a breach of a contract amounts to a taking, the claim must be settled in accordance with local laws by local courts or tribunals.

  However, in BITs as well as in regional investment treaties, there is an increasing trend to include contracts, especially in the form of concessions, in the definition of investments so that, where there is a breach of such contracts, such a breach would fall within the definition of an expropriation or other measure similar to it and would become compensable in terms of the treaty. The dispute resolution provisions of these treaties would require the submission of these claims to arbitration by an international tribunal. There is a considerable body of arbitral jurisprudence that accepts this position.
- **Funds transfer.** A significant interaction occurs between the issue of taking of property and that of the free and unhindered transfer of funds. Where an investment has been expropriated and compensation is paid to an investor by the host country, such a remedy

would be worthless unless the investor was able to transfer the sum of compensation out of the host country. Hence, the right of free transfer of funds may often include the free transfer of amounts paid by way of compensation for expropriated assets belonging to the foreign investor. An example of a typical provision dealing with this issue can be found in the BIT between Chile and Norway (1993). By article 5 (1) (e): "Each Contracting Party shall allow without delay the transfer of payments ... in a freely convertible currency, particularly of compensation for dispossession or loss described in Article 6 of this Agreement" (UNCTAD, 1998a, p. 77). In other agreements, this issue is dealt with by the expropriation provision itself.

- **Dispute settlement (investor-State and State-State).** Because disputes are caused by State interference with foreign investment, the interaction between takings and dispute settlement becomes very relevant in IIAs. A number of issues are particularly important:
  - **Takings provisions.** The article on takings usually contains a provision that the taking and the assessment of compensation must be reviewed by a national tribunal. This is sometimes included in the form of a due process requirement. The provision is inserted as a protection for a foreign investor. Its genesis may also be in the "local remedies" rule which requires a foreign investor to exhaust all local remedies.[40] Unless this is done, no State responsibility can arise and therefore a home country cannot espouse the claim of the foreign investor. This gives the host country an opportunity of settling a dispute through its own tribunals.[41]
  - **Diplomatic protection.** Almost all IIAs facilitate diplomatic protection by providing for subrogation so that home country insurance agencies may pay out the claims of a foreign investor and the home country could stand in the investor's place to pursue its claims. Once the claim is espoused, the normal procedures of inter-State dispute settlement are used to settle the dispute.
  - **Arbitration.** Whereas reference in the IIAs to the first two procedures is confirmatory of existing customary international law, IIAs adopt novel solutions in devising arbitration as a method of dispute settlement. The now widely used method of creating standing in the foreign investor itself was a novelty when first employed. But provisions in modern regional and bilateral treaties have gone even further by vesting a virtual right to compulsory arbitration in a foreign investor. The early IIAs (usually BITs) that adopted this strategy confined this right to arbitration to the International Centre for Settlement of Investment Disputes (ICSID). But more recent treaties, including regional treaties like NAFTA, permit a choice to a foreign investor of using either ICSID or *ad hoc* arbitration. Expansive interpretations have been placed by ICSID tribunals on these treaty provisions in claiming jurisdiction not only in respect of takings but also in respect of acts resulting in State responsibility.[42] These trends resulting from IIAs and developments in arbitration mean that regulatory policies and interferences with foreign investment resulting from their application can be reviewed by international tribunals. Control by a host country on foreign investment through implementation of policy may, as a result is curtailed.

Conclusion: Economic and Development Implications and Policy Options

The classical instances of takings -- nationalizations or expropriations -- have greatly influenced the development, interpretation and application of the takings clauses in IIAs. Progressively however, the ambit of takings provisions has moved beyond the classical cases, and now attempts to include all direct and indirect takings that, from the investor's point of view, are tantamount to nationalization or expropriation, that is, result in substantial loss of control or value of a foreign investment.

Given the broad scope of the typical takings clause, and looking beyond the classical category of takings, there is growing concern and controversy that the potential expanse of the takings clause might encroach on too large a category of regulatory measures that can potentially interfere or otherwise affect the property rights of a foreign investor, or diminish the value of the foreign investment (regulatory takings). Clearly, those takings that can be characterized as criminal law penalties, resulting from the violation of laws of a host State, are not compensable under customary international law. The problem remains, how to address other measures, not clearly covered under existing customary law, given the difficulty of making precise classifications of measures and takings and clear distinctions among the various types of measures. The challenge of adequately protecting the investor from takings may conflict with the concerns of national regulators in discharging their duties, and promoting economic development or serving other objectives. IIAs are also becoming instruments that reflect national and global interests in a variety of social issues. Thus, the issue also concerns non-governmental organizations, some of which are involved with issues that transcend national boundaries such as the environment and human rights. They are particularly concerned that an open-ended international legal requirement of compensation could have a chilling effect on national regulatory activity.

Whether in the case of the classical category of takings or concerning more recent issues related to regulatory takings, there is substantial accord about some fundamental issues. Takings need to be for a public purpose, on a non-discriminatory basis, under due process of law, and accompanied by payment of compensation. As illustrated in section II, there remains, however, some diversity with respect to the standard of compensation that should be applicable. Increasingly, the general trend reflects the use of a standard that requires the payment of "prompt, adequate and effective" compensation. Nevertheless, there remains abundant practice of employing provisions that provide for some flexibility on the issue of determining the amount of compensation. Such provisions are generally based on standards like "just" or "appropriate" compensation. Thus while the requirement for payment of compensation is now generally regarded as a settled issue, its application illustrates that a variety of policy options still need to be considered today.

The following discussion first examines policy options that have recently been thrown into the national and international arena as the issue of regulatory takings continues to take increasing prominence. It then illustrates a number of other policy considerations relevant to some still rather controversial issues relating to the standard of compensation in case of a taking. Finally, and based on the above, an illustration of drafting models is provided.

A. Defining a taking: policy options

The task of negotiating and drafting a clause on takings requires from a negotiator to engage in the concomitant attempt to address, among others, the important issue of what constitutes a taking. There are a number of policy options that may be considered. The main ones are identified below.

1. A comprehensive definition

As already noted, it is today likely that countries would agree that the coverage of the takings clause should be broad enough to maximize the protective effect of the IIA. It would thus typically include in its scope both direct and indirect expropriations, or use similar formulations intended to include all measures having effects equivalent to expropriations of the "classical" kind. However, the effect of an all encompassing formulation, without more, could be interpreted to include within the ambit of the takings clause all governmental acts (and omissions) that interfere with a foreign investment. It may be desirable, therefore, to examine other possible options, so as to exclude certain regulatory takings from the reach of the takings clause.

2. A narrow definition

One option is to tailor narrowly the takings clause so that it only covers the classical instances of direct takings, that is, nationalizations or expropriations. This would provide limited protection for the investor, and maximum regulatory discretion for Governments.

Theoretically, the scope of such a clause could be broadened to include any taking, under whatever name or in whatever form, that is intended to deprive investors of their property. Intent is not, however, a useful or workable test, the motivation behind governmental action being by definition complex and difficult to determine with precision. In fact, intent is relevant only in highly exceptional cases, where it is possible to show that a Government had abused its powers, by acting for a purpose other than the one it had invoked.

3. Interpretative provisions

Under this option, IIAs could include an interpretative provision, either within the takings clause or separately, that seeks to clarify whether or not a regulatory measure triggers the takings clause and, thus, its requirement of compensation. This clarification could, for example, address the regulatory activity in question, or the effects of the measures on property rights. A variation of the former approach was discussed in the MAI negotiations, where the Ministerial statement on the MAI sought to clarify that the intention of the parties was not to include, in the scope of the expropriation and compensation draft provisions, "the normal, non-discriminatory exercise of regulatory powers by governments" (OECD, 1998b, p. 1). Thus, while the broad scope of the takings provision could remain, it would be understood that it is not intended to cover some types of regulatory activity or effects.

Since there are no express exclusionary provisions as to specific regulatory activities or effects under this option, there would necessarily be reliance on some appropriate mechanism to determine whether or not a particular measure is intended to be covered by the interpretative provision. Therefore, areas of uncertainty would exist on the part of both national regulators and investors, until a number of cases were considered under the appropriate mechanism.

4. Carve-out provisions

This approach would include the identification and carving-out of certain areas of regulatory activity from the ambit of the takings clause. Here, for example, a provision could expressly address measures taken to protect the environment and exclude them from the coverage of the takings clause. The issue would then arise on safeguarding against regulatory abuses. A right to an international review of the regulatory measures could be provided and, depending on the type of review mechanism and access, agreement may be desirable upon standards of review of governmental measures.

A related issue would be considered here. When countries enter into international obligations, they typically provide for their implementation within their national legal systems. This might pose a potential problem of conflicts between different international obligations, where, for example, under an environmental treaty, a State is obligated to take certain measures that amount to a regulatory taking, and thus be required to pay compensation therefore. A variation under this option could provide for the consideration of other potentially conflicting international obligations in the IIA, and the establishment of a hierarchy to determine whether and how the takings clause would be applicable as to these obligations in the case of a conflict.

5. International reviews

This approach would essentially leave the determination on whether or not a particular taking is compensable to a case-by-case review. Thus, the compensability of all regulatory takings would be subject to review. Here, there is no need to make any *a priori* classification between types of measures or takings. However, an international review mechanism would be provided for to decide whether or not a particular taking triggers the takings clause. Access to this mechanism could be made available only to States. The rationale is that States would be prudent in assessing the compensability of regulatory takings, as each State has an interest in exercising its own right to regulate.

B. Standard of compensation: policy options

The discussions on the issue of compensation in the earlier sections of this chapter reveal three factors.

- In case of a compensable taking, there exists a tension between the host country's need to infringe upon the property rights of a foreign investor, and the need to ensure that the investor is adequately compensated in the event of such infringement. On the one hand, a host country should not be put in a position to forego or delay the development of its national objectives or the restructuring of its economic sectors that might entail takings. On the other hand, investors who would suffer loss of their property rights should not further suffer inadequate or delayed compensation.
- There is no unanimity when it comes to the determination of compensation and the calculation of the value of affected property. As previously illustrated in section I, none of the various terms currently in use have become generally accepted definitions in this regard under international law. The use of

terminology incorporating the Hull formula, for example, implies that the compensation would only include market value whereas terms like "just" or "appropriate" compensation tend to imply a certain flexibility in reaching the value of compensation due.

- Terms such as "just" or "appropriate" are often employed in a context silent on other critical considerations such as the time frame within which payment is to be made, the type of currency in which payment is made, and the transferability of the compensation paid. Even the Hull formula variations may sometimes be ambiguous in this regard, though, by contrast, they usually imply that since compensation would be promptly paid it would be freely transferable from the host country, thus further implying that the currency in which payment is made is freely convertible.

Therefore, irrespective of the compensation formula employed, some of these foregoing factors need individual consideration and raise a number of policy options with regard to the standard of compensation in IIAs.

1. Determination of the value of compensation

The typical starting point is the calculation of the value of the affected property using market value based methods. Such methods include the going concern value, asset value (including declared tax value) and book value. At the same time, it is important that the selected method addresses issues such as depreciation and damage to property.

It is also important to know that once a specific method is indicated in an IIA, it might be difficult to use other legitimate methods. Therefore, to retain flexibility, the provision of an IIA could simply require that the value of property could in any case be calculated in accordance with generally recognized principles of valuation.

The value of the affected property, once calculated, could be the sole consideration in determining the amount of compensation. However, other equitable principles might have to be reflected in the IIA takings provisions. For example, market value based methods might not leave scope for recoupment of funds necessary to rehabilitate property, such as expenditures to clean hazardous wastes dumped on the property. Other considerations that might be taken into account include past practices, the depletion of natural resources and environmental damages (either recoupment costs or damages to the wider environment). On the other hand, including equitable principles within the provisions on the standard of compensation might raise controversy. Firstly, equitable principles are not universally accepted; they are creations of specific jurisprudence. Secondly, their introduction would necessitate a clarification of whether or not they only would be used to reduce the amount of compensation (as in the case of environmental damages) or if, for example, they could also be used to increase the amount of compensation (as in the case of attaching a value to the training of the labour force or diffusion of technology effected by the investor to the benefit of the host country).

2. Limitation on the time frame within which payment is made

An IIA may provide that budgetary or foreign exchange severe limitations might be justification for delaying payment, subject to payment of reasonable interest. As previously indicated, these limitations should not deter or delay the host country's pursuance of its development objectives or the restructuring or of its economic sectors. The flexibility that is required could be attained by IIA provisions that provide for delaying payment under conditions of adequate guarantees that the investor would receive the compensation in the near future.

3. Type of currency in which payment is made

The range of options available are from the requirement of payment in a specific hard currency (e.g. United States dollars) to payment in the local currency of the host country. A requirement of payment in a specific hard currency is often regarded by host countries as unduly restrictive. Firstly, it does not allow the host country to use other freely convertible currency in its foreign exchange reserves, or places transaction costs on the host country by requiring it to exchange to the indicated hard currency. Secondly, the host country could not use advantageous arbitrage rates in foreign exchange markets to reduce its exposure with regard to the payment of compensation to a given investor.

It could also be argued that, where there exists a private banking system including a foreign exchange market in the host country, together with no transfer restrictions, there is no reason why the host country should pay in any other currency than its own. This is so, even if the local currency is not fully convertible, so long as private foreign exchange enterprises in fact operate in the host country.

Amongst the range of options in this regard are, therefore, IIA provisions that guarantee the requirement that compensation be paid in a freely convertible currency, without specifying the currency and leaving room for the possibility that the compensation could be in the local currency.

4. Transferability of compensation paid

The same factors mentioned above as in relation to the time frame within which payment is made are relevant here. Flexibility could be attained by allowing exceptions to the general "freely transferable requirement for budgetary or foreign exchange limitations, subject to adequate protection of the investor for loss of interest and currency rate fluctuations that the delay in repatriation of funds might entail.

C. Drafting models

Besides the important issues of determining what constitutes a compensable taking in the first place, and then the standard of compensation, the other issues relating to requirements for a taking to be lawful — including the need for a public purpose, non-discrimination and the due process of law of course — remain relevant to the drafting of a clause on taking. In that regard, three main models of takings clauses that attempt to cover the principal relevant issues can be identified. Clearly there will be variations of these three models, depending on the particular circumstances of the States negotiating an IIA.

1. High protection for investment model

If a host country believes that foreign investment is important to fuel its economic development it will provide wide guarantees against takings in the hope that such guarantees will result in greater flows of foreign investment. States adopting such a view would subscribe to a model of IIA that will provide wide protection against takings. The typical clause on takings in the high protection for investment model includes the generally accepted requirements for a taking to be lawful:

- public purpose;
- non-discrimination;
- due process of law; and
- payment of compensation.

In addition, such a model has the following features:

- a taking is broadly defined, so as to cover all kinds of assets, as well as direct and indirect takings;
- it includes stringent requirements for payment of compensation. The payment should be prompt, adequate and effective, that is to say, compensation which must be:
  (a) paid without delay;
  (b) equivalent to the fair market value immediately before the expropriation; and
  (c) fully realizable and freely transferable.

The protective effect of this model is enhanced if, in the other provisions of the IIA:

- the initial definition of investment is very wide, covering not only physical property but intangible property like patents and know-how, shares in stocks of companies, contracts like concession agreements in the natural resources sector and the new type of "property" brought about by regulatory controls -- licences and permits necessary for a foreign investor to operate;
- dispute resolution provisions giving standing to a foreign investor to invoke arbitration against a host country at its option.

Such a model restricts sovereign control over foreign investment to the extent that a host State not only is not free to take at will property belonging to foreign investors but must conform to severe limitations on its ability to regulate foreign investments. As such this model forms the basis of IIAs that seek primarily to further the goal of protection of investments. The dispute resolution provision in this model might be of concern to the host country as it could transfer issues relating to the legitimacy of regulatory measures to a non-national tribunal. Home countries may prefer this model to the extent that it provides increased protection to their foreign investors, although they may be concerned that their own regulatory measures may be contested before international tribunals and their courts are bypassed. From the point of view of developing countries following this model, the limitation of sovereign powers is balanced by the conviction that a liberal regime would result in economic development.

2. High host country discretion model

The typical clause in this model would also include certain general requirements for a taking to be lawful:

- public purpose;
- non-discrimination;
- due process of law; and
- payment of compensation.

At the same time, in this model, such requirements would be accompanied by the following features of the takings clause:

- a narrow definition of the assets to which the takings clause applies;
- a narrow definition of takings, limiting them to the classical cases of expropriation or nationalization, not including measures of equivalent effect;
- provision for fair and just (or appropriate) compensation, as provided for in national law, with the host country having the right to determine the quantum of compensation and the terms of payment;

Here the host country provides the basic minimum protection against a taking. This will also mean that in the other provisions of the IIA:

- the definition of investment is relatively narrow, referring to specific physical assets and other interests in the IIA; and
- the dispute settlement provision provides for arbitration but permits it only if there is a specific arbitration provision in the contract; inter-State arbitration on investment issues is possible only after exhaustion of local remedies by the investor.

The high host country discretion model least restricts sovereign control over foreign investment. The model does not give any more protection than is given by existing customary international law. Some may even argue that customary international law gives a higher standard of protection than this model. This model presupposes that the regulatory authorities charged with screening and approving of investments function in an effective manner and avoid excessive interference with the operation of the enterprises involved.

3. Intermediate model

This model contains the basic features found in both the other models, that is to say:

- public purpose;
- non-discrimination;
- due process of law; and
- payment of compensation.

In addition, this model may contain some or a combination of the other features that distinguish "high protection" and "high host country discretion" models. A major difference could be that the definition of "investment" is qualified by a clause to the effect that only "approved investments" or investments made "in conformity with the laws and regulations of the host country" are covered by the agreement's protection provisions. The former formulation implies that a screening mechanism is in operation, while the latter formulation gives full scope for regulatory intervention in foreign investments and makes it clear that regulatory takings are not to be protected by the expropriation provisions of the treaty. Thus, the expropriation provision could be as extensive as that in the high protection for investment model, but the provision protects only approved investments or investments made according to a host country's laws and regulations. Compulsory arbitration between host State and investor, at the instance of the investor, may also be permitted, since this possibility would only apply to investments that have been specifically approved or made consistently with host country laws.

The important characteristic of such a model is that it is a dynamic one. It allows for a type of governance that would permit foreign investment to meet the desired development goals of a host country. At the same time, it provides safeguards to a foreign investor against unjustified takings. The model leaves the State with the power to legislate in order to protect the environment, human rights or other desirable public policy goals. At the same time, it ensures that a foreign investor, being desirous of protection against State interference, keeps to the goals behind the regulatory legislation of the host country. It may be relevant in this model to strengthen further the exclusion of regulatory takings by making specific exclusionary provisions relating to the environment and other areas such as tax, exchange controls and punitive measures.

***

The issue of taking of property has historically been a contentious one. At present, however, the prospect of mass nationalizations or expropriations, characteristic of many investment disputes during the twentieth century, has greatly diminished. As knowledge of the benefits of foreign direct investment has increased, and fear of exploitation by foreign investors has declined, the need for the extreme sanction of nationalization or expropriation has lessened. However, the function of IIAs is to protect investors and investments against the economic neutralization of their assets. Provisions on takings will therefore continue to be included, even if the need for them seems, at times, remote; and a number of policy options remain particularly relevant to the issue of the standard of compensation.

At the same time, the chapter also emphasizes that, within this changed situation, the major issues surrounding takings have also shifted. In particular, the need remains, in cases that fall short of outright takings, to reconcile the preservation of assets belonging to foreign investors and the role of the State as a regulator of the economy, even in a more liberal economic environment. In this context the chapter has also outlined options for effecting a balancing of such interests.

Notes

1 Much of the arbitral jurisprudence on creeping expropriations was produced by the Iran-United States Claims Tribunal, where the issue of creeping expropriation has been considered in several cases. They are surveyed in Aldrich, 1996.

2 There were State interferences in alien property before. But, the history of large-scale takings begins only with the socialist takings and takings in pursuance of social reform. For analyses of takings that have occurred, see Burton and Inoue, 1984. The authors found 1,857 cases of takings between 1960 and 1977.

3 The standard is referred to as the "Hull standard" or formula as it was contained in a letter of the then Secretary of State, Cordell Hull to the Government of Mexico (Kunz, 1940).

4 One of the most discussed in the literature is the Indonesian nationalization of Dutch property. It attracted much litigation in Europe. See for example McNair, 1959; Domke, 1960; Sornarajah, 1986b.

5 The doctrine began life in the form of economic self-determination in a General Assembly resolution in 1952 (res. 626 (VII) 21, December 1952); see Hyde, 1956, p. 854. The early resolutions linked self-determination with permanent sovereignty over natural resources (see res. 1314 (XIII) 1958). The resolution that had unanimous support was resolution 1803 (XVII) of 14 December 1962. It had no negative votes as it represented a compromise between the different views of States. While the doctrine was recognized and appropriate compensation was to be paid in the event of nationalization, thus representing a victory for the position of the developing countries, the resolution required that "foreign investment agreements freely entered into by or between sovereign States shall be observed in good faith", thereby securing the interests of the developed countries (Schwebel, 1963, pp. 463-469).

6 The resolution on a New International Economic Order was passed by the Sixth Special Session of the General Assembly; res. 3201 (S-VI) 1974. The Charter of Economic Rights and Duties of States which is contained in General Assembly res. 3281 (XXIX) 1974 had, in its article 2(2)(c), the controversial proposition that issues of compensation should be settled by national courts only. This was in fact an assertion of the Calvo doctrine. (The "Calvo doctrine" denotes the idea that foreign investors are, or ought to be, required to settle their foreign investment disputes exclusively in the courts of the host State.) France, Germany, Japan, United Kingdom and the United States refused to accept this provision. Later resolutions retreated from this position.

7 The Libyan nationalizations of United States oil companies in 1973 are the last major example. They resulted in leading arbitral decisions on the subject: BP v. Libya, 1973; Texaco v. Libya, 1973; and Liamco v. Libya, 1977.

8 The possibility of large-scale nationalizations recurring is contemplated in the literature; see Penrose, et al., 1992.

9 On "tolerable" takings, see Higgins, 1982.

10 For further discussion of the dispute, see Zedalis, 1996; Graham, 1998; and Soloway, 1999.

11 For example, the Russian nationalizations after the October Revolution.

12 For example, the Chilean nationalization of its copper industry; or the Iranian nationalization of its oil industry.

13 The *Restatement of the Law: The Foreign Relations Law of the United States* points out in its commentary that, for these purposes, "...public purpose is broad and not subject to effective reexamination by other states" (American Law Institute, 1987, p. 200). The European Court of Human Rights, considering the issue of taking in violation of the right to property under the first protocol of the European Convention on Human Rights, has held that it will "respect a national legislature's judgement as to what is in the public interest ... unless that judgement is manifestly without reasonable foundation" (James v. United Kingdom, 1986, p. 123).

14 The consequence of an illegal taking is that reparation will not be confined to the making good of the loss alone but additional factors such as loss of future earnings could be taken into account in calculating the damages owed to a foreign investor (BP v. Libya, 1973).

15 For example, an earlier Chinese position of an absence of a requirement to compensate has changed; China has recognized an obligation to compensate in several bilateral investment treaties, and its present position is to accept that compensation should follow takings of foreign property, though the exact standard of compensation is left in doubt (Chew, 1994).

16 The last part of the requirement creates a significant interaction with the issue of funds transfer. See further section III below.

17 There is no standard definition of "appropriate compensation"; see Sornarajah, 1994.

18 For an overview of the issue of compensation, see UNCTAD, 1998a, pp. 67-71.

19 A study of takings in the context of domestic law that adverts to the difficulty of distinguishing between different types of takings is contained in Epstein, 1985; a recent survey of the law on takings in the United States is contained in Alexander, 1996. Because of the increasing prevalence of regulatory takings in the international sphere, there would be a tendency to transfer arguments in the domestic sphere into the international sphere.

20 There is further authority for this category of non-compensable regulatory takings. The *Restatement of the Law: The Foreign Relations Law of the United States* recognizes this category: "A state is not responsible for loss of property or for other economic disadvantage resulting from bona fide general taxation, regulation, forfeiture for crime, or other action of the kind that is commonly accepted as within the police power of states..." (American Law Institute, 1987, p. 201).

21 There is rich case law on whether regulatory takings are compensable and the basis on which such compensation, if any, should be assessed. See Mellacher v. Austria, 1990; Fredin v. Sweden, 1991; further see Jacobs and White, 1996. For a problem concerning regulatory takings, see Mobil Oil v. New Zealand, 1989.

22 For these arguments, see Graham, 1998.

23 There is reference to the due process requirement in the judgment of the International Court of Justice in the ELSI Case, 1989, at para. 128, where the Court said that "...a wilful disregard of due process of law, an act which shocks, or at least surprises, a sense of juridical propriety" will amount to a denial of justice. There is also reference to a pre-taking due process requirement in Amco v. Indonesia, 1992. This requirement was based on the view that due process is a general principle of international law. A contrary view expressed is that the authority for such a proposition was not adequately canvassed in the award (Sornarajah, 1995b).

24 For a comprehensive study on modern BITs, see UNCTAD, 1998a.

25 For example, article 5 of the United Kingdom model BIT (1991) reads : "Investments of nationals or companies of either Contracting Party shall not be nationalised, expropriated or subjected to measures having effect equivalent to nationalisation or expropriation...." (UNCTAD, 1996a, vol. III, p. 188). (Unless otherwise noted, the texts of the BITs mentioned in this study may be found in the collection of BITs maintained by the International Centre for Settlement of Investment Disputes (ICSID) (ICSID, 1970—), and at www.unctad.org/iia. Similarly, unless otherwise noted, all instruments cited herein may be found in UNCTAD, 1996a and 2000.)

26 In developed systems, ownership is regarded as a bundle of rights a person has against others. These ideas have been developed more fully in the context of United States constitutional law on taking of private property (Michelman, 1967; Epstein, 1985).

27 See Vandevelde, 1992, appendix A-1 for the full text of the model BIT; the United States-Zaire BIT (1984) also contains this provision.

28 See for example, Council of Canadians, "Under the MAI it would be considered a form of expropriation if the federal government or a province moves to enact new laws to protect the enviornment, wilderness, species or natural resource prodution" (Council of Canadians, 1998, p. 1).

29 "Subject to the requirement that such measures are not applied in a manner which would constitute a means of arbitrary or unjustifiable discrimination between countries where the same conditions prevail, or a disguised restriction on international trade, nothing in this Agreement shall be construed to prevent the adoption or enforcement by any contracting party of measures: ... (b) necessary to protect human, animal or plant life or health ... (g) relating to the conservation of exhaustible natural resources if such measures are made effective in conjunction with restrictions on domestic production or consumption." ... (United Nations, 1950, p. 262).

30 "Nothing in this Chapter shall be construed to prevent a Contracting Party from adopting, maintaining or enforcing any measure otherwise consistent with this Chapter that it considers appropriate to ensure that investment activity in its territory is undertaken in a manner sensitive to environmental concerns" (UNCTAD, 1996a, vol. III, p. 81).

31 In the broader context of an Expert Group Meeting of the UNCTAD Commission on Investment, Technology and Related Financial Issues, dealing with international investment agreements, the Agreed Conclusions noted similarly: "that flexibility, including with regard to a Government's normal ability to regulate, can be reflected, *inter alia,* in the objectives, content, implementation and structure of IIAs" (UNCTAD, 1999b, p.2).

32 The possibility of such a review is raised in Mobil Oil v. New Zealand, 1989.

33 NAFTA specifically excludes environmental measures from the scope of the taking provisions. But, the issue arises as to whether environmental

regulation is the only sphere of regulation that should be excluded.

34 In a few cases (Brazil-Venezuela (1995), Ecuador-Paraguay (1994), Peru-Paraguay (1994) BITs) the more general expression "just compensation" is used. In most cases however, in relation to the value of the expropriated investment, the terms "market value", "fair market value", or "genuine value" immediately before the expropriatory action was taken or became known, is stipulated.

35 For an interpretation of the provision in the Energy Charter Treaty, see Norton, 1996 and Sornarajah, 1996.

36 The increasing usage of the Hull standard may not be conclusive for, despite such use in many other instruments, some arbitral tribunals have regarded the standard in treaties covering disputes before them as indicating a mere starting point for the calculation of the compensation that is finally to be awarded. In the Shahin Shane Ebrahimi Claim, a dispute covered by a Friendship, Commerce and Navigation treaty using the Hull standard, Judge Gaetano Arangio-Ruiz concluded that considering the scholarly opinions, arbitral practice and tribunal precedents, once full value of the property has been properly evaluated, the compensation to be awarded must be appropriate to reflect the pertinent facts and the circumstances of each case (Shahin Shane Ebrahimi v. Iran, 1995).

37 The use of regulatory measures on environmental grounds is subject to review as the Ethyl case shows.

38 This was an objection raised against the MAI by environmental groups.

39 The authority supporting this view is canvassed in Sornarajah, 1994.

40 See for example, the CARICOM Guidelines for use in the Negotiation of Bilateral Treaties.

41 The International Court of Justice, considering a Friendship, Commerce and Navigation treaty, held in the ELSI case that the rule on the exhaustion of local remedies must be deemed as incorporated in the treaty even in the absence of any specific reference to it in the treaty.

42 AAPL v. Sri Lanka, 1990.

Chapter 9. Transfer of Funds*

Executive summary

By establishing a host country's obligation to permit the payment, conversion and repatriation of amounts relating to an investment, a transfer provision ensures that, at the end of the day, a foreign investor will be able to enjoy the financial benefits of a successful investment. While all of the existing multilateral agreements that liberalize and protect investment contain transfer provisions, the features of these provisions vary, depending on the overall purpose of the agreement and the scope of the other obligations that the agreement establishes. For example, the Articles of Agreement of the International Monetary Fund (the Fund's Articles) establish a general prohibition on the imposition of restrictions on payments and transfers for current international transactions. While this obligation protects the free transferability of income derived from an investment, it does not cover the transfer of the proceeds of liquidation. In contrast, the Organisation for Economic Co-operation and Development' s (OECD) Code of Liberalisation of Capital Movements requires the free transfer of all amounts relating to international investments, including investments made by a non-resident in the host country, and investments made by the host country's residents abroad.

Notwithstanding these variations, all of the principal multilateral agreements permit countries to impose restrictions on transfers in circumstances where a member is confronted with a balance-of-payments crisis. However, they require that these restrictions be temporary and applied in a manner that does not discriminate among the other signatories to the agreement. These "balance-of-payments derogation" provisions reflect a recognition that, while restrictions on transfers will generally not be the preferred means of addressing balance-of-payments crises, in certain circumstances they may be necessary.

In addition to these multilateral agreements, a number of regional and bilateral investment agreements have, as their primary purpose, the protection of existing foreign investment. The transfer obligations under these agreements are comprehensive and, in many cases, detailed. With certain notable exceptions (such as the North American Free Trade Agreement (NAFTA)), most of these agreements do not, however, allow for the imposition of restrictions on transfers for balance-of-payments reasons.

The absence of balance-of-payments derogation provisions in most bilateral and regional agreements raises the question of whether such provisions are, in fact, entirely inconsistent with the principle of investor protection, which is the overarching objective of many of these agreements. In that context, the chapter discusses the various disadvantages of restrictions, including their lack of effectiveness over the long term and the negative impact they can have on a country's future access to capital markets. However, it concludes that, in certain circumstances, countries may need to rely on restrictions as a complement to their own adjustment efforts and external financial assistance. The inclusion of a balance-of-payments derogation provision in the draft text of the OECD's Multilateral Agreement on Investment (MAI) -- generally regarded as a draft agreement that establishes a high standard of investment protection -- demonstrates the degree of consensus that has been achieved with respect to this issue.

Introduction

Given their economic significance, the features of provisions dealing with the transfer of funds are the subject of considerable scrutiny when an international investment agreement (IIA) is negotiated or interpreted. From the perspective of a foreign investor, an investment can hardly be considered protected unless the host country has committed itself to permit the payment, conversion and repatriation of amounts relating to the investment in question. In the light of the importance of transfer obligations to foreign investors, a country wishing to attract investment stands therefore to benefit from the inclusion of a comprehensive and sufficiently detailed transfer provision. But a host country may also seek qualifications, the most important of which relates perhaps to the ability of the country to impose

* The chapter was written in 2000 by Sean Hagan, Assistant General Counsel, International Monetary Fund (IMF). The final version has benefited from comments received from Gerald Helleiner, Robert Ley and Antonio Parra. The opinions expressed are those of the author and do not necessarily reflect the views of the IMF or

restrictions on transfers in response to balance-of-payments crises.

This chapter discusses the treatment of transfers under existing international agreements and, in that context, identifies issues that are of particular relevance in the consideration of IIAs. As will be seen, this analysis will often transcend the developing/ developed country dichotomy. For example, given the growing importance and volatility of international capital movements, developed countries cannot be considered immune to severe balance-of-payments crises, as has been borne out by the experience of the past several years. While the imposition of exchange restrictions may normally not be the preferred response to such a crisis, a country facing a sudden and severe depletion of foreign exchange reserves arising from massive capital outflows cannot rule out the possibility of imposing such restrictions for a temporary period while corrective economic policies take hold. Any IIA therefore needs to address this contingency, irrespective of the stage of development of its signatories.

The chapter is organized as follows. Section I identifies the key issues that arise in the design of a transfer provision. Section II analyses the treatment of transfers under existing international agreements. While the first part of this section discusses the treatment of transfers under existing multilateral agreements, the second part analyses the transfer provisions of those bilateral and regional agreements whose primary purpose is that of protecting existing investment and, in some cases, admitting new investment. Drawing on the comparative analysis set forth in section II, section III identifies the important relationship between transfer provisions and the other provisions of international agreements. Finally, section IV analyses the most important economic policy issues that need to be addressed when considering the design of a transfer provision, namely the existence and scope of a derogation provision that, among other things, allows a country to impose restrictions when confronted with a balance-of-payments crisis.

Section I
Explanation of the Issue

As noted in the Introduction, the primary purpose of a transfer provision is to set forth a host country's obligation to permit the payment, conversion and repatriation of the funds that relate to an investment. The key issues that arise in the design of a transfer provision can be divided into two categories. The first category relates to the scope of the general obligation undertaken by the host country; this category includes issues relating to the types of transfers that are covered by the transfer provision and the nature of the obligation that applies to these transfers. The second category relates to the principal exceptions and qualifications to this general obligation, the most important of which relate to a derogation for economic reasons.

A. Scope of the general obligation

1. Types of transfers covered

The types of transfers protected under an agreement largely depend on the type of investments covered and the nature of the obligations that apply to these investments.

With respect to the different types of investments, if an agreement only covers *inward* investment (i.e. investment made in the host country by investors of foreign countries), the transfers covered typically include funds that are needed to make the initial investment by the foreign investor and the proceeds of any such investments, including profits and the proceeds of any sale or transfer. These are the types of transfers that are of primary importance in most bilateral and regional investment agreements. However, if an agreement also covers outward investment (i.e. investment made in other countries by the nationals or residents of the home country), it typically also covers funds needed by such nationals to make such outward investment. As will be discussed in this chapter, the requirement to allow for outward transfers by both foreign investors and the country's own investors (which is provided for in some multilateral agreements) can have important foreign exchange implications for the host country.

Regarding the nature of the obligations that apply to these investments, differences in this area have an important impact on the scope of the transfers covered. For example, if an agreement covers the admission of a *new* investment (which is not the case with most bilateral agreements), the transfers protected typically include inward transfers needed to make the initial investment. In addition, a key question is the extent to which the agreement establishes obligations regarding the treatment of *existing* investments. For example, while the OECD Capital Movements Code[1] establishes obligations regarding the ability of a foreign investor to liquidate an investment, many bilateral and regional agreements also establish obligations regarding the way a host country treats an investment prior to liquidation. Thus, for example, where an agreement requires compensation for destruction of an investment as a result of civil strife, such compensation would be covered by the transfer provision.

2. Nature of the obligations

The obligation that applies to transfers is normally of an absolute rather than of a relative nature. This distinguishes it from the national treatment obligation that normally applies to the admission and treatment of investment. Specifically, while the latter obligation ensures that foreign investors are treated no less favourably than a host country's own nationals, the transfer obligation may actually provide the foreign investor with preferential treatment, as is the case with other investment protection obligations (e.g. expropriation).

With respect to the various elements of the obligation, the transfer obligation requires the elimination of restrictions not only on the ability of an investor to receive and repatriate amounts relating to investments, but also on the ability of the investor to convert the currency prior to repatriation. Key issues in this area relate to the type of foreign currency that the investor is entitled to convert into and the applicable rate of exchange.

B. Exceptions

Perhaps the most critical issue that arises in the design of a transfer provision in IIAs is whether or not a qualification to the general obligation described above needs to be made that effectively excuses the host country from performing its obligations on the basis of its economic circumstances. While multilateral agreements generally provide for such a derogation, most regional and bilateral agreements do not, out of a concern that these qualifications would undermine the principle of investor protection, which is the overriding objective of most of these agreements.

The principal economic derogation provisions can be divided into two categories. The first sets forth the conditions under which a host country can impose *new* restrictions on a temporary basis for reasons relating to balance of payments and macroeconomic management ("temporary economic derogation"). The second category permits the host country to maintain *existing* restrictions that would otherwise not be permitted, on the grounds that the economy of the host country is not yet in a position to eliminate these restrictions ("transitional provisions").

1. Temporary derogation

Any discussion of the merits of a temporary derogation provision must begin with an analysis of the economic costs and benefits of liberalization. Over the years, the global economy has benefited from the global transfers of savings that have been associated with the growth of international investment flows. For economic policy makers, however, the expansion of international investment has presented new challenges. The volatility of certain types of capital flows, in particular, can be disruptive in a number of respects. Large surges of *capital outflows* can exacerbate a country's balance-of-payments problems by making it more difficult for the country to implement adjustment policies that are designed to correct the underlying problem. Surges in *capital inflows* can also complicate the tasks of policy makers, particularly where the inflows are of a short-term nature.

In circumstances in which a country that has eliminated restrictions on a broad range of investments is confronted with the type of crises discussed above, the extent to which restrictions on transfers can play a constructive role in the resolution of these crises is limited for a number of reasons. First, one of the dangers of such restrictions could be that a country facing a crisis may rely upon them as a substitute for policy adjustments, which will often be necessary in the light of the new external environment. Second, the imposition of restrictions by a country that has benefited from access to international capital markets may jeopardize such access in the future or, at a minimum, make it more expensive. Moreover, there is a risk that it may have contagion effects in other emerging markets and contribute to an intensification of a crisis. Third, when restrictions are imposed in an economy that has grown accustomed to the free movement of capital and where, accordingly, capital markets are relatively well developed, controls will have limited effectiveness, since they will quickly be circumvented through sophisticated techniques of financial engineering.

Nevertheless, there may be circumstances where the temporary reliance on restrictions may be necessary. As will be discussed in this chapter, the resolution of balance-of-payments problems normally requires both the implementation of appropriate adjustment policies and external financing. However, there may be situations in which, for example, outflows are so large that the extent of adjustment required and the magnitude of the official financing needed far outstrip both the adjustment capacity of the country and the amount of external financing that can be obtained. In these circumstances, and as evidenced in most multilateral agreements, there may be a need to impose restrictions on a temporary basis while economic adjustment efforts take hold.

Given the limited -- but important -- role that restrictions on transfers may play, care must be taken to ensure that any temporary derogation provision carefully circumscribes the conditions under which new restrictions may be imposed. Most derogation provisions contain some mechanism to ensure that the restrictions are of a temporary basis and also require that restrictions be of a nondiscriminatory nature. As will be discussed, whether restrictions may be permitted to apply to certain transfers but not to others raises a number of complex issues, given the fact that, in the midst of a crisis, a country may not have the capacity to make such distinctions.

2. Transitional provisions

The temporary derogation issues discussed above are of particular relevance for countries that have already liberalized foreign investment but need to maintain adequate flexibility regarding the temporary reimposition of restrictions in times of a balance-of-payments or macroeconomic crisis. However, multilateral agreements also contain provisions that allow a host country to maintain restrictions that are in place upon its accession to an agreement. These provisions are normally designed to address situations in which a host country's economy may not yet be prepared for full liberalization and where the continued maintenance of restrictions may, in fact, contribute to macroeconomic and balance-of-payments stability.

In the light of the purpose of these provisions, one of the critical questions is whether the protection provided by such provisions should, in fact, be transitional. In other words, should a country be required to phase out these restrictions once the economic weaknesses that justified them disappear? As will be seen, multilateral agreements differ in this regard.

Section II
Stocktaking and Analysis

A. Multilateral agreements

1. The Articles of Agreement of the International Monetary Fund

The Articles of Agreement of the International Monetary Fund (the "Fund") (IMF, 1976) constitute an international treaty and the Fund's charter. As will be seen, while the obligations established under the Fund's Articles serve to liberalize investment flows in a number of important respects, it is not an international investment agreement as such.

Although the Fund's Articles enumerate a number of purposes for the Fund, two of them are of particular relevance for this chapter:

- The establishment of a multilateral system of payments in respect of current transactions between members of the Fund and in the elimination of exchange restrictions which hamper the growth of world trade (Article I(iv)).
- The provision of financial assistance to Fund members so as to enable them to resolve balance-of-payments crises without resorting to measures destructive of national or international prosperity (Article I(v)).

These two purposes should be viewed as self-supporting. Specifically, by providing financial support to a member that is adopting appropriate measures to resolve its balance-of-payments problems, the Fund reduces the need for the member to rely on exchange restrictions as a means of responding to the crisis in question. Indeed, as will be discussed, the relationship between external financial support and exchange restrictions is a key issue when considering the design of a transfer provision within IIAs.

To enable the Fund to achieve the purpose of establishing a multilateral system of current payments, the Articles establish obligations that must be observed by all Fund members, while also providing for specific exceptions to these obligations. The most relevant of these obligations and exceptions are described below.

a. Restrictions

Under Article VIII, Section 2(a), of the Fund's Articles, members may not, absent Fund approval, "impose restrictions on the making" of payments and transfers for current international transactions (IMF, 1976). For purposes of understanding the extent to which this obligation serves to protect transfers relating to foreign investments, the following observations may be made with respect to its meaning. "

- "*Current*". As defined in the Articles, payments arising from "current" transactions include not only payments relating to trade and services but also a number of investment-related payments. Specifically, they include: all income arising from investments, including interest on loans and other debt instruments, net of any income tax that may be levied by the country from which the payment is to be made; and a "moderate amount" for amortization of the principal of loans (or other debt instruments) or for the "depreciation of direct investments" (Article XXX(d)) (IMF, 1976). Accordingly, investment-related payments that fall outside the Fund's definition of current payments (and, therefore, are not subject to a member's obligations) include payments arising from the liquidation of either the original capital or any capital appreciation. Indeed, Article VI, Section 3, of the Articles specifically provides that members are free to impose restrictions on capital transfers.
- "*International transactions*". The meaning of the term "international transactions" derives from the Fund's mandate regarding the balance of payments of its members. Since the transactions that affect a member's balance of payments are normally those entered into between residents and non-residents, it is these transactions that are treated as "international" for purposes of this obligation. Since the foreign affiliate of a foreign investor is considered a resident of the host country where it is incorporated, this definition has important implications with respect to the degree of investment protection that the Funds Articles provide. Specifically, transactions between a foreign affiliate and other companies located in the host country (and any payments arising from these transactions) would constitute transactions between two residents and, therefore, would not be considered "international" within the meaning of this provision. However, the repatriation of profits by the foreign affiliate to its non-resident parent firms would be "international" within the meaning of the Fund's Articles.
- "*The making of payments and transfers*". By covering the "making of payments and transfers" relating to current international transactions, this obligation embraces two different circumstances. First, members are not permitted to restrict a resident from making a current "payment" to a non-resident. Second, in circumstances where this payment is made within the jurisdiction of the resident, the member may not restrict the non-resident from making a "transfer" of the proceeds of this payment from the jurisdiction in question. It is important to note, however, that in both of these cases the obligation only extends to *outward* payments and transfers relating to investments. Since this provision applies to the "making" -- but not the "receipt-- of current payments and transfers, members are free to restrict their residents from receiving payments and transfers from non-residents. Accordingly, while this provision protects the ability of a non-resident to repatriate certain proceeds of an investment, it does not ensure that the non-resident can execute payments and transfers associated with the making of investments, i.e. it does not liberalize *inward* payments and transfers associated with the making of new investments.
- "*Restriction*". The type of international current payments and transfers covered by this provision having been identified, the final issue relates to the nature of the obligation that extends to these payments. The key principles may be summarized as follows.
  First, any governmental action, whether of a formal or informal nature, that impedes the making of current international payments and transfers constitutes a restriction. Thus, even if payments and transfers are permitted, a governmental measure gives rise to a restriction if it increases their cost or subjects them to an unreasonable burden or delay.

  Second, limitations on the ability of a resident or non-resident, as the case may be, to purchase foreign exchange for the purpose of making the payments or transfers in question constitute a restriction. For this purpose, the type of foreign exchange that must be made available has generally been understood as including either the currency of the non-resident or a currency that the non-resident can readily convert into its own currency.

Third, limitations imposed on the ability of residents to enter into underlying current transactions generally do not constitute restrictions. Thus, for example, a member is free under the Articles to impose restrictions on the making of imports. Moreover, if it does impose such a prohibition, it may also restrict the making of any payments and transfers associated with the import since the Articles do not require members to permit payments and transfers associated with illegal transactions. The application of the above principle has the consequence that, as a general rule, a member wishing to restrict the availability of foreign exchange for balance-of-payments reasons may do so under the Articles as long as the restriction is imposed on the underlying transaction rather than the payment and transfer. Accordingly, it has been the *nature* of the measure (i.e. whether it is a trade measure, which limits the underlying transaction, or an exchange measure, which limits payment or transfer) rather than the *purpose* or the *effect of the measure* that is determinative.

Fourth, the concept of a restriction requires the imposition of a governmental measure upon a third party. Thus, if a Government defaults on its own external obligations (e.g. it fails to make interest payments on a loan to which it is a party), this action is considered proprietary rather than governmental in nature and, therefore, does not give rise to a restriction.

b. Multiple currency practices

Under Article VIII, Section 3, of the Articles (IMF, 1976), members are prohibited engaging in "multiple currency practices". This obligation provides an important form of investment protection in that it generally provides that the rate at which a resident and a non-resident purchase foreign exchange when making a payment or transfer may not, as a result of governmental action, deviate significantly from any market rate that prevails in the country in question.[2] However, members obligations regarding multiple currency practices under the Fund's Articles are limited in at least two important respects.

First, as noted above, the Articles provide that members may impose restrictions on capital transfers. In the light of this provision, members have been permitted to impose official rates for foreign exchange transactions that are associated with capital payments and transfers. Thus, applying the definition of "current payments" contained in the Articles, while the authorities would be precluded from establishing a special exchange rate for the repatriation of profits, they would be free to impose a special rate for the repatriation of the original capital or capital appreciation.

Second, members are only precluded from establishing a special rate for certain current payments in circumstances in which the exchange rate for other current payments is, in fact, a legal rate. The authorities are not required to ensure that the exchange rate offered corresponds to an illegal black market rate. Accordingly, if the authorities establish an official exchange rate that is required to be utilized for exchange transactions associated with all current payments and transfers, that rate will not give rise to a multiple currency practice even if the official rate is not determined by market forces.

c. Transitional arrangements

When the Articles of Agreement entered into force in 1944, most of the original members were not in a position to adhere to the above obligations because of severe weaknesses in their balance of payments. For example, the Exchange Control Act of the United Kingdom, enacted in 1948, imposed comprehensive controls on current international payments and transfers. So as to enable the Fund to be an organization of broad membership, the drafters of the Articles provided for transitional arrangements that enabled members to "maintain and adapt to changing circumstances" exchange restrictions and multiple currency practices in existence at the time of membership that would otherwise be subject to the Fund's jurisdiction (Article XIV, Section 2) (IMF, 1976). It was only in the late 1950s and early 1960s that most of the Fund's original European members were in a position to eliminate measures that were protected by these transitional provisions. The process of liberalization has quickened over the past ten years for all other members: of the Fund's 182 members, only 34 continue to maintain restrictions under the transitional arrangements.

It should be noted that the transitional provisions differ in important respects from the "standstill" of "grandfather" provisions that are often found in other multilateral agreements. For example, the obligation does not require a strict standstill since the relevant provision allows the member to "adapt to changing circumstances" restrictions that were in place when it became a member. This provision has been interpreted as allowing a member to relax, intensify or vary a restriction that it already applies to payments and transfers of a particular current international transaction. The imposition of a restriction on previously unrestricted payments and transfers would not be an "adaptation" and would therefore not be protected by the transitional provisions.

In a different respect, however, the Fund's transitional provisions are less generous than the typical standstill or grandfather provision. Specifically, the period of time during which a member may avail itself of these arrangements is not open-ended: Article XIV gives the Fund the authority under exceptional circumstances to make representations to a member that conditions are favourable for the general or partial abandonment of restrictions that have been protected by these provisions. Given the purpose of the transitional arrangements, discussed above, conditions would be favourable when the Fund is of the view that the member's balance of payments is sufficiently strong that continued reliance on the restrictions is no longer justified. [3]

d. Temporary balance-of-payments derogation and financial assistance

The second principal exception to the general obligations described above is the provision of the Fund's Articles that permits members to impose new restrictions with the prior approval of the Fund. The criteria for approval are not set forth in the Articles themselves. Rather, as in many other instances, the criteria have been developed through the adoption of "approval policies" by the Fund's Executive Board. Under the Fund's principal approval policy, exchange measures that have been imposed for balance-of-payments reasons will be approved if they are temporary and do not discriminate among Fund members. The requirement that the measure be temporary (approval is normally granted for up to a one-year period) is designed to ensure that members do not rely on exchange restrictions as the principal means of addressing balance-of-payments difficulties. Rather, if the problem is not one that will automatically correct itself within a short period of time, members are expected to introduce the necessary macroeconomic, exchange rate or structural adjustment policies that will address the underlying causes of the difficulties. However, since such policy measures may take some time to take hold, it is recognized that reliance on exchange restrictions may be necessary for an interim period. Regarding the criterion of non-discrimination, this is dictated by the mandate of the Fund to promote a multilateral -- rather than regional or bilateral -- system of payments and transfers.

Perhaps the design of the Fund's approval policy can be best understood in the context of the policies it applies regarding the use of its financial resources. As noted earlier, the Fund's financial assistance enables members to reduce their reliance on exchange restrictions. It does so in two ways. First, the Funds resources normally support an economic adjustment programme that is designed to address a balance of payments problem. Second, the foreign exchange provided by the Fund can assist members in dealing with their external problems, either by reducing the size of the balance of payments deficit or by building up the member's foreign exchange reserves, or both. Although the amount of assistance actually provided by the Fund may be relatively modest in comparison with the members needs, the fact that the Fund is supporting an economic adjustment programme is intended to "catalyse" financial assistance from other sources. In some cases, however, the size of the problem is such that the combination of external financing and strong economic adjustment may be insufficient to enable the member to weather the immediate crisis. It is in these circumstances that temporary exchange restrictions may be necessary. Unless these restrictions are imposed on a non-discriminatory basis, however, it may prove difficult for a member to receive adequate financing from a broad range of sources. As will be discussed in section IV, these principles are also of relevance when considering the possible design of a temporary balance-of-payments derogation provision under IIAs.

2. The OECD Liberalisation Codes

Under the OECD Convention, OECD members are required to "pursue their efforts to reduce or abolish obstacles to the exchange of goods and services and current payments and maintain and extend the liberalisation of capital movements" (Article 2(d)) (United Nations, 1960). As a means of implementing this obligation, the OECD has adopted two legally binding codes, the Code of Liberalisation of Capital Movements (the "Capital Movements Code") and the Code of Liberalisation of Current Invisible Operations (the "Current Invisibles Code") (collectively, the "OECD Codes"). Taken together, these two Codes serve to liberalize a broad range of transfers relating to investments. As a means of understanding the scope and nature of the Codes' transfer provisions, it is useful to take into consideration the following general features of these instruments.

From an investment perspective, the scope of coverage of the OECD Codes is considerably broader than that of the Fund's Articles and, in some respects, also broader than the typical foreign investment agreements discussed in the following subsection. First, the transfer provisions of these Codes, taken together, cover all proceeds of investments, unlike the Fund's Articles. Second, the Capital Movements Code requires the liberalization not only of the proceeds derived from an investment but also of the making of the investment itself. In this important respect, therefore, the Capital Movements Code serves not only to protect existing investment but also to liberalize the admission of new investment. As will be seen, many of the bilateral and regional agreements discussed in the next subsection do not cover admission. Third, the investment liberalization obligations of the Capital Movements Code extend not only to the ability of non-residents to make investments in a host country, but also to the ability of a country's residents to make investments abroad. In this latter respect, the liberalization obligations of the Capital Movements Code are also broader than the typical foreign investment agreements discussed in the next subsection, which only liberalize inward investments and, accordingly, allow host countries to retain control of the outward investments -- and related transfers -- of their own residents.

Notwithstanding the broad scope of the OECD Codes, they are limited in one important respect: as with the Funds Articles, they focus exclusively on transactions and transfers between residents and non-residents, i.e. cross-border investments. Thus, while the Capital Movements Code and the Current Invisibles Code serve to enable a non-resident to establish a foreign affiliate in a host country and also ensure that the profits and capital of the affiliate can be repatriated to the parent firm, they do not establish obligations regarding the ongoing treatment of foreign affiliates, i.e. they do not create what are generally referred to as "post-establishment" obligations, obligations that are considered a critical feature of investment protection. As will be discussed in the next subsection, such obligations are normally found in IIAs and also shape the design of the transfer obligations found in these agreements.

a. The scope of the transfer obligations

Given the comprehensive coverage of the OECD Codes, as described above, the scope of the transfer obligations in these agreements is very broad. These obligations may be summarized as follows:

- With respect to investments made by a non-resident, the Capital Movements Code requires that members permit the non-resident to transfer from abroad the funds that are necessary to make such investments. As noted in the previous section, the Fund has no jurisdiction over such inward transfers.
- Regarding the outward transfer of amounts that a non-resident has earned on investments made in the territory of a member, the Current Invisibles Code covers all income arising from such investments (including dividends, interest and royalties and fees arising from licensing agreements involving intellectual property rights). The Capital Movements Code covers all other amounts, i.e. the original capital, capital appreciation and all principals on loans.
- Since the Capital Movements Code liberalizes the making of investments by residents abroad, it requires that residents be permitted to transfer abroad the amounts that are necessary to make these investments. As noted above, such transfers are covered under neither the Fund's Articles nor the foreign investment agreements discussed in the next subsection.

Although the types of transfers that are covered under the OECD Codes are considerably broader than those covered by the Fund's Articles, the principles that apply for purposes of determining when a transfer is restricted are similar. Thus, as under the Fund's Articles, the obligation to permit a transfer includes the obligation to avoid restricting the availability of foreign exchange that is needed for that purpose. Moreover, even if the transfer is not prohibited, a restriction arises if a governmental measure causes unreasonable delay, costs or other constraints on the making of the transfer. As under the Fund's Articles, members may maintain controls for the purpose of verifying the authenticity of the transfer or to otherwise prevent the evasion of their laws and regulations. Thus, for example, members may require that transfers be made through authorized agents and may also impose withholding taxes on payments to non-residents. Finally, proprietary measures (i.e. limitations that the government imposes on transfers relating to its own transactions with non-residents) are excluded.

Although the OECD Codes cover both underlying transactions and associated transfers, the nature of the obligation that applies to these two different operations is not identical. With respect to underlying transactions, the principal obligation is essentially that of national treatment, i.e. while the authorities may restrict transactions, they may not do so if the restriction results in transactions among residents being treated more favourably than transactions between residents and non-residents. Thus, while the authorities may, for example, prohibit the issuance of commercial paper in the domestic market generally, they may not permit such issuances to resident purchasers but restrict sales to non-residents. In the case of transfers, however, such a relative standard is not applied. Even if the authorities impose an across-the-board limitation on the availability of foreign exchange that serves to restrict all types of transfers (whether made by residents or non-residents), this non-discriminatory exchange restriction still gives rise to a restriction on transfers to the extent that it actually limits, for example, the transfer of the proceeds of a non-resident's investment abroad.

b. Reservations

Similar to the approach followed under the Fund's Articles, the OECD Codes permit members to maintain restrictions, including restrictions on transfers, that were in existence when the country became a member of the OECD. Such restrictions are grandfathered through "reservations" that are lodged by the country upon membership. These reservations are subject to periodic "peer reviews" which are designed to promote their progressive elimination. After a country's admission to the OECD, new restrictions on most transactions and transfers may only be imposed in certain circumstances (discussed below). However, restrictions on certain transactions (and their related transfers) may be imposed at any time through the lodging of reservations. These latter transactions are currently limited to financial operations that are considered short-term in nature, including money market and foreign exchange operations, negotiable instruments and non-securitized claims and financial (non-trade-related) credits. The generous treatment of these transactions is attributable to their volatility and, accordingly, their potentially adverse impact on the macroeconomic and balance-of-payments stability of OECD members.

c. Temporary derogation

As noted above, new restrictions may only be imposed on most items in specified circumstances. Consistent with the policies developed by the Fund under its Articles, the OECD Codes provide that members may impose restrictions "If the overall balance of payments of a Member develops adversely at a rate and in circumstances, including the state of its monetary reserves, which it considers serious" (Article 7(c) of both of the OECD Codes) (UNCTAD, 1996a, vol. II). However, unlike under the Fund's Articles, restrictions do not require approval by the relevant organ (in this case the Council) before they are imposed. Rather, the OECD Codes provide that a member may take the initiative to introduce restrictions for balance of payments reasons, but that they must be promptly notified to the OECD, where they are examined. Continued maintenance of these restrictions requires a decision by the Council based on an evaluation of whether the member is taking adequate economic adjustment measures to address the underlying balance-of-payments problems.

Another important difference between the temporary derogation provisions under the Capital Movements Code and the approval policies of the Fund is that derogation under the Capital Movements Code also applies to inward transfers. As noted above, unlike the Fund's Articles, the Capital Movements Code requires that a member permit non-residents to make investments in its territory and, in that context, to permit all inward transfers associated with such investments. As has been recently demonstrated, in some cases large surges of capital inflows may complicate the task of exchange rate and macroeconomic management. In particular, if a member's exchange rate and interest rates are broadly appropriate, a large surge in capital inflows may involve disruptive adjustments that are inconsistent with longer-term stability. In these circumstances, restrictions on capital inflows may be justified. The ability of countries to impose restrictions on such capital inflows is covered under Article 7(b) of the Capital Movements Code, which allows for the temporary imposition of controls if the liberalized operation in question results "in serious economic and financial disturbance" not caused by balance-of-payment difficulties (UNCTAD, 1996a, vol. II).

Because the Capital Movements Code, unlike the Fund's Articles, covers both underlying transactions and associated transfers, the scope of the temporary derogation is not limited to restrictions imposed on transfers; it also covers measures that restrict the underlying transactions. The coverage of underlying transactions is particularly necessary in the case of inflows, where restrictions are normally imposed at that level. For example, if the authorities wish to restrict inflows arising from the acquisition by non-residents of domestic securities, they will normally restrict the actual purchase of the securities (the underlying transaction). They will generally avoid permitting the non-resident to enter into the transaction but then restrict the ability of the non-resident to transfer the funds necessary to make the payment.

As in the case of the Fund's Articles, the OECD Codes provide that any restrictions imposed by a member be applied in a manner that does not discriminate among other signatories to the treaty. It should also be noted that the OECD Codes provide that "Members shall endeavour to extend the measures of liberalization to all members of the International Monetary Fund" (Article 1(d) of both the OECD Codes) (UNCTAD, 1996a, vol. II).

3. The General Agreement on Trade in Services

The General Agreement on Trade in Services (GATS), which entered into force on 1 January 1995, is a multilateral agreement that focuses on the liberalization of trade in services. Nonetheless, given the broad range of services covered under the agreement, it has the potential to liberalize investments and, in that context, also serves to protect the transfers associated with such investments.

More specifically, one of the "modes of delivery" covered under the GATS is the cross-border supply of services. Since the GATS covers financial services, liberalizing the supply of cross-border services liberalizes investments in those cases in which the investment is an integral part of the service itself. For example, to the extent that a member restricts its residents from borrowing from non-residents, a member's commitment to allow banks of other members to provide cross-border lending services to its nationals would require a relaxation of this restriction. Similarly, if a member also makes a commitment to permit non-resident banks to provide cross-border deposit services, such a commitment would require the member to liberalize restrictions it may have imposed on the ability of residents to hold accounts abroad. In these respects, the GATS serves to liberalize the making of both inward and outward investments.

A second "mode of delivery" covered under the GATS involves the "establishment" of a commercial presence by a foreign service provider in the territory of a member. Accordingly, the liberalization of this mode of delivery could serve to liberalize restrictions on the making of foreign direct investment (FDI). In view of the broad scope of services covered under the GATS, this could be of considerable significance, given that approximately 60 per cent of FDI flows are estimated to be in service industries (UNCTAD, 1999a).

Notwithstanding the breadth of its coverage, the structure of the GATS is such that the extent to which investments and their associated transfers are actually covered depends on the outcome of negotiations. The GATS is a framework agreement, attached to which are schedules negotiated individually with each member and setting forth the extent to which it commits itself to liberalizing a particular industry. Under this approach, a member only makes a commitment with respect to a service industry if it has made a "specific commitment" with respect to the industry in its schedule. This approach contrasts with that of the Fund and the OECD Codes, where members incur obligations with respect to all transactions and payments and transfers covered, but find protection through transitional arrangements (in the case of the Fund) or reservations (in the case of the OECD Codes).

a. Scope of payments and transfers covered

The GATS provides that, subject to important exceptions (discussed below), members must refrain from imposing restrictions on international payments and transfers associated with the current and capital transactions that are covered by the specific commitments made by that member. Given the coverage of the cross-border trade in services described in the previous section, this rule would serve, for example, to liberalize both the interest and principal portion of loan repayments made by a consumer to a foreign bank. Moreover, both inward and outward transfers relating to the service committed are covered where the cross-border movement of capital is an essential part of the service itself. Thus, a member must permit the non-resident bank to disburse the amount it has agreed to lend to a local consumer; the consumer must also be free to transfer the amounts it wishes to deposit with a non-resident bank.

Regarding commitments made with respect to trade in services through establishment, the member is obligated to allow all related inflows of capital into its territory that are necessary to enable the enterprise to establish a commercial presence. However, regarding the treatment of outflows arising from the activities (e.g. repatriation of profits or liquidation of the enterprise), a determination of whether a restriction on such inflows would be precluded depends on whether they would be considered "inconsistent" with the commercial presence commitment. Although there has been no formal interpretation of this provision in that context, there do not appear to have been such restrictions on scheduled commitments to date.

b. Derogation and relationship with the Fund's Articles

When the GATS was negotiated, it was recognized that any derogation for restrictions imposed on payments and transfers would need to take into consideration members rights and obligations under the Fund's Articles so as to ensure that the two treaties did not give rise to conflicting rights and obligations for a very similar (i.e. almost universal) membership. As a consequence, the relevant provisions of the GATS (Articles XI and XII) respect both the Fund's jurisdiction and its mandate in the area of balance of payments assessment. Although these provisions have never been the subject of authoritative interpretation, their substance can be summarized as follows.

First, regarding restrictions on current payments and transfers, Article XI of the GATS ensures that the exercise by a member of its rights under the Fund's Articles to impose or maintain such restrictions does not give rise to a breach of a members' obligations under the GATS. Thus, if a restriction has been temporarily approved by the Fund for balance of payments reasons, or is maintained under the Fund's transitional arrangements, the restriction is automatically consistent with the member s obligations under the GATS. Conversely, the GATS is precluded from permitting a signatory to impose a restriction on a current payment relating to a commitment under the GATS if such restriction is not consistent with the Fund's Articles because, for example, it has not been approved by the Fund.

Second, with respect to derogation for restrictions imposed on capital movements, the Fund plays a more limited role, reflecting the fact that the Fund does not have approval jurisdiction over restrictions on capital payments and transfers. With one exception, discussed below, derogation for such restrictions appears to be covered under Article XII of the GATS, which sets forth the conditions upon which a member may impose restrictions "in the event of serious balance of payments and external financial difficulties or threat thereof, " (UNCTAD, 1996a, vol. I). As can be seen from the text of Article XII, some of these conditions are similar to the approval criteria that are applied by the Fund and under the OECD Codes (e.g. non-discrimination and temporariness). The conditions set forth in the GATS are more numerous and detailed, however, and are clearly drafted to limit the possibility that this balance of payments derogation provision (which is designed to address a crisis in the entire economy) is used to justify restrictions that may, in fact, be imposed to protect a particular industry. Thus, while members may give priority to the supply of services that are more essential to their economic or development programmes, such restrictions are not adopted or maintained for the purpose of protecting a particular service industry.

Third, similar to the OECD Codes, but unlike the Fund's Articles, the GATS does not require that restrictions be approved before they are introduced. Rather, when a member invokes Article XII as the basis for the imposition of a restriction, it is required to notify the General Council of the WTO and to "consult" with the Balance of Payments Restrictions Committee appointed by the Council so as to give this Committee the opportunity to determine whether -- and for how long -- the imposition of restrictions is justified under this provision. In that context, Article XII provides that, in such consultations, all statistical findings regarding a member's balance of payments position shall be accepted; conclusions made by the Committee are to be based on the Fund's assessment of the balance of payments and external financial situation of the member.

Finally, it is unclear from the text of Article XII whether a derogation is also intended to apply to restrictions on capital inflows; the resolution of this issue will need to await a formal interpretation of the provision. As noted in the discussion of the OECD Codes, restrictions on inflows are normally imposed on the underlying transaction rather than the payments and transfers associated with such transactions. Although Article XII is clearly broad enough to cover restrictions imposed on transactions and transfers, there has not been a formal interpretation as to whether the phrase "balance of payments and external financial difficulties" (UNCTAD, 1996a, vol. I) is broad enough to cover the type of macroeconomic difficulties that members experience with capital inflows.

B. Bilateral and regional investment agreements

1. General considerations

Although the transfer provisions of the agreements discussed in the previous section serve, to a greater or lesser extent, to protect investments, the primary purpose of these agreements is not the protection of investment. In contrast, investment protection is one of the central objectives (and, in some cases, the only objective) of bilateral and regional investment agreements.

As with the agreements reviewed in the previous section, the treatment of transfers under bilateral and regional investment agreements is shaped by the objectives of these agreements and, more specifically, by the other obligations that they establish. Thus, before analysing in detail the design of transfer provisions under these agreements, it is useful to highlight how the scope of these other obligations shapes the treatment of transfers.

First, these agreements normally require a host country to liberalize the full range of investments made by the treaty party's investors. However, they do not require the host country to liberalize international investments made by its own residents. Thus, these agreements serve to liberalize inward, but not outward, investments, in contrast to the OECD Codes, which liberalize both. Accordingly, they do not require the liberalization of transfers associated with such outward investments.

Second, the protection of investment provided by bilateral and regional investment agreements is not limited to the right of the investor to liquidate and repatriate the proceeds of the investment. Rather, such agreements typically establish a number of obligations regarding the manner in which a host country must treat the investment in question prior to such liquidation and outward transfer of the proceeds. Thus, while the manner in which a host country treats, for example, the operations of a foreign affiliate generally goes beyond the scope of the OECD Capital Movements Code, which focuses on cross-border investments (i.e. investments between residents and non-residents), the standard of such treatment is the very essence of bilateral and regional investment agreements. For this reason, the latter are viewed as a particularly effective instrument for the protection of FDI, i.e. investment that involves the establishment of a local presence by the investor. As will be discussed in greater detail below, the scope of the transfer provisions of most foreign investment protection agreements specifically takes into consideration the existence of a broad array of other investment protection obligations.

Third, as in the case of the OECD's Capital Movements Code, the nature of the transfer obligation needs to be distinguished from the general national treatment obligation that applies to the general treatment of investment. Specifically, while the latter obligation ensures that foreign investors are treated no less favourably than a host country's own nationals, the transfer obligation actually provides foreign investors with preferential treatment, as is the case with other investment protection obligations (e.g. expropriation, protection from strife).

Fourth, although the scope of investment protection provided under bilateral and regional investment agreements is of particular applicability to FDI (as noted above), the scope of investment covered under most of these agreements is not technically limited to this type of investment. For example, many bilateral investment treaties contain a very expansive, asset-based definition that would include all the types of cross-border investments that are covered by the OECD Capital Movements Code.

Fifth, while bilateral and regional investment agreements typically protect investments that have already been made, only some of them establish firm legal obligations with respect to the admission of new investment, as is provided for in the OECD Capital Movements Code and, to a lesser extent, in the GATS. Thus, as will be seen, not all the transfer provisions of such agreements specifically liberalize transfers that are necessary in order to make new investments.

2. The treatment of transfers

Although the overall treatment of transfers under bilateral and regional investment agreements is shaped by the general considerations discussed above, the specific design of these provisions varies from agreement to agreement. In certain respects, these differences reflect varying drafting approaches: while some provisions express the transfer obligation in general terms, others do so inconsiderable detail, with an illustrative list of the type of transfers that are covered and a carefully defined convertibility obligation. As will be seen, however, the variations may also be attributable to the fundamentally different bargains that have been struck by the signatories to the respective agreements. In that regard, the key issues that arise when negotiating an investment agreement are the types of transfers to be covered; the scope of the convertibility requirement that applies to these transfers; and the nature of the limitations, exceptions and derogations that apply to the transfer obligation. Each of these issues will be discussed in turn.

a. Types of transfers protected

The types of transfers protected under the transfer provisions normally contained in bilateral and regional investment agreements may be described as falling into three general categories.

The **first category** consists of the *outward transfer of amounts derived from or associated with protected investments.* Assuming that the investment in question is covered under the agreement (some investment may be specifically excluded), a very comprehensive transfer provision will normally include:

(i) "returns" on investments, which are normally defined as including all profits, dividends, interest, capital gains, royalty payments (arising from the licensing of intellectual property rights), management, technical assistance or other fees or returns in kind;

(ii) proceeds from the sale or liquidation of all or any part of the investment;

(iii) payments under a contract including a loan agreement (including payments arising from cross-border credits) ; and

(iv) earnings and other remuneration of personnel engaged from abroad in connection with an investment.

Several comparative observations can be made with respect to the above category of transfers. First, it includes all transfers that are covered under the OECD Codes, i.e. all capital and income derived from an international investment. Second, like the Fund's Articles, it includes earnings of foreign personnel that are employed in connection with an investment. Although such transfers are clearly not "derived" from an investment (hence the use of the term "associated with an investment") their coverage is generally considered an important feature of investment protection: in the absence of such coverage, a foreign investor may not be able to attract foreign labour to be employed in connection with its investment, which could undermine its viability. Third, by including transfers "in kind", the comprehensive transfer provisions of bilateral and regional investment agreements are broader than both the OECD Codes and the Funds Articles, which only include monetary payments.

Finally, it should be noted that, as under the Fund's Articles and the OECD Codes, a protected transfer may involve a single operation, in which, for example, the borrower situated in the host country wishes to make an international payment of interest to the foreign investor located abroad. As noted in the previous section, such an operation is described as a "payment" under the Fund's Articles. Alternatively, a foreign investor may first receive the interest payment from the borrower in the territory of the host country and then transfer the proceeds of the payment outside the territory. The subsequent repatriation of the proceeds by the foreign investor in this case is described as a "transfer" under the Fund's Articles.

The **second category** of transfer covered under transfer provisions consists of the *outward transfer of amounts arising from the host country's performance of other investor protection obligations under an agreement.* The transfers falling within this category are outward transfers of payments that the Government of a host country is required to make to the foreign investor pursuant to other investment protection provisions contained in an agreement. If the investment agreement is comprehensive, these payment obligations consist of the following, none of which are provided for in the OECD Codes or the Fund's Articles:

(i) payments received as compensation for a host country's expropriation of the investment;
(ii) payments received as compensation for losses suffered by an investor as result of an armed conflict or civil disturbance ("protection from strife");
(iii) payments arising from the settlement of disputes; and
(iv) payments of contractual debts owed by the Government of a host country to the foreign investor.

The **third category** of transfer consists of the *inward transfer of amounts to be invested by a foreign investor*. There are, in fact, two types of inward transfers that fall into this category. The first type are those that are made for purposes of making a new investment; the second type are those that are made to develop or maintain an existing investment (e.g. increased capitalization of a foreign affiliate). Almost all foreign investment agreements cover the latter type, on the basis that the right of an investor to provide additional infusions of capital into an existing investment is an important attribute of investment protection. However, only those agreements that require the host country to admit new investments include the first type of transfers in the transfer provisions. Most bilateral investment agreements do not include such admission obligations.

b. Convertibility requirement

Under the Fund's Articles and the other agreements discussed in the previous sections, an international transfer is considered restricted if the authorities of a host country restrict either the availability or the use of the foreign exchange that is required to make the transfer in question. Although this principle is incorporated into the transfer provisions of most investment agreements, the specific nature of the obligation tends to vary. There are two issues of particular importance in this regard.

The first issue relates to the *type of foreign currency that must be made available* for the transfer to take place. Although investment agreements generally attempt to incorporate the principle that the currency to be made available must be "freely convertible" or "freely usable", many of them fail to define what these terms actually mean. Into what currencies should foreign investors be able to convert the foreign currency that is being made available to them? Where must a foreign currency be used in order for it to qualify as a "freely usable" currency and what type of transactions are relevant for making this assessment? In order to avoid uncertainty in this regard, some agreements using the above terms have defined them by relying on the definition of "freely usable currency" contained in the Fund's Articles, namely a currency that the Fund determines is, in fact, widely used to make payments for international transactions and is widely traded in the principal exchange markets (Article XXX(f)) (IMF, 1976). Exercising the authority provided under the Articles, the Fund's Executive Board has identified the currencies that, until otherwise decided, meet this definition: the United States dollar, the Japanese yen, the British pound and the euro. Following the Fund even further in this regard, some investment agreements have actually identified these currencies as being freely usable currencies for purposes of their transfer provisions. While this approach creates a degree of certainty, it may also be too rigid given the fact that the Fund's definition of freely usable currency is not a permanent one. For this reason, the most appropriate approach may be to provide that transfers may be made available in a freely usable currency "as defined by the Fund from time to time".[4]

The second issue that arises in this area relates to the *exchange rate at which the foreign currency is to be made available at the time of the transfer*. Although most investment agreements apply the general rule that the foreign investor should be able to purchase the necessary foreign currency at the market rate of exchange prevailing on the date of the transfer, many of them do not address the contingency that, in some cases, there may not be such a market rate. Specifically, in circumstances in which a country relies on exchange restrictions, it is possible that the Government mandates a rate of exchange for all foreign exchange transactions. Such official rates often overvalue the local currency for the purpose of subsidizing payments for certain imports and are accompanied by a surrender requirement which will force exporters to sell the foreign exchange proceeds of exports to the Government at this overvalued rate. To take into account these circumstances, some investment agreements provide that, in circumstances in which a market rate does not exist, the foreign currency must be made available at the rate prescribed under the applicable regulations in force. Going one step further, the most sophisticated transfer provisions provide for the contingency that the exchange control regulations may set forth multiple rates of exchange, with the applicable rate depending on the type of transaction involved. In these circumstances, an agreement can provide that the foreign investor receives the most favourable rate.

c. *Limitations, exceptions and temporary derogation*

As discussed below, the exceptions and limitations to a host country's obligations regarding transfers under an investment agreement are generally consistent with the exceptions and limitations that exist under the multilateral agreements discussed in the previous section. In most cases, however, the scope for temporary derogation is considerably narrower.

(i) Taxes

The Fund's Articles preclude a member from imposing restrictions on international payments of "net income". As discussed earlier, this has been interpreted as permitting income taxes arising from a payment to be deducted before the payment is effected. The transfer provisions of most investment agreements provide for a similar limitation, the difference being that these agreements also allow for the deduction of capital gains taxes, reflecting the fact that, unlike the Fund's Articles, these agreements cover both capital and current payments.

(ii) Reporting and screening

The obligation to permit transfers does not require a host country to abandon measures that enable it to ensure compliance with those laws and regulations that are otherwise consistent with the host country's obligations under an investment agreement. For example, as discussed earlier, the transfer obligations of investment agreements do not preclude a host country from maintaining restrictions on the ability of its own residents to make investments abroad. Thus, when a resident seeks to purchase foreign exchange, the host country may request written evidence of the purpose of the payment before providing the foreign exchange so as to assure itself that the foreign exchange is not, in fact, going to be transferred by the resident for the purpose of making its own outward investment (e.g. the making of a deposit in an offshore bank account). While these and other types of reporting and screening requirements are generally permitted under investment agreements, comprehensive agreements also contain language to the effect that such reporting requirement should not give rise to "undue delays" in the making of transfers and should otherwise not be used by a host country as a means of avoiding the transfer obligations set forth in the agreement.

(iii) Adjudicatory proceedings and enforcement of creditor rights

The transfer provisions of many investment agreements provide that transfers may be restricted to satisfy judgements arising from adjudicatory proceedings in a host country or as a means of protecting creditor rights. What type of situations are these exceptions to the general transfer obligation trying to address? With respect to adjudicatory proceedings, a foreign investor may become the defendant in civil, administrative or criminal proceedings within a host country and, if these proceedings result in the issuance of a monetary judgement against the investor, the proceeds of amounts derived from the foreign investor's investments may be attached and, in those circumstances, the investor would be restricted from making the necessary transfer. In this situation, the above-described exception enables the host country to effect such an attachment without violating its transfer obligation.

Regarding the protection of creditor rights, the primary purpose of this second exception is to ensure that the operation of a host country's insolvency laws does not give rise to a breach of the host country's transfer obligations. For example, if a host country's liquidation or reorganization laws are activated with respect to a local company (as a result of a petition filed by a creditor or by the debtor), all assets of the company may be frozen, including amounts that the company may owe to a foreign investor (e.g. payment on a loan). Not only do the insolvency laws restrict the making of such payments, but also they may give the administrator of the insolvency proceedings the authority to nullify earlier payments that may have been made to the extent that, for example, such payments are considered to have unfairly benefited the recipient at the expense of other creditors.

The above exceptions are often qualified by a proviso that states that these measures must result from the non-discriminatory application of the law. In some respects, this proviso may be considered unnecessary since restrictions that are exempted under this provision must still satisfy the general obligation of national treatment that would still apply to these restrictions.

(iv) Temporary derogation

A notable feature of the agreements discussed in the previous section is that they all contain provisions that specifically allow for the imposition of restrictions on transfers in circumstances in which a host country is confronted with a balance-of-payments crisis. In contrast, most bilateral and regional investment agreements do not contain such provisions. For example, only a very small proportion of the nearly 1,800 bilateral investment treaties in existence specifically allow for temporary balance-of-payments derogation. Of the regional agreements in force, only the North American Free Trade Agreement (NAFTA) contains such a provision. The general absence of temporary balance of payments derogation provisions may be attributable to the general perception that these agreements are generally designed to protect FDI. Since this type of investment is generally not volatile, signatories may therefore not view temporary balance of payments derogation as being a necessary safeguard. Two observations can be made regarding this explanation. First, irrespective of the primary purpose of bilateral investment agreements, their definition of investment is typically broad enough to include investments other than FDI. Second, as will be discussed in the next section, when a country is forced to impose restrictions in the context of a balance of payments crisis, it will find it difficult to exclude -- at least at the outset of the crisis -- any form of transfer from the restrictions, including transfers associated with inward FDI.

The balance-of-payments derogation provision of NAFTA is relatively elaborate and, when compared with the provisions contained in the agreements discussed in the previous section, is noteworthy in at least two respects.

First, the type of treatment provided under the derogation provision of NAFTA varies according to the type of transfer restricted. Specifically, if the restriction is imposed on transfers relating to *financial services* (which, as noted in the discussion of the GATS, can give rise to investments), the restriction must be temporary, non-discriminatory and consistent with the Fund's Articles. Accordingly, if it falls under the Fund's jurisdiction but is not approved by the Fund, it will not qualify for derogation. However, if it is imposed on transfers relating to any other type of investment covered under NAFTA, it only qualifies for derogation if it satisfies additional criteria. The more generous treatment afforded to restrictions imposed on transfers relating to financial services is attributed to the fact that the financial flows associated with such services (e.g. inter bank deposits), being more volatile, may be more destabilizing from a balance of payments perspective. Accordingly, it was considered appropriate for the signatories to have greater latitude regarding their ability to impose restrictions on these measures.

Second, in one important sense, the degree to which NAFTA relies on the Fund is broader than either the GATS or the OECD. Specifically, if a restriction meets the criteria described in the previous paragraph, NAFTA also requires that the host country "enter into good faith consultations with the IMF on economic adjustment measures to address the fundamental underlying economic problems causing the difficulties; and adopt or maintain economic policies consistent with such consultations" (Article 2104(2)(b) and (c) (NAFTA, 1993). Since consultations regarding an adjustment programme normally take place in the context of a member's request for the use of the Fund's financial resources, NAFTA relies not only on the Fund's jurisdiction but also its financial powers. The Fund's role in this area will be discussed further in the next section.

Section III Interrelationships

As has been demonstrated in the previous section, the treatment of transfers under existing international agreements is largely shaped by the overall objectives of an agreement and, more specifically, by the design of the other obligations that it establishes. As a means of distilling these relationships, it is possible to identify two categories of provisions that directly affect the treatment of transfers: provisions that specify the type of underlying investments that are to be covered under the agreement; and provisions that specify the nature of the obligations that will apply to these investments.

A. Types of investments

As has been illustrated by the review of the relevant agreements in the previous section, an investment agreement protects a transfer if the transfer in question is associated with an underlying investment that is covered under the agreement. Thus, for example, if the types of investment that are required to be admitted and/or protected only include direct investment, transfers relating to other types of investment do not benefit from protection under a transfer provision.

The scope of the transfer provision also depends on whether an agreement covers both inward and outward investment. One of the important features of the bilateral and regional investment agreements discussed in the previous section is that they only establish obligations with respect to a host country's treatment of *foreign* investors (i.e. investors of other signatories). In contrast to the OECD Capital Movements Code, they do not set forth obligations with respect to a country's treatment of its own investors. From a developing country perspective, this limitation can be an important one. Specifically, one of the principal reasons why many developing countries enter into investment agreements is to obtain the foreign exchange that accompanies such investment. Since a commitment that permits foreign investors to repatriate the proceeds of their investments is a necessary means of attracting such investment, a host country is normally willing to relax its exchange controls to the extent necessary to achieve this purpose. However, the very shortage of foreign currency that makes foreign investment attractive also makes it difficult for a host country to allow its own residents to invest their foreign exchange abroad. Not surprisingly, restrictions on the ability of residents to purchase foreign exchange in connection with overseas investment (e.g. the establishment of foreign bank accounts, the purchase of foreign securities, the acquisition of foreign real estate) are often the last element of exchange control to be removed by a country as its overall balance of payments position improves.

The relationship between the types of underlying investments that are covered and the scope of the derogation provision that allows for the imposition of restrictions on transfers is more complicated. For example, with respect to temporary restrictions imposed for balance of payments reasons, it may seem reasonable to assume that the need for derogation increases to the extent that the underlying investment covered is broad enough to include, for example, short-term, cross-border flows (e.g. interbank credits), which are the most volatile and, therefore, the most problematic in terms of macroeconomic and balance of payments management. But experience demonstrates that a country facing a balance-of-payments crisis may find it difficult to exclude certain types of transfers (including transfers relating to FDI) from the scope of its exchange control regime. Accordingly, the relationship between temporary balance of payments derogation and the scope of investments covered may, in fact, be somewhat limited. This issue is discussed in greater depth in the following section.

B. Nature of obligations

The design of the transfer obligation depends on the nature and scope of the obligations that apply to the types of investment that are covered. Two issues are of particular importance in this regard.

First, does an agreement establish firm obligations with respect to the admission of investments? As discussed in the previous section, while the OECD Capital Movements Code contains such obligations, most bilateral and regional investment agreements do not. If an admission obligation is to be established, the transfer obligation would need to encompass the inward transfer of amounts that are needed to make the initial investment. While it is true that countries wishing to restrict the inflow of capital normally impose the restriction at the level of the underlying transaction rather than transfers associated with these transactions, failure to cover inward transfers explicitly under an agreement could create the risk that a signatory may try to circumvent its admission obligation by imposing the control on the transfer rather than on the underlying transaction.

Second, does an agreement establish investment protection obligations other than the transfer obligation? The premise of the bilateral and regional investment agreements reviewed in section II is that a host country is only able to attract FDI if it also makes undertakings with respect to the treatment of this investment once it has been made. Thus, in addition to guaranteeing the free transfer of the proceeds of an investment, an agreement also, for example, typically provides for compensation following either expropriation or civil strife. Moreover, in some cases, an agreement establishes obligations regarding a host country's repayment of any debt that it may have contracted with a foreign creditor. Unlike the general national treatment obligation that also exists in investment agreements, these investment protection obligations (including the transfer provision) actually result in the foreign investor receiving more favourable treatment than a host country's own investor. If an investment agreement is to provide for such comprehensive investment protection, it is appropriate for the transfer provision to provide specifically for the free transfer of amounts that have been received as a result of a host country's performance of these investment protection obligations.

Section IV
The Design of a Transfer Provision: Key Economic Policy Issues

While there are a number of important decisions that need to be made when designing a transfer provision, the issue that has the greatest impact on the economic policy of a host country is the existence and scope of a provision that allows for derogation from the general transfer obligation. From the analysis contained in the previous sections, it is clear that bilateral and regional agreements establish a framework that places considerable emphasis on the protection of investment, particularly when compared with the multilateral agreements currently in existence. One of the key differences in this respect is the fact that, while the multilateral agreements discussed contain relatively comprehensive derogation provisions, most bilateral and regional agreements (with some important exceptions) do not contain such clauses. Does this signal that investor protection is incompatible with derogation?

This section of the chapter first discusses the merits of a temporary derogation clause, before making some observations regarding the possible need for some type of transitional arrangements for countries that are not yet in a position to liberalize all investments immediately, a need that is particularly relevant for developing countries. It then concludes with a brief discussion of the draft text of the MAI. As will be seen, the relevant provisions of the MAI text provide evidence of a growing recognition that investor protection and derogation are not mutually exclusive concepts.

A. Temporary derogation: a limited role for restrictions

When a country that has eliminated restrictions on a broad range of investments is confronted with a balance-of-payments crisis, to what extent can the reimposition of restrictions play a constructive role in the resolution of this crisis? Given the magnitude of the balance-of-payments crises that have faced both developed and developing countries over the past several years, the debate on the efficacy of controls has recently intensified. While an exhaustive analysis of the costs and benefits of restrictions is beyond the scope of this chapter, there are a number of considerations that are of particular relevance to the treatment of transfers under IIAs.

First, one of the biggest dangers of restrictions is that a country facing a crisis may rely upon them as a substitute for necessary policy adjustments. Even in circumstances where it has maintained appropriate macroeconomic policies, a country that is trying to weather a crisis arising from a large withdrawal of capital normally has no choice but to introduce corrective macroeconomic and, in some cases, structural policies in order to adapt itself to the new external environment. To the extent that the adoption of corrective polices is delayed by the reliance on restrictions, this delay can make the eventual adjustment more painful.

Second, the damage caused by the imposition of restrictions can be considerable. For a country that has benefited from access to capital markets, the imposition of restrictions may jeopardize such access in the future or, at a minimum, make it more expensive. This is particularly the case where restrictions impede the types of transfers that are normally covered under investment agreements, i.e. when they prevent residents from performing their contractual obligations to non-residents or when they prevent non-residents rom repatriating the proceeds of their investment. Moreover, such action may trigger a flight of residents' capital. Finally, investors may perceive such measures as a signal that other countries may also rely on controls as a means of dealing with difficulties and, as a result, the controls may have "contagion" effects, i.e. they may prompt foreign investors to withdraw their capital from other countries in the region or, more generally, from all developing countries.

Third, when restrictions are imposed in an economy that has grown accustomed to the free movement of capital and where, accordingly, capital markets are relatively well developed, controls are likely to have limited effectiveness. While, for an initial period, the restrictions may serve their purpose, over time their effectiveness is likely to erode as the private sector, through financial engineering techniques, discovers the means to circumvent them. This is particularly the case with restrictions on outflows.

Notwithstanding the above considerations, there are circumstances in which the temporary reliance on restrictions may be necessary. As noted earlier in this chapter, the resolution of balance of payments problems normally requires both the implementation of appropriate adjustment policies and external financing. In circumstances in which the crisis has undermined market confidence and, therefore, a country's access to capital markets, such financing is provided by the official sector, normally led by the Fund. Such financing is designed to tide the country over until corrective economic policies take hold and market confidence is restored. As has been recently demonstrated, however, this formula may not be sufficient in circumstances in which the outflows are so large that the extent of adjustment required and the magnitude of the official financing needed far outstrip both the adjustment capacity of the member and the amount of financing that can be provided by the Fund and other official creditors.

What choices are available in these circumstances? In many, but not all, cases the primary problem is the maturity structure of a country's short-term debt. In these circumstances, a country tries to convince creditors to maintain their exposure, e.g. by agreeing to roll over their credit lines. Another -- more difficult -- option is to persuade creditors to agree upon a restructuring that will result in longer maturities (coupled, perhaps, with a government guarantee). If such *ex ante* attempts to restructure are not successful, however, a country may have no choice but to impose restrictions as a component of its overall adjustment programme. A number of observers are of the view that, in these circumstances, a restructuring of external debt -- whether done on a voluntary or involuntary basis -- also has broader systemic benefits. Specifically, to the extent that a crisis has been precipitated by imprudent lending by foreign investors, forcing them to bear some of the burden in its resolution provides an important means of ensuring that they fully understand and measure the risks of their international investment decisions, thereby limiting imprudent lending in the future.

The considerations that are relevant for purposes of determining when restrictions may be necessary, as described above, also provide guidance as to how such controls should be designed and implemented. In this regard, several issues are of particular importance in the design of a temporary balance of payments derogation provision:

- Restrictions should be temporary. As discussed above, if a country is facing a crisis, the primary purpose of controls should be to give the country a breathing space until corrective policies take hold. Moreover, experience demonstrates that controls can become less effective the longer they are in place.
- Restrictions should be imposed on a non-discriminatory basis, as is required under all of the relevant multilateral agreements discussed earlier. As noted above, a critical feature of a country's strategy to resolve a balance of payments crisis is to mobilize external financing, both from the Fund and from other multilateral and bilateral creditors. Such a "burden sharing" strategy within the international community would be severely undermined if restrictions were imposed with respect to the investors of certain countries but not others.

The question of whether restrictions should differentiate between certain types of transfers raises a number of complex issues. Clearly, if an IIA only covers foreign investment, the imposition of controls that only apply to outward investments (and associated transfers) by residents would be beyond the scope of the framework and, therefore, would not require derogation. Moreover, as discussed earlier, such a limited application of restrictions would, from a policy perspective, limit the disruption of the country's access to financial markets that otherwise would arise from the imposition of restrictions on transfers relating to inward investment. But should restrictions only apply to transfers relating to certain types of foreign investment? For example, given the volatility of short-term investment (portfolio equity investment and short-term debt), there may be merit in trying to limit restrictions to transfers relating to such debt. IIAs could express such a "prioritization" in a number of different ways. First, as with outward investment made by residents, such investments could be excluded from the coverage of the framework altogether. Alternatively, while short-term investment could be included, the derogation provision could afford more generous treatment to controls on such transfers, as appears to be the case under NAFTA.

In considering this issue, it should be borne in mind that, in the midst of a crisis, countries often are not able to make distinctions as to which types of transfers are to be restricted. This is due in part to the fact that, if such an attempt is made, foreign investors operating in a well-developed financial market quickly find a means of taking advantage of these distinctions so as to circumvent the restrictions. For this reason, it may be necessary for the derogation provision of an IIA to apply the same standard for all restrictions that are covered under the agreement, but with the requirement (similar to the one found in the GATS) that the measures be no more restrictive of foreign investment than is necessary to address the crisis that required their imposition.

Regarding the possibility of excluding certain types of investment from the scope of an agreement (e.g. short-term debt), such an exclusion would not, in and of itself, obviate the need for a balance-of-payments derogation provision since, as noted above, a country responding to a sudden and massive outflow of capital may find it difficult to avoid imposing restrictions with respect to all transfers, at least for an initial period. It is notable that, under the OECD Capital Movements Code, the signatories of which are the world's most developed countries, the balance-of-payments derogation clause is applicable to all types of investment, including for example FDI. As will be noted below, while it may be appropriate for an IIA to make distinctions as to different types of investment, these distinctions may be more relevant to the pace at which a relatively restrictive economy should liberalize; they may be of less relevance when discussing how a relatively open economy should react to a balance-of-payments crisis.

What of the design of a temporary derogation provision to address macroeconomic problems caused by inflows rather than outflows? The imposition of restrictions on inflows would normally only be justified for macroeconomic reasons in circumstances where a sudden -- and potentially reversible -- surge in inflows threatens to disrupt macroeconomic and exchange rate policies that are broadly appropriate for the country in question over the medium term. However, to the extent that this surge of inflows is not temporary, this would normally signal that the resolution of the problem requires an adjustment of macroeconomic policies. For this reason, the criteria applicable to restrictions on outflows are also of relevance for restrictions on inflows, namely that they be temporary and non-discriminatory. It is important, however, to distinguish this analysis from that which addresses the question of when a country with a restrictive system should liberalize restrictions on inflows. This latter question, which is of critical importance, will now be addressed.

B. Transitional provisions

Issues relating to the need for, and design of, a temporary derogation are of primary relevance for a host country that has already liberalized foreign investment but needs to maintain adequate flexibility regarding the temporary reimposition of restrictions in times of balance of payments or macroeconomic crises. But what of the countries that have not yet liberalized their restrictions on foreign investments? Viewed from a balance of payments and macroeconomic perspective, what benefit, if any, is to be gained by the continued maintenance of a restrictive system and what implications would the maintenance of the system have for the design of any liberalization obligations under IIAs?

These are questions of critical importance for developing countries that are weighing the cost and benefits of eliminating restrictions on foreign investment. At the outset, it needs to be recognized that one of the biggest drawbacks to restrictions -- the extent to which they are effective -- is not as problematic in circumstances in which a host country has never liberalized foreign investment, particularly short-term investment. In these circumstances, financial markets are typically relatively undeveloped, and the problem of circumvention, which makes the reimposition of restrictions in a previously liberal market so difficult, is not as acute. While the continued maintenance of restrictions by relatively closed economies may involve costs in that they may deny the country the opportunity to utilize foreign savings as an engine of growth, they can be ineffective.

Even if effective, what role, if any, do they have in promoting macroeconomic and balance of payments stability? While the economic benefits of international investment for developing countries point to liberalization as an objective, recent international financial crises also serve to demonstrate that it is an objective that countries should not necessarily try to achieve overnight, or at least not until certain preconditions have been met. The precondition of macroeconomic stability is relatively undisputed: a liberalized system, in some respects, imposes greater demands on policy makers since it requires them to correct the financial imbalance that they were able to suppress for an extended period through reliance on restrictions. However, recent financial crises have also demonstrated that, if the regulation of a host country's financial sector is inadequate, the consequence of this inadequacy is exacerbated by liberalization and may precipitate large balance-of-payments crises. For example, in the absence of appropriate prudential regulations, financial institutions that are in a position to access international capital markets may take inappropriate risks, including the accumulation of a large volume of unhedged, short-term liabilities. The fact that the State normally provides the financial sector with some form of financial safety net can exacerbate this problem by creating "moral hazard": financial institutions may be encouraged to take even greater risks on the assumption that, if necessary, they will be "bailed out" by the State. When international market sentiment does begin to shift, experience demonstrates that those investors who were willing to extend large amounts of short-term credit to the banking system will be the first investors to "head for the exits" and withdraw their investments, often leaving the financial sector (and, as a consequence, the rest of the economy) in distress.

To address the issue of risk management that is magnified by the liberalization of investment, adequate prudential regulations need to be supplemented by other reforms. One of the reasons why capital flows give rise to crises is attributable to "asymmetries" in information, which may lead to imprudent lending in the first instance and a large, excessive and herd-like withdrawal in the second instance. For this reason, liberalization should be preceded by, or at least go hand in hand with, measures that serve to reduce these inefficiencies, including the introduction of adequate accounting, auditing and disclosure requirements in both the financial and corporate sector.

For all of the above reasons, in order to maximize the benefits of international investment and minimize the associated risks, it is critical that liberalization be appropriately "sequenced" with reforms in the financial system that serve to ensure that the risks incurred can be appropriately managed. Until such reforms have been put in place, restrictions on foreign investment, particularly short-term investment, can play a constructive role.

What implications does the above analysis have for the design of IIAs? On one level, the issue of "sequencing" liberalization is not directly applicable to the treatment of transfers. The restrictions that play the most important role in maintaining stability while the regulatory framework for the financial system is being developed are restrictions on inflows. And, as discussed earlier in the chapter, these are normally imposed at the level of the underlying transaction rather than the associated transfer. Indirectly, however, the treatment of these restrictions is of considerable relevance: to the extent that adequate safeguards are not put in place to guard against the incurring of unsustainable risks, any ensuing balance of payments crisis arising from a loss in market confidence raises the issue of the need for restrictions on outflows, which includes restrictions on transfers.

Given the fact that the most volatile type of foreign investment is of a short-term nature, one means of addressing the need for sequencing is to exclude such flows from the coverage of an IIA altogether, thus enabling signatories to maintain restrictions on the making of such investments for as long as they wish. Such an approach is complicated by the fact that, as a result of the development of financial engineering techniques, the distinction between short-term, medium-term and long-term debt is becoming increasingly blurred. Alternatively, while such investments would not be excluded, they could be protected by some form of transitional arrangements that would enable them to be maintained until a signatory has put in place alternative, non-restrictive means of limiting the risk of such investments, of the variety discussed above. The advantage of the latter approach is that it would avoid throwing the proverbial "baby out with the bath water". To the extent possible, therefore, IIAs should find a means of pacing the liberalization of these investments in line with the circumstances of each host country, while avoiding the risk of such flexibility being used as a means of unnecessarily delaying beneficial liberalization.

C. Investment protection and derogation in a multilateral context: the example of the MAI

The draft MAI serves to demonstrate the growing recognition that derogation -- or at least temporary derogation -- is neither inconsistent with the objective of investor protection nor an issue that is only of relevance to developing countries. One of the objectives of the negotiators of the MAI was to negotiate an agreement that establishes the highest standards of investor protection. In that regard, most bilateral agreements -- the provisions of which provided important precedents during the negotiations -- do not include balance-of-payments derogation provisions.

But it was precisely because the MAI was intended to be more than a bilateral investment treaty that the inclusion of a balance-of-payments derogation provision was eventually accepted in the text. Two considerations were of particular importance in that regard. The first may be described as a concern for "jurisdictional coherence". Although the text of the MAI was negotiated at the OECD, it was envisaged that developing countries would become signatories. In that context, it was recognized that a situation needed to be avoided in which two treaties with potentially the same universal membership contained provisions that could give rise to conflicting rights and obligations. The conflict could arise with the Fund's Articles because the Fund's jurisdiction includes many investment-related transfers, such as the repatriation of investment income. Thus, if the Fund were to approve a restriction imposed by a country on the repatriation of profits of an investment, would such approval exempt it from its obligations under the MAI? As noted in a previous section of this chapter, the drafters of the GATS effectively addressed this issue by specifically providing in that agreement that restrictions approved by the Fund would be consistent with a signatory's obligations under the GATS.

The second consideration related to the potential impact of unrestricted investment flows on a signatory's balance of payments, as discussed in detail above. In brief, while there was a general recognition that unrestricted capital flows can be very beneficial to individual countries and the world economy in general, the MAI negotiators also recognized that the volatility of these flows (many of which fall outside the Fund's jurisdiction) can also be detrimental to a country's balance-of-payments position. In these circumstances, it would be necessary to ensure that restrictions are applied in a non-discriminatory manner.

The above considerations ultimately shaped the design of the balance-of-payments derogation provision that is contained in the draft MAI. With respect to restrictions imposed by a signatory on transfers that fall within the Fund's jurisdiction, the MAI text provides that Fund approval renders such restrictions consistent with the signatories' obligations under the MAI. Interestingly, where the restrictions fall outside the Fund's jurisdiction, the Fund's determination that the measures satisfy the criteria set forth in the MAI (which include temporariness and non-discrimination) would have the same result. The prominent role of the Fund in the implementation of the derogation provisions reflects the fact that the Fund is charged with both assisting countries in the design of programmes that address balance-of-payments problems and providing the financial assistance that is necessary to support these programmes. As noted earlier, when a country faces a balance-of-payments crisis there is a very close relationship between issues relating to the need for restrictions, the degree of economic adjustment and the amount of external financing.

Notes

1 Unless otherwise noted, all instruments referred to here are contained in UNCTAD, 1996a or 2000.

2 Pursuant to a decision of the Fund's Executive Board, a multiple currency practice only arises if the action by a member or its fiscal agencies, in and of itself, gives rise to a spread of more than 2 per cent between the buying and selling rates for spot exchange transactions between the member's currency and any other member's currency (see Decision No. 6790-(81/43), adopted on 20 March 1981, as amended (IMF, 1999)).

3 It should be noted that the failure by a member to act upon such a representation by the Fund would not give rise to a breach of obligation under the Articles and, therefore, could not result in compulsory withdrawal from the Fund. However, the Articles specify that a member's failure to take such action can result in the Fund declaring the member ineligible to use the Fund's financial resources (Article XIV, Section 3).

4 While the transfer provisions of many investment agreements rely on the Fund's concept of freely usable currency, this concept is not, in fact, relied on by the Fund for the application of its own transfer provision. As was noted earlier, under the Articles the emphasis is on the non-resident's own currency; more specifically, a member imposes a restriction on a current international payment or transfer if it restricts the non-resident from transferring either its own currency or a currency that the non-resident can readily convert into its own currency. In contrast, the concept of freely usable is relied on by the Fund for other, unrelated purposes.

Chapter 10. Transparency*

Executive summary

The aim of this chapter is to examine how transparency issues have been addressed in international investment agreements (IIAs) and other relevant instruments dealing with international investment.

The chapter identifies some of the main issues that influence State and corporate approaches to the question of transparency in international investment relations (section I). First, it is necessary to identify the potential addressees of a transparency obligation. The chapter takes a novel approach and addresses the nature and extent of transparency obligations in IIAs and other international instruments as they apply to all three participants in the investment relationship – the home country, the host country and the foreign investor. In this respect, the addressees of transparency requirements depend on the objective and scope of the transparency provision in question and, more generally, on the nature of the agreement that contains the transparency provision.

Secondly, the content of the transparency obligation needs to be delimited. The key issue here concerns the degree of "intrusiveness" of transparency obligations, which in turn principally depends on the selection of items of information to be made public. A third key issue concerns the modalities employed to implement transparency, which may involve, for example, the exchange of information or the publication of relevant government measures. Further issues characterizing transparency provisions in IIAs concern the time limits for meeting transparency requirements and the exceptions to transparency obligations.

Section II reviews the various ways in which transparency requirements are addressed in IIAs, focussing on the key issues identified in section I. Section III highlights points of interaction between transparency, on the one hand, and other general issues addressed in IIAs (i.e. those covered in other chapters), on the other. Finally, in the conclusion, the chapter briefly examines the significance of different approaches to transparency for economic development in individual countries and considers the various options open to negotiators when drafting transparency provisions. The most basic choice is whether to include or to exclude provisions on this subject. Where the former choice is made, further alternatives exist as to how to deal with each of the issues identified in section I.

Introduction

The concept of transparency is closely associated with promotion and protection in the field of international investment. In the present context, transparency denotes a state of affairs in which the participants in the investment process are able to obtain sufficient information from each other in order to make informed decisions and meet obligations and commitments. As such, it may denote both an obligation and a requirement on the part of all participants in the investment process.

Although issues concerning transparency have long been of concern to States and transnational corporations (TNCs), they have often been addressed as matters of national law. Even today, this may still be true, as transparency questions arise in the context of the relationship between one foreign investor and one State, with the national legislation of the State being of particular relevance. In recent years, however, questions concerning transparency have also assumed prominence in a number of bilateral, regional and multilateral treaties. Transparency issues relevant to the investment process have also found a place in a variety of instruments of more general scope. Hence, the instruments to be considered in this chapter include treaties and other documents concerning for example illicit payments, environment and corporate social responsibility; however, these specific subjects are not reviewed in this chapter due to their coverage in other chapters in the present volumes.

Transparency provisions in an IIA are usually formulated in general terms imposing requirements on all parties to the agreement. However, such provisions have traditionally been viewed as imposing obligations on host countries alone, perhaps because host country measures are

---

* The chapter was prepared in 2003 by Federico Ortino on the basis of the conceptual approach set out in Sauvant, 2002. It benefited from a background paper prepared by Stephen C. Vasciannie. The final version reflects comments received from Joachim Karl, Peter Muchlinski and Christoph Schreuer.

usually viewed as one of the major determinants of foreign direct investment (FDI). Despite this perception, however – and if not expressly limited in this manner – general transparency provisions appear to impose obligations upon both the host country and the home country. This is so because home countries too, typically have measures in place that affect investment flows.

Similarly, the traditional application of the transparency concept can be extended to corporate entities – the third participant in the investment relationship. Although this issue has traditionally been dealt with under the heading of "disclosure", several examples exist in which "transparency" requirements have been imposed specifically on TNCs.

This is an area in which traditional interpretations of international legal obligations as well as the addressees of such obligations need to be examined with a view towards a more inclusive approach to transparency.[1] In particular, while the traditional approach in international law has been concerned primarily with inter-State relations, and has not sought to enunciate rules that are specifically addressed to, and are directly binding upon, individuals (including corporate entities), more recently there has been a discernable tendency for international law, and especially for treaty law, to set out rules that have a direct bearing on individuals and corporations. Given this development, and the increasing interest in corporate disclosure and accountability, there may be an increased belief that transparency obligations in IIAs should apply to corporate actors as well as to countries. Accordingly, this chapter will address the nature and extent of transparency obligations in IIAs as they apply to all three participants in the investment relationship – home country, host country and foreign investor.

A second key issue concerns the degree of intrusiveness of transparency obligations in IIAs, i.e., the impact that such obligations have on national policies. The degree of intrusiveness principally depends on the items of information, both of a governmental and corporate nature, that are to be made available (policies, laws, regulations, administrative decisions, etc., as well as corporate business information).

A third key issues relates to the modalities that may be employed in order to provide such information, which include, for example, the exchange of information, the publication as well as the notification of relevant measures. Further key issues relate to other variables that characterize transparency provisions. These include the time limits for meeting transparency obligations and the exceptions or safeguards to such obligations.

The main task of the chapter is to analyze and take stock of the various ways in which transparency requirements are addressed in IIAs, focussing on the key issues identified above. This exercise is ultimately aimed at an examination of the various options open to negotiators when drafting transparency provisions in IIAs and at a brief review of the significance of these options for economic development.

Section I
Explanation of the Issue

As a general term that is broadly synonymous with openness, transparency connotes the idea that any social entity should be prepared to subject its activities to (public) scrutiny and consideration.

The overriding aim of transparency in relation to FDI policy is to enhance the predictability and stability of the investment relationship and to provide a check against circumvention and evasion of obligations, by resort to covert or indirect means. Thus, transparency can serve to promote investment through the dissemination of information on support measures available from home countries, investment conditions and opportunities in host countries and through the creation of a climate of good governance, including, for example, a reduction of the likelihood of illicit payments in the investment process. In addition, transparency is important for treatment and protection as without it, these cannot be assessed. Transparency is also necessary for the monitoring of disciplines, restrictions, reserved areas, exceptions and the like, that are provided for in IIAs. Equally, the extension of transparency obligations to corporate disclosure can help to protect the interests of host countries and home countries, as well as other stakeholders. For instance, with regard to host countries, corporate disclosure may enhance a country's ability in the formulation and management of its policies in company, environmental and labour matters; with regard to home countries, corporate disclosure may facilitate *inter alia* the application of fiscal and competition laws. Finally, the need for transparency is a logical corollary to certain established assumptions about the legal knowledge of individuals affected by the law, in particular that ignorance of the law is no defence.

The issue of transparency, as developed in IIAs, concerns a number of specific matters. First, it is necessary to identify the potential addressees of the transparency obligation. As noted in the Introduction, these are not only host countries, but also home countries and investors. The review of practice set out in section II below examines the extent to which current agreements and other international instruments create obligations for each of these addressees. In this respect, the addressee of transparency requirements may depend on the objective and scope of a transparency provision and, more generally, on the nature of the agreement that contains the transparency provision.

In the area of international investment, typically, the need for transparency is viewed from the perspective of foreign investors. Thus emphasis is usually placed on the desire of foreign investors to have full access to a variety of information in a host country that may influence the terms and conditions under which the investor has to operate. At the same time, however, transparency issues may also be of particular concern to the host country in an investment relationship. At the broadest level of generality, the host country may wish to have access to information about foreign investors as part of its policy-making processes and for regulatory purposes. If the foreign investor is exempt from providing information on its operations to the host country, this will naturally not only undermine the capacity of the host country to assess the nature and value of the contribution being made by particular foreign investors, but also restrict its capacity to assess the appropriateness and effectiveness of its regulatory framework. Also, still at the level of generality, transparency questions may arise with respect to the home country of the foreign investor. The latter may wish to acquire information about the operations of the investor in other countries, both for taxation purposes and as a means of assessing whether the foreign investor is acting in accordance with the home country's legal rules and policies that have extraterritorial reach. Similarly, the host countries and the foreign investor may want to have access to information concerning home country measures designed to promote development oriented outward FDI (UNCTAD, 2003, chapter VI, section A).

Second, the content of transparency obligations needs to be delimited. Although the trend in investment relations is supportive of greater disclosure on the part of both governments and enterprises, there is the question of the degree of "intrusiveness" of such action, i.e. what, precisely, to make transparent. The scope of a transparency obligation is determined by the precise items of information to be made public by the relevant addressees. In relation to governmental information, the range of items includes, at the least intrusive level, general policies that may be of importance to investment. This is followed, in terms of increasing intrusiveness, by laws and regulations and administrative rulings and procedures. Specific administrative decisions pertaining to individual cases are still more intrusive as they concern directly identifiable applications of policies, laws and regulations to individual cases. The same applies to the information relating to a proposed law or regulation, which may be disclosed to afford interested parties the possibility to express their views on such a proposal before its final adoption. On the other hand, judicial proceedings in open court are subject to a general duty of reporting in an open society; thus, a duty to disclose their content may be relatively unintrusive, as it is part of a general commitment to the rule of law. An additional issue that arises in this connection concerns the cost of transparency, as it may impose a significant financial and administrative burden on developing countries, and least developed countries in particular.

In relation to corporate information, the range of items depends on a distinction between traditional disclosure for the purposes of the correct application of national company, fiscal and prudential laws (e.g. anti-competitive conducts, transfer pricing, financial system stability) and newer items of "social disclosure" which are not always required under national laws, but which can serve to inform specific groups of stakeholders other than shareholders, as to the operations of the company in question, so that they can better understand the effects of its operations upon their vital interests. The latter type of information may be more intrusive, as it deals with a wider range of information than is traditionally required of corporations, and may require a greater devotion of time, expertise and resources to be delivered than mere financial information, which a company needs to compile as a matter of normal business management. The range of other stakeholders interested in such information includes potentially employees, trade unions, consumers, and the wider community as represented by governmental institutions at the local, regional and national levels.

It should be noted that the development of transparency obligations in IIAs could create conflicting approaches to the degree of intrusiveness required to achieve the policy aims in question. For instance, a host developing country may require a broad duty of disclosure on the part of TNCs, while particular TNCs may prefer to restrict the level of information they are required to divulge publicly concerning their financial and technical operations. Thus the precise degree of intrusiveness is an issue of some delicacy, and it is not easy to draw a clear line as to the appropriate level of transparency. What is clear, however, is that this line has shifted over the past decade or two in the direction of more transparency.

A third issue relates to the different types of mechanisms that can be used to implement a transparency obligation. Here, the emphasis is not so much on *what* items of information should be disclosed (which may be listed as part of the transparency provision to which the mechanism in question applies) but *how* this disclosure should occur. This may have a direct bearing upon the content of a transparency obligation, as each modality entails a different degree of commitment to the process of disclosure thereby affecting the quality of the disclosure provided. (Compare, for example, an obligation to consult and exchange information and an obligation to make the same information unilaterally available to the public.) In particular, four different modalities stemming from past and present IIA practice can be identified. These are:

- consultation and information exchange,
- making information publicly available,
- answering requests for information, and
- notification requirements of specific measures that need to be notified to the other party or to a body set up for the purpose under the agreement.

In each case, the modality can be:

- voluntary or mandatory;
- reciprocal and based on mutual agreement to disclose or a unilateral obligation involving disclosure by one party only;
- an *ad hoc* obligation or part of a continuing and repeated process.

The weakest obligation would be a voluntary, mutually agreed *ad hoc* exchange or disclosure requirement while the strongest one would be a mandatory, unilateral and continuing obligation to disclose. In between, a number of variables can be devised based on these basic parameters of choice. Once again, these several forms of transparency requirements may be imposed both upon countries and/or corporate investors.

A fourth issue is that of the timing of disclosure. The time limits set in an IIA for making information available or for meeting transparency requirements will also have a bearing on the content of the transparency obligation, as this will determine the speed with which the disclosure is to take place. Usually, the shorter the period of disclosure the more demanding will the obligation be. However, with regard to a requirement to make public or notify a draft law or regulation in order to afford interested parties the possibility to comment on such draft instruments, the degree of intrusiveness will increase with the length of time available to comment, as this may permit for a more searching disclosure process to be undertaken.

A fifth issue relates to the possible safeguards and exceptions to transparency obligations that can be put into place to take into account difficulties in the implementation of such obligations or with their degree of intrusiveness. Such exceptions/ reservations will serve to reduce the overall impact of the transparency obligation in question. Exception can fall into a number of broad categories:

- *National security and defence.* Countries are likely to make transparency obligations subject to exceptions based on their vital national security and defence interests. In some instances, foreign investors with investment projects in different countries may be prohibited from disclosing aspects of operations in one country to representatives of another country for national security reasons.
- *Law enforcement and legal processes.* When a matter is the subject of judicial process or under investigation by a State, limits may be placed on the availability of information to third parties so as to protect the integrity of that process. Both countries and private entities participating in such procedures may benefit from this restriction.
- *Internal policy deliberations and premature disclosure issues.* Both government and private entities will, of necessity, engage in internal deliberations before taking policy decisions on a wide range of questions pertaining to investment. Where this is not inconsistent with a public policy right of

information, such deliberations could be excluded from a transparency obligation.

- *Intrusiveness in the duty to inform.* It may be a matter of discussion whether States should be required to provide information on the status of investment applications or to reveal each stage in the deliberative process (at the legislative and administrative levels) concerning foreign investment.
- *Protection of commercially confidential information or information that may affect the privacy rights of individuals.* This obligation will be primarily placed upon countries rather than corporate or other private actors, who are the principal beneficiaries of this restriction. In this connection, the need to protect intellectual property is increasingly accepted as a basis for restricting transparency.

* * *

Section II
Stocktaking and Analysis

Traditionally, references to transparency in IIAs have been quite limited. Even today many such agreements, especially at the bilateral level, do not include references to transparency in their terms (UNCTAD, 1998a, p. 85). This approach is exemplified by the model bilateral investment treaties (BITs) of the United Kingdom and the Federal Republic of Germany.[2] In these model treaties, it is expressly or implicitly acknowledged that foreign investors shall be subject to national laws and regulations; but, there is no requirement that these laws and regulations be published.[3] A number of regional instruments share similar features. For example, the Agreement on Promotion, Protection and Guarantee of Investments among Member States of the Organisation of the Islamic Conference, which entered into force in 1986, provides various safeguards for foreign investors, but does not include a reference to transparency.

However, more recent IIAs have sought expressly to incorporate transparency requirements. These requirements differ depending on certain key features, such as the addressees, the scope of transparency, the mechanisms employed to implement transparency, the time-limits and the exceptions to transparency obligations. This section analyses in more detail existing IIAs dealing with transparency by focussing in particular on these issues.

A. Addressees

Transparency provisions in IIAs are usually formulated in general terms, imposing requirements on every party to the agreement. Unless otherwise specified, such general provisions arguably impose obligations upon both host and home countries to ensure that their conduct under the IIA is in accordance with transparency obligations. And, of course, provisions can deal with TNCs. But certain provisions are clearly drafted so as to impose obligations upon the host country alone or as targeting investors. At the same time, there do not appear to be any cases where transparency provisions are imposed exclusively on home countries. In this respect, the addressee of transparency requirements may depend on the objective and scope of a transparency provision and, more generally, on the nature of the agreement that contains the transparency provision. As already mentioned, transparency is essentially a means to other ends in investment policy, and this is also reflected in the addressees of transparency provisions in IIAs.

1. Transparency provisions addressing all parties to an IIA

Generally speaking, transparency obligations arise out of the reciprocal character of all provisions in IIAs and so are formulated to cover any contracting party. Accordingly, it can be argued that all transparency requirements and provisions that are expressly spelled out are applicable to both the host and the home country of a foreign investor. In this connection, there are two main types of provisions that apply to both home and host countries:

First, certain transparency obligations apply to all parties to an IIA as a matter of logic. For example, exchange of information and consultation requirements, as well as requirements to notify "lists of exceptions", apply to any party to an investment agreement simply because of the nature of these requirements. With regard to exchange of information and consultation, this is exemplified by the model BITs of both Egypt and Indonesia: the former indicates that "the Contracting Parties" may periodically consult on investment opportunities to determine where investments may be most beneficial (article 2.3); the latter indicates that "either Contracting Party" may request consultations on any matter concerning the agreement, and that such requests are to be given sympathetic consideration (article XII.1).[4] A good example of a transparency requirement related to the possibility of listing exceptions is the 1997 BIT between Canada and Thailand. While article II(3) (a) requires each contracting party to permit the establishment of an investor of the other contracting party on a national treatment basis, article IV(3) permits each contracting party to make or maintain measures inconsistent with article II(3) (a) within the sectors or matters listed in Annex I to the Agreement itself. In order to render such lists of exceptions operational and transparent, article XVI(1) of the BIT between Canada and Thailand provides that:

> "The Contracting Parties shall, within a two year period after the entry into force of this Agreement, exchange letters listing, to the extent possible, any existing measures that do not conform to the obligations in subparagraph (3)(a) of Article II, Article IV or paragraphs (1) and (2) of Article V."

Secondly, there are other transparency obligations that apply to both host and home countries as a matter of law. For example, an obligation "to make laws and regulations *pertaining to investment* publicly available" applies not only to the laws and measures of the host country but also to those of the home country, since both host and home country laws potentially *pertain* to investment. Accordingly, the obligation to make laws publicly available may extend to the laws of both the host and home countries. For example, article II.5 of the revised model BIT of the United States of America stipulates that:

> "Each Party shall ensure that its laws, regulations, administrative practices and procedures of general application, and adjudicatory decisions, that pertain to or affect covered investments are promptly published or otherwise made publicly available".[5]

Similarly, article XIV of the 1999 BIT between Canada and El Salvador provides that:

> "Each Contracting Party shall, to the extent practicable, ensure that its laws, regulations, procedures, and administrative rulings of general application respecting any matter covered by this Agreement are promptly published or otherwise made available in such a manner as to enable interested persons and the other Contracting Party to become acquainted with them."

This exact provision can also be found in the 2003 free trade agreement between Singapore and the United States (article 19.3).

As explained above, the general reference to laws and regulations "respecting any matter covered by this Agreement" or "that pertain to or affect covered investments" suggests that the transparency obligations contained in the two above-mentioned instruments apply to both host and home countries.[6] In other words, since it may be possible that foreign investment is *affected* by the regulatory framework of *both* the host and home countries, any transparency obligations, formulated in these terms, should thus cover laws and regulations of both countries involved.[7] Although this reading appears logical, there is a tendency of interpreting these types of transparency obligations as covering host countries only. This may perhaps be explained on the simplistic and incorrect view that only host countries measures affect FDI.

2. *Transparency provisions imposed on the host country alone*

As suggested above, transparency requirements may also be imposed exclusively on the host country. This occurs often within BITs, since there is a perception that some host country measures in particular affect negatively the establishment and operation of foreign affiliates.

This approach may clearly be found in the 1988 BIT between Australia and China imposing various transparency requirements on the contracting parties. Article VI provides that:

> "Each Contracting Party shall, with a view to promoting the understanding of its laws and policies that pertain to or affect investments in its territory of nationals of the other Contracting Party:
> (a) make such laws and policies public and readily accessible; [...]"

By expressly limiting the subject-matter of the transparency obligation to laws and policies pertaining to the investment *in each country's territory of nationals of the other contracting party*, such provision clearly applies only to host country measures. In other words, this means that the obligation to make laws and policies public will apply to Australia and China in their capacity as the host country.

Recent developments in model texts of BITs also show a trend to include explicit transparency obligations on the host country. This is exemplified by article 15 of the 2001 model BIT of Finland. It reads as follows:

> "Each Contracting Party shall promptly publish, or otherwise make publicly available, its laws, regulations, procedures [...] *which may affect the investments of investors of the other Contracting Party* in the territory of the former Contracting Party" [emphasis added].

Article 2.3 of the 2000 model BIT of Peru requires each contracting party to "publicize and disseminate laws and regulations related to investments of investors of the other Contracting Party".

A very similar approach is also taken in the amended Association of Southeast Asian Nations (ASEAN) Agreement for the Protection and Promotion of Investment. Article III-B of the revised version of the Agreement, signed in September 1996, incorporates a provision on "Transparency and Predictability" requiring each contracting party to ensure the provision of up-to-date information on all laws and regulations pertaining to foreign investment *in its territory*. Similarly, the transparency provision of the Asia-Pacific Economic Cooperation (APEC) Non-binding Investment Principles requires all "Member economies" to make publicly available "all laws, regulations, administrative guidelines and policies *pertaining to investment in their economies*" [emphasis added].

3. *Transparency on the part of corporate entities*

Notwithstanding the fact that most IIAs, whether bilateral, regional or multilateral, do not refer to corporate disclosure duties, there is an increasing number of IIAs that specifically require TNCs to disclose certain information or that give governments the right to collect specific information directly from foreign investors. Given that each country has the sovereign right to pass legislation governing investors in its territory, provisions to this effect are, strictly speaking, superfluous. However, transparency provisions in IIAs may clarify that nothing in a particular treaty is meant to undermine each country's regulatory sovereignty in this respect. They indicate moreover the parties' clear knowledge that matters pertaining to transparency raise important issues for the relations between a country (especially a host country) and investors.

Where an investment treaty does not specify transparency requirements for foreign investors, this does not necessarily mean that foreign investors are exempt from such requirements. On the contrary, most investment instruments, and in particular BITs, expressly confirm that foreign investors are at a minimum subject to the laws and regulations of the host country (e.g. article 2 of the model BIT of Jamaica; article 2 of the model BIT of Malaysia; article 2 of the model BIT of The Netherlands; article 8 of the BIT between the Republic of Korea and Sri Lanka; and article 10 of the BIT between China and New Zealand). It thus follows that foreign investors need to adhere to applicable transparency rules in force in the host country. Under national law, however, it is not always clear under what conditions disclosure duties exist (box II.1).

With regard to transparency provisions expressly attributing to the State the authority to gather information from foreign investors, several examples exist in IIAs. Article 17-09 of the 1990 Treaty on Free Trade between Colombia, Mexico and Venezuela, which entered into force in 1995, ensures that each State party, notwithstanding national and most-favoured-nation (MFN) treatment obligations, may require an investor of another party to provide information about the particular investment, consistent with applicable laws in the State party. Article 1111 (2) of the NAFTA takes a similar approach by granting each State party, notwithstanding the national and MFN treatment obligations, the right to "require an investor of another Party, or its investment in its territory, to provide routine information concerning that investment solely for informational or statistical purposes."[8]

A variety of other investment instruments follow a different approach: corporate disclosure is not simply recognized as a State's prerogative, but it is required. One of the more detailed formulations of this approach is contained in the draft United Nations Code of Conduct on Transnational Corporations (draft United Nations Code). Although these provisions have never assumed legal force, they can serve as precedent, especially because they were acceptable to most countries (UNCTC, 1988b, p. 16). Paragraph 44 of the draft United Nations Code stated in part that:

> "Transnational corporations should disclose to the public in the countries in which they operate, by appropriate means of

communication, clear, full and comprehensible information on the structure, policies, activities and operations of the transnational corporation as a whole. [...]"

The disclosure provisions of the draft United Nations Code were justified partly on the grounds that they could lead to improvements in the comparability of information disclosed by foreign investors relying on different accounting and reporting practices in various jurisdictions with divergent expectations (UNCTC, 1988b, p. 17).

Box II.1. Corporate disclosure duties under national law and *Klöckner v. Cameroon*

One issue addressed by the ICSID arbitral tribunal in this case (ICSID Case No ARB/81/2) concerned whether Klöckner, a corporate investor party to various contractual arrangements for the construction and operation of a turnkey plant, owed a duty of disclosure to the Government of Cameroon, where no duty of corporate disclosure was specified (a) in any relevant treaty between Cameroon and the Federal Republic of Germany (the home country of Klöckner), (b) between the parties to the various contracts and (c) under national law. The tribunal found that in the circumstances of the case a duty of full disclosure existed under national law, since "the principle according to which a person who engages in close contractual relations, based on confidence, must deal with its partner in a frank, loyal and candid manner is a basic principle of French civil law", the source of the major principles of Cameroonian law. The failure of Klöckner to divulge particular items of financial and commercial information to the Government, as Klöckner's joint venture partner, helped to relieve the Government of liabilities claimed by Klöckner.

The ensuing decision by an *ad hoc* committee annulling the arbitral award in *Klöckner v. Cameroon* emphasised the problematic issues of relying simply on national law. Among the stated grounds for annulment, the *ad hoc* committee noted that the arbitral tribunal was at fault in not identifying the rules of French or Cameroonian law justifying the existence of a duty of corporate disclosure between joint venture partners in the circumstances of the case. For the *ad hoc* committee, it was not enough to presume the existence of a rule requiring corporate disclosure simply from general principles of law.

The approach taken by the *ad hoc* committee gives little support for the view that corporate disclosure requirements may be implied from the relationship between investors and host countries, even where both are parties to a commercial joint venture.

Source: UNCTAD, based on ICSID Award of 21 October 1983, *Journal du droit international*, 111 (1984), p. 409-421; *Ad hoc* Committee Decision of 3 May 1985, *Journal du droit international*, 114 (1987), pp. 163-184.

Even after the recent changes, the wording of the OECD Guidelines on Multinational Enterprises (OECD Guidelines), imposing disclosure requirements on "enterprises", reflects substantially the approach on corporate disclosure taken in the draft United Nations Code. This suggests that both capital-exporting and capital-importing countries are not averse to corporate transparency. Corporate transparency under the OECD approach, for instance, benefits host countries by enhancing their information base; simultaneously, though, the broadening of the host country's information base may also reduce some of its suspicion and fear towards foreign investors. Codes such as the OECD Guidelines can help to improve investor-State relations, and thus improve the prospects of foreign investors (Wallace, 1994, p. 210).[9]

The recommendations advanced in the OECD Guidelines have been supplemented by the OECD Principles of Corporate Governance (OECD Principles), approved in May 1999. Expressly designed to assist both OECD member countries and non-members in examining and developing their legal and regulatory frameworks for corporate governance, the OECD Principles include, among other things, a framework on corporate disclosure and transparency suggesting that all companies – and not only TNCs – should be required to disclose all material matters regarding the corporation. More recently, a set of guidelines for businesses worldwide to ensure their compliance with international human rights treaties and conventions ("draft Norms on the Responsibilities of Transnational Corporations and Other Business Enterprises With Regard to Human Rights") was adopted by the United Nations Sub-Commission for the Promotion and Protection of Human Rights. These draft Norms, which contain an explicit requirement to recognize and respect transparency and accountability obligations, apply not only to TNCs but also to private businesses (see E/CN.4/Sub.2/2003/12/ Rev.2, 13 August 2003).

In addition to treaty provisions, the duty of corporate disclosure has also received support from various non-governmental organizations (NGOs) as well as business organizations. This development underlines the fact that the activities of foreign investors in host countries are likely to affect not just governments, but also private persons in both home and host countries. The draft NGO Charter on Transnational Corporations (published in 1998 by the People's Action Network to Monitor Japanese Transnational Corporations Abroad) and the International Right To Know (IRTK) campaign calling on United States companies doing business abroad for more public disclosure, transparency and accountability,[10] are indicative of one line of opinion among NGOs.

Numerous transparency initiatives also stem from business organisations. In order to improve greater transparency in payments and contributions made by companies (as well as revenues received by governments) for natural resource extraction, the 2003 draft Voluntary Compact of the Extractive Industries Transparency Initiative (EITI) includes *inter alia* certain commitments by companies with regard to the publication and report of any transfer of funds or the payments of a tax, dividend, royalty, and fee.[11] Moreover, the Association of British Insurers has put forward in 2003 Disclosure Guidelines on Socially-Responsible Investment, taking the form of disclosures, which institutions would expect to see included in the annual report of listed companies.[12]

B. Items of information

A first point of variation in IIAs concerns the identification of the items of both governmental and corporate information that are to be made available pursuant to an investment agreement. Although the range of possibilities with regard to the items of information subject to the transparency provisions in IIAs is substantial, certain general points are discernible.

1. Governmental information

Almost all IIAs that impose a transparency obligation upon States apply it to the "laws and regulations" of the States party to the agreement. This seems to constitute one of the least intrusive items of information subject to the transparency obligation in IIAs, for two major reasons:

- The terms "laws" and "regulations" are viewed as referring to measures of general application usually requiring further implementing legislation; thus these measures might not in themselves be seen as constituting a significant concern for FDI.
- Laws and regulations are usually subject to disclosure requirements under national laws, independently of IIAs obligations; this excludes in turn the need for any further actions to ensure compliance with international obligations.

Several of the IIAs that contain transparency provisions also include a reference to "procedures",[13] "administrative procedures"[14] and/or "administrative rulings".[15] There are also cases in which the reference to "laws and regulations" is accompanied by a reference to both "administrative procedures" and "administrative rulings",[16] or to both "procedures" and "administrative rulings".[17] With regard to "administrative procedures", transparency obligations may also extend to criteria and procedures for applying for or renewing relevant investment authorizations, as well as to deadlines for processing applications.[18] This type of procedural transparency enhances the ability of foreign investors to operate in a host country. However, transparency on these items of information, dealing with specific administrative procedures and decisions pertaining to individual cases, also involves a higher degree of intrusiveness as it concerns directly identifiable applications of laws and regulations to individual cases and might involve extra financial costs.

Relevant to the discussion is also the question of the type of approach one might have with regard to the listing of the items of information in an IIA: is the reference to laws, regulations and administrative procedures enough or should other items of governmental information be specifically included in the transparency obligation in order for all relevant information to be covered? Arguably, the laws, regulations and administrative procedures of the parties to an agreement cover the range of items that are legitimately of interest to a foreign investor. On this view, matters such as international agreements or judicial decisions of national courts would fall within the scope of the term "laws", as long as one interprets this term in a broad manner. Similarly, the reference to administrative procedures would also include any administrative practices that are not clearly expressly addressed in the laws, regulations and administrative procedures of the State. (See box II.2 for two different approached followed by the WTO with regard to the issue of the items of information.)

Although this argument carries some force, a number of investment agreements contain broader formulations that expressly include, next to laws and administrative procedures, reference to judicial decisions and/or international agreements. Thus, for example, the model BIT of Finland includes transparency provisions applicable to "laws, regulations, procedures and administrative rulings and judicial decisions of a general application as well as international agreements" (article 15.1).[19] A similar formulation can be found in article 67 of the 2002 Free Trade Agreement between the European Free Trade Association (EFTA) States and Singapore, which includes "international agreements that may affect the operation of this Agreement" within the scope of the transparency obligation. For some countries, the reference to international agreements would possibly be superfluous, given that in some constitutional arrangements treaties properly concluded are automatically part of the municipal law of the State. But this is not true for all countries. Bearing in mind the possibility that in some cases treaty provisions on investment may be different from local law provisions, this approach could provide an additional layer of confidence for foreign investors.

Box II.2. Items of information subject to transparency obligations in the WTO

The identification of the items of information subject to transparency in the WTO follows two different approaches. Article 63 of TRIPS, reflecting the majority practice in investment agreements, lists expressly the several items to be covered by the transparency provision. It states that:

> "Laws and regulations, and final judicial decisions and administrative rulings of general application, made effective by a Member pertaining to the subject matter of this Agreement [...] shall be published, or where such publication is not practicable, made publicly available, in a national language, in such a manner as to enable governments and rights holders to become acquainted with them. Agreements concerning the subject matter of this Agreement which are in force between the government or a governmental agency of a Member and the government or a governmental agency of another Member shall also be published."

On the other hand, article III of the GATS does not specify a list of the items that need to be published by each member; rather, it stipulates, in broad language, that "all relevant measures of general application which pertain to or affect the operation of this Agreement" shall be published or made public.

Evidently, both approaches are intended to be comprehensive. However, while the approach taken by the GATS may be favoured because of the flexibility it embodies, it may as well be subject to the criticism that it is too vague.

Source: WTO, 2002.

Several BITs signed by Canada adopt a similar approach listing a broad range of governmental information in their transparency provisions. For example, in the 1991 BIT between Argentina and Canada, article XI provides for a duty of consultation between the parties, and indicates that, in the course of such consultations, information may be exchanged on the impact that "the laws, regulations, decisions, practices or procedures, or policies" of the other contracting party may have on investments covered by the agreement.[20] The draft Multilateral Agreement on Investment (MAI) also indicated that policies not expressed in laws, regulations and related instruments that could affect the operations of the MAI should also be published or made public. In this regard, it should be emphasised that, although "policies" appear to constitute one of the least intrusive items of governmental information, they are only rarely included in transparency obligations in recent IIAs.

A few recent IIAs contain transparency obligation with regard to *draft* laws and regulations. These obligations usually require parties to make public or notify their proposed laws or regulations with the view of affording interested parties the possibility to comment on such laws and regulations before they are formally adopted. In NAFTA, article 1802 provides that "to the extent possible, each Party shall: (a) publish in advance any such measure it proposes to adopt; and (b) provide interested persons and Parties a reasonable opportunity to comment on such proposed measures." Although this approach may not amount to a binding obligation to publish information in advance, for it is qualified by the phrase "to the extent possible", it is an example of how requirements of prior notification and comment work together.

Generally, provisions contemplating the advance publication of investment measures are exceptional and represent a greater degree of intrusion than some countries are willing to accept. Publication of draft laws and regulations provides States as well as foreign investors with the opportunity to express their views on investment initiatives, and thereby to influence the decision-making process. However, host countries could advance at least two sets of objections with regard to this type of obligation:

- Host countries may view a requirement of advance publication as undermining their sovereign right to discuss and decide on investment rules without formal intervention by foreign investors and home countries.

- In cases in which there is a power imbalance between host and home countries, the weaker host country may fear undue influence on its legislative and administrative decision-making processes. However, it may also be true that undue influence on legislative and administrative processes may nevertheless be imposed on host countries independently from the existence of any requirement of advance publication. On the contrary, the lack of any transparency provisions in this regard may contribute to this influence being exercised away from the eyes of other stakeholders and the public in general.

Furthermore, article 3 of chapter VI on "Transparency-Related Provisions" of the 2000 Free Trade Agreement between the United States and Viet Nam also provides for nationals of the parties, and not only to State parties, "the opportunity to comment on the formulation of laws, regulations and administrative procedures of general application that may affect the conduct of business activities covered by this Agreement".[21]

Transparency requirements that tend to enhance the level of participation of foreign actors (whether States or private parties) in national legislative processes have recently been extended to national administrative proceedings in particular by granting any persons directly affected by such a proceeding "a reasonable opportunity to present facts and arguments in support of their positions prior to any final administrative action, when time, the nature of the proceeding, and the public interest permit".[22] Furthermore, this type of transparency requirement (aimed at broadening the participation of interested parties) has also been introduced for purposes of international dispute settlement. For example, in the context of its investor-State dispute settlement provisions, the 2003 Free Trade Agreement between Chile and the United States provides that:

> "The tribunal shall have the authority to accept and consider *amicus curiae* submissions from a person or entity that is not a disputing party (the 'submitter'). The submissions shall be provided in both Spanish and English, and shall identify the submitter and any Party, other government, person, or organization, other than the submitter, that has provided, or will provide, any financial or other assistance in preparing the submission" (article 10.19, paragraph 3).[23]

A final issue to consider in this section deals with the circumstance that, as already noted in the section dealing with the addressees of transparency requirements, in many IIAs, the particular items of governmental information covered by transparency requirements may be a matter of legal assessment. Most agreements requiring transparency – in respect of the publication of laws and in other ways – apply transparency rules to matters "pertaining to investment", "relevant to investment", or "affected by" investment. This raises the question of where the boundary line is to be drawn between investment matters *per se*, and other matters that touch and concern investment in a remote or indirect manner. On a broad interpretation, transparency rules concerning investment mean that rules concerning the environment, taxation and employment are also subject to transparency requirements, for each of these items are linked in some sense to investment. On a more narrow interpretation, however, only those rules directly applicable to investment matters will be subjected to transparency rules. In this regard, the attempt should be noted in the recent Free Trade Agreement between Chile and the United States to limit the scope of transparency requirements by qualifying the otherwise broad term "affect": article 20.3, paragraph 1, of this Agreement specifies that the duty to notify applies with respect to any measures "that the Party considers might *materially* affect the operation of this Agreement or otherwise *substantially* affect the other Party's interests under this Agreement" [emphasis added].

Similarly, the scope of the transparency requirements may depend on whether the relevant provisions make reference to rules "relevant to foreign investment",[24] rules "affecting this Agreement",[25] or rules "respecting any matter covered by this Agreement".[26] Although terms such as "relevant" or "respecting" appear to be broader than the term "affecting", much would depend on the actual interpretation of the different terminology employed in IIAs.

Finally, from the perspective of developing countries, the question of costs may be a significant factor in determining the material scope of provisions concerning transparency. Usually, the obligation to provide information requires countries to act promptly, and where this covers a broad range of items, some developing countries may encounter problems. It is however difficult to argue that transparency must be sacrificed simply because countries cannot afford publication.

Accordingly, although the cost factor is not always entirely ignored, it tends not to be given much weight. The more recent United States model BIT requires transparency in respect of "laws, regulations, administrative practices and procedures of general application, and adjudicatory decisions". The reference to general application in this provision provides some scope for flexibility with regard to transparency, since it means that a country will not be pressed to undertake the presumably costly exercise of making public or publishing practices and procedures that affect only small groups of individuals. Implicit in this approach, however, is the notion that individuals affected by localized regulations or practices will have access to information on such regulations or practices.

2. Corporate information

A few cases exist in which transparency provisions pertaining to TNCs in IIAs are formulated in very general terms, without any clear indication of the type of corporate information that need to be disclosed. For example, the 1990 Treaty on Free Trade between Colombia, Mexico and Venezuela employs general language. Article 17-09 of this Treaty ensures that each State party, notwithstanding national and MFN treatment obligations, may require an investor of another party to provide information about the particular investment in accordance with applicable laws in the State party. Similarly, the draft MAI merely contains the possibility for a contracting Party to require an investor of another contracting Party or its investment to provide "routine information concerning that investment solely for information or statistical purposes."[27] However, the reference to *routine* information and the specification that such information is only for *information* or *statistical* purposes seem to imply that the information subject to the transparency obligation in the MAI deals mainly with business-related information dealing with the structure and operation of the corporate entity.[28]

In other IIAs, the transparency obligation imposed on TNCs provides for a more detailed list of items of information that need to be disclosed. While traditionally such obligations have required the disclosure of mainly business and financial information, more recently the scope of these provisions has been extended to other broader social, environmental and ethical concerns.

An example of the more traditional, relatively less intrusive approach is the draft United Nations Code suggesting that a large amount of information, including both financial and non-financial items, should be made available by the TNC to the country in which it operates. This information deals principally with business information. As to financial matters, TNCs should provide *inter alia* the following:

(a) a balance sheet;
(b) an income statement, including operating results and sales;
(c) a statement of allocation of net profits or net income;
(d) a statement of the sources and uses of funds;
(e) significant new long-term capital investment;
(f) research and development expenditure.

As to non-financial matters, the items to be provided by the TNC should include *inter alia* the following:

(a) the structure of the transnational corporation, showing the name and location of the parent company, its main entities, its percentage ownership, direct and indirect, in these entities, including shareholdings between them;
(b) the main activities of its entities;
(c) employment information including average number of employees;
(d) accounting policies used in compiling and consolidating the information published;
(e) policies applied in respect of transfer pricing.

All information provided should, as far as practicable, be broken down according to geographical area or on a country-by-county basis, and by major line of business, depending on the nature of the TNC's operations and its significance for the areas or countries concerned. In addition, it was expressly acknowledged that the information to be provided should, as necessary, be in addition to information required under the laws, regulations and practices of the host country.

Along the same lines, the draft NGO Charter on Transnational Corporations (the draft NGO Charter) provides that the information publicized shall include at least the following:

(1) names and addresses of the local corporation and the investing corporations including the parent company, the form and breakdown of the investments, the fond [*sic*] or nature of the business relationship such as technology transfers and related local and overseas business entities;
(2) the contents of the major businesses, the financial statements including the balance

sheet and the revenue statement and other relevant information of the local corporation;

(3) the number of employees, working conditions and the information on the labour and management relationship of the local corporation and;

(4) the pricing policy for merchandise/ commodity transfers among the affiliates and other related companies.

In the context of establishment agreements, the Economic Community of West African States, in Protocol A/P1/11/84 relating to Community Enterprises, provides that all enterprises that have been admitted to the status of Community Enterprise shall:

(a) submit progress reports, annual balance sheets and audited accounts to the relevant authorities of the Member States involved in the project;

(b) furnish the Member States and the Executive Secretariat with information relating to the fulfilment of the conditions of any permit and the extent to which benefits and permits have been utilised; [...]

(d) inform the Executive Secretariat of any intended deviations from or difficulties in the implementation of the terms of an Approval Agreement, so as to enable any necessary re-assessment to be made between the parties to the Approval Agreement.

The more recent and potentially more inclusive approach to corporate disclosure may be found in the OECD Principles. Next to the information relating to business matters (such as material information on their financial and operating results, share ownership and voting rights, issues concerning employees, and governance structures), the OECD Principles go further by stipulating that all companies – and not only enterprises involved in foreign investment – be required to provide information on each of the following:

- company objectives (including commercial objectives, policies relating to business ethics, the environment and other public policy commitments);
- members of the board and key executives, together with their remuneration;
- material foreseeable risk factors: these may include risks that are not specific to a particular area or industry, dependence on commodities, financial market risk, risk related to derivatives and off-balance sheet transactions, and risks pertaining to environmental liabilities;
- material issues regarding other stakeholders. So, apart from reporting on issues concerning employees, the company should be required to make public material affairs concerning creditors, suppliers, local communities, and other stakeholders, as appropriate.

Following the 2000 revision, the OECD Guidelines combine disclosure requirements of both business and non-business information. According to the OECD Guidelines, the main items of information to be disclosed include the financial and operating results of the company, major share ownership and voting rights, members of the board and key executives (and their remuneration) and material issues regarding employees and other stakeholders (part III, paragraph 4). In addition, however, paragraph 5 of part III of the OECD Guidelines encourages enterprises to communicate information that could include (a) value statements or statements of business conduct intended for public disclosure including information on the social, ethical and environmental policies of the enterprise and other codes of conduct to which the company subscribes, (b) information on systems for managing risks and complying with laws, and on statements or codes of business conduct and (c) information on relationships with employees and other stakeholders.

This expanded approach to the items of corporate disclosure is also found in instruments stemming from several NGOs (box II.3).

Box II.3. Items of information subject to corporate disclosure

The Disclosure Guidelines on Socially-Responsible Investment put forward in 2003 by the Association of British Insurers (ABI) indicate the items that listed companies are expected to include in their annual reports. They focus principally on information dealing with social, environmental and ethical matters.

With regard to disclosure relating to the board, the ABI Guidelines provide that the company should state in its annual report whether the board: (1) takes regular account of the significance of social, environmental and ethical (SEE) matters to the business of the company; (2) has identified and assessed the significant risks to the company's short and long term value arising from SEE matters, as well as the opportunities to enhance value that may arise from an appropriate response; (3) has received adequate information to make this assessment and that account is taken of SEE matters in the training of directors; (4) has ensured that the company has in place effective systems for managing significant risks, which, where relevant, incorporate performance management systems and appropriate remuneration incentives.

/...

Box II.3 (concluded)

With regard to disclosures relating to policies, procedures and verification, the ABI Guidelines require that the annual report should: (1) include information on SEE-related risks and opportunities that may significantly affect the company's short and long term value, and how they might impact on the business; (2) describe the company's policies and procedures for managing risks to short and long term value arising from SEE matters and, if the company has no such policies or procedures, provide reasons for their absence; (3) include information about the extent to which the company has complied with its policies and procedures for managing risks arising from SEE matters; and finally (4) describe the procedures for verification of SEE disclosures. The verification procedure should be such as to achieve a reasonable level of credibility.

The International Right to Know campaign also calls for broad disclosure requirements by United States, companies including specific environmental and labour information concerning their foreign operations. For example, corporations would be required to provide information about the number of workers injured or killed in work-related accidents, workers' exposure to hazardous substances, child labour, forced labour and discrimination in the workplace. Corporations would also be obligated to disclose security arrangements with military, paramilitary or private security forces, as well as human rights complaints brought by local communities.

Source: http://www.abi.org.uk/ and http://www.irtk.org/.

C. Modalities

A third point of variation in IIAs deals with the issue of "modalities", that is the different types of transparency mechanisms that may be employed in order to further transparency. The emphasis here is on the manner in which disclosure should occur, rather than on the items of information to be disclosed.

1. Consultation and exchange of information

Many IIAs contain provisions either encouraging or mandating consultation and/or exchange of information between parties to an IIA. When parties agree to cooperate and exchange information, this is likely to enhance transparency in foreign investment. To that extent, the willingness of a country to participate in consultations may be regarded as a component of the degree of transparency offered by that country, under an IIA. The main objective of this type of transparency mechanism is the reciprocal promotion of investment flows. Several examples may be found in current IIAs. In the 1993 BIT between the People's Republic of China and Lithuania, article 11 stipulates that:

> "1. The representatives of the two Contracting Parties shall hold meetings from time to time for the purpose of:
> (a) reviewing the implementation of this Agreement;
> (b) exchanging legal information and information concerning investment opportunities;
> (c) resolving disputes arising out of investments [...];
> (d) forwarding proposals on promotion of investment [...];
> (e) studying other issues in connection with investments [...]".

Under the terms of this provision, there is an undertaking for each party to consult and to exchange information. However, as regards transparency in terms of the provision of information concerning laws, regulations and investment procedures, it is to be noted that this provision does not compel transparency. Specifically, the provision stipulates that meetings shall be held for the exchange of legal information and related matters, but there is no particular rule to the effect that the legal information exchanged must include an authoritative or timely statement of the investment laws and procedures of the State; rather, the existence of the consultative mechanism may be seen as a means of encouraging transparency, without compelling it.

In some cases, too, consultation is recommended, but not required, by investment agreements. This is exemplified by the model BITs of both Egypt and Indonesia. The former indicates that contracting parties may periodically consult on investment opportunities to determine where investments may be most beneficial (article 2). The latter indicates that either party may request consultations on any matter concerning the agreement, and that such requests are to be given "sympathetic consideration" (article XII(1)). The model BIT of The Netherlands also contemplates that sympathetic consideration should be given to requests for consultations over matters concerning the interpretation or application of the investment agreement. Although all these provisions do not amount to a duty to consult, they suggest a partial acknowledgement of the importance of consultations among the parties concerned.[29]

2. *Making information publicly available*

As far as this modality is concerned, points of variation may be noted by reference to past and current IIA practice.

A first point of variation depends on whether the IIA contains simply a requirement "to make information public" or whether it clearly includes a publication requirement. In the earlier versions of its model BIT, the United States' preference was simply for a provision requiring the parties to the treaty to "make public" their investment-related rules. Accordingly, article II (7) of the 1984 revised text of the United States Prototype Treaty concerning the Reciprocal Encouragement and Protection of Investment read as follows:

> "Each Party shall make public all laws, regulations, administrative practices and procedures, and adjudicatory decisions that pertain to or affect investments" (UNCTC, 1988a, annex V).

This wording is identical to the formulation used in the 1983 draft of the United States model agreement, and it has been incorporated into the respective provisions on transparency in United States BITs with Turkey (article II (9)), Grenada (article II (7)), Argentina (article II (6)), the then Czechoslovakia (article II (7)), and Kyrgyzstan (article II (7)), among others.[30] It is also used, *verbatim*, in article 2 of the 1991 BIT between Malaysia and the United Arab Emirates (UNCTAD, 1998a, p. 85).[31]

By contrast, more recent United States model BITs contain modified language on the question under consideration. In both the 1994 and 1998 versions of the prototype treaty, for example, article II (5) stipulates that:

> "Each Party shall ensure that its laws, regulations, administrative practices and procedures of general application, and adjudicatory decisions, that pertain to or affect covered investments are promptly published or otherwise made publicly available".

One apparent point of contrast between the 1984 United States model and the more recent United States models concerns the difference between "making information public" and "publishing it". Where an investment agreement requires parties to make public certain items of information, this may be satisfied as long as the State makes those items of information available, i.e. it is a restriction against secrecy. In all likelihood, it requires the information to be in written form, but it does not imply that the information should be widely available (UNCTAD, 1998a, p. 85). In contrast, if an agreement requires the parties to publish particular items of information, this implies that the information will be in printed form and widely distributed. In the more recent United States model BITs, however, the publication requirement may take either of two alternatives, for the States have the option either to publish the information or to make it otherwise publicly available. In practice, therefore, there may be no real difference between the "make public" approach, on the one hand, and the combined "publish or make public" approach, on the other.[32]

Another approach to the question of making State information available to foreign investors is reflected in the 1996 revised version of the ASEAN Agreement for the Protection and Promotion of Investments, where the new article III-B on "Transparency and Predictability" provides as follows:

> "Each Contracting Party shall ensure the provision of up-to-date information on all laws and regulations pertaining to foreign investment in its territory and shall take appropriate measures to ensure that such information be made as transparent, timely and publicly accessible as possible".

In practical terms, there might not be much difference between the approach followed in the ASEAN Treaty and that featuring in the United States model BITs. The former combines two obligations, namely, the obligation to ensure the provision of up-to-date information, and the obligation to take appropriate measures to ensure that the information be made as publicly accessible as possible. Together, these obligations may constitute the basis for a duty among the State parties to disseminate widely information concerning investment-related laws and regulations. At the same time, however, it should be noted that the mandate requiring such information to be made "as publicly accessible as possible" is inherently subjective.

To reduce the subjectivity and thus uncertainty of these types of transparency provisions, certain IIAs have stipulated more fully how the transparency requirement may be met in particular instances. In this regard, the International Monetary Fund (IMF)/World Bank Guidelines on the Treatment of Foreign Direct Investment (IMF/World Bank Guidelines) serves as a useful point of reference. Paragraph 8 of article III on "Treatment" of the IMF/World Bank Guidelines contemplates a duty on the part of each State to take "appropriate measures" to promote accountability and transparency in its dealings with foreign investors. In addition, however, paragraph 6 of article II of the IMF/World Bank Guidelines concerning the admission of foreign investors gives a more specific form to the transparency obligation. This paragraph indicates that:

> "Each State is encouraged to publish, in the form of a handbook or other medium easily accessible to other States and their investors, adequate and regularly updated information about its legislation, regulations and procedures relevant to foreign investment and other information relating to its investment policies [...]".

Although this approach gives an indication of the formula that may enhance the accessibility of legislation and other investment-related material, at the same time, it does not contemplate that the use of a handbook or other easily accessible medium should be set out as a legal requirement in IIAs.

Another method of ensuring clarity in respect of the publication requirement is incorporated in the 1988 BIT between Australia and China, where article VI, after providing that each party shall make laws and policies on investment public and readily accessible, states further that, if requested, each party shall provide copies of specified laws and policies to the other party (article VI (b)), and shall consult with the other party in order to explain specified laws and policies (article VI (c)).[33]

A further point of variation deals with whether the duty to make laws publicly available is limited in order to take into account the issue of feasibility and cost. For example, article 6 of the BIT between Australia and Laos indicates that:

> "Each Contracting Party shall, with a view to promoting the understanding of its laws that pertain to or affect investments in its territory by nationals of the other Contracting Party, make, *to the best of its ability*, such laws public and readily accessible" [emphasis added].

By limiting the transparency obligation through reference to the best of each party's ability, this provision implies sensitivity to the technical capacity and costs of making laws public.[34] At the same time, however, a certain degree of vagueness in determining the best of a country's ability remains.[35]

With regard to multilateral agreements, the GATS specifies the manner in which information is to be made available that reflects the overall structure of the WTO scheme and, at the same time, takes into account some of the concerns that affect investment interests generally. Article III of the GATS reads in its relevant part as follows:

> "1. Each Member shall publish promptly and, except in emergency situations, at the latest by the time of their entry into force, all relevant measures of general application which pertain to or affect the operation of this Agreement. International agreements pertaining to or affecting trade in services to which a Member is a signatory shall also be published.
>
> 2. Where publication as referred to in paragraph 1 is not practicable, such information shall be made otherwise publicly available."

The duty to "publish promptly" therefore does not arise when publication is "not practicable", although even in this case, the information shall nevertheless be made "publicly available". This provision could allow developing countries lacking the financial resources to publish all measures of relevant application the opportunity to argue that in some circumstances they are not obliged to meet the full costs of publication (including the wide dissemination of certain material). This possibility may be undermined, however, by the vagueness implicit in the criterion of practicability. Article III of the GATS does not indicate whether the criterion is to be applied by the State independently, with reference to foreign investors, or with reference to objective standards from within the GATT framework. Accordingly, it will be difficult to identify, *a priori*, when a country will not be obliged to publish relevant information concerning investments in service industries.

Finally, publication mechanism may be used in order to impose on countries an obligation to disclose draft laws and regulations with the aim of affording other interested parties the possibility to comment on such proposals before they are formally adopted.[36] As noted in the section on the items of information, this type of advance publication requirements is exceptional and represents a greater degree of intrusion than some members are willing to accept.

With regard to transparency obligations on investors, a contrast in the binding force of such obligations may be noted for example by comparing the draft United Nations Code and the OECD Principles, on the one hand, and the draft NGO Charter on the other. While both the draft

United Nations Code and the OECD Principles provide that TNCs "should" disclose to the public relevant business information (paragraph 44 and article IV, respectively), the draft NGO Charter states, as a general principle, that each TNC "must" publicize to the public in its host countries detailed information concerning the company's organizational structure, business activities and management conditions (paragraph 7 of part II). In particular, the draft NGO Charter specifies that the information so provided "shall" include at least a breakdown of investments undertaken, financial statements of the local entity (including a balance sheet and revenue statement), labour information, and the pricing policy of the company. Moreover, the TNC "must" provide all relevant information on its business activities where required by local governments, authorities and general public of the place where it operates as well as its labour union (paragraph 8 of part II). Elsewhere, the draft NGO Charter also indicates that each TNC shall freely disclose information on its environmental policy (paragraph 13 (3) of part II).

3. *Answering requests for information*

A third set of transparency provisions deals with the obligation to answer specific questions or provide information upon request.

Recent BITs contain such provisions, as for example, the model BIT of Austria. While paragraph 1 of article 4 imposes the duty to promptly publish or make publicly available laws, regulations, etc. affecting the operation of the Agreement, paragraph 2 of article 4 provides that:

> "Each Contracting Party shall promptly respond to specific questions and provide, upon request, information to the other Contracting Party on matters referred to in paragraph (1)."

Similar provisions can be found in several bilateral treaties that contain specific transparency provisions. For instance the 1997 BIT between Canada and Lebanon provides that, upon request by either party, "information shall be exchanged" on the measures of the other party that may have an impact on investments covered by the agreement (article XIV.2).[37] The 2003 Free Trade Agreement between Singapore and the United States also includes the obligation of each party, on request of the other party, to "promptly provide information and respond to questions pertaining to any actual or proposed measure, whether or not the other Party has been previously notified of that measure" (article 19.4, paragraph 2).

The right to require information is also extended by several IIAs to the State with regard to the foreign investor. Each party in the 1990 Treaty on Free Trade between Colombia, Mexico and Venezuela may "require an investor of another Party or its investment in its territory to provide information concerning that investment in accordance with the laws of that Party" (article 17-09). Likewise, as noted above, the NAFTA in its article 1111, provides, that "Notwithstanding Articles 1102 or 1103 [National Treatment and Most-Favoured-Nation Treatment], a Party may require an investor of another Party, or its investment in its territory, to provide routine information concerning that investment solely for informational or statistical purposes".

In addition to general obligations to provide information, some IIAs provide for the establishment of permanent enquiry or contact points charged with the duty to provide information on relevant matters. For example, article III of the GATS requires members to establish enquiry points to facilitate transparency, with each enquiry point providing information to other members in response to requests for specific information or in connection with information that is to be provided pursuant to the notification provisions. Generally, each enquiry point was to be established within two years of the entry into force of the agreement establishing the WTO. But this rule is not strictly applicable to developing countries, for whom "appropriate flexibility with respect to the time-limit within which such enquiry points are to be established may be agreed upon for individual developing country members" (article III:4 GATS).[38]

4. *Notification requirements*

A further form of transparency provision requires notification procedures. This type of transparency obligation is principally aimed at monitoring parties' compliance with regard to substantive obligations contained in IIAs. As noted above, regional and multilateral treaties oblige each State party in some cases to provide information to a central agency concerning actions taken by each party in respect of investment-related matters. This notification requirement does not usually exist in lieu of a duty to publish information; on the contrary, the duty to notify and the duty to publish information are frequently perceived as complementary means of promoting transparency.

Box II.4. The Havana Charter

The Havana Charter for an International Trade Organization (ITO), which was negotiated in 1948, is an early example of an investment-related instrument that incorporates a duty of notification. The Charter never entered into force, but its approach to notification merits brief consideration. Specifically, by virtue of article 50(3) of the Charter, each member of the proposed ITO was obliged to furnish the Organization, as promptly and as fully as possible, such information as the Organization may have requested either to address member State complaints or to conduct studies on trade and investment. Sensitive to the possible conflict between transparency and confidentiality, the duty of notification in article 50(3) was made subject to certain conditions.

In keeping with its monitoring objective, the ITO also required each member to report on action taken to comply with requests and follow through on recommendations of the Organization. Where action required or recommended by the Organization was not taken by a State, article 50(5) required each State party concerned to report on the reasons for inaction.

Source: UNCTAD.

In various respects, the broad template set out in the Havana Charter in the early post-World War II period is reflected in the WTO Agreements (box II.4). The TRIMs Agreement, for example, requires WTO members to notify the Council for Trade in Goods of all trade-related investment measures they are applying – whether general or specific – that do not conform with the Agreement. Thus, each non-conforming trade-related investment measure (such as local content requirements) notified to the Council was scheduled to be eliminated on a time-scale that accords preferential consideration to developing and least developed countries. The link between notification and the right to extend non-conforming measures may have served as an incentive for developing and least developed countries to report on such measures to the Council. In addition to transparency in respect of transitional arrangements, the TRIMs Agreement also requires each member State to notify the WTO Secretariat of the publications in which its trade-related measures may be found, including those applied by regional and local governments and authorities.

The GATS and the TRIPS Agreement also contain notification requirements designed to enhance centralized monitoring. Under the former, each member must promptly and at least annually notify the Council for Trade in Services of any new laws, regulations or administrative guidelines that significantly affect commitments on trade in services, or of any changes to existing provisions. Similarly, under the latter, members are obliged to notify the Council for TRIPS of all laws, regulations and final judicial decisions and administrative rulings that pertain to the matters concerning trade-related intellectual property rights.

The WTO notification provisions are designed primarily to give the Organization the means to monitor whether member countries are showing due deference to their obligations, and to administer the gradual abolition of particular exceptions to WTO requirements.[39] However, some developing countries may reasonably question whether the cumulative impact of notification requirements within the WTO system is unduly burdensome from a financial and bureaucratic standpoint. As discussed below, WTO law does take these concerns into account by providing for "exceptions" or "waivers" to notification requirements.

Notification requirements are imposed on States for the benefit of private investors as well as directly on private investors. With regard to the first type of requirements, certain IIAs contain obligations imposed on national administrative authorities to notify certain decisions taken of direct concern of investors. For example, article VI:3 of the GATS provides that "where authorization is required for the supply of a service [...], the competent authorities of a Member shall [...] inform the applicant of the decision concerning the application".[40]

A duty to notify may also apply directly to TNCs. In the Economic Community of West African States, Protocol A/P1/11/84, for example, provides that all enterprises that have been admitted to the status of Community Enterprises shall:

> "(d) inform the Executive Secretariat of any intended deviations from or difficulties in the implementation of the terms of an Approval Agreement, so as to enable any necessary re-assessment to be made between the parties to the Approval Agreement, (e) comply with such audit as may be requested by the Executive Secretary in collaboration with the relevant authorities of the Member State where they are located in order to ascertain compliance with the terms of the Approval Agreement; [...] (h) not fix or alter the prices

of its product or services without prior consultation with the Executive Secretariat and the competent authorities of the Member States where they are located".

These provisions emphasize at least two points: first, the duty to notify may include an obligation on corporate entities *vis-à-vis* both "central agencies" and "competent authorities of member States"; second, the duty to notify may be included in order to allow the parties to reassess previous agreements (sub (d)) as well as permit central agencies or states to participate to some extent in the decision-making process of the investor (sub (h)).

Similar transparency mechanisms have been applied to dispute settlement provisions in IIAs. There are a number of notification requirements surrounding the 1965 Convention on the Settlement of Investment Disputes Between States and Nationals of Other States, establishing the International Centre for Settlement of Investment Disputes (ICSID). These include the designation and notification by contracting states of the class or classes of disputes which it would or would not consider submitting to the jurisdiction of the Centre (article 25 of the ICSID Convention), and the designation and notification of courts or other authorities competent for the recognition and enforcement of awards rendered pursuant to the Convention (article 54).[41] These activities constitute an important contribution to transparency in the context of dispute settlement, in particular in light of the increasing role played by the ICSID in international investment disputes.

D. Timing

Bearing in mind current systems of communication, and the nature of competition in a liberalized economic environment, time is often of the essence in modern investment relationships. Thus, for example, the more recent BITs and free trade agreements entered into by the United States, the TRIMs Agreement, the Energy Charter Treaty (annex 1, article 20 (2)), and the draft MAI, all require the host country to publish its laws, regulations and related information "promptly", while the ASEAN treaty indicates that the information should be published in as timely a manner as possible, and the World Bank Guidelines recommend that a country's handbook of investment information should be "regularly" updated.

Other treaties, however, omit reference to timing considerations in respect of publication. Among these are the BIT between Haiti and the United States, and the TRIPS Agreement. Similarly, the BIT between Canada and Hungary, and that between China and Viet Nam, do not carry any reference to time in their provisions requiring consultation and sharing of information between the countries involved.

Where a treaty requiring information to be made public does not contain a reference to timing, the host country may have some degree of latitude, and may be inclined to assume that laws and regulations in place are binding on foreign investors even if they are yet to be made public. Likewise, because expressions such as "promptly" and "as timely as possible" are subjective in nature, the host country may not feel obliged to make its laws and regulations public immediately upon their entry into force. With these concerns in mind, some IIAs incorporate language that lends urgency to the duty to make laws and regulations public. Hence, article III of the GATS indicates that, in the normal course of events, all relevant measures (including laws and regulations) must be published at the latest by the time of their entry into force, and that this rule should apply save in emergency situations. Admittedly, the exception for undefined emergency situations reduces the force of the provision somewhat. But the intent is clear. And, in the case of litigation concerning the meaning of this provision, the onus is likely to be on the host country to demonstrate the existence of an emergency.

Similar timing provisions apply to TNCs. For example, Protocol A/P1/11/84 of the Economic Community of West African States requires Community Enterprises to submit on a regular basis progress reports, annual balance sheets and audited accounts.

More specifically, paragraph 44 of the draft United Nation Code (providing for certain transparency requirements on TNCs) states that the required information should be provided on a "regular annual basis, normally within six months and in any case not later than 12 months from the end of the financial year of the corporation". The same paragraph also provides that, where appropriate, a semi-annual summary of financial information should also be made available. Similarly, paragraph 7 of Part II of the draft NGO Charter provides that the required information on the corporate entity shall be "regularly publicised every six months in general or in exceptional cases, every year". In this regard, the specification on timing contained in the 1976 OECD Declaration on International Investment and Multinational Enterprises, as reviewed in 1991 (information by firms "should be published within reasonable time limits, on a regular basis, but at least annually"), should be compared with the 2000 OECD Guidelines on Multinational Enterprises which now contain no specific provision on the timing of the disclosure obligations.[42]

E. Exceptions

A last element relating to the content of transparency provisions in IIAs deals with safeguards or exceptions to transparency obligations. In section I, a number of considerations were advanced tending to support restrictions on the transparency principle. These considerations seek to determine the extent of intrusiveness that a transparency obligation may carry. Although this may be done by defining the scope of the transparency obligation itself (for example by limiting the items of information), IIAs have also used specified exception provisions in order to accomplish such goals.

A recent example of an IIA that includes extensive confidentiality safeguards is the 2003 Free Trade Agreement between Singapore and the United States. This Agreement contains both specific and general provisions protecting confidential information of parties to the Agreement, as well as corporate entities. In the chapter on Investment, article 15.13, paragraph 2, requires each party to protect "business information that is confidential from any disclosure that would prejudice the competitive position of the investor or the covered investment". In addition, article 21.4 provides for a general exception to disclosure obligations which states as follows:

> "Nothing in this Agreement shall be construed to require a Party to furnish or allow access to confidential information, the disclosure of which would impede law enforcement, or otherwise be contrary to the public interest, or which would prejudice the legitimate commercial interests of particular enterprises, public or private."

At the multilateral level, the ITO Charter, for example, was sensitive to the possible conflict between transparency and confidentiality. For this reason, the duty of notification in article 50 (3) was made subject to the proviso that:

> "any Member on notification to the Organization may withhold information which the Member considers is not essential to the Organization in conducting an adequate investigation, and which, if disclosed, would substantially damage the legitimate business interests of a commercial enterprise. In notifying the Organization that it is withholding information pursuant to this clause, the Member shall indicate the general character of the information withheld and the reason why it considers it not essential".

The balance struck in this provision is mainly in favour of disclosure, for the information to be withheld would have had to be both inessential to the ITO and its disclosure would have had to be substantially damaging to a particular commercial enterprise.

Today, WTO agreements incorporate certain exceptions to the duty of notification in order to take into consideration host countries' reluctance in certain cases to divulge confidential information with respect to particular measures. These safeguard provisions include:

- *Exceptions to notification requirements*. In order to preserve confidentiality, the TRIMs and TRIPS Agreements, and the GATS, all contain provisions that allow members to withhold some items of information. In the TRIMs Agreement, a note to article 5(1) on notification indicates that, where investment measures are applied under the discretionary authority of the State, the general notification requirement need not apply to information that would prejudice the legitimate commercial interests of particular enterprises. The TRIPS Agreement and GATS adopt a similar approach; in either case, the notification and other transparency requirements in the agreement are not applicable to confidential information, the disclosure of which "would impede law enforcement, or otherwise be contrary to the public interest, or which would prejudice legitimate commercial interests of particular enterprises, public or private" (article III *bis*, GATS).[43] The component of this exception allowing confidentiality on grounds of public interest raises issues of definition; for, it is possible to argue that, without qualification, an exception to transparency on the basis of public interest could give the host country a wide margin of discretion, and reduce considerably the scope of the notification provisions.

- *Waivers*. Under the TRIPS Agreement, there is express acknowledgement that some notification provisions may become onerous. Thus, with respect to each State party's duty to notify the Council for TRIPS about laws and regulations, the Council "shall attempt to minimize the burden on Members in carrying out this obligation and may decide to waive the obligation to notify such laws and regulations directly to the Council if consultations with WIPO on the establishment of a common register containing these laws and regulations are successful." This waiver possibility also applies to notification obligations for members arising from the terms of article 6*ter* of the Paris Convention of 1967. This approach is intended to reduce notification requirements for individual countries for which the information concerned is otherwise available. However, because the waiver possibility applies only to laws and regulations, while the notification requirement also includes final judicial decisions and administrative rulings of general application, the waiver covers only a portion of what is normally to be disclosed.
- *Time limits*. The transitional provisions of the TRIPS Agreement allowed developing countries the opportunity to delay the implementation of some TRIPS obligations (including duties as to notification) for five years from the date of entry into force of the WTO Agreements (article 65). This exception to the notification provisions of the TRIPS Agreement was also expressly made available for economies in transition (article 65.3). Article 66 of the TRIPS Agreement grants least developed country members a delay of ten years for the application of several TRIPS obligations, which can be extended by the Council for TRIPS for duly motivated reasons. Flexibility through the use of time limits is also exemplified by article III of the GATS, which was described above.

Turning to the question of exceptions related to corporate disclosure, the draft United Nations Code sets limit to such disclosure in the light of concerns often raised by foreign investors. Thus, paragraph 44 (penultimate sub-paragraph) states that:

> "The extent, detail and frequency of the information provided should take into account the nature and size of the transnational corporation as a whole, the requirements of confidentiality and effects on the transnational corporation's competitive position as well as the cost involved in producing the information".

This qualification – sensitive to costs, competitiveness and confidentiality – may have helped to make the terms of proposed paragraph 44 more acceptable to capital-exporting countries at the time of the deliberations on the draft United Nations Code. As is sometimes the case, however, the qualification is worded in very general terms, thus leaving open the question of how exactly it would apply in practice. The disclosure provisions in the OECD Guidelines on Multinational Enterprises, like those in the draft United Nations Code, are also limited by considerations of costs, business confidentiality and other competitive concerns.[44]

A further example may be found in the draft MAI. Although the draft MAI contains provisions clarifying that none of its other terms would prohibit State parties from applying transparency rules to foreign investors for information or statistical purposes, this provision is limited in two significant respects. First, the provisions of the draft MAI would not require any State party to furnish or allow access to information concerning the financial affairs and accounts of individual customers of particular investors or investments. And, second, these provisions would not require any State party to furnish or allow access to confidential or proprietary information. Included in this category of confidential or proprietary information is "information concerning particular investors or investments, the disclosure of which would impede law enforcement or be contrary to its laws protecting confidentiality or prejudice legitimate commercial interests of particular enterprises." Thus, under the draft MAI, it is envisaged that each contracting party would have the power legally to enforce disclosure rules with respect to foreign investors in its territory, but restrictions would apply to the items of information derived from foreign investors that the contracting party could reveal to other contracting parties.

The approach followed in the draft United Nations Code, the OECD Guidelines and the draft MAI may be contrasted with that adopted by the draft NGO Charter, which does not provide for exceptions to the principle of corporate transparency on grounds of confidentiality or otherwise.

* * *

This section has shown that a number of IIAs as well as related instruments have addressed the issue of transparency by imposing different sets of obligations on the three main participants in foreign investment, i.e. the host country, the foreign investor and the home country. Among these obligations, IIA practice includes the duty to make information publicly available, the obligation to answer requests for information, and notification and consultation requirements. Transparency being essentially a means to other ends in investment policy, the addressees, content and modalities of any transparency provision depend on the nature and objective of the particular international agreement under consideration. For example, agreements for the protection of investment, on the one hand, and investment liberalization agreements, on the other, do not address the same actors of the investment relationship (the former dealing mainly with the "host country", the latter with all "members" of the agreement); and if they do, the type of transparency provisions may differ (notification and monitoring requirements are usually more comprehensive in investment liberalization agreements than in investment protection agreements). With regard to corporate disclosure, the preceding survey has shown the diversity of approaches contained in IIAs and related instruments. For example, while traditionally transparency provisions imposed on investors have required disclosure of mainly business and financial information, more recently the scope of these provisions has been extended to other broader social, environmental and ethical concerns.

Section III Interaction with other Issues and Concepts

As a concept, transparency is essentially a mechanism by which information relevant to the parties of an agreement is made available. Accordingly, transparency considerations overlap significantly with various other issues and concepts that prevail in international investment practice. A summary of the main points of interaction between transparency and other issues and concepts discussed in the present volumes is set out in table 1.

The level of interaction between transparency and each of the following concepts is extensive:

Table 1. Interaction across issues and concepts

Issue	Transparency
Admission and establishment	++
Competition	++
Dispute settlement: investor-State	+
Dispute settlement: State-State	+
Employment	+
Environment	+
Fair and equitable treatment	++
Home country measures	+
Host country operational measures	+
Illicit payment	++
Incentives	++
Investment-related trade measures	+
MFN treatment	+
National treatment	+
Scope and definition	0
Social responsibility	++
State contracts	+
Taking of property	+
Taxation	+
Transfer of funds	+
Transfer of technology	+
Transfer pricing	++

Source: UNCTAD.
Key: 0 = negligible or no interaction.
+ = moderate interaction.
++ = extensive interaction.

- **Admission and establishment.** In keeping with international law, countries have traditionally retained for themselves the right to determine whether, and under what conditions, foreign investors may participate in the domestic economy. Generally, the putative investor, contemplating investment abroad, wishes to acquire information about the terms and conditions of admission and establishment and, for that purpose, needs information about the host country's regulatory framework in this area. In addition, the investor also would want to know the processes by which decisions concerning investment are made, and the criteria used for deciding which investments are to be granted approval (where a scheme requiring host country approval is in place). Before making an investment commitment, some foreign investors may wish to know that mechanisms for consultation between home and host countries on investment issues are in place.
- **Competition**. In recent years, various countries have entered into agreements designed to enhance the efficacy of their laws concerning competition between corporate

entities. It may be too early to speak of a typical agreement in this area, but some patterns are already discernible. For instance, in the Agreement between the European Communities and Canada, which entered into force in June 1999, fairly detailed provision is made for cooperation through notification, consultation and exchange of information, among other things. One underlying idea is that, where a party intends to take enforcement action to counter anti-competitive behaviour on the part of a corporation, it has to notify other parties that are likely to be significantly affected. The parties may undertake consultations on specific matters that have arisen, and in the course of enforcement activities may opt to work in coordination with each other. The parties also undertake to share information that enhances the application of their respective competition laws, though all information requirements are subject to confidentiality exceptions. Here again, the duty of transparency is not placed upon countries exclusively as home countries, but in particular cases such agreements concerning competition will place particular responsibilities on home countries for conduct carried out by their enterprises abroad.

- **Fair and equitable treatment**. Where a host country is obliged to grant fair and equitable treatment to foreign investors, it may be argued that this also implies a duty on the part of the host country to make public the laws, regulations and practices that are applicable to foreign investors. This would be implicit in the concept of fairness. For, if a foreign investor wishes to establish whether or not a particular host country action is fair and equitable, as a practical matter, the investor needs to ascertain the pertinent rules and practices that govern that country's action. The degree of transparency in the regulatory environment therefore helps to determine the extent to which a host country may be regarded as acting in accordance with the concept of fair and equitable treatment (Vasciannie, 2000). As is shown by the *Metalclad* controversy (box III.1), the precise relationship between transparency and fair and equitable treatment is ultimately determined by the terms of the given agreement.[45]

Box III.1. The NAFTA Metalclad case

In the case between Metalclad Corporation and Mexico, the Arbitral Tribunal constituted under Chapter Eleven of the NAFTA found that:

"74. NAFTA Article 1105(1) provides that 'each Party shall accord to investments of investors of another Party treatment in accordance with international law, including fair and equitable treatment and full protection and security'. For reasons set out below, the Tribunal finds that Metalcald's investment was not accorded fair and equitable treatment in accordance with international law, and that Mexico has violated the NAFTA Article 1105(1).

75. An underlying objective of NAFTA is to promote and increase cross-border investment opportunities and ensure the successful implementation of investment initiatives (NAFTA Article 102(1)).

76. Prominent in the statement of principles and rules that introduces the Agreement is the reference to 'transparency' (NAFTA Article 102(1)). The Tribunal understands this to include the idea that all relevant legal requirements for the purpose of initiating, completing and successfully operating investments made, or intended to be made, under the Agreement should be capable of being readily known to all affected investors of another Party. [...]

99. Mexico failed to ensure a transparent and predictable framework for Metalclad's business planning and investment. The totality of these circumstances demonstrates a lack of orderly process and timely disposition in relation to an investor of a party acting in the expectation that it would be treated fairly and justly in accordance with the NAFTA. [...]

101. The Tribunal therefore holds that Metalclad was not treated fairly or equitably under the NAFTA and succeeds on its claim under Article 1105."

The Government of Mexico successfully challenged this finding in a review of the award in accordance with Article 1136 of NAFTA before the Supreme Court of British Columbia. It was held that the Tribunal had gone beyond its jurisdiction by relying on Article 102(1) to include transparency obligations. Transparency was not an objective of NAFTA but was listed in Article 102(1) as one of the principles and rules contained in NAFTA through which the objectives were elaborated. While the principles of national treatment and MFN treatment were contained in Chapter 11 of NAFTA, transparency was not. Given that the Tribunal could only determine whether rights under Chapter 11 had been breached it did not have jurisdiction to arbitrate claims in respect of alleged breaches of other provisions of NAFTA. Therefore, while, as a general proposition, it may be argued that transparency forms part of the fair and equitable treatment principle, its actual operation as a binding obligation depends on the precise terms and structure of the IIA in question.

Source: UNCTAD, based on ICSID Case No. ARB(AF)/97/1, in International Law Materials, 40 (2001), pp. 36-40; Supreme Court of British Columbia, in *British Columbia Law Reports*, 89 (2001), pp. 359-366.

- **Illicit payments.** Generally, the main methods of tackling the problem of illicit payments at the international level have involved considerable reliance on transparency (see chapter 20 in volume II; also Sornarajah, 1990). Consequently, the extent of interaction between both concepts is substantial. There are several examples of international instruments employing transparency provisions to combat corruption. The Inter-American Convention against Corruption, which entered into force in 1997, exemplifies this approach with regard to transparency in at least two respects. First, by virtue of article X, each party is required to notify the Secretary General of the Organization of American States when it adopts legislation to combat transnational bribery and illicit enrichment, with the Secretary General being obliged to transmit this information to other parties. Second, article XIV requires each of the parties to afford to each other "the widest measure of mutual assistance" in the gathering of evidence and in the preparation of legal proceedings against corruption, and to participate in cooperative efforts to prevent, detect, investigate and punish corruption. Broadly similar rules that allow for the cross-border sharing of information concerning corrupt activities are also incorporated in the OECD Convention on Combating Bribery of Foreign Public Officials in International Business Transactions and in the Council of Europe's Criminal Law Convention on Corruption, while United Nations General Assembly resolutions, including Resolutions 51/191 and 52/87, exhort States to undertake international cooperative efforts in this area (see more recently, the United Nations Convention against Corruption, adopted on 31 October 2003 at the fifty eighth session of the General Assembly by resolution A/RES/58/4). Strictly speaking, these instruments are not concerned exclusively with investment matters. In practice, countries are obliged to act in accordance with principles of transparency to combat bribery and corruption and, in some instances, will be among States with the means to gather substantial information for this purpose. The 1992 World Bank Guidelines on the Treatment of Foreign Direct Investment (guideline III, section 8) also use the promotion of transparency as a tool for the prevention and control of corrupt business practices. The relationship between transparency and the fight against corruption has also been at the core of NGOs activities. For example, Transparency International seeks to curb corruption by mobilizing a global coalition to promote and strengthen international and national "Integrity Systems". Its work includes business advocacy, awareness raising, monitoring, and national Integrity Systems building.
- **Incentives**. The majority of IIAs that specifically address the issue of transparency do so in general terms. It is therefore not always clear whether the resulting transparency obligations extend to incentives. The usual formulation is to refer to laws, regulations, procedures and administrative practices of general application in respect to any matter covered by the IIA in question, coupled with the obligation that these are promptly published or otherwise made available to interested parties. To the extent that incentives provisions are contained in such instruments, the transparency obligation extends to them as well. Beyond that, certain agreements make an explicit connection between incentives and transparency. Thus, the section on Investment Incentives in the draft MAI included a provision that expressly applied the transparency provision in the draft MAI to investment incentives. In other instruments, transparency in the operation of investment incentives is placed on a hortatory basis. Thus, the OECD Declaration on International Investment and Multinational Enterprises, paragraph IV (International Investment Incentives and Disincentives), states, inter alia, that member countries will endeavour to make measures concerning investment incentives and disincentives "as transparent as possible, so that their importance and purpose can be ascertained and that information on them can be readily available". In a similar fashion, Article 160 of the Treaty Establishing the Common Market for Eastern and Southern Africa addresses the need for the member States to undertake "to increase awareness of their investment incentives, opportunities, legislation, practices, major events affecting investments and other relevant information through regular dissemination and other awareness–promoting activities." The SCM Agreement contains mandatory, detailed transparency provisions

dealing with incentives. For example, article 25 of this Agreement requires members to notify subsidies covered by the Agreement in order to enable other members to evaluate the trade effects and to understand the operation of the notified subsidy programmes. Article 22 also requires members to notify and make publicly available the initiation of an investigation on the legality of subsidy programmes of other members, providing clearly the types of information to be included in the public notice.

- **Social responsibility**. In investment law, the idea underlying the concept of corporate social responsibility is the notion that TNCs should seek in their operations to promote the economic and social interests of host and home countries in the course of their activities (chapter 18 in volume II). Several components of social responsibility interact in significant ways with the concept of transparency. For instance, if TNCs are required to adhere to ethical business standards and to promote and protect human rights, there must be means by which transnational activities in these areas are assessed and verified by the wider public; for this to occur, the activities of TNCs must be transparent and open. Similarly, if TNCs are required to show due regard for environmental, labour and consumer concerns, there will need to be adequate means of communication between TNCs and the various stakeholders, as well as methods by which actions on the part of TNCs may be verified (Muchlinski, 1999). Transparency as a means of promoting social responsibility may be achieved by the use of national legislation, but in some instances, the force and direction of national laws may need to be strengthened by international agreements and policy pronouncements.
- **Transfer pricing**. The methods by which TNCs place a value on goods, services and other assets transferred from one country to another but within the same corporate structure has raised important accounting and management problems for both governments and corporations (see chapter 19 in volume II). Transfer pricing questions interact with issues of transparency in a number of ways. For one thing, if home and host governments fear that a TNC may rely on invoicing methods that do not reflect the market value of goods and services being transferred within the corporate structure, they may monitor intra-company transfers by requiring transparency on the part of the company, under taxation law and also under the law concerning funds transfer from the particular jurisdiction. Indeed such probity on the part of the TNC is also required by the OECD Guidelines section on Taxation. At the same time, however, for reasons of efficiency, TNCs need information about the applicable laws concerning taxation and funds transfers, and will thus require transparency as to laws in both home and host countries. Also, bearing in mind the risks of illicit payments in this area, the emerging treaty rules concerning corruption that require transparency on the part of home and host countries are relevant.

Conclusion
Economic and Development Implications and Policy Options

The concept of transparency is applicable to the three main sets of participants in the international investment process. Accordingly, the present chapter has examined transparency issues from the different perspectives of the host country, the home country and the foreign investor. For all three sets of investment participants, the question for consideration here is whether, and to what extent, different approaches to transparency may influence the development prospects of countries participating in IIAs.

This question has no straightforward answer, for a variety of reasons. First, there is the familiar point that transparency is only one of a number of factors that influence development possibilities for countries or companies. Thus, even where the most rigorous standards of transparency are enforced, it will be difficult to state that this has contributed to, or retarded, the investment process. To illustrate, a developing host country may have a transparent FDI framework, but the laws and regulations that it publishes widely happen to have features that are inimical to investment promotion. Indeed, the country in question may simply have too few locational advantages to be a worthwhile investment destination. In such cases, there will be no direct relationship between transparency and the development prospects of the country concerned. The converse may also be true, namely that a developing country that has a non-transparent FDI framework may have natural advantages as an investment location making the risk of investment worthwhile.

Secondly, the impact on development prospects of different approaches to transparency may be difficult to discern because transparency is still largely perceived as an issue for national law. In most cases, in which there is a reference to transparency in an IIA, this reference is meant to reinforce the national law treatment of the subject. To be sure, several concepts in IIAs share this feature, so that, for instance, treatment standards for foreign investors in BITs are often meant to supplement or confirm national law approaches. However, in the case of transparency, this characteristic is especially pronounced because almost all countries maintain, in principle, that transparency is important. With this in mind, some countries argue that, as transparency is included in their legal systems as a matter of course, there is no need for transparency issues to be included in IIAs. Thus, the absence of a provision on transparency in an investment agreement may not be fully indicative of a country's attitude towards transparency. Similarly, even where an investment agreement does incorporate provisions on transparency, the strictures in the agreement are likely to be somewhat general, leaving scope for countries to indicate more detailed rules on transparency in their national law. Again, this underlines the difficulty in assessing the extent to which the transparency provisions in an IIA may actually influence the investment process in regard to a particular country.

Thirdly, the impact that specific approaches to transparency in IIAs may have is sometimes obscured by the fact that some agreements incorporate more than one approach to transparency. For instance, a host country may accept a legal duty to publish its laws and regulations, and simultaneously accept a duty to consult with some other countries on investment matters. If the host country is successful in attracting FDI, the particular contribution made either by the country's broad acceptance of transparency, or by the country's acceptance of one form of transparency as against the other, will almost certainly be beyond calculation.

Fourthly, administrative and cost factors should be borne in mind. Efforts to ensure transparency – whether in the form of information-disclosure or consultation – involve administrative costs (WTO, 2002, p. 14), a burden particularly for developing countries with scarce resources. Administrative costs of maintaining transparency may also be high with duties to notify, provision of information and response to requests.

Fifthly, transparency obligations imposed with regard to home country measures may enhance the information capacity of both the host country and the foreign investor since such measures play a role in promoting FDI, generally and development-oriented FDI more specifically. Similarly, disclosure requirements imposed on TNCs may be beneficial to both host and home countries. The latter may wish to acquire information about the operations of the investor in other countries for example for taxation purposes and as a means of assessing whether a foreign investor is acting in accordance with its own rules and policies that have extraterritorial reach. The former will want to have access to information concerning TNCs in order to strengthen its capacity to assess the nature and value of the contribution being made by particular foreign investors, as well as to assess the effectiveness of its national policies and regulations.

In light of the preceding discussion the following policy options present themselves:

A. No reference to transparency

Although transparency is not a major determinant of FDI, as a general proposition, foreign investors do expect a certain degree of transparency, especially from host countries. Since foreign investors may regard the absence of legal rules compelling transparency in host countries unfavourably, this option might not be ideal to enhance a country's image among foreign investors and to a certain extent weakens their prospects for improving inward capital flow.

In fairness, however, this is not to suggest that reliance on an approach that makes no reference to transparency necessarily conveys hostility to transparency, or to foreign investors more generally. Much will depend on the circumstances of each case. More specifically, a country may support this option for reasons that do not reflect its perspective on the importance of transparency in practice. A country may, for instance, accept investment agreements without a reference to transparency because it believes that this type of transparency is inherently an issue for national law, and may thus be best addressed by domestic legislation. This, in itself, makes no negative statement as to the need to ensure transparency safeguards in the interests of foreign investors. Moreover, a country may accept the omission of a treaty reference to transparency on the assumption that this type of transparency is implicitly incorporated in all agreements which provide for fair and equitable treatment for foreign investors. In this case, too, silence on the question of transparency ought not to be construed as hostility to foreign investment.

Similarly, depending on the circumstances of the case, a lack of transparency provisions dealing with home country measures and foreign investors' activities may, on the one hand, restrict the investment-promotion potential of the former measures and, on the other, impede both host and home countries' capacity to implement and monitor their national policies and laws.

B. Reference to transparency

1. *Addressees*

When transparency requirements are incorporated into IIAs, there may exist at least three different options with regard to the addressees of such requirements.

Option 1. Reference to all State parties to an IIA.

A transparency requirement that is imposed on all State parties to an IIA means that such a requirement is applicable not only to host countries but also to home countries. It thus makes sure that the regulatory framework for FDI of the home country, including any measures for the promotion of FDI to developing countries, is subject to transparency as is the regulatory framework of host countries (UNCTAD, 2003). In this respect, the scope *ratione personae* (the addressees) of a transparency obligation may often depend on its actual drafting and on the related issue of the scope *ratione materiae* (the items of information that are subject to transparency). In addition, reference to all parties to an IIA means that home countries might be called to provide information for purposes of assisting host countries in the conduct of their regulatory policies such as, for example, tackling corruption and promoting economic competition (UNCTAD, 2003, p. 156). This comprehensive approach would also enhance the investment-promotion features of home country measures in as much as it would provide potential investors with the necessary information.

Option 2. Specific reference to host country.

A transparency requirement imposed on host countries only is narrower in coverage than the requirement in option 1. If a country wishes to make a clear statement to the effect that it is hospitable to FDI, it may consider adopting this option. By acknowledging a legal obligation on the part of the country to comply with transparency requirements in different ways, this option should, subject to other investment considerations, encourage investor confidence. However, this option would have the same possible shortcomings signalled above with regard to the lack of transparency provisions dealing with home country measures.

Option 3. Specific reference to corporate entities.

The inclusion of specific transparency obligations on corporate entities would ensure broad access to information, in particular by the host country. This would in turn facilitate the planning and monitoring responsibilities of both host and home governments, for example, in the fields of taxation, company, competition and labour regulations. In addition, having regard to trends in favour of corporate social responsibility, host countries that place obligations of transparency on TNCs would also be able adequately to assess the evolving relationship between particular foreign investors and the wider public affected by their operations in the host country.

However, disclosure requirements in IIAs are not always supported by foreign investors or by capital-exporting countries. For one thing, disclosure requirements in an IIA may imply a possible discrimination of foreign investors (in violation of the national treatment obligation) if they are imposed on them only (i.e. if the domestic law of the host country does not include similar requirements). For another, foreign investors may fear that such requirements are really the foundation for unduly intrusive disclosure rules and regulations under national law. Furthermore, where mandatory corporate disclosure rules are placed in investment instruments, they may not – in the view of foreign investors – incorporate appropriate protection for information to be safeguarded from public scrutiny on grounds of confidentiality or otherwise. Mandatory disclosure requirements in investment agreements may therefore be regarded as a factor that may deter foreign investors, though the extent to which they may actually deter such investment will vary from case to case.

2. *Items of information*

Transparency requirements incorporated into IIAs may display a different degree of intrusiveness depending first of all on the items of information that are subject to such requirements. Different options may be available depending on whether the transparency requirements deal with governmental or corporate information.

a. Governmental information

With regard to governmental information, at least four different basic options may be envisaged. These could be used alone, or on a combined basis so as to increase the types of information that have to be disclosed under the transparency obligation:

Option 1. The first option is to include a transparency obligation with regard to "general policies" pertaining or affecting investment.

Option 2. A broader option, and one that would be more intrusive would be to add "laws and regulations" and "administrative procedures" to the relevant items of information subject to transparency.

Option 3. In order to supplement the scope of the information subject to transparency, a third option would be also to include explicit reference to "judicial decisions" and "international agreements" pertaining or affecting investment.

Option 4. A further, more intrusive option would be to add specific "judicial procedures", "administrative practices" and/or "administrative decisions" on individual cases to the transparency obligation.

Option 5. A final option would be to include a transparency obligation with regard to "draft" or "proposed" laws and regulations, in order to give other interested parties the possibility to comment on such draft laws or regulations before their finalization.

The key issue here concerns with the extent of intrusiveness a country (host or home) is comfortable with.

There is also a related issue, that of costs. Countries (and particularly, developing countries) may realistically fear that a duty to publicize every item of legal information could become burdensome and, indeed, even developed countries do not publicize every low level administrative or judicial decision that may affect investment in particular communities. This factor, however, may be overcome by a country's commitment to make some items of information public (without publishing it), so that foreign investors will have access even to information of specific scope in appropriate instances.

In practice, there may be questions about the treatment of items of confidential information, but these issues do not undermine the basic point that core items of information concerning the operation of the host country's legal regime for investors need to be placed in the public domain if that country wishes to promote investor interest. Public disclosure of laws, regulations and administrative practices allows foreign investors to assess different regimes for fairness and non-discrimination, and tends to reduce opportunities for petty corruption and arbitrary behaviour within countries, factors that have bearing on the investment climate. Public disclosure of laws, regulations and administrative practices, too, allows investors to obtain information that may be relevant to their locational decision. Such disclosure may also facilitate the promotional strategies of host countries seeking to attract FDI by providing them with information that can then become an integral part of promotion strategies geared towards particular countries.

b. Corporate information

With regard to corporate information, two general options may be envisaged.

Option 1. A first option would be to require disclosure of business and financial information only. This would include information relating to the structure of the corporation and its main activities, as well as information relating to financial matters such as the balance sheet, income statement, statement of sources, significant new long-term capital investment, etc.

Option 2. A second, and more modern and inclusive, option would be to require, in addition to business and financial information, disclosure of information on company policies relating to business ethics, the environment and other public policy commitments.

As noted above, corporate information is important for both home and host countries to be able to formulate and manage their national policies and laws, whether dealing with development, taxation or environmental issues. Within the context of an IIA this may apply with greater emphasis depending on whether or not transparency requirements already exist in the national laws of the countries concerned. Where the actual disclosure requirements are widely drawn, countries may be allowed to gather information about commercial plans, opportunities and prospects of particular foreign investors, information which could enhance, on the one hand, host countries' capacity to benefit more from FDI and, on the other, home countries' ability to improve development-oriented FDI measures. While foreign investors frequently do not support broad mandatory disclosure requirements that include business and non-business information, this may ultimately be beneficial also for foreign investors at least where governments make use of the information collected in a manner that is receptive to investors' interests. In any event, the inclusion of safeguards or exceptions to transparency requirements (e.g. to protect confidential information), as explained below, constitutes an option addressing some of these concerns.

3. *Modalities*

Different degrees of intrusiveness may also depend on the types of mechanisms that are employed to further transparency. In this regard, several options are available, which may also be used concurrently. In each case the commitment could be mandatory or voluntary. Clearly, where the latter approach is taken, the burden of compliance on countries is much lesser than in the case of a mandatory obligation. The discussion continues on the assumption that a binding obligation is to be taken, as this is where the most significant issues of intrusiveness lie.

Option 1. Consultation and exchange of information.

Where such a commitment is mandatory, some countries may consider that they do not have the administrative and technical capacity to undertake frequent rounds of consultations on matters that, ultimately, may be of little practical consequence. This suggests that the duty to consult could be framed to include the notion that consultations shall take place following specified intervals, or that the time interval between rounds of consultation should be reasonably spaced.

Option 2. Making information publicly available.

Information could be made publicly available, whether through formal publication or by simply allowing interested parties access to relevant information. This type of transparency mechanism is basic to the investment relationship. Moreover, this option does not seem to involve any problematic issues per se, since it is often the case that such obligations exist already under national laws. However, depending on the items of information that are required to be made public, even this mechanism may become more controversial (see above B.2).

As noted above, publication requirements may also be imposed on countries with regard to draft laws or regulations with the aim of affording interested parties the opportunity to express their views before the formal adoption of these laws and regulations. This is the most intrusive type of publication requirement. Although it is based on the general idea that broader participation of all interested parties to the regulatory process might contribute to the final result, such a mechanism may also be seen as compromising a country's sovereign right to discuss and decide on investment rules without intervention by "external" parties (whether host, home countries or private investors). This is especially true in case of a broad power imbalance between the countries involved.

Option 3. Answering requests for information.

A third option may be to provide a duty to answer requests for information stemming from any of the other parties to an IIA. Although this option may be seen as more burdensome than the previous two, it would be advancing FDI flows in the sense that it may help countries as well as investors to obtain relevant information more easily.

Option 4. Notification.

A further option involves a requirement to notify general or specific actions taken by each party in respect of investment-related matters and/or changes to the regulatory framework affecting investment. These types of transparency requirements are usually specified in multilateral schemes, such as those set out in WTO agreements, in which a central agency is mandated to monitor the degree of country compliance to agreed rules. Acceptance of the duty to notify is therefore part of a wider package of rules, and if a country wishes to continue enjoying the benefits of the relevant multilateral scheme, it will need, as a matter of law, to adhere to the notification requirements. In the light of the possible costs and technical capacity problems involved in complying with detailed notification requirements, some multilateral schemes have sought to incorporate flexibility in the interests of developing countries and economies in transition by allowing certain exceptions to notification, waivers and/or relaxed time periods for satisfying notification rules.

Notification requirements may be imposed on States with the specific aim to guarantee procedural transparency in administrative proceedings directly affecting foreign investors. While this option enhances investors' information and thus their ability to operate efficiently in a host country, this type of transparency obligation also involves a higher degree of intrusiveness as it might require a greater administrative burden and extra financial costs. Foreign investors may also want for administrative transparency obligations to be imposed on home countries in order to make sure that any administrative proceedings in the home country affecting outward FDI (e.g. taxation, financial assistance, promotion schemes) be carried out in a fair and impartial manner. Similar arguments are applicable with regard to notification requirements imposed directly on TNCs.

4. Timing

The issue of timing also offers certain options.

Option 1. No timing provision.

Of course one option is not to include any time obligations within the transparency provision. That would give the country the maximum discretion as to when to disclose the information required under the transparency provision. However, it could also be seen as a license to treat compliance with that obligation rather lightly.

Option 2. Inclusion of timing provision.

On the other hand, should such a provision be decided upon, two main approaches to this issue can be discerned:

a. General timing clause

This offers no specific dates or deadlines by which the transparency obligation has to be fulfilled. Rather, it requires a general commitment to the prompt publication, or to making available, the items of information that have been included under the transparency obligation. A further variation of this approach is to have a commitment to a regular submission and/or updating of the required information, but without a specified deadline.

From a development perspective such a general commitment has the advantage of allowing for a measure of discretion and policy space as to the process of compliance with the transparency obligation. This may be important for a country that wishes to show a commitment to effective and regular disclosure of information under its transparency obligation, but which does not wish to be bound by strict deadlines, possibly due to concerns about the resource implications of such a commitment. Equally, where the addressee of this general approach is a corporation, it too would benefit form a wider discretion as to time for compliance. Such an approach might be particularly helpful for small and medium-sized enterprises. On the other hand, large TNCs could be expected to have the resources to comply with strict deadlines where these are required.

b. Specific deadlines

A number of ways can be used to establish specific deadlines for compliance with the transparency obligation. These include compliance:

- by the date of entry into force of the policy measure, law, regulation or administrative decision, as the case may be;
- by a specific date in the calendar year;
- by the lapse of a specific period of time from the chosen point in time from which that period is to be measured. For example, six months after the date of the annual budget statement of a country or the date of the publication of a company's annual financial statement; for regular reporting or notification commitments, these can be specified at particular periods of the calendar year, for example, annually, half-yearly, quarterly and the like.

The common development implication of such measures is that they will place a greater burden of compliance upon the home or host country addressee of the obligation than a more flexible period. On the other hand, such a commitment will show a degree of seriousness in the country's approach to transparency. In relation to corporate addressees, while small and medium-sized enterprises might find such deadlines relatively burdensome, larger firms should not. However, effective regulation may depend on effective and timely disclosure of information regardless of firm size. Thus such deadlines may be of value in ensuring regulatory compliance.

5. Exceptions

As noted in section I, a number of policy reasons exist for expressly limiting the transparency obligation. In this light the following options present themselves:

Option 1. No exceptions.

A transparency obligation could be made absolute and unconditional. This would show a significant commitment towards such a principle. However, it would be perhaps unrealistic to expect countries or corporations to accept such a wide ranging commitment, given the vital issues that exceptions to transparency commitments entail. Thus exceptions are more likely to be put into place than not.

Option 2. Exceptions to the transparency obligation.

The main exceptions to this obligation are:

- Exclusion of information on public interest or national security grounds on the part of the addressee government.
- Exceptions to a notification requirement of certain items of information.
- Waiver of the duty to disclose in cases in which the item of information is otherwise available, as where another international agreement requires its disclosure.
- The protection of confidential information obtained in the course of governmental activities, on the part of a country addressee, or by a corporation in the course of its business operations.
- Exclusion of commercially sensitive information, or the content of intellectual property rights or secret know-how, in the possession of the addressee corporation.

The precise implications of such exceptions on development are hard to discern, especially as their purpose is not directed at this precise issue. They are aimed more at making the parameters of the intrusiveness of the transparency obligation acceptable within the boundaries of essential public policy and national security goals for countries, while for firms they seek to protect their sources of comparative advantage. In addition a general principle of confidentiality is needed to ensure that the transparency obligation is not abused through the disclosure of information that has been obtained by countries or corporations in confidence and in good faith. To the extent that essential public policy goals are not undermined through unconditional disclosure it could be said that such exceptions preserve the policy space needed by, in particular, developing host countries, in furthering their economic development policies. In addition, an assurance of confidentiality for firms may reduce the risk of compliance with disclosure regulations and so enhance their effectiveness as policy tools for development.

A final possibility that has not yet appear to have been used in IIA provisions is to provide for a capacity exception for small and medium sized enterprises that may be unable to meet all the requirements of full transparency and disclosure.

Option 3. Development exceptions.

In this connection a further possible option arises, namely, whether special, development oriented exclusions should not be added to a transparency provision. At least two such exceptions can be envisaged:

- Transitional provisions that exclude the transparency obligation (or certain parts thereof) for developing and/or least developed countries for a specified time after entry into force of the IIA in question, so as to allow for time to adapt to the demands of compliance with the full obligation.
- Capacity based exceptions that limit the scope of transparency (or parts thereof) for countries that cannot sustain the administrative and financial burdens of full compliance.

Such provisions could also be used in conjunction with technical assistance provisions requiring such cooperation from developed home countries in ensuring that developing and least developed host countries can meet the standards required by a transparency obligation.

* * *

From the foregoing discussion, it is clear that the inclusion of transparency provisions in IIAs offers a range of possibilities as to the addressees, the type or scope of information covered, the modalities for the delivery of the information, the timing of transparency disclosures and any relevant exceptions. On the other hand, there is a growing understanding, based on lengthy national policy experience, that transparency in the conduct of FDI policy, and transparency on the part of private investors, are conducive to the development of an effective, open and accountable system of economic activity that is particularly conducive to economic development. The use of appropriately formulated transparency obligations in IIAs can enhance this process by complementing national policies and by ensuring the acceptance of transparency as an increasingly valuable principle of international economic co-operation that may acquire the status of a general legal obligation.

Notes

1 See Sauvant, 2002.

2 Unless otherwise noted, all instruments cited herein may be found in UNCTAD, 1996a, 2000, 2001, 2002a and 2004b; the texts of the BITs mentioned may be found in the collection of BITs maintained online by UNCTAD at www.unctad.org/iia.

3 The approach in the model BIT of the United Kingdom is actually borne out in BITs completed between the United Kingdom and various countries: see, for example, the BITs between the United Kingdom and Dominica (1987), Bolivia (1988), China (1988) and the Russian Federation (1989).

4 See also article 11 of the 1997 model BIT of The Netherlands, and article 12 of the 1994 model BIT of the People's Republic of China.

5 See also article 5 on "Transparency" of chapter IV on "Development of Investment Relations" of the 2000 free trade agreement between the United States and Viet Nam.

6 See further below section B (1) on items of information subject to transparency obligations.

7 Very similar provisions are also contained in plurilateral and multilateral instruments such as the Organisation for Economic Co-operation and Development (OECD) draft Multilateral Agreement on Investment (draft MAI) (paragraph 1 of the section on "Transparency"), the Energy Charter Treaty (article 20(2) of Annex 1), the North American Free Trade Agreement (NAFTA) (article 1802.1), the 1961 OECD Code of Liberalisation of Capital Movements (Article 11(a)), and the 1992 International Monetary Fund (IMF)/World Bank Guidelines on the Treatment of Foreign Direct Investment (Guideline II, Section 6). Moreover, several agreements of the World Trade Organization (WTO) contain transparency provisions applying to all parties without distinction: for example, article X of the General Agreement on Tariff and Trade (GATT), article 6.1 of the Agreement on Trade-Related Investment Measures (TRIMs Agreement), article III of the General Agreement on Trade in Services (GATS), article 63 of the Agreement on Trade-Related Aspects of Intellectual Property Rights (TRIPS), article 7 and Annex B of the Agreement on Sanitary and Phyto-sanitary Measures (SPS Agreement), and article 10 of the Agreement on Technical Barriers to Trade (TBT Agreement).

8 The draft MAI contains provisions clarifying that none of its other terms would prohibit State parties from applying transparency rules to foreign investors. In the section on Transparency of Part III concerning treatment of investors, the draft MAI states that "(n)othing in this Agreement shall prevent a Contracting Party from requiring an investor of another Contracting Party, or its investment, to provide routine information concerning that investment solely for information or statistical purposes." However, certain restrictions would apply to the items of information derived from foreign investors that the contracting party could reveal to other contracting parties. See below the sub-section addressing the "content of transparency provisions".

9 In the Joint Declaration in the 2002 Association Agreement between Chile and the European Union, parties remind their TNCs "of their recommendation to observe the OECD Guidelines for Multilateral Enterprises, wherever they operate" (UNCTAD, 2003, p. 167).

10 The specific objective of the IRTK campaign is to require United States companies to report to agencies of the Government of the United States and then to disclose to the public specific environmental and labour information concerning their operations abroad. See <http://www.irtk.org>.

11 See <http://www.dfid.gov.uk/>.

12 See <http://www.abi.org.uk/>.

13 Article 4 of the 2001 model BIT of Austria.

14 Article 5(b) of the 1998 Framework Agreement of the ASEAN Investment Area (AIA).

15 Article 15 of the 2001 model BIT of Finland.

16 Article 2 of the 2002 Agreement between Japan and the Republic of Singapore for a New-Age Economic Partnership.

17 Article XIV of the 1997 BIT between Canada and Lebanon and article 19.3, paragraph 1, of the 2003 FTA between Singapore and the United States.

18 See article 20.4 of the 2003 FTA between Chile and the United States and article VI:3 of the GATS.

19 The Convention Establishing the European Free Trade Association (EFTA) (article 51) and the draft MAI (paragraph 1 of the section on Transparency) also follow this approach.

20 Similar provisions may be found in the 1991 BIT between Canada and Hungary (article X), and the 1999 BIT between Canada and El Salvador (article XIV). In the latter treaty, however, there is no reference to "policies".

21 See also article 20 of the 2000 Free Trade Agreement between the European Community and Mexico with regard to the financial service sector and annex B, paragraph 5, of the SPS Agreement.

22 Article 20.4(a) of the 2003 Free Trade Agreement between Chile and the United States.

23 For a similar approach with regard to the dispute settlement mechanism of the WTO, see further Mavroidis, 2002.

24 See International Monetary Fund (IMF)/World Bank Guidelines on the Treatment of Foreign Direct Investment.

25 See paragraph 1 of the section on Transparency in Part III of the draft MAI.

26 See the 1997 BIT between Canada and Lebanon (article XIV.1) and the 2003 Free Trade Agreement between Chile and the United States (article 20.2, paragraph 1).

27 See paragraph 3 of the section on "Transparency" in Part II.

28 For an example that adopts a combination of the two above-mentioned approaches, see article 1111(2) of NAFTA which stipulates as follows: "a Party may require an investor of another Party, or its investment in its territory, to provide routine information concerning that investment solely for informational or statistical purposes" and "(n)othing in this paragraph shall be construed to prevent a Party from otherwise obtaining or disclosing information in connection with the equitable and good faith application of its law."

29 See also the Partnership and Cooperation Agreements entered into by the European Communities and other States, which provides for cooperation to establish stable and adequate business law and conditions, and to exchange information on laws, regulations and administrative practices in the field of investment and to exchange information on investment opportunities in the form of, *inter alia*, trade fairs, exhibitions, trade weeks and other events. See for example, article 47 of the 1995 Partnership and Cooperation Agreement Establishing a Partnership between the European Communities and their Member States, of the one Part, and the Kyrgyz Republic, of the other Part.

30 Some BITs between the United States and other countries modify the language of the 1984 United States model to clarify that the duty to make information public refers to those laws, regulations and the like that concern the investments of nationals of either State. This drafting clarification may be superfluous. See, e.g., the BITs between the United States and Haiti and Cameroon, respectively.

31 In 1992, Vandevelde reported that, in negotiations between the United States and various other countries on this particular wording, there were no objections on principle. Vandevelde, 1992, p. 207.

32 For a wording similar to the one in the 1994 model BIT of the United States see also paragraph 1 of the section on "Transparency" of the draft MAI indicating that: "Each Contracting Party shall promptly publish, or otherwise make publicly available, its laws, regulations, [...]".

33 This approach, also followed in the BIT between Australia and Papua New Guinea, is not reflected in some other BITs involving Australia. For example, the Hungarian and Polish BITs with Australia provide that the parties shall make their laws and policies on investment "public" and "readily accessible", respectively, but omit reference to specific means of clarification.

34 See also the BIT between Senegal and the United States which adopts the language of article II (7) of the 1984 model text, but adds that the pertinent information needs to be made public only "by existing official means". Similarly, article II (6) of the BIT between Morocco and the United States requires laws and regulations to be made public, but specifies that administrative practices and procedures, as well as adjudicatory decisions, "can be consulted" by investors of either party. Vandervelde, 1992, p. 208.

35 Similar issues may be emphasized in the BIT between Canada and Thailand where article XVI (1) expressly provides that each contracting party shall publish or make available "to the extent practicable" laws, regulations, procedures and administrative rulings of general application.

36 See article 1802 of NAFTA and article 3, chapter VI, of 2000 Free Trade Agreement between United States and Viet Nam.

37 Also see the transparency provisions of the draft MAI.

38 The 2003 Free Trade Agreement between Singapore and the United States also contains several provisions requiring the establishment of contact points (e.g. articles 11.5, 17.4, 18.7 and 19.2). See also the Implementation Procedures of the OECD Guidelines for Multinational Enterprises (part I of the Decision of the OECD Council in June 2000).

39 There may be cases in which the burden of collecting specific information is attributed to an agency or organization. An example of such a type of transparency mechanism is found in the 1980 Unified Agreement for the Investment of Arab Capital in the Arab States. Article 18 (4) provides that the Economic Council has the faculty to collate and coordinate the reports, information, statements, legislation, regulations and statistics relating to investment, the fields of investment, the sectors open to investment and the preconditions for investment in such sectors in the States parties.

40 See also article 20.4 (a) of the 2003 Free Trade Agreement between Chile and the United States.

41 See http://www.worldbank.org/icsid.

42 Paragraph 1 of part III on "Disclosure" simply states that "[e]nterprises should ensure that timely, regular, reliable and relevant information is disclosed [...]."

43 The formulation in article 63 (4) of the TRIPS Agreement adopts this form of words; but, of course, it applies to a different set of items for disclosure. In respect of requests for information from other members (not, strictly speaking, a notification function), article 6 (3) of the TRIMs Agreement requires a State to treat enquiries with sympathetic consideration; it allows the State to withhold such information on terms similar to those applicable in the TRIPS Agreement and the GATS.

44 See the first paragraph of part III on "Disclosure". In this regard, it should be noted that in the previous version of the OECD Guidelines, there was no reference to "competition concerns" (see the first paragraph of the section on "Disclosure of Information".

45 In this regard the evolution of the ASEAN Agreement for the Protection and Promotion of Investment should be noted. While in its original form this Agreement contained no express language on the provision of information by host countries to foreign investors, the revised version

of the Agreement, signed in September 1996, does incorporate a provision on "Transparency and Predictability", even though the original version of the ASEAN Treaty did incorporate a provision guaranteeing fair and equitable treatment for foreign investors in article IV(2).

Chapter 11. Dispute Settlement: State-State*

Executive summary

Provisions concerning the settlement of investment disputes are a central feature of international investment agreements (IIAs). The present chapter deals with such provisions as they pertain to State-to-State disputes. Such disputes are relatively rare, in that the bulk of investment disputes arising under IIAs involve investor-State disputes. These are the subject of chapter 12.

The following principal issues raised by State-to-State dispute settlement provisions provide the focus for discussion throughout the chapter and are specifically discussed in section I. First, the types of disputes that could trigger a State-to-State procedure need to be identified. State-to-State disputes can arise out of either the exercise of diplomatic protection on the part of the home State of the investor (though this is increasingly rare given the existence of investor-State dispute settlement provisions that give direct rights of action to the investor) or as a result of a dispute over the interpretation or application of the IIA. Secondly, the procedures governing dispute settlement mechanisms need to be considered. These involve: negotiations and consultations which are nearly always required as a preliminary step in the dispute settlement process; ad hoc inter-State arbitration, which is most prominently featured in IIAs; permanent arbitral or judicial arrangements for dispute settlement; and political or administrative institutions whose decisions are binding. Third, the applicable standards for the settlement of disputes need to be agreed. This issue raises the further question of which law is to govern the resolution of the dispute at hand. Fourth, the nature and scope of outcomes of dispute settlement mechanisms need to be addressed and, fifth, compliance with dispute settlement awards. The substantive provisions of IIAs that cover each area are examined in section II of this chapter.

Section III of the chapter considers the various interactions that exist between the present topic and others that arise in the context of IIAs. The most significant one is between State-to-State and investor-State dispute settlement. As regards other areas of interaction, two main categories of such interactions can be identified. First, there are provisions in IIAs, the interpretation or application of which could normally be expected to be directly at issue. These include the scope of coverage and definitions of investors and investments, admission and establishment commitments and obligations concerning standards of treatment (fair and equitable treatment, most-favoured-nation treatment, and national treatment), host country transfer of funds, and the taking of property. Second, there are those interactions that would result, either directly if certain topics are expressly addressed in IIAs, or indirectly in so far as measures relating to such topics would give rise to issues with respect to the topics in the first category identified above. These include competition law and investment-related trade measures; employment, environmental and tax laws and regulations; State contracts; incentives; illicit payments; transfer of technology; and measures taken by an investor's home country with respect to the social responsibility of investors or in response to transfer pricing.

Finally, the last section considers the various options open to negotiators when drafting State-to-State dispute settlement clauses. The most basic choice is whether to include or to exclude provisions on this subject. Where the latter choice is made further alternatives exist as to how to deal with each of the issue areas identified in sections I and II. These are laid out in detail in the last section.

Introduction

A. International investment disputes and their settlement: An overview

Every foreign direct investment (FDI) transaction entails a trilateral relationship involving a host

* The chapter is based on a 2003 manuscript prepared by Amazu Asouzu and Mattheo Bushehri. The final version reflects comments received from Nils-Urban Allard, Joachim Karl, Mark Koulen, Ernst-Ulrich Petersmann, M. Sornarajah and Americo Beviglia-Zampetti.

State, a foreign investor and the latter's home State. Inherent in the concept of State sovereignty lies the notion that a State has the power – which can be qualified in an IIA – to admit foreigners within its territory and to regulate their activities, as well as to protect its nationals abroad from acts contrary to international law. Thus, within the context of the regulation and protection of the investment activities of transnational corporations, disputes might arise between States or between States and investors.

Investment-related disputes between States could arise from various governmental measures that affect cross-border economic activities, some of which are addressed in IIAs. IIAs put into place frameworks consisting of general and specific undertakings and obligations by the States party to such agreements that determine the scope, extent and manner of their involvement with the cross-border investment activities of their nationals. The genesis of State-to-State (or "inter-State") disputes in IIAs can be traced either to issues that arise directly between the signatories of IIAs, or to issues that first arise between investors and their host States, but then become inter-State disputes.

It should be noted at the outset that, by comparison with investor-State disputes, State-to-State disputes in the field of investment, which have gone to third party settlement, are few and far between. Thus, experience of such disputes is relatively limited. The present chapter should be read in the light of this fact. This situation requires some clarification. It is true to say that, in a certain sense, even a dispute between an investor and a State that arises under an IIA contains an inter-State element, in that the investor is a national of another State party to the IIA, and that State might even have been involved in attempts to negotiate an amicable settlement of the dispute. Nonetheless, such a dispute remains an investor-State dispute albeit one arising out of an IIA agreed between States.

The main explanation for the lack of State-to-State investment disputes lies in the manner in which foreign investment law has developed in recent decades. That development is marked by the move from the era of Friendship, Commerce and Navigation (FCN) treaties, and investment treaties that pre-dated the establishment of the International Centre for Settlement of Investment Disputes (ICSID), in which the investor had no right to institute proceedings against a host State, to the current era where the investor has direct rights to do so under many investment agreements. Such agreements often contain a dispute settlement clause permitting the investor to bring a claim before an international arbitral tribunal or before ICSID. Similarly, regional agreements may provide for direct rights of this type before regional dispute settlement bodies. Such agreements give ascendancy to the investor, who is the principal beneficiary of rights contained in agreements entered into between States. In this context, it is to be expected that the principal disputes will be between the investor and the host State, not between the State contracting parties to an IIA.

B. A typology of State-to-State investment disputes

A classification of the types of inter-State disputes that could arise under an IIA is difficult, as each agreement needs to be considered in the light of its scope, objectives and purposes. While any classification would therefore be, to some extent, arbitrary, it might nevertheless be useful to distinguish inter-State investment disputes as follows:

- The bulk of disputes that arise between States under IIAs are "investment disputes". Broadly speaking, they relate to investments covered under an IIA that have been subjected to adverse governmental measures by a host country.T[1] To the extent that these measures run counter to the provisions of an IIA,[2] they could give rise to inter-State disputes, in that the home country of the investor may wish to bring a claim directly against the host country on the basis of its right of diplomatic protection exercised on behalf of the investor by reason of their home country nationality. This is, however, an unlikely situation in that, where investor-State dispute settlement procedures are available, it is likely that the investor will bring a claim directly against the respondent State without the intervention of its home country. In such a case, diplomatic protection may well be excluded by agreement of the States parties to the IIA, in that the investor-State dispute settlement provisions will contain a clause to that effect, which comes into operation as soon as the investor brings a claim against the host country. It should be noted that such disputes could also include in their underlying subject matter other agreements (usually referred to as "investment agreements" or "State contracts") that grant certain entitlements to foreign investors with respect to public assets, enable foreign investors to enter into certain specific investments, or grant certain ancillary interests to foreign investors upon which they might rely to establish or acquire an investment, so long as the investors and investments are covered by an IIA. Apart from the category of investment disputes, other investment-related disputes that might arise include situations involving armed conflict or civil disturbances, in so far as a government has agreed to provide protection to covered investment in such circumstances.

- Inter-State disputes might also arise in cases that do not appertain to particular investments, such as the application of an IIA within the territory of its signatories. These types of cases would, on balance, remain exceptional. However, given that international rule-making in areas that address investment issues is on the rise in various settings, inter-State disputes could arise in relation to this diffusion concerning the hierarchy of different IIAs between the same countries that address the same investment issues.
- Furthermore, where IIAs seek to reduce government involvement, management and regulation in national economic sectors or open them to foreign investment, provisions may be included that allow a widened scope of one country's policies and legislation affecting investments to be subject to scrutiny by other States party to those IIAs. Such provisions could be coupled with further obligations undertaken by the signatories to take or refrain from taking specified measures affecting the establishment and operations of investments. In such cases, inter-State disputes could develop on the basis of these undertakings alone, without specific reference or connection to a particular investment dispute. In these circumstances, a concrete factual situation involving an investor would no longer be necessary for a dispute to arise. The dispute is thus one between two regulators, each having promised to take or refrain from taking certain measures that are presumed to affect investments adversely, which concerns not what was done to a specific investor, but simply whether or not there has been compliance with the letter and spirit of their mutual obligations. An example of such a dispute could arise over a "no lowering of standards" clause where one State alleges that the standards contained in the regulatory laws covered by the clause have been lowered by another State contracting party to the IIA in question.

C. Dispute settlement arrangements in IIAs: issues and objectives

Inter-State disputes and their settlement, arising within the context of IIAs, involve processes that are, to a large extent, addressed by dispute settlement arrangements (DSAs) therein. Such arrangements in IIAs give rise to a number of general considerations. First, while mutually agreed standards and rules in IIAs set forth the undertakings, rights and obligations of their signatories, like all other agreements, IIAs cannot be drafted in such a way as to foresee all possible contingencies and eventualities. Moreover, disagreements could develop as to the precise nature and scope of those undertakings, rights and obligations. Thus, the need might arise for their interpretation and application in specific contexts and factual situations. Indeed, it is not uncommon that the solution to a particular dispute would require the development of still more detailed criteria or ancillary rules.

Second, in national systems, compulsory procedures exist within the jurisdictions of various official fora that could be initiated to handle such matters should there be no provisions on dispute settlement in an agreement. By contrast, there is a lack of compulsory dispute settlement fora within the international system at large.[3] In these circumstances, the involved parties must ensure that they can settle the dispute amicably and peacefully.[4] Otherwise, the absence of such arrangements could lead to the settlement of a dispute on the basis of the relative power of the parties involved rather than on the merits of their claims. Equally, lack of appropriate DSAs might result in unilateral decision-making on disputed matters by the parties, thus setting off an unsound chain reaction, which could lead to the termination of mutually beneficial relations between the signatories, or perhaps even an escalation of the dispute into a higher-level political conflict.[5] DSAs provide for mutually acceptable fora that allow for certain decision-making mechanisms and procedures, which the parties agree to engage should a dispute arise within the context of an IIA, thereby reducing the scope for recourse to unilateral acts by the parties.

Third, as with many international agreements, it might not be practicable (or desirable) to put into place complex rules that set forth highly detailed provisions in certain substantive areas covered by IIAs. In those circumstances, the development and growth of a set of standards and rules in particular substantive areas covered under an IIA could be delegated to when issues arise in specific contexts, by leaving the detailed formation, interpretation and application of rules to a case-by-case review. The latter issue is of increasing significance given that IIAs increasingly involve the internationalisation of matters that have traditionally belonged within the sphere of national policy-making, including the exercise of domestic jurisdiction to regulate matters such as the environment, labour standards and the competitive structure of national markets. DSAs contribute to this rule-making process by providing the mechanisms for case-by-case reviews.

Fourth, the objectives of IIAs can be considered effective only where DSAs are incorporated into "packages" that ensure, to the extent possible, that the agreed upon rights and obligations provided for in IIAs are realizable. DSAs complete and make effective such rule-based systems by allowing for a challenge and review process vis-à-vis measures and practices of all actors involved in the FDI relationship.

The conception of arrangements for the settlement of inter-State disputes in IIAs involves careful deliberations on certain fundamental notions concerning the purposes for which DSAs are established. In this connection, first, a primary purpose is to ensure that, when disputes arise, a pre-determined set of procedures will be available to the parties, the engagement of which will result in a final, authoritative decision that will fully settle the matter. Second, the purposes and objectives behind DSAs appertain not only to the settlement of particular disagreements concerning the interpretation, implementation or application of the provisions in IIAs, but also the avoidance of conflict. The latter implies two ideas: first, that prior to a measure being taken by a Government that might affect a foreign investment covered by an IIA, there should be a notification and discussion with regard to the proposed measure; and second, that prior to resort to particular dispute settlement mechanisms provided for in IIAs, there should be discussions intended to avoid recourse to such mechanisms.

In sum, the purposes and objectives behind the establishment of DSAs include a contribution to the avoidance, management and settlement of State-to-State disputes. In order for DSAs to achieve these objectives, effective structures – processes, mechanisms and procedures – must be agreed to and provided in IIAs. The general processes encompass two extremes: either ensuring the close control by the disputing parties of the settlement procedures and decisions that might effect the outcome; or their limited control and influence over procedures and decisions that affect the final results. The mechanisms under which States retain control are negotiations, consultations, fact-finding, good offices, conciliation and mediation, and those under which there is practically no control over the final outcome are arbitration, judicial settlement or other third party decision-making mechanisms. Third party dispute settlement procedures could still involve two decision-making models: non-binding and binding outcomes.

In the following section, the main issues that arise in the negotiation of IIAs concerning DSAs will be considered.

Section I
Explanation of the Issue

State-to-State dispute settlement provisions in IIAs are textually diverse. The practical implications of arrangements on the settlement of inter-State investment disputes flow from the choices and agreements made during the negotiation of IIAs. In this connection, the main issues concerning DSAs that arise within the context of the negotiation of IIAs are the following:

- the scope of disputes that could trigger DSAs;
- the procedures governing dispute settlement mechanisms;
- the applicable standards for the settlement of disputes;
- the nature and scope of outcomes of dispute settlement mechanisms; and
- compliance with dispute settlement awards.

A. The scope of disputes that could trigger DSAs

The nature and scope of the type of disputes that could be submitted under the provisions of a DSA determine its effectiveness. At the same time, there may be a need to strike a balance between the expectation of the parties to an IIA as to how certain issues will be addressed should a dispute arise. In these circumstances, it is recognized that, on the one hand, no dispute should be left outside the scope of the DSA, while, on the other hand, not all disputes are amenable to settlement through the same dispute settlement mechanisms. This balance is particularly important in terms of emerging issues that go beyond protection afforded by IIAs in the classical instances of nationalizations and direct and indirect expropriations, and that involve the exercise of domestic jurisdiction to regulate matters such as the environment, labour standards and the competitive structure of national markets.

The determination of the nature and scope of disputes that trigger the DSA in an IIA thus first involves the task of the determination of how a dispute or matter that gives rise to a dispute is defined in DSA provisions. Second is the analysis of the extent to which a given question is to be addressed by the mechanisms included in the DSAs. In this regard, "matters" involve either the interpretation or the application of the provisions of the IIA, or both. A related issue that completes the analysis is whether or not there exist any limitations on recourse to a DSA, which will, by definition, circumscribe the types of disputes that could be submitted thereto.

The typical formulations for DSAs refer to "disputes" (other terminology used are "differences", "divergences", "matters" or "questions") concerning or arising out of IIAs, without providing a formal definition of what is meant by the terminology. Thus, the first issue that might arise in a dispute is whether or not a genuine dispute exists that would trigger the DSA, which absent a definition, would need to be defined.[6] In most instances, the term will, absent express indications to the contrary, be defined to cover as broad a range of disagreements between the parties as possible. It should be noted that a "legal dispute" could be considered as a term of art, and connotes a particular set of circumstances between States. These include first, that a claim could be formed under international law, which means that the claim should be based upon an act or omission that gives rise to State responsibility. Second, the claim must be rejected, or there must be a disagreement as to its disposition. The third element, which is not universally agreed upon, is that the subject matter of the claim must be disposable through the application of international law, as evidenced by recourse to one or more of its accepted sources. In this way, legal disputes are sometimes differentiated from "political disputes".

If they appear in an IIA, "matters" or "questions" are intended to cover a much wider set of issues than "disputes". Thus, in some IIAs, consultations may be available although there is no "dispute" between States as to the interpretation or application of a provision. A proposed measure or action could be the subject of consultations between the parties in areas of serious controversies so as to avoid or prevent a dispute from arising between the parties and to facilitate its settlement when it arises. It has also been observed that the term "divergences" (which appears in German bilateral investment treaties (BITs)) would include, in addition to legal disputes, any questions where a gap in an agreement has to be filled by a third party (binding advice) or where facts have to be ascertained by an outsider (fact-finding commission) (Peters, 1991).

A given dispute, matter or question may relate to the "interpretation" or "application" of an IIA. The phrase "interpretation and/or application", when appearing in an IIA, is an all-encompassing formulation that mostly relates to issues or actions after the agreement has entered into force between the contracting parties. "Interpretation" is the determination of the meanings of particular provisions of an agreement in concrete or proposed situations. "Application" relates to the extent to which the actions or measures taken or proposed by the contracting parties comply with the terms of an agreement, its object and purpose. In practice, there is a large degree of overlap between the purport of "interpretation" or "application." A question of the application of an agreement will involve a question of its interpretation, and the interpretation of an agreement may be warranted by an action taken or proposed by a contracting party with respect to the subject-matter of the agreement. Assessing the effects or implications of actions or measures taken or proposed by a contracting party with respect to the subject-matter of an agreement necessarily entail an interpretation thereof.

Thus, the nature and type of issues and the particular context within which they have arisen determine the scope of issues that could trigger the DSA in an IIA. Unless particular types of disputes are intended to be left outside the purview of the DSA in an IIA, the terminology typically used provides for a relatively wide scope of subject-matter, albeit that different processes, mechanisms or procedures might be applicable to different issues.

A parallel consideration is when certain matters covered by an IIA lie outside the scope of its DSA. This arises especially either where a particular exception is provided for (for example, as to measures taken on the grounds of national security), or where alternative DSAs (such as investor-State provisions) are also included in IIAs. On the former issue, States might be reluctant to allow for another party to challenge certain measures. As to the latter, where parallel DSAs exist, the question arises whether or not they could be simultaneously utilized. To the extent that the same issues are considered, and given the view that investor-State DSAs allow for a "de-politicization" of a dispute that would otherwise have to be resolved through inter-State channels, use of one DSA should preclude the concurrent engagement of another. There are in any event three possibilities: to allow concurrent resort to the DSAs; to restrict resort to only one DSA by requiring an election between the DSAs; or to limit resort to the DSAs, for example, by providing that only issues that are not being considered under investor-State procedures could be brought under the State-to-State DSA.

B. Dispute settlement mechanisms and their procedures

The mechanisms and procedures for the settlement of disputes determine, to a large degree, the manner and extent of control that the parties have over the outcome of the dispute settlement process. In their DSAs pertaining to inter-State issues, IIAs predominantly provide for the initiation of dispute settlement processes through bilateral means. Some IIAs require that these bilateral attempts for the settlement of disputes must be engaged in as a pre-condition of having resort to third-party decision-making processes. The types of bilateral and third-party mechanisms typically provided for in inter-State DSAs include:

- negotiations and consultations;
- *ad hoc* inter-State arbitration, which is most prominently featured in IIAs;
- permanent arbitral or judicial arrangements for dispute settlement; and
- political or administrative institutions whose decisions are binding.

1. Negotiations and consultations

DSAs typically first provide for mechanisms that utilise bilateral decision-making processes for dispute settlement, such as negotiations and/or consultations. A prevalent formulation refers to "diplomatic channels". Other formulations refer to "negotiations", "consultations", or both. All three formulations essentially involve a negotiation process.[7] This is not surprising, since settlement of disputes through diplomatic negotiations and/or consultations have historically been the most common means of dispute settlement between States (Eyffinger, 1996). Negotiations could resolve all but the most intractable disputes and, in the more complicated cases, they can assist to narrow the issues to more manageable proportions or prepare them for resolution by the formal binding third party processes.

Consultations may appear in an IIA as distinct from negotiations. However, the former is, in a way, an integral part, if not a variety, of the latter. The distinction between them, if any, seems to be a question of degree and intensity in, and the timing of, the discussions (exchange of views) between the disputing parties. Provisions for consultations in IIAs are nevertheless useful (UNCTAD,1998a; Kirgis, 1983; Sohn, 1994). At the pre-dispute stage, DSAs could create an obligation to consult on matters – not necessarily involving a dispute in the narrow sense – pertaining to an agreement. This may enable the parties to supply and exchange information and learning for the purposes of avoiding the emergence of a dispute. There are also provisions for consultations that encompass other contexts such as the review and implementation of an IIA. These have regulatory functions and could promote meaningful co-operation between the contracting parties. In this connection it is worth noting that the Dispute Settlement Understanding of the WTO requires consultations as a preliminary step in the dispute settlement process applicable to trade disputes arising between Members under the WTO Agreements (Article 4) (WTO, 1994).

Negotiations and consultations are normally conducted on an ad hoc basis, even within an institutional setting. Their inherent flexibility does not easily make these mechanisms susceptible to any rigid procedural frameworks. Typically, the only procedural matter that is pre-determined with respect to these mechanisms is the timeframe within which they are to begin and end.

2. *Ad hoc arbitration*

Party autonomy is the basic rule in the establishment of an arbitral tribunal (which may be a single individual or a group of individuals as may be appropriate). It is essentially an adjudicative process by a tribunal, except that the procedures for the establishment of the arbitral tribunal are effected either by the agreement of the disputing parties when a dispute arises (*compromis*), or by the operation of provisions negotiated previously and incorporated into DSAs (standard rules and procedures).

These procedures normally address the following tasks:

- selection of arbitrators, the place, venue and the official language for the proceedings;
- determination of the terms of reference for the arbitral panel; and
- institution of time limits for the conduct of the arbitration proceedings and the promulgation of working rules for the panel and the parties, such as rules on the submission of case-briefs, arguments and evidence.

3. *Permanent arbitral and judicial institutions*

In contrast to ad hoc arbitral tribunals, governments may choose to utilise the rules, procedures and facilities of specialised institutions for the arbitration of their disputes. The only arbitral institution that provides for the settlement of State-to-State disputes under its auspices is the Permanent Court of Arbitration (PCA). Other institutional systems, for example, ICSID and the International Chamber of Commerce (ICC), are geared to the settlement of investor-State disputes. Indeed, ICSID procedures expressly exclude State-to-State disputes from their jurisdiction, in that the ICSID Convention is limited to the settlement of disputes between a contracting State and a national of another contracting State. The resort to a permanent institution with pre-determined procedural rules for choosing the members of the arbitration panel and its proceedings might secure savings in terms of the time and resources committed to searching for potential candidates to be selected as an arbitrator, drafting an ad hoc arbitration agreement (or comparing and negotiating on proposed drafts from each involved party), looking for a convenient venue, and establishing a suitable set of procedural rules.

Although featured less frequently in IIAs, States always have the option of referring their disputes arising from such agreements to standing judicial tribunals, such as the ICJ or to standing regional judicial tribunals, if they have jurisdiction. In addition to the advantages accounted for with respect to institutional arbitration, the members that would constitute the judicial panel are known, which will dispense with the necessity of choosing the members of the panel. Moreover, the position, prestige and influence offered by standing judicial tribunals might encourage States to decide to submit their disputes to them, with the hope that those virtues will enhance the legitimacy of the awards and ensure complete and speedy compliance. It should be noted, however, that one advantage of referring disputes to arbitration would be that the members of their panels might have more of an expertise on the specific subject matters involved as compared to sitting members of the judicial tribunals, which may explain the infrequent reference of disputes in IIAs to judicial bodies.

4. *Permanent political institution for dispute settlement*

The third-party settlement mechanism provided for in a DSA could be a political body or an organ of an international organization. Recourse to such institutions has caused concern that their decisions may be political and incapable of achieving binding effects on the parties (Peters, 1991; Sohn, 1976). In particular cases, it is argued that political considerations might creep into what should essentially be limited to legal and commercial issues. Nevertheless, there are permanent institutions with internal dispute settlement means that could instil finality to disputes. An example would be the Senior Economic Officials Meeting of the Association of South-East Asian Nations (ASEAN) Investment Agreement. Equally the Dispute Settlement Body of the WTO has the power to adopt a WTO Panel (or as the case may be an Appellate Body) Report within 60 days of its circulation to members unless, in the case of a Panel Report, a party to the dispute formally notifies the Dispute Settlement Body of its decision to appeal to the Appellate Body or the Dispute Settlement Body decides, by consensus, not to adopt the report (Article 16) (WTO, 1994). Thus the winning party has a right to the adoption of a Report as it can block the consensus required for its non-adoption by not adhering to the consensus reached by the other members.

C. Applicable standards for the settlement of disputes

This is an important issue concerning DSAs. Absent provisions in an applicable treaty (or a subsequent arbitration agreement), it is for the disputing parties in their negotiations or the tribunal to determine what laws, standards or principles are to be applied to the matters in dispute. To be sure, the starting point (which does not require an express reference) is having regard for the rights and obligations provided for in the IIA itself, as well as in other relevant treaties between the parties. However, IIAs do not provide for all rules, standards or principles that might be applicable to a dispute. For example, in the light of increasing recognition of the complexities involved with regulatory measures (which are typically still not expressly addressed in IIAs) that affect foreign investment and that might trigger the provisions of an IIA, what standard of discretion should the adjudicator of a dispute apply with respect to the issue of whether or not protection should be afforded to covered investments against such measures?

Where the issue is provided for, reference is typically made to rules of (international) law. In some instances, however, this indication creates rather than solves problems in that their recognition is conditioned by requiring that all parties to the dispute must accept the particular principles or rules of international law. In addition to these legal standards, equitable principles (*ex aequo et bono*) and procedural standards might also be considered in DSAs.

When issues concerning an IIA arise between its signatories, their successful settlement turns in part on whether or not the standards that are to be applied have been considered by and between the parties involved. On the one hand, given that disputes could arise within a variety of contexts relative to IIAs, it is difficult to agree on the controlling standards before a dispute arises. On the other hand, there could be general agreement as to the applicable standards, which would provide parameters for the decision-makers as to what criteria should be applied in reaching a decision. Generally, these standards pertain to defining the nature and extent of the rights and obligations undertaken in the IIAs, which is a question of interpretation, or to the conformity of (proposed) measures undertaken by the parties thereto vis-à-vis those rights and obligations, as defined, which is an issue of application.[8]

This issue deserves careful consideration.[9] The main question is whether or not all types of disputes could (and should) be settled with reference to one standard (e.g. general rules of international law, within which vast lacunae exist). Alternatively, could the provision for, and application of, different standards to differing disputes in various contexts provide for a more appropriate means of dispute settlement? For example, when considering the issue of national treatment, what standards are to be applied to a particular programme of affirmative action designed to embrace more of the native population of a country into its cultural industries? Present national treatment standards in most IIAs would not permit such discrimination, and excluding national treatment for cultural industries might not be an acceptable solution. In addition, there need to be safeguards in relation to any exceptions clause, so that it would not be abused. Presently, there exist no rules of international law that could provide a solution. This must be considered in the context of establishing mutually acceptable standards that would be applicable should a dispute arise in relation to measures to implement and administer such programmes. This is of crucial importance in relation to the development needs and concerns of countries.

D. Nature and scope of outcomes of dispute settlement mechanisms

With respect to bilateral processes of negotiation and consultation provided for in DSAs, the outcome would normally be a settlement agreement. In most instances, this would be unproblematic. The agreement would be, by definition, binding upon the parties thereto, and its nonperformance would entail State responsibility under international law. However, in a situation in which a particular regime is established by an IIA involving a number of States (such as a regional agreement), there may be certain considerations that could render the agreement unacceptable, in the light of the purposes and objectives of the regime as a whole. Other States that are members of the regime may object to an agreement that, for example, provides for a looser application of its provisions between two parties, on the grounds that such an agreement would endanger the discipline imposed by the IIA.

Awards or judgements rendered through a tribunal are, by and large, binding upon the parties. In fact, it is this very feature that provides for a final decision on the settlement of a dispute. Once a State agrees that an award shall be binding, its non-compliance with the award entails State responsibility. Thus, as with settlement agreements, inter-State arbitration is likewise unproblematic, yet the special considerations regarding particular regimes equally hold here.[10] In this connection, the finality of the awards, or recourse to an appeals process, deserves consideration.[11] Clearly, if binding arbitration is said to have the merits of final and speedy settlement of the dispute, then any review or appeals process is an anathema. However, as the reach of IIAs goes beyond the traditional issues of nationalization and expropriation, and where DSAs provide for compulsory, binding, rule-based adjudication of disputes based on legal standards and rigid rules of procedure, the possibility of a genuine error in the determination of the dispute becomes more serious, when looked at from the point of view of compliance. Thus, an appeals procedure may be required to allow for a reconsideration of the case where an error is alleged to have occurred at first instance. This approach has been adopted in relation to inter-State trade disputes arising out of the WTO Agreement and its Annexes. The Dispute Settlement Understanding (DSU) of the WTO provides for an appeal from a WTO Panel ruling to the Appellate Body on issues of law covered in the Panel Report and legal interpretations developed by the Panel. The Appellate Body may uphold, modify or reverse the legal findings and conclusions of the Panel (DSU, Article 17 (6) and (13)) (WTO, 1994).

E. Compliance with dispute settlement awards

Compliance issues can be viewed from the standpoint of the parties to an inter-State dispute, the beneficiaries of IIAs, or the international system at large. In the final analysis, however, two factors must be considered. The first is the legitimacy of the final decision concerning the settlement of a dispute, and the ability of the parties to comply with the terms of such decision. In this respect, negotiated settlements derive their legitimacy from the fact that the disputing parties enjoy a large degree of control over claims or matters involved and the settlement process. Tribunals derive their legitimacy from the agreement of the parties, their independence and impartiality, and their focus on the rule-based system of rights and obligations that allows them to assess the merits of the claims on an objective basis.

The second factor to be considered – notwithstanding the foregoing and the fact that non-compliance is not historically an intractable feature of international relations – is how to avoid disputes that might arise in the event that a State does not comply with the final decision. In such circumstances, while the original dispute has been settled, another dispute might arise concerning the response to noncompliance, since under present international law, only unilateral decision-making structures or actions are available to respond to non-compliance with awards. In this connection, the procedures for establishing noncompliance – and the range, scope and manner of remedies – could be addressed.

In the following section, this chapter will consider the foregoing issues as they have featured in different IIAs, and document and analyse how the particular DSA provisions would contribute to the attainment of their attendant objectives.

Section II Stocktaking and Analysis

This section, after providing a brief historical perspective on settlement of inter-State investment disputes, takes stock of the manner in which IIAs have dealt with the main issues enumerated in section I concerning DSAs. It furthermore analyses the individual provisions discussed in terms of the purposes and objectives behind the conclusion of IIAs, i.e. their contribution to the avoidance, management and settlement of State-to-State disputes.

As State-to-State disputes involve the principal participants in the international legal order, rules that have been shaped through time concerning dispute settlement need to be analysed in the light of both the basic expectations within that order and the realities of power and governance structures that shape the relations therein. Moreover, rules developed on dispute settlement must pass the additional test of legitimacy and validity relative to those actors that the order seeks to organize. Traditionally, inter-State investment disputes were (and in the absence of IIAs would still be) resolved under rules of customary international law, which is not without its own attendant problems relative to the subject matter. For example, the lack of international legal personality by foreign private persons under customary international law has meant that only their national States could espouse a claim on their behalf through "diplomatic protection" (Wetter,

1962; Higgins, 1994; Muchlinski, 1999; UNCTAD, 1998a).[12]

In exercising diplomatic protection on behalf of its injured national, a protecting State may resort to an international claim through arbitration or before an international tribunal, should there be consent on the part of the other State involved. Otherwise, protection may involve some unilateral acts of self-help such as diplomatic protest and reprisals, though the latter raise complex questions as to their legality (see the Naulilaa case (ADPILC, 1927-1928) and the Air Services Agreement case (RIAA, 1978); see also the United Nations Reports of International Arbitral Awards).

Attempts by States to address issues concerning the settlement of investment-related disputes through treaty practice could be traced back to the post-1945 Friendship, Commerce and Navigation (FCN) treaties. FCN treaties contained only provisions for State-to-State disputes arising out of their interpretation or application. Sometimes, provisions were also included for consultations on "matters affecting the operation" of a particular treaty. The dispute settlement arrangements in FCN agreements, despite their differing drafting patterns, lengths or scope, were substantively uniform in implications. Typically, they proceeded from bilateral mechanisms such as consultations or diplomacy, to third party mechanisms, which in their case was always submission of a dispute to the ICJ.[13] For example, article XIV of the 1966 Treaty of Amity and Economic Relations between the United States of America and the Togolese Republic provides:

> "1. Each Party shall accord sympathetic consideration to, and shall afford adequate opportunity for consultation regarding, such representations as the other Party may make with respect to any matter affecting the operation of the present Treaty.
>
> 2. Any dispute between the Parties as to the interpretation or application of the present Treaty, not satisfactorily adjusted by diplomacy shall be submitted to the International Court of Justice, unless the Parties agree to settlement by some other pacific means" (United Nations Treaty Series, 1969).

Despite their substantive uniformity, the dispute settlement arrangements in FCN treaties had some drawbacks or weaknesses (Vandevelde, 1988). The FCN treaties differed from modern IIAs, as the latter are specifically directed at the protection and promotion (encouragement) of foreign investment and typically include State-to-State DSAs.

A. The scope of disputes that could trigger DSAs

The expressions used to define the types of issues or disagreements that could trigger the recourse to such mechanisms need to be analysed individually to see what definitions could be derived from the terminology used with respect to such issues or disagreements, and how they are limited not only in terms of their definitions, but also in relation to their role in resolving questions that arise from the substantive provisions of the IIA. Nevertheless, two general models may be mentioned.

The first model, an example of which is article VIII of the 1994 United States model BIT, provides in one provision that:

> "The Parties agree to consult promptly, on the request of either, to resolve any disputes in connection with the Treaty, or to discuss any matter relating to the interpretation or application of the Treaty or to the realization of the objectives of the Treaty."[14]

Thus, under this model, DSAs, at one stroke, provide for consultations with respect to "disputes" or "matters". The scope of the disputes is wide, in that they need only be "in connection with the Treaty". The scope of matters (other than disputes) is similarly wide, as all that is needed is that they relate to the interpretation or application of the BIT, or to the realization of its objectives. The three instances, put together, would cover the widest possible range of issues that might arise from the agreement. By providing for both a wide definition and scope of the types of circumstances that could trigger the DSA, this model would contribute to the avoidance of disputes, by expressly providing for a process to tackle any concerns that might arise for any of the parties.

A variation of the first model is indicated, for example, by articles 9(1) and 10 of the Chilean model BIT, which provides in two provisions that:

> "The Contracting Parties shall endeavour to resolve any difference between them regarding the interpretation or application of the provisions of this Agreement by friendly negotiations", and
>
> "The Contracting Parties shall consult at the request of either of them on matters concerning the interpretation or application of this Agreement."

Under this approach, there is a bifurcation of disputes and matters, both of which should be resolved through bilateral settlement processes: the scope of disputes and matters are wide, as they both relate to the interpretation or application of the agreement. The effect of this model would be, in the final analysis, the same as the first.

The second model, as illustrated in article 9(1) of the Swiss model BIT, provides simply that "Disputes between Contracting Parties regarding the interpretation or application of the provisions of this Agreement shall be settled through diplomatic channels". Here, a somewhat narrower definition exists, in that a dispute needs to have formed as to the interpretation or application of the agreement, before the DSA could be triggered.

The first model expressly addresses the issue of dispute avoidance by creating an obligation – triggered at the insistence of any one of the parties – to consult and negotiate on matters that might not be disputed at the time.[15] By contrast, in the second model, dispute avoidance would depend more on the awareness of the parties that concerns related to the IIA exist, and on their mutual goodwill to address those issues before they come to form the basis of disputes. Moreover, from an investment protection perspective, where matters have arisen within the context of IIAs – for example, on the creation of a regulatory framework affecting a particular industry – inefficiencies related to the operations of enterprises could arise if these concerns are not promptly addressed. Specifically, where goodwill is lacking, one party could engage in dilatory practices in addressing the concerns of the other, on the grounds that no dispute has arisen in connection to the IIA, as the proposed regulatory framework is not yet set in place.

The scope of disputes that could trigger a DSA in an IIA has, in some instances, been limited, either on procedural or substantive bases.

First, this issue concerns circumstances in which alternative dispute settlement procedures have been made available, and that the election to use one removes the availability of the other. In this connection, a clear example is in relation to diplomatic protection in investor-State disputes concerning those countries that are party to the 1965 Convention on the Settlement of Investment Disputes between States and Nationals of other States (ICSID Convention). Article 27(1) of the ICSID Convention states:

> "No Contracting State shall give diplomatic protection, or bring an international claim, in respect of a dispute which one of its nationals and another Contracting State shall have consented to submit or shall have submitted to arbitration under this Convention, unless such other Contracting State shall have failed to abide by and comply with the award rendered in such dispute."

This issue is also reflected in the BIT practices of some countries. For example, the "preferred" article 8(4) of the 1991 model BIT of the United Kingdom, entitled "Reference to International Centre for Settlement of Investment Disputes", provides that:

> "Neither Contracting Party shall pursue through the diplomatic channel any dispute referred to the Centre ..."

unless there is a determination that ICSID has no jurisdiction to decide the matter, or the other party has failed to comply with the decision of the arbitral panel formed under the auspices of the Centre.

Another example is provided by the NAFTA agreement, where in some areas (such as the prohibition of TRIMs) the parties have recourse to both NAFTA's State-to-State DSA under its Chapter 20, and to the procedures under the understanding on rules and procedures governing the settlement of disputes, Annex 2 to the Agreement Establishing the WTO (WTO Agreement). In such circumstances, NAFTA's Chapter 20, entitled "Institutional Arrangements and Dispute Settlement Procedures", in its Article 2005(1), provides that disputes that arise in connection to both treaties, subject to certain considerations, "may be settled in either forum at the discretion of the complaining Party" (Canada, Mexico and United States, 1992). However, paragraph (6) of the same article restricts such election by stating that once the dispute settlement procedures have been initiated under either treaty, "the forum selected shall be used to the exclusion of the other", except that the respondent could force the recourse to NAFTA's Chapter 20 with respect to environmental and conservation agreements under Article 104 of NAFTA, and certain aspects of Sanitary and Phytosanitary Measures (NAFTA, Chapter 7) or Standards-Related Measures (NAFTA, Chapter 9) (Canada, Mexico and United States, 1992).

Second, IIA provisions sometimes provide for circumstances in which the parties cannot challenge certain measures, which but for the existence of those circumstances would have been subject to the DSA therein. One example is the reference found in United States BITs related to the non-application of the BIT to measures taken for the protection of the United States' own essential security interests. This provision would not, on its own, provide for a bar on the operation of the DSA, for a dispute might arise as to whether or not a genuine threat exists to the United States, essential security interests. However, when coupled with another provision – as evidenced by paragraph 8 of the Protocol to the 1992 United States-Russian Federation BIT, which states: "whether a measure is undertaken by a Party to protect its essential security interests is self-judging" (ILM, 1992) – the matter is then rendered as not subject to review, and hence, could not trigger the DSA (Vandevelde, 1993). The NAFTA uses a similar technique under its Chapter 11 (Investment). Article 1138 (2) provides in its relevant part that "the dispute settlement provisions of ... Chapter Twenty shall not apply to the matters referred to in Annex 1138.2". Annex 1138.2 in turn provides, among other things, that the "decision by the National Commission on Foreign Investment ("Comisión Nacional de Inversiones Extranjeras") [of the Government of Mexico] following a review pursuant to Annex I, page IM4, with respect to whether or not to permit an acquisition that is subject to review, shall not be subject to the dispute settlement provisions of ... Chapter Twenty", the State-to-State DSA in NAFTA.

Another example of limitations on the scope of disputes that trigger DSAs pertain to particular substantive provisions in IIAs, which have been extracted from the scope of disputes. In this connection, Article XIII (1) of the 1994 United States model BIT provides that "No provision of this Treaty shall impose obligations with respect to tax matters ...", except that with respect to expropriation, the provisions of the agreement's State-to-State DSA would still apply. Thus, the only possibility for challenging tax measures would be where a claim is made that the measure is tantamount to expropriation.

The foregoing review makes clear that the majority of IIAs provide for the coverage of a wide range of issues under their DSAs. Minimally, all disputes that arise in relation to IIAs are covered. In most cases, all matters connected with an IIA, with which the parties are concerned, could trigger its DSA. The availability of such a wide range of issues contributes not only to the settlement of inter-State disputes, but also to their avoidance. In this connection, it should however be noted that at times this wide scope has been limited, through either procedural or substantive restrictions.

B. Dispute settlement mechanisms and their procedures

DSAs typically provide first for bilateral mechanisms for dispute settlement, such as negotiations or consultations, and if they should be unsuccessful, then for third-party mechanisms like arbitration, which will provide the parties to IIAs, in most cases, with a final, binding decision.

1. Negotiations and consultations

While there is diversity in the drafting of DSAs in this respect (box 1), the significance lies in the fact that they all establish an obligation that the parties involved in a dispute must first engage in negotiations, before resorting to third-party means.

Thus, where matters have arisen in relation to an IIA, compulsory consultations or negotiations could provide for the objective of dispute avoidance. As regards a dispute that has already arisen, consultations or negotiations could clarify the disputed issues for the parties involved, and provide for a mutually acceptable solution.

Box II.1. Obligation to negotiate

"Disputes between the Contracting Parties concerning the interpretation or application of this Agreement should, if possible, be settled through the diplomatic channel."
The UK model BIT, Article 9 (1).

"The Contracting Parties shall endeavour to resolve any dispute between them connected with this Agreement by prompt and friendly consultations and negotiations."
Article 11 (1) Australia/Lao People's Democratic Republic 1994 BIT.

"Contracting Parties shall endeavour to settle disputes concerning the application or interpretation of this Treaty through diplomatic channels."
The Energy Charter Treaty, Article 27 (1) (Waelde, 1996a).

"Disputes or differences between the Contracting Parties concerning interpretation or application of this agreement shall be settled through negotiations."
The Asian-African Legal Consultative Committee (ALCC) Model (A) BITs, Article 11 (1).

"B. CONSULTATION, CONCILIATION AND MEDIATION
1. Consultations
a. One or more Contracting Parties may request any other Contracting Party to enter into consultations regarding any dispute between them about the interpretation or

/...

Box II.1 (concluded)

application of the Agreement. The request shall be submitted in writing and shall provide sufficient information to understand the basis for the request, including identification of any actions at issue. The requested Party shall enter into consultations within thirty days of receipt of the request. The requesting Contracting Party shall provide the Parties Group with a copy of the request for consultation, at the time it submits the request to the other Contracting Party.
b. A Contracting Party may not initiate arbitration against another Contracting Party under Article C of this Agreement unless the former Contracting Party has requested consultation and has afforded that other Contracting Party a consultation period of no less than 60 days after the date of the receipt of the request."
Article B (1)(a) and (b), Multilateral Agreement on Investment (MAI), Draft Negotiating Text, 24 April 1998.

Source: UNCTAD.

Negotiation processes do not easily lend themselves to "proceduralization". Thus, the procedures for negotiations under DSAs are left almost entirely to the parties. An exception is evidenced by article 2006(5) of NAFTA, which provides:

> "The consulting Parties shall make every attempt to arrive at a mutually satisfactory resolution of any matter through consultations under this Article or other consultative provisions of this Agreement. To this end, the consulting Parties shall:
> (a) provide sufficient information to enable a full examination of how the actual or proposed measure or other matter might affect the operation of this Agreement;
> (b) treat any confidential or proprietary information exchanged in the course of consultations on the same basis as the Party providing the information..." (Canada, Mexico and United States, 1992).

Moreover, a few IIAs include in their DSAs that negotiations should be through ad hoc or standing institutions. For example, article 12 (1) of the 1980 BIT between the Belgo-Luxembourg Economic Union and Cameroon provides that disputes between the parties "shall, as far as possible, be settled by a mixed Commission, composed of representatives appointed by the Contracting Parties" (United Nations Treaty Series, 1982). Similarly, the Economic Partnership Agreement between Mexico and the EU of 1997 provides for a Joint Committee to which disputes shall be referred in the first instance for consultations. The Joint Committee has 30 days from the delivery of the request for consultations to arrive at a decision. However, the parties to the dispute remain free to submit the dispute to arbitration if, after 15 days from the date after the Joint Committee has been seized of the request for consultations, the legal issues arising between the parties have not been resolved (Articles 38-39). Should the parties decide upon arbitration, the procedures specified in Articles 39-43 will apply.

In some instances, IIAs provide for a timeframe within which negotiations must take place, usually six months.[16] Where no timeframes exist, DSAs provide that each party could end negotiations by requesting that the third-party settlement processes begin. Finally, it should be noted that some recent bilateral agreements between the United States and other countries concerning the development of trade and investment relations contain only a consultation clause, but do not provide for full dispute settlement procedures.[17]

2. *Ad hoc arbitration*

Where parties could not reach a mutually acceptable solution to their disputes through negotiations, most IIAs, and in particular almost all BITs, provide for recourse to ad hoc arbitration (box 2). With regard to the establishment of an arbitral tribunal, DSAs take into consideration the will and participation of the contracting parties, without allowing any of them to control unilaterally the appointment procedure, to stop or delay the establishment of a tribunal, or its operations once it is established.

Box II.2. *Ad hoc* arbitration model

"If a dispute between the Contracting Parties cannot thus [diplomatic channel] be settled within six (6) months from notification of the dispute, it shall, upon the request of either Contracting Party, be submitted to an arbitral tribunal."
Article 9 (2) Estonia/Israel 1994 BIT

"Any dispute between the Contracting Parties as to the interpretation or application of the present Agreement not satisfactorily adjusted by diplomacy, shall be referred for decision to an arbitration board..."
Article 13 (2) Japan/China 1988 BIT

Source: UNCTAD.

Thus, a typical clause can be found in the Chile model BIT (article 9.3):

"The Arbitral Tribunal shall be formed by three members and shall be constituted as follows: within two months of the notification by a Contracting Party of its wish to settle the dispute by arbitration, each Contracting Party shall appoint one arbitrator. These two members shall then, within thirty days of the appointment of the last one, agree upon a third member who shall be a national of a third country and who shall act as the Chairman. The Contracting Parties shall appoint the Chairman within thirty days of that person's nomination."[18]

For a panel to be established, a number of issues are typically subject to the agreement of the parties, which are sometimes provided for in the DSA, in various forms and degrees of detail (box 3). The first issue is the selection of the arbitrators. Most IIAs provide for three (and in a few instances five) members, an odd number being required to prevent a deadlock. The paramount consideration concerning the make-up of the panel is the balancing required between subject matter expertise, familiarity with the particular circumstances that affect the parties involved, and the overall impartiality of the panel. Most IIAs do not provide for specific subject matter expertise. However, article 2010(1) of NAFTA states: "All panellists shall meet the qualifications set out in Article 2009(2)". The latter article requires that "Roster members shall:

(a) have expertise or experience in law, international trade, other matters covered by this Agreement or the resolution of disputes arising under international trade agreements, and shall be chosen strictly on the basis of objectivity, reliability and sound judgment;
(b) be independent of, and not be affiliated with or take instructions from, any Party; and
(c) comply with a code of conduct to be established by the Commission" (Canada, Mexico and United States, 1992).

IIAs almost universally provide that each party selects, within a prescribed time period, one arbitrator. In most instances, parties select an arbitrator who is their own national. This practice has been questioned, and arguments can be made as to whether or not more relevant factors, such as conflicts of interest on the basis of, for example, close personal or financial links with the parties involved in the underlying dispute, should not affect the selection process (Peters, 1991). However, it could also be argued that the selection of parties who are nationals of the disputing parties could ensure that the panel includes members who have intimate knowledge of special circumstances prevalent in those countries.

Box II.3. Establishment of arbitration tribunal

"If a dispute is not resolved by such means within six months of one Contracting Party seeking in writing such negotiations or consultations, it shall be submitted at the request of either Contracting Party to an Arbitral Tribunal established in accordance with the provisions of Annex A of this Agreement …"
Article 11 (2) Australia/Lao People's Democratic Republic 1994 BIT

"Annex A

PROVISIONS FOR THE ESTABLISHMENT OF AN ARBITRAL TRIBUNAL FOR THE SETTLEMENT OF DISPUTES BETWEEN THE CONTRACTING PARTIES

(1) The Arbitral Tribunal referred to in Article 11 shall consist of three persons appointed as follows:
  (a) each Contracting Party shall appoint one arbitrator;
  (b) the arbitrators appointed by the Contracting Parties shall, within sixty days of the appointment of the second of them, by agreement, select a third arbitrator who shall be a national of a third country which has diplomatic relations with both Contracting Parties;
  (c) the Contracting Parties shall, within sixty days of the selection of the third arbitrator, approve the selection of that arbitrator who shall act as Chairman of the Tribunal.
(2) Arbitration proceedings shall be instituted upon notice being given through the diplomatic channel by the Contracting Party instituting such proceedings to the other Contracting Party. Such notice shall contain a statement setting forth in summary form the grounds of the claim, the nature of the relief sought, and the name of the arbitrator appointed by the Contracting Party instituting such proceedings. Within sixty days after the giving of such notice the respondent Contracting Party shall notify the Contracting Party instituting proceedings of the name of the arbitrator appointed by the respondent Contracting Party.
(3) If, within the time limits provided for in paragraph (1) (c) and paragraph (2) of this Annex, the required appointment has not been made or the required approval has not been given, either Contracting Party may request the President of the International Court of Justice to make the necessary appointment. If the President is a national of either Contracting Party or is otherwise unable to act, the Vice-President shall be invited to make the appointment. If the Vice-President is a national of either Contracting Party or is unable to

/…

Box II.3. (continued)

act, the Member of the International Court of Justice next in seniority who is not a national of either Contracting Party shall be invited to make the appointment.

(4) In case any arbitrator appointed as provided for in this Annex shall resign or become unable to act, a successor arbitrator shall be appointed in the same manner as prescribed for the appointment of the original arbitrator and the successor shall have all the powers and duties of the original arbitrator.

(5) The Arbitral Tribunal shall convene at such time and place as shall be fixed by the Chairman of the Tribunal. Thereafter, the Arbitral Tribunal shall determine where and when it shall sit.

(6) The Arbitral Tribunal shall decide all questions relating to its competence and shall, subject to any agreement between the Contracting Parties, determine its own procedure.

(7) Before the Arbitral Tribunal makes a decision, it may at any stage of the proceedings propose to the Contracting Parties that the dispute be settled amicably. The Arbitral Tribunal shall reach its award by majority vote taking into account the provisions of this Agreement, the international agreements both Contracting Parties have concluded and the generally recognised principles of international law.

(8) Each Contracting Party shall bear the costs of its appointed arbitrator. The cost of the Chairman of the Tribunal and other expenses associated with the conduct of the arbitration shall be borne in equal parts by both Contracting Parties. The Arbitral Tribunal may decide, however, that a higher proportion of costs shall be borne by one of the Contracting Parties …"

Annex A Australia/ Lao People's Democratic Republic 1994 BIT

"2. If the Contracting Parties cannot reach an agreement within twelve months after being notified of the dispute, the latter shall upon request of either Contracting Party, subject to their relevant laws and regulations, be submitted to an arbitral tribunal of three members. Each Contracting Party shall appoint one arbitrator, and these two arbitrators shall nominate a chairman who shall be a national of a third state having diplomatic relations with both Contracting Parties at the time of nomination."

Article 12 Belarus/Iran 1994 BIT

Source: UNCTAD.

After the selection of the first two arbitrators, it is for them to nominate a third, with the proviso that the nominee be the national of a third country.[19] The almost uniform insistence that the third arbitrator be from a third country would seem to be the countervailing element in the selection process, with which the parties could ensure the panel's overall impartiality. Furthermore, the fact that both parties involved in the dispute must then confirm the nomination also provides for a safeguard that if either party is uncomfortable with the proposed composition, they would have a chance to request a change, although, as will be further discussed below, none of the parties have the power to avoid the establishment of the panel.

In the event that any one of the parties fails to make the requisite appointments for any reason, almost all DSAs provide for an appointing authority, whose involvement could be elicited by a request from the other party to the dispute. For example, article 8(4) of the Chinese model BIT provides that "If the arbitral tribunal has not been constituted within four months from the receipt of the written notice requesting arbitration, either Contracting Party may, in the absence of any other agreement, invite the President of the International Court of Justice to make any necessary appointments. If the President is a national of either Contracting Party or is otherwise prevented from discharging the said functions, the Member of the International Court of Justice next in seniority who is not a national of either Contracting Party... shall be invited to make such necessary appointments". Again, the prestige, office and, in particular, nationality requirement of the appointing party are intended to ensure impartiality in both the process of selection and the composition of the panel.

Second, the parties need to agree on what questions the panel should decide, and the nature of, as well as the form in which it would render, its decision. These could be agreed in advance (standard terms of reference), provided for in a separate arbitration agreement when specific disputes arise (*compromis*), or left to be determined by the panel. For example, article 2012(3) of NAFTA provides that "Unless the disputing Parties otherwise agree within 20 days from the date of the delivery of the request for the establishment of the panel, the terms of reference shall be: 'To examine, in the light of the relevant provisions of the Agreement, the matter referred to the Commission (as set out in the request for a Commission meeting) and to make findings, determinations and recommendations as provided in Article 2016(2)'" (Canada, Mexico and United States, 1992).

Where provided for in the DSA or the *compromis*, the terms of reference could be general, which would give the arbitral panel a relatively high degree of latitude with respect to what issues are to be argued and determined, as well as the form in which they would render their decision. Parties could, on the other hand, mandate that only certain narrowly defined issues are considered, or that the panel should make only findings of fact or law. Several examples exist concerning terms of reference of arbitrators in inter-State disputes that, while they do not involve investment-related issues, are nonetheless instructive. For example, in the New Zealand-France arbitration arising out of the Rainbow Warrior case,[20] the United Nations Secretary-General was asked specifically not to decide whether New Zealand was justified in the detention of the French agents, although he was asked to determine the manner and length of any future detention. The significance of the issue of the terms of reference is demonstrated through the Alabama Claims case,[21] where the arbitration proceedings were almost aborted because the parties had not previously agreed on the type of damages that the panel could award, and during the proceedings, disagreed on whether it could award indirect damages, in addition to direct damages.

Third, the parties would consider the operational rules and procedures of the panel. Most IIAs leave the determination of the working rules and procedures to the panel. For example, article 8(5) of the Chinese model BIT provides, in its relevant part, that "The arbitral tribunal shall determine its own procedure."

Some DSAs provide for time frames within which the arbitral proceeding should be completed. For example, Article X (3) of the United States model BIT states: "Unless otherwise agreed, all submissions shall be made and all hearings shall be completed within six months of the date of selection of the third arbitrator, and the arbitral panel shall render its decisions within two months of the date of the final submissions or the date of the closing of the hearings, whichever is later".

An alternative to the provision of rules and procedures concerning the establishment and the operations of the ad hoc arbitral panel is for the parties to agree to refer, in part or in whole, to provisions of a comprehensive pre-established set of rules, such as the Arbitration Rules of the United Nations Commission on International Trade Law (UNCITRAL rules). For example, article 27 (3) (f) of the Energy Charter Treaty provides:

> "(f) In the absence of an agreement to the contrary between the Contracting Parties, the Arbitration Rules of UNCITRAL shall govern, except to the extent modified by the Contracting Parties to the dispute or by the arbitrators. The tribunal shall take its decisions by a majority vote of its members."[22]

Another alternative would be for the States involved to submit their dispute to be settled under the auspices of specialized institutions such as an inter-State claims commission of which the Iran-United States Claims Tribunal is a leading example.

3. Permanent arbitral and judicial institutions

One of the very few inter-governmental arbitration institutions that is self-standing (i.e. is not part of the institutional arrangements of a subject-specific treaty) is the Permanent Court of Arbitration at The Hague, which was born out of the 1899 and 1907 Hague Conventions for the Pacific Settlement of International Disputes. Other specialized institutions offering arbitration services are typically geared towards private cases or government-private party cases. These include the International Court of Arbitration of the ICC and ICSID. DSAs have seldom provided for the submission of inter-State disputes to institutional arbitration, if the institutional arrangements have been outside the framework of the IIA.

In contrast, some IIAs, most of which are at the regional level, have established institutional arrangements for the settlement of inter-State disputes. An example is Chapter 20 of NAFTA, which provides for elaborate institutional arrangements for the settlement of inter-State disputes. As noted previously, the issues that are covered under these arrangements are the same as those that arise for ad hoc arbitration, but which are pre-arranged within the rules and procedures of the institutional arrangements.

Recourse to permanent, self-standing inter-governmental judicial bodies such as the ICJ is always a possibility. In principle, where States that are parties to a dispute have accepted the jurisdiction of the ICJ, and their acceptance provides, on a reciprocal basis, subject-matter jurisdiction to the ICJ, then the matter could be adjudicated by the World Court.[23]

However, in some instances, DSAs specifically provide for the submission of the dispute to the ICJ. For example, the inter-State DSA of the ICSID Convention, in its article 64, provides that "Any dispute arising between Contracting States concerning the interpretation or application of this Convention which is not settled by negotiation shall be referred to the International Court of Justice by the application of any party to such dispute, unless the States concerned agree to another method of settlement".

Some DSAs create permanent judicial bodies that have competence over disputes that arise between the parties in connection with the specific IIA. An example is the Andean Subregional Integration Agreement (Cartagena Agreement), which provides, in its article 47, for the resolution of disputes between its member States as follows:

> "The resolution of disputes that may arise due to the application of the Andean Community Law, shall be subject to the provisions of the Charter of the Court of Justice" (OAS, 1996b).

Article 42 of the Charter of the Court of Justice of the Andean Community, in turn, provides the Court with exclusive jurisdiction over inter-State disputes by stating that:

> "Member Countries shall not submit any dispute that may arise from the application of provisions comprising the legal system of the Andean Community to any court, arbitration system or proceeding whatsoever except for those stipulated in this Treaty"
> (Andean Community, 1996).

Perhaps the leading example of such a system is that established under the European Union (EU) Treaty, which places the European Court of Justice at the heart of State-to-State dispute settlement in relation to the provisions of that treaty. Thus, by Article 227 of the EU Treaty, a member State that considers that a member State has failed to fulfill an obligation under this treaty may bring the matter before the Court of Justice. Before that is done the complainant member State shall bring the matter before the European Commission, which shall deliver a reasoned opinion after each of the States concerned has presented its own case and its observations on the other party's case both orally and in writing. Where the Commission has not delivered an opinion within three months of the date on which the matter was brought before it, the absence of such an opinion will not prevent the matter from being brought before the Court of Justice. This procedure has been rarely invoked as member States have tended to prefer the European Commission to act against member States under its own powers to bring an action for failure to fulfill an obligation under the EU Treaty (Weatherill and Beaumont, 1999).

Similar to institutional arbitration, judicial fora have established, time-tested rules and procedures for the conduct of the proceedings. Their constitutional documents provide for their terms of reference, or as is referred to in legal terms, for their "competence" and "jurisdiction". Moreover, the members of the judiciary are pre-selected and, therefore, issues similar to the selection of arbitrators seldom arise.

4. Permanent political institution for dispute settlement

In addition to permanent judicial institutions, DSAs might provide recourse to a political organ for third-party settlement of disputes. An example was provided by article IX of the 1987 Agreement Among the Governments of Brunei Darussalam, Indonesia, Malaysia, the Philippines, Singapore and Thailand (member States of ASEAN)for the Promotion and Protection of Investments, which stated:

> "1) Any dispute between and among the Contracting Parties concerning the interpretation or application of this Agreement shall, as far as possible, be settled amicably between the parties to the dispute. Such settlement shall be reported to the ASEAN Economic Ministers (AEM).
>
> 2) If such a dispute cannot thus be settled it shall be submitted to the AEM for resolution."[24]

Article 4 of the 1996 Protocol replaced the preceding text of Article IX of the ASEAN Investment Agreement with the following: "The provisions of the ASEAN Dispute Settlement Mechanism shall apply to the settlement of disputes under the agreement". The ASEAN Dispute Settlement Mechanism in turn provides for panel procedures established by the Senior Economic Officials Meeting (SEOM) to assist it in ruling on the dispute.[25] Article 7 of the Dispute Settlement Mechanism states that "The SEOM shall consider the report of the panel in its deliberations and make a ruling on the dispute within thirty (30) days from the submission of the report by the panel..." (ASEAN, 1996). Thus, the permanent political body SEOM has the task of ruling on inter-State disputes that arise from the ASEAN Investment Agreement (Mohamad, 1998).[26]

Typically, political bodies do not have established rules and procedures concerning settlement of disputes. Thus, as in the case of ad hoc arbitration, the procedures and methods concerning recourse to and the functioning of political bodies are elaborated in DSAs. For example, with reference to disputes arising from the WTO Agreement on TRIMS, article IV of the Agreement Establishing the WTO provides in paragraph (2) that "There shall be a General Council composed of representatives of all the Members, which shall ... carry out the functions assigned to it by this Agreement...", and further provides in its paragraph (3) that "The General Council shall convene as appropriate to discharge the responsibilities of the Dispute Settlement Body provided for in the Dispute Settlement Understanding. The Dispute Settlement Body may have its own chairman and shall establish such rules of procedure as it deems necessary for the fulfilment of those responsibilities" (WTO, 1995).[27]

This examination suggests that IIAs almost uniformly provide in their DSAs for dispute settlement first through consultation and negotiation procedures, and then through some type of third-party mechanism, such as arbitration (be it ad hoc or institutional), or permanent tribunal (be it judicial or political). The rules and procedures to be followed concerning, for example, the selection of the third-party decision-makers, their terms of reference, and their working rules and procedures – where provided for with sufficient detail and clarity – help reduce the scope of disagreements when these mechanisms are employed. This prevailing model, in principle, could provide States with the means of avoiding disputes, and contribute to the management of their relations when disputes arise, by providing a predetermined, clear and uncontroversial course of action. At the same time, it could provide the confidence that, where agreement can not be reached in a particular dispute, an impartial (and relatively quick) settlement would nonetheless be obtained through definitive rulings concerning the interpretation or application of the provisions of IIAs, which should signify a secure and predictable investment environment.

C. Applicable standards for settlement of disputes

Where DSAs have addressed the subject of applicable standards – almost uniformly in relation to settlement through arbitration – they have typically made reference, albeit in varying formulations, to sources from which such standards could be derived, including the provisions of the IIA, other measures or agreements by the parties, and international law.

The provisions of the IIA are an indispensable source, which does not require explicit mention. However, they are sometimes referred to expressly, though not exclusively, in IIAs. For example, article 11(6) of the Argentina-El Salvador 1996 BIT provides that:

> "The tribunal shall decide on the basis of the provisions of the Agreement, legal principles recognized by the Parties and the general principles of international law" (OAS, 1997).

Box. II.4. Provisions on applicable law

"Any dispute between the Parties concerning the interpretation or application of the Treaty, that is not resolved through consultations or other diplomatic channels, shall be submitted upon the request of either Party to an arbitral tribunal for binding decision in accordance with the applicable rules of international law."
Article 10 (1) United States/Bahrain 1999 BIT.

"(5) The tribunal shall decide on the basis of this Agreement and other relevant agreements between the two Contracting Parties, rules of International Law and rules of Domestic Law. The forgoing provisions shall not prejudice the power of the tribunal to decide the dispute *ex aequo et bono* if the Parties so agree."
Article 12 (5) Netherlands-Nigeria 1992 BIT.

"(g) The tribunal shall decide the dispute in accordance with this Treatyand applicable rules and principles of international law;"
Article 27 (3) (g) Energy Charter Treaty.

Source: UNCTAD.

Generally, provisions of IIAs that establish standards are most-favoured-nation, national, and fair and equitable treatment clauses, as well as the clause on the taking of property. The various formulations of, and the issues that arise in relation to, such standards have been reviewed in other chapters in this volume, and will not be repeated here. Some IIAs include a particular standard in their DSAs[28] in reference to negotiations, namely a standard of "direct and meaningful" negotiations. Here, an arbitral panel might be asked to decide whether or not negotiations were "meaningful", and perhaps even be required to rule on whether or not the arbitration could proceed, if it finds that negotiations were not meaningful. The other measures or agreements by the parties that could serve as sources from which standards are derived are often placed at issue under a separate provision in an IIA. An example is article XI of the United States model BIT, which states:

> "This Treaty shall not derogate from any of the following that entitle covered investments to treatment more favourable than that accorded by this Treaty:
> (a) laws and regulations, administrative practices or procedures, or administrative or adjudicatory decisions of a Party;
> (b) international legal obligations; or
> (c) obligations assumed by a Party, including those contained in an investment authorization or an investment agreement."

Clearly, in the deliberations on applicable standards, this type of provision would require consideration of additional sources other than the IIA. In relation to applicable standards, a problem could arise with regard to the possible differing contexts within which the "more favourable" treatment is provided. The majority of favourable treatment clauses envision "like situations", whereas the exemplified article provides for an absolute standard to be applicable.

The reference to international law is, as noted previously, far from uniform. For example, while article 9(6) of the Chilean model BIT states that:

> "The arbitral tribunal shall reach its decisions taking into account the provisions of this Agreement, the principles of international law on this subject and the generally recognized principles of international law...",

article 8(5) of the Chinese model BIT requires that:

> "The tribunal shall reach its award in accordance with the provisions of this Agreement and the principles of international law recognized by both Contracting Parties."

Notwithstanding the theoretical distinction between rules and principles, the Chilean formulation seems to refer to a combination of standards to be derived from the treaty, the rules of international law on the subject applied as *lex specialis*, and generally recognized principles of international law. The Chinese formulation, however, creates a problem in that the applicable standards would need to be derived not only from the treaty provisions, in itself relatively unproblematic to the extent that such derivation is possible, but also from principles of international law recognized by both parties. Presumably, if both parties to the dispute do not recognize a particular principle of international law that the arbitral tribunal considers to be relevant, that principle must be discarded.

Still other sources of applicable standards are provided for in some Dutch BITs. For example, article 9(6) of the 1987 Netherlands/Sri Lanka BIT states that "The tribunal shall decide on the basis of respect for the law ... The foregoing provisions shall not prejudice the power of the tribunal to decide the dispute *ex aequo et bono* if the Parties so agree" (United Nations Treaty Series, 1987). The first sentence provides that standards could also be derived from relevant national laws, and the second increases the scope beyond legal considerations, and concerns a balancing on equities (what is fair or reasonable) as between the parties to a dispute.

D. Nature and scope of outcomes of dispute settlement mechanisms

Successful negotiations secure settlement agreements, which are, by definition, binding upon the signatory States. This derives from a fundamental principle of international law, *pacta sunt servanda*, which in this context translates itself into an obligation on the part of a State to comply with that to which it has agreed. With regard to BITs, there are no major impediments as to the scope of negotiated settlement agreements. With regional IIAs, however, and those that establish particular integration or liberalization regimes, there might be some limitation on the scope of settlement agreements. For example, article 2006 (5) NAFTA provides:

> "The consulting Parties shall make every attempt to arrive at a mutually satisfactory resolution of any matter through consultations under this Article or other consultative provisions of this Agreement. To this end, the consulting Parties shall ... (c) seek to avoid any resolution that adversely affects the interests under this Agreement of any other Party" (Canada, Mexico and United States, 1992).

Most IIAs provide in their DSAs that the decisions resulting from the engagement of third-party dispute settlement mechanisms, such as ad hoc arbitral tribunals, are to be reached by majority voting, and are binding upon the parties to the dispute. Article 11 (iv) of the AALCC Model BIT

(A) provides a typical example by providing that "The arbitral tribunal shall reach its decision by majority of votes. Such decision shall be binding on both the Contracting Parties...". In some instances, however, arbitral decisions do not have a binding effect, as illustrated by article 2018(1) NAFTA: "On receipt of the final report of a panel, the disputing Parties shall agree on the resolution of the dispute, which normally shall conform with the determinations and recommendations of the panel, and shall notify their Sections of the Secretariat of any agreed resolution of any dispute" (Canada, Mexico and United States, 1992). Thus, it is up to the disputing NAFTA parties to settle their dispute; and, while the panel decision is influential, it is not necessarily conclusive of the matter and, hence, is non-binding.[29]

On the other hand, in the absence of such specific provisions, which may render the award of a panel non-binding until it is adopted by a political body, it may be presumed that any arbitral award properly made under the authority of a dispute settlement clause in an IIA will be legally binding. In this connection, it should be noted that the discretion of an arbitral panel with respect to the type of ruling or award that it could make is generally wide in BITs. Indeed, the majority of BITs are silent on the issue, thus leaving it for the panel to decide the scope of its award.

E. Compliance with dispute settlement awards

The majority of IIAs and BITs, almost uniformly, are silent on this issue. At times, however, the decision of an arbitral tribunal is immediately neither final nor binding on the disputing parties, but its implementation will be the basis upon which the dispute between the parties will be resolved or settled. Non-compliance thereafter is dealt with by sanctions in the forms of compensation to the prevailing party or the suspension of benefit of an equivalent amount as awarded by the panel (e.g. article XV (6) of the BIT between Canada and Trinidad and Tobago). Some provide for steps that monitor and report the progress made with respect to compliance. However, under both the NAFTA and the WTO, sanctions are provided for in the case of non-compliance. For example, article 2019 of NAFTA provides:

> "1. If in its final report a panel has determined that a measure is inconsistent with the obligations of this Agreement or causes nullification or impairment in the sense of Annex 2004 and the Party complained against has not reached agreement with any complaining Party on a mutually satisfactory resolution pursuant to Article 2018(1) within 30 days of receiving the final report, such complaining Party may suspend the application to the Party complained against of benefits of equivalent effect until such time as they have reached agreement on a resolution of the dispute.
>
> 2. In considering what benefits to suspend pursuant to paragraph 1:
>
> (a) a complaining Party should first seek to suspend benefits in the same sector or sectors as that affected by the measure or other matter that the panel has found to be inconsistent with the obligations of this Agreement or to have caused nullification or impairment in the sense of Annex 2004; and
>
> (b) a complaining Party that considers it is not practicable or effective to suspend benefits in the same sector or sectors may suspend benefits in other sectors.
>
> 3. On the written request of any disputing Party delivered to the other Parties and its Section of the Secretariat, the Commission shall establish a panel to determine whether the level of benefits suspended by a Party pursuant to paragraph 1 is manifestly excessive..."

* * *

On the basis of this examination of the substantive provisions in IIAs dealing with dispute settlement issues, the next section will consider the foregoing issues in their relationship with other issues arising in IIAs.

Section III
Interaction with other Issues and Concepts

Of the various interactions that exist between the present topic and others that arise in the context of IIAs, a significant one is between State-to-State and investor-State dispute settlement. IIAs are agreements between States, and any commitments entered into are, in the final analysis, opposable only by their signatories. Under this perspective, inter-State DSAs provide for the general and final methods of the settlement of international investment disputes. The foregoing notwithstanding, IIAs increasingly establish rights for foreign investors to challenge directly the measures of their host countries through a variety of dispute settlement mechanisms. Investor-State dispute settlement arrangements therefore provide for alternative means of settling particular investment disputes (see chapter 12). This section will, however, highlight some of the interactions with respect to the topic of investor-State dispute settlement.

As regards other areas of interaction, State-to-State dispute settlement arrangements provided for in IIAs make effective the rights and obligations contained in such agreements. As such, the topic of dispute settlement can potentially interact with all other substantive and procedural matters covered in an IIA that might give rise to a question or disagreement. To some extent, therefore, the degrees of interaction with other issues are determined by the matters that are typically covered by IIAs, as well as by their substantive nature. For purposes of analysis, it is useful to classify individual topics within relevant groupings, and to consider the interactions in terms of groups of issues, rather than by an item-by-item analysis.

In relation to relevant groupings of issues, two main categories can be identified. First, there are topics that are typically included as provisions in IIAs, the interpretation or application of which could normally be expected to be directly at issue. These include the scope of coverage and definitions of investors and investments; admission and establishment commitments and obligations concerning standards of treatment (fair and equitable treatment, most-favoured-nation treatment, and national treatment), host country operational measures, transfer of funds, and the taking of property.

Second, there are those interactions that would result, either directly if certain topics are expressly addressed in IIAs, or indirectly in so far as measures relating to such topics would give rise to issues with respect to the topics in the first category identified above. These include competition law and investment related trade measures; employment, environmental and tax laws and regulations; State contracts; incentives; illicit payments; transfer of technology; and measures taken by an investor's home country, with respect to the social responsibility of investors, or in response to transfer pricing. It should be noted that, while these topics are not currently principal, recurring features of IIAs, some of them (such as environmental measures) could be considered as emerging issues, which could indirectly interact with DSAs in IIAs.

Table 1. Interaction across issues and concepts

Issues	State-to-State dispute settlement
Admission and establishment	++
Competition	+
Dispute settlement: investor-State	++
Employment	+
Environment	+
Fair and equitable treatment	++
Funds transfer	++
Home country measures	+
Host country operational measures	++
Illicit payments	+
Incentives	+
Investment-related trade measures	+
Most-favoured-nation treatment	++
National treatment	++
Scope and definition	++
Social responsibility	+
State contracts	+
Taking of property	++
Taxation	+
Transfer of technology	+
Transfer pricing	+
Transparency	0

Source: UNCTAD.

Key: 0 = negligible or no interaction
+ = moderate interaction
++ = extensive interaction

- **Investor-State dispute settlement arrangements.** Where both State-to-State and investor-State DSAs are present in IIAs, together they can provide a framework to ensure the fullest implementation of an IIA. However, whilst most State-to-State dispute procedures in IIAs refer to ad hoc processes to which both parties have equal access, in the investor-State arrangements, there are mixtures of both ad hoc and institutional processes, access to which may be had either equally or at the preference of the investor.
  Once the national of either contracting party validly submits a dispute to an investor-State procedure, such election could be, in some cases, exclusive. Thus, no other national or international procedures remain open to the disputing parties (either the State or the investor), including either arbitration under any other system or regime, or, the State-to-

State dispute settlement procedures under the particular IIA. For example, the draft MAI, Part V, C1b (on State-to-State Dispute Settlement Procedures) provides:

"A Contracting Party may not initiate proceedings under this Article for a dispute which its investor has submitted, or consented to submit, to arbitration under Article D [dealing with investor-to-State dispute settlement procedures], unless the other Contracting Party has failed to abide by and comply with the award rendered in that dispute or those proceedings have terminated without resolution by an arbitral tribunal of the investor's claim."

The interconnection between investor-State arbitration and State-to-State dispute settlement is also manifest where the range of disputes that could be submitted to either mode of dispute settlement do not overlap. For example, under Article 64 of the ICSID Convention, the scope of inter-State disagreements extends to any dispute arising between contracting States concerning the interpretation or application of the ICSID Convention, while Article 25, its counterpart concerning investor-State issues, includes only a legal dispute arising directly out of an investment. This makes clear that contracting States cannot enter into disputes with each other under the ICSID Convention over specific investor-State disputes that have been brought under Article 25. They may only enter into disputes concerning the interpretation or application of the Convention itself, whereupon they are required to reach a negotiated settlement. Failure to do so will open the possibility of a referral of the dispute to the International Court of Justice, or to another method of settlement agreed to by the parties. Thus Article 64 ensures that the ICJ will not be used by contracting States as an appellate body against decisions of ICSID tribunals, or to challenge the competence of such a tribunal to hear the case before it.

- **Scope and definition.** The scope of the coverage of an IIA is established by the interaction between all its provisions in light of the definitions clause. The wider the definitions of certain concepts and issues in an IIA, for example, "nationals", "investments", "investor", the more susceptible it is to disagreements as to the inclusion of particular instances of such concepts or issues. Far-reaching definitions would constitute a limitation on a host country's investment-related measures. Such measures might be incompatible with treaty commitments; but, more importantly, the threat of challenges to these measures under DSAs might prove to have a chilling effect on legitimate governmental regulation. On the other hand, a more detailed, carefully considered set of definitions of those concepts or issues would ensure predictability for both States and investors as to particular issues that are covered by IIAs, and those that fall outside their respective coverage, and hence, also outside of the scope of DSAs.

  This is more prominent in those models that define "investment disputes" as a dispute between a party and a national or company of the other party arising out of or relating to:

  (a) an investment agreement between that party and a national or company;

  (b) an investment authorization granted by that party's foreign investment authority to such national or company; or

  (c) an alleged breach of any right conferred or created by the treaty with respect to an investment.

  Ordinarily, in the first instance, the dispute may involve a host country and an investor. The home country might only become engaged if the investor is unjustifiably denied the remedy available under the investor-State dispute settlement procedure; if the tribunal under the investor-State dispute settlement procedure declines jurisdiction for one reason or another (for example, because the investment does not come within the definition of protected investment although the concerned investor is a national of one contracting State); or when the right violated is also a breach of the IIA (for example, a State purporting to withdraw its unilateral consent to submit to arbitration expressed in the IIA after a covered investment was made on the basis of the subsistence of that consent or to pre-empt a pending claim by an investor).

  Any of the above could amount to or lead to "a dispute" between the host country party and the home country party concerning the interpretation or application of the IIA.

- **Admission and establishment.** Where an IIA guarantees rights of entry and establishment by the respective nationals of the contracting parties, an action of a State restricting such

admission in violation of such rights may lead to a dispute concerning the interpretation or application of the IIA between the host country and the home country of the covered investors, though it is more likely that the investor will bring a claim against the host country if the IIA provides for investor-State dispute settlement. On the other hand, where an IIA does not provide such a positive guarantee, the refusal to grant a right of entry and establishment to an investor from another contracting State cannot be the basis of any dispute, whether between the contracting parties themselves, or between the investor and the State refusing entry and establishment.
An IIA that applies to investments made in the host country before it entered into force would cover all investments in the host country of the nationals of the treaty partner. An action taken by the host country may not only be a violation of a right assured to the private investor by the IIA but would also amount to its violation therefore leading to a dispute under the State-to-State dispute settlement provision of the IIA.

- **Standards of treatment**. The standard of fair and equitable treatment in an IIA contained in a State-to-State dispute settlement arrangement would give negotiators or adjudicators the opportunity to assess whether an impugned action against an investor would withstand the commitments undertaken by a State in that respect (e.g. compensation for expropriation). The availability of, or access to, an independent and neutral binding third party procedure enhances the value and potency of this standard in a dispute situation. If a State action is below the fair and equitable standard, it could constitute a breach of the IIA in that specific area, thereby justifying a finding of responsibility against the concerned contracting State.
The interaction with national treatment provisions in an IIA would be relevant in those countries that do not have relatively adequate provisions on a particular subject in their treaties with the home country of the investor when compared with what is obtainable within the national legal system. The national treatment standard expects a host country to extend to foreign investors treatment that is at least as favourable as the treatment that it accords to national investors in like circumstances (UNCTAD, 1999c). In that case, a foreign investor might expect a treatment as favourable as compared with what is obtainable nationally and, in the process of using the available national treatment standard, might implicate the international responsibility of the host country. For example, if there is no provision in an IIA for the settlement of investor-State disputes as in the 1988 BIT between Bangladesh and Thailand, an investor could insist on using the national procedure in that instance as it is the more favourable and effective in obtaining redress from an injury in the host country. If, in the course of utilising the national procedure, an investor suffers a denial of justice below the fair and equitable standard, the treaty-based remedy of diplomatic protection through the State-to-State dispute settlement procedure in an IIA could be availed automatically. The fair and equitable treatment and the national treatment standards could complement each other in this way.
The national treatment standard could merge with the most-favoured-nation (MFN) standard to implicate the State-to-State dispute settlement arrangement in an IIA. Both standards have a very strong link and interaction in avoiding discrimination against foreign investors. The MFN standard involves comparability of favourable rights with respect to third countries with which a particular country has concluded an IIA containing a more favourable standard. If a country has both the national and the MFN standards in its IIA, the MFN standard might be relied upon to call in a more effective State-to-State dispute settlement regime where a denial of justice at the national level below the fair and equitable standard has occurred. Assuming that the BIT with the claimant State has only the primary stage of dispute settlement procedure in it, as in the BIT between Egypt and Indonesia, the MFN clause might enable the more favourable of the dispute settlement arrangements in the BITs to which the host country is a party with other countries to be invoked in the circumstance.
- **Taking of property**. The taking of property (assuming that it qualifies as a covered investment under an IIA), contrary to the conditions stipulated in the provision covering such takings, could constitute a breach of the IIA and thus lead to a dispute concerning the interpretation or application of the obligation

of the State taking the action under the IIA to pay compensation as stipulated. The interaction between this issue and State-to-State dispute settlement is more fully discussed in the chapter on taking of property, and will not be further considered here.

Conclusion: Economic and Development Implications and Policy Options

The process of foreign investment can create disagreements and disputes between the various actors involved. There is, therefore, little doubt for the need to have in place procedures for the settlement of investment disputes. This is so regardless of the level of development of the host country in question. Equally, it is clear that disputes will arise not only over specific investments between investors and host countries, but that the wider implications of such disputes, on the evolution of the treaty-based framework for investment that IIAs are seeking to create and develop, can, in their turn, create questions and differences that might need some kind of formal resolution. This is particularly true of issues pertaining to the general interpretation and application of the substantive provisions and procedures established by IIAs. Such disputes are of the type that are more likely to be dealt with at the State-to-State level.

A further issue to be borne in mind, when considering the development implications of dispute settlement mechanisms, is the paramount need to ensure the primacy of swift, efficient and amicable methods of dispute settlement. This is the best guarantee of long-term stability in investment relations. Therefore, the majority of dispute settlement clauses and systems that are found in IIAs stress the value of this type of approach, and expect informal means of settlement to be used in the first instance. Indeed, dispute settlement clauses and systems are there to deal with the generally rare disputes that cannot be easily disposed of through amicable means. On the other hand, major disagreements can and do occur. Thus, the proper conduct of more serious investment disputes must be ensured.

The system of dispute settlement to be chosen must provide effective means for the resolution of differences between the parties and, crucially, it must be fair to both parties, and to be perceived as such. In this connection, State-to-State disputes concerning investment issues bring with them many development implications. In particular, the way in which an IIA is interpreted and applied may have significant implications for the conduct of investment policies on the part of developing host countries. Thus it is essential that State-to-State dispute settlement systems offer sufficient flexibility to be sensitive to development concerns. This may require procedures that ensure adequate coverage for the development implications of the various positions taken by the States party to the dispute in question. Equally, such procedures must provide for full "equality of arms" as between developed and developing countries parties to a dispute so that superior resources or experience do not, in themselves, result in the development dimension of the dispute being incompletely heard and analysed.

Equally, State-to-State investment disputes arise in the context of investment relationships between a private commercial party and a State administration or agency. Thus, a public interest and policy element is present. This cannot be wholly disregarded as against the commercial interests of the private party, nor, indeed, can the legitimate interests and expectations of the commercial party always take second place to the public interest. This may be especially the case where private property rights are protected as fundamental individual rights (as for example under the European Community Treaty) or human rights (as for example under Article 1 of the First Protocol to the European Convention on Human Rights) against a "taking" by a government through administrative action. The dispute settlement system must therefore be sensitive to both kinds of interests and to the claims that they might generate in the course of a dispute.

Against this background, and in the light of the preceding discussion, a number of policy options present themselves for consideration in the drafting of State-to-State dispute settlement clauses in IIAs.

A. No Reference to State-to-State dispute settlement

At the most basic level it is possible to decide not to include any reference to dispute settlement in an IIA. This option is not usually found in practice. A central purpose of many IIAs is to place a guarantee of dispute settlement into legally binding terms through the use of such an agreement. The effect is to create an international legal obligation to settle disputes between a host country and other countries parties to an IIA in accordance with the procedures laid down in that agreement.

In relation to investor-State disputes, when the host country has a well-structured and generally accepted internal legal order, a reference to dispute settlement in an IIA could be thought of as unnecessary. The internal laws and practices of a host country may be seen as sufficiently protective of the rights and obligations of both a private investor and a host country, so as not to need further determination in an international agreement. By contrast, where State-to-State disputes are concerned, the particular features of the internal legal order of the host or, indeed, home country are unlikely to influence the need for some type of dispute settlement system to be used by the contracting State parties to an IIA.

In such cases, silence on State-to-State dispute settlement would mean that the parties will rely on traditional methods of international dispute settlement to deal with any disputes that might arise. This may give rise to uncertainty over the applicable method of dispute settlement to be used and will require further negotiation between the State parties to a dispute as to how to deal with that eventuality. The main advantage of including a clause on State-to-State dispute settlement in an IIA is that the contracting parties will know ex ante what types of dispute settlement methods are open to them and how they should be activated and pursued, though the degree of coverage and procedural detail may vary from agreement to agreement, as will be shown below.

B. Reference to State-to-State dispute settlement

In the light of the practice detailed in section II, a number of options arise in relation to how the principal issues identified in section I should be dealt with by the terms of the State-to-State dispute settlement clause in an IIA.

(a) The scope of disputes that could trigger State-to-State dispute settlement procedures

Option 1: General formulations as to scope

There appears to be little practical difference in the effects of the various formulations that have been used to delineate the scope of disputes that could be covered under State-to-State dispute settlement provisions. As noted in section II, some agreements refer to prompt consultations on any dispute or matter arising from an agreement. It is a formulation aimed at dispute avoidance and possesses the advantage of informality and flexibility as to the subjet-matter of the dispute that may be dealt with through this procedure. This may be particularly useful for a developing country party that may not have the resources to engage in extensive formal dispute settlement procedures.

Other agreements provide dispute settlement procedures only in relation to the interpretation and application of the substantive and procedural provisions of the agreements. This formulation would appear to restrict disputes that come within the State-to-State dispute settlement provisions to those arising directly out of the agreements themselves. In practice, however, the range and scope of disputes that could be fairly described as arising out of the interpretation and application of the provisions of IIAs is quite wide. Equally, such a formulation will not rule out the primacy of informal, negotiated methods of dispute settlement.

Option 2: Removal of certain substantive measures from the State-to-State dispute settlement provisions

A variant of this approach is to remove certain substantive measures from review under the State-to-State dispute settlement provisions, for example national security issues, national FDI screening decisions or tax measures that do not amount to expropriatory measures. Such an approach can offer a degree of flexibility over which areas of an IIA should be excluded from the dispute settlement system in the agreement. These may reflect vital national public policy issues. Indeed, this approach could be adapted to exclude specific industries or sectors as well, where a State feels this to be necessary.

Option 3: The avoidance of concurrent proceedings

As noted in section II, certain IIAs have added a specialized clause to their State-to-State dispute settlement provisions which ensures that there will be no concurrent proceedings before other fora where the State-to-State dispute settlement procedure has been instituted. Usually, such provisions prevent States from commencing State-to-State dispute proceedings over a matter that is already subject to investor-State proceedings under the investor-State dispute settlement provisions of the agreement in question. In addition such clauses may provide rules for determining which of more than one available forum should take precedence in State-to-State proceedings.

(b) Dispute settlement mechanisms and their procedures

(i) Treatment of negotiations

Here a number of options arise in relation to the extent to which the States parties to the dispute are obliged to pursue a negotiated settlement.

Option 1: Hortatory provision

The parties may exhort the use of negotiated settlement techniques without making these mandatory. The formulation in this case would use wording such as "shall endeavour to" or "should" when referring to the use of negotiated informal methods of dispute settlement. Such a formulation does not, however, absolve a State from undertaking negotiations prior to moving on to third-party methods of dispute settlement. It requires that States make a genuine effort to negotiate or consult. Where this is a pre-condition to binding third-party settlement, failure to negotiate or consult will mean that the pre-condition would not have been met, even though the language used is hortatory in nature.[30]

Option 2: Mandatory provision

Here the parties are obliged to use negotiated settlement techniques before proceeding to more formal means of dispute settlement. Such clauses typically use mandatory language in that the parties "shall" or "must" use informal methods.

Option 3: Specific procedural requirements

In addition to the issue of whether the parties are obliged to use informal methods first, other requirements by which the dispute should be handled can be included in the relevant provision. For example, as noted in section II, there may be information requirements pertaining to the exchange of relevant information between the parties to a dispute, rules regarding permissible time limits or requirements to use ad hoc or specific standing institutions for the purposes of mediation, good offices or conciliation.

(ii) Mode of dispute settlement

Under this heading the parties to an IIA must decide on the types of procedures that will be made available to disputing State parties to the agreement and on the effects of the parties making a choice of a particular mode of dispute settlement, where such choice is available.

Option 1: Ad hoc arbitration

As shown in section II, the majority of agreements opt for mandatory ad hoc arbitration between the State parties to a dispute upon the failure of an informal negotiated settlement of the dispute. There is a wide discretion on the part of negotiators as to the amount of detail to be inserted as concerns the procedures to be followed. However, as indicated in section II, a number of issues can be addressed with varying degrees of specificity:

- Appointment of arbitrators and arbitral panels.
- Determination of the subject-matter of the arbitration which can be done, in part by the general provisions of the agreement, as described in (a) above, but which also needs more specific determination in relation to the dispute at hand either by the parties themselves or by the arbitral panel.
- Operational rules and procedures to be used by the arbitral panel. These issues are mostly left to the panel's discretion but may include mandatory provisions such as, for example, rules on time limits applicable to the stages of the proceeding or references to the use of pre-established arbitral rules such as the UNCITRAL Arbitration Rules.

Option 2: Reference to the Permanent Court of Arbitration

In the alternative to ad hoc international arbitration, an IIA could refer to the Permanent Court of Arbitration as the forum before which the State parties to a dispute could present their case. This is not a common approach.

Option 3: Reference to specific institutional procedure under the IIA

As discussed in section II, certain regional agreements have included specialized institutional arrangements for the settlement of disputes for both investor-State and State-to-State disputes. These could be used as an exclusive mode of dispute settlement. They offer the advantages of a predictable and specialized organ that is devoted to settling disputes under an agreement. This is particularly useful in relation to newly established investment regimes in regions in which no precedent exists for this type of arrangement, or as between State parties that are at different levels of development and which might require a degree of specialized understanding of the particular issues raised by the investment regime in question for their national policies and practices. This is also the approach used in relation to the multilateral trade arrangements before the WTO.

Option 4: Recourse to international judicial bodies

In the absence of ad hoc arbitration or specific institutions dealing with dispute settlement, the parties may seek recourse to the established international judicial forum of the ICJ for the settlement of disputes under an IIA. This approach has the advantage of involving the main expert international judicial body, set up specifically to adjudicate upon inter-State disputes, in the settlement of disputes arising under the IIA in question.

The most significant drawback of this approach may be the fact that the ICJ is a general court of international law and does not, as such, specialize in disputes such as those arising out of the interpretation or application of investment agreements. That is not to say that the ICJ could not discharge this task. Indeed, that would be not only incorrect as a matter of history, in that disputes between States over the terms of international economic agreements have been brought before the Court, but also a slight on the legal expertise available on the bench of the ICJ in such matters. On the other hand, the procedure before the ICJ is that of a full judicial, as opposed to a more informal arbitral, tribunal and proceedings may take too much time in relation to the nature of the dispute arising under the agreement.

Option 5: Recourse to regional judicial bodies

In the case of regional economic groupings, State-to-State disputes concerning the application of regional treaty provisions to investment issues may be taken to a specialized regional court set up to deal with such disputes. Unlike the more general ICJ, such judicial tribunals may be set up as specialized courts with a primary jurisdiction over economic issues arising out of regional economic agreements. They may also be tasked with the development of a coherent and consistent jurisprudence concerning the interpretation and application of the agreement in question. Therefore recourse to such a tribunal may form an essential part of the economic policy aims of the States parties to the agreement, making recourse to such a tribunal a necessary element of the economic order sought to be created. On the other hand, in common with other judicial tribunals, their procedure is likely to be more time consuming and expensive than informal arbitration. Accordingly this option is not likely to be used in relation to more informal investment agreements that do not constitute a part of a wider-ranging regional economic integration arrangement.

Option 6: Recourse to a permanent political institution

This option allows for an institutionalized political approach to State-to-State dispute settlement. The advantage here is of a more discretionary mode of dispute settlement, not bound by the formalities of third party adjudication, but offering third party decision-making. The major disadvantage is that such a system is not predictable or certain in the outcome of disputes, as each dispute is treated on its own merits in the light of the overall objectives of the parties to the agreement. Thus, decisions are not made in accordance with the usual rules and practices of due process that third party arbitral and judicial bodies must adhere to, nor are they necessarily limited to the issues raised by the disputing parties, as the wider interests of the parties as a whole are on the minds of the decision-makers.

Certain further qualifications may be placed upon the use of the above options:

- The agreement in question may mandate the use of only one of the above. Indeed, as already pointed out, most IIAs opt for mandatory ad hoc arbitration on the failure of informal dispute settlement methods.
- An agreement may offer a choice of dispute settlement mode from among a range of alternatives based on the above six options.
- In the latter case, the parties may wish to insert a clause ensuring that the chosen mode becomes exclusive, so as to avoid duplication of proceedings and procedures and so as to allow for a degree of finality based on the outcome of the selected mode of dispute settlement.
- The parties may consider whether to offer another mode of dispute settlement upon the outcome of the application of another mode. For example, the award of an ad hoc arbitral tribunal might be subjected to review for error, or even to full appeal, by a judicial body specified in the agreement; in specialized institutional arrangements an initial decision could be subjected to an appeal process by an appellate body established under that system.

(c) Applicable law for dispute settlement

In this connection, as shown in section II, the majority of IIAs refer to standards recognized by various sources of law, including national laws, regulations and administrative practices, international law, the provisions of the IIAs themselves and other measures or agreements to which the parties adhere. There are no hard and fast alternatives in this context. It is therefore difficult to provide clear alternative options. However, in principle, the following options could be developed:

Option 1: Silence on applicable law

This approach would require the arbitral tribunal itself to determine the applicable standards. This is not usual practice. If the arbitral tribunal is to decide on this issue then an express provision making this clear would be preferable to silence, as this could create space for further disagreement between the disputing States as to precisely which standards apply, thereby adding fuel to the underlying dispute and thereby increasing its scope. In the absence of any provision on this matter, it is safe to say that applicable principles of international law, which bind States regardless of any treaty provisions between them, will apply to the dispute. This is particularly important in relation to the interpretation of the IIA provisions, which should conform to the requirements of Articles 31 and 32 of the Vienna Convention on the Law of Treaties, which deal with the rules of treaty interpretation and which have been uniformly and generally held to represent customary international law in this field by successive WTO Panels and Appellate Bodies (Cameron and Gray, 2001).

Option 2: Reference to specific sources of standards

As shown in section II, a number of variations are possible though in the majority of cases a reference to international law appears almost ubiquitous. No examples have been found in IIAs where national law alone is referred to as the sole source of standards. Any such reference will usually be qualified by reference to applicable principles of international law. From the examples in section II the following variants have been identified:

- Reference to international law alone.
- Reference to the IIA itself and to international law.
- Reference to the IIA, international law and to rules of domestic law.
- Reference to the IIA, international law and to "principles of law recognized by the Parties".

The reference to international law may take numerous forms and may not always show full agreement between the parties as to what the content of the international law applicable to the issue should be. The examples of the Chilean and Chinese BITs mentioned in section II illustrate that problem.

Some further variations are also possible:

- A reference to sources, such as other international agreements or investment contracts, that contain more favourable treatment standards for investors.
- A reference to settlement ex *aequo et bono*.

The arrangements for the settlement of inter-State disputes would contribute to the management of investment relations between countries, and to investor expectations with regard to a secure and predictable investment environment in those countries, only to the extent that the applicable standards are carefully considered and to some extent foreseeable by the parties concerned. In this connection, it should be mentioned that use of concepts and standards, such as national treatment, for which established jurisprudence exist, could be useful. Conversely, the inclusion of general or vague standards, such as fair and equitable treatment, which are themselves capable of creating disputes as to their meaning, scope and coverage, should be considered together with explanatory notes that set out clear guidelines for decision-makers in case of disputes.

(d) Nature and scope of outcomes of dispute settlement

Here at least two options present themselves:

Option 1: Silence on the issue

This is the usual approach in BITs. It gives a wide discretion on these matters to the arbitral tribunal itself.

Option 2: Specific provisions

Such provisions usually assert that the award of the arbitral tribunal shall be binding on the parties. In regional or multilateral arrangements, a specific provision detailing the force of the panel award and its effect on third party States may be necessary so as to determine whether they have any rights or obligations arising out of the award such as, for example, to treat it as a binding precedent.

(e) Compliance with awards

Here there are two possible approaches: the first is to leave the issue of how to exact compliance to the parties, while the second is to provide expressly for sanctions in the event of non-compliance with the award by the losing party. This may take the form of compensation for loss and/or the right to take counter-measures by the winning State party to the dispute.

****

The foregoing discussion has shown the significant choices that arise in relation to the development of an effective State-to-State dispute settlement mechanism in IIAs. While raising many intricate technical issues, it should not be thought that such a system is always at the centre of the dispute settlement provisions of an IIA. Current practice has tended to extend dispute settlement provisions to cover investor-State disputes and it is fair to say that this type of dispute is likely to be the more common in relation to the application and interpretation of IIA provisions. In that sense, State-to-State procedures may be regarded as secondary to investor-State procedures in agreements where both types of dispute settlement are catered for. On the other hand, some IIAs may only provide for State-to-State dispute settlement, especially where the main aim behind the agreement is the development of an inter-State order for the regulation of FDI in which investor protection rights may be of a "soft law" or hortatory character. In such cases, the main types of disputes will relate to the interpretation and application of general provisions in the agreement, without reference to specific disputes involving actual investors. Thus, State-to-State dispute settlement provisions may be ubiquitous in all IIAs, even though their actual significance may vary between agreements.

Notes

1 The classic cases involve the de facto termination of the property rights of an investor in its investment, examples of which are nationalizations and direct and indirect expropriations. These measures have their history in disputes concerning diplomatic protection under customary international law, but now are the subject of specific provisions under IIAs.

2 Governmental measures include all legislative, regulatory or administrative acts (encompassing practices) or omissions.

3 Under current international law, no State can be compelled to engage in any dispute settlement mechanism without its consent. Furthermore, no dispute settlement structure exists that provides for the submission of all types of disputes. Thus, unlike domestic systems of governance, DSAs in international relations do not feature in the overall governance structure of international relations. Notwithstanding the foregoing, the organization of the International Court of Justice (ICJ) under the auspices of the United Nations could be regarded as a move towards the establishment of a compulsory and comprehensive DSA within the governance structure of the international system. However, it is arguable that regional dispute settlement systems, such as the European Court of Justice, are examples of a system of mandatory dispute settlement as the member States of the grouping accept that membership entails submission to the authority of the tribunal in question. Another example would be the WTO dispute settlement mechanism under the Dispute Settlement Understanding (DSU) (WTO, 1994) to which all Members of the WTO must adhere as part of their membership obligations.

4 In these circumstances, international law requires States to attempt to settle the dispute using any means agreeable to both, so long as those means exclude measures that might endanger international peace and security.

5 However, it should also be noted that unilateralism is not always detrimental to the relationships formed by IIAs. The legitimacy of such practices depends on the purposes and objectives of the State that resorts to unilateralism, and whether or not those purposes and objectives were anticipated within the context of the IIA. For example, a State might wish to be the sole arbiter of whether certain measures fall within the scope of an exception clause negotiated in the IIA. Equally, recourse to unilateral acts needs to be considered in terms of non-compliance of one party with the final decision that settles a dispute. Regardless of which dispute settlement mechanism renders the final decision concerning the dispute, compliance with the final decision – be it a negotiated agreement or a tribunal award – is always an issue since the international system lacks enforcement procedures and mechanisms. To the extent that an IIA has covered these and similar issues, any attempt to act unilaterally would make a travesty of the DSAs contained therein. If, however, DSAs do not address such issues, then a State remains free to engage in unilateralism.

6 The interpretation of an IIA is governed by customary rules of international law concerning treaty interpretation, as codified in the 1969 Vienna Convention on the Law of Treaties

(Vienna Convention on the Law of Treaties, 1969, pp. 875-905).

7 The issue could arise as to whether or not "consultations" and "negotiations" imply qualitatively different processes, especially where DSAs provide that should matters concerning the IIA develop, parties must consult, and where disputes have developed, the parties must negotiate. In this connection, while the alternative usage might imply a subtle difference in the stages within the dispute process, the basic process involved in both is an exchange. It could be noted in this regard that consultations might not involve striking a bargain, whereas negotiations do. The matter might be of philosophical interest, but remains outside the scope of this paper.

8 The issue of the application of a measure – especially where the question goes beyond whether or not a measure constitutes a well-described act that is prescribed by the IIA – may require an examination involving the characterization of the host-country's measures and their effects, and sometimes even the motives behind their initiation. In these circumstances, it could be of crucial importance that the parties to IIAs determine the applicable standards on the level of scrutiny that is afforded to the decision-maker in a dispute settlement mechanism.

9 Where DSAs are silent on this subject, it is generally accepted that, as regards the interpretation of the provisions of a treaty, the customary rules of international law, as recorded in the 1969 Vienna Convention on the Law of Treaties (Vienna Convention on the Law of Treaties, 1969), would apply. However, in connection with standards on treaty application, the parties involved in bilateral means of dispute settlement may need to reach agreement on those standards, such agreement at times being a prerequisite to reaching an acceptable solution to the dispute. In the case of third-party means of dispute settlement, it would be left for the tribunal to decide the matter, which might thereby add to the issues in dispute.

10 It should be noted that not all disputes involve questions of law. In some cases, an award might be limited by agreement to a determination of facts in controversy, after which the parties would negotiate a settlement on the basis of the tribunal's findings.

11 In the case of settlement agreements, the element of review is embodied in a request for renegotiation of the agreement.

12 Diplomatic protection is a distinct and absolute right of the claimant State to be exercised at its exclusive discretion, which absent other arrangements, could leave an investor without any remedies in relation to measures that have adversely affected its investment. Other problems related to the espousal of an investor's claim under customary international law are that the nature of the subject-matter that can be protected may be limited and the rules regulating its exercise may be cumbersome; for example, a State will not espouse a claim on behalf of its national unless requested to do so by such national, usually after the latter has exhausted the available local remedies in the State alleged to have caused the injury in question. Another example of such issues under customary international law is the need to establish the link of nationality with the claimant State and, in the case of a dual national, for that nationality to be recognized by other interested States, and the establishment of a genuine link (a dominant and effective nationality) between the private person and the State whose nationality the latter claims to possess.

13 The contracting parties also reserved the freedom to choose any other peaceful means of dispute settlement on which they might subsequently agree.

14 Unless otherwise noted, all instruments cited herein may be found in UNCTAD, 1996a, 2000 and 2001; the texts of the BITs mentioned in this chapter may be found in the collection of BITs maintained by ICSID (ICSID, 1972–), or at www.unctad.org/iia.

15 In some cases, the duty to consult between the parties could also serve as an essential instrument of joint policy formulation, implementation and monitoring by governments. For example, article 12 of the Chinese model BIT requires that consultations take place between the representatives of the two parties on matters related to the implementation of the agreement, exchange of legal information, resolving investment disputes, investment promotion and other investment-related issues.

16 See for example, article 9 (2) of the Chilean model BIT; article 11 (2) of the French model BIT; article 4 (a) of the United States Overseas Private Investment Corporation (OPIC) draft Investment Incentive Agreement; and article 4 (a) of the United-States-Egypt Investment Incentive Agreement. The United States-Jordan Agreement on the Establishment of a Free Trade Area of 2000 provides for a period of 90 days: article 17(c).

17 See, for example, the agreements between the United States and: Turkey, article 5; Egypt, article 5; Ghana, article 7; Nigeria, article 7.

18 See too the Cambodia model BIT, article IX; the Iran model BIT, article 13; and the Peru model BIT, article 9. It is interesting to note that NAFTA provides for a novel selection procedure, whereby the parties are required to create first a roster of potential panelists by appointing, through consensus, up to 30 individuals. The selection process is then reversed in that the parties are to endeavor to agree on the chairperson of the panel. If there is no agreement, one of the disputing

parties (chosen by lot) will select a chairperson from the roster, with the proviso that the selecting party must select a person who is not its citizen. Thereafter, each party to the dispute is required to select two panelists who are citizens of the other disputing party from the roster (Articles 2009-2011 NAFTA) (Canada, Mexico and United States, 1992).

19 In the case of China, the nationality proviso further requires that the third country have diplomatic relations with the parties to the dispute.

20 Rainbow Warrior, 1986.

21 Wetter, 1962.

22 Another example is provided for in article X(2) of the United States model BIT.

23 The ICJ has adjudicated a limited number of investment-related cases, including the case concerning the Chorzów factory (Germany v. Poland) (PCIJ, 1928); the Nottebohm case (Liechtenstein v. Guatemala) (ICJ, 1955); the Barcelona Traction, Light and Power Company Limited (Belgium v. Spain) (ICJ, 1970); and the case concerning Elettronica Sicula S.p.A. (ELSI) (United States v. Italy) (ICJ, 1989b).

24 On 12 September 1996, a Protocol to amend the 1987 agreement between the ASEAN member countries changed the name of the agreement to "The ASEAN Agreement for the Promotion and Protection of Investments" (Article 1 of the Protocol to Amend the Agreement Among the Governments of Brunei Darussalam, The Republic of Indonesia, Malaysia, The Republic of The Philippines, The Republic of Singapore, And The Kingdom of Thailand for the Promotion and Protection of Investments, hereinafter the "ASEAN Investment Agreement").

25 Articles 4 through 7 of the 1996 ASEAN Protocol on Dispute Settlement Mechanism. (ASEAN, 1996).

26 Another example of recourse to a permanent political body can be found in the Convention Establishing the Multilateral Investment Guarantee Agency (MIGA) which, in its article 56(a), provides that any question of interpretation or application of the Convention among members of MIGA shall be submitted to the Board for its decision.

27 In the case of WTO members, Annex 2 to the WTO DSU) was negotiated inter se, which is an ample document that describes, in detail, the functions and responsibilities of the WTO General Council when it sits as the Dispute Settlement Body, and the integral rules and procedures concerning the settlement of disputes.

28 See Turkey's BITs with Austria, the Netherlands, Switzerland, and the United States.

29 It will be noted (and more fully discussed below) that non-compliance with non-binding decisions might nevertheless lay the basis for suspension of benefits or other authorized remedial measures in an IIA.

30 For a discussion see ICSID, 1999b.

Chapter 12. Dispute Settlement: Investor-State*

Executive summary

The present chapter is concerned with the settlement of investment disputes between States, on the one hand, and private parties, on the other. Generally speaking, this is an area of investment practice that has prompted a broad range of legal issues, and a substantial number of approaches to tackle them. While in theory this issue is of importance for both the host State and the foreign investor, in practice it has more significance for the foreign investor. When a foreign investor enters the territory of a host country, that investor is usually inclined to seek protection in the form of specified treatment standards – such as most-favoured-nation treatment, national treatment and fair and equitable treatment – as well as guarantees on matters such as compensation for expropriation and the right to transfer capital, profits and income from the host State. These rights are often embodied in particular provisions of bilateral investment treaties, or in regional or multilateral instruments on particular aspects of investment.

It is evident, however, that treatment standards and guarantees are of limited significance unless they are subject to a dispute-settlement system and, ultimately, to enforcement. Accordingly, the importance of dispute-settlement mechanisms for issues between a host State and an investor is readily discernible. Indeed, this is a point often made by both foreign investors and host countries. For the former, the security of foreign investment will turn not only on specified safeguards, but also on the assurance that these safeguards are available on a non-discriminatory and timely basis to all foreign investors. Conversely, the host country wishes to ensure that, in the event of a dispute with foreign investors, it will have the means to resolve the legal aspects of that dispute expeditiously and taking into account the concerns of the State, as well as those of foreign investors.

Against this background, the present chapter examines the main aspects of investor-State dispute settlement from the perspective of both the investor and the host State. Considerable attention is paid to the different venues available for resolving investment disputes. Investors and capital-exporting countries representing them have often maintained that disputes between host States and investors should be resolved in accordance with international third party dispute-settlement procedures. Such procedures are said to encourage investor confidence and security and help to create the appearance and reality of fairness in the dispute-settlement process. In contrast, some capital-importing countries have traditionally maintained that private foreign investors are not entitled to privileged treatment in dispute settlement and should be required to resolve their disputes in the national courts of the host country.

These two basic models suggest that States negotiating investor-State dispute settlement mechanisms have a number of options when considering dispute-settlement provisions in international investment agreements. Reference to dispute-settlement procedures can be omitted from an investment agreement; reference to dispute-settlement procedures can grant exclusive jurisdiction to the courts and tribunals of the host State, or at least state a clear preference for such national approaches; reference to dispute-settlement procedures can be in keeping with the consensual approach which offers the parties a choice between national and international systems and methods of dispute settlement and, in exceptional cases, it can provide for compulsory recourse to international dispute settlement. Each model carries distinct implications for the investor and for the host country. These are considered in section IV of the chapter.

At the procedural level, investor-State dispute settlement raises a number of issues concerning the most appropriate technique for dispute settlement, with an emphasis on the use of the most speedy, informal and effective method; the procedure for the initiation of a claim; the establishment and composition of arbitral tribunals, should this method of dispute settlement be chosen; the admissibility of the claim before such a

---

* The chapter is based on a 2003 manuscript prepared by Peter T. Muchlinski and Stephen C. Vasciannie. The final version reflects comments received from Nils Urban Allard, Joachim Karl, Mark Koulen, Ernst-Ulrich Petersmann, Christoph Schreuer and M. Sornarajah.

tribunal; the applicable procedural and substantive law to be applied by such a tribunal to the conduct and resolution of the dispute; the extent to which the award of such a tribunal can be regarded as final; the enforcement of arbitral awards; and the costs of using such dispute settlement mechanisms. With particular reference to international investment agreements (IIAs), this chapter considers these issues in order to highlight the main approaches that are available to host States and investors in the prevailing economic environment. This reference to procedural matters does not imply that such matters are all of equal importance, but the question of how dispute settlement procedures are developed is of significance to the drafting of investor-State dispute settlement clauses.

Introduction

The growth in international trade and investment as a means of creating new economic opportunities in the global economy, for both developed and developing countries, has led to the rise of IIAs that seek to regulate a range of issues related to foreign investment. In this context, special consideration has been given to the concerns of both foreign investors and host countries with respect to dispute-settlement procedures. The vast majority of bilateral investment treaties (BITs) – as well as some regional agreements and other instruments – contain provisions for the settlement of disputes between private parties and the host State, and of disputes between States arising from investment. (For a documentation of the rise of the number of investment disputes, see UNCTAD, 2004c.)

The distinction between investor-State and State-to-State disputes is used to provide an ordering principle for the discussion of this extensive topic in the present volume. Thus, two chapters – covering, respectively, each set of relationships – are provided.

Traditionally, dispute settlement under international law has involved disputes between States. However, the rise of private commercial activity undertaken by individuals and corporations engaged in international trade and/or investment has raised the question whether such actors should be entitled to certain direct rights to resolve disputes with the countries in which they do business. Under customary international law, a foreign investor is required to seek the resolution of such a dispute in the tribunals and/or courts of the country concerned. Should these remedies fail or be ineffective to resolve a dispute – be it that they lack the relevant substantive content, effective enforcement procedures and/or remedies or are the result of denial of justice (see Brownlie, 1998, ch. XXII) –, an investor's main recourse is to seek diplomatic protection from the home country of the individual or corporation concerned. This is explicable on the basis that, by denying proper redress before its national courts, the host State may be committing a breach of international law, where such denial can be shown to amount to a violation of international legal rules.[1] Furthermore, generally only States can bring claims under international law, given that they are the principal subjects of that system. Private non-State actors lack the requisite international legal personality and so must rely on this indirect means for the vindication of their legal rights.

However, the remedy of diplomatic protection has notable deficiencies from an investor's perspective. First, the right of diplomatic protection is held by the home country of the investor and, as a matter of policy, it may decide not to exercise this right in defence of an investor's claim. The home State may choose not to pursue the investor's claim for reasons that have more to do with the broader international relations between the home and host countries than with the validity of the investor's claim. Second, even if the home country successfully pursues an investor's claim, it is not legally obliged to transfer the proceeds of the claim to its national investor (Jennings and Watts, 1992; Brownlie, 1998). Third, in the case of a complex transnational corporation (TNC) with affiliates in numerous countries (each possessing, in all probability, a different legal nationality) and a highly international shareholder profile, it may be difficult, if not impossible, to state accurately what the firm's nationality should be for the purposes of establishing the right of diplomatic protection on the part of a protecting State.[2]

Furthermore, there are practical limitations on the process of diplomatic protection. This system requires even relatively small claims to be pursued through inter-State mechanisms, meaning that investor-State disputes on particular points may be conflated into State-to-State disagreements. As a matter of business strategy, neither the investor nor the host country may wish this to occur, as it could have implications for future economic arrangements among investors, and for relations between the home and host countries concerned – implications that may be quite out of proportion to the claim in issue. Given these difficulties, foreign investors often decline diplomatic protection where they have the option of securing remedies more directly by means of investor-State dispute-settlement mechanisms. In addition, capital-importing countries may wish to avoid the inconvenience of diplomatic protection by investors' home States by agreeing to direct settlement procedures with investors.

The kinds of disputes that may arise between an investor and a host State will often involve disagreements over the interpretation of their respective rights and obligations under the applicable investment agreement. In addition, they may involve allegations unrelated to the contract such as, for example, the failure to provide treatment according to certain standards or failure to provide protection required by treaty or customary law (see generally Sornarajah, 2000). Such disputes rarely lead to full litigation, and normally are settled by mutual and amicable means. Much will depend on the condition of the relationship between the investor and the host State. Where both parties wish the relationship to continue and to develop, the resolution of disputes should prove possible with little recourse to the kinds of systems of dispute settlement provided for in IIAs. Indeed, the existence of an effective third-party settlement procedure may prevent the breakdown of negotiations over a dispute by ensuring that parties do not attempt to get away with unreasonable or inflexible demands. However, in certain cases, disputes may be incapable of mutually satisfactory resolution by way of amicable discussion and negotiation. Where this is the case, the parties have a number of options for dealing with the dispute. These are discussed in section I below.

Dispute-settlement provisions in IIAs are mainly concerned with providing methods for resolving more serious cases of disagreement. In this context, IIAs may offer an avenue for the resolution of investor-State disputes that allow significant disagreements to be overcome and the investment relationship to survive. Equally, where the disagreement is fundamental and the underlying relationship is at an end, the system offered by an IIA might help to ensure that an adequate remedy is offered to the aggrieved party and that the investment relationship can be unwound with a degree of security and equity, so that the legitimate expectations of both parties can, to some extent, be preserved. IIAs perform an essential risk-reducing function that may allow for more confidence on the part of investors and host States in the conduct of their investment relationships.

These functions of investor-State dispute settlement should not be taken as suggesting that this issue is unproblematic. Several areas of controversy exist. First, there is a continuing debate over whether it is appropriate to use international arbitration as a means of dispute settlement where this may weaken national dispute-settlement systems. Second, the application of international minimum standards for the treatment of aliens and their property is by no means universally accepted (Sornarajah, 1994, 2000). Third, not only developing countries but also, it seems, developed countries may view the process of international dispute settlement in this field with some suspicion. This can be seen from, for example, academic, judicial and political criticism of recent North American Free Trade Agreement (NAFTA) arbitration awards (De Palma, 2001; Foy and Deane, 2001) and from the significant disagreements that remained over the form and contents of the investor-State dispute-settlement provisions during the Multilateral Agreement on Investment (MAI) negotiations at the Organisation for Economic Co-operation and Development (OECD) (see chapter 26 in volume III).

Section I
Explanation of the Issue

At the outset, it is essential to place the issue of investor-State dispute settlement within its wider context. The settlement of any dispute, not just investment disputes, requires the adoption of the most speedy, informal, amicable and inexpensive method available. Hence, in recent years, the stress has been on the use of so-called "alternative dispute-resolution" mechanisms, i.e. those methods of dispute settlement that seek to avoid the use of the procedures provided by the public courts of a country, or, in international law, of an international court. Usually they include direct methods of settlement through negotiation, or informal methods that employ a third party, such as the provision of good offices, mediation or conciliation.[3] Arbitration may also be seen as an alternative dispute-resolution mechanism, although it is arguable that, given the high degree of legal control over the means and modalities of arbitration in municipal and, to a lesser extent, international law, its practical conduct may be only marginally different from that of a court proceeding (Merills, 1998; Asouzu, 2001, pp. 11-26). However, as far as the international settlement of investment disputes is concerned, from an investor's perspective arbitration is a more accessible method of dispute settlement than diplomatic protection, given that their lack of international personality does not bar them from direct participation.[4] Recourse to an international court such as the International Court of Justice (ICJ) is effectively barred, given the lack of standing for non-State actors, although investor-State disputes could be brought before regional courts such as the European Court of Justice or the European Court of Human Rights, where non-State actors have direct rights of audience under the treaties that establish these judicial bodies.

In light of the foregoing discussion, the most important question to make clear is that the first step in the resolution of any investment dispute is the use of direct, bilateral, informal and amicable means of settlement. Only where such informal means fail to resolve a dispute should the parties contemplate informal third-party measures such as good offices, mediation or conciliation. The use of arbitration should only be contemplated where bilateral and third-party informal measures have failed to achieve a negotiated result. Indeed, this gradation of dispute-settlement methods is commonly enshrined in the dispute-settlement provisions of IIAs, as will be demonstrated in section II of this chapter. However, the bulk of the chapter will concentrate on the rules and practices surrounding arbitration, as this method of dispute settlement has generated the most detailed international treaty provisions in practice.

The choice of a dispute-settlement method is only one of the choices that an investor and State may have to make when seeking to resolve a dispute. Another central question for consideration concerns the forum for the resolution of such a dispute. In keeping with traditional perspectives, some developing capital-importing countries – particularly some Latin American States – have historically maintained that disputes between an investor and a host State should be settled exclusively before the tribunals and/or courts of the latter (referred to as the Calvo Doctrine; see further Shea, 1955). This viewpoint was manifested not only in the domestic legislation of individual countries; it also prevailed in certain regional agreements that prohibited member States from according foreign investors more favourable treatment than national investors, demonstrating a clear preference for dispute settlement in domestic courts. The United Nations Charter of Economic Rights and Duties of States of 1974[5] also adopted such an approach. However, while this approach remains an important precedent, it will be shown that the practice of developing countries and economies in transition has moved away from it in recent years. Most recent BITs concluded by such States provide for some type of international dispute-settlement mechanism to be used in relation to investment disputes. Nonetheless, this remains a controversial issue for negotiations leading to IIAs, as a balance needs to be struck between host country and international dispute settlement. Local settlement is convenient and there is a continuing need to recognize the validity of properly conceived and drafted national investment laws – and other applicable laws and regulations – as a legitimate and valuable source of rights and obligations in the investment process.

In contrast with the above-mentioned approach, foreign investors have traditionally maintained that, as regards developing countries, investor-State disputes should be resolved by means of internationalized dispute-settlement mechanisms governed by international standards and procedures, with international arbitration at its apex. This position is supported largely by arguments concerning the apparent fairness inherent in relying upon independent international arbitrators, rather than upon national courts that may be subject to the influence of the executive in host countries. Host countries may perceive such an emphasis on internationalized systems of dispute settlement as a sign of little confidence, on the part of investors, in their national laws and procedures, which may or may not be justifiable in a given case. However, the willingness to accept internationalized dispute settlement on the part of the host country may well be motivated by a desire to show commitment to the creation of a good investment climate. This may be of considerable importance where that country has historically followed a restrictive policy on foreign investment and wishes to change that policy for the future. In so doing, the host country can be entitled to expect that the internationalized system is itself impartial and even-handed with both parties to the dispute.[6]

Assuming that the investor and host State choose to adopt an international system of dispute settlement, a series of further choices arise. The first again concerns method. Where the parties have tried and failed to resolve their differences informally and to reach a negotiated settlement, the next choice concerns whether the parties wish to pursue *ad hoc* or institutional arbitration.

Ad hoc arbitration depends upon the initiative of the parties for their success. The parties must make their own arrangements regarding the procedure, the selection of arbitrators and administrative support. The principal advantage of *ad hoc* dispute settlement is that the procedure can be shaped to suit the parties. However, there are numerous problems associated with *ad hoc* arbitration. First, the process is governed by the arbitration agreement between the parties. Its content depends on the relative bargaining power of the parties. The stronger party may therefore obtain an arrangement advantageous to its interests.[7] Second, it may be impossible to agree on the exact nature of the dispute, or on the applicable law. Third, there may be difficulties in selecting acceptable arbitrators who can be relied on to act impartially and not as "advocates" for the side that had selected them. Fourth, the proceedings may be stultified by inordinate delay on the part of one side or both, or through the non-appearance of a party. Finally, there may be a problem in enforcing any award before municipal courts should they decide that the award is tainted with irregularity, or because the State party to the proceedings enjoys immunity from execution under the laws of the forum State. These difficulties – which may be particularly acute in the case of developing country parties to investor-State disputes – have led to the use of institutional systems of arbitration.

An institutional system of arbitration may be a more reliable means of resolving a dispute than an *ad hoc* approach, especially as it is likely to have been devised on a multilateral level and so may show greater sensitivity to the interests of developing countries. Once the parties have consented to its use, they have to abide by the system's procedures. These are designed to ensure that, while the parties retain a large measure of control over the arbitration, they are constrained against any attempt to undermine the proceedings. Furthermore, an award made under the auspices of an institutional system is more likely to be consistent with principles of procedural fairness applicable to that system and so is more likely to be enforceable before municipal courts. Indeed, recognition may be no more than a formality. Two systems in particular appear suitable for use in investment disputes between a host State and a foreign investor: the conciliation and arbitration procedures available under the auspices of the International Centre for Settlement of Investment Disputes (ICSID) and the International Chamber of Commerce (ICC) Court of Arbitration.

The ICSID system is the only institutional system of international conciliation/arbitration specifically designed to deal with investment disputes and will receive closer scrutiny in section II below. Apart from ICSID, ICC arbitration clauses have been used in IIAs, resulting in ICC arbitration in the event of a dispute. However, one of the criticisms lodged against the ICC Court of Arbitration as a forum for the resolution of foreign investment disputes is that, being primarily a centre for the resolution of commercial disputes between private traders, it has relatively little experience in the complexities of long-term investment agreements involving a State as a party. This may account for the observation that ICC arbitration clauses are used relatively infrequently in international economic development agreements. Nonetheless, the evidence of the actual use of the ICC Court of Arbitration in disputes involving Governments or State-owned enterprises is by no means negligible. Accordingly, this criticism of the ICC should not be overstated (Muchlinski, 1999, p. 539).

In the case of institutional systems, a further distinction should be made between regional and multilateral systems. A number of regional international commercial arbitration centres have been established, especially in developing regions, that may be of value in relation to investor-State disputes. Though these cater mainly to disputes between private parties, and will not therefore be studied in detail, their existence cannot go unnoticed in the present chapter, given their potential to develop as possible venues for the settlement of investor-State disputes (Asouzu, 2001, chapters 2-3).

Once the choice between *ad hoc* and institutional arbitration has been made, further issues must be determined, either by the parties to the dispute themselves when *ad hoc* procedures are chosen, or by the constitutive instrument that governs the institutional system chosen by the parties for the resolution of their dispute. In particular, the following matters must be addressed:

- *Procedure for initiating a claim.* Under *ad hoc* procedures, the parties must agree on a method for initiating the claim. An institutional system prescribes a procedure. The principal aim of this procedure is to show that the dispute is submitted with the consent of the parties in accordance with any required procedural rules. It often involves a preliminary examination of the complaint by the secretariat attached to the system concerned, so that it may be assessed for admissibility, although it must be stressed that the tribunal itself is normally the final judge of admissibility.

- *Establishment and composition of the arbitral tribunal.* Clearly, a basic question that needs to be determined is who sits on the tribunal, who is eligible to sit and in what numbers should they sit.
- *Admissibility.* In *ad hoc* procedures, the parties must decide for themselves which claims they submit to the tribunal. In institutional systems, by contrast, there are rules on admissibility. In particular, the dispute must come within the jurisdiction of the tribunal:
    - *ratione materiae* in that it must be one connected with an investment;
    - *ratione personae* in that it is brought by an investor and/or a country that is entitled to use the institutional system concerned against a respondent investor or country that is capable of being sued under such system;
    - *ratione temporis* in that the dispute must have arisen at a time when the parties were legally entitled to have recourse to the system concerned.
- *Applicable law.* In cases of international arbitration, two choice of law questions arise: which law governs the procedure of the tribunal and which substantive law governs the resolution of the dispute. In *ad hoc* procedures, the parties need to determine these issues. These may already have been determined by the investment agreement governing the investor-State relationship, typically reflecting the relative bargaining position of each party. However, such agreements may at times be unclear or even be silent on these important questions, especially where the parties cannot accept each other's preferred governing law or laws. In such cases, the parties need to agree on the choice of law issues in the arbitration agreement that founds the tribunal and its jurisdiction. Much depends again on the relative bargaining positions of the parties, as the choice of a particular procedural or substantive law may confer advantages to one party over another (Sornarajah, 1994, pp. 332-338). By contrast, institutional systems specify rules on the choice of law issue in their constitutive instrument. In the first place, the choice of procedural law is resolved by the applicability of the rules and procedures of the institutional system itself. These can be found in the constitutive instrument and in supplementary rules of procedure produced by that system. As regards the choice of substantive law, preference is usually given to the parties' own choices in these matters, where the investment agreement concerned makes clear what these choices are. Where such clarity is absent, the applicable provision governs the determination of that question. Nonetheless, the main guiding principle concerning applicable law is the principle of party autonomy in choice of law matters, whether under an institutional or *ad hoc* system of arbitration.
- *Finality of the award.* A very important aspect of dispute settlement through third-party adjudication is that the resulting award is the final determination of the issues involved. However, to allow an award to stand where there is evidence of errors on the face of the record, or some suggestion of impropriety, would defeat the very purpose of such a dispute-settlement technique. Accordingly, in the case of *ad hoc* awards, these may be regarded as unenforceable by reason of error of law, or procedural impropriety, under the municipal law of a country that is requested to enforce the award. By contrast, institutional systems of arbitration may provide procedures for the review of an award by another panel of arbitrators. Equally, as is the case with the World Trade Organization's (WTO) State-to-State dispute-settlement mechanism, an appellate body might be set up with the right to review an original decision for errors of law (see Article 17(6) of the Dispute Settlement Understanding of the World Trade Organization (WTO, 1994)). Furthermore, should one party to the dispute fail to take part in the procedure, provisions for default or *ex parte* proceedings may prevent the frustration of the award.
- *Enforcement of awards.* Where a dispute is resolved in national courts, the particular court concerned also has the means to ensure that its decision is executed by agents of the State with respect to persons and property within the State. By contrast, in cases of internationalized

ad hoc arbitration, the arbitral tribunal has no direct powers of enforcement *vis-à-vis* either the investor or the host country in respect of persons and property in the host country. Naturally, this prompts the need for special award-enforcement mechanisms, which are briefly described in section II. If such enforcement mechanisms are not in place, or if they are inadequate, then both the investor and the host State may find that a successful claim before an arbitral tribunal could lose its financial significance: there are no means of enforcing the tribunal's decision. In order to remedy this possible outcome, institutional systems of arbitration may provide for the automatic enforcement of awards, made under their auspices, by the courts of all the countries that are parties to the system, subject only to specific rules concerning immunities of sovereign property from attachment in enforcement proceedings.

- *Costs*. A further procedural issue concerns the allocation of costs in a dispute settlement proceeding between an investor and the host State. Generally, the costs of an arbitration are borne by the losing party on the basis of costs agreed by the parties at the outset of the proceeding. On the other hand, where institutional systems of arbitration are used, such costs may be pre-determined by the administrative organs of that system. However, as will be shown in section II, even under an institutional arrangement the parties concerned can still exercise considerable discretion when allocating costs.

Section II
Stocktaking and Analysis

This section of the chapter uses the range of choices discussed in section I as the basis for a review of the types of dispute-settlement clauses that may be included in IIAs. The structure and content of such clauses will be considered in the context of current and historical practice and in light of their impact on investor-State disputes. From a negotiator's viewpoint, the main concern is the extent to which a dispute-settlement provision preserves or limits party choice in these matters. This depends on a number of policy variables that are discussed more fully in section IV below. For now, it suffices to indicate examples of clauses and provisions that serve either to preserve or to control party choice in the relevant areas. The discussion will focus in the main on institutional approaches to dispute settlement, rather than on *ad hoc* methods, as the former are referred to in the bulk of international instruments in this field. As noted in section I, where *ad hoc* arbitration is used the parties themselves determine most of the issues surrounding the process and these determinations are not normally controlled by IIA provisions. Nonetheless, IIAs may offer the parties some guidance on the procedures that can be followed under *ad hoc* arbitration and intergovernmental organizations (most notably UNCITRAL) have offered standardized rules of dispute settlement. Thus, attention will also be paid to these developments where relevant.

A. Encouragement of informal, negotiated settlement

At the outset it should be noted that the majority of dispute-settlement clauses in IIAs relating to investor-State disputes mandate the use of informal methods of dispute settlement in the first instance. Recourse to informal methods will, hopefully, lead the investor and host State towards an amicable, negotiated settlement of their differences. As was noted in section I, the requirement for consultation or negotiation is valuable to States not only because it helps to defuse tensions in some instances, but also because it may underline the amicable spirit in which most States hope to conduct their investment relations (UNCTAD, 1998a, p. 88). Furthermore, the obligation to negotiate and consult before initiating the other means of dispute settlement is not to be taken lightly: it is an obligation of substance and context. The parties to the dispute must negotiate in good faith.[8]

At the bilateral level, the model BITs of capital-exporting countries such as Germany (1991) (Article 11(1)), Switzerland (1995) (Article 8(1)) and France (1999) (Article 8) all expressly envisage that consultation or negotiation should precede adversarial proceedings.[9] Among capital-importing countries, BITs such as those between China/Viet Nam (1992) (Article 8(1)), Argentina/Bolivia (1994) (Article 9(1)) and Brazil/Chile (1994) (Article VIII(1)) also exemplify this approach. In some instances at the bilateral level, the duty to negotiate or consult is implicit in the dispute settlement provision. For example, Article 8 of the 1991 United Kingdom model BIT stipulates that, if an investor-State dispute should arise and "agreement cannot be reached within three months between the parties to this dispute through pursuit of local remedies or otherwise", then conciliation or arbitration may be instituted.

At the interregional level, although some of the earlier efforts of capital-exporting countries to formulate treaties on investment did not refer to amicable settlement (including the Abs-Shawcross and OECD BIT drafts), the draft MAI does (Abs and Shawcross, 1960; see also chapter 5 in volume III). Specifically, Article V(D)(2) of the draft MAI indicates that each investor-State dispute "should, if possible, be settled by negotiation or consultation", and then envisages other solutions involving judicial settlement. It is arguable that the use of the term "should" – as distinct from "shall" – implies that the duty to negotiate or consult does not rise to the level of a legal obligation. However, this may be a matter of little practical significance in most cases, as both parties to a dispute, acting in good faith, will wish to proceed amicably in the first instance. At the regional level, this issue also arises with respect to the NAFTA: Article 1118 of that agreement states, in full, that: "The disputing parties [in an investor-State dispute] should first attempt to settle a claim through consultation or negotiation".

Where provision is made for an amicable settlement of disputes, time limits are often countenanced as a means of facilitating the interests of both protagonists, although time limits are not always specified. Usually, the time limits range from three months[10] to 12 months.[11] More recently, a six-month period appears to have become commonplace, as exemplified by Article 34(2) of the New Zealand/Singapore Economic Partnership Agreement of January 2001.

Finally, it should be noted that the World Bank system of investment dispute settlement, under the 1965 Washington Convention on the Settlement of Investment Disputes Between States and Nationals of Other States (ICSID Convention), provides for conciliation as well as arbitration. The system offers an international form of third-party, nonbinding, dispute settlement, in which the role of the conciliators is "to clarify the issues in dispute between the parties and to endeavour to bring about agreement between them upon mutually acceptable terms" (Article 34 (1)). If the parties reach agreement, the Conciliation Commission set up under the Convention draws up a report noting the issues in dispute and recording that the parties have reached agreement. If the parties do not agree, the Commission draws up a report recording its failure to bring the parties to agreement (Article 34(2)).[12] Two points should be noted in relation to ICSID conciliation procedures. First, the procedure is not completely informal and parties must follow prescribed rules. Second, it is rarely used. Furthermore, on a more general level, it should be noted that the ICSID Convention's main effect on disputes is to lead to the settlement of most cases that are submitted to arbitration or conciliation (Schreuer, 2001, pp. 811–812).

B. Venue

As noted in section I, apart from the initial question of whether a dispute can be settled amicably, the first main question that the parties to a dispute must answer concerns venue. In other words, should a dispute be dealt with by national dispute-settlement methods – centred upon the host State party to the dispute and the procedures that it offers – or by an international approach to dispute settlement? In the latter case, there is a choice between *ad hoc* and institutional systems. The implications of these different choices on the content of dispute-settlement clauses deserves consideration and will be done in three stages: first, the possibility of using clauses that restrict party choice to dispute settlement in the host State will be considered; second, the basic features of provisions that offer an internationalized dispute settlement system will be described; and third, the nature and content of choice of venue clauses in IIAs will be mapped out.

1. National dispute settlement in the host country

In accordance with the principle of national sovereignty over activities occurring on the territory of a State, most countries have traditionally maintained that investor-State disputes should be resolved in their national courts. In its strict formulation, this position means that foreign investors ought not, in principle, to have the option to pursue investor-State disputes through internationalized methods of dispute settlement.

This approach has been exemplified in historical practice by the provisions of certain Latin American investment instruments. For example, by Articles 50 and 51 of Decision No. 24 of the Commission of the Cartagena Agreement (1971) pertaining to foreign investment:

> "Article 50. Member countries may not accord to foreign investors treatment more favourable than to national investors.
>
> Article 51. No instrument pertaining to investment or to the transfer of technology may contain a clause removing disputes or conflicts from the national jurisdiction and competence of the recipient country, or permitting subrogation by States of the rights and actions of their national investors".

The rule in Article 51 of Decision No. 24 indicated the Commission's disapproval of internationalized dispute settlement by prohibiting outright legal instruments which allowed access to any form of adjudicatory mechanisms outside the host country. This level of antipathy towards third party dispute settlement was also reflected, for instance, in the national constitutions of some Latin American countries and in the resistance that Latin American countries[13] initially maintained to the consensual approach included in the ICSID Convention (Szasz, 1971).

Beyond Latin America, this perspective also influenced the attitude of other countries during the 1970s. Thus, the United Nations Charter on Economic Rights and Duties of States, which was adopted by the General Assembly on 12 December 1974, emphasises that each State has the right "to regulate and exercise authority over foreign investment within its national jurisdiction in accordance with its laws and regulations and in conformity with its national objectives and priorities". It also states that, in the case of disputes concerning compensation as a result of nationalization or expropriation, such disputes should be settled "under the domestic law of the nationalizing State and by its tribunals, unless it is freely and mutually agreed by all States concerned that other peaceful means be sought on the basis of the sovereign equality of States and in accordance with the principle of free choice of means" (Article 2.2(a) and (c)). The priority of national measures is apparent. However, it should also be noted that States are given the freedom to use other means of resolving compensation disputes. Thus, the Charter certainly cannot be interpreted as prohibiting the use of internationalized measures, merely not advocating them.

Before negotiations on the draft United Nations Code of Conduct on Transnational Corporations were discontinued, the provisions of the Code concerning dispute settlement remained subject to considerable controversy. The influence of the Latin American negotiating perspective – and of some other developing capital-importing countries – was evident in various draft provisions of the Code. For example, one of the later versions of Article 57 stipulated as follows:

> "[Disputes between States and entities of transnational corporations, which are not amicably settled between the parties, shall/should be submitted to competent national courts or authorities in conformity with the principle of paragraph 7. Where the parties so agree, such disputes may be referred to other mutually acceptable dispute settlement procedures.]".

From the perspective of the Group of 77, the group representing the negotiating position of the developing countries, this provision – including the reference to paragraph 7 of the draft Code of Conduct – was meant to reinforce the point that dispute settlement is mainly an issue for national courts. Where there is agreement, other forms of settlement may be acceptable, but the draft Code of Conduct [14] should, in the Group of 77's perspective, emphasize the primacy of national courts (Robinson, 1985, p. 13).

It would be misleading, however, to focus solely on the practice and perspectives of Latin American countries concerning national court jurisdiction in the period leading up to the end of the 1970s. Since that period, Latin American countries have generally reconsidered their approach. Hence, at the bilateral level, Latin American countries that had traditionally eschewed BITs, mainly because of reservations concerning dispute settlement, have become parties to a number of such treaties. Furthermore, on becoming parties to such treaties, Latin American countries have not, as a rule, avoided dispute-settlement provisions that contemplate internationalized dispute settlement (OAS, 1997). In this regard, the 1994 Chilean model BIT provides an important example of this change. Specifically, Article 8 indicates that the investor and host country should enter consultations in respect of any dispute, but, if such consultations fail, the investor may submit the dispute either:

"(a) to the competent tribunal of the Contracting Party in whose territory the investment was made; or

(b) to international arbitration of [ICSID]".

The extent of the change in Latin American perspectives in this area can be seen in a willingness in their relations with each other to accept the *lex specialis* on dispute settlement in BITs. For example, the BITs between Chile and

Ecuador (1993) (Article X), Argentina and Bolivia (1994) (Article 9), Colombia and Peru (1994), Ecuador and El Salvador (1994) (Article X) and Brazil and Venezuela (1995) (Article 8) are testimony to the notion that international arbitration is becoming accepted as part of the contents of investor-State dispute settlement clauses. This change of policy is also reflected at the regional level. The States involved in Decision No. 24 of the Commission of the Cartagena Agreement have revised the policy inherent in Articles 50 and 51, quoted above. Now, by virtue of Decision 291 (1991), the members of the Andean Community accept that they shall each apply the provisions of their domestic legislation in settling disputes between foreign investors and the State (Article 10).

Apart from prohibiting international dispute settlement outright, a preference for national dispute settlement in the case of investor-State disputes can be preserved by including dispute-settlement provisions that require local remedies to be exercised before an international claim can be pursued. For example, according to the Caribbean Community (CARICOM) Guidelines for use in the Negotiation of Bilateral Treaties (1984), each CARICOM State, in considering investor-State dispute-settlement provisions, should seek to ensure that "resort to arbitration would only be permitted after all national remedies have been exhausted". Broadly in keeping with this guideline, Article 9 of the (1987) BIT between Jamaica and the United Kingdom contemplates ICSID conciliation or arbitration proceedings for investor-State disputes, but also envisages that local remedies should be exhausted as a precondition for internationalized third party intervention. In its relevant part, Article 9 reads:

> "If any such [investor-State] dispute should arise and agreement cannot be reached between the parties to the dispute through pursuit of local remedies in accordance with international law then, if the national or company affected also consents in writing to submit the dispute to the Centre [ICSID] for settlement by conciliation or arbitration under the [ICSID] Convention, either party may institute proceedings. ...".

It should be noted, however, that Jamaica has moved away from requiring the exhaustion of local remedies as a precondition for resort to arbitration in more recent agreements.[15]

The approach requiring prior exhaustion of local remedies is also taken in other cases. For example, Model B of the Asian-African Legal Consultative Committee Revised Draft of Model Agreements For Promotion and Protection of Investments (1985) reads as follows:

> "If any dispute or difference should arise between a Contracting Party and a national, company or State entity of the other Contracting Party, which cannot be resolved within a period of ______ through negotiations, either party to the dispute may initiate proceedings for conciliation or arbitration *after the local remedies have been exhausted"* (emphasis added).

In some cases, although it is envisaged that local remedies are to be exhausted before external arbitration or conciliation is pursued, time limits are placed on the local remedies requirement (UNCTAD, 1998a; Schreuer, 2001, pp. 390-393). Here, then, even if the courts or other tribunals within the host country are still considering a particular dispute, once the fixed term period is reached, the investor may forego the local proceedings. As noted above, time limits tend to range from three months, as suggested in the 1991 United Kingdom model BIT (Preferred Article 8), to eighteen months, as in the 1995 Italy/Jamaica BIT (Article 9(3)). Naturally, the rate at which domestic proceedings are completed varies from country to country, but where the time limit is as short as three months, it can be maintained that the value of the need to exhaust local remedies is undermined: most domestic legal systems require more than three months for judicial processes to be completed.

In several instances, bilateral and regional instruments that include investor-State dispute-settlement provisions remain silent on whether the disputant investor has an obligation to exhaust local remedies. From the numerous examples in this regard, the 1991 German and 1995 Swiss model BITs, NAFTA and the 1967 OECD Draft Convention on the Protection of Foreign Property may be mentioned. For each such agreement that has entered into force, the question is whether one may infer that the investor must exhaust local remedies before proceeding to international third party settlement. Arguably, it should not be possible to exclude so basic a rule of customary international law without express words. Some support for this view may be garnered from the decision of the Chamber of the International Court of Justice in the case concerning *Elettronica Sicula S.p.A.(ELSI) (United States v. Italy)* (ICJ, 1989b). In this case, the Chamber of the Court considered, *inter alia*, whether a foreign investor was required to exhaust local remedies before the investor's home country could pursue an international claim with the host country concerning an alleged breach against the investor. The Friendship, Commerce and Navigation Treaty (FCN) in question provided for international arbitration between the two States, but was silent on the need to exhaust local remedies. Did this mean that the local remedies rule was not applicable? The Chamber of the International Court of Justice responded in the negative. The majority judgment maintained:

> "The Chamber has no doubt that the parties to a treaty can therein either agree that the local remedies rule shall not apply to claims based on alleged breaches of that treaty; or confirm that it shall apply. Yet the Chamber finds itself unable to accept that an important principle of customary international law should be held to have been tacitly dispensed with, in the absence of any words making clear an intention to do so" (ibid., paragraph 50).

Admittedly, the ELSI case was directly concerned with whether local remedies needed to be exhausted before a State-to-State arbitration could be commenced. But this does not mean that the approach quoted above should be disregarded; there would seem to be no reason in principle to reject the Chamber's pronouncement with respect to investor-State disputes. To support this conclusion, it may also be noted that, although the 1967 OECD draft Convention was silent on the local remedies rule in investor-State matters, the OECD Commentary (OECD, 1963) on the point treated State-to-State and investor-State disputes in the same way. In Comment No. 9 on Article 7 concerning both types of disputes, the Commentary maintained that:

> "Nothing in the Convention, whether in this or any other Article, affects the normal operation of the Local Remedies' rule. The rule implies that all appropriate legal remedies short of the process provided for in the Convention must be exhausted..." (ibid., p. 261).

The need to observe the local remedies rule may apply at least for IIAs concluded before the establishment of ICSID, in that they would not refer to that system of dispute settlement. The ICSID Convention explicitly excludes the local remedies rule, unless a State contracting party expresses a reservation to preserve the operation of the rule under Article 26 of the Convention. Also, as a matter of policy, there may be some reason for requiring exhaustion of local remedies in investor-State disputes even where the governing instrument makes no express reference to local remedies. Most investor-State disputes are prompted at least in part by issues arising within the host country. Where the host country has in place a modern system of law, it may reasonably believe that, where no express provision has been made to override national jurisdiction, such local issues should be determined within the local court system. This approach shows respect for the host country's judicial system.

On the other hand, as far as investor-State dispute settlement is concerned, the understanding of many negotiators is that the formulations used in BITs, unless otherwise explicitly expressed, normally imply that the contracting States have dispensed with the requirement that local remedies must be exhausted (Schreuer, 2001, pp. 390-396; Peters, 1997, pp. 233-243).[16] This view is confirmed by the provisions of Article 26 of the ICSID Convention, which is discussed in detail in the next sub-section. Furthermore, the FCN Treaty between the United States and Italy, which was at issue in the ELSI case, did not contain an investor-State dispute settlement clause providing for direct investor access to international arbitration, effectively dispensing with the requirement to exhaust local remedies. Given that many of today's IIAs contain both State-to-State and investor-State dispute settlement clauses and that the latter routinely provide for direct access by the investor to international arbitration, it may be open to question whether the interpretation applied by the ICJ to the FCN treaty would stand in relation to contemporary forms of investment agreements. The distinction between an agreement providing for direct investor access to international arbitration and one without such a provision, was not taken by the ICJ in that case. Yet it may be a significant difference affecting the proper approach to the local remedies rule where an agreement is silent on this issue, but provides for such direct investor access to international arbitration.

2. International dispute settlement

a. Ad hoc dispute settlement

Ad hoc forms of dispute settlement have been used relatively little in recent years. Nonetheless, certain developments under the auspices of UNCITRAL and the Permanent Court of Arbitration deserve brief mention.

Although the UNCITRAL Arbitration Rules (1976) do not constitute an institutional system for international dispute settlement, they can be viewed as a possible improvement to *ad hoc* international arbitration and may be of some value in disputes between foreign investors and host States. Their primary aim is to harmonize the rules used in commercial arbitration, providing an optional and generally acceptable system of procedural norms for the conduct of such arbitrations. In relation to foreign investment disputes, although the UNCITRAL Arbitration Rules do not provide the institutional back-up available under the ICC and ICSID systems, they can remove some of the difficulties associated with *ad hoc* arbitration by basing it on internationally acceptable procedures.

The Permanent Court of Arbitration has also produced Optional Rules for Arbitrating Disputes Between two Parties of which only one is a State. These Rules, which are similar in structure and content to the UNCITRAL Rules, provide a framework for the conduct of an arbitration between a State and a private party with the assistance of the International Bureau of the Permanent Court. They are not limited to any particular type of dispute and so could be used in relation to investment disputes. They are entirely voluntary in character, with the International Bureau acting purely as an administrative aid to the arbitration. The Rules are thus not a fully-fledged institutional system of arbitration, but offer parties to an *ad hoc* arbitration a model to use as the arbitration agreement between them. The Optional Rules cover all the important procedural questions that need to be addressed by the parties when establishing an arbitral tribunal, the conduct of its proceedings and for the making and enforcement of an award.

b. Institutional dispute settlement

It was mentioned in section I that the only system of institutional dispute settlement specifically designed to deal with investor-State disputes is that provided for under the auspices of the World Bank, the ICSID. The specific procedural requirements for the use of this system are contained in the ICSID Convention. These will be considered in detail below. For now, the main concern is to describe the provisions used by the ICSID Convention to develop an internationalized model of investor-State dispute settlement.

The international character of ICSID dispute settlement is emphasized by the provisions of Articles 26 and 27 of the ICSID Convention. Article 26 of ICSID Convention states:

> "Consent of the parties to arbitration under this Convention shall, unless otherwise stated, be deemed consent to such arbitration to the exclusion of any other remedy. A Contracting State may require the exhaustion of local administrative or judicial remedies as a condition of its consent to arbitration under this Convention."

Two points arise from this provision. First, as soon as the parties give consent to the conduct of an arbitration under the ICSID Convention, that renders any other remedy unavailable. This relates, in particular, to remedies in national law. Thus, ICSID arbitration is an exclusive procedure, subject to the prior consent of the parties, unless otherwise stated. Second, the State party retains a degree of sovereign control over the availability of ICSID arbitration by being able to require the prior exhaustion of local remedies. In effect, this reverses the rule of customary international law, in that the inapplicability of that rule is presumed in the absence of an express statement by the State party to the dispute (Schreuer, 1997a, pp. 196-197). Such a statement can be made at any time up to the time that consent to arbitration is perfected as, for example, in a BIT offering consent to ICSID arbitration, in national investment law or in the investment agreement with the investor party to the dispute. The requirement cannot be introduced retroactively once consent to ICSID arbitration has been perfected (Schreuer, 1997a, p. 198). In practice, States almost never insist on the exhaustion of local remedies.[17]

Article 27 of the ICSID Convention addresses the relationship between ICSID Arbitration and the remedy of diplomatic protection:

> "No Contracting State shall give diplomatic protection, or bring an international claim, in respect of a dispute which one of its nationals and another Contracting State shall have consented to submit or shall have submitted to arbitration under this Convention, unless such other Contracting State shall have failed to abide by and comply with the award rendered in such dispute."

This provision ensures that diplomatic protection is excluded as a possible remedy once the parties have both consented to submit the dispute to ICSID. It is insufficient to offer ICSID arbitration through a clause in an IIA for this effect to be achieved. The international character of ICSID arbitration is further emphasized by the Convention's provisions on applicable law, which will be considered in sub-section C (d) below.

c. Choice of venue clauses

As outlined above, certain provisions in international instruments define the kinds of venue that may be chosen in order to resolve international investment disputes. The next question is what type of clause should be used to outline the nature and scope of the choices available to the parties to an IIA? By the 1990s, with changing attitudes to foreign direct investment (FDI), there was a marked shift towards arrangements that accept that foreign investors are entitled to a measure of choice concerning which dispute-settlement procedures to follow should they have a grievance against the host State (Parra, 1997).

This shows a marked contrast to the position prior to the adoption of the ICSID Convention in 1965, when the investor had no right to bring a claim against a host State. Now the investor appears to have such a right, as part of the choice of dispute-settlement means offered to investors in IIAs. However, despite this change, it should be borne in mind that the major principle underlying choice of venue is party autonomy and that this doctrine is followed in IIAs even where investor choice is offered.

For example, at the regional level, under Section V of the draft MAI, a foreign investor was given the choice of submitting disputes to one of following:

- any competent court or administrative tribunal of the host country;
- any dispute settlement procedure agreed upon prior to the dispute arising; or
- by arbitration, under the ICSID Convention; the ICSID Additional Facility; the UNCITRAL Arbitration Rules; the Rules of Arbitration of the ICC.

Two additional features of the draft MAI warrant attention. First, investment disputes would have been subject to time limits. Thus, pursuant to Article V(D)(4), an investor could submit a dispute for resolution under the dispute-settlement procedures at any time 60 days after the date the host country received a notice of intent from the investor, providing this was no later than five years from the date the investor acquired, or should have acquired, knowledge of the events giving rise to the dispute. Second, the draft MAI stipulated, as a general rule, that neither the host country nor the investor could withdraw its consent to international arbitration (Article V(D)(5)). According to the draft MAI, at the time when the host country becomes a party to the MAI, it could indicate that its acceptance was conditional on the investor being unable to pursue the same dispute through both arbitration and other dispute-settlement procedures (Article V(D)(3)(b)).[18]

At the regional level, too, the dominant trend is towards foreign investor choice of venue. For example, NAFTA Article 1120 indicates that foreign investors shall have the right to submit a claim against the host country in one of the following ways:

- under the ICSID Convention, provided that both the disputing State and the home country of the investor are parties to that Convention;
- under the Additional Facility Rules of the ICSID, provided that either the disputing State or the home country of the investor, but not both, is a party to the ICSID Convention; or
- under the UNCITRAL Arbitration Rules.

The claimant must give the host country 90 days notice of its intention to submit a claim (Article 1119). Here, too, except in certain specified instances, the claimant may not insist upon arbitration while pursuing other means of dispute settlement with respect to the same dispute (Article 1121).

This pattern is also evident in the Energy Charter Treaty. Specifically, Article 26 of that treaty allows foreign investors from a contracting party to submit investment disputes for adjudication to any one of the following:

- the courts or administrative tribunals of the host country party to the dispute;
- proceedings in accordance with any applicable, previously agreed dispute-settlement procedure; or
- arbitration under the ICSID Convention; under the ICSID Additional Facility; before a sole arbitrator or *ad hoc* arbitration tribunal established under UNCITRAL Arbitration Rules; or under the Arbitration Institute of the Stockholm Chamber of Commerce (Articles 26(2) to (5)).

All parties to the Energy Charter Treaty accept the basic dispute-settlement requirements, but the treaty also allows States to make access to arbitration conditional upon the termination of all other dispute-settlement proceedings (Article 26(3)(b) and Annex ID). States may also opt to exclude a general commitment to observe their contractual obligations from the ambit of arbitral proceedings (Article 26(3)(c) and Annex IA).

Some BITs also offer foreign investors the choice of venue in instances of a dispute. Though their actual provisions on this issue vary on points of detail, the basic thrust is for host countries to guarantee third-party settlement as one option available to foreign investors in their territory. Thus, by way of example, the model BITs of Germany (1991), the United Kingdom (1991), the United States (1994 as revised 1998), Switzerland (1995) and France (1999) – as well as actual treaties completed by these countries with developing countries[19] – include provisions allowing for the arbitration of investor-State disputes as a matter of course. Equally, the model agreements of certain developing countries and economies in transition follow this approach.[20]

On the other hand, free investor choice may be accompanied by an equivalent freedom of choice for the host country party to the investment dispute. Thus, by Article 12(2) of the Iranian model BIT:

> "In the event that the host Contracting Party and the investor(s) can not agree within six months from the date of notification of the claim by one party to the other, either of them may refer the dispute to the competent courts of the host Contracting Party or with due regard to their own laws and regulations to an arbitral tribunal of three members. ..."

The arbitral tribunal in question is of an *ad hoc* nature, with each party selecting an arbitrator, who will then select the umpire of the tribunal. The arbitration will be conducted in accordance with UNCITRAL rules (Article 12(5) and (6)). The Peru model agreement, Article 8, also provides for either the investor from the other contracting party or the host contracting party to submit the dispute to a competent tribunal of the host contracting party or to ICSID, should settlement of the dispute in a friendly manner prove impossible after six months. Once that choice has been made it cannot be undone by either party.[21]

The broad impact of BITs in this area is also evident in the fact that a significant proportion of the 2,099 BITs concluded as of 1 January 2002 provide for arbitration (UNCTAD, 2002b). So, for example, in one survey of 335 BITs in force at the beginning of 1992, it was found that 334 contained provisions for arbitration (Khalil, 1992). Of the treaties surveyed, 212 required arbitration under ICSID procedures either as the only, or as one of the methods of dispute settlement. This pattern has continued, so that today many BITs establish that the foreign investor shall have the option to use ICSID procedures or another form of internationalized arbitration, for the settlement of investment disputes.

Finally, brief attention should be given to some common formulations in BITs on the issue of dispute settlement. As noted, many of these instruments contemplate arbitration by ICSID, under the ICSID Additional Facility, or on an *ad hoc* basis. Not all references to ICSID arbitration necessarily mean that ICSID will have jurisdiction in particular cases. This is so because the ICSID Convention grants jurisdiction to that arbitral mechanism only where the parties to the particular dispute give their consent in writing to ICSID arbitration.[22] The question, therefore, is whether certain formulations used in BITs give rise to ICSID jurisdiction (Sornarajah, 1986a).

Some of the formulations often encountered in this regard include:

- *Type 1.* Cases where the dispute-settlement provision seeks to create a unilateral offer of consent of the host country to ICSID adjudication in anticipation of any future dispute. It is exemplified by the Preferred Article 8 (1) in the 1991 model BIT of the United Kingdom:

  > "Each Contracting Party hereby consents to submit to the International Centre for the [sic] Settlement of Investment Disputes [...] for settlement by conciliation or arbitration under the Convention [...] any legal dispute arising between that Contracting Party and a national or company of the other Contracting Party concerning an investment of the latter in the territory of the former".[23]

- *Type 2.* Cases where the BIT establishes an obligation on the part of both State parties to accept ICSID jurisdiction once requested to do so by the investor from the other contracting State party. One example of this type is to be found in Article XII of the Agreement on Economic Cooperation signed between the Netherlands and Uganda in 1970, which stipulated that:

  > "The Contracting Party in the territory of which a national of the other Contracting Party makes or intends to make an investment, shall assent to any demand on the part of such national to submit, for conciliation or arbitration, to [the ICSID],

any dispute that may arise in connection with the investment".

Although this provision never entered into force, in that the 1970 agreement itself never entered into force, it offers an interesting formulation that could be considered in the drafting of BITs.

- *Type 3.* Cases where the mandatory "shall" is used in a manner that indicates that disputes are to be subject to ICSID jurisdiction, but where this result is not necessarily achieved. In this category, the contracting parties typically agree that any investor-State dispute "shall, upon agreement between both parties, be submitted for arbitration by [ICSID]" (1979 Sweden/Malaysia BIT, Article 6). This provision acknowledges the possibility that the parties to the dispute might eventually conclude agreements accepting ICSID jurisdiction, but it does not, by itself, constitute that acceptance (Dolzer and Stevens, 1995, p. 132).
- *Type 4.* A number of BITs, particularly some concluded by the Netherlands, rely on the following form of words: "The Contracting Party in the territory of which a national of the other Contracting Party makes or intends to make an investment, shall give sympathetic consideration to a request on the part of such national to submit for conciliation or arbitration, to [ICSID],..." (1979 Netherlands/Kenya BIT, Article XI).

  Clearly, although this type of provision may have some moral authority, it does not constitute consent to ICSID arbitration. However, it may imply "an obligation not to withhold consent unreasonably" (Broches, 1982, p. 67).

C. Determination of procedural issues

Assuming that the parties elect international arbitration, this raises a number of further procedural questions. As already noted, where *ad hoc* procedures are chosen the parties themselves must agree on these issues. Some guidance may be obtained from the use of standard model rules outlined above, should the parties wish to use them. By comparison, the ICSID Convention lays down a comprehensive international system for investor-State dispute settlement through the establishment and operation of ICSID. Given its prominence as a precedent, most of the issues raised in this section will be discussed with reference to the provisions of that Convention, though reference is also made to the provisions of the UNCITRAL Arbitration Rules and the Permanent Court of Arbitration Optional Rules for arbitrating disputes between a private and a State party. Finally, it should be stressed that not all of the ensuing issues are of equal importance. They are presented here in a sequence that reflects the order in which these issues are often laid out in international instruments dealing with arbitration. In particular, it should be emphasized that questions relating to the applicable law not only affect the procedure of the tribunal in question, but also impact upon the content of the substantive law used by the tribunal to resolve the dispute.

1. Procedure for the initiation of a claim

The first step in commencing an arbitration procedure is the initiation of a claim by the complaining party. Under the ICSID Convention, this is done by the notifying the Secretary-General of ICSID of a request for arbitration, who thereupon sends a copy of the request to the respondent party. The request must contain information on the issues in dispute, the identity of the parties and evidence of their consent to ICSID arbitration in accordance with the rules of admissibility (on which see below). The Secretary-General is empowered to make a preliminary examination of the request to ensure that it is *prima facie* admissible, though the final right of decision on this question rests with the arbitral panel. Provided that the request is admissible, the Secretary-General will then register the request, notifying the parties the same day. Proceedings are deemed to have commenced from the date of registration (Article 36, ICSID Convention).

By contrast, the procedure under the UNCITRAL Arbitration Rules is a bilateral process. Proceedings are initiated by the claimant through a notice of arbitration to the respondent. Arbitral proceedings are deemed to commence on the date on which the notice of arbitration is received by the respondent (Article 3). The notice must comply with the content requirements contained in Article 3 of the UNCITRAL Arbitration Rules. The provisions of the Permanent Court of Arbitration Optional Rules for arbitrating disputes between a private and a State party are identical in these requirements to the UNCITRAL Arbitration Rules. It should be noted, however, that both sets of Rules make clear that when a State party agrees to arbitration under the Rules, this constitutes a waiver of sovereign immunity – though a waiver of immunity relating to the execution of an award must be explicitly expressed (Permanent Court of Arbitration Optional Rules, Article 1(2)).

2. Establishment and composition of the arbitral tribunal

The usual practice in international arbitrations is for the parties to choose between a sole arbitrator or an arbitration panel of uneven number, usually three. One problem with *ad hoc* procedures has been the inability of the parties to agree on a number or on a selection of arbitrators. Accordingly, the UNCITRAL Arbitration Rules and the Permanent Court of Arbitration Optional Rules provide procedures for the appointment of arbitrators in the absence of agreement between the parties after the lapse of a specified time period (see Articles 5-8 of each instrument). Given that each arbitrator is selected by a party, the other party retains rights of challenge (see Articles 9-12 of each instrument). Provision is also made for replacement of arbitrators and for a repeat of hearings where this is required (Article 14 of each instrument).

The ICSID Convention provisions offer a more institutionalized approach (Articles 37-38). While agreement between the parties is still the first principle of procedure, should they fail to agree on the number and appointment of arbitrators, the chairperson of the Administrative Council of ICSID (the President of the World Bank) shall appoint the panel members. Panel members will be appointed from persons nominated by the parties, provided they conform to the qualities listed for members of the ICSID Panel of Arbitrators in Article 14(1) of the ICSID Convention. Where the chairperson makes the nomination, this is limited to the members of the standing Panel of Arbitrators. The majority of the arbitrators shall be nationals of States other than the States or nationals party to the dispute, unless the parties agree otherwise (Article 39, ICSID Convention).

3. Admissibility

In *ad hoc* procedures, the parties must decide for themselves which claims they submit to the tribunal through their statement of claim and defence. The jurisdiction of the tribunal also rests on the terms of the arbitration agreement between them. However, the arbitral tribunal has the power to rule that it is not competent to decide the issue on the basis of the terms of that agreement. This is a preliminary question that must be raised no later than the statement of defence or of counter-claim. This approach is maintained in the UNCITRAL Arbitration Rules and in the Permanent Court of Arbitration Optional Rules (Article 21 of each instrument).

Institutional systems, by contrast, have rules on admissibility. In particular, a dispute must come within the jurisdiction of the arbitral tribunal, as defined in the constitutive instrument setting up the system. In this regard, the ICSID Convention has provisions covering the admissibility of claims – these can be regarded as the cornerstone of this dispute-settlement system. The provisions have been developed through the interpretative jurisprudence of successive ICSID Tribunals into a complex and technical body of procedural law, though it must be stressed that each Tribunal is free to interpret the Convention as it sees fit, there being no doctrine of precedent under the ICSID Convention. However, earlier decisions on admissibility undoubtedly form persuasive precedents upon which the parties and subsequent Tribunals may rely. It is neither possible nor necessary to examine this jurisprudence in detail for the purposes of the present chapter, it being sufficient merely to describe the main requirements of admissibility. Nonetheless, it is necessary for any negotiator of an IIA to remember that, in offering ICSID as a dispute-settlement option, the agreement in question automatically applies the procedural law of the ICSID Convention to the disputes covered by the IIA.[24] As noted in section I, to be admissible a request for arbitration must fulfil the following requirements: it must be admissible as regards subject matter (jurisdiction *ratione materiae*); the parties to the dispute must be entitled to use ICSID procedures and have the standing to answer claims under these procedures (jurisdiction *ratione personae*); and the request must be admissible at the time it is made (jurisdiction *ratione temporis*).

***a. Admissibility* ratione materiae**

Before the provisions of the ICSID Convention are considered, it is necessary briefly to review practice in other IIAs. The most common approach in this regard is for the relevant treaty to stipulate that the dispute must be a legal dispute, that it must concern an investment issue and arise from it. A typical form of words can be found in Article 9 of the 1994 BIT between Lithuania and the Netherlands (UNCTAD, 1998a), which reads in the relevant part:

> "Each Contracting Party hereby consents to submit any legal dispute arising between that Contracting Party and an investor of the other Contracting Party concerning an investment of that investor in the territory of the former Contracting Party to the International Centre for the [sic] Settlement of Investment Disputes ..."

Here the connection established is that the dispute must be one "concerning an investment", but other formulations are commonplace (UNCTAD, 1998a, p. 91). For instance, BITs may provide that the dispute in question must be "relating to" an investment (1995 BIT between Australia and the People Democratic Republic of Laos), "in connection with" an investment (1992 China-Viet Nam BIT), "with respect to" an investment (1995 Swiss model BIT), or "regarding" an investment (1994 Chilean model BIT). The Asian-African Legal Consultative Committee Revised Draft of Model Agreements for Promotion and Protection of Investments can be placed in this category as well; these instruments provide for dispute settlement for "any dispute or difference that may arise out of or in relation to investments made" in the host country's territory by a foreign investor (models A and B).

In some cases, an IIA that gives rise to the jurisdiction of the relevant tribunal contemplates both disputes arising under the agreement itself, and disputes arising under other specified agreements or in other specified circumstances. Thus, the draft MAI included two different types of investor-State disputes for settlement – namely, disputes arising under the MAI itself (Article V(D)(1)(a)) and disputes arising under either an investment authorization or a written agreement between a host country and an investor (Article V(D)(1)(b)(i) and (ii)). This is also the approach taken in United States' BITs. Article IX of the 1994 United States model BIT (as revised in 1998), which sets out the pertinent rules for "investment disputes", indicates that:

> "For purposes of this Treaty, an investment dispute is a dispute between a Party and a national or company of the other Party arising out of or relating to an investment authorization, an investment agreement or an alleged breach of any right conferred, created or recognized by this Treaty with respect to a covered investment."

The ICSID Convention applies the following formulation in Article 25(1):

> "The jurisdiction of the Centre shall extend to any legal dispute arising directly out of an investment, between a Contracting State (or any constituent subdivision or agency of a Contracting State designated to the Centre by that State) and a national of another Contracting State, which the parties to the dispute consent in writing to submit to the Centre. When the parties have given their consent, no party may withdraw its consent unilaterally."

The dispute must be "legal" and must arise directly out of the "investment". The first requirement seeks to differentiate between a conflict of interests and a conflict of rights. Only the latter comes within the jurisdiction of the Centre. Thus, the parties must show that the dispute relates to the scope of a legal right or obligation, or the nature of reparation to be paid for breach of a legal obligation (Schreuer, 1996, p. 339). In general, this requirement has not caused many problems before ICSID Tribunals.[25]

The second requirement has been defined broadly so that "investment" includes, in essence, any outlay of capital by at least one party. Furthermore, it is not limited to FDI in cases where the treaty involved provides that portfolio investment is covered by the definition of investment (ICSID, 1998). Whether the subject matter of the dispute arises out of an "investment" is a matter to be decided on a case-by-case basis and the views of the parties are not decisive. Equally, if jurisdiction is based on an arbitration clause referring to ICSID, the definition of "investment" in that agreement will not be binding on the ICSID Tribunal, as it reflects the specific agreement of the parties, although it is likely that the definitions in the BITs will meet the Convention's objective requirements (Schreuer, 1996, pp. 362-363). As to the requirement that a dispute "arises directly" out of an investment, this is also a matter for decision on the facts of each case. It introduces a requirement that the dispute has a clear and real connection to the investment and is not an unrelated ancillary transaction. In practice, this may be a hard distinction to draw, as an investment relationship typically gives rise to many transactions, some of which are closely related in an economic sense to the main investment agreement while others are rather more remote from it.[26]

b. Admissibility ratione personae

This question does not arise in relation to *ad hoc* internationalized arbitration as the parties themselves define the tribunal's personal jurisdiction by agreeing to submit to the proceeding. However, in relation to institutional arbitration (or indeed conciliation), it is a central issue. Thus, with respect to the ICSID Convention, as noted above, Article 25(1) requires:

- *first*, that the parties be State contracting parties to the ICSID Convention and the national of another State contracting party (see further Schreuer, 2001, pp. 141-168, 265-334; Asouzu, 2001, chapter 9; Amerasinghe, 1974); and
- *second*, that they both consent to ICSID jurisdiction (see further Schreuer, 1996, pp. 422-492; Asouzu, 2001, chapter 10).

As to the nature of the parties to the dispute, the State contracting party can appear in person or can designate any governmental agency or constituent sub-division to appear as parties in their own right. It must be a party to the Convention at the time the dispute is submitted to the Secretary-General of ICSID (ICSID Convention, Articles 68, 70, 73). As for the other party to a dispute, it must be a national of a contracting State party other than the host State party to a dispute. It can be a natural or juridical person. A natural person must possess the nationality of a contracting State party on the date on which the parties consent to submit the dispute to ICSID and on the date the dispute is registered by the Secretary-General.

The nationality requirements of a juridical person are not as strict. Under Article 25 (2)(b) of the ICSID Convention, "national of another Contracting State" means:

> "any juridical person which had the nationality of a Contracting State other than the State party to the dispute on the date on which the parties consented to submit such dispute to conciliation or arbitration and any juridical person which had the nationality of the Contracting State party to the dispute on that date and which, because of foreign control, the parties have agreed should be treated as a national of another Contracting State for the purposes of this Convention."

The first case covers a juridical person possessing a nationality other than that of the contracting State party to the dispute. The second case deals with the common situation in which the locally incorporated affiliate of a foreign parent company is a party to a dispute with the contracting State in which it is incorporated. Given that the affiliate possesses the nationality of the respondent host State, it would be easy for the latter, in the absence of Article 25(2)(b), to avoid jurisdiction before ICSID by invoking that fact. Thus, the ICSID Convention allows the locally incorporated affiliate to assert foreign control, in order to satisfy the nationality requirements needed for ICSID juristiction to apply. However, to do so the affiliate must show that the host contracting State agreed that it should be treated as a national of another contracting State – for example, by specifically recognizing its foreign ownership and control in an investment authorization and confirming that actual foreign control exists (ICSID, 1994; Schreuer, 2001, pp. 292-324; and Asouzu, 2001, pp. 273-300).[27]

As to consent to ICSID jurisdiction, the State party to the ICSID Convention and the foreign investor must provide written consent that they each submit to the jurisdiction of ICSID. Being a State party to the Convention is not sufficient for the Centre to have jurisdiction; for ICSID jurisdiction, an additional, voluntary, submission must be made to the Centre. At the time that the ICSID Convention was being negotiated, capital-importing countries were not generally prepared to accept compulsory jurisdiction for investor-State disputes, so the ICSID approach represents an attempt to balance the divergent perspectives of these countries and those of capital-exporting countries (Schwarzenberger, 1969).

Other ICSID provisions underline the consensual character of this Convention. So, for example:

- Article 25(4) allows each State party to notify ICSID of the class or classes of disputes that it "...would or would not consider submitting to the jurisdiction of the Centre. ...";
- the seventh preambular paragraph of the Convention declares that: "...no Contracting State shall by the mere fact of its ratification, acceptance or approval of this Convention and without its consent be deemed to be under any obligation to submit any particular dispute to conciliation or arbitration"; and
- Articles 28 and 36 respectively require that requests for conciliation or for arbitration shall expressly indicate that the relevant parties have given consent for those procedures.

Offers of consent (if not, indeed, actual consent, depending on the terms of the instrument in question) may be found in a number of sources.

These include: the terms of the dispute-settlement clause in the master investment contract itself; in a series of documents constituting the legal basis of the investment relationship in cases in which more than a single document exists; in the national legislation of the host contracting State; and in BITs (see further Schreuer, 1996, pp. 422-492; Asouzu, 2001, chapter 10). For present purposes, it is enough to recall the types of formulations mentioned above which are commonly found in BITs and relate to the choice of venue for dispute settlement.[28]

Consent to submission to international arbitration was unconditional for contracting Parties to the draft MAI, reflecting the practice of many other treaties. Together with the submission of the dispute by the investor to ICSID arbitration – or to other systems of arbitration mentioned in the investor-State dispute settlement provisions of the draft MAI – this constituted the consent required to establish jurisdiction over the dispute in question.

c. Admissibility ratione temporis

This requirement is again mainly relevant to institutional systems of arbitration or conciliation. In *ad hoc* procedures, there may be time limits laid down for submission of claims and defences, but these are not bound by any law that limits action – unless the parties decide to apply such a law, or stipulate that time is of the essence regarding a submission's admissibility.

In relation to ICSID proceedings, as noted above, the parties to a dispute must be legally entitled to have recourse to that system on the grounds that the dispute was registered at a date when both parties were, respectively, a contracting State party and a national of another contracting State.

4. Applicable law

As noted in section I, in an international arbitration two choice of law questions arise: which law is to govern the procedure of the tribunal and which substantive law will govern the resolution of the dispute.

a. Applicable procedural law

In *ad hoc* procedures, the parties need to determine these issues. These may already have been determined by the investment agreement governing the investor-State relationship. However, such agreements may at times be unclear or even be silent on these important questions, especially in cases in which the parties cannot accept each other's preferred governing law or laws. In such cases, the parties need to agree the choice of law issues in the arbitration agreement that founds the tribunal and its jurisdiction. One solution here is for the parties to adopt standard rules for the conduct of international arbitration, such as those provided for in the UNCITRAL Arbitration Rules or the similar rules adopted by the Permanent Court of Arbitration Optional Rules. These Rules become the "procedural law" of the arbitration, though they remain subject to any rules of law applicable to the arbitration from which the parties cannot derogate. In this way, *ad hoc* arbitration can come closer to institutional systems, where the choice of procedural law is resolved by the applicability of the rules and procedures of the institutional system itself. Thus, in relation to ICSID, these are found in the constitutive instrument and the supplementary rules of procedure produced by ICSID to govern conciliation and arbitration proceedings.

b. Applicable substantive law

As regards the choice of substantive law, preference is usually given in both *ad hoc* and institutional systems to the parties' own choices in these matters, where such choices are clear from the investment agreement concerned. However, where such clarity is absent, *ad hoc* and institutional systems may take different paths.

In the case of *ad hoc* arbitration, standardized rules of arbitration include an applicable law clause. Thus, Article 33 of the UNCITRAL Arbitration Rules and Article 33 of the Permanent Court of Arbitration Optional Rules both state:

> "1. The arbitral tribunal shall apply the law designated by the parties as applicable to the substance of the dispute. Failing such designation by the parties, the arbitral tribunal shall apply the law determined by the conflict of laws rules which it considers applicable.
>
> 2. The arbitral tribunal shall decide as *amiable compositeur* or *ex aequo et bono* only if the parties have expressly authorized the arbitral tribunal to do so and if the law applicable to the arbitral procedure permits such arbitration.
>
> 3. In all cases, the arbitral tribunal shall decide in accordance with the terms of the contract and shall take into account the usages of the trade applicable to the transaction."

This provision re-emphasizes party control over choice of substantive law and the governing force of the contract between them in its commercial context. It also reflects arbitral practice by allowing the tribunal to apply relevant conflict-of-laws rules to decide on the applicable law in the absence of party consent, or to decide without reference to a specific system of law where the parties have authorized a decision on the basis of the principles stated in paragraph 2. Where the latter option arises, the arbitration is decided on the basis of what the tribunal considers fair and equitable in the circumstances of the case, paying regard to the contract and to the laws and practices to which it is most closely associated.

As regards institutional systems of arbitration, Article 42(1) of the ICSID Convention deals with the applicable substantive law as follows:

> "(1) The Tribunal shall decide a dispute in accordance with such rules of law as may be agreed by the parties. In the absence of such agreement, the Tribunal shall apply the law of the Contracting State party to the dispute (including its rules on the conflict of laws) and such rules of international law as may be applicable."

This provision establishes an order of preference as to the applicable law. First, the Tribunal will apply the rules of law agreed by the parties. In the absence of such agreement, the law of the contracting State party to the dispute – including its conflict-of-laws rules (which may, in turn, point to the law of another State as the applicable law) will be applied. Finally, the Tribunal will turn to any applicable rules of international law. This reference to international law has been interpreted by subsequent ICSID Tribunals to mean that the law of the contracting State party to a dispute will apply so long as it is consistent with rules of international law (Shihata and Parra, 1994). Similarly, where the parties make an express choice of a national law as the applicable law, this too will be subject to review in accordance with applicable rules of international law (Schreuer, 1997b, pp. 473-487; Muchlinski, 1999, pp. 549-551). Where the applicable national law is consistent with international law an ICSID Tribunal can decide the case by reference to that domestic law alone (ICSID, 1987). By contrast, a tribunal acting under Chapter 11 of NAFTA is bound to apply the provisions of NAFTA, the applicable rules of international law and interpretations of the NAFTA Free Trade Commission (Article 1131 NAFTA). A NAFTA tribunal would exceed its jurisdiction if it decided a claim solely on the basis of domestic law (Foy and Deane, 2001, pp. 306-307).

5. Finality of awards

As is the case with any third-party adjudication, whether conducted through a court or an arbitral body, international arbitral proceedings must comply with certain basic procedural requirements that ensure a full and fair hearing of each party's case, a properly reasoned award that is correct in both factual and legal analysis and a hearing that is conducted by a professionally competent and impartial tribunal. Accordingly, both *ad hoc* and institutional systems of arbitration must observe such fundamental requirements of due process and fairness in order to provide effective and legitimate means of dispute settlement.

In relation to *ad hoc* arbitration, failure to observe such requirements may result in the unenforceability of the award under the national laws of States before whose tribunals such enforcement is sought. An international arbitral award that fails to comply with the requirements of fairness and due process will usually be unenforceable, as this would offend against the public policy of the forum State.[29] In some jurisdictions this might lead to the award being annulled.[30] In practice, it may not be easy to ensure that such rights are observed if the parties cannot agree to include certain procedural standards in the arbitration agreement, either by reference to an applicable procedural law or through specific provisions in the agreement itself. In order to avoid this possible problem, the UNCITRAL Arbitration Rules and the Permanent Court of Arbitration Optional Rules set down standardized procedural requirements for the proper conduct of the arbitration and for the making of a fully reasoned award (UNCITRAL Rules 1976 and Permanent Court of Arbitration Optional Rules, Section III Articles 15-30 and Section IV Articles 31-37 (both instruments)). However, both instruments are silent on enforcement, although it is safe to say that, where an award is governed by the provisions of these instruments and the requirements stated therein are followed, that award will almost certainly be accepted as complying with the essential requirements of fairness, due process and reasoned decision making.

The draft MAI included a provision stressing that any award made under its provisions would be final and binding between the parties to the dispute and should be carried out without delay by the party against whom it was issued, subject to the post-award rights granted under the arbitral systems used to make the award (draft MAI, Dispute Settlement, Section D). Thus, the draft MAI envisaged that the issue of finality would be governed by the applicable rules of the arbitration system chosen by the parties for resolving their dispute.

In the case of institutional arbitration, the approach of the ICSID Convention is similar, in that it also contains provisions dealing with the proper conduct of arbitral proceedings (see further ICSID Convention, Chapter IV, Articles 36-49). However, the ICSID Convention goes beyond *ad hoc* systems by including provisions on the interpretation, revision and annulment of the award (see, for a detailed analysis, Schreuer, 2001, pp. 856-1075). These provisions permit either party to request a review of the award of an ICSID Tribunal where:

- a dispute arises between the parties as to the meaning or scope of an award, in which case either party may request an interpretation of the award by the tribunal that rendered it or, if this is not possible, by a new tribunal (ICSID Convention, Article 50);
- new facts arise that decisively affect the award and which were unknown to the tribunal and to the party seeking to introduce the new facts, and that the latter's ignorance was not due to negligence. In such a case, that party can apply within specified time limits to request revision of the award by the tribunal that rendered it or, if this is not possible, by another tribunal (ICSID Convention, Article 51);
- either party feels there are grounds for annulment of the award (ICSID Convention, Article 52).

This last situation calls for further elucidation. By Article 52, either party may request annulment of the award where one or more of the following grounds of annulment are alleged to exist:

(a) that the Tribunal was not properly constituted;
(b) that the Tribunal has manifestly exceeded its powers;
(c) that there was corruption on the part of a member of the Tribunal;
(d) that there has been a serious departure from a fundamental rule of procedure; or
(e) that the award has failed to state the reasons on which it is based.

The application must be made within 120 days after the date on which the award was rendered, or within 120 days of the discovery of any alleged corruption and, in any case, within three years of the date of the award (ICSID Convention Article 52 (2)).

The annulment request is made to the Secretary-General of ICSID, who will forward it to the chairperson, who, in turn, will appoint an *ad hoc* committee of three persons to review the award. These persons must be different from the members of the Tribunal that rendered the award, they must not be of the same nationality as any such member or of the State party to the dispute or of the State whose national is a party to the dispute, nor must they have acted as conciliators in the same dispute (ICSID Convention, Article 52(4)). If an award is annulled, either party may request that the dispute be submitted to a new Tribunal.

This procedure is in essence a review procedure, not an appeal procedure (Caron, 1992). An appeal procedure, such as that used under the Dispute Settlement Understanding of the WTO, permits a challenge to an arbitral award on the basis not only of procedural defects, but also as regards the substance of the decision where this shows a defect in law – for example, the evidence was not properly reviewed by the tribunal. While the distinction between a review and an appeal of a decision is at times hard to draw, the main difference lies in the fact that an appellate body can not only nullify an award for procedural defects, but can go further and substitute its own decision for that of the first tribunal. By contrast, the *ad hoc* committee under ICSID rules can only annul the decision of the Tribunal on one or more of the narrow grounds provided for in Article 52, thereby freeing the parties to decide whether either one of them wishes to submit the dispute afresh to a newly constituted Tribunal.[31] In practice this has led to some prolongation of disputes and to calls for a revision of the ICSID Convention in order to ensure greater finality of awards (Feldman, 1987; Redfern, 1987). Finally, it should be noted that, by Article 53 of the ICSID Convention, the award of an ICSID Tribunal is binding on the parties and is not subject to any appeal or to any other remedy, except those provided for in the Convention.

It should also be noted that, under ICSID Convention rules, the delivery of a binding award is not proscribed where a party fails to appear. The ICSID Convention provides for decisions in default of a party appearing, subject to certain procedures aimed at encouraging that party to appear (ICSID Convention Article 45).

6. Enforcement of awards

If an investor-State dispute has been submitted to a local court in a host country for final settlement, then enforcement issues should not raise any special problems. This is so because the local court with jurisdiction over the issue also has enforcement jurisdiction in the normal course of events.

Where, however, an investor-State dispute is submitted to international arbitration, certain issues of enforcement may arise in practice. In the first place, an investor naturally wishes to have the arbitral award enforced to its full extent even though the arbitral tribunal will, in all likelihood, not have the ultimate means of enforcement available to domestic courts. To address this consideration, Article 54(1) of the ICSID Convention stipulates, *inter alia*, that:

> "Each Contracting State shall recognize an award rendered pursuant to this Convention as binding and enforce the pecuniary obligations imposed by that award within its territories as if it were a final judgment of a court in that State. ..."

One result of this provision is that if ICSID arbitration is used, each State party to the ICSID Convention is required to enforce the resulting arbitral award in its territory (Schreuer, 2001, pp. 1098-1140). In some circumstances, however, a party to the ICSID Convention may not carry out enforcement as a result of the interplay between the provisions of Article 54 and Article 55. Article 55 stipulates that:

> "Nothing in Article 54 shall be construed as derogating from the law in force in any Contracting State relating to immunity of that State or of any foreign State from execution."

Consequently, if a court of the State in which enforcement is sought takes the view that it is being called upon to enforce an award contrary to the principle of sovereign immunity, it may decide against enforcing the award. This is exemplified by the decision of the District Court for the Southern District of New York in *LETCO v. Liberia* (ICSID, 1987), in which the court relied expressly on Article 55 in holding that, on the facts, certain Liberian property was immune from execution (Schreuer, 2001, pp. 1141-1180).

Another well-established method for the enforcement of arbitral awards is through the United Nations Convention on the Recognition and Enforcement of Foreign Arbitral Awards (the New York Convention). Under this Convention, which applies to the recognition and enforcement of awards made in foreign territory, arbitral awards are to be recognized in accordance with the rules and procedures of the State in which enforcement is sought, and under specified terms and conditions. In practice, however, the scope of the New York Convention is limited by the fact that parties to the Convention are often only prepared to enforce arbitral awards made in the territory of other State parties. Article I(3) of the New York Convention entitles parties to follow this course of action.

A second limiting factor to enforcement under the New York Convention is that, in some countries, enforcement against the respondent State may be limited by the Act-of-State doctrine or the plea of sovereign immunity (UNCTAD, 1998a). This possibility arises largely because Article V(2)(b) of the New York Convention allows the State in which recognition and enforcement is sought to refuse such recognition and enforcement if this would be "contrary to the public policy of that country". The Act-of-State doctrine, which indicates a policy of judicial self-restraint mainly in the United States, may arguably prompt the view that it is contrary to public policy to exercise enforcement jurisdiction with respect to the actions taken by a foreign State within its own territory. In similar fashion, it is open to argument that considerations of public policy may prevent a party to the New York Convention from enforcing an arbitral decision against a foreign sovereign without regard to the principle of sovereign immunity.

In the event that a particular country is party to neither the ICSID nor the New York Conventions, then it may not be legally obliged to enforce an award. As a means of addressing this problem, some BITs contain provisions which stipulate that an arbitral award shall be enforceable in the territory of each party to the given bilateral agreement (Article VI, 1992 United States/Russia BIT). Similarly, some BITs provide for mutual enforcement of awards pursuant to the domestic laws of the host State party (Article 7(5), 1992 Lithuania/Sweden), (UNCTAD, 1998a).

Each of the possibilities noted in this section – those of the ICSID and New York Conventions and of individual BITs – creates an obligation under international law for the relevant State parties to enforce certain third-party decisions. It should be noted, however, that these possibilities do not necessarily reflect obligations in the national law of the State parties. In some jurisdictions, the treaty obligations of the State automatically become a part of the national law; in such jurisdictions, the enforcement obligations accepted by the State would automatically apply within the State. In other jurisdictions, however, the enforcement obligations derived from relevant treaties need to be expressly incorporated in local legislation in order to be applicable as part of the national law (Jennings and Watts, 1992).

7. Costs

In *ad hoc* arbitration it is usual for the costs to be determined by agreement of the parties or by the arbitral tribunal itself. The UNCITRAL Arbitration Rules and the Permanent Court of Arbitration Optional Rules both opt for the latter approach, leaving the determination of costs to the tribunal (UNCITRAL Rules Article 38; Permanent Court Rules Article 38). As to the question of which party bears the costs, practice is not uniform. The possible options include: equal sharing of costs, the "loser pays" principle, or apportionment at the discretion of the tribunal. The UNCITRAL Rules and the Permanent Court of Arbitration Optional Rules both follow the "loser pays" approach (UNCITRAL Rules, Article 40; Permanent Court Rules, Article 40), while the ICC Rules of Arbitration 1998 follow the tribunal-discretion approach (Article 31(3), Schreuer, 2001, pp. 1224-1225).

Under institutional systems of arbitration costs are determined in accordance with the applicable procedural rules. Thus, the ICSID Convention leaves the determination of charges for the use of ICSID facilities to the Secretary-General in accordance with the applicable regulations, while each Conciliation Commission or Arbitral Tribunal shall determine the fees and expenses of its members within the limits prescribed by ICSID rules (ICSID Convention, Articles 59-60). However, the parties are not precluded from agreeing in advance with the Commission or Tribunal concerned upon the fees and expenses of its members (ICSID Convention Article 60(2)). As to the apportionment of costs, in conciliation proceedings before ICSID the costs are shared equally between the parties, while in ICSID arbitrations the apportionment of costs are determined by the Tribunal as part of the award, unless the parties otherwise agree (ICSID Convention Article 61). Where the parties decide to reach their own agreement on the apportionment of costs, they cannot reduce or withdraw their overall financial obligation towards ICSID by such agreement (Schreuer, 2001, p. 1222).

Section III Interaction with other Issues and Concepts

The issue of dispute settlement is fundamental to the balance of the relationship between a foreign investor and a host country. It follows that there is substantial interaction between investor-State dispute settlement and a broad range of other issues and concepts that arise in investment practice. A summary of the extent to which this interaction is likely to occur in practice is set out in table 1.

Table 1. Interaction across issues and concepts

Issue	Investor-State dispute settlement
Admission and establishment	++
Competition	+
Dispute settlement: State-State	++
Employment	+
Environment	+
Fair and equitable treatment	++
Home country measures	+
Host country operational measures	+
Illicit payments	+
Incentives	+
Investment-related trade measures	+
Most-favoured nation treatment	+
National treatment	++
Scope and definition	++
Social responsibility	+
State contracts	++
Taking of property	++
Taxation	+
Transfer of funds	+
Transfer of technology	+
Transfer pricing	++
Transparency	+

Source: UNCTAD.
Key: 0 = negligible or no interaction.
+ = moderate interaction.
++ = extensive interaction.

- **Scope and definition**. IIAs take divergent positions on the actual definition of the terms "investment" and "investor", as they seek to define forms of investment and the types of investors that are covered by each agreement.

Generally, the definition of "investment" depends on the types of assets that could fall within the meaning of the term. However, in some cases it refers mainly to the underlying transaction involving the particular assets. "Investor" is defined in relation to the criteria to be used for determining whether a particular entity is to have rights and duties in an investment agreement.

As noted in section II above, some IIAs identify the types of investor-State disputes within their ambit by reference to matters "concerning investment", matters "in connection with investment" and so forth. At the same time, other IIAs provide for investor-State dispute settlement in respect of disputes under a particular IIA, or in other specified circumstances. In each case, however, there is a link between a particular form of "investment" and the use of dispute-settlement mechanisms, whether through third-party arbitration or otherwise. Accordingly, there is a strong correlation between the definition of the term "investment" and the range of matters that are subject to investor-State dispute settlement. A significant degree of correlation also exists between the definition of "investor" and the circumstances in which investor-State dispute settlement may arise. Specifically, a claimant in an investor-State dispute will, almost certainly, need to satisfy the definition of an investor in the relevant IIA in order to pursue a legal claim against a host country.

In some cases, an entity may satisfy the definition of an "investor" (or a "national", or some other entity eligible to make a claim), but the claim may be barred on grounds of nationality. Many IIAs, including NAFTA, the Energy Charter Treaty, and numerous BITs, specify rules concerning the nationality of claimants and the circumstances in which "investors" satisfy the requirements of nationality in order to make a claim. In each particular investor-State dispute, therefore, it must be considered whether a foreign investor meets the nationality criteria in order to bring a valid claim. In the case of corporate entities, factors such as the claimant's country of incorporation or the country where it has its headquarters will be used to determine nationality.

- **Admission and establishment**. Various IIAs specify the circumstances in which foreign investors may become participants in the economy of a host country. The criteria for admission and establishment may include, among other things, minimum capital requirements, reinvestment requirements and/or requirements concerning joint venture participation with locals. Almost invariably, too, an investor is required to comply with the national laws, national security and public policy of the host country as conditions of entry.

  Investor-State dispute-settlement procedures may enhance rights of admission and establishment by providing the mechanism by which investors may challenge a host country's decision concerning which investments are entitled to treaty rights and benefits in that host country. That is the effect of an extension of an IIA to the pre-entry stage of an investment when combined with the investor-State dispute-settlement provision in the agreement. Examples of such an approach include NAFTA and the draft MAI, as well as the Draft Supplementary Treaty to the Energy Charter Treaty.

  In some cases, however, the putative investor may not have access to investor-State dispute-settlement mechanisms because treaty rights are not made applicable to pre-investment activities in the host country. So, for instance, Article 10 of the Asian-African Legal Consultative Committee Revised Draft of Model Agreements for Promotion and Protection of Investments contemplates rights to foreign investors in relation to "investments made in [the host State's] territory". Here, an investor's right to dispute settlement is active only after the time of investment: admission and entry questions are not subject to dispute resolution under the treaty. A similar approach has been adopted in BITs concluded by Canada – for example, the BIT concluded between Canada and Thailand in 1997 (Article II (4)) or the BIT concluded between Canada and Lebanon in 1997 (Article VI of Annex I on Exceptions) (Canada, 2002).

- **National treatment**. The guarantee of national treatment – meaning in this context that a foreign investor is entitled at least to the same level of treatment accorded to national investors in the host country – is an important feature of modern investment treaty practice. In the context of investor-State dispute issues, national treatment means that a foreign investor should have access to the same avenues of dispute settlement available to national investors. Given that host countries are usually willing to have FDI matters considered by local courts, modern treaty practice is furnished with numerous instances in which both national and foreign investors have access to the same domestic jurisdiction. As discussed in section II above, foreign investors frequently seek access to internationalized means of settlement in the form of arbitration or conciliation that may not be available to national investors. To this extent, an entitlement to investor-State dispute settlement may be regarded as an exception to the notion that foreign investors must be given the same treatment as national investors in all respects. In this case it is better to see the treatment accorded to the foreign investor as being in line with the concept of "no-less-favourable-treatment". Here a host country may give preferential treatment to foreign investors compared to the treatment it accords to comparable national investors, but not less than it affords national investors.

- **Fair and equitable treatment**. Most modern multilateral, regional and bilateral investment instruments contain the assurance that foreign investors shall receive "fair and equitable" treatment with respect to their operations in a host country. There has been some disagreement as to the precise meaning of this assurance. Some suggest that it is equivalent to the international minimum standard, while others argue that it simply means that fairness and equity, in their plain meaning, should be accorded to foreign investors.

  Most treaties that contemplate fair and equitable treatment also provide for third-party settlement of investor-State disputes. Third-party procedures can enhance the fair and equitable standard by allowing investors to have their claims about unfair or inequitable treatment considered by tribunals operating outside the control of the host country. In addition, because disputes about what constitutes fair and equitable treatment may involve the different economic perspectives of a host country and investor, third-party settlement may provide some assurance to investors that their views on fairness and equity will be given due consideration. More generally, if there were to be no dispute-settlement mechanism for investor-State disputes – whether through third-party mechanisms or otherwise – there would be no judicial or independent means by which an investor would be able to have its perspective on fairness and equity assessed.

- **Transfer pricing**. Issues of transfer pricing are essentially concerned with how one may establish prices for goods, services, know-how and intellectual property transferred across borders within the corporate structure of a particular TNC. Where these transfers occur, the pricing of the items transferred is a significant factor in determinating possible tax revenues for the host country. For this reason, host countries have an interest in ascertaining the transfer price used by TNCs, and in ensuring that this price is determined on a reasonable basis. For transfer pricing issues, investor-State dispute-settlement mechanisms provide a host State and foreign investor with some assurance that there is an independent avenue for assessing their divergent viewpoints, should such differences occur. Dispute-settlement provisions are therefore often provided for in bilateral tax treaties.

- **Taking of property**. One of the primary concerns of an investor in a foreign country is the vulnerability of the investment to a "taking" by the host State. Such taking may assume diverse forms, ranging from relatively minor interference by a host country with respect to the investor's assets, to the complete appropriation of such assets, possibly as part of a broad scheme of nationalization of foreign property. In any event, a taking by a host country can give rise to questions of both municipal and international law and sometimes prompts the need for investor-State dispute settlement. Indeed, historically investor-State disputes on this issue have been at the heart of this area of international law. Disputes over whether a taking has occurred or whether sufficient compensation has been paid for a taking generally fall within the scope of typical investor-State dispute settlement provisions. This is true for multilateral, regional and bilateral instruments. Thus, most of the dispute-settlement provisions reviewed in Section II above are fully applicable to questions concerning takings. However, some IIAs also contemplate specific dispute-settlement rules for matters concerning expropriation and compensation. So, for instance, the Asian-African Legal Consultative Committee Revised Draft of Model

Agreements for Promotion and Protection of Investments makes provision for investor-State disputes in general in Article 10, but it also expressly stipulates that disputes concerning the "determination of compensation or its payment" shall be referred either to an independent judicial or administrative tribunal under the host country's laws, or in accordance with any agreement between an investor and a host country for third-party arbitration (Article 7). Similarly, the 1994 Chinese model BIT makes general provisions for dispute settlement in the courts of the host country, but it further contemplates that disputes concerning the amount of compensation for expropriation "may be submitted at the request of either party to an *ad hoc* arbitral tribunal". These provisions implicitly acknowledge the important role that dispute-settlement provisions play in the area of takings. Finally, even where there is a general provision on investor-State dispute settlement that is applicable to takings, some BITs also indicate that takings should be assessed in accordance with "due process of law" in the host country. This has been interpreted to mean that the taking and assessment of compensation must be considered by a national tribunal of the host country, as a precondition for submission to third-party arbitration.

- **State contracts**. Particularly with respect to large scale projects in the mining and petroleum sector, but also in areas such as telecommunications, transport, power supply and related fields, foreign investors sometimes enter a host country under the terms of a contract between themselves and a host country. Such State contracts normally stipulate matters such as choice of law, the applicable tax regime and the terms and conditions concerning the operations of an investor. In addition, they frequently contain provisions on what should occur in the event of an alleged breach of a contract and, in this regard, the trend is for conflict resolution through arbitration. In some cases, therefore, foreign investors that are parties to a State contract have rights of access to third-party dispute resolution not only by virtue of any relevant treaty instrument, but also under the terms of a State contract (Mann, 1990).
- **Dispute settlement: State-State**. Under customary international law, when foreign nationals suffer loss and damage in a host country and receive no adequate remedy from the courts of the host country or otherwise, those foreign nationals may seek diplomatic protection from their home country (Jennings and Watts, 1992). Specifically, an aggrieved national may request the home country to espouse a claim against the host country in respect of the damages originally suffered by the national. If the home country pursues this claim, it will be doing so on its own behalf and international law does not require the home country to transfer any sums received for damages to the aggrieved national (Jennings and Watts, 1992; Brownlie, 1998). Nevertheless, it is clear that, when a State espouses the claim of one of its nationals in this context, the resulting State-to-State dispute-settlement proceedings depend substantially on the particular dispute that the foreign national (the investor) originally had with the host country. Thus, the State-to-State dispute is a derivative of the original investor-State disagreement. In addition, investor-State disputes are sometimes linked to State-to-State disputes by way of subrogation (Dolzer and Stevens, 1995, pp. 156-164). In some home countries, agencies of a State are prepared to grant financial guarantees against non-commercial risks (such as the risk of expropriation) to investors of their nationality who invest in foreign territory. Under the principle of subrogation, if a State agency makes payment to a foreign investor in respect of a foreign investment dispute, the State or agency may then assume the rights of the foreign investor in the dispute with the host country. This principle is recognized in most recent BITs. Finally, some agreements take into account the possibility that the same claim by an investor may constitute the basis for both investor-State and State-to-State dispute-settlement proceedings (UNCTAD, 1998a). To avoid this occurrence, some BITs that contain both types of dispute-settlement provisions expressly provide that, if a dispute has been submitted to investor-State mechanisms, then that submission automatically serves as a bar to the same claim being presented for State-to-State resolution. Where, however, the investor-State tribunal finds that it does not have jurisdiction with respect to a particular claim, or where the tribunal's judgement has not been respected by the host country, then,

under the terms of some BITs, the claim is not barred from State-to-State procedures – see for example Article 12(4), 1995 Australia/Lao People's Democratic Republic BIT.

Conclusion: Economic and Development Implications and Policy Options

The process of foreign investment can create disagreements and disputes between the various actors involved, and as such there is little doubt that procedures for the settlement of investment disputes are needed. This is so regardless of the level of development of the host country in question. However, there is less of a consensus on the precise nature of those procedures. In this regard, there may be a greater choice of approach (and more flexibility in the alternatives open in relation to procedural detail) than might at first appear. In relation to the economic development process of developing countries, there has been a tendency to polarize choice around two basic models of dispute settlement: national approaches and international approaches. Though much of the practice in IIAs, reviewed in section II above, echoes this tendency, the present section places these approaches into a wider context of choice and flexibility, illustrating the full range and complexity involved in drafting dispute-settlement clauses in IIAs.

A further issue to be borne in mind, when considering the development implications of dispute-settlement mechanisms, is the need to ensure the primacy of swift, efficient and amicable methods of dispute settlement. These are the best guarantee of long-term stability in investment relations. Therefore, to give primacy to more legalistic and formal third-party methods of dispute settlement may be to limit party flexibility unduly. Nonetheless, it must be stressed that, although the majority of dispute-settlement clauses and systems found in IIAs seem to deal with this type of approach, they do not represent the only alternative. Indeed, such clauses and systems are there to deal with the rare disputes that cannot be easily resolved through amicable means. On the other hand, major disagreements can and do occur. Thus, the proper conduct of more serious investment disputes must be ensured.

The implication is that the dispute settlement system chosen must provide effective means for the resolution of differences between the parties and, crucially, must be fair to both parties and be perceived as such. Investor-State disputes arise between a private commercial party and a State administration or agency and as such include a public interest and policy element. This cannot be wholly disregarded against the commercial interests of the private party, nor, indeed, can the legitimate interests and expectations of the commercial party always take second place to the public interest. The dispute-settlement system must therefore be sensitive to both kinds of interests and to the claims that they might generate in the course of a dispute.

Against this background and in the light of the preceding discussion, a number of policy options can be considered in drafting investor-State dispute settlement clauses in IIAs. These options arise in relation to the major choice that parties to IIAs must make – namely, whether to include dispute-settlement clauses in an agreement or not. Should the former approach be taken, two further choices arise; first, which venue to choose and how far there should be room to choose; second, what types of procedural rules should apply.

A. No reference to investor-State dispute settlement in an agreement

At the most basic level it is possible to decide not to include any reference to dispute settlement in an IIA. This option is not usually found in practice. A central purpose of many IIAs is to place a guarantee of dispute settlement into legally binding terms through the use of such an agreement. The effect is to create an international legal obligation to settle disputes between a host State and investors from other States party to an IIA in accordance with the procedures laid down in that agreement.

On the other hand, when the host country has a developed and generally respected internal legal order, a reference to dispute settlement in an IIA could be thought of as unnecessary (although this has not always dissuaded investor home countries of from insisting that dispute settlement clause be included in an IIA). The internal laws and practices of a host country may be seen as sufficiently protective of the rights and obligations of both a private investor and a host State not to need further determination in an international agreement.

B. Reference to investor-State dispute settlement in an agreement

1. Choice of venue

Here a number of major options present themselves:

Option 1: Exclusivity of national dispute-settlement methods in a host country

This option involves the exclusive jurisdiction of national courts and represents the end of the spectrum that gives greatest control to host countries. From the perspective of foreign investors, this approach suggests possible vulnerability: a host country could modify its rules on investment or a change of government could lead to a change in attitude towards foreign investors. However, a host country may believe that the application of national law is the option that is most compatible with its notions of national interest. In addition, a host country may believe that its national laws are inherently fair and just and that if investors come to the host country, they should be prepared to accept the host country's law, just as much as they accept other aspects of the host country.

In support of such a policy, it might be said, as a political matter, that a foreign investor should be accorded treatment equal to that granted to nationals of the host country (Rogers, 1978); to grant an investor the right to third-party dispute settlement amounts, in effect, to placing the foreign investor in a privileged position *vis-à-vis* national investors. In addition, it might be said that since foreign nationals usually invest in a host country for their own commercial reasons, these investors should be prepared, on the basis of equality with nationals, to accept the national courts of the host country (Shea, 1955). In short, investors should be expected to take the investment climate of the host country as a whole, including its judicial system.

Option 2: International dispute settlement is subject to a requirement of prior exhaustion of local remedies in a host country

This approach allows for some degree of host State control over the process of dispute settlement, in that an investor is not free to pursue internationalized remedies until they have exhausted all local avenues of dispute settlement in a host country. A possible variant could be a requirement to use regional dispute-settlement systems to which the host country is a party, before fully international dispute-settlement systems are followed.

Option 3: Non-binding preference for national dispute settlement

Another approach may be to state a preference for national dispute-settlement in a host country, but to avoid making this preference legally binding on investors. This approach might be useful for countries in which there may be some resistance to international dispute settlement, but where such an option is deemed necessary to attract investors.

Option 4: Choice of national or international dispute settlement

As noted in section II, choice of venue clauses in IIAs are tending towards an "investor choice model", in that the choice of venue, whether national or international, is offered to investors, coupled with a unilateral offer to respect that choice on the part of the State party to an IIA. This approach is sometimes interpreted as creating a compulsory internationalization of investment disputes at the whim of an investor. In practice, however, investor choice is still bounded by many restrictions. For example, should investors choose host country dispute settlement, they are bound by the rules and practices of the host country's legal system. Should an investor choose international dispute settlement, then the active consent of the host country is still required. In relation to *ad hoc* dispute settlement, no procedure can begin without the agreement of both parties to submit to such methods in an arbitration or conciliation agreement. In relation to institutional systems, the host country party must still consent in accordance with the applicable rules that seek to determine when valid consent has been given. As noted in section II, in relation to ICSID arbitration or conciliation, the contracting State party to a dispute must agree in writing to the registration of any dispute brought against it by an investor. This may be done in an investment agreement or in national law. In either case, the investor must still accept that offer by requesting those proceedings. Furthermore, the request must come within the terms of the unilateral prior-consent given by the State party.

It should also be borne in mind that, as shown by reference to the Iranian and Peruvian Model BITs in section II, the choice of dispute settlement method can be extended to the host country party to the dispute. As a matter of principle, offering choice of method to the investor does not exclude the possibility of offering the same choice to the host country. It is up to the host country to decide, when negotiating an investment agreement, whether it wishes to offer free choice of means to the investor alone – by expressing a unilateral commitment to accept the investor's choice in the terms of the agreement – or to reserve similar freedom for itself. Should the latter approach be taken, it would effectively preserve the host country's discretion to impose its method of dispute settlement on the investor, at least where it initiates a claim against the investor.[32] Although this may not be a common occurrence, it does emphasize the possibility that the investor may be a respondent rather than a claimant and that the host country may wish to enjoy the same freedom of choice of dispute-settlement method that current practice offers to the investor.

Option 5: Compulsory international dispute settlement

In principle, it is possible to conclude a dispute-settlement clause that makes international dispute settlement the only available option. However, such clauses are virtually non-existent in current IIA practice in the context of investor-State dispute settlement. Such a clause might be of use in relation to a host country that has no existing means of dispute settlement available at the national level. Thus, its existence would suggest a highly exceptional situation, such as a complete breakdown of internal governance in a host country, resulting from either internal or international conflict. Such an approach is more reminiscent of inter-state mixed claims commissions, which may arise out of such cases and which may be charged with the administration of a State-to-State lump sum settlement agreement. One example may be the Iran-United States Claims Tribunal, which heard *inter alia* claims by United States nationals for compensation against loss of their property during the Iranian revolution. Such examples can be said to fall outside the normal concerns of IIAs, which tend not to cover such cases, even in clauses covering loss due to civil unrest or commotion (see chapter 8).

Option 6: Establishment of a specialized dispute settlement body under the investment agreement itself

A further possible alternative is for the parties to an IIA to establish a specialized dispute-settlement body under the agreement, with the purpose of creating a forum for the settlement of investment disputes between investors from States that are contracting parties to the agreement and other contracting parties that are hosts to the investment undertaken by the investor in question. One example of such a body, discussed in section II, is the NAFTA investor-State dispute-settlement system. In addition to the above-mentioned provisions of NAFTA, it should be added here that the Free Trade Commission established by the NAFTA contracting parties also has a special role to play in the investor-State dispute-settlement system under that Agreement. The Commission is empowered to make "Notes of interpretation" on investment issues arising under Chapter 11 of NAFTA. By Article 1131 (2) of NAFTA, these "Notes" are binding on subsequent arbitral tribunals established in accordance with Section B of Chapter 11. As such, they offer a means of ensuring consistency and clarity of interpretation of Chapter 11 among NAFTA tribunals. However, such an approach can limit the freedom of a tribunal to determine the dispute before it in a manner that it sees fit. Thus, the "Notes of interpretation" system introduces an element of control over the range of admissible interpretations of NAFTA investment provisions that tribunals may use.

2. Choice of procedure and procedural rules

Following the specific issues discussed in section II, a number of policy options present themselves when drafting the procedural aspects of the investor-State dispute-settlement clause in an IIA.

a. Choice of dispute-settlement method

As stated in both sections I and II of this chapter, it may be essential to prioritize amicable negotiated solutions to disputes between investors and States. Accordingly, the first sentence or paragraph of any dispute-settlement clause should address the desirability of using such methods in the first instance. This may be done through mandatory language, creating an obligation to use such methods before being able to resort to formal, third-party decision-making methods such as arbitration. Alternatively, the parties may be urged to resort to informal methods, but without compulsion. The former approach may be useful to ensure that disputes do not become more serious by requiring negotiation and restraint from the parties in their approach to their dispute. The latter method may offer greater freedom of choice for the parties to go straight to arbitration, with the attendant risk that this might escalate a dispute.

b. Procedure for initiating a claim

Here, the main choice lies between the various methods of dispute settlement available to an investor and a State party under the relevant IIA. As such, it is an issue closely related to the choice-of-venue clause. What needs to be borne in mind is that, where an IIA allows for the choice of a particular dispute-settlement method or system, then the making of that choice implies acceptance of the procedures for initiating a claim under the chosen method or system. Thus, for example, if ICSID arbitration is an option under an IIA, the parties' choice of that system entails the application of ICSID rules concerning the initiation of the claim.

It is possible for the parties to an IIA to include specific rules on the procedure for initiating a claim, such as, for example, the need for written consent. However, the effect of including such rules in an IIA when also including one or more of the existing dispute-settlement methods and systems must be carefully considered, in order to avoid uncertainty. Usually, party choice on procedural issues is respected, but a given system may have certain basic mandatory rules on the initiation of a claim from which the parties cannot derogate. Thus, any specific requirements in an IIA relating to the initiation of a claim should aim to be compatible with any mandatory rules on this matter that exist in the methods and systems listed as available to the parties to the IIA in question.

c. Establishment and composition of the arbitral tribunal

This issue also needs to be considered in the light of applicable rules of any method or system of dispute settlement parties may chose to include in an IIA's dispute-settlement clause. Nonetheless, some basic choices exist in regard to the establishment and composition of the arbitral tribunal. First, the parties to an IIA may wish to allow for full party choice on its establishment and composition, or they may defer to the rules on this matter that apply under any of the methods or systems of dispute settlement included in the dispute-settlement clause. Second, the parties to an IIA may wish to decide whether party choice on the composition of the tribunal should extend to the number, qualifications and nationality of the members, or be subject to certain mandatory rules stated in the dispute-settlement clause in the IIA in question. If the latter approach is taken, then the compatibility of such rules with those of any methods or systems of dispute settlement included in an IIA must be taken into account – although party choice will usually be respected, as shown in section II.

d. Admissibility

The terms relating to the admissibility of a dispute are subject to the same caveat as above – namely that there be compatibility with existing rules operating under available methods and systems of dispute settlement mentioned in the dispute-settlement clause. Nonetheless, the following matters may be considered for inclusion in the terms of that clause:

- Whether the subject matter of an admissible dispute will be restricted in any way or whether it will be left open to the parties to submit any dispute. Restrictions on admissibility can be based on specific criteria – such as a requirement that the dispute be a legal dispute arising out of an investment covered by an IIA – or limited to certain classes of investment dispute, such as those arising over compensation in the case of expropriation.
- Whether there should be a restriction as to the persons or parties that may be permitted to bring claims under a dispute-settlement clause of an IIA, or to appear as respondents to those claims – for example, by allowing only States parties to an agreement and nationals of other States parties to the agreement to do so. Such a provision may also require a clarification of who such a party or national is. It may also need to address the standing of indirect third parties, such as parent companies located in a State that is not a party to an IIA, but which own or control affiliates that are incorporated in a host State that is party to the IIA. Similarly, the issue of party consent to the use of a particular method or system of dispute settlement may need to be dealt with by including specific rules on who is able to give such consent. Whether to include specific rules covering the time at which a dispute can be brought and the criteria that makes a party eligible to submit a dispute at that time.

e. Applicable law

The parties to an IIA may wish to specify rules on the choice of applicable procedural and substantive laws that should apply to disputes between investors and States, although this is again subject to the same caveat on compatibility that runs through this whole section. The usual approach would be to respect party choice in these matters, although there may be certain mandatory rules that apply in the case of institutional systems. For example, as noted in section II, in relation to the applicable substantive law ICSID applies the national law of the State party to the dispute on the basis of party choice. In the absence of such choice Article 42(1) of the ICSID Convention is used to determine the choice of law, but that law will be subject to the corrective application of international law should the national law in question be found to diverge from international law. It may not be possible for the parties to an IIA to exclude this approach should they choose to use ICSID arbitration.

f. Finality of awards

The parties to an IIA may wish to determine whether any award made under an IIA will be final or whether it can be the subject of further proceedings. Thus the parties may determine that the award be:

- Final with no possibility of further review at the international level. It should be noted that such a clause would probably be ineffective if it sought to exclude review at the national level by a national court, as clauses that purport to exclude review of arbitral awards at the national level may be regarded as contrary to public policy before the courts of the State in question.
- Subject to review for interpretation, or in light of the discovery of new facts, procedural errors or excess of powers, all of which may lead to annulment of an award. This is the ICSID model of review, and it is incorporated into an IIA that offers party choice of ICSID arbitration.
- Subject to full appeal to an appellate body. This is the WTO model as applicable to inter-State disputes arising out of the WTO Agreement and its Annexes in accordance with the WTO Dispute Settlement Understanding (WTO, 1994).[33] Although no existing agreement contains such an approach, it could be adapted for investor-State disputes in future IIAs.

g. Enforcement of awards

The parties may choose between a number of enforcement approaches, although again much depends on the choice of the dispute-settlement method or system and the specific rules that it provides for in this matter. In essence, the parties may choose between:

- Bilateral enforcement in accordance with the terms of a BIT between them.
- Enforcement in accordance with the New York Convention – which may be termed a "mutual harmonization" approach – whereby the parties agree to leave enforcement of any award made under an IIA to their national courts, which in turn apply the principles of that Convention. This approach assumes that the parties to the IIA are also parties to the New York Convention and that the award is not made under any other institutional system that has its own rules of enforcement, most notably the ICSID system under the ICSID Convention.
- Enforcement under the ICSID system – which may be termed a "mandatory multilateral enforcement" approach – whereby all contracting parties to the ICSID Convention agree to enforce validly-concluded ICSID Tribunal awards without any further review.

However, given that disputes of the kind discussed in the present chapter involve a State party, where an award is made against that party, it may still rely on any applicable rules of international law that render sovereign property immune from the satisfaction of any award made against a State. These rights to immunity from execution can, in principle, be waived by a State contracting party within the provisions of an IIA, but this practice very rarely happens (Schreuer, 2001, pp. 1165-1175). Indeed, as noted in section II, they are expressly preserved in both the New York and ICSID Conventions.

h. Costs

Here the choice is between party determination of costs and determination by a third party, which may be either the arbitral tribunal or, in the case of an institutional system, its administrative organs acting in accordance with pre-determined rules on costs. However, even in an institutional system there may be choice between the applicable institutional rules and party determination.

As to apportionment, the choices are between equal apportionment between the parties, full payment of costs by the losing party or apportionment by discretion of the tribunal. These choices may be particularly significant in relation to developing country parties, which may have limited resources available to satisfy the costs of an international arbitral procedure. Thus, the parties may need to consider carefully the relative ability of each party to bear costs. It should be noted that ICSID fees and expenses are pre-set and so offer a degree of predictability and certainty concerning the ultimate cost of proceedings (Schreuer, 2001, pp. 1212-1215).

Finally, in relation to the costs associated with arbitration under IIAs, countries might wish to consider whether it would be possible to set up a fund to assist developing and in particular least developed countries to meet the costs of such procedures, bearing in mind that the investor may be a TNC with significant resources at its disposal that cannot be matched by the State party for the conduct of a dispute. Such a fund would address an important aspect of procedural due process, which is inherent in any effective dispute-settlement system.

* * *

Given the foregoing considerations, host countries need to consider carefully which of the above-outlined options to pursue. For example, in the highly competitive world market for FDI, countries that seek such investment may be inclined to accept international dispute settlement because this could be perceived as an incentive to attract foreign capital.

However, one needs to keep in mind that the principal determinants in the FDI decision-making process are of an economic nature, once an enabling regulatory environment is in place. Thus, factors such as market size, economic growth, the quality of the infrastructure and the availability of skills typically bear most heavily on the decision (UNCTAD, 1994). For example, China, a host country that ranks highly in a number of these variables, has generally not allowed internationalized third-party adjudication for all investor-State disputes. Rather, China's 1994 model BIT contemplates national court jurisdiction for most disputes, raising the option of internationalized arbitration only in cases concerning compensation for expropriation. Given China's size and economic prospects, China does not feel obliged to comply fully with investor preferences in this area of practice. The approach taken by China illustrates that, although the regulatory framework for FDI (including provisions for dispute settlement) may influence capital flows, it is only one of a number of determinants of foreign investment. These determinants vary significantly from one host country to another, in turn influencing the particular significance that investors may attach to the strength of dispute-settlement procedures.

Furthermore, as the infrastructure of legal systems and dispute-settlement mechanisms evolves and becomes more sophisticated in all countries and regions that seek inward FDI, the availability of good quality localized dispute-settlement mechanisms may encourage their increased use (Asouzu, 2001). However, the most important factor to stress is that investors and the countries in which they operate need to do their utmost to avoid disputes in the first place and, should a dispute arise, use the least confrontational approach possible to arrive at its resolution. To ensure this, the preservation of choice for both parties and the recognition of their legitimate interests and expectations are important. These are the ultimate goals towards which the dispute-settlement provisions of IIAs should strive.

Notes

1 See Azanian v. United Mexican States, International Centre for Settlement of Investment Disputes (ICSID) (ICSID, 1999a).

2 Indeed, under international law, it may not even be acceptable to "lift the corporate veil" and determine the nationality of the corporation by reference to the nationality of its principal controlling shareholders, as opposed to the nationality of its seat or place of incorporation which is the accepted standard; see Barcelona Traction case, International Court of Justice (ICJ, 1970).

3 The concept of negotiation as a technique of dispute settlement used directly by each party is self-explanatory and requires no further definition. However, the other terms used in the text have some specialized connotations and may be defined as follows: good offices involves the use of a third party to liaise with the disputing parties and to convey to each party the views of the other on the dispute. The third party plays no part in suggesting solutions to the dispute. By contrast mediation and conciliation involve the third party in a more active role, in that it may intervene with suggestions as to how the dispute might be resolved, thereby helping

the disputing parties towards a negotiated settlement. In practice it may be difficult to differentiate between mediation and conciliation on a functional basis and the two terms can be used interchangeably (Asouzu, 2001, p. 20). However, they differ from arbitration in that the third party has no right or authority to determine the resolution/outcome of the dispute independently of the parties.

4 It has also been said that dispute resolution through international arbitration may be preferred by foreign investors due to a possible distrust of the court system of the host State and the choice of a forum in which the investor will feel more comfortable. See further text below and Sornarajah, 2000.

5 Unless otherwise noted, all instruments cited herein may be found in UNCTAD, 1996a, 2000 or 2001.

6 Such impartiality has at times been questioned (Dezaly and Garth, 1996).

7 This problem could be mitigated by the use of United Nations Commission on International Trade Law (UNCITRAL) Arbitration Rules in *ad hoc* procedures. See further below.

8 In *Tradax Helles SA v. Albania* (ICSID, 1999b) the ICSID Tribunal held that it was not necessary to decide whether a provision in Albanian law for an amicable settlement practice before recourse to a domestic court or administrative tribunal also applied to the procedure for recourse to ICSID arbitration because, in any event, Tradax had made a good faith effort to settle amicably.

9 Unless otherwise indicated, the texts of the BITs mentioned in this chapter may be found in the collection of BITs maintained by ICSID (ICSID, 1972) and at www.unctad.org/iia.

10 See for example the 1993 Denmark/Lithuania BIT Article 8(2) and the 1991 United Kingdom model BIT, Preferred Article 8.

11 As exemplified by the 1994 Indonesia/ Republic of Korea BIT Article 9(2), the 1987 Association of South-East Asian Nations (ASEAN) Treaty Article X(1) and also by the 1991 BIT between Argentina and Chile Article 10(1).

12 For the applicable procedural rules see the ICSID Convention, Chapter IV, and the ICSID Conciliation Rules.

13 On the issue of national laws and disputes-settlement among member States of the Andean Commission, see Wiesner, 1993.

14 Paragraph 7 of the Chairperson's text of the draft Code of Conduct of 1983 reads as follows: "An entity of a transnational cooperation is subject to the jurisdiction, laws, regulations and administrative practices of the country in which it operates" (Robinson, 1985, p. 13).

15 See, for example, the Jamaica-United States Agreement of 1994, ArticleVI.

16 However, some experts would dispute this approach and attach primacy to the local remedies rule and the above interpretation of the ELSI case. See, for example, Sornarajah, 2000.

17 Only one country, Israel, had, at the time of its ratification of the ICSID Convention in 1983, made a notification to ICSID requiring the exhaustion of local administrative or judicial remedies. This reservation was withdrawn in 1991 (Schreuer, 2001, p. 391).

18 A similar approach, which promotes certainty in the dispute-settlement process, is reflected in some bilateral agreements, including the 1994 model BIT of the United States. Article IX(3)(a) of that BIT gives an investor the right to pursue arbitration, provided that the investor has not already submitted the dispute to national courts or administrative tribunals of the host country, or in accordance with any other applicable, previously agreed procedures.

19 See for example Article 4, Chapter IV, of the United States-Viet Nam Agreement on Trade Relations, 2000.

20 See for example the Cambodia model agreement, Article VIII and the Croatia model agreement, Article 10.

21 There is at least one example of a host country bringing a claim against a foreign investor before ICSID: see Gabon v. Société Serete SA (ICSID, 1976). That case was settled by agreement of the parties in 1978.

22 For this reason, Mann suggests that, if a private investor wishes to be assured of ICSID jurisdiction, that investor should seek to obtain the host country's written submission to ICSID jurisdiction in the agreement inter se (Mann, 1990, p. 244).

23 A provision of this type was used as the basis for establishing ICSID jurisdiction in the first ICSID arbitration brought pursuant to a BIT in *Asian Agricultural Products Ltd. (AAPL) v. Republic of Sri Lanka*, Award of the Tribunal dated 21 June 1990 (ICSID, 1990). For commentary, see Vasciannie, 1992. This formulation is also used in Article XII of the 2000 BIT concluded between the Netherlands and Uganda.

24 For further analysis of the law of ICSID relating to admissibility of claims, see Schreuer, 1996; Schreuer, 2001, pp. 82-344.; Delaume, 1984; and Amerasinghe, 1974.

25 See Fedax v. Venezuela (ICSID, 1998).

26 For example, a dispute with caterers, supplied by the host State, over the supply of food to workers on an investment project is unlikely to "arise directly out of an investment" even though, but for the investment, the contract for the supply of food would not be concluded with the caterers. On the other hand, in some circumstances it might – for example where the investment project is in a remote location that can only be supplied by a host country's military catering unit, without which the

workforce would go unfed. For a full discussion, see Schreuer, 1996, pp. 348-355, and Schreuer, 2001, pp. 113-121.

[27] To ensure clarity on this issue, ICSID has drafted its Model Clause 7 which states: "It is hereby agreed that, although the Investor is a national of the Host State, it is controlled by nationals of name(s) of other Contracting State(s) and shall be treated as a national of [that]/[those] State(s) for the purposes of the Convention" (ICSID, 1993).

[28] Such unilateral offers of consent to ICSID procedures on the part of host States parties to the ICSID Convention, and, indeed, under other IIAs as noted above, have led some tribunals and experts to assert that it is now possible to institute arbitration "without privity" that is, without the prior conclusion of a bilateral agreement to submit a specific dispute to ICSID arbitration. See ICSID, 1990, and Paulsson, 1995.

[29] See for example New York Convention on Recognition and Enforcement of Foreign Arbitral Awards, Article V, which lists the main grounds for refusal to recognize and enforce an arbitral award, including on public policy grounds. See further next sub-section.

[30] See for example Sections 33 and 34 of the Swedish Arbitration Act of 1999 (International Legal Materials, 1999).

[31] However, the contrast between review and appeal may be hard to draw even in relation to ICSID procedures, as Article 52(c) allows for annulment on grounds that the Tribunal has manifestly exceeded its powers. This may raise questions about the substance of the decision itself, though in principle excess of powers is a procedural issue.

[32] Indeed mutual freedom of choice over dispute-settlement methods can only work where that freedom is reserved for the claimant. Otherwise the agreement would in effect offer a power of veto over the claimant's choice on the part of the respondent, thereby negating the very freedom that is sought to be guaranteed.

[33] See further the preceding chapter.

References

Abs, Hermann and Hartley Shawcross (1960). "The proposed convention to protect private foreign investment: a round table: comment on the draft convention by its authors", *Journal of Public Law,* 9, pp. 115-132.

Agosin, Manuel R. and Francisco J. Prieto (1993). "Trade and foreign direct investment policies: pieces of a new strategic approach to development?", *Transnational Corporations,* 2, 2 (August), pp. 63-86.

Aldrich, G.H. (1996). *The Jurisprudence of the Iran-United States Claims Tribunal* (Oxford: Clarendon Press).

Alexander, G.S. (1996). "Ten years of takings", *Journal of Legal Education*, vol. 46, pp. 586-596.

Alston, Philip (1979). "The right to development at the international level", in Jean Dupuy, ed., *The Right to Development at the International Level*, Workshop, The Hague, 16-18 October 1979 (The Hague: Sijthoff & Noordhof), pp. 99-126.

"Amco Asia Corporation v. Republic of Indonesia" (Amco v. Indonesia) (1992), *International Law Reports*, vol. 89, pp. 366-661.

Amerasinghe, C.F. (1974). "Jurisdiction *ratione personae* under the Convention on the Settlement of Investment Disputes between States and Nationals of Other States", *British Yearbook of International Law,* Vol. 47, pp. 227-267.

American Journal of International Law (AJIL) (1908). "Convention respecting the limitation of the employment of force for the recovery of contract debts", *American Journal of International* Law, vol. 2, pp. 81-85.

American Law Institute (1987). *Restatement of the Law: The Foreign Relations Law of the United States*, vol. 2 (Minnesota: American Law Institute Publishers).

Andean Community (1996)."Charter of the Court of Justice of the Andean Community" (Peru: Andean Community Secretariat) http:www.comunidad andina.org/normativa/tratprot/moditrib.htm).

Annual Digest of Public International Law Cases (ADPILC) (1927-1928). "Portugal v. Germany (The Naulilaa case)", vol. 4, pp. 526-527.

Asante, Samuel, K.G. (1979). "Traditional concepts *versus* developmental imperatives in transnational investment law", in Jean Dupuy, ed., *The Right to Development at the International Level*, Workshop, The Hague, 16-18 October 1979 (The Hague: Sijthoff & Noordhof), pp. 352-369.

________ (1989). "The concept of the good corporate citizen in international business", *ICSID Review – Foreign Investment Law Journal*, 4, pp. 1-38.

"Asian Agricultural Products Ltd. v. Republic of Sri Lanka" (AAPL v. Sri Lanka) (1990), *International Legal Materials*, vol. 30, pp. 577-655.

Asouzu, A. (2001). *International Commercial Arbitration and African States* (Cambridge: Cambridge University Press).

Association of South-East Asian Nations (ASEAN) (1996). "Protocol on dispute settlement mechanism" (Jakarta: ASEAN Secretariat), (http:www.asean.or.id/ economic/dsm.htm).

________ (1998). "Framework Agreement on the ASEAN Investment Area", http://www.asean.or.id/ economic/aem/30/frm_aia.htm.

Baxter, R.R. (1970). "Treaties and custom", *Recueil des Cours* (The Hague: Academy of International Law), vol. 129, pp. 24-105.

Bernal, Richard L. (1998). "Small developing economies in the World Trade Organization" (December, 1998), mimeo..

Blanpain, R (1979). *The OECD Guidelines for Multinational Enterprises: Labour Relations Experience and Review 1976-1979* (Kluwer: Deventer).

Borchard, E.M. and W. H. Wynne (1951). *State Insolvency and Foreign Bondholders* (New Haven, Connecticut: Yale University Press).

"BP Exploration Company (Libya) v. Government of the Libyan Arab Republic, Judgement" (BP v. Libya) (1973), *International Law Reports*, vol. 53, pp. 297-388.

Broches, Aron (1972). "The Convention on the Settlement of Investment Disputes between States and Nationals of other States", *Hague* Academy *Recueil des Cours,* vol. 130, pp. 331-410.

________ (1982). "Bilateral investment protection treaties and arbitration of investment disputes", in Schultsz, J.C. and van den Berg, A.J., eds., *The Art of Arbitration: Essay on International Arbitration: Libe Amicorum Pieter Sanders* (Boston: Kluwer), pp. 63-72.

Brownlie, Ian, ed. (1992). *Basic Documents on Human Rights* (Oxford: Clarendon Press).

________ (1998). *Principles of Public International Law* , 5th ed. (Oxford: Clarendon Press).

Burton, F. and H. Inoue (1984). "Expropriations of foreign-owned firms in developing countries: a cross-national analysis", *Journal of World Trade Law* , vol. 18, pp. 396-414.

Cameron, James and Kevin R. Gray (2001). "Principles of international law in the WTO Dispute Settlement Body", *International and Comparative Law Quarterly* , vol. 50, part 2, pp. 248-298.

Cameron, P.D. (1983). *Property Rights and Sovereign Rights: The Case of North Sea Oil* (London: Academic Press).

Cameron, Rondo (1997). *A Concise Economic Histor y of the World* (New York: Oxford University Press).

Canada (1998). "The definition of investment in existing international investment instruments", Submission to WTO Working Group on the Relationship between Trade and Investment (Geneva:WTO), mimeo..

Canada (2002). Department of Foreign Affairs and International Trade. Regional and Bilateral Agreements. http://www.dfait-maeci.gc.ca/tna-nac/fipa_list-e.asp.

Canada and Chile (1997). "Free trade agreement", *International Legal Materials*, vol. 36, pp. 1067-1192.

Canada, Mexico and the United States (1992). North American Free Trade Agreement. *International Legal Materials*, vol.32 No. 2, March 1993, pp. 289-296; and *Organization of American States*; Internet: http/www.sice.oas.org/trade/nafta/env/9141.stm.

________ (1993a). "North American Agreement on Environmental Cooperation Between the Government of Canada, the Government of the United Mexican States and the Government of the United States of America". *Organization of American States*; Internet: http/www.sice.oas.org/trade/nafta/env/9141.stm.

________ (1993b). "North American Agreement on Labour Cooperation Between the Government of Canada, the Government of the United Mexican States and the Government of the United States of America". *Organization of American States*. Internet: http/www.sice.oas.org/trade/nafta/env/9141.stm.

Canada - United States (1988). "Free trade agreement", *International Legal Materials*, vol. 27, pp. 271-402.

Chew, P. K. (1994). "Political risk and U.S. investments in China: chimera of protection and predictability?", *Virginia Journal of International Law*, vol. 34, pp. 615-683.

Christie, G.C. (1962). "What constitutes a taking of property under international law?", *The British Yearbook of International Law* , vol. 38, pp. 307-316.

Conklin, David and Donald Lecraw (1997). "Restrictions on foreign ownership during 1984-1994: developments and alternative policies", *Transnational Corporations*, 6, 1 (April), pp. 1-30.

Corrales, Werner (1999). "The space for development policies in international investment agreements", Presentation at the Inter-regional Symposium on International Investment Agreements and Their Implications for Development (Caracas, 6-8 December), mimeo.

Council of Canadians (1998). "The Multilateral Agreement on Investment (MAI) and our environment" (Ottawa: Council of Canadians), mimeo..

Council of Europe (CoE) (1950). "European Convention for the Protection of Human Rights and Fundamental Freedoms", *United Nations Treaty Series*, vol. 213, pp. 221-271. The Convention was subsequently amended by Protocols Nos 3, 5, and 8 which entered into force on 21 September 1970, 20 December 1971 and 1 January 1990 respectively; Internet: http://www1.umn.edu/humanrts/instree/z17euroco.html

________ (1965). "European Social Charter", *Council of Europe Treaty Series* No. 35; revised in Strasbourg, May 1996; Internet: http://www.coe.fr/eng/legaltxt/163e.htm.

________ (1999). "Criminal Law Convention on Corruption" (Strasbourg: Council of Europe) (http://www.coe.fr/eng/legaltxt/173e.htm).

De Castro, J. and K. Uhlenbruck (1997). "Characteristics of privatization: evidence from developed, less-developed and former Communist countries", *Journal of International Business Studies,* 28, pp. 123-143.

De Palma, A. (2001). "How NAFTA makes the rules", *International Herald Tribune, 13 March.*

Delaume, G.R. (1984). "ICSID arbitration: practical considerations", *Journal of International Arbitration,* Vol. 1, pp. 101-125.

Denza, Eileen and Shelagh Brooks (1987). "Investment protection treaties: United Kingdom experience", *International and Comparative Law Quarterly*, vol. 36 (Fall), pp. 908-923.

Dezaly, Yves and Bryant G. Garth (1996). *Dealing in Virtue: International Commercial* Arbitration and the *Construction of* a *Transnational Legal Order* (Chicago and London: University of Chicago Press).

Documents on American Foreign Relations (1948). "Economic Agreement of Bogota", R. Dennett and R. Tuner, eds., (Princeton: Princeton University Press).

Dolzer, Rudolf (1986). "Indirect expropriation of alien property", *ICSID Review: Foreign Investment Law Journal*, vol. 1, pp. 41-65.

________and Margrete Stevens (1995). *Bilateral Investment Treaties* (The Hague: Martinus Nijhoff).

Domke, M. (1960). "Indonesian nationalization measures before foreign courts", *American Journal of International Law*, vol. 54, pp. 305326.

Dore, J. (1996). "Negotiating the Energy Charter Treaty", in Thomas Waelde, ed., *The Energy Charter Treaty* (London: Kluwer Law International), pp. 137-155.

Dunning, John H. (1993). *Multinational Enterprises and the Global Economy* (Wokingham: Addison-Wesley).

________ and Rajneesh Narula (1996). "The investment development path revisited: some emerging issues", in John H. Dunning and Rajneesh Narula, eds., *Foreign Direct Investment and Governments* (London: Routledge), pp. 1-41.

Economic Community of West African States (ECOWAS) (1996). "Revised treaty", *International Legal Materials*, vol. 35, pp. 660-697.

Eden, Lorraine (1996). "Thc emerging North American investment regime", *Transnational Corporations* 5, 3 (December), pp. 61-98.

Epstein, R. (1985). *Takings: Private Property and the Power of Eminent Domain* (Cambridge: Harvard University Press).

European Commission (EC) (1975). "First Convention of Lomé", *The Courier*, African-Carribean-Pacific-European Community, No. 31 (Special Issue), March 1975. The text of the First Lomè Convention appears also in *International Legal Materials*, vol. XIV, number 3, May 1975, pp. 595-640.

________ (1979). "Second Convention of Lomé", *The Courier*, African-Carribean-Pacific-European Community, No. 58 (Special Issue), November 1979. The text of the Second Lomè Convention appears also in *International Legal Materials*, vol. XIX, number 2, March 1980, pp. 327-640.

________ (1985). "Third Convention of Lomé", *The Courier*, African-Carribean-Pacific-European Community, No. 89, January-February 1985. The text of the Third Lomè Convention appears also in *International Legal Materials*, vol. XXIV, number 3, May 1985, pp. 571-652.

________ (1990). "Fourth Convention of Lomé", *The Courier*, African-Carribean-Pacific-European Community, No. 120, March-April 1990.The text of the Fourth Lomè Convention appears also in *International Legal Materials*, vol. XXIX, number 4, July 1990, pp. 783-901.

________ (EC) (1997). *Communication on Certain Legal Aspects Concerning Intra-EU Investment* (Brussels: European Commission).

European Communities (1998). "Agreement Establishing an Association between the European Communities and Their Members States, of the One Part, and the Republic of Latvia, of the Other Part", *Official Journal of the European Communities*, L026, 2 February 1998, pp. 3-225.

European Union (1997). "Treaty on European Union", as amended by the Treaty of Amsterdam, *Official Journal, C 340, 10.11.1997*, pp. 145-172; Internet: http://ue.eu.int//Amsterdam/en/amsteroc/en/treaty/main.htm.

Eyffinger, Arthur (1996). *The International Court of Justice 1946-1996* (The Hague: Kluwer Law International).

Fatouros, A. A. (1961). "An international code to protect private investments: proposals and perspectives", *University of Toronto Law journal*, vol. 14, pp. 77-102.

________ (1962). *Government Guarantees to Foreign Investors* (New York and London: Columbia University Press).

________, ed. (1994). *Transnational Corporations: The International Legal Framework,* United Nations Library on Transnational Corporations, vol. 20 (London: Routledge on behalf of the United Nations).

Feldman, M.B. (1987). "The annulment proceedings and the finality of ICSID arbitral awards", *ICSID Review: Foreign Investment Law Journal,* Vol. 2, pp. 85-110.

Fennell, WWA. and J.W. Tyler (1993). "Trade-related investment measures", in T.P. . Stewart, ed., *The GATT Uruguay Round: A Negotiating History* (1986-1992) (Deventer-Boston: Kluwer).

Flores Caballero, R., et al. (1976). Justice *economique internationale: contributions a I'etude* de la Charte des droits et des *devoirs* economiques des Etats (Paris: Gallimard).

Foighel, Isi (1957). *Nationalization: A Study in* the Protection *of Alien Property in International Law* (London and Copenhagen: Stevens).

Foy, P.G. and Deane, R.J.C. (2001). "Foreign investment protection and investment treaties: recent developments under Chapter 11 of the North American Free Trade Agreement", *ICSID Review: Foreign Investment Law Journal,* Vol. 16, pp. 299-331.

Ganesan A. V. (1998)." Reflection of development-friendly elements in international investment agreements" (Geneva: UNCTAD), mimeo..

General Agreement on Tariffs and Trade (GATT) (1986a). *The Tokyo Round Agreements: The Texts* (Geneva: WTO).

________ (1986b). "Ministerial Declaration on the Uruguay Round" (MIN.DEC), 20 September 1986 (Geneva: WTO).

________ (1994). "The Fourth ACP-EEC Convention of Lomé". Decision of 9 December 1994, document L./7604, of 19 December 1994 (Geneva: WTO).

Gestrin, Michael and Alan M. Rugman (1994). "The North American Free Trade Agreement and foreign direct investment", *Transnational Corporations,* 3, 1 (February), pp. 77-95.

________ (1996). "The NAFTA investment provisions: prototype for multilateral investment rules?", in OECD, *Market Access After the Uruguay Round* (Paris: OECD), pp. 63-78.

Graham, E.M. (1998). "Regulatory takings, supernational treatment and the multilateral agreement on investments: issues raised by non-governmental organizations", *Cornell International Law Journal*, vol. 31, pp. 599-614.

Guzman, A.T. (1998). "Why LDCs sign treaties that hurt them: explaining the popularity of bilateral investment treaties", *Virginia Journal of International Law* , vol. 38, pp. 639-688.

Haquani, Z. (1979). "Le droit au development: fondements et sources", in Jean Dupuy ed., *The Right to Development at the International Level*, Workshop, The Hague, 16-18 October 1979 (The Hague: Sijthoff & Noordhof), pp. 22-69.

Higgins, R. (1982). "The taking of property by the state: recent developments in international law", *Hague Academy Recueil des Cours*, vol. 176, pp. 259-348.

________ (1994). *Problems and Process: International Law and How We Use It* (Oxford and New York: Clarendon Press).

Horn, Norbert, ed. (1980) "Legal problems of codes for conduct for multinational enterprises", *Studies in Transnational Economic Law*, (Kluwer: Deventer/The Netherlands Antwerp-Boston-London-Frankfurt).

Hyde, J.N. (1956). "Permanent sovereignty over wealth and natural resources", *American Journal of International Law*, vol. 50, pp. 854-867.

International Centre for Settlement of Investment Disputes (ICSID) (1972-), *Investment Treaties* (Dobbs Ferry, NY, Oceana).

________ (1976). "Gabon v. Société Serete SA", ICSID Case No. ARF/76/1, http//www.worldbank.org/icsid/cases/conclude.htm.

________ (1987). "LETCO v. Liberia, United States District Court (USDC)", *International Legal Materials* , Vol. 26, pp. 95-701.

________ (1990). "Asian Agricultural Products Ltd (AAPL) v. Republic of Sri Lanka", *International Legal Materials* , vol. 30, pp. 577655.

________ (1993). *ICSID Model Clauses* (Doc.ICSID/5/Rev.2., February 1, 1993), reproduced in *ICSID Review: Foreign Investment Law Journal*, Vol. 10, pp. 134-151.

________ (1994). "Vacuum Salt Products Limited v. Ghana", ICSID Case No. ARB/92/1, *ICSID Review: Foreign Investment Law Journal*, Vol. 9, pp. 71-101.

________ (1997). "American Manufacturing and Trading Inc. v. Republic of Zaire", *International Legal Materials,* vol. 36, pp. 1534-1561.

________ (1998). "Fedax N.V. v *The Republic of Venezuela*", Case ARB/96/3, July 11, 1997, *International Legal Materials*, vol. 37, pp. 1378-1398.

________ (1999a). "Azanian v. United Mexican States", ICSID Case No. ARB(AF)/97/2, (November 1), *ICSID Review: Foreign Investment Law Journal,* Vol. 4, pp. 538-575.

________ (1999b) "Tradax Helles SA v. Albania", ICSID Case No. ARB/94/2, *ICSID Review: Foreign Investment Law Journal,* Vol. 14, pp. 161-196.

International Court of Justice (ICJ) (1955). "Nottebohm Case (Liechtenstein v. Guatemala), Judgement", *International Court of Justice Reports*, 1955 Report, pp. 4-65.

________ (1969). "North Sea Continental Shelf Cases" (Federal Republic of Germany v. Denmark, Federal Republic of Germany v. Netherlands), Judgment, *International Court of Justice Reports* , 1969 Report, pp. 3-357.

________ (1970). "Barcelona Traction Light and Power Company Limited (Belgium v. Spain), Judgement", *International Court of Justice Reports*, 1970 Report, pp. 3-357.

________ (1989a). Acts *and Documents concerning the Organization of* the *Court,* No. 5: Charter *of* the *United* Nations, Statute *and Rules and Other* Documents (Netherlands: International Court of Justice), International Court of justice publication, Sales No. 575.

________ (1989b). "Elettronica Sicula S.p.A.(ELSI) (United States of America v. Italy) judgement", *International Court of Justice Reports*, 1989 Report, pp. 15-121.

International Labour Office (ILO) (1998). *ILO Declaration on Fundamental Principles and Rights at Work and Its Follow-up* (Geneva, Switzerland: International Labour Office).

International Law Reports (ILR) (1951). "Petroleum Development Limited v. Sheikh of Abu Dhabi, Judgement", *International Law Reports*, vol. 18, 1951 Report (Cambridge: Grotius Publications), pp. 144-164.

________ (1953). "Ruler of Qatar v. International Marine Oil Company Limited, Judgement", *International Law Reports*, vol. 20, 1953 Report (Cambridge: Grotius Publications), pp. 534-547.

________ (1963). "Saudi Arabia v. Arabian American Oil Company (ARAMCO), Judgement", *International Law Reports*, vol. 27, 1963 Report (Cambridge: Grotius Publications), pp. 117-233.

________ (1967). "Sapphire International Petroleum Limited v. National Iranian Oil Company, Judgement", *International Law Reports*, vol. 27, 1967 Report (Cambridge: Grotius Publications), pp. 117-233.

International Legal Materials (ILM) (1992). "Russian Federation-United States: Treaty concerning the encouragement and reciprocal protection of investment", *International Legal Materials*, vol. 31, no. 4, pp. 794-799.

________ (1999). "The Swedish Arbitration Act of 1999 (SFS 1999:116)", *ILM*, Vol. 6, pp. 1663-1673.

International Monetary Fund (IMF) (1976). "International Monetary Fund: proposed second amendment to the Articles of Agreement of the International Monetary Fund", *International Legal Materials*, vol. 15, pp. 546-590.

________ (1993). *Balance of Payments Manual* (Washington, DC.: IMF).

________ (1999). *Selected Decisions, 24th Issue* (Washington, D.C.: IMF).

Jackson, J.H. (1997). *The World Trading System: Law and Policy of International Economic Relations*, 2nd ed. (Cambridge: MIT Press).

Jacobs, F. G. and R. C. White (1996). *The European Convention on Human Rights* (Oxford: Oxford University Press).

"James v. United Kingdom" (1986), *European Human Rights Reports*, vol. 8, pp. 123-164.

Jennings, R., and A. Watts (1992). *Oppenheim's International Law*, Vol. I (Harlow, Essex: Longman).

Jiménez de Aréchaga, E. (1968). "International responsibility", in Sorensen, ed. *Manual of Public International Law* (New York: MacMillan), pp. 531-603.

Juillard, Patrick (1994). "L'Evolution des Sources du Droit des Investissments", *Recueil des Cours* , *Hague Academy of International Law* (The Hague: Sijthoff & Noordhoff), pp.11-215.

Karl, Joachim (1996). "Multilateral investment agreements and regional economic integration", *Transnational Corporations,* 5, 2 (August), pp. 19-50.

Katzarov, K. (1960). *Theorie* de la *nationalisation* (Neuchatel: La Baconniere).

Kemper, R. (1976). *Nationale Verfügung über natürliche Ressourcen and die neue Weltwirtschaftsordnung der Vereinten Nationen* (Berlin: Duncker and Humblot).

Khalil, Mohamed I. (1992). "Treatment of foreign investment in bilateral investment treaties", *ICSID Review - Foreign Investment Law Journal*, 7 (Fall), pp. 339-383.

Kindleberger, Charles P. (1993). *A Financial History of Western Europe* (New York: Oxford University Press).

Kirgis, L. Frederic Jr. (1983). *Prior Consultation in International Law: A Study of State Practice* (University Press of Virginia).

Kline, John M. and Rodney D. Ludema (1997). "Building a multilateral framework for investment: comparing the development of trade and investment accords", *Transnational Corporations,* vol. 6, pp. 1-31.

Konoplyanik, A. A. (1996). "The Energy Charter Treaty: a Russian perspective", in Thomas Waelde, ed., *The Energy Charter Treaty* (London: Kluwer Law International), pp. 156-178.

Kramer, Stefan (1989). "Die Meistbegünstigung", *Recht der internationalen Wirtschaft,* 6, pp. 473 - 481.

Kudrle, Robert T. (1995). "Canada's foreign investment review agency and United States direct investment in Canada", *Transnational Corporations,* 4, 2 (August), pp. 58-91.

Kunz, J. (1940). "The Mexican expropriations", *New York University Law Quarterly Review* , vol. 17, pp. 327-345.

Kuusi, Juha (1979). *The Host State and the Transnational Corporation: An Analysis of Legal Relationships* (Westmead: Saxon House).

Levy, T. (1995). "NAFTA's provision for compensation in the event of expropriation: a reassessment of the 'prompt, adequate and effective standard' ", *Stanford Journal of International Law*, vol. 31, pp. 423-453.

"Libyan American Company v. Government of the Libyan Arab Republic" (Liamco v. Libya) (1977), *International Law Reports*, vol. 62, pp. 141-236.

Lillich, Richard B., ed. (1983). *International Law of* State *Responsibility for Injuries* to *Aliens* (Charlottesville, Virginia: University Press of Virginia).

Lin, L. and R. Allison (1994). "An analysis of expropriation and nationalisation risk in China", *The Yale Journal of International Law*, vol. 19, pp. 135-186.

Mann, F.A. (1990). "British treaties for the promotion and protection of investments". In *Further Studies in International Law* (Oxford: Clarendon Press), pp. 234-251.

Mattoo, A. (1997). "National treatment in the GATS: corner-stone or pandora's box?" *Journal of World Trade*, 31, pp. 107-135.

Mavroidis, P. (2002). "*Amicus curiae* briefs before the WTO: much ado about nothing", in A. von Boddandy, et al. (eds.), *European Integration and International Co-ordination: Studies in Transnational Economic Law in Honour of Claus-Dieter Ehlermann* (The Hague and London: Kluwer Law International), pp. 317-330.

McNair, A. (1959). "The seizure of property and enterprises in Indonesia", *Netherlands International Law Review* , vol. 6, pp. 218-256.

Meagher, Robert F. F. (1979). An *International Redistribution of Wealth and Power: A Study of the Charter of Economic Rights and Duties of States* (New York: Pergamon).

Mendes, E. (1981). "The Canadian National Energy Program: an example of assertion of economic sovereignty or creeping expropriation in international law", *Vanderbilt Journal of Transnational Law* , vol. 14, pp. 475-507.

Merills, J.G. (1998). *International Dispute Settlement,* 3rd ed. (Cambridge: Cambridge University Press).

Metaxas, Spyro A. (1988). *Entreprises* transnationales et codes *de conduite:* cadre *juridique* et questions d' effectivite (Zurich: Schulthess).

Michelman, F. (1967). "Property, utility and fairness: comments on the ethical foundations of just compensation law", *Harvard Law Review* , vol. 80, pp. 1165-1258.

"Mobil Oil v. New Zealand" (1989), *ICSID Reports*, vol. 4, pp. 140-244.

Mohamad, Rahmat (1998). "ASEAN's protocol on dispute settlement mechanism: a rule-based or political approach?", *International Trade Law and Regulation*, vol. 4, pp. 47-54.

Muchlinski, Peter T. (1995). *Multinational Enterprises and the Law* (Oxford: Blackwell Publishers).

________ (1996). "A case of Czech beer: competition and competitiveness in the transitional economies", *Modern Law Review,* 59, pp. 658-674.

________ (1999). *Multinational Enterprises and the Law* (Oxford and Cambridge: Blackwell).

North American Free Trade Agreement (NAFTA) (1993). "The North American Free Trade Agreement", *International Legal Materials,* 32, 2, pp. 289-456, and 32, 3, pp. 605-799.

Norton, P. (1996). "Back to the future: expropriation and the Energy Charter Treaty", in T.W. Waelde, ed., *The Energy Charter Treaty: An East-West Gateway for Investment and Trade* (London: Kluwer), pp. 365-385.

Nurick, R. (1998). "The multilateral agreement on investment: potential impacts on local economic development and poverty issues in the UK" (London:Oxfam), mimeo..

Nurkse, Ragnar (1954). "International investment to-day in the light of nineteenth-century experience", *The Economic Journal: The Journal of the Royal Economic Society*, vol. 64, pp. 744-758.

Nwogugu, E.I. (1965). *The Legal Problems of Foreign Investment in Developing Countries* (Manchester: Manchester University Press).

O'Connell, D.P. (1970). *International Law, Vol. II* (London: Stevens & Sons).

Organisation for Economic Co-operation and Development (OECD) (1963). "Draft Convention on the Protection of Foreign Property: text with notes and comments", *International Legal Materials*, Vol. 2, pp. 241-267.

________ (1967). "Council Resolution of 12 October 1967 on the Draft Convention on the Protection of Foreign Property", *International Legal Materials*, vol. 7, pp. 117-143.

________ (1985). *National Treatment for Foreign-Controlled Enterprises* (Paris: OECD).

________ (1989). *Trade in Services and Developing Countries* (Paris: OECD).

________ (1992). *The OECD Declaration and Decisions on International Investment and Multinational Enterprises: 1991 Review* (Paris: OECD).

________ (1993). *National Treatment for Foreign Controlled Enterprises* (Paris: OECD).

________ (1994). *National Treatment for Foreign-Controlled Enterprises* (Paris: OECD) Working Papers, vol. II, No. 34.

________ (1995). *Introduction* to *the OECD* Codes *of Liberalisation of Capital Movements and Current Invisible Transactions* (Paris: OECD).

________ (1996a). "Convention on Combating Bribery of Foreign Officials in International Business Transactions and Related Instruments" (Paris: OECD), document DAFFE.IME/BR (97) 20.

________ (1996b). *Benchmark Definition of Foreign Direct Investment* (Paris: OECD).

________ (1998a). "The MAI Negotiating Text (as of 24 April 1998)", http://www.oecd.org/daf/cims/mai/negtext.htm.

________ (1998b). "Ministerial statement on the Multilateral Agreement on Investment (MAI)", *OECD News Release,* doc. SG/COM/NEWS/ (98)50, 28 April (Paris: OECD).

Organization of American States (OAS) (1961). "Economic Agreement of Bogota, 2 May 1948", *Organization of* American States *Treaty* Series, No. 21.

________ (1996a). "Inter-American convention against corruption" (Washington, D.C.: OAS), mimeo. (httttp:www.oas.org/EN/PROG/ J U RID ICO/corr-eng. htm).

________ (1996b). "Codification of the Andean Sub-Regional Integration Agreement (Cartagena Agreement)" (Washington, D.C.: OAS) (http:www.sice.oas.org/trade/junac/carta_ag/cartag 2e.asp).

________ (1997). "Working Group on Investment, OAS/IDB/ECLA Tripartite Committee: Free Trade Area of the Americas: investment agreements in the western hemisphere: a compendium" (Washington D.C.: OAS).

________ (1998). "Ministerial Declaration of San José Summit of the Americas", Fourth Trade Summit Meeting; Internet (http://www.sice.oas.org/FTAA/Costa(minis_e.st).

Paasivirta, E. (1990). *Participation of States in International Contracts and Arbitral Settlement of Disputes* (Finland: Finnish Lawyers Publishing Company).

Parra, Antonio R. (1992). "Principles governing foreign investment, as reflected in national investment codes", *ICSID Review Foreign Investment Law Journal*, 7 (Fall), pp. 428-452.

________ (1995). "The scope of new investment laws and international instruments", *Transnational Corporations*, vol. 4, 3 (December), pp. 27-48.

________ (1997). "Provisions on the settlement of investment disputes in modern investment laws, bilateral investment treaties and multilateral instruments on investment", *ICSID Review: Foreign Investment Law Journal,* Vol. 12 (fall), pp. 287-364.

Pattison, Joseph (1983). "The United States-Egypt bilateral investment treaty: a prototype for future negotiation", *Cornell International Law Journal,* 16, pp. 305-339.

Paulsson, J. (1995). "Arbitration without privity", *ICSID Review: Foreign Investment Law Journal,* Vol. 10, pp. 232-257.

Penrose, E., G. Joffe and P. Stevens (1992). "Nationalisation of foreign-owned property for a public purpose: an economic perspective on appropriate compensation", *The Modern Law Review* , vol. 55, pp. 351-367.

Permanent Court of International Justice (PCIJ) (1928). "Case concerning the factory of Chorzów, judgement", Series A, no. 17, case no. 13, pp. 4-65.

Peters, Paul (1991). "Dispute settlement arrangements in investment treaties", *Netherlands Yearbook of International Law*, vol. 22, pp. 91-161.

________ (1997). "Exhaustion of local remedies: ignored in most bilateral investment treaties", *Netherlands International Law Review,* Vol. XLIV, pp. 233-243.

Preiswerk, Roy (1963). *La protection des investissements prives dans les traites bilateraux* (Zurich: Ed. Polygraphiques).

Puri, Hardeep and D. Bondad, (1990). "TRIMs, development aspects and the General Agreement", in UNCTAD, *Uruguay Round: Further Papers on* Selected Issues (New York: United Nations), United Nations publication, pp. 55-77.

Puri, Hardeep and Philippe Brusick (1989). "Trade-related investment measures: issues for developing countries in the Uruguay Round", in UNCTAD, *Uruguay Round: Papers on* Selected Issues (New York: United Nations), United Nations publication, pp. 203-219.

Raby, J. (1990). "The investment provisions of the Canada-United States free trade agreement: a Canadian perspective", *American Journal of International Law*, vol. 84, pp. 394-443.

Rainbow Warrior (New Zealand v. France) (1986). *International Law Reports*, vol.74, pp. 241-277.

Redfern, D.A. (1987). "ICSID – losing its appeal?", *Arbitration International,* Vol. 3, pp. 98-110.

Reich, Robert (1991). *The Work of Nations: Preparing Ourselves for 21st Century Capitalism* (New York: Vintage Books).

Robinson, Patrick (1985). "The June 1985 reconvened special session on the code", *The CTC Reporter*, 20, pp. 11-14.

________(1998). "Criteria to test development Friendliness of International Investment Agreements", *Transnational Corporations,* 7, 1, April 1998, pp. 83-89.

Rogers, W.D. (1978). "Of missionaries, fanatics and lawyers: some thoughts on investment disputes in Latin America", *American Journal of International Law*, Vol. 72, pp. 1-16.

Rosenberg, D. (1983). *Le principe* de souverainete des Etats *sur leurs* ressources *naturelles* (Paris: Librairie Generale de Droit et de Jurisprudence).

Rubin, Seymour J. and Gary C. Hufbauer, eds. (1984). *Emerging Standards of International Trade and Investment: Multinational Codes and Corporate Conduct* (Totawa, New Jersey: Rowman and Allanheld Publishers).

________ and Don Wallace Jr., eds. (1994). *Transnational Corporations and National Law.* United Nations Library on Transnational Corporations, vol. 19 (London: Routledge on behalf of the United Nations).

Sacerdoti, Giorgio (1972). *I Contratti* tra Stati e *Stranieri nel Diritto Internazionale* (Milano: Giuffre).

________ (1997). "Bilateral treaties and multilateral instruments on investment protection", Academy *of International Law, Recueil des Cours,* vol. 269, pp. 257-460.

Sauvant, Karl P. (2002). "Transparency", UNCTAD presentation at the Meeting of the WTO Working Group on the Relationship between Trade and Investment, 18-19 April 2002, DITE/IPCB/IA/PUB/2002/14.

________ and Victoria Aranda (1994). "The international legal framework for transnational corporations", in A.A. Fatouros, ed., *Transnational Corporations: The International Legal Framework United Nations Library on Transnational Corporations*, vol. 20 (London: Routledge), pp. 83-115.

Schreuer, C. (1996). "Commentary on the ICSID Convention: Article 25", *ICSID Review: Foreign Investment Law Journal,* Vol. 11, pp. 318-323.

________ (1997a). "Commentary on the ICSID Convention: Article 26", *ICSID Review: Foreign Investment Law Journal,* Vol. 12, pp. 151-158.

________ (1997b). "Commentary on the ICSID Convention: Article 42", *ICSID Review: Foreign Investment Law Journal,* Vol. 12, pp. 398-417.

________ (2001). *The ICSID Convention: A Commentary* (Cambridge: Cambridge University Press).

Schwarzenberger, G. (1969). *Foreign Investments and International Law* (London: Stevens & Sons).

Schwebel, S. (1963). "The story of the U.N.'s declaration on permanent sovereignty over natural resources", *American Bar Association Journal*, vol. 49, pp. 463-469.

Seidl-Hohenveldern, Ignaz (1961). "The Abs-Shawcross draft convention to protect private foreign investment: comments on the round table", *Journal of Public Law,* vol. 10, pp. 100-112.

Shahin, Magda (1999). "Provisions in the WTO Agreements relevant to investment", Presentation at the Regional Symposium on International Investment Agreements and their Implications for Arab Countries, (Cairo: May 17-18 1999.), mimeo..

"Shahin Shane Ebrahimi v. Government of the Islamic Republic of Iran" (Ebrahimi v. Iran) (1995), *American Journal of International Law,* vol. 89, pp. 385-389.

Shea, Donald R. (1955). *The Calvo Clause:* A Problem *of Inter-American and International Law and*

Diplomacy (Minnesota: University of Minnesota Press).

Shihata, Ibrahim F. (1993). *Legal Treatment of Foreign Investment: The World Bank Guidelines* (Dordrecht/Boston/London: Martinus Nijhoff Publishers).

________ (1994), "Recent trends relating to entry of foreign investment", *ICSID Review - Foreign Investment Law Journal*, 9 (Spring), pp. 47-70.

________ and A. Parra (1994). "Applicable substantive law in disputes between States and private foreign parties: the case of arbitration under the ICSID Convention", *ICSID Review: Foreign Investment Law Journal*, Vol. 9, pp. 183-213.

Sohn, Louis B. (1976). "Settlement of disputes relating to the interpretation and application of treaties", *Recueil des Cours*, vol. 150, pp. 195-294.

________ (1994). "The use of consultations for monitoring compliance with agreements concluded under the auspices of international organizations", in Niels Blokkers and Sam Muller, eds., *Towards More Effective Supervision by International Organizations: Essays in Honour of Henry G. Schermers*, vol.1 (Dordrecht/Boston/London: Martinus Nijhoff Publishers), pp. 65-115.

Soloway, J. (1999). "Environmental trade barriers under NAFTA: the MMT fuel additives controversy", *Minnesota Journal of Global Trade,* vol.8 (1), pp. 55-95.

Sornarajah, M. (1986a). "State responsibility and bilateral investment treaties", *Journal of World Trade Law*, Vol. 20, pp. 79-98.

________ (1986b). *The Pursuit of Nationalized Property* (London: Martinus Nijhoff).

________ (1990). *International Commercial Arbitration: The Problem of State Contracts* (Singapore: Longman Singapore).

________ (1994). *The International Law on Foreign Investment* (Cambridge: Cambridge University Press).

________ (1995a). "Protection of foreign investment in the Asia-Pacific economic co-operation region", *Journal of World Trade,* 29, pp. 105-129.

________ (1995b). "ICSID involvement in Asian foreign investment disputes", *Asian Yearbook of International Law* , vol. 4, pp. 69-98.

________ (1996). "Compensation for nationalization: the provision in the European Energy Charter Treaty" in T.W. Waelde, ed., *The Energy Charter Treaty: An East-West Gateway for Investment and Trade* (London : Kluwer), pp. 386-408.

________ (2000). *The Settlement of Foreign Investment Disputes* (The Hague: Kluwer).

South Centre (1997). *Foreign Direct Investment, Development and the New Global Economic Order* (Geneva: South Centre).

Szasz, P. (1971). "The investment disputes convention and Latin America", *Virginia Journal of International Law*, Vol. 11, pp. 256-265.

"Texaco Overseas Petroleum Company v. The Government of the Libyan Arab Republic" (Texaco v. Libya) (1973), *International Law Reports*, vol. 53, pp. 389-512.

The Oxford English Dictionary, 2nd ed. (1989). (Oxford: Clarendon Press).

Umbricht, Ralph (1979). "Right to development", in Jean Dupuy, ed., *The Right to Development at the International Level* (The Hague: Sijthoff & Noordhoff), pp. 94-97.

United Nations (1948). "Universal Declaration on Human Rights", document A/RES/217 A (III), of 10 December 1948 (New York: United Nations).

________ (1950). "General Agreement on Tariffs and Trade", *United* Nations *Treaty* Series, vol. 55, pp. 194-305.

________ (1951). "Treaty of Friendship, Commerce and Navigation between the United States of America and the Italian Republic", *United Nations Treaty Series* , vol. 71, pp. 172-220.

________ (1959). "Convention on the Recognition and Enforcement of Foreign Arbitration Awards", Reservations available on the Internet Website of the *Multilateral Treaties Deposited with the Secretary-General* - TREATYI-XXII--1asphttp://untreaty.un.org:80//ENGLISH/ bible...rnetbible/part1/chapter XXII/treaty1.asp.

________ (1960). "Convention on the Organisation for Economic Cooperation and Development, with supplementary protocols (Nos. 1 and 2)", *United Nations Treaty Series,* vol. 888, pp. 179-199.

________ (1961). "Treaty of Friendship, Commerce and Navigation between the United States of America and the Italian Republic-Agreement supplementing the above treaty", *United Nations Treaty Series* , vol. 80, pp. 326-334.

________ (1964). "International Convention for the Protection of Performers, Producers of Phonograms and Broadcasting Organisations, Done at Rome on 26 October 1961", *United Nations Treaty Series*, vol. 496, pp. 43-96.

________ (1969). "Vienna Convention on the Law of Treaties", United Nations document A/CONF.39/27(23 May 1969), *United Nations Treaty Series,* vol. 1155, pp. 331-353.

________ (1972). "Paris Convention for the Protection of Industrial Property of March 20, 1883", *United Nations Treaty Series*, vol. 828, pp. 305-388.

________ (1979). "Convention on Long-Range Transboundary Air Pollution" *United Nations Treaty Series*, vol. 1302 (1992) (New York: United Nations), pp. 217-245.

________ (1980a). "United Nations Convention on Contracts for the International Sale of Goods", *United Nations Treaty Series*, vol. 1489 (New York: United Nations), p. 3.

________ (1980b). "Berne Convention for the Protection of Literary and Artistic Works of

September 9, 1886", *United Nations Treaty Series*, vol. 1161, pp. 3-73.

________ (1980c). "Patent Cooperation Treaty, Done at Washington June 19, 1970", *United Nations Treaty Series*, vol. 1160, pp. 232-482.

________ (1980d). "Strasbourg Agreement Concerning the International Patent Classification of March 24, 1971", *United Nations Treaty Series*, vol. 1160, pp. 483-522.

________ (1982). "International Convention on the Harmonization of Frontier Controls of Goods", *United Nations Treaty Series*, vol. 1409 (New York: United Nations), p.3.

________ (1983). "United Nations Convention on the Law of the Sea", *The Law of the Sea*, (New York: United Nations), Sales No. E. 83.V.5.

________ (1986a). "Declaration on the Right to Development", General Assembly Resolution 41/128, 4 December 1986, *Official Records of the General Assembly: Forty-First Session,* Supplement No. 53 (A/41/53) (New York: United Nations).

________ (1986b). "Agreement between the Government of the People's Republic of China and the Government of the Kingdom of Thailand for the Promotion and Protection of Investments", *United Nations Treaty Series,* vol. 1443, pp. 31-68.

________ (1992a). "United Nations Framework Convention on Climate Change", document A/AC.237/18 (New York: United Nations).

________ (1992b). *The Rio Declaration on Environment and Development* (New York: United Nations), United Nations publication, Sales No. E.93.I.11.

________ (1997). "Kyoto Protocol to the United Nations Framework Convention on Climate Change", United Nations document FCCC/CP/1997/7/Add.1 (New York: United Nations).

United Nations Centre on Transnational Corporations (UNCTC) (1978). "Transnational corporations: certain modalities for implementation of a code of conduct in relation to its possible legal nature", Report of the Secretariat, United Nations document E/C.10/AC.2/9, 22 December (New York: United Nation).

________ (1988a). *Bilateral Investment Treaties* (New York: United Nations), United Nations publication, Sales No. E.88.II.A.1.

________ (1988b). *The United Nations Code of Conduct on Transnational Corporations. UNCTC Current Studies* (London: Graham & Trotman).

________ (1990a). *Key Concepts in International Investment Arrangements and Their Relevance to Negotiations on International Transactions in Services* (Current Studies Series A, no. 13) (New York: United Nations), United Nations publication, Sales No. E.90.II.A.3.

________ (1990b). *Transnational Corporations, Services and the Uruguay Round* (New York: United Nations), United Nations publication, Sales No. E.90.II.A.11.

________ (1991). *World Investment Report 1991: The Triad in Foreign Direct Investment* (New York: United Nations), United Nations publication, Sales No. E.91.II.A.12.

________ and United Nations Conference on Trade and Development (UNCTAD) (1991). *The Impact of Trade-Related Investment Measures on Trade and Development: Theory, Evidence and Policy Implications* (New York and Geneva: United Nations), United Nations publication, Sales No. E.91.II.A.19.

United Nations Commission on Transnational Corporations (1984). "Outstanding issues in the draft Code of Conduct on Transnational Corporations" (New York: United Nations), United Nations document, E/C.10/1984/S/5, mimeo..

United Nations Conference on Trade and Development (UNCTAD) (1993). *World Investment Report 1993: Transnational Corporations and Integrated International Production* (New York and Geneva: United Nations), United Nations publication, Sales No. E.93.II.A.14.

________ (1994). *World Investment Report 1994: Transnational Corporations, Employment and the Workplace* (New York and Geneva: United Nations), United Nations publication, Sales No. E.94.II.A.14.

________ (1995). *World Investment Report 1995: Transnational Corporations and Competitiveness* (New York and Geneva: United Nations), United Nations publication, Sales No. E.95.II.A.9.

________ (1996a). *International Investment Instruments: A Compendium,* vols. *I, II and III* (New York and Geneva: United Nations), United Nations publications, Sales Nos. E.96.II.A.9, 10 and 11.

________ (1996b). *World Investment Report 1996: Investment, Trade and International Policy Arrangements* (New York and Geneva: United Nations), United Nations publication, Sales No. E.96.II.A.14.

________ (1996c). *Incentives and Foreign Direct Investment* (New York and Geneva: United Nations), United Nations publication, Sales No. E.96.II.A.6.

________ (1996d). *The TRIPS Agreement and Developing Countries* (New York and Geneva: United Nations), United Nations publication, Sales No. 96.II.D.10.

________ (1996e). "A Partnership for Growth and Development"(Geneva: UNCTAD), United Nations document, No. TD/378.

________ (1997). *World Investment Report 1997: Transnational Corporations, Market Structure and Competition Policy* (New York and Geneva: United Nations), United Nations publication, Sales No. E.97.II.D.10.

________ (1998a). *Bilateral Investment Treaties in the Mid-1990s* (New York and Geneva: United Nations), United Nations publication, Sales No. E.98.1l.D.8.

________ (1998b). *World Investment Report 1998: Trends and Determinants* (New York and Geneva: United Nations), United Nations publication, Sales No. E.98.1l.D.5.

________ (1998c). *The Financial Crisis in Asia and Foreign Direct Investment: An Assessment* (Geneva: UNCTAD), United Nations publication, Sales No. GV.E. 98.0.D.29.

________ (1998d). *Handbook on Foreign Direct Investment by Small and Medium-sized Enterprises: Lessons from Asia* (New York and Geneva: United Nations), United Nations publication, Sales No. E.98.II.D.4.

________ (1999a). *World Investment Report 1999: Foreign Direct Investment and the Challenge of Development* (New York and Geneva: United Nations), United Nations publication, Sales No. E.99.II.D.3.

________ (1999b). "International investment agreements: concepts allowing for a certain flexibility in the interest of promoting growth and development", Note by the UNCTAD Secretariat", TD/B/COM.2/EM.5/2.

________ (1999c). "Report of the Expert Meeting on International Investment Agreements: Concepts Allowing for a certain Flexibility in the Interest of Promoting Growth and Development: Note by the UNCTAD Secretariat", /TD/B/COM.2/EM.5/3, of May 1999.

________ (2000). *International Investment Agreements: A Compendium*, vols. IV and V (New York and Geneva: United Nations), United Nations publication, Sales Nos. E.00.II.D.13 and E.00.II.D.14.

________ (2001). *International Investment Instruments: A Compendium*, vol. VI (New York and Geneva: United Nations), United Nations publication, Sales No. E.01.II.D.34.

________ (2002a). *International Investment Instruments: A Compendium*, vols. VII, VIII, IX and X (New York and Geneva: United Nations), United Nations publications, Sales Nos. E.02.II.D.14, 15, 16 and 21.

________ (2002b). *World Investment Report 2002: Transnational Corporations and Export Competitiveness* (New York and Geneva: United Nations), United Nations publications, Sales No. E.02.II.D.4.

________ (2003). *World Investment Report 2003. FDI Policies for Development: National and International Perspectives* (New York and Geneva: United Nations), United Nations publication, Sales No. 03.II.D.8.

________ (2004a). *World Investment Report 2004: The Shift Towards Services* (New York and Geneva: United Nations), United Nations publication, Sales No. 04.II.D.33.

________ (2004b). *International Investment Instruments: A Compendium*, vols. XI and XII (New York and Geneva: United Nations). United Nations publication, Sales Nos. E.04.II.D.9 and E.04.II.10.

________ (2004c). "International investment disputes on the rise", *Occasional Note* (29 November), UNCTAD/WEB/ITE/IIT/2004/2.

________ (forthcoming). *The REIO Exceptions in MFN Treatment Clauses. UNCTAD Series on International Investment Policies for Development* (New York and Geneva: United Nations).

________ and the World Bank (1994). *Liberalizing International Transactions in Services: A Handbook* (New York and Geneva: United Nations), United Nations publication, Sales No. E.94.II.A.11.

United Nations Department of Economic and Social Development, Transnational Corporations and Management Division (UN/DESD/ TCMD) (1992). *World Investment Report 1992: Transnational Corporations* as *Engines of Growth* (New York: United Nations), United Nations publication, Sales No. E.92.II.A.24.

United Nations Economic and Social Council (UN-ECOSOC) (1956). "Financing of economic development: the international flow of private capital, 1953-1955", United Nations document E/ 2901, mimeo.

________ (1957). "Financing of economic development: the international flow of private capital, 1956", United Nations document E/3021, mimeo.

________ (1990). "Development and economic co-operation: transnational corporations" (New York: United Nations), United Nations document, E/1990/94, mimeo..

United Nations General Assembly (UNGA) (1997). "United Nations Declaration against Corruption and Bribery in International Commercial Transactions (resolution No. 51/191)", *Resolutions adopted by the General Assembly during its Fifty-first session*, vol. 1: 17 September - 18 December 1996. General Assembly Official Records, Supplement No. 49 (A/51/49) (New York: United Nations), pp. 176-177.

________ (1998). "International Cooperation against Corruption and Bribery in International Commercial Transactions (resolution No. 52/87)", *Resolutions and Decisions adopted by the General Assembly during its Fifty-second session*, vol. 1: 16 September - 22 December 1997. General Assembly Official Records, Supplement No. 49 (A/52/49) (New York: United Nations), pp. 211-212.

United Nations Treaty Series (UNTS) (1969). "Treaty of Amity and Economic Relations (United States and Togo)", UNTS, vol. 680, no. 9677, pp. 159-178.

________ (1982). "Belgo-Luxembourg Economic Union and United Republic Cameroon: Convention concerning the reciprocal promotion and protection of investments", UNTS, vol. 1284, no. 21155, pp. 132-143.

________ (1987). "Agreement between the Kingdom of the Netherlands and the Democratic Socialist Republic of Sri Lanka for the promotion and protection of investments", UNTS, vol. 1458, no. 24654, pp. 70-74.

United States Treaty Series. "General Convention of Peace, Amity, Navigation and Commerce Between the United States of America and the Republic of Colombia of October 3, 1824", 1776-1949 Report, pp. 855-864.

Vandevelde, Kenneth (1988). "The bilateral investment treaty program of the United States", *Cornell International Law Journal*, 21, pp. 201-276.

________ (1992). *United States Investment Treaties: Policy and Practice* (Deventer, Netherlands: Kluwer).

Vasciannie, Stephen C. (1992a). "Bilateral investment treaties and civil strife", *Netherlands International Law Review*, Vol. 39, pp. 332-354.

________ (1992b). "The Namibian foreign investments act: balancing interests in the new concessionary era", *ICSID Review - Foreign Investment Law Journal*, 7 (Spring), pp. 114-140.

________ (2000). "The fair and equitable treatment standard in international investment law and practice", *British Year Book of International Law*, vol. LXX, pp. 99-164.

VerLoren van Themaat, P. (1981). *The Changing Structure of International Economic Law* (Dordrecht: Martinus Nijhoff).

Vienna Convention on the Law of Treaties (1969). *American Journal of International Law*, vol.63, no. 4, pp. 875-903.

Virally, Michel (1974). "La Charte des droits et devoirs economiques des Etats, notes de lecture", *Annuaire Francais de Droit International,* vol. 20, pp. 55 - 77.

Waelde, Thomas W., ed. (1996a). *The Energy Charter Treaty: An East-West Gateway for Investment and Trade* (London, The Hague and Boston: Kluwer Law International).

________ (1996b). "International investment under the 1994 Energy Charter Treaty", in Thomas Waelde, ed., *The Energy Charter Treaty* (London: Kluwer Law International), pp. 251-320.

Walker, Herman Jr. (1957-1958). "Modern treaties of friendship, commerce and navigation", *Minnesota Law Review*, vol. 42 (April), pp. 805-824.

Wallace, Cynthia (1983). *Legal Control of the Multinational Enterprise* (The Hague: Martinus Nijhoff).

________ (1994). "Control through disclosure legislation: foreign multinational enterprises in industrialized States", in S.J. Rubin and D. Wallace (eds.), *Transnational Corporations and National Law* (London and New York: Routledge), pp. 200-235.

Weatherill, Stephen and Paul Beaumont (1999). *EU Law* (London, Penguin Books, third edition).

Weston, B. (1975). "Constructive takings under international law: a modest foray into the problem of creeping expropriation", *Virginia Journal of International Law* , vol. 16, pp. 103-175.

Wetter, J. Gills (1962). *The International Arbitral Process*, vol.1, pp. 27-173.

Wiesner, E. (1993). "ANCOM: a new attitude toward foreign investment?", *University of Miami, Inter-American Law Review*, Vol. 24, No. 3, pp. 435-465.

Wilson, Robert R. (1960). *United States Commercial Treaties and International Law* (New Orleans: Hauser Press).

Wint, Alvin G. (1993). "Promoting transnational investment: organizing to service approved investors", *Transnational Corporations*, 2, 1 (February), pp. 71-90.

World Bank (1992). *Legal Framework for the Treatment of Foreign Investment, Volume 1: Survey of Existing Instruments* (Washington, DC: World Bank).

World Development Movement (1998). "The impact of the Multilateral Agreement on Investment on local government in the UK" (London: WDM), mimeo.

World Trade Organisation (WTO) (1994). "Understanding on rules and procedures governing the settlement of dispute (DSU)", *International Legal Materials,* Vol. 33, pp. 112-135 and www.wto.org.

________ (1995). *The Results of the Uruguay Round of Multilateral Trade Negotiations: The Legal Texts* (Geneva: WTO).

________ (1996a). *Trade and Foreign Direct Investment* (Geneva: WTO).

________ (1996b). "Decision on Maritime Services" (Geneva: WTO), document S/L/24, 3 July 1996.

________ (1997)."European Communities -- Regime for the Importation, Sale and Distribution of Bananas", (WT/DS27/AP/R), adopted on 25 September 1997 (Geneva: WTO).

________ (1998). "Bilateral, regional, plurilateral and multilateral agreements", WTO Secretariat Document no. WT/WGTI/W/ 22, 22 January, mimeo..

________ (1999). "Technical Note on the Accession Process", Note by the Secretariat (WT/ACC/7) of 10 March 1999 (Geneva: WTO).

________ (2002). "Transparency: note by the secretariat", Working Group on the Relationship between Trade and Investment, doc. WT/WGTI/W/109, 27 March, mimeo, http://docsonline.wto.org/.

Wyatt, D. and A.
Community Law,
Maxwell).

Youseff, Hesham (19
treatment for devel
South Centre, Trade
and Equity (T.R.A.D
South Centre), mime

Zacklin, Ralph (1979). "
international level: sc

n Dupuy ed., in
velopment at the
he Hague, 16-18
ff & Noordhof),

individuals in
w: NAFTA
of International